BIOGRAPHICAL
DICTIONARY
OF
MARXISM

BIOGRAPHICAL
DICTIONARY
OF
MARXISM

Edited by

ROBERT A. GORMAN

Greenwood Press
Westport, Connecticut

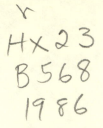

Library of Congress Cataloging in Publication Data
Main entry under title:

Biographical dictionary of marxism.

   Includes bibliographies and index.
   1. Communists—Biography—Dictionaries.
2. Socialists—Biography—Dictionaries.   I. Gorman,
Robert A.
HX23.B568   1986   335.43′092′2 [B]   84-29016
ISBN 0-313-24851-6 (lib. bdg.)

Library of Congress Catalog Card Number: 84-29016
ISBN: 0-313-24851-6

First published in 1986

Greenwood Press
A division of Congressional Information Service, Inc.
88 Post Road West
Westport, Connecticut 06881

Printed in the United States of America

∞

The paper used in this book complies with the
Permanent Paper Standard issued by the National
Information Standards Organization (Z39.48-1984).

10 9 8 7 6 5 4 3 2 1

For Jane, Emily, Michael, Linda, Netzach, and Nechemya

Contents

Preface

This volume contains biographical essays for over 210 Marxian philosophers and activists from almost fifty nations on five continents. Whereas the *Biographical Dictionary of Neo-Marxism*—also published by Greenwood Press—encompasses nontraditional philosophical variations of Marxian theory, this book focuses only on materialist or orthodox Marxism. Since most contemporary Marxists and Marxist parties are materialist, the problem of deciding who to include has been vexing. Two factors have particularly complicated the selection process. First, once materialist Marxism is established in the work of its seminal theorists, very little else of philosophical interest or significance is produced. And second, orthodox parties everywhere are represented by ideologues committed to rationalizing, justifying, and occasionally modifying Marxian theory to meet current national or regional conditions. Although these intellectual efforts may be interesting, they rarely transcend in significance the narrow geographical and temporal interests involved, and they are simply too numerous to all be included here. This dictionary will therefore concentrate almost equally on philosophy and strategy. Seeking to minimize the risk of redundancy, I have included only the major theoretical formulations of materialist Marxism as well as the significant and influential applications of materialism to concrete national conditions. One consequence is the extensive coverage given Third World Marxists, whose practical contributions have retooled materialist Marxism for the postcolonial liberation struggles in Africa, Asia, and Latin America—without, however, altering its philosophical base.

As in the *Biographical Dictionary of Neo-Marxism*, the final list of entrants herein has been formulated, debated, and ultimately approved by at least three indigenous scholars from each nation or region represented. I am certain that it is a fair and representative sampling of twentieth-century materialist Marxian thought and praxis.

In the introductions to both books I have tried to define carefully relevant terms and explain the criteria by which names are included and excluded. Nevertheless, some entrants rudely blur these distinctions. Where a nonmaterialist's impact on Marxist theory or praxis is noteworthy, or the editorial decision regarding exclusion problematic, I have listed the name alphabetically with the notation "See the *Biographical Dictionary of Neo-Marxism.*" An asterisk in the text indicates that a separate entry is listed (alphabetically) in this book for the preceding name; a dagger, that an entry can be found in the *Biographical Dictionary of Neo-Marxism.* The designation "n.a." means relevant information is either unavailable or purposely withheld at the subject's request.

In addition to the biographical essays, five group entries have been judged crucial to understanding Marxian theory and practice either within a nation or internationally. These include the Clarté group in France, the Tribunists in Holland, and the First, Second, and Third Internationals. Members who are considered significant in their own right are also given separate entries.

The bibliographies that follow each essay are intended as guides to further reading rather than as exhaustive compilations. They are divided into two parts: paragraph A lists relevant primary works; paragraph B, useful secondary material. When secondary readings are judged inferior or are nonexistent, paragraph B has been omitted. Where politics rather than theorizing distinguish an entrant, paragraph A is omitted. Wherever possible, English translations of original works are used.

This biographical dictionary, like its companion, offers students and scholars of Marxism a useful and handy resource. Organized alphabetically, essays on major twentieth-century materialist Marxists—with bibliographies—are quickly located. The introduction examines the meaning of philosophical materialism and historically situates Marx's version. Allen Wood's biographical essay on Marx offers a materialist interpretation of Marx's lifework that stresses the origins and meaning of historical materialism. The List of Names by Nationality (Appendix) encourages area specialists to relate both materialist theorizing and Marxian liberation movements to the diversity of national and regional cultures, facilitating cross-cultural comparison and analysis. Finally, the index lists all individuals, groups, and institutions, as well as key phrases, which are matched with their appropriate author(s).

I enthusiastically applaud those scholars from countries throughout the world who have given their limited time and unlimited energy and knowledge to formulating lists and writing essays. Their consistently high-quality work is, for me, the tresaure at rainbow's end. I am also indebted to the chorus of translators, typists, and assorted aides whose contributions have been timely and invaluable. Cynthia Harris provided expert guidance in addition to solving a bevy of practical problems. Douglas Gall's editorial skills and general knowledge carefully smoothed the edges. The joy of being with my family would have been more than enough, even without the extra care, help, and encouragement they have given me throughout these years of occasionally frustrating work. I owe them more than words can tell.

BIOGRAPHICAL
DICTIONARY
OF
MARXISM

Introduction

With contemporary Marxism splintered into categories ranging from nihilism to theology and including almost the entire spectrum of bourgeois philosophical alternatives, it is perhaps wise for intellectuals to remind themselves that its first, most politically successful, and still most acknowledged version is based on materialism. Materialist Marxism has become the philosophical rationale of mainline Communist parties throughout the world, daily shaping the beliefs and actions of millions of workers and peasants. In the following pages we will examine the meaning of materialism, reconstruct a materialist reading of Marx, and distinguish between Marxism and neo-Marxism.

MATERIALISM

Materialism, which has a long and rich history in Western philosophy dating from the Ionian school in ancient Greece, perceives valid knowledge as existing objectively at a level removed from common-sense thinking. Reality, in other words, exists only as matter: properties that scientific and everyday experience ascribe to physical bodies. Science must utilize observed facts to unearth their material substratum, excavating a world that molds our empirical experiences.

Although materialism originated in ancient Greece and matured in the early Stoic period, its social influence peaked during the Renaissance, when scholars like da Vinci and Galileo devised an experimental method emphasizing measurement of observable physical relationships without recourse to primary forms, essences, or divinities. This new thought system was philosophically expressed by Descartes, from whom the modern usage of the term "materialism" is derived.

Although a medievalist in attributing the universal cause and substance of all physical movement to God, Descartes in his philosophical writings described reality as thinking substance (mind) and extended substance (matter), a dichotomy that shaped modern Western philosophy. Henceforth, an idealist is one who denies ontological reality to matter; a materialist to mind. Yet despite Descartes's metaphysical dualism, as a physicist he was a rigid materialist, perceiving organic and inorganic nature as qualitatively identical and relating plant and animal behavior to the functioning of machines. Philosophy from this perspective depends on physics and chemistry. The significance of Descartes's other pillar of reality—mind—is soon obliterated by this material logic. Mechanical explanations are applicable to both mental and social phenomena. Mechanistic materialism, born in Descartes's physics, perceives human beings as nothing more than complex physical mechanisms.

In England, Francis Bacon and especially Thomas Hobbes systematized the materialist study of human and social behavior. Hobbes described the motion of irreducible particles as the prime source of substance and change. Geometry, mechanics, physics, ethics, and politics are scientific to the extent they trace the effects of motion in nature, mind, and society. John Locke asserted that ideas and knowledge are derived from experience and reflection, which Condillac and Helvétius later reduced to sensations. French Enlightenment philosophy, especially Diderot and Holbach, explored how the movement of matter generates consciousness. Diderot in particular argued that the quality or degree of human consciousness is determined by the complexity of material surroundings, in the same manner as sound or light copies the quality and quantity of matter from which it is composed.

Early nineteenth-century materialism strove toward the perfection of man through his reasoned manipulation of nature. This is not surprising since materialism presupposes that decent, knowledgeable people can be mechanically propagated by apposite conditions. Speaking practically, this means reorienting society toward the people's welfare, initiating concrete reforms to create desirable surroundings. Justice grows from a science of human welfare. First utopian and then scientific (Marxian) socialism appeared as nineteenth-century fruits of philosophical materialism. By the twentieth century, materialism was associated primarily with Marxism, while the non-Marxist, mechanistic brand was gradually absorbed by the methodology of empirical science.

MARXIAN MATERIALISM

The most immediate and direct materialist influence on Marx was Ludwig Feuerbach. In the early 1840s Germany was rife with Hegelian idealism, with variations ranging from the Young (or Left) Hegelian radicals on the left of the political spectrum to the more orthodox conservatives on the right. Feuerbach, who was himself once an Hegelian, emphasized the reactionary, undesirable social consequences of abstract—particularly religious—ideas. In the context of Germany's unquestioned Hegelianism, he became a beacon of materialist rationalism. In his *Lectures on the Essence of Religion* (1848), Feuerbach argued that religion and idealism generally were symbols of ignorance and weakness, reflecting our inability to comprehend and control nature. As knowledge increased, Feuerbach anticipated the demise of both abstract thinking and its social consequences: poverty, exploitation, and inequality. Rationality alone would guarantee social peace and complete freedom.

Feuerbach's materialist critique of German idealism, unexceptional when compared to British and French Enlightenment thought, was radical and exciting in Germany. Marx's own early flirtation with Hegel was quickly tempered by his reading of Feuerbach. Although Marx eventually rejected Feuerbach's own rather naive assumptions regarding enlightened, rational human beings, Marx's early writings (1842–45) expanded the notion of religious alienation and critically examined Hegel's blatant idealism.

Marx's materialism emerged first in his earliest published writings in the journal *Rheinische Zeitung* (1842–43), where he began reflecting on matter's influence on social behavior. In the article "Defense of the Moselle Correspondent," Marx noticed the "objective character" of politics, and the fact that social behavior "can be determined with almost the same certainty as a chemist determines under which external conditions given substances will form a compound.[1] Here, inchoately, is the materialist emphasis on concrete factors lying hidden in society's substructure.[2]

In the introduction to *A Critique of Hegel's Philosophy of Right* (1843), Marx criticized the utopian socialist belief in an irresistible ideal that, cognitively experienced, alters consciousness and liberates humanity. Marx foresaw human progress as an aspect of history's objective telos, making an unconscious historical tendency a conscious one.[3] For Marx, there are no mystical subjective qualities, only material processes bending minds toward history. Scientific socialism must expose these concrete forces. "In demanding that . . . [workers] give up illusions about this condition, we demand that they give up a condition that requires illusion. . . . The criticism of heaven is thus transformed into criticism of earth, the criticism of religion into criticism of law, and the criticism of theology into the criticism of politics."[4]

Even the *1844 Manuscripts*, often cited by nonmaterialists as evidence of Marx's own idealism, envisioned exploitation and alienation as necessary and even positive historical occurrences, unavoidable benchmarks in history's evolution to pure communism.[5] The compelling account of human alienation is intended by Marx as a vivid illustration of the quality of life experienced in one kind of society, i.e., at a capitalist stage of material development. Although man and woman are "active," "sensuous," and capable of creative labor, they are also "suffering, conditioned and limited creature[s], like animals and plants."[6] Alienation, in brief, is an impersonal condition equally affecting all exposed subjects and is embedded in material factors that "condition" and "limit" us.

The Holy Family (1844–45) ties historical progress to the contradictions that accompany capitalist production. The concrete modes of human reproduction negate themselves by breeding and cultivating classes that will eventually reshape these economic processes. Capitalism, for example, simultaneously generates the need for wage labor and the alienated, oppressive life style that workers endure, thus assuring its own downfall. Oppressed workers, on the other hand, need capitalists to survive, but in surviving realize that they can live better without capitalists. Subjugated classes, in brief, eventually seize and alter the extant mode of production in order to satiate their own needs. Each mode of production spawns an exploited class that it cannot do without, assuring its own destruction as the exploited inevitably become exploiters, who then create ideas and institutions that rationalize and protect their newly acquired hegemony. As matter historically unfolds through negation and revolution, there are corresponding movements in philosophy and social organization. The history of ideas depends on the history of production.[7]

Just as capitalism created the proletariat, who will carry history to communism, so the philosophy of materialism—which flourished in capitalism—will evolve into a theoretical rationale for worker rebellion and communism. Since materialism presumes that men and women are products of matter, then human potential is realized only when matter (e.g. society) is made human. "If man is formed by circumstances, then his circumstances must be made human."[8] This, Marx argued, is possible only in communism, where real material human needs are satiated, not merely the selfish urge to profit. Materialism is thus an authentic philosophical expression of working-class interests. Its own evolution from a mechanistic doctrine that turns humans into homunculi and rationalizes bourgeois science to a dialectical philosophy guaranteeing human freedom and creativity— what Marx called in the tenth *Thesis on Feuerbach* the "humanizing" of materialism—will be described in later works.

It is *The German Ideology* (1846), however, that materialist Marxists usually point to as Marx's and Engels's* most convincing early statement. In refuting the popular argument that mental aberrations cause social injustice and human alienation, Marx expounded his theory of historical materialism, his materialist science of history.

Asserting that human beings are extensions of nature who must battle to survive in inhospitable surroundings, Marx traced the origin of society to humanity's efforts at collectively creating and using the tools needed to extract sustenance from nature. Human history, for Marx, is the totality of those actions by which we produce in the material world to satisfy changing needs. "What . . . [individuals] are . . . coincides with their production, both with what they produce and how they produce it. The nature of individuals thus depends on the material conditions of their production."[9] Oppression originates when humanity begins producing more than it consumes and one group appropriates the excess goods produced by others. The forms of appropriation Marx called the "relations of production," including property relations, the social division of labor, and the organs of exchange and distribution. The means and relationships of production comprise society's material base. As technology develops, new forms of appropriation become feasible. In brief, society's base or substructure comprises the technical level of productive forces as well as the relationships involved in production, exchange, and distribution.

One's position in the base determines class, which in turn conditions one's perception of reality. The dominant economic class owns and controls society's productive apparatus, appropriating excess goods and distributing them to maximize their own interests. Their enormous wealth generates leisure activities (e.g. writing, worshiping, drawing, playing) that intellectually justify their dominance. Culture is therefore interpreted by Marx as the ideas and institutions by which a society defines itself and rationalizes the dominant class's hegemony. The level of productive forces and the social relations of production, distribution, and exchange determine all facets of a culture. "The ruling ideas are nothing more than the ideal expression of the dominant material relations, the dominant material relations grasped as ideas."[10] Cultures, however, also rise and fall in history. Hence human history can be explained by its patterns of technological innovation and the social forms taken by divided labor and property. First came the "primitive" world, with its tribal-owned property. Next, the "ancient" world, with communal and state-owned property. The "feudal" world was characterized by private estates and the beginnings of landed property. Finally, the modern "capitalist" world is marked by private ownership of land and factories, and the initiation of wage labor. Each successive historical stage represents a higher level of productive technology, encompassing foraging, hunting, farming, and modern commodity production. Each successive stage also embodies a new, more technically sophisticated division of labor.

Only communism will abolish the division of labor, which Marx and Engels saw as the first cause of social oppression. With workers controlling the productive apparatus—deciding what to produce and how to produce it—labor will no longer be estranged from workers' creative potentials. Our current sophisticated technology will generate personal fulfillment and social justice, ending capitalism's reification of commodities, private property, and wealth. But such dramatic changes can occur only after capitalism's human residue, that is, its impoverished and angry class of workers, has ripened. Moreover, these changes can survive only through a productive apparatus that efficiently and effectively satisfies workers' material needs. Finally, they require a world market in which all countries are economically interdependent. The proletariat, a worldwide class, must mature and rebel collectively. In sum, capitalism's maturing productive capacity produces an increasingly large and volatile class of workers, who experience material and cultural exploitation and eventually rebel. Revolution materializes when society's productive forces conflict with its relations of production.

Despite the human costs and benefits of this revolutionary process, Marx and Engles nevertheless argue that such violent and emancipatory activities are part of history's impersonal evolution. As matter evolves, as productive forces are transformed from ancient to modern proportions, the voices of discontent will simultaneously grow louder. Each productive mode, as it technically matures, will generate a disaffected class whose material needs will finally be satisfied only through a revolutionary transformation of the base. Consequently, at certain historical junctures revolutions occur regardless of subjective personalities or feelings. They are as natural and inevitable as a sunrise. Our eager expectations each morning are the *result* of matter's undeniable process, not its cause. Similarly, revolutions are fought because matter makes such battles, and their accompanying rhetoric, inevitable. The proletariat's understanding and evaluation of capitalism is purely practical, inseparably linked to their activities. Ethics, practical activity, and history's necessary material process comprise an irreducible totality. Human energy is "conditioned by the circumstances in which men find themselves, by the productive forces already acquired, by the social form which exists before they do, which they do not create, which is the product of the preceding generation.''[11] Marx's harsh critique of utopian socialism, particularly in *The Poverty of Philosophy* (1847) and *The Communist Manifesto* (1848), is based on the latter's naive moral and economic ideals, which ignore history's innate propensities.

Historical materialism, in sum, sees reality—including human perceptions and ideals—unfolding impersonally. Technology determines society's productive capacity, conditioning relations of production. This economic base consists of antagonistic classes, which appear historically when human labor is appropriated. Culture reflects the base. Antagonistic economic classes, therefore, produce social classes with opposing interests, expressed in conflicting ideologies. Society's institutions and ideas reflect the interests of its dominant economic class. When material conditions ripen, oppressed classes seize the means of production and replace existing institutions—including the state—with their own. Workers are thus destined to achieve economic and cultural hegemony, which will emerge concretely as communism.

Particularly after 1846, Marx emphasized the engine of this historical process: the dialectical quality of matter, its innate tendency to negate itself. Dialectics thus became, for Marx, an aspect of materialism. Each mode of production internally contains its own negation. As substructures mature, inequities grow, and oppressed classes cognitively and physically congeal and finally seize the means of production. History, therefore, necessarily unfolds through conflict and progressive change, culminating in proletariat hegemony and, ultimately, the abolition of classes altogether.[12] The dialectic, as part of matter, is impersonal and determining, an inexorable law of evolution generating negation, revolution, and progress. The science of historical materialism presupposes the philosophical worldview later called dialectical materialism.

For the materialist Marx, empirical reality is a multidimensional process, encompassing past and future as well as a present in which seemingly unrelated phenomena are in fact intertwined. Dialectics perceives each concrete society as a progressive synthesis of past contradictions and as a portent of new antagonisms, and each reflective individual as defined by objective matter. Reality exists of opposites coexisting in dynamic, tense unity.

Grundrisse (1857) analyzes the multifaceted contradictions between free and equal consumers and capitalism's drive for profit, the source of worker exploitation, oppression, and alienation. It powerfully conveys the fluid, dynamic, contradictory nature of society. Marx now perceived dialectics as a total social process of change, historic (diachronic) and spatial (synchronic), with observable features shaped by stages of economic development. Each aspect of society (economic, political, social, aesthetic, legal, and so on) comprises a moment of the total whole constantly interacting, defining, and influencing others. Consequently, concrete levels of social intercourse are neither independent nor identical. In a narrower sense, each aspect of the economy (production, distribution, exchange, and consumption) is similarly defined by its interactions with every other economic aspect, as well as with the noneconomic totality. The emerging picture is multidimensional and alive, where "everything that has a fixed form ...appears as merely a moment, a vanishing moment, in this [social] movement."[13]

For Marx, bourgeois liberty, equality, and legalism simultaneously obscure and justify the hideous conditions found in capitalist factories. Eventually, *Grundrisse* argues, the antagonism between worker and capitalist will negate empirical reality, the underlying contradiction will be suspended, and the totality will turn into its opposite—with identities and contradictions at a new, more progressive level. The hordes of specialists who accompany capitalism are incapable of perceiving this social totality in its separate parts. Conversely, mechanistic (nondialectical) materialism's overly simplistic, deductive theories obliterate the totality in a haze of abstract generalizations. Dialectics alone can reassemble the parts into a coherent whole that will simultaneously explain the past and present and generate the future. Dialectics grasps matter's dynamic total movement within which particulars are only incomplete moments.

Capital examines empirically capitalism's concrete developmental processes, conceptualizing each separate phase within an impersonally functioning dialectical material totality.

MARXISM AND NEO-MARXISM

The dialectical materialist version of Marxism is undoubtedly the most popular brand of contemporary radicalism. Its intellectual lineage goes from Marx to Engels, Kautsky,* Plekhanov,* Bukharin,* Lenin,* Mao,* and the legions of activists associated with orthodox Marxist-Leninist parties throughout the world. Materialists emphasize history's impersonal necessity and the inevitability of proletarian rebellion. Particularly since the publication of Lenin's *Philosophical Notebooks* in 1914, however, there is a small but lively effort to revitalize materialism dialectically, reasserting the subjective moment of the material totality. Both orthodoxy and neo-orthodoxy, however, presuppose the epistemological priority of matter and anchor history in matter's predictable, dialectical patterns. As the reader will quickly notice, most Marxian theorists, particularly those from the Third World, where practical concerns usually outweigh theoretical speculation, unquestioningly accept materialism. Their important contributions deal primarily with organizing and mobilizing effective revolutionary movements. They seek, in other words, to read the material components of their time and place accurately and to push history toward its progressive, inevitable dénouement.

This book vividly illustrates that there is ample room in materialist Marxism for divergent, often conflicting, opinions regarding the social and political roles of the Communist Party, apt strategies for revolutionary national workers' parties, and the quality of political life in socialism. Materialist Marxism thus encompasses democrats and totalitarians, those emphasizing the vanguard role of urban workers and those relying on revolutionary peasants, those favoring violent confrontation and those who are more cautious. What it cannot tolerate, however, is epistemological disagreement. At that point, where debate over strategy and tactics evolves into philosophical disagreement, Marxism is transformed into what we now call neo-Marxism, that is, into nonmaterial versions of Marxism. Disputes proliferate among Marxists regarding the revolutionary potential of electoral politics in specific capitalist states, for example. When such tactical debates turn theoretical, and when the materialist worldview is shattered by visions of the autonomy of politics, the state, or human consciousness, then materialist Marxism has been transformed into neo-Marxism.[14]

The following essays depict this century's foremost Marxian theoreticians as well as Marxian activists and politicians who have influenced the subsequent evolution of Marxian theory in their own nations or regions. They all subscribe to both the materialist principles outlined above and the materialist reading of Marx proffered by Allen Wood in his fine essay. The exclusion of so many luminaries of the left—Adorno,† Lukács,† Gramsci,† Sartre,† Marcuse,† etc.— indicates the alarming number of Marxian intellectuals who have abandoned their materialist heritage.

NOTES

1. Karl Marx, "Defense of the Moselle Correspondent," in *Selected Writings*, ed. David McLellan (London: Oxford University Press, 1977), p. 24. Hereafter cited as *KMSW*.

2. In this respect see also "The Law on Thefts on Wood," in ibid, pp. 20–22.

3. In Karl Marx, *Early Writings* (New York: Vintage Books, 1975), pp. 256–57. Hereafter cited as *KMEW*.

4. Marx, *A Critique of Hegel's Philosophy of Right*, in ibid., pp. 244–45.

5. See Marx, *Economic and Philosophical Manuscripts*, in ibid., pp. 322–34.

6. Ibid., p. 329.

7. Marx, *The Holy Family*, in *KMSW*, pp. 135–52.

8. Ibid., p. 155.

9. Karl Marx and Friedrich Engels, *The German Ideology* (Moscow: Progress, 1976), p. 37.

10. Ibid., p. 67.

11. Marx, "Letter to Annenkov" (1846), in *KMSW*, p. 192.

12. In the *Critique of the Gotha Programme* (Moscow: Progress, 1971), Marx recognized the need for an intermediary period between the proletarian revolution and the advent of true socialism. In this transition period economic rights are proportionate to labor and the proletariat organize themselves into a "dictatorship of the proletariat" to

abolish class distinctions forcefully and develop the economy. The full promise of communism is realized only when the productive forces are fully developed.

   13. Marx, *Grundrisse: Foundations of the Critique of Political Economy* (New York: Vintage Books, 1973), p. 712.

   14. See this author's *The Biographical Dictionary of Neo-Marxism*(Westport, Conn.: Greenwood Press, 1986), for a listing of major neo-Marxists. See also *Neo-Marxism— The Meanings of Modern Radicalism* (Westport, Conn.: Greenwood Press, 1982).

Biographies of Marxists

A

ADHIKARI, GANGADHAR   (1898–1981). Born in India in 1898, Gangadhar Adhikari was a member of the central leadership of the Communist Party of India from 1933 to 1981. His thesis, in 1942, on "Pakistan and the Right of Indian Nationalities, Including Muslim-Majority Nationalities, to Self-Determination to the Point of Secession," introduced notable innovations to the "Indian paradigm" of Marxian social theory that continue to remain influential and under debate.

Marxian social theory focuses on the dominant phenomenon of the emergence and disintegration of social classes, of their combination, recombination, and conflict, as being endemic in social situations. But it concedes that these dominant phenomena are conditioned or refracted by various major and minor epiphenomena, especially of politicized religion and politicized nationalism. Indeed, Marxian social and political theory, initially regarded by Indians as Eurocentric and exoteric, has penetrated the ideology and politics of the Indian subcontinent through a series of encounters with some peculiarly Indian epiphenomena first encountered there. One such encounter in recent times was forced on Indian Marxists in 1940. A nascent professional, mercantile, and rich landowning peasant Muslim bourgeoisie, and Muslim landlords in Muslim-majority areas, enriched by "primary accumulation" during war and a pervasive food crisis (including famine in Bengal), and desirous of becoming an industrial bourgeoisie, staked a claim to a sovereign Indian Muslim state (or states) in the Muslim-majority provinces of colonial India. Adhikari's 1942 "Pakistan thesis" articulated an Indian Marxian response to this demand for Pakistan that, for the first time, recognized the Hindu–Muslim dichotomy in Indian society as a major epiphenomenon. In the process, it recognized, also for the first time, the epiphenomenon of several Indian "nationalities" in place of the integral Indian "nation," till then regarded by Marxists as well as non-Marxists as the major manifestation of politicized nationalism in India. Adhikari held that the "Pakistan demand" was mystical and obscurantist in form and used by the political instrument of the politicized Muslim religion in India, the All-India Muslim League, to split the actual and potential unity of the exploited workers, peasants, and urban petit bourgeoisie of India. But, he maintained, there was a "rational kernel" inside this mystical shell. According to him this "rational kernel" could be identified on the basis of Marxian theory by recognizing the crystallization of a multiplicity of Indian nationalities, each having an urge for freedom and self-determination to the point of secession in an India freed from British colonial rule. Among these, the "Muslim-majority nationalities" had reached a point where they were insisting on the exercise of their right to secede, although only at the end of the antifascist world war in which both Britain and India were then involved. Indian Marxists, Adhikari argued, must uphold their right to secede, just as they had, until then, supported the right of the integral Indian nation-in-the-making to secede from the British Empire and establish a sovereign Indian state. The notable innovations Adhikari's 1942 thesis made can be set out in bold relief by comparison with two earlier, standard versions of the "Indian paradigm" of Marxian social theory.

In Marx's 1853–57 paradigm the "social formation" of precolonial and early colonial India is identified as a species belonging to the genus of the "Asiatic mode of production," with its "superstructure" or "civil society" of "Oriental despotism." It was distinguished from others belonging to the same genus by being divided into occupational and hierarchical classes that had "petrified" into castes, whose members were engaged in both agricultural and manufacturing crafts. These castes were locked in an unchanging or slowly changing equilibrium prevailing within, as well as between, villages, which were like disconnected autonomous units of Indian society. Their self-sufficiency (due to the absence of long-distance trade) was based on an intravillage, or even an intrahousehold union of agriculture and industry maintained by limited production and direct exchange of commodities (without the intervention of merchants). In this paradigm, Adhikari's two major preoccupations, i.e., the Hindu–Muslim dichotomy and the formation of a multiplicity of Indian nationalities rather than of one integral Indian nation, have no place except as minor, ephemeral epiphenomena. They were artificially incubated, Marx thought, by the *divide et impera* Indian strategy adopted by Anglo-Scottish mercantile monopoly capital, which was too weak to capture state power in their home territory. Nevertheless, it was in search of state power in a foreign country, in order to break up forcibly the Indian variant of the Asiatic mode of production entrenched in India. But the Hindu–Muslim dichotomy and multiplicity of Indian nationalities that the East India Company sought to foster had no deep and permanent roots in precolonial or early colonial Indian society, according to Marx. This was because of the absorption, by a process of Indianization, of the impact of waves of Muslim invasions as well as of internal (e.g. anti-Hindu but also anti-Muslim Sikh) dissidence by a superior Indian civilization acting through the Brahmin priestly class. Furthermore, Marx thought that the dialectics of the destructive-regenerative-conservative modernization process resulting from the impact of superior British bourgeois civilization would, especially after the defeat of the Indian

revolt of 1857–59, finally eliminate whatever Hindu–Muslim dichotomy or multiplicity of contending Indian nationalities it had initially incubated.

Lenin's* 1920 essentially Indocentric Marxian colonial paradigm was an extension of his theory of rival monopoly capitalist imperialisms engaged in struggles to redivide a world, especially the colonial and semicolonial countries of
the world, which they had already first divided up among themselves. It focused
on the epiphenomenon of the making, by an on-going economic and political
revolutionary process, of an integral Indian nation (ignoring altogether the possible crystallization of many Indian nationalities as a parallel or contradictory
process). In this paradigm, too, but for somewhat different reasons, the Hindu–
Muslim dichotomy is noticed as an unimportant epiphenomenon in India. It is
now downgraded as having been incubated artificially by a dialectical interre-
lation of conflict and collusion between the Pan-Islamic appeals of a dying
theocratic Turkish imperialism, on the one hand, and British imperialism facing
a multiclass economic and political upsurge in India, with the Hindu–Muslim
conflict being temporarily in abeyance during the Khilafat movement, on the
other. In this paradigm, the focus is on a somewhat ambidextrously identified
dichotomy and differentiation within an integral Indian nationalism, involving
the ''bourgeois-democratic nationalists'' on the one hand and the ''nationalist
revolutionaries'' on the other.

The foregoing would seem to establish conclusively Adhikari's credentials as
an innovator of the Marxian paradigm for Indian society. However, the verdict
on the success of the predictions made on the basis of this innovation must be
a mixed one. True, politicized Hindu–Muslim dichotomies, raised to a fever
pitch by the Muslim League, involved semirevolutionary violence directed against
the British colonial power and also the instigative or reactive violence of the
Muslim urban, and to some extent rural, masses against Hindus (and Sikhs) of
all classes. This led to the establishment of a single, sovereign state of Pakistan
in a divided India in 1947. But the longer-term outcome has been seemingly
irrevocable splits of the Bengali-speaking and Punjabi-speaking nationalities of
precolonial India, with the emergence, with the East Bengali Muslims as the
nucleus, of a full-fledged Bangladeshi Muslim-majority nation, and a demo-
graphically even more homogeneous Punjabi Muslim nationality dominating
Pakistan after the secession of Bangladesh. The verdict must also be mixed on
Adhikari's prescriptions for advancing the overall cause of communism as a
political force in the Indian subcontinent by upholding the claims of politicized
religious nationalisms to nationhood. Where such claims have led to the birth
of new nations or nationalities splitting all classes, political communism had
either receded (e.g. in Bangladesh) or still failed to arrive (e.g. in present-day
Pakistan). Political communism has also receded, seemingly irrevocably, first
in Tamil Nadu, and then in Andhra. In the former it lost a working-class foothold,
in the latter strongly politicized Communist-led Andhra nationalist peasant bases;
in both cases it retreated before militant, intensely politicized, semireligious
''little nationalisms.'' On the other hand, through successful politicization of

communism as a new kind of "popular religion," communism has become
entrenched, seemingly irreversibly, as the dominant political force among Indian
Bengalis (in the Indian states of West Bengal, Tripura, and parts of Assam),
with the backing of an economically weak, nascent, Indo-Bengali national
bourgeoisie.

BIBLIOGRAPHY:

A. *National Unity Now, in People's War* (Bombay, 1942); "Resolution of the Central
Committee of the CPI on Pakistan and National Unity" (drafted by G. Adhikari in 1942),
pp. 168–70, in *Documents of the History of the Communist Party of India*, ed. M. B.
Rao, vol. 7 (New Delhi: People's Publishing House, 1976); "Resolution of the Central
Committee of the CPI on the Muslim League" (drafted by G. Adhikari in August 1943),
p. 171, in ibid.; "Party Letter" (drafted by G. Adhikari in October 1943), p. 172, in
ibid.

B. Aron Bose, *Political Paradoxes and Puzzles* (Oxford: Clarendon Press, 1977).

ARUN BOSE

AGUILAR MONTEVERDE, ALONSO   (birthdate n.a.). An economist,
Alonso Aguilar Monteverde studied at New York University and Columbia
University in 1945–46, before joining the faculty of the School of Economics
of the National Autonomous University of Mexico (UNAM). He also served as
coordinator of the Executive Commission of the Mexican Liberation Movement
(MLN), founded in 1961 as a part of the independent left in Mexico that operates
within the official single-party system. The MLN program advocated radical
reforms and favored the Cuban Revolution.

Aguilar Monteverde's written works are a mixture of polemics that ruthlessly
attack the capitalist order and sophisticated surveys of the roots of both Mexican
and Latin American underdevelopment. An example of the former is his *Latin
America and the Alliance for Progress* (1963), which, although correctly alerting
readers to the difference between the purported rationale for the Alianza and the
actual implementation and results of the short-lived experiment, often lowers
itself to *ad hominem* attacks: "All we have received from North America is
pressure, interference, low prices, McCarthyism, gifts with strings attached,
investments which pervert our development and put brakes on our progress, as
well as rhetoric in defense of free enterprise and the so-called Free World"
(p. 29). Aguilar Monteverde states that Latin America should rely less on foreign
capital and ideas and more on its own efforts.

In *Teoría y política del desarrollo latinoamericano* (1967), he criticizes the
direction that economic integration has taken and considers "planning" primarily
a device to obtain foreign financing. Advocating a "genuine proletarian alternative," Aguilar Monteverde is critical of Mexico's ruling party, the Partido
Revolucionario Institucional (PRI).

BIBLIOGRAPHY:

A. *Latin America and the Alliance for Progress* (New York: Monthly Review Press, 1963); *Teoría y política del desarrollo latinoamericano* (Mexico: Instituto de Investigaciones Económicas, UNAM, 1967).

CARL A. ROSS and ALLEN WELLS

AI SIQI   (1910?–1966). A Chinese Marxist-Leninist theoretician, Ai Siqi was born in Tengchong, Yunnan Province, and as a young man studied in Japan. He emerged in Shanghai in the early 1930s as a prolific writer on Marxist-Leninist philosophy. He joined the Chinese Communist Party (CCP) in 1935 and in 1937 went to Yan'an, where he became part of the "think tank" Mao Zedong* was assembling in the area of philosophy and theory. After the Communist victory in 1949, Ai held a variety of influential positions in the intellectual-cultural field, although he never achieved high party rank. A frequent contributor to *Study*, *Red Flag*, and other CCP journals, he died in early 1966 just prior to the Cultural Revolution.

Ai Siqi is important in the history of Chinese communism for two interrelated reasons: He did much to popularize Marxist-Leninist philosophy in a distinctly Chinese idiom; and he helped Mao establish his reputation as a leading theorist in China and abroad. Ai made his reputation in the mid-1930s as a vigorous writer, editor, and translator of Marxist-Leninist philosophy in a popular and accessible style. His best-selling book, *Philosophy for the Masses* (1934), was a pioneering attempt to explain Marxism-Leninism in a format that used familiar Chinese historical, philosophical, and cultural concepts. In particular, he argued that foreign ideas like dialectical materialism could be more readily assimilated by the Chinese public if they were conveyed in Chinese literary forms such as traditional historical epics or contemporary regional drama rather than Western-derived formats. For an entire generation of young Chinese, the writings of Ai Siqi were their earliest introduction to the intricacies of Marxist-Leninist theory, and in later years prominent CCP leaders testified to Ai's impact on their intellectual development.

After becoming a theoretical advisor to Mao Zedong, Ai Siqi worked with Chen Boda,* Hu Qiaomu, and others to assist Mao in formulating a body of doctrine that would draw on his practical experience in the Chinese Revolution and yet be consistent with the broader Marxist-Leninist tradition in the Soviet Union and the international Communist movement. He was thus closely associated with the idea of the "Sinification of Marxism" and the effort to portray the "thought of Mao Zedong" as the creative synthesis of Marxism-Leninism and Chinese revolutionary practice. As such, Ai argued, Mao's thought was a development of and not a deviation from the European and Soviet theoretical traditions. Although the term "Sinification of Marxism" has been phased out of Party usage, Mao's thought has been retained as the "guiding ideology" of the CCP up to the present time.

Ai Siqi has left behind a substantial body of writings, most of which have not been translated into English. This is true of his most influential work, *Philosophy for the Masses*, which has been reprinted many times. Ai has not yet been the subject of a major study, so information on his life and writings must be pieced together from a variety of sources in Chinese and in Western languages.
BIBLIOGRAPHY:

A. *Philosophy for the Masses* (Shanghai: n.a., 1934).

RAYMOND F. WYLIE

AIDIT, DIPA NUSANTARA   (1923–1965). D. N. Aidit was born on 30 July 1923 at Belitung, Sumatra, Indonesia. He attended technical school in Jakarta and was a student during the Japanese occupation of Indonesia. In the Indonesian August revolution of 1945, Aidit played a leading role in student circles, helping to form the Angkatan Pemuda Indonesia (API). In 1946 he became secretary of the People's Democratic Front (FDR), a popular front organization of the Indonesian Communist Party (PKI). Following the defeat of the Communist Party led by Musso* in the revolt of 1948, Aidit fled abroad, visiting Vietnam and China. Returning to Indonesia in 1950, he rapidly assumed control of the PKI, becoming first a member of the Politburo and then first secretary of the PKI. In 1951 he became secretary general of the Party and retained this post until his murder in 1965, following a military *coup d'état*.

Under Aidit's guidance, the PKI moved quickly in the 1950s to eschew revolutionary violence and to identify itself formally with militantly political but essentially constitutional and parliamentary means of coming to power. In this respect, the strategy the PKI pursued under Aidit's leadership between 1951 and 1965 in many ways resembled what was to become "Eurocommunism." The Party participated in elections and parliamentary life, avoided overtly class positions, and adopted a national ideological orientation. The PKI also attempted to maintain an independent position in the developing Sino–Soviet dispute, although it endorsed Indonesia's ever closer diplomatic partnership with China in the early 1960s.

Aidit in his own writings showed himself to be the theoretical pioneer of the path the Party chose to follow. Above all, Aidit showed himself adept in harmonizing the PKI's program with the theories of President Sukarno, with whom the Party, for tactical reasons, had to all intents and purposes developed a politically symbiotic relationship. As well as explaining its nationalist appeal and "national" character, Aidit also stressed the PKI's equality with and independence from all other Communist parties. The close relationship that the PKI maintained with President Sukarno was later blamed by Party dissidents as being partly responsible for the defeat and liquidation of the Party after the September 1965 coup led by General Suharto.

BIBLIOGRAPHY:
   A. *A Short History of the Communist Party of Indonesia* (New Delhi: People's Pub-
lishing House, 1955); *Indonesian Society and the Indonesian Revolution* (Djakarta: Jajasan
Pembaruan, 1958); *Set Afire the Banteng Spirit! Ever Forward, No Retreat* (Peking:
Foreign Languages Press, 1964).
   B. Rex Mortimer, *Indonesian Communism Under Sukarno: Ideology and Politics,
1959–1965* (Ithaca: Cornell University Press, 1974).

MICHAEL C. WILLIAMS

ALLENDE GOSSENS, SALVADOR   (1908–1973). Salvador Allende Gossens was born in Valparaíso, Chile, on 26 July 1908. He came from an anticlerical
family tied to the Masons and the reformist Radical Party. Salvador Allende
began studying medicine at the university in 1926. There he became president
of the medical students and vice-president of the national Student Federation of
Chile. He spearheaded student protests against the dictatorship of Carlos Ibáñez
in 1931. After imprisonment for political activism, Allende received his medical
degree in 1932. Upon the death of his father that same year, the young doctor
vowed to dedicate his life "to social struggle." To carry out that mission, he
helped found the Socialist Party of Chile in 1933 in Valparaíso, where he was
working for the public health service. Elected to the national Chamber of Deputies
in 1937, Allende resigned that seat in 1939 to become Minister of Health in the
Popular Front government (1938–41).
   When the Socialists became disenchanted with participation in increasingly
conservative multiparty governments, Allende and Raúl Ampuero† led the intraparty rebellion. For the first of two times, Allende became secretary general
of the party in 1943. He withdrew it from governmental responsibilities and
argued for greater dedication to proletarian conquests. Rather than devoting
himself to internal party affairs, however, Allende built his career in the national
Senate, to which he won election in 1945, 1949, 1953, 1961, 1965, and 1969.
He also became vice-president of that legislative body in the 1940s and president
in the 1960s. As his party turned away from coalitions behind centrist reformers
and instead aligned electorally with the Communists, Allende emerged as the
perennial presidential candidate of the Marxist forces.
   He initiated those independent Marxist bids for the presidency in 1952 with
a token campaign backed by small segments of the Socialist and Communist
parties. That symbolic effort, dubbed the People's Front, fetched only 6 percent
of the ballots cast. Thereafter, the reunification of the splintered Socialists and
their formation with the full Communist Party of an enduring electoral partnership
known as the Popular Action Front (FRAP) set the stage for a more concerted
drive in 1958. In his second presidential race, Allende captured 29 percent of
the national electorate, narrowly losing to the right-wing nominee, Jorge Ales-
sandri, who finished with 31 percent. In 1964, Allende increased his tally to 39
percent of the votes, but the alliance of rightist and centrist groups behind
Christian Democrat Eduardo Frei (56 percent) denied him victory. When the

right, center, and left each posted candidates in 1970, Allende finally triumphed with 36 percent of the electorate. The first Marxist president ever so elected in Latin America, he took office as the head of the Popular Unity coalition, comprised of Socialists, Communists, Radicals, and minor groups of social democrats and left-wing Christian democrats.

Vowing to lead Chile toward socialism through representative, democratic institutions, President Allende legally transferred the means and fruits of production from wealthy Chileans and foreigners to workers and peasants. He nationalized copper and other foreign-owned industries, expropriated most of the banks, redistributed the vast majority of agricultural lands from large owners to farmworkers, and increased the share of national income accruing to wage and salary earners. As production fell and inflation soared, Chilean society and politics polarized. Despite mounting hostility from the United States and from domestic rightist and centrist opponents, the Popular Unity increased its electoral base to 44 percent in the midterm congressional showdown in March 1973. Thereafter the opposition consummated plans for a military *coup d'état*, which resulted in the death of Salvador Allende on 11 September 1973. The subsequent dictatorship of Army General Augusto Pinochet set out to obliterate Marxism and democracy in Chile.

Throughout his long political career, Allende remained Marxist in orientation, but he was a practitioner rather than an ideologist. A fervent nationalist, he believed that Chile's democratic traditions opened up a uniquely peaceful route to socialism. That experiment and its destruction continue to stir controversy around the world.

BIBLIOGRAPHY:

A. *La realidad médico-social chilena* (Santiago: Ministerio de Salubridad, 1939); *Su pensamiento político* (Santiago: Quimantú, 1972).

B. Regis Debray, *The Chilean Revolution* (New York: Pantheon, 1971); Ian Roxborough et al., *Chile: The State and Revolution* (New York: Holmes & Meier, 1977); Paul Sigmund, *The Overthrow of Allende and the Politics of Chile, 1964–1976* (Pittsburgh: University of Pittsburgh Press, 1977); Paul W. Drake, *Socialism and Populism in Chile, 1932–52* (Urbana: University of Illinois Press, 1978); Arturo Valenzuela, *The Breakdown of Democratic Regimes: Chile* (Baltimore: Johns Hopkins University, 1979).

PAUL DRAKE

ALMARAZ PAZ, SERGIO   (1928–1968). In his short life Sergio Almaraz became one of the most popular writers on the Bolivian left, attracting a following well beyond the ranks of the Communist Party (PCB), which he had helped establish and of which he remained a militant for most of his life. His reputation was established in 1952 and 1953, when as a student leader he became a forceful member of the union leadership and critic of the Trotskyists.* Yet his primary contribution lay in his accessible and incisive writing on the effects of the metropolitan economy on Bolivia. Although Almaraz developed no new theories of substance in Marxist economics, he proved capable of applying this method to the case of Bolivia with an empirical rigor and openness of style that has never since been matched. Moreover, he displayed a remarkable ability to capture the broader social and subjective characteristics of economic organization in a backward capitalist state in an expansive and acute analysis that is at times almost poetic in resonance. The political essays of his later years show a distancing from the PCB and growing sympathy for the armed struggle, although his reputation remains firmly based on the critique of petit bourgeois nationalism and its inexorable concessions to metropolitan pressures.

BIBLIOGRAPHY:

A. *El petroleo en Bolivia* (La Paz: Editorial Juventud, 1957); *El poder y la caida* (La Paz: Editorial Los Amigos de Libro, 1966); *Requiem para una república* (La Paz: Biblioteca de Marcha, 1969); *Para abrir el diálogo: Ensayos 1961–67* (La Paz: Ediciones Los Amigos del Libro, 1979).

JAMES DUNKERLEY

ALMEYDA MEDINA, CLODOMIRO (b. 1923). Clodomiro Almeyda Medina was born in Santiago, Chile, on 11 February 1923. After receiving his law degree from the University of Chile, he worked there as a professor in political science and sociology. He also practiced journalism. Joining the Socialist Party of Chile in 1940, he became one of its leading intellectuals and a member of the Central Committee from 1948 on. Almeyda served as Minister of Labor (1952–53) and of Mines (1953) under President Carlos Ibáñez (1952–58). After brief duty as secretary general of his party, Almeyda won election to the national Chamber of Deputies during the years 1961–65. When fellow Socialist Salvador Allende* became president of Chile (1970–73), Almeyda filled the posts of Minister of Foreign Relations, of Defense, and of Interior. Following the overthrow of Allende's Popular Unity government by the armed forces, Almeyda went into exile, principally in Mexico. There he became executive secretary of the Popular Unity and secretary general of a divided Socialist Party.

Within his party, Clodomiro Almeyda consistently advocated a Marxist Revolution cast in a nationalist, anti-imperialist mold. He opposed slavish imitation of Western European or Soviet ideologies or political systems. In his quest for models applicable to Chilean conditions, Almeyda was attracted to Peronism at the start of the 1950s, Titoism* by the middle of that decade, and Maoism* and Castroism* by the early 1960s. Since then he has supported a Marxist-Leninist position for his Socialist Party.

BIBLIOGRAPHY:

A. *Reflexiones políticas* (Santiago: Prensa Latinoamericano, 1958).

B. Ernst Halperin, *Nationalism and Communism in Chile* (Cambridge: Cambridge University Press, 1965)

PAUL DRAKE

ALVAREZ DEL VAYO, JULIO (1891–1975). Devoted since early youth to journalism and travel, Julio Alvarez visited Paris and spent a year in London before the declaration of war caught up with him at a German university. From there he went to the United States, where he spent two years taking courses at Columbia University and writing articles for *El Liberal* in Madrid. After the war he traveled through Europe as a correspondent for *La nación* of Buenos Aires. Upon his return to Madrid he married a Swiss woman whose brother was another newspaper man, Luis Araquistain,* director of *España*. Alvarez worked for this magazine as well as for the newspaper *El sol*, which sent him to Zurich. Because of his international experience and his Latin American connections, he was named the first ambassador to Mexico by the Spanish Republic. Upon his return to Spain he and Luis Araquistain led the thrust to the left of the Spanish Youth as well as the labor leaders headed by Francisco Largo Caballero.* It was precisely the intellectuals and journalists who gathered around *Leviathan*, together with the youths and the radical wing of the General Confederation of Workers, who shaped the leftist tide of Spanish socialism from early 1934 and also proposed the rupture of the alliance with the Republican parties. Alvarez del Vayo then assumed the role of a bridge between the Communist Party and the "Socialist Youth," in which the latter was absorbed by the former. He was appointed minister of state by Largo Caballero. From this position he was able to reinforce the ties with the Soviet Union. Although Juan Negrin* did not confirm him, he was appointed commissioner general of an army already amply controlled by the Communist Party. After the April 1938 crisis, he again became minister of state. While in exile, Alvarez del Vayo remained faithful to Negrin and close to the Communists until they accepted participation in the government formed by Geral. In 1947 he organized España Combatiente (a group made up of *negristas* of different sorts), but without any success. Negrin himself preferred to keep the Executive Committee of the Partido Socialista Obrero Española (PSOE) (who were faithful to him) against that of the moderates or "*prietistas*," who had expelled him from the party.

Alvarez del Vayo called himself "the last optimist." In 1950, after abandoning definitely the symbols of his party, which was internally torn between *negristas* and *prietistas*, he formed the Spanish Socialist Union, made up of dissidents from France and North Africa. In 1964 he formed a Spanish Front for National Liberation and established relations with the Frente Revolucionario Antifascista Patriotica (FRAP), which operated within Spain as an organization of Marxist-Leninist masses who had split from the Spanish Communist Party (PCE). The FRAP, of which Alvarez del Vayo was president, attained notoriety toward the end of Franco's era because of its aim: to accelerate the downfall of the regime by means of armed force.

He died in Geneva, unable to witness the end of *franquismo*, on 3 May 1975. He did not contribute anything significant to Marxist theory in his writings, limiting himself to exalting the optimism of the gallant fighter.

BIBLIOGRAPHY:

A. *Freedom's Battle* (New York: Knopf, 1940); *The Last Optimist* (London: Putnam, 1950); *China Triumphs*, New York: Monthly Review Press, 1964); *Give Me a Combat* (Boston: Little, Brown, 1973).

B. Fernando Claudin, *The Communist Movement, from Comintern to Cominform* (New York: Monthly Review Press, 1975); Paul Preston, *La destrucción de la democracía en España* (Madrid: Siglo XXI, 1977); Santos Juliá, *Oregenes del Frente Popular en España* (Madrid: Siglo XXI, 1979).

SANTOS JULIÁ

ANDRADE RODRIGUEZ, JUAN   (1897–1981). Juan Andrade Rodriguez, a founder-member of the Spanish Communist party (PCE), was a leading left Communist figure during the 1920s and 1930s. Born on 3 February 1897 in Madrid, he began his political career at the age of fourteen as a member of the Juventudes Radicales. After joining the Grupo de Estudiantes Socialistas in 1916, Andrade quickly acquired a reputation as a talented writer and propagandist and eventually became the editor of *Renovación*, the central organ of the Federacion de Juventudes Socialistas (FJS). The Russian Revolution aroused a great deal of enthusiastic support from the socialist youth movement, inspiring many, including Andrade, to embrace an ultrarevolutionary perspective. The founding of the Comintern in 1919 gave fresh impulse to these young radicals, who began increasingly clamoring for the Partido Socialista Obrero Española (PSOE) to adhere to the new organization. When it became apparent that the majority of Socialists were unwilling to do this, Andrade, along with Ramón Merono García, Vicente Arroyo, and other prominent members of the national committee of the FJS, spearheaded a drive to transform the FJS into a Communist Party. Their plans finally crystallized in April 1920, when they formed the Partido Comunista Español (PCE). The schism within the socialist movement was more than just a conflict of generations; it owed a great deal to deep-seated ideological differences. Andrade himself was typical of those in the PCE: he wanted to break decisively with the reformist tradition of the PSOE, which he argued had resulted in the embourgeoisement of the Spanish proletariat, and to adopt a revolutionary course of action modeled on the Bolshevik experience.

A year later another dissident group, the Terceristas (those who supported the Comintern), emerged within the PSOE. Led by distinguished activists such as Virginia Gonzalez, Oscar Perez Solis, and Manuel Nuñez Arenas, this faction seceded from the PSOE in April 1921 to create the Partido Comunista Obrero Español (PCOE). At first the two Communist parties were decidedly hostile toward each other, largely because Andrade and the PCE generally dismissed the PCOE as a party of "old reformists" who were incapable of being revolutionary. Under pressure from the IKKI (Executive Committee of the Comintern), however, the two groups agreed to merge in November of that year to form the Partido Comunista d'España (PCE). From the outset, Andrade and others who believed that the fusion had been weighted in favor of the PCOE created problems for the new Party by organizing an opposition faction known as Oposición Comunista Española (OCE). Unity in the Party was finally restored at the second PCE congress held in July 1923, when Andrade was reinstated on the Executive Committee and made editor-in-chief of the Party's mouthpiece, *La antorcha*.

During the six-and-a-half-year reign of Primo de Rivera's military dictatorship (1923–30), Andrade devoted his time to writing, occasionally serving as a correspondent for the Comintern papers, *The International* and *International Correspondence*, and working for various publishing firms as a translator and editor. Throughout this period, Andrade's relations with the PCE itself had grown increasingly strained chiefly because he objected to the "bolshevizing" (centralizing) of the Party under José Bullejos, who had assumed the leadership of the Party in 1925. Andrade's personal and political disagreements with the Executive Committee led to his resignation from the editorial board of *La antorcha* in 1926 and, finally, to his expulsion from the PCE in 1928.

Following the collapse of Primo's dictatorship, Andrade resumed his activities in the Communist movement, but this time as a member of the recently formed Trotskyist* Left Opposition faction. Since 1928 he had been in contact with "Henri Lacroix" (Francisco García Lavid), Andreu Nin,* and other Spanish Trotskyists (or Bolshevik-Leninists, as they were then called) living abroad who were interested in developing a Spanish section of the Left Opposition. In February 1930, Lacroix, with the assistance of Spanish emigrés from Belgium, France, and Luxembourg, formally constituted the Oposición Comunista Española (OCE) in Liège, Belgium. That spring, the OCE transferred its headquarters to Madrid, where Lacroix and Andrade began directing its activities. Like Trotsky, they believed that the primary task of the OCE in Spain was to establish unity within the badly splintered Communist movement—which, including the OCE faction, was now split into four distinct tendencies—and thereby create a mass revolutionary party of the working classes.

From 1932 onward, Andrade began following a political trajectory that brought him increasingly into conflict with Trotsky. His first significant deviation from Trotskyism came in March 1932, when he collaborated with Nin in converting the OCE into an independent political party, the Izquierda Comunista d'España (ICE). Trotsky opposed this move most of all because it amounted to a rejection of his tactic of "factionalism," whereby the OCE was to be used as a vehicle for reforming the PCE's ideological orientation. For Nin and Andrade, however, it was self-evident that factionalism of this sort would be ineffectual in the PCE, not only because its antidemocratic slogans and "scissionist" tactics among the labor unions had served to isolate the Party from the masses, but also because the PCE's rigidly authoritarian infrastructure was itself impervious to outside criticism. The issue of factionalism resurfaced two years later, but with more resounding implications than before. Then, Trotsky insisted that the ICE adopt the tactic developed by the French Trotskyists known as the "French turn" (later called "entryism"), by which the Party would dissolve itself and enter the PSOE as a faction. Yet Andrade and Nin were unequivocally opposed to the idea, arguing, as before, that Trotsky's strategy did not have universal applicability. Upon announcing their position on this question in *Comunismo* in September 1934, they effectively severed their official ties with Trotsky and the Left Opposition movement.

In passing it should be emphasized that although Andrade had broken with Trotsky over issues concerning strategy and tactics, he never went so far as to renounce his ideological commitment to Trotskyism. In fact, his writings throughout the 1930s reflect a deep intellectual indebtedness to Trotsky's own social and political theories. He subscribed, for instance, to the Trotskyist concept of permanent revolution. According to this, the Spanish revolution would not pass through distinct stages—as the Stalinists* maintained—but rather would be a continuous process in which the democratic and socialist revolutions would be combined. Andrade also shared Trotsky's aversion to bureaucracy, and he even dedicated a book-length study on the subject to his mentor entitled, *La burocracía reformista en el movimiento obrero* (1935).

In 1935 the ICE decided to join forces with the much larger independent Marxist party of Joaquín Maurín,* the Bloque Obrero y Campesino (BOC). The two groups formally merged in September of that year, forming the Partido Obrero de Unificación Marxista (POUM), of which Maurin was made secretary general and Andrade was chosen to preside over the Party's operations in Madrid. The next few months saw the rise of the Popular Front alliance, in which nearly every left-wing party of importance, including the POUM, participated. The Popular Front policy itself, which represented the general strategy of the Comintern after September 1935, called for collective resistance to the growing threat of fascism by means of a political alliance between the parties of the liberal segment of the bourgeoisie and the working classes, respectively. Predictably, the POUM's decision to adhere to the Popular Front provoked a venomous reply from Trotsky, who accused both Nin and Andrade of betraying the proletariat for the sake of a political alliance with the bourgeoisie. On the other hand, they defended the POUM's action on the grounds that to have done otherwise would have meant isolating the Party from the strong prodemocratic movement among the masses. In any case, during the elections of February 1936, Maurín was the only POUM candidate to win a seat in the Cortes.

Following the outbreak of civil war in July, Andrade transferred to Barcelona, the center of revolutionary activity on the Republican side, where he immediately began writing leading articles for the POUM's principal organ, *La batalla*, and also was appointed to the Party's Executive Committee. From the outset, Andrade was recognized as the leading spokesman of the left wing of the Party. Among other things he advocated the creation of a popular army organized along the lines of the Red Army in the Bolshevik Revolution. This was to be composed of people's militias—as opposed to a professional standing army—which was to be headed by Marxist-dominated soldiers' committees. Because he, like the POUM generally, believed that the war and revolution were inextricably bound up with one another, Andrade stressed that the army's primary task was to consolidate the revolutionary gains of the working classes. When it became apparent that the revolution itself was being subordinated to the war effort, Andrade's revolutionary rhetoric grew increasingly strident. By the spring of 1937, Andrade and the POUM began urgently calling for a Frente Obrero Revolutionario, or alliance among the ultra-left groupings, in the hope of restoring the proletariat's ascendancy over the course of events.

The POUM's revolutionary drive climaxed during the notorious May events of 1937. The events themselves, which revolved around the issue of the revolutionary gains in Catalonia since July 1936, involved open street fighting between the forces of revolution, as represented by the POUM and the anarchosyndicalist organizations, Confederación Nacional del Trabajo (CNT) and Federación Anarquista Ibérica (FAI), on the one side, and those who sought to roll back their movement, the Communist-controlled Partit Comunista Unificat de Catalunya (PSUC) and the middle-class republican Esquerra of Luis Companys on the other. By the seventh of May the revolutionaries had been defeated, thus bringing to an end a revolutionary process begun ten months earlier. Because the POUM was vehemently anti-Stalinist and because many of those sitting on its Executive Committee, including Nin, Andrade, and Julian Gorkin, had once been Trotskyists, the Party was vigorously persecuted by the Communists under the Negrin government. Meanwhile, an international campaign was launched by organizations such as the Independent Labour Party of Great Britain that aimed to expose the persecution of the POUM as a Communist conspiracy. Despite these efforts, though, Nin was taken to Alcala de Henares (near Madrid), where he was eventually murdered by the Communists, while Andrade and other prominent POUMists were tried as traitors in October 1938. Even though they were acquitted of treason, they received long prison terms for their role in the May events.

Andrade managed to escape from prison just days before Francoist troops occupied Barcelona. He then fled to France, where he helped to build an exile base for the POUM. Under the Vichy regime, Andrade was again persecuted by the authorities: he was convicted, without grounds, of being an agent of the Comintern and subsequently incarcerated until 1944. After the war he took up residence in Paris, where he resumed his activities as a journalist.

BIBLIOGRAPHY:

A. *China contra el imperialismo* (Madrid: Ediciones Oriente, 1928); *La burocracia reformista en el movimiento obrera* (Madrid: Ediciones Gleba, 1935); Preface in Andreu Nin, *Los problemas de la revolución española, 1931–7* (Paris: Ruedo ibérico, 1971); *Apuntes para la historia del PCE* (Barcelona: Hacer, 1979); *La revolución española día a día* (Madrid: Editiones Júcar, 1979).

B. Gerald Meaker, *The Revolutionary Left in Spain, 1914–1923* (Stanford: Stanford University Press, 1974); Andrés Suárez, *El proceso contra el POUM* (Paris: Ruedo ibérico, 1974); Francesc Bonamusa, *Andreu Nin y el moviemiento communista en España, 1930–1937* (Barcelona: Hacer, 1977); Pelai Pagés, *El moviemiento trotskista en España, 1930–1935* (Barcelona: Hacer, 1978); Pelai Pagés, *Historia del Partido Communista d'España* (Barcelona: Hacer, 1978); Ronald Fraser, *Blood of Spain* (London: A. Lane, 1979).

GEORGE R. ESENWEIN

ARAQUISTAIN, LUIS   (1886–1959). For most of his life, Luis Araquistain oscillated within a narrow political spectrum of liberalism, Fabianism, and social democracy. However, during one period of his life, from 1933 to 1937, he seemed to be turning into a major Marxist thinker. This was not a view he shared. In later life, a dedicated anti-Communist and stricken with remorse for the consequences of the leftist radicalization of which he had been the main theorist, he dismissed his activity in those years as merely playing at Marxism. Despite his own hostile verdict and without going so far as to declare Araquistain an important, original, or creative Marxist on the world stage, it is in fact difficult to exaggerate the importance of Luis Araquistain in Spain in the mid-1930s. That is, in large measure, the consequence of the general poverty of Spanish Marxism. Even more so, it is connected with the particular political circumstances of the time. Araquistain effectively became the theoretician behind the Spanish Socialist leader, Francisco Largo Caballero,* at the moment when the traditional reformism of the Partido Socialista Obrero Español was crumbling in the face of right-wing authoritarian resistance to change.

Araquistain's personal transformation from Fabian to revolutionary was largely dictated by a spell as Spanish ambassador in Berlin in 1932 and 1933. Witnessing the rise of Nazism and its appalling consequences, he became an advocate of a united working-class revolutionary response to fascism. Before that time, however, Araquistain had been an advocate of the gradualist tactics of the British Labour Party. Joining the PSOE in 1911, he came to prominence as a journalist and novelist committed to liberal and progressive causes. He argued in favor of the Western Allies in World War I; he welcomed the Russian Revolution but felt it could not be emulated elsewhere. In the 1920–21 debate in the PSOE over affiliation to the Third International,* Araquistain opposed the twenty-one conditions because of their implications for party unity. In 1921, he left the party in protest at the splits and expulsions that followed the debates. In that year, he published one of his most characteristic works, *España en el crisol* (Spain in the Melting Pot), arguing in non-Marxist terms for the PSOE to contribute to the regeneration of Spain by means of the democratic revolution. Accordingly, he greeted the British Labour government in 1924 as an example to follow.

It came as no surprise that Araquistain rejoined the Socialist Party in 1930 and even less that he greeted with great enthusiasm the establishment of the Second Republic on 14 April 1931. At that time, the Socialists were taking part in government with considerable optimism. In particular, Francisco Largo Caballero as Minister of Labor entertained hopes of being able to alleviate the misery of the workers, and especially of the rural proletariat, by means of legislation. He appointed Araquistain, who had been elected deputy for Bilbao, to be Undersecretary of Labor and Social Welfare. Probably his only effective achievement from that period was to ensure that the new Spanish Constitution had as its first clause the statement, "Spain is a Republic of Workers of all classes." Otherwise, the experience was a dispiriting one for both the minister of labor and his second-in-command. The success with which a determined and aggressive right wing blocked all attempts at reform was gradually to alter the views of both about the efficacy of Socialist participation in bourgeois democracy.

In the case of Araquistain, the catalyst was his experience in Germany. The rise of Hitler convinced him of the futility of reformist tactics. In consequence, he decided that the only choice lay between fascist or socialist dictatorship. Largo Caballero had been pushed to the same conclusion by a combination of right-wing intransigence and of the rank-and-file militance that it provoked among his followers. Thus, through the pages of the journal *Leviatán* which he founded and directed, Araquistain set about creating the theoretical bases for the practical radicalization of Largo Caballero. It was at this time that Araquistain coined the phrase "the Spanish Lenin" to describe Largo Caballero. His most serious task was to discredit the right wing of the party led by Julián Besteiro,* and this he did in a series of articles that set out to establish the relationship between capitalism in crisis and fascism, while at the same time exposing the alleged banality of Besteiro's thought on the question. Rejecting what he denounced as the "pseudo-Marxism" of Besteiro and Karl Kautsky,* Araquistain reasserted the revolutionary nature of Marxism and the temporary need for the dictatorship of the proletariat.

By the highest standards, Araquistain's many articles in *Leviatán* tended to be somewhat journalistic and were occasionally contradictory. However, they assumed enormous importance within the Spanish Socialist Party. The right in Spain had built on its success in blocking reform between 1931 and 1933 by winning the elections of November 1933 and by going on to dismantle the few social reforms carried through by the PSOE. The rank and file, which bore the brunt of rightist policies, pressed for a more revolutionary policy, and Largo Caballero, at least at a rhetorical level, took up their cause within the party. This brought him into conflict with the more moderate leadership. Araquistain was thus to be at the forefront of a power struggle within the PSOE every bit as damaging as that which divided it in 1921. The issues now were the Bolshevization of the party and the adoption of Leninist tactics. No one argued these points with greater panache than Araquistain in the pages of *Leviatán* and in the left Socialist newspaper *Claridad*.

At first, the radicalization of the PSOE carried it nearer to the Communists, but Araquistain, like Largo Caballero, opposed the popular front policy both because it involved accepting a blanket strategy imposed by Moscow and because it meant further collaboration with bourgeois liberals. Ironically, popular frontism was to bring together the Communists and the right Socialists. Although Largo Caballero accepted it finally as an electoral device, he prevented the Socialist Party from either joining or forming a popular front government and thereby fatally undermined the Second Republic in the spring of 1936. In later years, Araquistain was appalled at what he and Largo had done. Similarly, he was shattered by the way in which the Communist Party effectively took over the entire Socialist youth movement under the guise of merger in April 1936.

Within a short time of the Spanish Civil War breaking out in July 1936, Araquistain had become strongly anti-Communist, although he still considered himself to be a revolutionary. While the Communists aimed to subordinate revolution to the winning of the war and thus bend everything to the will of the Party, Araquistain denounced this as counterrevolutionism. He argued instead that the trade union should be the instrument of revolutionary war. However, by the end of the war, the ruthless imposition of Stalinism* in Spain had so embittered him that his anti-Communist articles and pamphlets made increasingly less use of Marxist categories. In exile, until his death in Geneva in 1959, he returned to the social democracy and Fabianism that had characterized his early career.

BIBLIOGRAPHY:

A. *Entre la guerra y la revolución* (Madrid: n.a., 1917); *España en el crisol* (Barcelona: Minerva, 1921); *El ocaso de un régimen* (Madrid: España, 1930); *El derrumbamiento del socialismo alemán* (Madrid: Gráfica Socialista, 1933); *El pensamiento español contemporáneo* (Buenos Aires: Losada, 1962); Paul Preston, ed., *Leviatán (antologia)* (Madrid: Turner, 1976).

B. Raúl Morodo, "Introducción al pensamiento de Luis Araquistain," *Boletín informativo de ciencia politica*, no. 7 (1971); Marta Bizcarrondo, *Leviatán y el socialismo de Luis Araquistain* (Glashütten im Tarunus: Detlev Auvermann KG, 1974); Santos Juliá, *La izquierda del PSOE* (Madrid: Siglo Veintiuno, 1977); Paul Preston, "The Struggle Against Fascism in Spain: *Leviatán* and the Contradictions of the Socialist Left, 1934–1936," *European Studies Review*, 9, no. 1 (1979); Paul Preston, *The Coming of the Spanish Civil War* (New York: Methuen, 1983).

PAUL PRESTON

ARISMENDI, RODNEY   (b. 1913). The Uruguayan Rodney Arismendi was born on the Uruguayan–Brazilian border on 22 March 1913. He was a militant in the Uruguayan Communist Party (PCU) since his early youth. Here he distinguished himself as a doctrinaire ideologue. His actions show him to be a follower of the trends of the PCU. His exaggerated loyalty to Moscow led him, toward the end of the 1930s, to support the then secretary general, Eugenio Gómez, against the so-called Trotskyist* dissidents, and, in 1955, following the Twentieth Congress of the PCU, to become the leader of a new faction, which eventually ousted Gómez. He kept his position as secretary general of the PCU thereafter. Arismendi's actions rarely violated Uruguay's system of law, an exceptional accomplishment for a Communist leader in a Third World country. For twenty-seven years, between 1946 and 1973, Arismendi was, without interruption, a national deputy from the PCU to the Uruguayan Parliament. This situation changed after 1973, when the PCU was declared illegal. He was arrested shortly thereafter by the military and sent into exile. He has resided in Moscow since 1976.

Theoretically, Arismendi has always been an orthodox Marxist-Leninist, although he adapted the official rhetoric to the specific conditions found in Uruguay. He was thus perceived as an "official," pro-Moscow Communist leader in Latin America during the 1960s, in which he energetically defended revolutionary orthodoxy against the supporters of *foquismo* and the pro-China and neo-Trotskyite variants. Many Latin Americans remember very well his famous gesture of disapproval of Fidel Castro's* words, while the other delegates applauded Castro's criticism of the Soviet Union at the OLAS in 1967.

His intellectual output includes a large number of articles, some of which were later compiled into a book, written to justify and popularize the Party's daily political activities. In 1945 he published two articles that crystallize his theoretical contributions to Marxism. In "El materialismo histórico y la evolución histórica del Uruguay" Arismendi argued that, with the emergence of Batllism in the early twentieth century, Uruguay had passed from a feudal-colonial state into capitalism. In his opinion, therefore, Batllism represented the interests of Uruguay's national bourgeoisie. That same year he published "La filosofía del marxismo y el señor Haya de la Torre," in which he refutes the theoretical positions of this precursor of modern dependency theory, who tried to "Indoamericanize" traditional Marxist-Leninism.

Following the "defenestration" of Gómez in 1955, Arismendi led the PCU onto a new path. He iterated the need for a "single front" policy, which would expand the influence of the PCU, a policy he called a "gathering of forces." His first major political achievement came in 1967, when he founded the FIDEL (Frente Izquierda de Liberación), and organized an electoral coalition that united FIDEL with Christian Democrats, Socialists, and dissidents from the Blanco and Colorado parties, among whom were some unofficial spokesmen for the Tupamaros guerrilla group. This coalition obtained 18 percent of the vote nationally, but in Montevideo over 30 percent of the vote—thus becoming a significant political force in Uruguay.

Socially, Arismendi decided to reinforce Communist influence among labor unions by broadening their input into Party policy-making. The triumph of the Cuban Revolution eroded the anti-Communist opposition in Uruguayan labor unions, which had kept the labor group divided into Communists and "autonomous," or free groups. The year 1966 brought to a culmination this process, with the labor movement now structured into a single important entity: the Convención Nacional de Trabajadores (CNT), which was preeminently Communist. Arismendi was less successful organizing Uruguayan students, who were, for the most part, more radical than the PCU. Arismendi tried to justify the need for an alliance with middle-class groups. He argued that the bourgeoisie was composed of a layer "sold to imperialism." This segment of the middle class he considered irretrievable. The bourgeoisie also consisted of a "conciliatory layer," which despite conflicts with imperialism (normally identified with the United States) in the long run would be subservient to U.S. interests. This segment, too, is part of the enemy camp. Arismendi felt, finally, that the "national" layer of the bourgeoisie was the one that could be counted on for political support. Although it was almost indistinguishable from the conciliatory layer Arismendi nonetheless rather arbitrarily considered this group a Uruguayan middle class with interests opposed to those of the United States and sought to bring them into an alliance with workers and intellectuals that would be the social basis for the political "single front." Arismendi wanted the Communists to lead this coalition first to an anti-imperialist, populist phase, and then to socialism. In this strategy Arismendi opposed those on the right (e.g. Trias†), who denied PCU hegemony, and those on the left (e.g. Trotskyites like Jorge Abelardo Ramos*), who wanted to fight the bourgeoisie. After 1968 Arismendi speculated on the desirability and possibility of peaceful revolution in Uruguay. He believed that the Uruguayan democratic tradition permitted the PCU tactical flexibility. The Tupamaros ignored the specific conditions of Uruguay and were hence adventuristic and unwise in pursuing their petit bourgeois policy of armed struggle. Despite this, Arismendi's Party, clandestinely, prepared a small war apparatus, which had to be dismantled shortly after the Party and other fronts under its control were declared illegal.

Arismendi's recent expulsion to Moscow has minimized his influence among Uruguayans.

BIBLIOGRAPHY:

A. *Problemas de una revolución continental* (Montevideo: EPU, 1970).

B. Vivian Trias, *Uruguay hoy* (Montevideo: Banda Oriental, 1973).

JUAN RIAL

ARZE, JOSÉ ANTONIO (1904–1955). The most prominent and prolific of the generation of Marxist intellectuals to emerge from the crisis caused by the Chaco War (1932–35), Arze consistently defended a Moscow-oriented strategy against strong Trotskyist* and nationalist challenges. He elaborated and spread his ideas in San Simón University, Cochabamba, which became the base of his party, the highly popular Partido de la Izquierda Revolucionaria (PIR), which never finally affiliated itself to the international Communist movement. Arze was strongly influenced by the Communist Party of Chile while in exile and as a result remained a staunch advocate of the popular front strategy. This the PIR tried to put into effect in 1946, but with disastrous results as it allied with rightist forces and lost its dominant influence in the radical labor movement that now turned toward Trotskyism. Although he dubbed the Movimiento Nacional Revolucíonario (MNR), which took power after the 1952 revolution, "Nazi-fascist," this party recognized Arze's pioneering role on the left by putting him in charge of educational reform. In fact, Arze's major contribution lay in his sociological work, which, despite its reductionism and empiricism, was the first concerted attempt at rigorous Marxist analysis produced by the Bolivian left. Arze's studies are almost encyclopedic in style and his knowledge extremely wide ranging, but despite a number of insights and the variety of sources discussed, they fail to achieve the "total analysis of society" he sought, principally because of a trenchantly functionalist method and adherence to the theory of "stages." Although his political ideas were rejected by the new Communist Party (PCB, 1950), it continues to publish his work, still the clearest espousal of orthodox communism to be produced in Bolivia.

BIBLIOGRAPHY:
A. *Hacia la unidad de las izquierdas bolivianas* (Santiago: n.a., 1938); *Sociología Marxista* (Oruro: UTO, 1963); *Escritos literarios* (La Paz: Roalva, 1980); *Polémica sobre marxismo* (La Paz: Roalva, 1980).

JAMES DUNKERLEY

AVELING, EDWARD BIBBINS   (1849–1898). Edward Aveling was born at Stoke Newington, the fourth son of a Congregational minister. He was educated at Harrow, Taunton, and the University of London, where he won medals and scholarships as a medical student and from which he received a D.Sc. in 1876. He was also named to fellowships in the Linnaean Society and at University College and teaching positions at London Hospital and Kings College, London. From his undergraduate days he coached pupils for medical and scientific examinations to earn extra money. His female students were also reputed to be the first victims of his long career as a seducer. George Bernard Shaw noted that the fortunate ones lost only their deposits; the unlucky ones, their virtue and their microscopes. Aveling's marriage to Isabell Campbell Frank in July 1872 soon broke up, but they were never divorced. From 1879, he launched into a career as a publicist and lecturer for the National Secular Society, rising meteorically to be vice president of the NSS and even forming a temporary trinity with Charles Bradlaugh and Annie Besant, which soon however turned to bitter enmity. In 1879 he also launched a significant school of science classes at the Secularist Hall of Science. From 1882 to 1884 he served as an elected member of the London School Board. He seems to have met Eleanor Marx,* youngest daughter of Karl Marx,* at the British Museum Reading Room in 1883, shortly before Marx's death. By early 1884 Aveling and Eleanor Marx had joined H. M. Hyndman's* Democratic Federation, and Aveling began to produce socialist lectures and articles, even converting some of his secularist comrades. By the summer of 1884 Aveling and Eleanor Marx had ''set up'' together in a flat in Fitzroy Street. Their union, which Eleanor regarded as a marriage in principle even if it was impossible by law, lasted fourteen years. By late December they had swung onto the anti-Hyndman majority on the SDF, led by William Morris,† which soon seceded to form the Socialist League. In the background stood Friedrich Engels,* the adopted patriarch of the Marx family connection, hostile to Hyndman, warmly paternalistic to Eleanor, or ''Tussy'' as she was known, and hence endlessly forgiving to Aveling. Aveling had the gifts of a medicine show man. He was blithely unscrupulous about finances, mercilessly exploiting unsuspecting hoteliers, friends, political hosts, and colleagues. He inspired a loathing in many who came to know him. ''Nobody can be so bad as Aveling looks,'' remarked Hyndman. One of Aveling's closest friends experienced feelings of ''horror'' and ''dread'' toward him. At intervals Aveling wrote and produced plays with modest success. In June 1897 he suddenly and secretly married a young actress with whom he had been producing road shows. When Eleanor learned of it ten months later, she resolved upon suicide. He helped her procure poison, having previously shifted her will in his favor, and then left the house until she had killed herself. He outlived her by only four months.

Aveling's significance in the history of Marxism is threefold. Although he was regarded in some quarters after Engels's death as the leading interpreter of Marxism in Britain, his Marxist writings were not theoretically significant. But first, he was the cotranslator of the first English edition of *Das Kapital*, volume 1, which appeared in 1887. He had been adopted to assist Samuel Moore when Engels learned Hyndman was working on a translation. Eleanor Marx also worked hard on the volume, looking up quotations from the Parliamentary Bluebooks in order to avoid errors in retranslation. Second, he was one of many midwives of an independent labor party in Britain. The Avelings' Bloomsbury branch was expelled from the Socialist League in 1888, but they reconstituted it as the Bloomsbury Socialist Society and remained active by agitating in London's East End and by participating in the emergence of new unionism at the time of the Dock Strike. From 1890 the Avelings began to lead successful May Day demonstrations in London for an eight-hour day, the key issue in international labor politics at that time. Aveling's Legal Eight Hours and International Labour League was tiny, but the Avelings served as valuable links between the British new unionists and continental Marxists at the foundation of the Second International* in 1890. In the face of the employers' counteroffensive in the 1890s, the Avelings kept pressing for the formation of a British labor party. They were founding members of the Independent Labour Party at the Bradford Conference of January 1893. Aveling helped draft the party program, which emphasized the eight-hour day, social welfare measures, a graduated income tax, and collective ownership of the means of production. Both were elected to the original executive committee, but they soon fell out with Keir Hardie and were expelled from the ILP in 1894. After Engels's death in 1895, they were reconciled with Hyndman and rejoined the SDF. They were important links between British Marxists and the Second International and helped organize its London congress in 1896. Third, Aveling's relationship with Eleanor Marx, whatever sustenance it may have offered her, certainly drained her energies and ultimately caused her death, just as she was contributing mightily to the labor movement from which was soon to emerge the Labour Party.

BIBLIOGRAPHY:

A. Karl Marx, *Capital: A Critical Analysis of Capitalist Production*, trans. Samuel Moore and Edward Aveling and ed. Friedrich Engels, 2 vols. (London: Sonnenschein, 1887).

B. H. Pelling, *The Origins of the Labour Party 1880–1900*, 2d ed. (Oxford: Oxford University Press, 1965); C. Tsuzuki, *The Life of Eleanor Marx 1885–1898: A Socialist Tragedy* (Oxford: Oxford University Press, 1967); E. Royle, *Radicals, Secularists and Republicans: Popular Freethought in Britain, 1866–1915* (Manchester: Manchester University Press, 1980).

JOHN BOHSTEDT

AVELING, ELEANOR MARX   (1855–1898). Eleanor Marx was born in the Dean Street, Soho (London), flat where Karl Marx's* family lived from 1850 to 1856. Eleanor was the youngest of Marx's three daughters who survived to adulthood. When her only surviving brother died at the age of eight, soon after she was born, the family transferred their whole attention to Eleanor, who grew up a much-loved child, speaking both German and English, and lapping up stories spun by her father and tales from the classics. She was her father's pet: "Tussy is me," he once declared. She had little formal schooling, but the richest of Victorian home atmospheres suffused with politics and Shakespeare. As a teenager she twice traveled to France to visit her married sister, Laura Lafargue. The second time, the Paris Commune had just been crushed, and Eleanor and Jenny, her oldest sister, were arrested and detained overnight by French border police. She attended the London and The Hague conferences of the International Working Men's Association. She met many of the Communard refugees in London, including Hippolyte Prosper Olivier Lissagaray, a French Basque twice her age, with whom she became first fascinated and then engaged. In 1873, Eleanor taught briefly at Miss Hall's boarding school for girls at Brighton, but her unsettled emotional health forced her resignation. Her father objected to Lissagaray, but allowed her to see him and work with him on political work and on his classic *L'Histoire de la Commune de 1871*, which she later translated into English at his request. She also loved the theater and hoped in vain for a career on the stage. She regularly suffered bouts of serious depression and tension between duty and independence. Shortly before her father's death, she met Edward Aveling,* and in June 1884 she began to live with him as his wife, although she could not marry him since his broken marriage had not been legally ended. She remained his loyal partner until her death, despite the unhappiness his infidelities and financial irresponsibility caused her. When she learned on 31 March 1878, that he had secretly married a young actress, she decided to end her life. She took poison and died while Aveling left the house.

Eleanor was a devoted worker for the cause of socialism, both in collaboration with Aveling and in her own efforts. She did much to keep British Marxists in touch with continental movements by her personal friendships, organizational work, and articles in a series of socialist newspapers. With Aveling, she joined H. M. Hyndman's* Democratic Federation in early 1884, but by the end of the year, they had joined William Morris† and Ernest Belfort Bax† in the anti-Hyndman faction, which seceded to form the Socialist League. She took an active interest in W. T. Stead's campaign against prostitution in 1885. In a pamphlet on *The Woman Question*, the Avelings insisted that relations between the sexes would be distorted by property and capitalist ethics until a socialist revolution took place. Henrik Ibsen's *The Doll's House* was their favorite play, and they played an important part in introducing Ibsen to the English public as part of the movement in the late Victorian theater to criticize bourgeois institutions of marriage and property. Eleanor translated Ibsen's *Enemy of the People*, as well as Flaubert's *Madame Bovary* and some Norwegian short stories. She also aided Aveling in his work on the translation of the first volume of *Capital* by looking up original quotations in the Parliamentary Bluebooks.

It was in the excitement surrounding new unionism in 1889 that Eleanor most nearly came into her own. She worked hard for the strike committee of the great Dock Strike in August and spoke effectively to crowds in Hyde Park. That autumn and the following year she also worked hard for several unions of the unskilled in East London, especially helping mobilize women strikers. She particularly considered the Gasworkers "her union." She helped their general secretary, Will Thorne, with reports and accounts and tutored him in reading and writing. She was unanimously elected to the Gasworkers' Executive Committee and drafted most of their addresses and rules, which emphasized class struggles and solidarity and the rights of women as equal participants. With Aveling, she helped organize the early May Day demonstrations for the eight-hour day in the early 1890s, and they began to work for the establishment of an independent labor party, a project also dear to Engels's* heart. She and Aveling helped in the founding of the Second International,* Eleanor serving as a translator at the early conferences. The Avelings were elected to the original executive committee of the Independent Labour Party at its formation in 1893. Although they left the ILP in 1894, they rejoined the Social Democratic Federation in 1895, after Engels's death permitted a partial reconciliation with Hyndman. Eleanor was at her most effective in taking the Socialist message directly to the workers and came to be a popular speaker. But this vigorous phase of her work was cut short by her tragic death. Her biographer, Tsuzuki, concludes that "her contribution to the Socialist movement in England would have been greater if she had not been encumbered by her husband" (*Eleanor Marx*, p. 334), both because of the personal unhappiness his depravity caused her and because his reputation continually raised personal questions that poisoned all their political relationships. Yet she did perform yeoman service for the Socialist movement both with Aveling and on her own account, and while one might wish she had liberated herself like Ibsen's Nora, instead of remaining Karl Marx's daughter, dutiful to a fault, it is just possible that such a long union may have fulfilled, even for Eleanor, some personal needs.

BIBLIOGRAPHY:

A. With Israel Zangwill, *"A Doll's House" Repaired* (London, n.d.); with E. Aveling, *The Woman Question* (London: Sonnenschein, 1886); Hippolyte Prosper Olivier Lissagaray, *History of the Commune of 1871*, trans. Eleanor Marx Aveling (London: Reeves and Turner, 1886); Henrik Ibsen, *An Enemy of Society*, trans. Eleanor Marx Aveling (London: Camelot Classics, W. Scott, 1888); *The Working Class Movement in England: A Brief Historical Sketch* (London: Twentieth Century Press, 1896); Karl Marx, *Value, Price, and Profit, Addressed to Working Men*, ed. Eleanor Marx Aveling, (London: Sonnenschein, 1898).

B. C. Tsuzuki, *The Life of Eleanor Marx 1855–1898: A Socialist Tragedy* (Oxford: Oxford University Press, 1967).

JOHN BOHSTEDT

B

BAGÚ, SERGIO   (b. 1911). A renowned historian born and educated in Argentina, Sergio Bagú is also known for his early exposition of ideas about the relationship of the advanced capitalist nations to backward colonial areas. He taught for a number of years at the University of Buenos Aires while writing biographies on José Ingenieros and Mariano Moreno and studies of the economy of colonial society and of social structure of the colony. Writers of dependency often refer to Bagú as a precursor to their ideas during the 1960s.

During the middle 1940s Bagú developed his interpretation of colonial history while lecturing at U.S. universities. His central thesis was that capitalism had established itself early during the colonial period in Latin America, when Europe had dominated the international markets and shaped the structure of the colonial economies. He argued that the European metropolis would promote economic dependency of the colonies and that the feudal cycle of many parts of Europe was not particularly strong in the Iberian peninsula and therefore was unable to reproduce itself in Latin America.

He analyzed the elements of capitalism in terms of the accumulation of capital, financial capital, production for market, and commerce. He identified merchant capital in the mines of Mexico as early as the middle of the sixteenth century, and he showed that finance capital was in evidence at that time in credit arrangements among miners, merchants, large farmers, and slave traders.

BIBLIOGRAPHY:

A. *Economía de la sociedad colonial: ensayo de historia comparada de América Latina* (Buenos Aires: El Alteneo, 1949); *Argentina en el mundo* (Buenos Aires: Fondo de Cultura Económica, 1960); *El desarrollo cultural en la liberación de América Latina* (Montevideo: Centro Estudiantes de Derecho, Biblioteca de Cultura Universitaria, 1967); *Evolución histórica de la estratificación social en la Argentina* (Caracas: Instituto de Investigaciones Económicas y Sociales, 1969); *Argentina 1875–1975: Poplación, Economía, Seciedad, Estudio temático y bibliográfico* (Mexico City: Universidad Nacional Autónoma de México, 1978).

RONALD H. CHILCOTE

BALIÑO, CARLOS B.   (1848–1926). The first Cuban Marxist to attain national recognition, Carlos B. Baliño was brought up in a revolutionary tradition by his father Carlos J. Baliño, a strong opponent of Spanish colonialism. After working with Cuba's laboring masses, especially the tobacco workers, he traveled to the United States, where he affiliated with Samuel Gompers and the workers movement and wrote for various newspapers on Cuban liberation and the abolition of imperialism.

Baliño and nonsocialist José Martí founded the Cuban Revolutionary Party in 1892. After the Spanish-American War, he tried to popularize the idea that the break with Spain had not brought independence to Cuba since the United States dominated the island. In 1903 he organized the Socialist Propaganda Club, the first group to propagate formally Marxist ideas in Cuba. He remained active in the Socialist movement until 1925, when he, along with Julio Antonio Mella,* founded Cuba's Communist Party, which strove to abrogate the Platt Amendment inserted in Cuba's constitution at the end of the Spanish-American War at the insistence of the United States and which gave the latter the right to intervene in Cuban affairs.

Baliño's most significant written work *Verdades socialistas* (Socialist Truths) claimed art and literature for all, not just the privileged, stated that moral decay came from the system and could not be eliminated by reforms, condemned the idea of social evolution as contributing to people's willingness to accept their fate or to have faith, maintained that equality of conditions was not designed to strip people of individuality or to regulate their actions, and expressed a belief in the effectiveness of strikes in bringing justice to workers. The pamphlet, published in 1905, was the most articulate plea by a Cuban Marxist to that time and effectively related the plight of Cuba's laborers to that of their international comrades.

BIBLIOGRAPHY:

A. *Documentos de Carlos Baliño* (Havana: Departamento Collección Cubana de la Biblioteca Nacional José Martí, 1964); *Apuntes históricos sobre sus actividades revolucionarias* (Havana: Partido Comunista de Cuba, 1967); *Documentos y artículos* (Havana: Instituto de Historia del Movemiento Communista y de la Revolución Socialista de Cuba, 1976).

                                                                                    SHELDON B. LISS

BARAN, PAUL A.   (1910–1964). Paul Baran was born in Nikolaev, Russia, in 1910, but his family moved to Vilna (Poland) in 1921, and Baran remained a Polish citizen until he became a naturalized American during World War II. While his family returned to what was now the Soviet Union, Baran was finishing his gymnasium studies in Germany, where he joined the youth organization of the German Communist Party (KPD). In 1926 he studied economics in Moscow, but returned to Berlin two years later. By 1930 he left the KPD, disagreeing with the "Third Period" policy, and joined the Social-Democratic Party (SPD). He did research at the Frankfurt Institute for Social Research, working under F. Pollock†; he met R. Hilferding* and wrote for the latter's journal, *Die Gesellschaft*. Baran left Germany in 1933 for the Soviet Union but was expelled two years later; after a few years of work in a family business in Poland he went to the United States, where he remained the rest of his life. Following graduate work at Harvard, Baran worked successively for the Brookings Institution, the Office of Price Administration, and as a specialist on German, Soviet, and Polish affairs for the OSS. After the war he worked (under J. K. Galbraith) for the U.S. Strategic Bombing Survey in Germany and Japan. After a stint at the Commerce Department, he went to the New York Federal Reserve Bank. In 1949 he joined the Economics Department at Stanford University, where he taught until his death in 1964.

Baran was described, during his last fifteen years, as "probably the only Marxian social scientist teaching at a large American university." He made no secret of his political and theoretical convictions and was certainly fairly isolated within American academia at that time of cold war (although he was invited to serve as a consultant to the Rand Corporation during this time). In Paul Sweezy,* however, he found the closest of colleagues, politically and theoretically. Baran was closely associated with Sweezy's journal *Monthly Review* from its founding in 1949, and his last work, *Monopoly Capital*, which was to have an enormous impact on the new left not only in the United States but around the world, was written with Sweezy.

Baran's book *The Political Economy of Growth* (1957), contained most of the themes later developed in *Monopoly Capital*, in the earlier book presented as facets of a comprehensive political ideology. Baran's Marxism made no real use of Marx's theory of value or of the theory of accumulation and crisis deduced from it, but (as the title of his book suggests) combined elements of the neo-classical price theory of "imperfect competition" with the national income analysis of classical political economy. As with the latter, Baran raised the question of the causes and limits of economic growth, and his answer, starting from the distribution of income between labor and capital, focused on the use made by the latter of their share.

Baran's key concept was that of the "surplus," with which he replaced Marx's focus on surplus value. This concept had a double sense: as a measure, first, of the social product in excess of social consumption; and by way of its extension to the idea of the "potential surplus," as a measure of unused potential for production. Baran argued that while the competitive capitalism of the nineteenth century had fostered rapid growth of investment and so of national income, the restriction of output characteristic of monopoly leads to a slowdown in investment and a consequent need to "absorb" the redundant surplus in various forms of waste production, from advertising to war production. Thus monopoly capitalism is a system in stagnation.

With this Baran introduced a new idea within Marxist theories of imperialism, which had hitherto seen capitalism as a dynamic global system, with the currently underdeveloped countries doomed—in the absence of socialist revolution—to follow the example set by the developed. Given the domination of the world economy by the latter and their current condition of stagnation, Baran argued, the nations of the Third World will be prevented from experiencing the "competitive period" that makes growth possible. For them, as for the dominant capitalist areas, further liberation of the productive capacities of modern industry is possible only with socialism.

"Socialism" for Baran meant statist economic planning, and—despite his personal distance from the parties of the Third International*—Stalinist* Russia and Eastern Europe remained exemplary for him. Despite Stalin's personal excesses, his policy (utilization of agricultural surplus to build heavy industry) was the only correct path to an economic development on a worldwide scale sufficient for an eventual reduction of the hours of work and increase in material consumption.

Baran's prediction of a stagnant world economy was not borne out by the history of "monopoly capitalism," as the postwar period saw both a tremendous expansion of capitalism—in developed and underdeveloped areas alike—and a renewal of cutthroat competition on an international scale as this boom came to an end in the 1970s. His importance at the present time lies not so much in his analysis of modern capitalism as in his direction of attention to the analysis of the special conditions of underdeveloped countries and to the forces preventing their economic growth.

BIBLIOGRAPHY:

A. *The Political Economy of Growth* (New York: Monthly Review Press, 1957); *Marxism and Psychoanalysis*, Monthly Review Pamphlet, no. 14 (New York: Monthly Review Press, 1960); *Reflections of the Cuban Revolution*, Monthly Review Pamphlet, no. 18, (New York: Monthly Review Press, 1961); with Paul Sweezy, *Monopoly Capital* (New York: Monthly Review Press, 1966).

B. P. H. Sweezy and Leo Huberman, eds., *Paul Baran 1910–1964: A Collective Portrait* (New York: Monthly Review Press, 1965); Anthony Brewer, *Marxist Theories of Imperialism* (London: Routledge and Kegan Paul, 1980).

PAUL MATTICK, JR.

BARBUSSE, HENRI   (1873–1935). Born on the outskirts of Paris in 1873, Henri Barbusse followed the profession of his father, a journalist of rural origins, until 1914, during which time he published one light novel, *Les Suppliants*, and one more serious work, *L'Enfer*. He fought in World War I, joined the Socialist Party in 1916, and in the same year published his condemnation of war and its class injustices, *Le Feu*. The book was a striking antiwar success in a jingoistic age and gave Barbusse the moral leadership of pacifist left-wing youth. He used this authority to influence his fellow intellectuals toward pacifism and the Bolshevik Revolution. In May 1919 he wrote his famous appeal for the formation of an International de la Pensée and founded the journal *Clarté*.* The journal and its supporting group were named after the second of his war novels, in which he argued for a new type of proletarian justice based on the "rule of numbers." Although Barbusse left *Clarté* in 1923 because he felt it was too narrowly Communist and published *Les Enchainements*, which dealt almost exclusively with oppression, he remained a member of the French Communist Party (PCF).

After this he became increasingly active, becoming literary editor of *L'Humanité* in 1926 and publishing *Jésus* in 1927; a book which portrayed Christ as an early communist. A year later he founded the weekly *Le Monde*, which took a strong class struggle line, although it mellowed toward its end in 1935. In 1930 he attended the International Writers Conference at Kharkov, where he was attacked for bourgeois sentiments. He published a fairly orthodox critique of Zola in 1932 and organized the first world conference of intellectuals for peace at Amsterdam in the same year. Paul Vaillant-Coutourier,* Rolland, Gide, and he founded the Association of Revolutionary Writers, with its journal *Commune*, in 1932, and two years later he organized the second intellectuals' peace conference in Paris at the Salle Pleyel. The Amsterdam-Pleyel movement became an influential left-wing movement in Europe and provided a platform for the launching of the Popular Front in France. He died in 1935, just before the triumph of the Popular Front, which embodied his twin concepts of peace and mass mobilization for social justice. His ideas on Marxism fluctuated wildly during the interwar period, but he was immensely influential through his antiwar novels and his organization of the peace campaign.

BIBLIOGRAPHY:

A. *Under Fire* (New York: Dutton, 1917); *La Lueur dans l'abîme* (Paris: Clarté, 1920); *Light* (New York: Dutton, 1929).

B. J. Freville and J. Duclos, *Henri Barbusse* (Paris: Sociales, 1949); A. Vidal, *Henri Barbusse, soldat de la paix* (Paris: François Reunis, 1953); V. Brett, *Henri Barbusse, sa marche vers la Clarté, son mouvement Clarté* (Prague: Czech Academy of Sciences, 1963); N. Guessler, "Henri Barbusse and His 'Monde' (1928–35): Progeny of the Clarté Movement and the Review *Clarté*," *Journal of Contemporary History*, 11 (1976), pp. 173–97.

JOHN C. SIMMONDS

BARTRA, ROGER (b. 1940). Roger Bartra took the Ph.D. in sociology from the University of Paris. He is currently a researcher with the Institute for Social Research of the National University of Mexico and is a member of the Unified Socialist Party of Mexico. He was also a cofounder of the important Marxist journal, *Historia y sociedad*. Bartra's chief contributions to the development of Marxist thought are in two areas: his critical testing and elaboration of "the Asiatic mode of production"; and his equally critical and trenchant application of Marxism to the contemporary rural sector. In the first case, Bartra takes as his critical point of departure what he seems to see as a still dominant conceptualization within Marxism of the Asiatic mode of production. This concept refers to a "non-Western" social formation characterized by (1) the absence of private property, (2) the presence of economically self-sufficient village communities based on agriculture and handicrafts, (3) the despotic presence of a wholly dominant state authority based in an urban center, (4) the enforced payment of tribute from the rural sector to this urban center, and (5) the enforced dependence of this rural sector as a result of inimical geographical and climatic conditions, which necessitate irrigation and therefore large-scale hydraulic works, which only such a centralized state apparatus can construct and administer. For Marx,* Engels,* and much of later Marxist analyses, these features are found usually in Eastern and Middle Eastern societies, although the concept is also applied to Spain and pre-Columbian America.

At least three controversial points emerge within Marxism from this concept. First, there is the implication that, in contrast to the West, such societies are stagnant given the absence of the fundamental Marxist "motor of history," e.g., private property, class relations of production, and a disequilibrium between technology, nature, and production. Second, such societies are aberrations in the otherwise conventional Marxist transitions of history (slave, feudal, capitalist, etc.), and finally, the absence of any internal class conflict in these societies requires the need for an external imperialist/colonial intervention to restore them to a "proper" historical course.

Bartra sets out a revisionist position with respect to the basic tenets of the dominant sense of the Asiatic mode of production and is in disagreement with its implications, particularly the question of a paradoxical need for an external colonial force. His general critical position is best set out in his introductory essay and in the articles by various authors in his edited volume on this question (1969). However, he has also discussed the concept in an intriguing, if hypothetical, set of suggestions concerning the rise and the mysterious fall of the pre-Columbia city of Teotihuacan near what is now Mexico City during the years 200 B.C. to A.D. 700 (1975). Here we can find an exemplified statement of his revisionist stance. After setting out the archeological evidence, which at first glance defines this ancient city as an example of the Asiatic mode of production, Bartra offers a hypothetical reconstruction of its otherwise mysterious fall. He suggests that by focusing on the likely relations of production rather than environmental/climatic factors and on a ruling class that used an ideology of religion, we can understand the development of this city from a primitive agrarian economy to a society structured by despotic domination and tribute payment. By the same hypothetical analyses, he also posits the notion of an increasingly oppressed rural sector and a food crisis leading to "the first urban revolution in Meso-America." The chief upshot of both his theoretical and his historically grounded analyses is to question the dominant understanding of "Asian" societies as stagnant, requiring the need for external intervention.

Yet it is important to note that the principal active agent in Bartra's nonstatic hypothetical portrait of Teotihuacan is that ancient city's rural sector, its protopeasantry, for this sectorial concern continues in Bartra's work on the rural populace of today. He develops this concern with ethnographic and sociological data drawn largely from Mexico, although in his most seminal statement he suggests that his observations "may be generalized for Latin America and for some countries of the so-called Third World" (*Estructura agraria y clases sociales en México*, p. 14). In this work on contemporary Mexico, Bartra seems to have two principal concerns. First, he seriously questions the official ideology and practice of postrevolutionary Mexico, particularly in regard to its agrarian reform program. Bartra contends that the official policy of creating some government-owned communal lands for the Mexican peasantry disguises the increasing pauperization of those peasants and the ever expanding landless rural proletariat, which forms a reserve labor pool for both the rural and urban bourgeoisie (*ibid.*, pp. 22–52). Further, he takes issue with Marxist analysts like Rodolfo Stavenhagen,† who developed a seeming class analysis of Mexican rural society by using a model that establishes class stratification and presumably levels of exploitation on the basis of ownership of land (ibid.).

Thus, according to Bartra, it becomes possible for Stavenhagen to imply that small landholding peasants are, in some meaningful measure, "better off" than the landless rural proletariat. For Bartra *all* are in a proletarian state and are exploited in the capitalist relations of production that were historically formed in Mexico, regardless of their relationship to land. It is precisely this mystified relationship to land and the lack of focus on the relationship to capital that both misleads Stavenhagen and is used by the Mexican bourgeoisie to maintain its power.

BIBLIOGRAPHY:

A. *El modo de producción asiático: antología de textos sobre problemas de la historia de los paises coloniales* (Mexico City: Era, 1969); *Estructura agraria y clases sociales en México* (Mexico City: Era, 1974); *Marxismo y sociedades antignas* (Mexico City, Grijalbo, 1975).

JOSÉ LIMON

BASSOLS, NARCISO (1897–1959). Mexican law professor Narciso Bassols wrote on government organization, education, sociology, economics, and the philosophy of law. During the 1930s he collaborated with Vicente Lombardo Toledano* in running the socialist magazine *Futuro* and in founding the publishing firm Editorial Revolucionario. He also helped refugees from the Spanish Civil War get into Mexico, where many of them became mainstays of the country's liberal and left-wing intelligentsia. To help regenerate the Mexican Revolution, in the 1940s he became publisher of the periodical *Combate*, which defended the interests of Mexicans against foreign exploitation. By 1951 he considered Mexico's social and economic progress at a halt and helped found the socialist Partido Popular to restimulate the revolution that he felt was falling into the hands of the United States and to offset the Organization of American States' 1947 Rio Treaty of Reciprocal Assistance, which he believed put Latin America under a United States-led anti-Communist alliance.

Bassols served Mexico as Minister to Great Britain, France, and the Soviet Union, Minister of Interior, Minister of Treasury and Public Credit, and Minister of Education. As head of the Ministry of Education under Lázaro Cárdenas's government, he began a program of socialized education in order to free young Mexicans from the influence of the Church and to teach "scientific truth" in the schools. His educational program furthered the doctrine of equal distribution of wealth and took education away from clerical control.

He called Mexico's Indians the backbone of the agrarian sector and the primary cultural component of Mexican society. He believed that by preserving the Indians' spiritual structure, while initiating scientific technology, Mexico could foster a social revolution. He conceived agrarian legislation containing a magnificent defense of the juridical rights of labor, including Indians, based on Mexico's historical conditions. He supported the *ejido* (collective farm) as a control unit in Mexican life, a core from which emanated a sense of political, economic, and social unity. He pushed for transferral of the means of production from the landed aristocracy and foreign companies to the rural workers. His thoughts contributed significantly to the progressive land reforms of the Cárdenas administration (1934–40).

BIBLIOGRAPHY:

A. *Obras* (Mexico City: Fondo de Cultura Económica, 1964).

SHELDON B. LISS

BASU, JYOTI   (b. 1913). Born in India, Jyoti Basu is known primarily for his many-sided elaboration in practice (although not in theory) of a combination of Communist parliamentary and extraparliamentary political tactics aimed at establishing a seemingly indestructible Communist control over some of the levers of state-level political power in West Bengal (India). A pioneer in such politics in India since 1945, and still its most successful exemplar in 1984, Basu was elevated to the Central Committee of the Communist Party of India (CPI) for the first time in June 1950, resigned in December 1950, but rejoined in April 1951. He has been a member of the Central Committee and Politburo of the Communist Party of India (Marxist) (CPI[M]) since its foundation in 1964.

Initially distrustful of parliamentary politics as the politics of the "bourgeois talking-shops," Basu contested and barely won his first parliamentary election to the Bengal Legislative Assembly of colonial India. His intent was to extend and legitimize Communist control over a trade union in a reserved constituency of railway workers. He ran again in the first elections in the Indian subcontinent after independence in 1951. This time, too, his involvement in bourgeois parliamentary politics was primarily due to some "other" interests, i.e., reorganizing the Communist Party in West Bengal, which had been weakened organizationally by bitter internecine conflict in 1948–49 but had extended its mass political influence (which was fully capitalized in the Communist electoral successes in the 1951 elections). But by now he was a firm believer in Lenin's* recommendation that Communists must contest bourgeois elections to serve as tribunes of the people in order to expose parliamentary "cretinism" from within, so as to prepare the masses for participation in revolutionary antiparliamentary politics. Since then, more fully than any other Indian Communist, Basu has explored the scope as well as the limits of such a combination of Communist parliamentary with extraparliamentary political tactics. But because of grim and unanticipated political events involving clashes of almost equal severity with Congress "enemies," left party "allies," as well as explosive "Naxalite" Communist dissent originating within a newly formed CPI(M) in the 1960s and 1970s, these tactics have produced a bizarre outcome.

Over the years, the more effectively the West Bengali Communists exposed the parliamentary system from within and from without, the more decisively did the West Bengali highly politicized voter vote for them. But there was no matching advance of the Communist parliamentary and/or extraparliamentary presence in the rest of India, where (except in Tripura and perhaps in Kerala) there was a recession of whatever Communist political influence had existed. The result was that by 1983 the West Bengali Communists were the encircled but semipermanent political managers of a capitalist economy in West Bengal, which was a less developing fraction of an unevenly developing but dependent Indian capitalist economy. There are several causes of West Bengal's low rate of capitalist development. First, there is the extensive damage caused by the policies of successive central governments of the all-India bourgeoisie, which have led to a drain of reinvestible resources from West Bengal. This drain has been caused by its tax measures and also by statutory all-India price differentials, which have deprived West Bengal of its comparative advantage in coal and engineering products. On the other hand, denial to West Bengal of its due share of foreign aid received by the central government, and deficit spending by it, has weakened the West Bengal government's fiscal powers. Second, multinational and Indian monopoly concerns have shown, apparently on grounds of political realism, only minimal interest in investment in West Bengal, despite public overtures by Basu (acting on behalf of the West Bengal ministry as well as the central leadership of the CPI(M). These overtures have been made to them on the basis of the doctrine that until capitalist monopolies are eliminated everywhere in India, West Bengal under Communist control will compete with the bourgeois governments of other Indian states to attract them. Third, the CPI(M)'s "democratic" rich peasant bourgeois "allies" in West Bengal probably habitually reinvest less out of their profits as compared to the "democratic" rich peasant bourgeoisies of other Indian states. Fourth, repeated though somewhat half-hearted appeals have been made by Basu and others to the civil employees of the West Bengal government to step up production as a token of political support for their own government. But they have not agreed to do so—not even the workers and employees belonging to the CPI(M) or the trade unions led by it.

ARUN BOSE

BESTEIRO, JULIAN   (1870–1940). At least until the Civil War, and in some circles even to the present day, Julián Besteiro was considered to be Spain's leading theoretical Marxist. That inflated judgment rested largely on two things. First of all, Besteiro was a distinguished academic philosopher, holding the Chair of Logic at Madrid University, and as such he was one of the very few intellectuals in the prewar Spanish Socialist movement. Secondly, he was between 1925 and 1933 president of both the Partido Socialista Obrero Español and of the Unión General de Trabajadores. From those positions, he played an important role in numerous crucial debates, consistently basing his arguments on what he presented as the tenets of classical Marxism. However, few if any of his pronouncements extended beyond what is broadly known as Kautskyism,* and none could be classified as creative or original Marxism.

In his early life, Besteiro was a positivist in academic terms and a liberal republican in political life. He joined the Madrid Socialist group in 1912 and quickly became president of the union of professionals affiliated to the UGT. He became nationally famous in 1917 during the revolutionary general strike of that year, was imprisoned, and then, in the following year, elected to the Spanish Parliament as a deputy for Madrid. Thereafter, his positions became progressively less radical. During the debates on affiliation to the Third International,* he argued convincingly against acceptance of the twenty-one conditions and, without condemning the Soviet experience, postulated the inapplicability to Spain of the dictatorship of the proletariat.

In 1923 he won a scholarship to go to England to do research on the Workingmen's Educational Association. His time there in 1924 confirmed his incipient reformism, and he returned to Spain a convinced Fabian. In the meanwhile, Spain had been subjected to the military dictatorship of General Primo de Rivera. The Socialist movement was deeply divided over the issue of how to respond to the new regime. While there was broad agreement that it would be foolish to sacrifice the movement in any attempt to reestablish the corrupt monarchy, there were bitter polemics over the dictator's offer of collaboration in his labor machinery. While some PSOE leaders argued that the party should join the democratic opposition against the dictator, Besteiro successfully propounded collaboration. He used the argument that was to be the central plank of his political thought. From the premise that Spain was still a semifeudal country awaiting a bourgeois revolution, he erected a logic of apparent revolutionary purity, concluding that it was not the job of the Spanish working class to do the work of the bourgeoisie. In the meanwhile, the working class should take advantage of the opportunity offered by the dictator to build up its own strength.

This argument was persuasive and combined with the readiness of the trade union bureaucracy to reap the benefits of having a monopoly of state labor affairs. However, when the regime became increasingly unpopular in the economic downturn at the end of the 1920s, opinion within the PSOE turned against Besteiro. When antidictatorial opposition grew into a massive republican movement, which swept away the monarchy in the municipal elections of 12 April 1931, Besteiro was in a small minority in arguing against Socialist participation in the new regime. With the bulk of the movement anxious to use state power to introduce basic reforms, Besteiro's line that the working class should not be the cannon fodder of the bourgeoisie fell on deaf ears. At the Thirteenth Congress of the PSOE in October 1932, he lost the presidency of the party, although the use of the block votes of his supporters kept him the presidency of the UGT at its Seventeenth Congress.

In fact, the rank and file of the Socialist movement was moving rapidly away from the positions advocated by Besteiro. Right-wing intransigence radicalized the grass-roots militants, and the conclusion drawn by an influential sector of the leadership under Francisco Largo Caballero* was that the Socialists should get more rather than less control of the government. Besteiro continued to argue in virtually Menshevik terms that this could only be achieved by the unacceptable imposition of a Socialist dictatorship and that the movement should wait until the bourgeois stage of Spanish history had been exhausted. Such quietism in the name of strict classical Marxism earned him only an accusation of being a Kautskyist traitor to the movement.

Accordingly, he opposed the Socialist part in the revolutionary insurrection of October 1934, as a consequence of which his house was stoned by enraged members of the Socialist youth. Thereafter, the radicalizers or self-styled "Bolshevizers" within the party saw their first task as to destroy Besteiro's reputation. Their opportunity came in the spring of 1935. On 28 April, at a time when thousands of his comrades were in jail, Besteiro accepted entry into the Academy of Moral and Political Sciences with a speech on "Marxism and Anti-Marxism." This gave rise to a series of sarcastic articles by Luis Araquistain* in the journal *Leviatán*, which effectively undermined his standing within the party hierarchy. However, his popularity remained undiminished, and in the Popular Front elections of February 1936 he won the highest number of votes of any candidate in Madrid.

During the Spanish Civil War, Besteiro confirmed that popularity by refusing numerous opportunities to seek a safe exile. He was assiduous in the performance of his duties as a municipal councilor and turned down the offer of the Spanish Embassy in Argentina. He worked hard to bring about an early peace settlement, making various efforts during the coronation of George VI in London, at which he was Spanish representative. In early 1939 he joined the anti-Communist National Defense Junta of Colonel Casado in the hope of being able to seek an armistice. When Franco refused, Besteiro was one of the few senior political figures to choose to stay with his constituents rather than escape. He was tried by the Nationalists and imprisoned. He died of untreated blood poisoning in Carmona prison on 27 September 1940. The dignity and humanity of his behavior during the Civil War period have ensured that he is the most revered figure of Spanish socialism and perhaps explain the continuing interest in his thought.

BIBLIOGRAPHY:

A. Andrés Saborit, ed., *El pensamiento político de Julián Besteiro* (Madrid: Seminarios y Ediciones, 1974).

B. Andrés Saborit, *Julián Besteiro* (Buenos Aires: Losada, 1967); Marta Bizcarrondo, "Julián Besteiro: socialismo y democracia," *Revista de Occidente*, no. 94 (January 1971); Alberto Miguez, *El pensamiento filosófico de Julián Besteiro* (Madrid: Taurus, 1971); Emilio Lamo de Espinosa, *Filosofía y política en Julián Besteiro* (Madrid: Edicusa, 1973);

Ignacio Arenillas de Chaves, *El proceso de Besteiro* (Madrid: Revista de Occidente, 1976); Paul Preston, *The Coming of the Spanish Civil War* (New York: Methuen, 1983).

PAUL PRESTON

BISHOP, MAURICE RUPPERT   (1944–1983). Maurice Bishop was born 29 May 1944, in Grenada, West Indies. He attended secondary school in Grenada and later studied law at Gray's Inn in England during the 1960s. While in England, he was very active in the West Indian Students' Union. In 1970, Bishop returned home to Grenada after participating in the black power revolt in Trinidad. After his return, he opposed the government of Eric Gairy, the Grenadian who led the island to independence from Great Britain. In 1973, Bishop—together with Unison Whiteman, Sebastian Thomas, and other disgruntled Grenadians— formed the New Jewel Movement (NJM). This organization brought together several opposition political groups, including Whiteman's, which had been called JEWEL (Joint Endeavor for Welfare, Education, and Liberation). Although the fairness of elections during the 1970s has been questioned, the NJM failed to win an electoral majority during that decade. On 13 March 1979, faced with a reported threat of imprisonment and execution, Bishop and some forty other members of the New Jewel Movement revolted against the Gairy government. The Gairy regime collapsed the next day, and Bishop served as prime minister of Grenada until his death on 19 October 1983, at the hands of rivals within the New Jewel Movement.

Bishop's political philosophy drew heavily upon the Caribbean, African, and global events of the 1960s. As a student in London, he followed with great interest the struggle for independence among many African states and the civil rights movement in the United States. The writings of Nkrumah, Castro,* Guevara,* Malcolm X, and Franz Fanon† influenced him greatly. During the 1970s, Bishop watched closely the fate of Salvador Allende* in Chile and Michael Manley in Jamaica and felt that their experiences had much to teach the future leaders of Grenada. Bishop and his followers always called themselves socialists. Yet Bishop's attention after gaining power focused more on the problems of governing than on political theory. As a result, Bishop's principles reflected an eclectic mixture of ideas prominent among many political movements, particularly those on the left.

Bishop supported Third World solidarity and argued that the Eastern Bloc offered more to countries like Grenada than did the West, especially more than did the United States. Bishop did not support free elections or a critical press in Grenada, asserting that these institutions could be destructive for a country going through the early stages of a political revolution. His major concern as Grenada's prime minister was economic issues. For Bishop the state had to play a major, although not exclusive, role in reorganizing the island's dependent economy. Through the means of state farms and rural cooperatives, Bishop hoped to stimulate agricultural production, employment, and import substitution. Reducing Grenada's high rate of illiteracy was also a principal target of Bishop's government, and he borrowed extensively from the Cuban experience under Castro to eradicate it. Although tourism traditionally loomed large in Grenada's economy, Bishop tried to restructure this business in order to lessen Grenada's dependence upon affluent white tourists and to ensure that more vacation dollars remained in Grenada. To a great extent, Bishop viewed Cuba as the most appropriate model for Grenada to follow.

BIBLIOGRAPHY:

A. "Revolution in Grenada: An Interview with Maurice Bishop," *The Black Scholar*, 11 (January-February 1980), pp. 50-58.

B. W. Richard Jacobs and Ian Jacobs, *Grenada: The Route to Revolution* (Havana: Casa de las Americas, 1980).

JAMES A. LEWIS

BLAGOEV, DIMITUR   (1855–1924). Dimitur Blagoev holds the distinction of forming the first known Marxist group in tsarist Russia and creating the Communist Party of Bulgaria. Born in 1855 in what is today Greek Madeconia, Blagoev entered a seminary in Odessa in 1878, transferring to the University of St. Petersburg three years later. Already active in radical politics, Blagoev organized the first Russian social democratic group that same year. Two years later, in 1885, Blagoev returned to Bulgaria, publishing, in 1891, his first book (*What Is Socialism and Do We Have a Basis for It*), which introduced Marxist thought to the Bulgarian intelligentsia. Forming the first Bulgaria Social Democratic Party in 1891, Blagoev in 1903 reorganized his followers along lines suggested by Lenin,* creating the so-called Narrows (Tesnyaki) in the image of the Bolsheviks. In 1919 the Narrows took the name of the Communist Party of Bulgaria and received a quarter of the parliamentary vote that same year. In 1923 the Bulgarian Agrarian Party captured the majority of parliamentary votes, with the Bulgarian Communists registering only about one-third their 1919 total. In May 1924 Blagoev died, at a time when the fortunes of his party were at a low ebb. Not until 1947 would the Bulgarian Communist Party, in the presence of Soviet troops of occupation, gain power.

BIBLIOGRAPHY:

A. *Suchineniia* (Collected Works) (Sofia: Bulgarska Komunisticheska Partiia, 1957–64).

B. Joseph Rothschild, *The Communist Party of Bulgaria: Origins and Development, 1883–1936* (New York: Columbia University Press, 1959); Khristo Kristov and Kiril Vasilev, *Dimitur Blagoev: A Biographical Sketch* (Sofia: Bulgarska Komunisticheska Partiia, 1960).

MICHAEL BOLL

BLANCO GALDOS, HUGO   (b. 1935). Born in 1935 in Cuzco, Peru, of middle-class and socially active parents, Hugo Blanco in 1954 went to Argentina to study agronomy at the University of La Plata. Here he joined the Trotskyist* movement. Returning in 1956 to Lima, Peru, he worked in a textile factory and joined the Revolutionary Workers Party (POR), a Trotskyite group of the Peruvian section of the Fourth International. Sent by POR to Cuzco in 1958 to organize peasants, he began work as a tenant farmer. Because of his efforts, the number of peasant syndicates in the valley of La Convención grew from 6 in 1958 to about 132 in 1962. Hugo Blanco emphasized the establishment of schools, health clinics, and cooperatives to politicize the peasants and the use of strikes and the occupying of land to increase peasant power. In 1961 Blanco created FIR (Frente de Izquierda Revolucionaria) to extend the power of the syndicates. On 13 November 1962 Blanco organized and led a movement to protect a peasant who had threatened a landowner who had raped the peasant's daughter. In an exchange of gunfire a national guardsman was wounded. Increased guerrilla action in the region and continued violent occupation of land brought government intervention and eventual capture of Blanco on 29 May 1963. From 1963 to 1966 Blanco was held without trial in prison. Eventually brought before a military court, he was convicted of killing two members of the National Guard and sentenced to death. A worldwide defense campaign saved his life and the sentence was changed to twenty-five years, on the island prison of El Frontón. It was at El Frontón that he wrote *Land or Death*, which spelled out his theory of revolution. In December 1970 General Juan Velasco Alvarado declared a general amnesty for political prisoners and released Blanco in hope of obtaining increased credibility for his land reform program. Although much of the left supported the Velasco regime, Blanco refused to do so, advising the peasants to take advantage of the reforms but not to trust the regime. The reforms took land from large owners and compensated them, but it put agricultural production under government bureaucracy rather than peasant leadership. As a result of strikes and demonstrations, the government deported Hugo Blanco in 1971, and again in 1973, 1976, and 1978, and he took refuge in Mexico, Sweden, Chile, and Argentina, respectively. Increased popular dissatisfaction caused the military regime to call for a constitutional assembly election in June 1978. In December 1977, Parti Socialista Trabajadores (PST), Blanco's political party, joined with several small Trotskyite groups, some trade unions, peasant organizations, and a number of independent socialists to organize the Workers, Peasants, Students, and People's Front (FOCEP). From Jujuy, Argentina, Blanco, in exile, campaigned by mail and tape recordings for a seat in the General Assembly. Successful in his political campaign, he returned to Peru on 16 July 1978. In the election of 1978, leftist parties received almost 30 percent of the vote. FOCEP alone received more than 12 percent, owing to the huge vote for Blanco. Over 280,000 Peruvians cast ballots for him, giving him more than any other candidate of the left and the highest total among 1,200 candidates. In addition to Blanco, eleven other FOCEP candidates were elected, making it the third strongest group in the Assembly. Blanco's electoral success came despite his absence from the country, a ban on leftist campaign propaganda, and literacy requirements for voters. The FOCEP platform advocated repudiation of foreign debt, withdrawal from the OAS, massive public works to end unemployment, expansion of education and literacy that would take into consideration Indian culture, determination by peasants whether land should be held privately or communally, and dissolution of existing police and military forces. FOCEP, representing the Peruvian Trotskyite Revolutionary Workers' Party, hoped to lead the masses toward the overthrow of dictatorship and its replacement with a worker-peasant government. As of 1983, Blanco remains in the General Assembly and leader of his party.

As the biographical data indicate, Hugo Blanco is a practicing politician rather than a theoretician. His unique contribution lies in three areas: first, he is a Trotskyist-Leninist rather than a Marxist-Leninist, as most guerrilla leaders of Latin America are; second, he exhibits an unusually clear understanding of how to organize Indian peasants in Peru to obtain land through cooperative action; and finally, he provides a third alternative to gaining power for the masses. Arguing that guerrilla warfare on the Cuban model failed to convert the masses and that elections such as those in Chile did not give workers and peasants power because of violence and fraud, Blanco developed a strategy of local revolutionary action.

There are several revolutionary concepts that Blanco put into practice. Opposing activity that is merely propaganda, Blanco supported instead direct peasant occupation of land. The result of the class struggle was the emergence of the peasants as a "dual power"countering the landlords. To advance agrarian interests, Blanco argued, the oligarchy must be destroyed. Agrarian syndicates provided the basis of peasant power. Two parallel organizations supported the struggle for power: the party-directed militia, to which all campesinos belonged, and the guerrillas, which helped the militia. The power of government was to be replaced with that of the workers. He encouraged workers and peasants to build a disciplined revolutionary party, centralized and directed by the syndicates, to organize the masses and direct the armed struggle.

BIBLIOGRAPHY:

A. *El camino de nuestra revolución* (Lima: Revolutión Peruana, 1964); *Land or Death: The Peasant Struggle in Peru* (New York: Pathfinder Press, 1972).

B. Victor Villanueva, *Hugo Blanco y la rebelión campesina* (Lima: Juan Majía Baca, 1967); Richard Gott, *Guerrilla Movements in Latin America* (Garden City, N.J.: Doubleday, 1971), pp. 314–29; Harold Eugene Davis, *Revolutionaries, Traditionalists and Dictators in Latin America* (New York: Cooper Square, 1973), pp. 80-85.

VERA BLINN REBER

BORDIGA, AMADEO   (1889–1970). Amadeo Bordiga was born in Naples on 13 June 1889, and died in Formia on 24 July 1970. He gained a reputation between 1912 and 1918 as one of the principal socialist leaders in Naples and the nation. Of particular note are his rigorous polemic against reformism and social democracy and his strenuous struggle against Italy's intervention in the war. In opposition to Mussolini, at that time still a socialist and a supporter of intervention, Bordiga energetically affirmed antimilitaristic principles and above all argued for the identity between capitalism, democracy, and militarism. Having become the leader of the extreme left wing of the Italian Socialist Party (PSI) in December 1918, he waged a battle to make the PSI a revolutionary party, and he set in motion the struggle for the formation of a Communist Party (PCI) in collaboration with Lenin* and the Third Communist International,* but at times also at odds with them. The Congress of Livorno (January 1921) confirmed Bordiga's leadership. He cooperated with Gramsci,† in spite of differences regarding the role of workers' councils, which Bordiga considered weak, limited organisms. From 1921 to 1923 Bordiga was the head of the PCI, which was formed as a result of the split at Livorno, and his leadership within the Party was complete. But his differences with the Communist International over the politics of the "united front," his criticism of the Soviet politics of the NEP, the rise to power of fascism, and Bordiga's failure to understand its true nature all led to the disintegration of his leadership position. Arrested in February 1923 and released in October of the same year, he found a group in power (Togliatti† and Terracini had taken over) that did not support him in his ever more stubborn dispute with the Communist International; the break with the International was complete in the first months of 1925, and Bordiga was isolated at the Congress of Lyons, which signaled the supremacy of Gramsci and his *Theses*. In 1930 Bordiga was expelled from the Party, and from then on his activity was confined to ineffective protest and, in the second postwar period, to the minority activities of groups to the left of the PCI.

Bordiga interprets Marxism as a rigid and deterministic instrument of analysis of the historical process. For this reason there are specific revolutionary phases with respect to the cycles of capitalistic development, which can be represented in geometric terms. The revolutionary process is interpreted in an equally rigid manner, so that elimination of the structure of economic exploitation by means of political revolution guided by the Party must precede any change in the forms of governmental organization and the delegation of power. The revolutionary subject is also defined on the basis of a rigorous "objective" determination of class, from which all possibilities of interclass alliances are therefore excluded, as is also any mixture of social groups (for example, intellectuals are completely excluded from the prospect of a revolution). The guide for revolutionary workers is the Party, which Bordiga considers the working class itself as a subject. Bordiga considered the notion of individual consciousness to be "insidiously subjective." "The certain *coordinates* of the Communist revolution," states Bordiga ("Relatività e determinismo," an article written in 1955), "are written as valid solutions of demonstrated laws, in the space-time of History."

The central concept of this theoretical determinism is the "invariance of Marxism": in opposition to the distortions and the betrayals of reformism and revisionism, Bordiga maintains that it is necessary, on the basis of the "need of the movement to base itself on the inviolability of a body of doctrinal and programmatic tables," to assume "the defense of a Marxism which never creates anything new and constitutes a constellation of precise indestructible theses" (*Dialogato coi morti*, 1956).

BIBLIOGRAPHY:

A. *Struttura economica e sociale della Russia d'oggi* (Milan: Contra, 1966); *Amadeo Bordiga, Scritti scelti*, ed. Franco Livorsi, (Milan: Feltrinelli, 1975).

B. Andreina De Clementi, *Amadeo Bordiga* (Turin: Einaudi, 1971); Michele Fatica, *Origini del fascismo e del comunismo a Napoli* (Firenze: La Nuova Italia, 1971); Franco Livorsi, *Amadeo Bordiga* (Rome: Riuniti, 1976).

VITTORIO DINI

BORGE MARTINEZ, TOMÁS (b. 1930). Nicaraguan Minister of Interior and Sandinista political leader, Tomás Borge was born in the provincial city of Matagalpa on 13 August 1930. He began political activities against the Somoza dictatorship at the age of 13. When he was 16, he, Carlos Fonseca* and other schoolmates began to publish *El Espartaco* (later changed to *Revolutionary Youth*) and to study other revolutionary struggles. He was among a small group of university students who, in the late 1950s, began to study Marxist theory and who had some contacts with the Nicaraguan Socialist Party (the pro-Soviet Marxist party in Nicaragua). Inspired by the developing Cuban revolutionary movement, he, Carlos Fonseca, and a small group of other nationalists broke with the unrevolutionary orthodoxy of the Nicaraguan Socialist Party and began to wage guerrilla warfare against the Somoza dictatorship. In July 1961, Borge, Fonseca, and Silvio Mayoraga founded the Sandinista National Liberation Front (FSLN) to wage armed struggle against Somoza. Inspired by Augusto César Sandino's earlier fight against the U.S. Marines and the National Guard (1927–33) and by the increasingly radical Cuban Revolution, the young revolutionaries began to attack the state security forces. Borge was captured in one such engagement, imprisoned and brutally tortured for nine months. Sentenced to 180 years of prison for his "subversive" activities, he stayed behind prison walls until his Sandinista comrades negotiated his release in August 1978, when they captured the National Palace while the Nicaraguan Congress was in session.

He participated vigorously in the final months of the Sandinista struggle to overthrow the Somoza dictatorship and used his status as the sole surviving founding member of the FSLN to reunite the three Sandinista factions (Protracted Popular Warfare [GPP], Proletarian Tendency [TP], and Insurrectionists [Terceristas]) After the 1979 Sandinista victory, he emerged as an important political figure in the new revolutionary regime and was among those who charted the radical nationalist course in internal and external affairs that the revolutionary government followed.

As a member of the nine-person FSLN National Directorate he helped shape Nicaragua's innovative socialist ideology. While relying on (international)orthodox Marxism as a general theoretical framework, Borge insisted on the importance of national conditions in the formation of ideology and national practice. Thus Sandino and the lessons learned from his struggle against the U.S. Marines and Nicaraguan National Guard were equally important sources for thought and praxis, as were the experiences of the Nicaraguan people before, during, and after the revolution. Indeed, Sandinismo became the repository of national consciousness. Borge and the other Nicaraguan leaders never lost touch with their own fervent nationalism or the actual contributions of their own people. Their thought became an outstanding example of the new wave of revolutionary national Marxism that has swept through the Third World.

BIBLIOGRAPHY:

A. *Carlos, El Amanecer dejó de ser una tentación* (Managua: n.a., 1979); *Los Primeros pasos* (Mexico City: Siglo XXI, 1981); *Sandinistas Speak, Speeches, Writings, and Interviews with Leaders of Nicaragua's Revolution* (New York: Pathfinder Press, 1982); *La revolución combate contra la teología de la muerte; Christian Discourses of a Sandinista Comandante* (Bilbao: Tercer Mundo/Tercera Iglesia, Desclée de Brouwer, 1983); *El axioma de la esperanza* (Bilbao: Desclée de Brouwer, 1984).

HARRY E. VANDEN

BRECHT, BERTOLT   (1898–1956). Born on 10 February 1898 in the city of Augsburg, the playwright, poet, and literary theorist Bertolt Brecht wanted to do for theater what Marx* did for social science. While his aesthetic innovations include insightful formulations of what he called "epic," and later "dialectic" theater and new, scientific "distance-creating" techniques of acting, directing, and writing, his reputation among Marxists is based primarily on his entertaining and stimulating plays. These include *Mother Courage, St. Joan of the Stockyards, The Resistable Rise of Arturo Ui, Caucasian Chalk Circle, The Baden Learning Play, A Man Is a Man*, and *Galileo Galilei*. Brecht's oeuvre illustrates the dilemmas and contradictions of modern society, which he felt capitalism had polluted with economic exploitation and cultural dehumanization. His artistic call for revolution encouraged viewers to reconstitute a cooperative moral community in which working-class values would generate new ways of living, caring, and working together. Brecht's moral and aesthetic visions were a product of his life-long study of Marxian texts, his friendship with the Marxist luminaries Karl Korsch,† Fritz Sternberg,* and Walter Benjamin,† and most importantly the orthodoxy of the German Communist Party, which Brecht adopted as his own. He used this Marxian perspective to criticize what he perceived as the indefensible idealism of nonorthodox Marxists like Theodore Adorno† and George Lukács† (see his essay "Breadth and Variety of the Realist Way of Writing"). Ironically, Brecht's work was never popular in the Soviet Union. In his lifetime only *The Threepenny Opera* was produced by Soviet authorities. Brecht emigrated to America in 1933 to escape Nazism and lived in New York and Santa Monica. He failed miserably in his efforts at commercial success in the American theater. With his wife, the actress Helene Weigel, Brecht returned to Europe in 1950 to organize the Berlin Ensemble Company, and then toured France, Great Britain, Italy, and Poland, entertaining and mobilizing audiences with his own revolutionary praxis. He died in Berlin on 14 August 1956.

BIBLIOGRAPHY:

A. *Plays*, ed. Eric Bentley (New York: Grove Press, 1961); *Brecht on Theater*, ed. John Willett (New York: Hill & Wang, 1964); *Collected Plays*, eds. Ralph Manheim and John Willett (New York: Random House, 1971); *Poems 1913–1956*, eds. John Willett and Ralph Manheim (New York: Random House, 1976).

B. John Willett, *Theater of Bertolt Brecht*, 3d ed. (New York: New Directions, 1968); Frederic Ewen, *Bertolt Brecht* (New York: Citadel, 1970); John Fuegi, *The Essential Brecht* (Los Angeles: Hennessy & Ingalls, 1972); Klaus Volker, *Brecht Chronicle* (New York: Seabury, 1975); Karl H. Schoeps, *Bertolt Brecht* (New York: Ungar, 1977).

ROBERT A. GORMAN

BREITSCHEID, RUDOLF   (1874–1944). Rudolf Breitscheid was born in Cologne, the only child of a bookstore employee. Although his father died when he was still a youth, Breitscheid managed to attend a gymnasium and thereby qualify for the university. He eventually wrote his dissertation at Marburg on British land policy in Australia. Breitscheid took up journalism, working for the party press of the left-liberal Democratic Union as a reporter and foreign policy specialist. He joined the German Social Democratic Party (SPD) just before the war, and his antiwar views pushed him toward the party's left wing. Drafted in 1916, he was unable to attend the founding congress of the Independent Social Democratic Party (USPD) in 1917, but he nonetheless joined. After the revolution in November 1918 he served briefly as Prussian interior minister, but resigned with the other USPD ministers at the end of December. He then became a prominent parliamentary spokesman for the right wing of the USPD, until the reunification of the two socialist parties in 1922.

Although the SPD leadership distrusted many former USPD notables, Breitscheid moved up the party hierarchy with uncharacteristic quickness. He gained a position on the SPD's parliamentary executive in 1926 and became one of three delegation cochairmen in 1928. In 1931 he also achieved membership on the SPD Executive Committee. He did not have a strong personal following or political base within the organization itself, in part because he did not relate comfortably to many of his colleagues from working-class backgrounds. (Before his election to the Executive Committee in 1931 party cochairman Wels found it necessary to inform the party congress that Breitscheid had worked his way through the university.) Nonetheless, he was one of the main figures in the brain trust around Wels.

Breitscheid was the best SPD speaker in the Reichstag. He also had a sharp enough grasp of foreign policy to be assigned semi-official negotiating tasks by longtime Foreign Minister Gustav Stresemann. Breitscheid was one of the originators and most consistent proponents of the policy of "fulfillment" (*Erfüllungspolitic*), by which Germany would make a good faith effort to meet its reparations obligations, partly to convince Britain and France to lower the burden. He saw reconciliation with France as the most important goal of German foreign policy, and although dissatisfied with Germany's eastern boundary, he was willing to have Germany renounce the use of force to alter it. That was farther than Stresemann would go.

Breitscheid placed great importance on parliamentary control of the government. In 1929 he warned the SPD party congress against the possibility of a presidential dictatorship, supported by the presidential emergency powers under the constitution. But Breitscheid had no remedy to prevent parliamentary coalitions from collapsing, and he actually favored the SPD's withdrawal from the Reich government in March 1930. That was the last parliamentary government Germany would enjoy until after World War II. After Hitler gained power, Breitscheid found it logical that the experiment with authoritarian government had resulted in the triumph of the most authoritarian figure in Germany.

Breitscheid supported the SPD's policy of tolerating the nonparliamentary Brüning government in 1930–32 with serious reservations. He was concerned that the party might lose its hold on the masses by not opposing a government hostile to labor. He also tended to underestimate the danger and distinctiveness of the Nazis and to overestimate the divisions in the reactionary forces. At times he flirted with the notion that the SPD might defend the republic by means of "extraparliamentary action," but the party leadership chose to avoid this course. Nor was Breitscheid himself very much inclined to take to the streets. One day after Hitler's appointment as chancellor, Breitscheid delivered a speech to the SPD party council entitled "Readiness Is All important." He warned the SPD and the working class against a premature action. It was already too late. Breitscheid spent his last years fighting German fascism through word and deed. He was apprehended and arrested by the Nazis in 1942, and brutally murdered in Buchenwald concentration camp on 24 August 1944.

BIBLIOGRAPHY:

A. *Der Bülow-block und der liberalismus* (Munich: Reinhardt, 1908); *Antifaschistische Beiträge 1933–1939* (Frankfurt: Marxistische Blätter, 1977).

B. Peter Pistorius, *Rudolf Breitscheid 1874–1944* (Nuremberg: n.a., 1970)

RICHARD BREITMAN

BREZHNEV, LEONID ILYICH   (1906–1982). Leonid Brezhnev was the major political force in the collective leadership of the Soviet Union for nearly twenty years. The son of a steelworker, a man who became a metallurgical engineer in 1935, Brezhnev was also an apparatchik in the Ukraine, Moldavia, Kazakhstan, and the Russian Republic. He rose through the ranks because he was simultaneously a good Stalinist* and a follower of Stalin's young lieutenant, Nikita Khrushchev.* He became first secretary of the Communist Party of the Soviet Union (CPSU) in October 1964, when he and several others in Krushchev's Presidium moved to oust the leader. Unlike prior successions, however, this time the Central Committee expressly forbade the simultaneous holding of two particularly strong offices, the first secretaryship and the chairmanship of the Council of Ministers (prime ministership). Thus, Brezhnev shared power with several others through his peak years and was unable to displace Podgorny for thirteen years and Kosygin at all. Nonetheless, by 1971 he had established himself as the most important member of the leadership and partially overcame the Central Committee's restriction by acquiring the office of chairman of the Presidium of the Supreme Soviet in 1977 and by promoting his group from Dnepropetrovsk throughout the upper reaches of the Party and the government in the 1970s. He died in office in November 1982.

Brezhnev made some important modifications to the official doctrines promulgated under Krushchev. Although the 1961 Party program was not abandoned, the institutional innovations of Krushchev to put into effect the "state of all the people" and the "party of all the people" were reversed, and the overt criticism of the "cult of personality" became severely muted. In its place, the central concept became "developed" or "mature socialism." The current status of socialism was therein elevated to the baseline for the next several decades at least, for this concept implies that only gradualist, incrementalist changes in the existing structures of politics, society, and economics are needed for the building of communism. Indeed, the Party was to become even stronger, and the key indicators of the existence of the new society were rooted in increasing production, consumption, and political stability. This growth was to be rooted in the application of science and technology to the economy and everyday life, under the close supervision of the Party. The "scientific and technological revolution" (STR) was to be the driving material force consolidating the past gains of socialism in the Soviet Union.

STR was also to transform international relations. Although "peaceful coexistence" continued under Brezhnev's leadership, the perspective was both more cooperative and more confrontational. STR was seen as a global phenomenon that produced useful information and inventions in the West, and therefore it was to the benefit of socialism to increase its trade and technical cooperation with the United States and Western Europe. (Socialist superiority was preserved in the idea that socialist systems could use such knowledge and technology in far more efficient and socially desirable ways than capitalism. Therefore, capitalist inventors were providing the socialist world with even more advantages in the global competition of the two systems.) In addition, STR meant the development of military technologies that required conscious cooperation to constrain the arms race.

On the other hand, the "relaxation of tensions"—sometimes explicitly called "detente" by Brezhnev—was seen to involve even more intense competition in military and ideological matters. The Brezhnev interpretation of detente perceives an intensification of the Western propaganda war against Soviet legitimacy at home and in Eastern Europe that can only be countered by severe action against "so-called dissidents" who are seen either as mentally ill or as misled citizens who have accepted parts of bourgeois ideology. In addition, the armed might of the Soviet Union must be used to protect the gains of the revolution where bourgeois activity may produce "silent counterrevolution" (e.g. Czechoslovakia in 1968), unless indigenous party and military forces move first against "counterrevolutionary elements" (as in Poland in 1981).

This confrontation with international capitalism is also intensified in the Third World, where military means are used by the West and must be countered by more active support of "national revolutions" as they unfold against imperialism. This support may even go so far as the movement of Soviet troops to defend a government collapsing from "reactionary resistence," as in Afghanistan.

BIBLIOGRAPHY:

A. *On the Policy of the Soviet Union and the International Situation* (Garden City, N.Y.: Doubleday, 1973); *Following Lenin's Course* (Moscow: Progress, 1975); *Peace, Detente, and Soviet-American Relations* (New York: Harcourt Brace Jovanovich, 1979); *Memoirs* (Oxford: Pergamon, 1982).

B. John Dornberg, *Brezhnev* (New York: Basic Books, 1974); Robert H. McNeal, *The Bolshevik Tradition* (Englewood Cliffs, N.J.: Prentice-Hall, 1975); R. Judson Mitchell, *The Ideology of a Superpower* (Stanford, Calif.: Hoover Institution Press, 1982).

THOMAS OLESZCZUK

BROWDER, EARL   (1891–1973). Born in 1891 in Wichita, Kansas, Earl Browder could trace his family to Welsh settlers in Virginia in the 1600s. Raised in the Populist-Socialist tradition of the Midwest, he joined the Socialist Party in 1907. Converted to syndicalism a few years later, Browder became president of an A.F. of L. Bookkeepers' local. He opposed American involvement in World War I and spent more than two years in prison for violating the draft law. In 1920 he joined the Communist Party. For the next decade he served in a variety of Party positions, including American representative to the Profintern and General Secretary of the Chinese-based Pan-Pacific Trade Union Secretariat. Late in 1929 he was placed on the American Communist Party's Secretariat. He was appointed General Secretary in 1934 and continued to lead the Party until 1945. In 1936 and 1940 Browder was the Communist candidate for president of the United States.

During the popular front era (1936–39), Browder popularized the slogan, "Communism Is Twentieth Century Americanism" in an attempt to link the American revolutionary tradition to Marxism. During World War II he interpreted the dissolution of the Third Communist International* (1943) and the Teheran summit meeting of Allied leaders as signals that the United States and the Soviet Union would continue cooperating in the postwar world. He called for peaceful coexistence between capitalism and communism and in 1944 arranged the transformation of the Communist Party into the Communist Political Association, designed to work within the two-party system. One year later, following Soviet-inspired criticism of his "revisionism" by Jacques Duclos, a leading French Communist, Browder, refusing to recant, was deposed and the Party reconstituted. He was expelled in 1946. In later years Browder moved toward democratic socialism. He died in 1973.

BIBLIOGRAPHY:

A. *Teheran: Our Path in War and Peace* (New York: International, 1944).
RICHARD KLEHR

BUKHARIN, NIKOLAI I. (1888–1938). Nikolai Bukharin was born in Moscow in 1888 into a family of Russian intellectuals. Starting his radical activities during the 1905 Russian Revolution, Bukharin joined the Moscow branch of the Bolshevik Party the next year, being co-opted to membership in the Bolshevik Moscow Committee two years later. Having studied economics at Moscow University but arrested prior to graduation, Bukharin left Russia in 1911, soon making the acquaintance of the leading Russian emigrées abroad. In 1914, Bukharin wrote a major Marxist rebuttal (*The Economic Theory of the Leisure Class*) to the Austrian School of Economics, which had challenged the labor theory of value by suggesting that marginal utility better described the movement of prices under capitalism. In 1916 Bukharin arrived in New York, becoming editor of a Russian-language journal the following year. After the spring 1917 revolution, Bukharin returned to Moscow, becoming a member of the Executive Committee of the Moscow Soviet, a member of the Bolshevik Central Committee, and an editor of the Bolshevik journal, *Pravda*. Following the fall 1917 revolution, Bukharin insisted upon continuing the war against Germany by calling upon the broad masses of Russian toilers to carry the anti-imperialist struggle into the heart of Europe, a position condemned by Lenin* as "left-wing communism." In 1919 Bukharin was elected to the Executive Committee of the just-formed Third International,* and became chairman in 1926. Having shed his "leftist" tendencies, Bukharin, by 1926, was a firm supporter of the New Economic Policy, which favored a mixed economy as the best means for reconstructing Russia. With the termination of the New Economic Policy, Bukharin found himself increasingly at odds with the emerging dictatorship of Joseph Stalin.* Implicated in the purge trials of the mid-1930s, Bukharin was arrested as a "rightist" in 1937 for defending Kulak rights, advocating an evolutionary approach to accumulation and industrialization, opposing Party despotism and terror, and favoring a more open culture and free social science. He was anointed, by some, a forerunner of European social democracy and reformism, despite the fact that before 1921 he strongly advocated proletarian state control over all economic and political matters, including coercing peasants and militarizing workers. Bukharin was tried, convicted, and executed in 1938.

While there is little doubt as to Bukharin's wide-ranging and penetrating intellect, his main contribution to the Russian Marxist movement lay in his ability to propagate and defend the unquestioned tenets of orthodox Marxism for both the Russian intelligentsia and the Russian masses. His work *The Economic Theory of the Leisure Class* became the standard Soviet response to the challenges of the Austrian School of Economics, while his *ABC of Communism*, written with E. Preobrazhensky, introduced Marxist concepts to the citizens of Soviet Russia. Bukharin's *Historical Materialism: A System of Sociology* remains to this day one of the most lucid expositions of orthodox Marxist theory. His one curious theoretical contribution to Marxism is his use of the term "equilibrium" in describing Engels's* dialectical laws of nature. Society and nature are parts of a dynamic dialectical cycle of change, governed by Engels's three principles. Each successive stage, however, embodies a new level of temporary stability, a state of equilibrium where potential internal contradictions live but are not yet manifest. As they mature quantitatively, they disturb the equilibrium and produce a new qualitative level. History is reducible to a constant process of disturbing and restoring social equilibrium, Bukharin's "law of equilibrium." In the revised terminology, proletarian revolutionary forces mature and destroy capitalism's equilibrium, bringing forth a new proletarian state, which owns and controls production, exchange, and distribution. When pure communism is realized, social equilibrium is permanently restored, and a liberated society finally achieves its full material potential. Bukharin's focus on social equilibrium permits him, more than his orthodox predecessors, to calmly appreciate the accomplishments of capitalism and bourgeois social science, even though his belief in an objective material dialectic never wavered.

BIBLIOGRAPHY:

A. *The Economic Theory of the Leisure Class* (London: M. Lawrence, 1927); with E. Preobrazhensky, *The ABC of Communism* (Ann Arbor: University of Michigan Press, 1969).

B. Stephen F. Cohen, *Bukharin and the Bolshevik Revolution: A Political Biography, 1888–1938* (New York: Vintage, 1975.

MICHAEL M. BOLL and ROBERT A. GORMAN

C

CABRAL, AMILCAR (1924–1973). Amilcar Cabral was born in 1924 in Bafatá, Portuguese Guinea, of Cape Verdean parents. He was brought up in Cape Verde, where he attended the Liceu Gil Eanes in São Vicente. He finished his secondary schooling at the age of twenty. A year later he was awarded a scholarship enabling him to go to Lisbon to study agronomy. A brilliant student throughout, he graduated in 1952. That same year, after his marriage in 1951 to a Portuguese colleague, he left for Guinea to take up a position in the colonial civil service as an agricultural engineer. It is in Lisbon that Cabral, like many of his contemporaries, "regained" his consciousness of being African and acquired the Marxist political tools that he was later to use so effectively. This experience in Portugal was also crucial to his understanding of metropolitan society and its socio-economic and political contradictions, and to his analysis of the relevance of the colonial question to Portuguese politics. In 1953 he was asked to conduct the first comprehensive agricultural survey of Guinea—a unique opportunity for one who was to become a guerrilla leader. He had to leave Guinea in 1955 in large measure because of his political activities, and until 1959 he worked from Lisbon both as an agricultural consultant (traveling regularly to Angola, for example) and as an agronomist in a laboratory for phytosanitary control. He left Portugal clandestinely that year in order to take direct control of the Guinean nationalist party, the Partido Africano da Independência da Guiné e Cabo Verde (PAIGC), a party founded on one of his visits to Bissau in 1956. Thereafter his life is tied to that of the party he led. It is best divided into three periods. The first, 1960–64, Cabral devoted to the organization of a party capable of carrying out political mobilization in the countryside and to the training of party cadres. The second, 1964–69, was largely taken up by the increasingly successful development of guerrilla warfare, eventually leading to the PAIGC's control of about sixty percent of Guinea. The third, 1969–73, saw a determined attempt to develop the organization and reconstruction of the liberated area by means of an effective political, economic, and social infrastructure from the village level upward. The 1972 elections, held in the liberated territories, unique in the history of guerrilla wars, granted final political legitimacy to the political bodies, which were to declare independence, unilaterally, in September 1973. Sadly, Cabral had been assassinated a few months earlier (January 1973) by party members collaborating with the Portuguese. In April 1974 the Portuguese regime fell, and that same year Portugal recognized the independence of Guinea-Bissau. The Cape Verde Islands became independent in 1975, following a general election.

Cabral's body of writings is quite considerable and has had much influence in the Third World. In only thirteen years of active political life, he communicated ideas, many original, which derived directly from his experience as a nationalist leader. In terms of political practice, Cabral's greatest contribution was, first, the creation and development of a party in which the political control of the war was systematically maintained and, second, the adaptation of the principles of guerrilla warfare to an African context, where reference to class struggle, land tenure, or even nationalism was virtually meaningless. This required the ability to evolve an ideology of political mobilization that appealed to villagers without sacrificing the all-important principles of national unity and socialist reforms. The most unique aspect of Cabral's political strategy was his attempt to set up a political system in which the power of the party, conceived as an ideological vanguard, would be balanced by genuinely independent and popularly elected institutions (at national and local levels). The establishment of an elected National Assembly before independence was a key step in that direction, although Cabral's death in 1973, before the consolidation of those institutions, contributed to the difficulties experienced at independence in maintaining such a delicate balance.

Cabral's contribution to radical theory is important, perhaps even more because of its political impact than because of its place in the Marxist corpus. At the most general level, Cabral developed, in the tradition of Lenin* and Mao,* an analysis of social classes under colonial rule and of the relationship of these classes to both national liberation and revolution. Cabral was one of the first African leaders to recognize, within a Marxist perspective, the inadequacy of a class-based theory of political action in the colonial context. Neither the proletariat, insofar as it existed, nor the peasantry could lead the nationalist struggle and the revolution. Cabral's most original and perceptive contribution lies in his explicit analysis of the political role of the colonial petit bourgeoisie and of the dilemma facing a revolutionary movement led by a petit bourgeoisie. He argued that, within the historically specific context of colonial rule in which it is both necessary and possible for the colonial power to "create" a collaborating petit bourgeoisie, the leadership of the nationalist movement could only come from that class, artificial though it was, because it, more than any other, was situated at the juncture of the political, social, and cultural contradictions of colonial practice. The key to the political orientation of the nationalist movement and the prospect of its evolution into a revolutionary socialist party lay in the experience of the nationalist war and, ultimately (however nefarious it was politically) in the political mettle of that petit bourgeois leadership. Implicitly, then,

Cabral dared say what many Marxists reject, that the conditions under which a struggle for national liberation occurs may well not be revolutionary.

Cabral's view of a socialist revolution followed those who have looked to the countryside as the primer of development. His understanding of African rural society, of its lack of potential for collective forms of agriculture, and its resistance to rapid modernization, led him to reject simplistic models of collective rural development. His views, although specifically related to the context of a country like Guinea-Bissau, resembled certain Chinese policies in advocating self-sufficiency in food, improvement in the countryside through gradual socioeconomic transformation, and a slow rate of industrialization based on the available surplus from the agricultural sector. This would have to be achieved through moral and material incentives and political mobilization, not coercion. Although Cabral put a premium on economic independence, he did not conceive that a country like Guinea-Bissau could subsist in autarky, nor did he believe that all economic links with the capitalist world should be severed. His appeared very much as a pragmatic socialist strategy of what is sometimes termed a "moderate hue." Results since independence have not been encouraging, particularly in the rural sector, and it is obviously impossible to know how much better they might have been under Cabral's leadership.

Cabral's last and most systematic contribution to Marxist theory was his analysis of culture in the colonial context. He set culture firmly within the socioeconomic milieu out of which it had grown, rejecting thereby any notion of black or African specificity. His experiences in the countryside suggested to him that culture, as the expression of the "milieu's material reality," was both more resilient and more adaptable than either colonial myth or *déraciné* African thought, in their opposite ways, had believed. This implied, on the one hand, that national liberation could be based upon existing cultural patterns of resistance and that, on the other, modernization of thought as well as of structure could not proceed at a pace incompatible with the slow transformation of the existing cultural consciousness. Finally, Cabral's analysis of culture helped him to refine his portrait of the petit bourgeoisie, cultural hybrids requiring a pilgrimage back to their African sources before they could become effective, politically, as nationalists. But the difficulty of their "return to the sources" and the large body of writings that they produce in order to justify it was not an indication of their accurate perception of African culture (hence, Cabral's rejection of *négritude*) but simply a reflection of the depth of their alienation. Cultural *déracinement* was only transcended in political action.

BIBLIOGRAPHY:

A. *Revolution in Guinea* (London: Stage One, 1969); *Unity and Struggle* (London: Heinemann, 1970).

B. Lars Rudebeck, *Guinea-Bissau: A Study of Political Mobilisation* (Uppsala: Scandinavian Institute of African Studies, 1974); Mario de Andrade, *Amilcar Cabral* (Paris: Maspero, 1980); Basil Davidson, *No Fist Is Big Enough to Hide the Sky* (London: Zed

Press, 1981); Patrick Chabal, *Amilcar Cabral: Revolutionary Leadership and People's War* (Cambridge: Cambridge University Press, 1983).

PATRICK CHABAL

CARRERA DAMAS, GERMÁN   (b. 1930). Venezuelan historian Germán Carrera Damas has earned considerable respect among academicians as an essayist and editor who uses creative approaches to the study of history. He has been a leading Latin American advocate of stressing ideas in historical study, rather than the traditional narrative-chronological approach favored by the majority of historians in the region. He is best known for applying Marxist analytical techniques to the colonial and independence periods of his nation's history. To him independence was a class struggle pitting slaves against native-born whites, the latter against those born in Spain, and Venezuelans of mixed black and white blood against native whites. He contends that one cannot speak strictly of an ideology of emancipation, that the various participants in independence had diverse ideologies, and that one must view the era in terms of pluralistic dynamics for change.

He has also dispelled some myths about Venezuelan independence leader Simón Bolívar and has tried to eliminate the cult of "the Liberator" that has pervaded Venezuelan history. He questioned Bolívar's negative attitude toward the masses and contended that "the Liberator" has been made a hero by writers who have an extreme individualist concept of history and who have created a cult that has become an "opiate for the people," one whose functions have obscured a failure and postponed a disillusion. To him, Bolivarism is a hoax that deceives people into believing that independence brought liberty, equality, and fraternity to the masses in Venezuela, when it basically served the commercial bourgeoisie. He maintained that Bolivarism is predicated upon supernatural ideas and the concept of predestination, which tend to raise expectations beyond reality.

Carrera Damas has postulated a unique theory, which divides postindependence Venezuela into periods of commercial dependency (1821–1970s), absolute commercial dependency (1821–1960s), imperialist dependency (1870–1970s), modernizing imperialist dependency (1870–1930), monopolistic imperialist dependency (dependence on minerals, 1930–70), and the present era of thermonuclear revolution, which has changed the relations of dependency.

BIBLIOGRAPHY:

A. *Tres terras de historia* (Caracas: Universidad Central, 1961); *Historiografía marxista venezolana y otros temas* (Caracas: Universidad Central, 1967); *La dimensión histórica en el presente de América Latina y Venezuela* (Caracas: Universidad Central, 1972).

SHELDON B. LISS

CASTRO RUZ, FIDEL   (b. 1927). Born in Mayari, Oriente Province, Cuba, on 13 August 1927, Fidel Castro received a law degree from the University of Havana in 1950. On 26 July 1953, he led an attack by young radicals on the Moncada barracks in Santiago. The attack was a failure, and he was captured, tried, and sentenced to fifteen years in prison. He served two years before a general amnesty issued by the Batista government freed him. During 1955 and the first eleven months of 1956, he was in exile in the United States and Mexico. He returned to Cuba in December 1956 on the *Gramna* and began the guerrilla struggle that ended in the collapse of the Batista government on 31 December 1958. Castro has been the effective head of the Cuban government since February 1959. On 3 December 1976, he became the president of the Council of State. He is also president of the Council of Ministers, first secretary of the Cuban Communist Party, and commander-in-chief of the Revolutionary Armed Forces. He took charge of defense, interior, health, and culture, in January 1980.

Castro's impulse for revolution and the creation of the modern Cuban state derives from his sense of nationalism and anti-imperialism. His guerrilla force was, during its early months in the mountains of eastern Cuba, denounced by orthodox Marxists within the Cuban Communist Party (Partido Socialista Popular) as putchist. Castro believed that a revolutionary vanguard, in Cuba the July 26 Movement, could lead the masses to revolution without either being part of an existing Marxist-Leninist party or constituting themselves as one. In contradistinction to the reticence toward armed struggle of traditional Communist Parties in Latin America, Castro's July 26 Movement and the Partido de la Revolución Socialista (PRS), which was formed out of it in 1961, called for armed struggle throughout the region as the principal motor force to revolutionary change.

After declaring the Cuban Revolution a socialist one in 1961, Castro and his principal advisors attempted to lead Cuba toward a communistic society by the imposition of moral incentives in the economy and the bypassing of traditional economic stages (e.g. commodity exchange economy) on the road to socialism.
BIBLIOGRAPHY:

A. *History Will Absolve Me* (New York: Center for Cuban Studies, n.d.); *The World Economic and Social Crisis* (Havana: Council of State, 1983).

B. Lee Lockwood, *Castro's Cuba, Cuba's Fidel* (New York: Vintage Books, 1969); R. H. Bonachea, and N. P. Valdés, eds., *Selected Works of Fidel Castro*, 3 vols. (Cambridge: MIT Press, 1972); K. S. Karol, *Guerrillas in Power* (New York: Hill and Wang, 1970).

KELLY AINSWORTH

CAYETANO CARPIO, SALVADOR (b. 1919). Salvador Cayetano is leader of the Fuerzas Populares de Liberación Nacional-Farabundo Martí (FPL) and the Frente Farabundo Martí para la Liberación Nacional (FMLN) and was previously Secretary General of the Salvadorean Communist Party (PCS). An artisan and bakery worker by trade, Cayetano was in the 1950s and 1960s the most renowned of Salvadorean trade union leaders. His differences with the PCS over the Soviet invasion of Czechoslovakia and the "peaceful road to socialism" had great impact since he was Secretary General until 1969. Splitting with a sizable faction in April 1970, Cayetano established the FPL on the basis of the rejection of the Party's policy of strategic alliances with what it saw as a democratic "national bourgeoisie," its aversion to the armed struggle, and its failure to build a revolutionary base in the working class. The FPL adopted a Vietnamese-style armed strategy, the *"guerra popular prolongada,"* which envisaged an extended conflict of attrition and radicalization rather than short-term insurrection. Cayetano was also responsible for building parallel to the guerrillas a mass movement in the Bloque Popular Revolucionario, which grouped unions and popular bodies around the FPL's program but did not itself fight. This step proved highly successful and lent the FPL considerable force. Although previously critical of the Cuban Revolution in a number of aspects, Cayetano has from 1979 entered into close cooperation with the Havana government and visited many liberation movements both in and outside Latin America. A highly respected military commander, he has become the effective leader of the FMLN and is recognized to be on its left wing. His political writings are rather dogmatic and contrast a capacity for flexibility in the military field.

BIBLIOGRAPHY:

A. *Secuestro y capucha* (San Jose: Editorial Universitaria Centroamericana, 1980).

B. Mario Menéndez Rodríguez, *El Salvador: una auténtica guerra civil* (San Jose: EDUCA, 1980).

JAMES DUNKERLEY

CHEN BODA   (b. 1905). A Chinese Marxist-Leninist theorist and Chinese Communist Party (CCP) leader, Chen Boda was born into a poor peasant family in Huian, Fujian province, and studied at Sun Yat-sen University in Moscow during the years 1927–30. A Party member since 1927, he achieved prominence in Peking in 1936 when he advocated a "new enlightenment movement" as a vehicle for disseminating Marxist-Leninist ideas. In 1937 he went to Yan'an and soon emerged as Mao Zedong's* political secretary and a central figure in the "think tank" Mao was assembling to assist him in philosophy and theory. An effective polemicist, Chen was a key figure in the "rectification campaign" of 1942–44 and in the subsequent "Party history study campaign" that rationalized Mao's leadership of the CCP. He was elected to the Central Committee in 1945, and after nationwide victory in 1949 he held a number of important positions: appointed to the Politburo in 1956; became editor of *Red Flag*, the Party's leading theoretical journal, in 1958; and assumed the directorship of the central Party group that took charge of the Cultural Revolution in 1966. But in 1970, following his involvement in an alleged plot to overthrow Mao, Chen was abruptly arrested and imprisoned. In 1980, along with the so-called Gang of Four radical Maoist leaders, he was sentenced to a lengthy prison term.

A highly intense personality, Chen Boda was a capable theorist and effective writer who supported Mao Zedong's ideological claims and helped shape his ideas. Although he had studied in Moscow and was fluent in Russian, Chen displayed a notable interest in Chinese history and culture throughout his life. In the mid-1930s he argued that Marxist theory should be developed in line with

Chinese political and cultural realities and not be imposed according to foreign (i.e. Soviet) models. In early 1938, following his arrival in Yan'an, he advanced the proposition that the modern culture emerging in China should be "Sinified," i.e., that it should absorb new influences from the West but recast them in a distinctly Chinese form, as had been the experience with Buddhism in the past. Working from this basic idea, Chen and Mao formulated the concept of the "Sinification of Marxism," which Mao advanced in an important CCP report later that year. The actual term "Sinification of Marxism" generated a good deal of opposition from Soviet-oriented Party leaders, and it was gradually phased out by the mid-1940s. Yet the ideas it incorporated have remained central to the CCP's theoretical thrust up to the present time.

Working closely with Mao, Chen Boda and other theoretical advisers in Yan'an developed the concept of "Mao Zedong's thought" as representing the creative synthesis of Marxist-Leninist theory and Chinese revolutionary practice. "Mao Zedong's thought" first appeared in Party propaganda in 1943, and it has remained the "guiding ideology" of the CCP ever since, albeit at times honored in word more than in deed. Chen's role in promoting Mao's ideological preeminence and in providing historical and theoretical justification for it was immense. In a series of key writings between 1943 and 1953 Chen explicated Mao's thought, rationalized its historical development, and harmonized it with Stalin's* theoretical claims. Further, he argued that the Chinese Revolution was the most appropriate model for Marxist-Leninist movements in Asia, Africa, and Latin America, a claim that was eventually to generate hostility in Moscow and to contribute to the Sino-Soviet split in the early 1960s.

Like Mao himself, Chen Boda had an ambivalent attitude toward Chinese society. On the one hand, he admired China's history and culture and, on the other, grew increasingly impatient with the nation's continuing poverty and weakness. It is not surprising, then, that Chen was closely involved in most of Mao's radical social experiments under the new regime, beginning with his central role in drafting the constitution in 1953. In 1955 he was appointed to the Party's Rural Work Department, where he promoted agricultural cooperativization and introduced the concept of the "people's communes" in 1958. The communes, in combination with the Great Leap Forward the same year, posed an overt ideological challenge to the Communist Party of the Soviet Union (CPSU), and shortly thereafter Chen published several blistering criticisms of "Yugoslav revisionism" in a none too subtle attack on the Soviet leadership. In the early 1960s he worked with Mao in drafting the ensuing Sino-Soviet polemics, and in 1966, as noted previously, he was named director of the Party group that launched the Cultural Revolution. Despite its ultimate failure, the Cultural Revolution was a radical attempt to advance beyond Soviet experience in building socialism in a postrevolutionary situation. It was promoted as a "brand-new" development in the history of revolution and a "higher development" in Marxist-Leninist theory, of which Mao Zedong's thought was said to be the most advanced embodiment. In these and other ways Chen worked with Mao to restructure the foundations of Chinese society along Marxist-Leninist lines, at the same time maintaining a resolute and even defiant independence from the CPSU and the international Communist movement as a whole. Both men were fervent Chinese nationalists as well as Marxist-Leninists, and in many respects their lives were devoted to attempting—with only partial success—to harmonize these potentially conflicting orientations.

BIBLIOGRAPHY:

A. *Mao Tse-tung on the Chinese Revolution* (Peking: Foreign Language Press, 1951); *Stalin and the Chinese Revolution* (Peking: Foreign Language Press, 1953); *Notes on Mao Tse-tung's "Report on an Investigation of the Peasant Movement in Hunan"* (Peking: Foreign Language Press, 1954); *On the Ten-Year Civil War, 1927–1937* (Peking: Foreign Language Press, 1954); *Collected Writings of Ch'en Po-ta* [in Chinese] (Hong Kong: n.a., 1971)

B. Raymond F. Wylie, *The Emergence of Maoism: Mao Tse-tung, Ch'en Po-ta and the Search for Chinese Theory, 1935–1945* (Stanford: Stanford University Press, 1980).

RAYMOND F. WYLIE

CHEN DUXIU (1879–1942). A Chinese Marxist-Leninist theoretician and Chinese Communist Party (CCP) leader, Chen Duxiu was born into a scholar-official family in Huaining, Anhui Province, and received a formal classical education. He spent various periods of time in France (1907?–10) and Japan (most notably in 1913–15), where he became interested in Western political and social ideas. Upon returning to Peking he launched a radical magazine, *New Youth*, and almost overnight became a national figure in Chinese intellectual and political circles. In 1919 Chen went to Shanghai, where he met with Comintern agents and agreed to organize a Communist Party in China. The CCP was duly established in July 1921 with Chen as general secretary, but his leadership was beset with many difficulties, most notably the delicate task of maintaining the highly unstable CCP–Kuomintang united front. When the coalition finally collapsed in early 1927, Chen was removed from his position at an emergency meeting on 7 August, and he never again played a role of major importance in the CCP. He was expelled from the Party in 1929 and soon after became active in a small Trotskyist* organization and thus broke with Moscow as well. He spent the years 1932–37 in a Nationalist prison in Nanking; upon his release he abstained from political activity and died in relative obscurity in 1942.

As a transitional figure between traditional and modern China, Chen Duxiu has left a mixed theoretical legacy. He adopted an iconoclastic attitude toward Confucian social and cultural values at an early age and eagerly accepted much of Western, particularly French, culture as he understood it. At root he was not narrowly political, being perhaps more interested in fundamental social and cultural reform than in mere political change. For example, he popularized the slogans "Mr. Democracy" and "Mr. Science" as easily understood embodiments of more sophisticated ideas he felt the Chinese masses should grasp. Although Chen was progressive and internationalist in his personal attitudes, he had considerable difficulty in putting these qualities to constructive use. He remained deeply suspicious of Sun Yat-sen, for example, fearing that he was not sufficiently revolutionary and prone to compromise with the forces of conservatism. Likewise, he did not get along well with the various Comintern agents in China and, while accepting their political and financial support, resented their influence in the Chinese Party.

In fact, Chen Duxiu's conversion to Marxism-Leninism was rather sudden, and he did not have a deep understanding of either the theory or Bolshevik practice in the Soviet Union. And he was impatient by nature, eager for radical change despite the lack of clarity in his own views. Originally believing that China would pass quickly from feudalism to socialism without going through the intervening stage of capitalism, he reluctantly accepted the Comintern view that the bourgeois revolution was necessary. In the course of time he made this view his own and was alarmed at the sudden violent turn of the worker and peasant organizations under CCP control in 1925–27. Later, he espoused Trotsky's view that the proletarian revolution would develop in a continuous, uninterrupted fashion, albeit now on a worldwide basis rather than in China alone. In the meantime he adopted an increasingly gradualist view of the revolutionary process and castigated the CCP for its continued advocacy of armed rebellion under unfavorable circumstances, i.e., before a revolutionary situation "objectively" existed in China.

After his release from prison in 1937, Chen Duxiu urged the CCP to drop its armed opposition to the KMT and enter into a "genuine" united front in order to oppose Japan more effectively. In his final years he remained committed to socialism as the best system to achieve economic equality but argued that parliamentary democracy was essential to guarantee political and intellectual freedom. The Soviet Union, he pointed out, lacked such a parliamentary system, and in consequence absolute power had passed into the hands of an elite bureaucracy that denied basic rights to the common people. It is thus not surprising that Chen has been condemned in the official version of CCP history, and his rehabilitation is highly unlikely.

BIBLIOGRAPHY:

A. Chen Duxiu's writings, few of which have been translated into English, are scattered throughout the several important periodicals he edited, most notably *New Youth* (pre-Communist period) and *Guide Weekly* (Communist period). Many of his pre-Communist writings (1915–21) were reprinted in the *Ch'en Tu-hsiu wenxuan*, 4 vols. (Shanghai, 1922; Hong Kong, 1964).

B. Lee Feigon, *Chen Duxiu, Founder of the Chinese Communist Party* (Princeton: Princeton University Press, 1983).

RAYMOND F. WYLIE

CHEN YUN   (b. 1905). A leader of the Chinese Communist Party (CCP) and specialist in economic affairs whose views on the economics of socialist development are roughly analogous to those of Nikolai Bukharin* in the Soviet Union of the 1920s, Chen Yun was originally a typesetter who joined the Communist Party in Shanghai in 1925. There he became active in labor organizing for the Party and was a leader of the workers' uprising of 1927. After the bloody suppression of the uprising, he fled the city and toured the Soviet Union and several rural base areas before returning to Shanghai's Party underground. He later fled the Nationalist police in 1933 and reached the rural base area led by Mao Zedong* in south-central China. He participated in the first part of the Long March to the north China base area of Yenan, and after 1937 he held a series of high Party and government posts, gradually specializing in financial and economic administration in the base areas. By the early 1950s he was a leading economic official in the new regime and a member of the Party's Politburo. His opposition to both Maoist economic ideas as well as Soviet-Stalinist* models of development led to a loss of influence during the Great Leap Forward of 1958–60, but he was to reassert his ideas during the period of economic recovery that followed the disruptive Great Leap policies. His continued opposition to Maoist ideas led again to his political eclipse with the beginning of the Cultural Revolution in 1966. He played no political role until 1978, when his economic ideas were rehabilitated and placed at the center of the post-Mao regime's strategy for economic development.

Chen has become a symbol of moderate and pragmatic views of socialist development that reject both the rapid mass-mobilization approach of the Maoists and the Soviet-Stalinist pattern of highly centralized planning and emphasis on heavy industrial development. By the 1950s he was criticizing Maoist-inspired political campaigns as disruptive of orderly economic growth and Soviet methods as both inefficient and as leading to sectoral imbalances and bottlenecks. He argued in 1956 that the collectivization of industry and agriculture had proceeded too far and too fast to be manageable and efficient. In 1962 he even suggested that commune agriculture be decollectivized and plots of land be given to peasant households to work (these ideas were put into wide practice starting in 1978). In his active periods, he became a spokesman for the use of financial criteria and fiscal discipline in planning, instead of input–output balances and output targets; for priority of the development of agriculture and greater stress on the production of light industrial and consumer goods; for the use of limited market mechanisms to regulate economic activity outside of heavy industry, especially in subsidiary agriculture production; for better terms of trade for peasants in the official pricing system; and for tight reins on capital construction and a general emphasis on intensive growth (stress on increasing capital and labor productivity) rather than extensive growth (crash building of new plants). He was also an early advocate of trade ties with the West and economic independence from the Soviet Union. His ideas currently dominate China's search for a new path of economic development.

BIBLIOGRAPHY:

B. Nicholas R. Lardy and Kenneth Lieberthal, *Chen Yun's Strategy for China's Economic Development: A Non-Maoist Alternative* (Armonk, N.Y.: M. E. Sharpe, 1983);

David Bachman, *Chen Yun and the Chinese Political System*, China Research Monograph (Berkeley: Center for Chinese Studies, University of California, 1984).

ANDREW G. WALDER

CHIN PENG (1922–1980?). Chin Peng was born in Sitiawan, Perak, Malaysia, in 1922. He attended secondary school in Perak. He joined the Malayan Communist Party (MCP) in the late 1930s, becoming a senior official in Perak State by the age of twenty. He was an officer in the Malayan People's Anti-Japanese Army (MPAJA) in World War II and cooperated with the British in resistance against the Japanese. In 1945 he traveled to London with the "Victory Contingent" of the MPAJA and was awarded the Order of the British Empire for his military services against the Japanese in the war. In 1948 he became publisher of the official Communist Party paper, *The Democrat*. In 1947 he was elected chairman of the Politburo of the Malayan Communist Party following the disappearance of Lai Teck (Mr. Wright), previous Party leader and almost certainly a paid agent of British intelligence. The unmasking of Lai Teck is widely held to be the work of Chin Peng.

Chin Peng inherited leadership of a party whose social constituency was almost entirely working class, virtually unique among Asian Communist parties. He promulgated a program of action that would unite the Party behind the leadership. At a Central Committee meeting in March 1948, Chin Peng was officially confirmed as secretary general, and a "mass struggle" program against British imperialism in Malaya was announced. With the declaration of "the Emergency" by the British colonial authorities in June 1948, however, the MCP was forced into launching an armed struggle that of necessity had to be fought largely in the countryside or jungles, a strategy that the Party was on the whole ill prepared for.

In December 1955, Chin Peng led a MCP delegation in talks with the Malayan government to end the Emergency. These failed and guerrilla operations continued until 1960, when Chin Peng and some 500 guerrillas retreated into southern Thailand. In 1982 there were unconfirmed reports that Chin Peng had died two years earlier.

BIBLIOGRAPHY:

B. Gene Z. Hanrahan, *The Communist Struggle in Malaya* (Kuala Lumpur: University of Malaya Press, 1971); Anthony Short, *The Communist Insurrection in Malaya, 1948–1960* (New York: Crane Russell, 1975).

MICHAEL C. WILLIAMS

CLARTÉ. The group and its journal were founded on 19 May 1919 as an antiwar coalition of intellectuals who believed that Woodrow Wilson's peace proposals had been largely ignored by the statesmen of the Versailles Conferences because of the immense capitalist and nationalist pressure that had been brought to bear on them. Organized by Raymond Lefebvre, Henri Barbusse,* and Paul Vaillant-Coutourier,* it attempted to rally intellectuals of all nations against imperialist wars and the old capitalist regimes that inspired such wars. It gained early support from Romain Rolland, but during 1920 when the debate on the question of whether to join the Third International* was at its height in the French socialist movement, Barbusse led *Clarté* toward a strident advocacy of the new International and a vigorous criticism of social democracy, which lost the movement some of its wider support. By 1921 the newly formed French Communist Party (PCF) had a considerable influence on *Clarté*, and the journal's contributors were mainly younger writers of the left, such as the editorial board of Berth, Fourier, and Bernier. By 1922 even Barbusse was criticizing its "narrow" and "undignified" views, and he resigned from the governing council in 1923. He and Vaillant-Coutourier remained on the editorial board despite the fact that they were leading members of the PCF and by 1925 the journal had moved to Trotskyism.*

The attempted merger with Breton's surrealists to form *La Guerre civile* failed in the same year, but the groups of the left were not yet far apart, and the PCF published a joint surrealist/ *Clarté* manifesto—"La Révolution d'abord et toujours"—protesting against the war in Morocco, in the Party paper, *L'Humanité*. *Clarté* became more surrealist under its new editor Pierre Naville* (1926–28), who also gave it a Trotskyist emphasis, until he replaced it with *Lutte de classes* in 1928, a thorough-going Trotskyist and anti-Stalinist journal. *Clarté* did not have a wide influence or readership, but it provided an ever-changing and quite tolerant forum for many of the most important left-wing theorists of the early postwar period. Its original impulse came from Rolland's *Au dessus de la Melée* and Barbusse's *Le Feu*, giving it a distinctly humanistic pacifist tone, but its manifesto, *La Luer dans l'abîme: ce que veut le groupe Clarté*, written by Barbusse in 1919, was a simple Marxist statement based on the Soviet model. *Clarté* was indeed a nursery for Communist Party writers just as much as it was a platform for surrealists and Trotskyists and as such played an important part in the fermentation of left-wing theory in interwar France.

BIBLIOGRAPHY:

B. V. Brett, *Henry Barbusse, sa marche vers la Clarté, son mouvement "Clarté"* (Prague: Czech Academy of Sciences, 1963); A. Kriegel, "Naissance du mouvement Clarté" *Le Mouvement sociale*, no. 42 (January-March 1963), pp. 117–35; N. Racine, "The Clarté Movement in France 1919–1921," *Journal of Contemporary History*, 2, no. 2 (1967), pp. 195–208; G. Normand, "Henry Barbusse and His Monde (1928–35): Progeny of the Clarté Movement and the Review *Clarté*," *Journal of Contemporary History*, 11, no. 2–3 (1976), pp. 173–97.

                                                                    JOHN C. SIMMONDS

CODOVILLA, VICTORIO   (1894–1970). Born in Italy on 8 February 1894, Victorio Codovilla began his political life when he joined the Italian Socialist Party in 1911. One year later he emigrated to Argentina, where he later changed his nationality. As a member of the Argentine Socialist Party and its youth organization, he sided with radical critics of the party's reformist leadership.

Codovilla was also a founder and leader of the Federation of Commercial Employees, and in 1917 he joined the editorial board of the antiwar *La internacional*. During 1918 he took part in the creation of the breakaway Internationalist Socialist Party (PSI), which became the Argentine Communist Party (PCA) in 1920. A member of the PSI executive from the start and of the Central Committee and Politburo of the PCA from 1921, Codovilla along with Rodolfo Ghioldi* used the direct intervention of Moscow to help purge rival right- and left-wing tendencies, despite majorities for the left at PCA congresses. Codovilla and Ghioldi were in full control of the Party by 1927.

Victorio Codovilla was also treasurer of the South American Bureau and a member of the South American Secretariat of the Comintern in the 1920s. One of the Latin American Communist leaders closest to Stalin,* Codovilla was elected to the Comintern's International Control Commission at the end of its Sixth Congress (1928). Between 1930 and 1941 he was absent from Argentina, yet continued to control the PCA by using special envoys.

As "Medina," Codovilla became the Comintern's most senior representative in Spain, where the Young Socialists dubbed him "the eye of Moscow." Through organizing a purge in the Spanish Communist Party (PCE) shortly before the outbreak of civil war, he became the Party's effective director. He was partly responsible for the recruitment to the PCE of Socialist youth leader Santiago Carrillo.† After failing in a bid to get Francisco Largo Caballero* to agree to a fusion of the Socialist and Communist parties, Codovilla helped engineer the downfall of the Caballero government in 1937. In the same year he worked with the Soviet State Security Service (NKVD) in carrying out the bloody purge of Partido Obrero de Unificación Marxista (POUM) militants, anarchists, and non-Stalinist Communists.

Before returning to Argentina to become general secretary of the PCA in 1941, Codovilla toured the Caribbean and Latin America, purging local Parties as he went. He was in Mexico, supervising the replacement of the Mexican Party's leadership, when the exiled Leon Trotsky* was assassinated in 1940. Back in Argentina he was imprisoned for a year after the 1943 military coup. Codovilla, "a very fat man, bourgeois in manner and taste" (Thomas, *The Spanish Civil War*, p. 123), made regular trips to Moscow for party congresses, and in 1966 he eulogized the Communist Party of the Soviet Union (CPSU) at its Twenty-third Congress. In March 1963 he changed from being general secretary to president of the PCA, but his presidency soon became symbolic as a result of illness. He spent the last three years of his life in a Soviet hospital and died in Moscow on 15 April 1970 at the age of seventy-six. A Moscow street now bears his name.

Codovilla was not an independent thinker, and indeed he often condemned the original ideas of individuals when asserting the superiority of collective elaboration of the Party line. From the mid-1920s his position mirrored all the zigzags ordained by Moscow, and he was exceedingly zealous in glorifying Stalin* and the CPSU. Codovilla described the Soviet leader as "one of the greatest geniuses of humanity" and described Soviet agricultural policies as having always been "inspired by Stalinist humanist concepts" (*Un congreso de constructores del comunismo y de defensores de la paz mundial*, 2d ed. [Buenos Aires: Anteo, 1953], pp. 5, 16).

In applying Soviet perspectives to Argentina, Codovilla made few allowances for national peculiarities and steered his Party into opposing the two Argentine popular nationalist movements of the present century: Yrigoyenism and Peronism. Yrigoyen's plan to nationalize petroleum in the late 1920s was dismissed as demagogy, and he and his followers were branded "radical fascists." Far more damaging to the PCA was its dismissal of millions of workers as *peronazis* in the 1940s. Although Codovilla's Party made a minor shift in position to one of "constructive opposition" following Perón's establishment of diplomatic relations and sponsorship of trade with the Soviet Union, antifascist rhetoric resurfaced in attacks on Peronism after the anti-Peronist military coup of 1955. Labor support for the PCA, which had been significant during the 1930s, dwindled greatly as a result of the anti-Peronist posture adopted by Codovilla and other PCA leaders. Most of Codovilla's works take the form of published speeches and reports to congresses.

BIBLIOGRAPHY:

A. *Batir al nazi-peronismo para abrir una era de libertad y progreso* (Buenos Aires: Anteo, 1946); *Trabajos escogidos* (Buenos Aires: Anteo, 1972).

B. Robert J. Alexander, *Communism in Latin America* (New Brunswick, N.J.: Rutgers University Press, 1957); Jorge Abelardo Ramos, *Historia del stalinismo en la Argentina* (Buenos Aires: Rancagua, 1974); Hugh Thomas, *The Spanish Civil War*, 3d ed., rev. and enl. (Harmondsworth: Penguin, 1977); Burnett Bulloten, *The Spanish Revolution* (Chapel Hill: University of North Carolina Press, 1979).

                                                                RICHARD GILLESPIE

CONNOLLY, JAMES   (1868–1916). Born in Edinburgh, Scotland, of Irish parents in 1868, James Connolly was executed in Dublin, Ireland, in 1916 for his part in the leadership of the national insurrection known as the Easter Rising. Of Irish nationality, he remained a citizen of the United Kingdom of Great Britain and Ireland. A life-long socialist activist and propagandist in Scotland, England, Ireland, and the United States, Connolly worked mainly in manual jobs when he was not employed as a political or trade union organizer. He lived as a socialist, only to die as an Irish nationalist. His socialist career was exactly coterminous with the Second International* (1889–1914): he was part of the Marxist current of British socialism that emerged from the 1880s; and he became increasingly sympathetic toward laborism, the political expression of British trade unionism, concerned to secure labor representation on public bodies. During his life, British politics were dominated by the Home Rule era (1880s–1920s), when Ireland sought to secure self-government. This became part of the progressive program of British politics, despite opposition in Ireland from the Ulster Protestant minority and in England from conservative Tories who feared that the weakening of the union between Britain and Ireland would endanger the empire. Connolly favored Irish self-government, although his Irish nationalism had little practical implication for his socialism. When partition was threatened and self-government postponed because of World War I in 1914, Connolly was forced to act. In the last eighteen months of his life he moved into the camp of the revolutionary nationalists, becoming one of their leaders. He was a Marxist until the 1914 "transition" in his politics led to his flowering as a revolutionary nationalist. But he was no socialist apostate. He is best described as a Marxist and Irish nationalist, for he had come to see an Irish nation-state as a precondition for socialism in Ireland. When his Marxism failed to bring him to social revolution, Connolly advocated, for practical reasons, an Irish revolution without any necessary socialist content.

His life can be periodized: (1) 1868–82, Edinburgh childhood and early youth in an unskilled, working-class family, receiving a rudimentary, Catholic education; (2) 1882–89, soldier in the army and although the details are disputed, likely serving in Ireland; (3) 1889–96, socialist apprenticeship in Edinburgh, a member of the local section of the Social Democratic Federation and also the early Independent Labour Party, and Scotland's first socialist journalist; (4) 1896–1903, his "first Irish period," when he established the first Irish socialist party, the Irish Socialist Republican Party, and paper, the *Workers' Republic* (1898–1903), propagandizing socialism in a nationalist political culture; (5) 1903–10, his "American period," when he lived in and near New York City, joining and resigning the Socialist Labor Party, becoming an organizer in the Industrial Workers of the World, working for the Socialist Party, and also establishing the Irish Socialist Federation to propagate ethnic socialism to Irish-Americans; (6) 1910–16, his "second Irish period," when he worked as a political organizer and then trade union official in Belfast before moving, in October 1914, to Dublin, where he joined the revolutionary underground, helped build the Irish Citizen Army, and eventually established insurrectionary headquarters in Dublin's General Post Office (GPO) on Easter Monday 1916, thereby securing a place in Irish national history.

Connolly has been mythologized by post-1916 Irish nationalism and by post-1917 Soviet Marxism as, respectively, the socialist who made a stand for the Irish nation and the Irish Lenin* who acted on the Leninist principle of the right of nations to self-determination. Both myths cross-fertilize, the former eliding the socialist critique of Connolly's politics and the latter distorting his real contribution to international socialism. There was but one Connolly, but he drew on the separate traditions of Second International Marxism and Irish nationalism. Hence two Connollys can be detected in his work, in the unrelated and incompatible paradigms of class and nation.

Connolly was a propagandist not a theorist. His two major works—*Labour in Irish History* (1910) and *The Re-Conquest of Ireland* (1915)—show him as an organic intellectual of the working class who stressed agitation, not innovation. Marx* had bequeathed a theory that did not adequately explain the role nationalism would play in the impending worldwide proletariat revolution. Connolly's rather naive Marxist theorizing was internationalist to the core, but the center, which should have been filled by a Marxist interpretation of Irish politics and society, contained ony Irish nationalism. Connolly had abandoned the Irish question to a nationalist answer, an answer that, because of the inability of Irish nationalists to hegemonize all the popular classes in the country, has never come into being. As a Marxist he should have struggled systematically with how the restructuring of the Irish state would contribute to democratic life and advance the cause of socialism. There are only glimpses of this in Connolly's writings on Ireland, certainly not enough to establish an Irish Marxist tradition. Instead, Marxism and nationalism are sloppily intermingled. There are socialist challenges and polemics but no fundamental undermining of nationalist propositions.

When in 1916 Connolly marched into the GPO, his revolutionary nationalism amounted to a rejection of socialism and a threat to democracy. The Irish working class was divided on the question of self-government, between a Catholic Irish nationalism and a Protestant Ulster unionism. Neither bloc was democratic or socialist. Connolly did not seriously address the question of working-class division. He eventually set his socialism to one side, not consciously denying it, but not affirming either. The believer in working-class self-activity and independent working-class politics across the globe was now prepared to bank all on an insurrectionary conspiracy that, somehow, would ignite a national revolutionary mass movement.

If Connolly made an original contribution it was in the United States, in the industrial unionism of the Industrial Workers of the World. There, he addressed the questions of working-class strategy, how to replace capitalism with socialism, and how to utilize industrial and political action effectively. The Second International had been politically fatalistic, dismissing the importance of trade unionism in Western capitalist democracies. Connolly's support for industrial unionism in America drew on the writings of Daniel DeLeon,* but also on his own proletarian instincts, and allowed him to bring the masses into an active struggle for socialism. In America Connolly functioned as a Marxist pedagogue, struggling to unite theory and practice.

BIBLIOGRAPHY:

A. *Labor in Ireland*, 2 vols. (Dublin: Sign of the Three Candles, 1910–15); *Socialism and Nationalism* (Dublin: Sign of the Three Candles, 1948); *Labor and Easter Week* (Dublin: Sign of the Three Candles, 1949); *The Workers' Republic* (Dublin: Sign of the Three Candles, 1951); *Selected Political Writings* (London: Jonathan Cape, 1973).

B. C. Desmond Greaves, *The Life and Times of James Connolly* (London: Lawrence and Wishart, 1961); Carl Reeve and Ann Barton, *James Connolly and the United States: The Road to the 1916 Rebellion* (Atlantic Highlands, N.J.: Humanities Press, 1978); Bernard Ransom, *Connolly's Marxism* (London: Pluto, 1980).

AUSTEN MORGAN

CONSUEGRA HIGGINS, JOSÉ   (b. 1926). Colombian economist and professor, José Consuegra Higgins was born 28 March 1926, in Isabel López,

Atlántico. He received his Ph.D. in economics at the National University in 1951. In addition to dean of the faculties of economics at the University of the Atlantic and the University of Cartagena, Consuegra has held professorships in economic theory and political economy at numerous universities. Among the posts Consuegra has occupied are chief of regional planning, communal action, and urbanism in the Administrative Department of Planning and Technical Service and head of the National Council of Political Economy and Planning. Consuegra has authored many books on economic theory, population growth, interest, salaries, and inflation. He directs the journal *Revista desarrollo indoamericano*.

Among his many theoretical contributions, José Consuegra's most significant contributions to modern social theory evolve from his attempt to reconcile economic theory with the history of underdeveloped nations. He contends that economic principles advanced as universal have originated in developed countries and therefore do not hold true for underdeveloped countries. Consuegra analyzes traditional economic theories (including those of Marx*) within a materialist dialectical framework, and in the context of Colombian reality. Among his many theoretical contributions are his application of Lenin's* concepts of imperialism and monopolistic capital to Latin America, his discussion of Malthusian concepts on population increase, and his critique of Marx's theory of paper money. He makes no significant departure from Lenin's principles, but rather considers them perfectly suited to analyzing Latin American underdevelopment. He concludes that Colombian history bears out Lenin's assessment of the relationship between underdevelopment and the concentration of capital, role of banks, export of capital, latifundia, minifundia, structural problems of underdeveloped countries, and inequitable distribution of income. Consuegra also criticizes the Malthusian doctrine that population increases must be controlled because such increases result in a decrease in real wages, thereby impeding development. While acknowledging the fact that decreases in real wages do occur, Consuegra maintains that so-called Malthusian doctrines merely constitute another manifestation of imperialism. He argues that the fault lies not with the increase in the population but with capitalist exploitation. Finally, Consuegra uses Marxist analysis to criticize Marx's concepts of the theory of paper money. He asserts that Marx's principles are confusing, contradict the law of circulation, and "participate in the metalist and quantitative spirit of capitalism" (*Un nuevo enfoque de la teoría de la inflación*, pp. 11–12). Marx concludes that the product of prices and the rhythm of circulation determine the amounts necessary for circulation. Consuegra, using Lenin's analysis of the concentration of capital in the imperialistic stage, concludes that prices are determined by the monopolistic producers and that the quantity of money in circulation stretches to fit the need.

BIBLIOGRAPHY:

A. *Apuntes de la economía política* (Bogotá: Pensamiento Económica y Social, 1963); *Lenín y la América Latina* (Bogotá: Cruz del Sur, 1971); *El control de la natalidad como arma del imperialism* (Barranquilla: Ediciones de la Universidad del Atlantico, 1972);

Interés, dependencia y subdesarollo (n.p.: Ediciones Universidad de Córdoba, Universidad de Medellin, Universidad Simón Bolívar, 1975); *Un nuevo enfoque de la teoría de la inflación* (Bogotá: Tercer Mundo, 1976).

DAWN FOGLE DEATON

COOKE, JOHN WILLIAM (1920–1968). Born in La Plata, Argentina, on 14 November 1920 into an ardently Radical family of Irish origin, John Cooke was politically active right from his school days. During the 1930s he supported a nationalist wing of the Radical Party known as FORJA, and with most *forjistas* he transferred his allegiance to Peronism when it emerged in 1945. His father, Dr. Juan Isaac Cooke, was minister of foreign relations in 1945, the year that John William graduated as a lawyer. In the ensuing 1946 elections Cooke was elected to Congress at the age of twenty-five. He immediately made his mark by being the only Peronist deputy to oppose ratification of the Treaty of Chapultepec and the United Nations Charter, regarding both as threats to Argentine sovereignty. In 1951 he paid for his dissidence by not being readopted. Cooke briefly lectured in political economy at the University of Buenos Aires before becoming editor of the militant Peronist magazine *De Frente* (1954–55), which presented itself as the moral and political conscience of the Peronist movement.

After a coup was attempted in June 1955, Cooke was appointed to take charge of the Peronist Party in the federal capital, where he unsuccessfully called for a strategy of popular mobilization and armed resistance in the face of the approaching September coup. When the military seized power he created a resistance *comando* but was betrayed and arrested in October. Despite Cooke's imprisonment, Perón named him as resistance commander, a task he was able to fulfill more directly following an escape from Rió Gallegos to Chile early in 1957.

During 1958 Cooke made several trips into Argentina for clandestine meetings with resistance units and Intransigent Radical leader Arturo Frondizi. He was a signatory to the Perón–Frondizi pact of February of that year, although he clearly distrusted Frondizi's nationalist promises. As leader of the Resistencia Peronista Cooke promoted worker cadres and hard-liners in an effort to provide labor struggles with effective political leadership. In November 1958 he flew to Argentina to support an oil workers' strike, but was arrested at the airport and detained on a prison ship until the end of that year. Nevertheless, he was again present in Argentina when the Resistencia reached its peak in the "revolutionary general strike" of January 1959. When it failed, his dismissal was organized by conservative Peronist politicians while he was being hunted by the security forces.

Persecution in Argentina forced him into exile in 1960, and it was quite natural that the increasingly radical Cooke should find his haven in Cuba. There Cooke's revolutionary nationalism found a coherent overall framework in Cuban Marxism, and he developed a close personal friendship with Che Guevara.* He became totally identified with the Cuban Revolution and was soon active there as revolutionary instructor and as militiaman in Cuban army operations against counterrevolutionaries infiltrated into the Sierras of Escambray. Both of the early rural guerrilla efforts in Argentina, the Uturuncos and People's Guerrilla Army (EGP), came under his political influence, and he was directly involved in the establishment of guerrilla training camps in Cuba and Argentina.

Cooke was only able to return to Argentina after the lifting of a state of siege in October 1963, and his final years on the mainland were his most productive as a theoretician. He remained a committed supporter of Cuba and headed the Argentine delegations to the Tricontinental and OLAS conferences, but in the light of the early 1960s rural guerrilla failures he soon realized that the Cuban model of revolution could not be mechanically applied elsewhere in Latin America. In creating his own organization, Peronist Revolutionary Action (Acción Revolucionaria Peronista—ARP) in the mid-1960s, Cooke demonstrated that his main concern was with a radicalization of the broad Peronist movement, rather than isolated armed initiatives of the *foquista* variety.

The death of Cooke came in 1968, just before the public emergence of the organizations such as the Montoneros and People's Revolutionary Army (ERP) and before the germs of a radical Peronism, which he had done so much to promote, crystallized into a powerful revolutionary tendency. His major works were not published until at least three years after his death (although his articles were available earlier). Ideologically, his posthumous influence was greater than his influence while alive. By 1973 Cooke's books had become second only to those of Perón in the best-selling Peronist book league. Young Peronists who believed that Peronism could or had become a revolutionary movement eagerly bought them. Most militants became acquainted with his ideas, though, through politically selective excerpts from his work. Within the Peronist left those who most seriously studied his thought were members of the small *alternativista* groups, such as Peronismo de Base, which hoped to build an "independent working-class alternative."

Cooke's personal wish was to die fighting like Che Guevara and Camilo Torres.* Instead he died in bed of an incurable cancer, by a strange quirk of history on 19 September 1968, the same day as guerrillas of the embryonic Peronist Armed Forces (FAP) were captured at Taco Ralo, Tucumán.

Although Cooke's parliamentary speeches reveal an early familiarity with Marxist ideas and some agreement with Marx's* vision of capitalism's character, his approximation to Marxism did not reach fruition before his exile in Cuba. The transition from militant Peronism to Marxism was eased by a recognition, even during the early years when his desired revolution was anti-oligarchic and anti-imperialist, that only the proletarian base of the Peronist movement had revolutionary potential, whereas the bureaucratic leadership of the movement was prone to temporization and compromise with its political enemies. As he became more radical the national revolution became increasingly bound up with a struggle for socialism.

From Cuba, Cooke decried the anti-Communist position of Peronist leaders in Argentina and argued that national liberation could never be consolidated without a social revolution. He presented Peronism and Castroism* as national variations of a common continental revolutionary struggle, for although he appreciated that Peronism's social composition differed from that of the Cuban anti-Batista alliance, he believed that Peronism was open to radicalization. Cooke always accepted the reality of Peronism's multi-class composition, but after the Cuban Revolution he insisted that the nonbourgeois sectors had to lead the movement, replacing the bureaucratic and at most reformist leadership of the movement inside Argentina.

Cooke's analysis of the revolutionary process presented class struggle as being waged within the Peronist movement as well as in Argentine society at large. Peronism had its limitations as a revolutionary movement, but would not disappear simply by negation but by integration into a new synthesis as the class struggle developed. Cooke was in agreement with those Marxists who stressed the need to build a revolutionary party, but he considered that this would develop out of the rank and file and left wing of the Peronist movement, not independently of it. Not surprisingly, he became the main theoretician of the Peronist left, albeit one whose example was to produce more epigones than followers in practice.

As for strategy and tactics, Cooke saw a role for guerrilla warfare, adapted to Argentina's urban condition, in the confrontation with the armed might of the state. However, his writings were less militaristic than those of Carlos Marighela* and Régis Debray.† Guerrillas could play an acceleratory role in the revolutionary process, but the latter could only reach a successful conclusion if armed struggle went hand in hand with mass struggles and led to a mass insurrection. Although revolution was to be made primarily by the working class, guerrilla warfare could help the masses see that revolution was a real possibility and thus persuade them to join the struggle.

Arguably the weakest aspect of Cooke's theories lay in his appraisal of Perón and estimation of his potential as the movement's leader. For a long time, influenced by the exiled Perón's radical-sounding pronouncements of the 1960s, Cooke relied upon Perón to make the major changes necessary for a revolutionary restructuring of the movement. He acknowledged no political differences with his leader until 1962 and as late as 1964 was hoping that Perón would shift his "revolutionary base" from Madrid to Havana. Clearly he had some illusions in Perón's alleged "left turn," although there was also the tactical element of Cooke being unable to question sharply a man whose leadership was unquestioned by the working class. Only in 1967 in one of his last articles, "La revolución y el peronismo," did Cooke finally come to a class judgment of Perón as the main asset of bourgeois democratic politics in Argentina.

Moreover, there was an air of unreality about Cooke's contention from 1959 onward that, although bourgeois groups were incapable of leading a revolutionary process, they might still play a subordinate role in a worker-led struggle for national and social liberation. Both this idea and the illusion of Perón as a revolutionary were to feature prominently in the ideology of the Peronist left, which had unduly high revolutionary expectations when Perón returned to Argentina in 1973.

BIBLIOGRAPHY:

A. *El peronismo y el golpe de estado* (Buenos Aires: Acción Revolucionaria Peronista, 1966), also published as *Peronismo y revolución* (Buenos Aires: Granica, 1971); *Apuntes para la militancia* (Buenos Aires: Schapire, 1973); *La lucha por la liberación nacional*, 2d ed. (Buenos Aires: Granica, 1973), including "La revolución y el peronismo"; Juan Domingo Perón and J. W. Cooke, *Correspondencia Perón–Cooke*, 2 vols., 2d ed. (Buenos Aires: Granica, 1973).

B. Donald C. Hodges, *Argentina, 1943–1976: The National Revolution and Resistance* (Albuquerque: University of New Mexico Press, 1976); R. H. C. Gillespie, "John William Cooke and Early Peronist Left Ideology," in "The Peronist Left" (Ph.D. thesis, University of Liverpool, 1979).

RICHARD GILLESPIE

CORTESI, LUIGI   (b. 1929). Born in 1929 in Bergamo, Italy, Luigi Cortesi is currently professor of contemporary history at the University of Naples. He was director of the Feltrinelli Library from 1956 to 1959, and founded together with Stefano Merli the *Rivista storica del socialismo* (1958–67), which played a major role in counterposing to the Italian Communist Party's (PCI's) interpretation of history a Leninist* perspective sympathetic to the Bordiga* left. Cortesi has been a constant critic from the left of the PCI's "politics of national unity" and has investigated the historical and theoretical roots of the Party's reformist strategy, tracing them back to the defeat of the Bordiga left and the accession of Gramsci† to leadership of the party.

BIBLIOGRAPHY:

A. *La rivoluzione leninista* (Bari: DiDonato, 1970); *Le origini del P.C.I.* (Bari: Laterza, 1972); *Gramsci e Togliatti: nascita di una strategia* (Rome: Bulzoni, 1984).

LAWRENCE GARNER

D

DALTON GARCIA, ROQUE   (1935–75). Although never a major innovator in the field of Marxist theory, Roque Dalton, who was born in El Salvador in 1935, must be considered a major figure in the Latin American revolutionary movement if only for the sheer scope of his activities. A significant and prolific poet, novelist, sensitive and analytical historian, resourceful political thinker and Party militant, he in many respects represented the "new man" projected by the Cuban regime with which he had such close ties. Joining the Salvadorean Communist Party (PCS) in 1957, he was for a decade a model militant celebrated more for his literary endeavors than directly political contributions. His poetry evidences a fine yet resourceful articulation of revolutionary ideals with social realism, expressed in rich and subtle language. His historical writing also demonstrates a consistent propensity to reconsider doctrinal readings of events as well as an appreciation of subjective factors.

His break with the PCS in 1969 came when he was living in Cuba and had developed strong leanings toward the armed struggle, sympathy for the "Vietnamese road," and a close interest in the writings of Vo Nguyen Giap.* Although he never advocated the strategy of the *guerra popular prolongada* supported by the Fuerzas Populares de Liberación Nacional-Farabundo Martí (FPL) of Salvador Cayetano,* his position was implicitly quite close to it. Instead, he rejected the *foco* theory for that of a "mass line" of an antifascist front, led by the working class and peasantry but incorporating much wider sectors. Returning to El Salvador to engage in military activity in 1972, Dalton was killed by some of his own comrades in a sordid internal struggle, which led his followers to split to form a new group, the FARN. This pointless and tragically early death deprived the Salvadorean left of one of its most talented figures of recent decades.
BIBLIOGRAPHY:

A. *Miguel Mármol* (San Jose: Editorial Universitaria Centroamericana, 1972); *Pobrecito poeta que era yo* (San José: Editorial Universitaria Centroamericana, 1976); *Las historias prohibidas del Pulgarcito* (Mexico: Siglo XXI, 1980).

JAMES DUNKERLEY

DAMODARAN, K.   (b. 1912). Damodaran was born in India in 1912, and was educated at Zamorin College, Kozhikode, in the state of Kerala, and at

Kashi Vidya Pith, Banaras. He joined the freedom struggle under Gandhi's leadership in 1930 and was imprisoned many times. He became a member of the All India Congress Committee, the decision-making body of the Indian National Congress, during the 1930s and also secretary of the state wing of the Congress Party in Kerala State during 1939. He was a member of the Communist Party as early as 1935. Like many Indian Communist leaders of that time, he joined the Congress Party first, was then attracted to socialist ideas, and finally joined the Socialist Party, which provided a legal front for the banned Communist Party. He was editor of the local Malayalam-language weekly *Nava Yugam* (New Age) from 1951 to 1964, and was a member of the literary body in Kerala known as the Sahitya Academy from 1956 to 1961. He wrote several books and published articles both in English and in his mother tongue Malayalam. Damodaran was also a short story writer and playwright. He was versed in the many schools of Indian philosophy and was able to apply his knowledge of Marxism when interpreting ancient and modern Indian philosophies.

Like most Marxists in India, he must be considered "orthodox," since apart from occasional criticisms of the Party's line he did not generate any new theoretical concepts. Nevertheless, the Twentieth Party Congress of the Soviet Union and the de-Stalinization that followed came as a rude shock to Damodaran, who was probably one of the very few Indian orthodox Marxists who "did not believe in the Stalinist* falsification of history in which Trotsky* was depicted as an imperialist spy and a fascist agent" (Damodaran's answers to questions put by *New Left Review* in September-October 1975).

His contribution to Marxism, however modest, is important because he (along with D. Kosambi,* W. Ruben, and D. Chattopadhyaya) tried to integrate Marxist thought with indigenous Indian philosophy. Damodaran claimed that Heraclitus was not alone among the ancients as a founder of dialectical thinking. The ancient Hindus, he argued, were also pioneers in the application of dialectical method, even though Hinduism and Western philosophy are conceptually quite different. Damodaran's comparative studies analyzed India's idealistic, materialistic, and monistic ways of thinking, and the various social movements that came in their wake, from his dialectical materialist perspective. He shows how in the Upanishads, the most ancient of Hindu scriptures, for example, the Hindus recognized the continuity of change in the universe. Similarly, he traced the changes in Indian thought from idealism to materialism and related these to India's intensifying class distinctions. The rise of Indian materialism, the so-called Lokayat philosophy, was viewed in the context of the rise of Brahminism and its theological priesthood. The medieval Bhakti movement, which arose in the wake of the great Vedantic guru Ramanuja, similarly reflected the philosophical interests of the lower classes. Despite the socio-economic roots of these Indian philosophies, Damodaran also recognizes—as any orthodox Marxist must—their essentially conservative, supportive social consequences. His message, finally, is that Marxism in India must be enriched by the Indian philosophical tradition.

BIBLIOGRAPHY:

A. *Indian Thought: A Critical Survey* (New Delhi: Asia Publishing House, 1967); *Man and Society in Indian Philosophy* (New Delhi: Peoples' Publishing House, 1970).

B. The Damodaran Memorial Committee, ed., *Prospects of Left Unity* (New Delhi: Enree, 1979); *National and Left Movements in India* (New Delhi: Vikas Publishing House, 1980).

K. SESHADRI

DAS GUPTA, PROMODE   (1910–1982). Born in India in 1910, Promode Das Gupta was a dour, often abrasive exemplar of the Communist "organization man." With Jyoti Basu,* Das Gupta helped organize the Communist Party of India (Marxist) (CPI[M]) and worked hard to make it the top-ranking party in a government coalition of left parties in West Bengal State (India). He played a key role as an organization man turned ideologue in the split in the Communist Party of India (CPI) in 1964 on the fundamental issue of whether Indian Communists should follow a policy of "unity and struggle" with the bourgeois Congress Party or adopt instead a political struggle against the bourgeois Congress regime in order to establish working-class hegemony over Indian politics through a strong nonrevisionist Communist Party.

During the troubles of the CPI(M) in West Bengal, Das Gupta clashed with Jyoti Basu, with Harekrishna Konar (who forged an alliance of Communists and rich peasants in West Bengal's biggest district, Burdwan), and with the explosive Naxalite Communist movement. An early disagreement was caused by Das Gupta's initiative in a ruthless drive to eliminate the Naxalites from the CPI(M) organization solely for violation of Party discipline when, obviously, wider ideological-political issues were involved. A struggle against those West Bengal Communists who did not join the CPI(M), but stayed with the CPI, peaked during the early stages of the "Emergency" declared in India in 1975–77 by the central Congress government, when belief in the tactic of "unity and struggle" made the CPI temporarily extend its support to the Emergency. But a few years before his death Das Gupta gave his consent to the readmission of the CPI to the West Bengal left front headed by the CPI(M), after it had unambiguously abandoned the policy of "unity and struggle" with the Congress and adopted a policy of "basic opposition" to the Congress regime in India. There was no similar rapprochement with any of the Naxalite factions.

Das Gupta's singular achievement was to give organizational support to West Bengali Communists to penetrate almost every pore of West Bengali society before, during, and after the CPI(M) captured power in West Bengal State, through a combination of parliamentary and extraparliamentary political action and a thoroughgoing organizational consolidation. The aim was to capture what Antonio Gramsci† referred to as the "molecules of the civil society." The "molecules" of the civil society "captured" in this way, and controlled somewhat like cogs in a vast democratic-centralist bureaucratic machine, were heterogeneous in nature. They included politicized trade unions and peasant associations, but also intensely politicized clubs and professional associations, extending even to exlandlord "old rich" members of the governing bodies of educational institutions, bar libraries, etc. Layers of society hitherto untouched by organized communism, such as police and prison personnel, also came within the ambit of this relentless drive. Das Gupta is not known, however, to have been familiar with Gramsci's work. He seems to have rediscovered the Gramsci strategy independently and applied it in practice. His crowning achievement was the electoral capture of more than half the village-level elective bodies, or *gram panchayats*.

There is every chance that these efforts have established a distinctive multi-class civil society based on a Bengali Communist subculture, to match, say, the dominant Bengali civil society of Bangladesh (based on a Bengali Muslim bourgeois subculture), or the dominant Tamilian civil society centered in Tamil Nadu (India), which is based on an anti-Brahmin, irredentist bourgeois subculture. The formation of a new civil society requires both continuity and discontinuity with the dominant cultural-political traditions of the larger civil society within which it is born. In the 1970s and 1980s Basu and Das Gupta staked a claim to continuity by labeling the popular but non-Communist Ram Mohun Roy and Subhas Bose precursors of the modern Bengali Communist cultural, social, and political tradition. On the other hand, a bold step toward a break in continuity was the replacement of the traditional Bengal school primer by a new elementary school textbook that has been collectively written by little-known authors selected by the CPI(M)-led left front ministry. The new primer focuses more sharply and clearly than did its predecessor on the contemporary class structure and class struggles in West Bengali society. Similarly, a bold step has been taken to establish the culture of West Bengal communism by extending state patronage for the education of Santal (tribal) schoolchildren of West Bengal in the Santali language, written in a newly designed *alchiki* script (in place of the Bengali script earlier in use).

ARUN BOSE

DAVIS, ANGELA YVONNE   (b. 1944). Angela Davis is a black American political activist and social scientist who was born on 26 January 1944 in Birmingham, Alabama. She worked with the philosopher Herbert Marcuse† at Brandeis University, from which she received her A.B. degree in 1965. First alerted to the problem of racism by an explosion in a Baptist Sunday school classroom that killed several of her Birmingham acquaintances, Ms. Davis became radicalized through contact with Algerian students during a junior year abroad while still at Brandeis. In 1965 she returned to Europe to study philosophy under the guidance of the Marxist Theodore Adorno.† However, when intensified civil protest broke out in the United States, she transferred to the University of Southern California at San Diego in order to engage in political activity and to resume her studies with Marcuse. She earned her M.A. in philosophy from that university in 1968, and by 1969 had fulfilled all requirements for the Ph.D.

except the dissertation. While at San Diego she helped organize the Black Students' Council, pressured for an experimental college for minorities, and worked with the Black Conference, a militant community organization.

After participating in a workshop sponsored by the Student Non-Violent Coordinating Committee, Davis moved to Los Angeles to become further involved in the Los Angeles SNCC, and later with the Black Panther Party and the Che-Lumumba Club, an all-black group affiliated with the Communist Party U.S.A. The major purpose of the latter, according to Davis's *Autobiography*, was to carry Marxist-Leninist ideas to the black liberation struggle. She joined the Communist Party itself in July 1968. A trip to Cuba made in 1969 confirmed, for Davis, the affinity of the black and Third World liberation movements.

Also in 1969 Davis first came to public notice when she was dismissed from her teaching position in the Department of Philosophy at the University of California at Los Angeles by Governor Ronald Reagan because she was a Communist. Although she was reinstated by court order, in 1970 the Board of Regents successfully terminated Davis's university appointment, citing as evidence of unfitness her speeches in behalf of the Soledad Brothers, under indictment for the murder of a tower guard at Soledad Prison. While engaged in the defense of the Soledad Brothers, Davis became involved with George Jackson, one of the accused who was later killed while allegedly attempting to escape from San Quentin Prison. His letters to Davis can be found in Jackson's book, *Soledad Brother* (1970).

On 7 August 1970 George Jackson's younger brother Jonathan, using several guns registered in Davis's name, took hostages during a trial at the Marin County Courthouse in San Rafael, supposedly in an attempt to ransom the Soledad defendants. In the ensuing shootout Judge Harold Haley and Jonathan Jackson, among other persons, were killed. On the basis of her ownership of the guns, Davis was sought by the state of California as a co-conspirator in the murder and kidnapping. Later, when she went into hiding, the Federal Bureau of Investigation placed her on its Ten Most Wanted list. Davis was arrested in New York City and extradicted to California, where she was held without bail until 1972. By this time her case had attracted attention and protest throughout the world. On 4 June 1972 a jury acquitted Davis on all counts raised against her. Upon her release she organized the National Alliance Against Racist and Political Repression to call attention to "political" prisoners in the United States, many of whom were poor, minorities, and women. Her edited anthology, *If They Come in the Morning* (1971), includes material on her own and other cases in which Davis was politically involved. Davis now teaches courses in women's studies and black philosophy and aesthetics at San Francisco State University.

Davis espouses the classic Marxist position that production and reproduction constitute the two key processes in society and that the course of a revolution can be judged according to the changes taking place in the status of women and of the working class. However, in the United States racism, along with sexism, has been used to exploit working people for the benefit of capitalist economic interests. The nineteenth-century women's suffrage movement—as well as its current feminist counterpart—has failed to link the phenomena of racism, sexism, and class exploitation, and hence has remained a captive of bourgeois ideology. Furthermore, according to Davis, by concentrating mainly on the plight and emancipation of women as a sex, feminism has failed to take into account the identity of black and working-class women with their men, or to challenge the capitalist class, the primary source of power and oppression. Thus feminism has had a limited appeal outside the white middle class.

The black woman, used as slave labor, as a breeder of white men's property, and as an object for the expression of their sexual desire, has historically constituted the most oppressed segment of capitalist society; simultaneously, the myth of the black matriarch has facilitated the emasculation and oppression of black men by whites. Rather than acquiesce in their fate, in fact black women under slavery "worked for and protected their families, fought against slavery, and were beaten and raped, but never subdued" (*Women, Race and Class*, p. 19). In the process they have created and passed on "a legacy spelling out standards for a new womanhood" (ibid., p. 19), which includes sexual equality with men.

According to Davis, black women must challenge bourgeois family structures and the general role of women in American society, but in the context of a "total" socio-economic revolution, which includes an assault on the racist and exploitative capitalist order, domestically and abroad. Such a women's liberation movement would contribute toward the emancipation of blacks from racist oppression. It would also assist in the destruction of the myths concerning black women and men that the white capitalist class has used to divide the black community. Davis's ultimate goal is the creation of a nonracist socialist society in which socialized child care and industrialized household services are available to all working people.

BIBLIOGRAPHY:

A. *Angela Davis: An Autobiography* (New York: Random House, 1971); *If They Come in the Morning: Voices of Resistance* (New York: Third Press, 1971); *Women, Race and Class* (New York: Random House, 1981).

KAREN ROSENBLUM-CALE

DELEON, DANIEL   (1852–1914). Daniel DeLeon was born 14 December 1852 on the island of Curaçao to Sephardic Jewish parents. His background is shrouded in mystery and controversy. He apparently attended the University of Leyden and came to the United States in 1872, receiving a law degree from Columbia University in 1878. After practicing law in Texas, he became a lecturer at Columbia. His first involvement in politics came during Henry George's 1886 campaign for mayor of New York. Two years later, Edward Bellamy's *Looking Backward* converted him to socialism. Shortly afterward, he embraced Marxism and joined the Socialist Labor Party. Within a few years his energy, intelligence, and capacity for intrigue and polemics enabled DeLeon to gain control of the SLP. It remained the preeminent Marxist party in America only until 1899, when his policies and behavior led to the formation of the Socialist Party. DeLeon played a role in the founding of the Industrial Workers of the World. When he died in 1914, the SLP was a tiny sect, which it has remained to this day.

DeLeon's major theoretical contributions to Marxism came in his discussion of the road to power. He resolutely opposed making immediate political or economic demands upon the capitalist state. Unions that fought for shorter hours or higher wages were inevitably corrupted; their leaders became "labor lieutenants" of capitalism. Strikes should be inspirational movements on the road to socialism. By the same token, DeLeon opposed political reform. As long as capitalist political parties held power, workers could expect nothing from them. Only a socialist revolution could better their lot. The electoral and industrial struggles had to proceed simultaneously. DeLeon envisaged a syndicalist society organized around industrial unions.

BIBLIOGRAPHY:

B. L. Glenn Seretan, *Daniel DeLeon: The Odyssey of an American Marxist* (Cambridge: Harvard University Press, 1979).

RICHARD KLEHR

DENG XIAOPING   (b. 1904). Deng Xiaoping is known as a practical leader, with little interest in questions of theory or the visionary promises of socialism. This image is accurate. Since he joined the Communist Party in the early 1920s while a student in France, Deng has distinguished himself as an organization man, a planner of day-to-day activities, and an advocate of efficient development. His writings and speeches, to the extent that they display a concern for theory, do so not to confront problems of revolution and socialism but in order to legitimize narrowly defined political and economic goals. There is little evidence that theory for Deng has ever served as anything but an instrument in the service of organizational efficiency.

Deng's significance in the Chinese Revolution is obvious. During the revolutionary struggle he distinguished himself as an organizational expert. After 1949, he emerged gradually as an advocate of efficiency in the cause of state building and economic development. By the time of the Cultural Revolution, he stood out as the foremost opponent of Mao Zedong* and the Cultural Revolutionaries. Since Mao's death in 1976, he has reemerged to launch China in a new direction of development. Policy changes he has instituted since then have been described in China and abroad as a "second revolution." Deng's significance, however, reaches beyond the confines of socialism in China, both in its worldwide impact and in what it reveals about the fate of socialism in the twentieth century. Deng's status as the leader of the largest socialist country in the world places him in a position to shape the meaning of socialism in the world. Although he has not written on socialism, his policies as a leader provide a "text" that speaks more clearly than any abstract treatise might.

Under Deng, socialism has been defined as an ideology of national development. The role of the Communist Party, in this conception, is a managerial one. The Party must guide the efficient management and development of social resources; at the same time it must check against, and control, tendencies that interfere with efficiency. This requires suppression, on the one hand, of revolutionary demands for egalitarianism. To achieve this end, the Party must be made into a coherent bureaucratic organization capable of acting in unity and discipline.

Deng's "second revolution" is reminiscent of the "second revolution" under Stalin* in the Soviet Union, which replaced revolutionaries with managers in the Party. In a basic sense, it is closer to the idea of "democratic centralism" than the "mass line" policies of Mao Zedong, which had sought closer integration of Party and people. Deng's conception of socialism as an instrument of national political and economic development is justified by a dependency-corporatist interpretation of Marxism. The task of revolution, in this view, is to liberate the nation from foreign economic and political domination and to launch an autonomous course of national development under the guidance of a state controlled by the Party. What this view shared with Marxism is its opposition to capitalism; but the future it envisions is not so much socialist as it is non-capitalist. The egalitarian-democratic vision of socialism is replaced in this notion of socialism with an administrative conception of economic and political activity that presupposes a hierarchical social organization. Indeed, Deng's approach to socialism in China makes room for the incorporation of capitalist elements into economic development as long as these elements remain under state control.

Deng is today the most powerful person in China, although he has scrupulously refrained from assuming the formal prerogatives of power.

BIBLIOGRAPHY:

A. *Den Xiaoping wenxuan* (Selections from the works of Deng Xiaoping) (Beijing: n.a., 1983).

B. Chi Hsin, *Teng Hsiao-ping: A Political Biography* (Hong Kong: Cosmos Books, 1978).

ARIF DIRLIK

DESAI, AKSHYAY KUMAR RAMANLAL   (b. 1915). Akshyay Desai was born on 31 May 1915 at Nadiad, Gujarat, western India, into an upper-caste Hindu, Brahmin family. His father was a renowned literary figure in Gujarat who also served in various official capacities in Baroda State. A. R. Desai took his primary and secondary education at several places in Gujarat, as his father was transferred from one place to another for administrative duties. He graduated as a social science major from the University of Bombay. He also earned a law degree and a Ph.D. in sociology from the University of Bombay in 1946. He began his academic career as a lecturer in sociology at his alma mater in 1946 and officially joined the Department of Sociology as a lecturer in 1951. He became a professor and head of the department in 1969, and retired from the university in 1976. Desai was then appointed a senior fellow and a national fellow of the Indian Council of Social Science Research in 1973–75 and 1981–

83, respectively. He was the president of the Indian Sociological Society for 1980 and 1981. Desai was active in the student movement during his college days and in the trade union and the Kisan movements since the 1930s. He was also a member of the Communist Party of India during the period between 1934 and 1939, but he opposed the Party for supporting the war efforts of the British government and resigned in protest. During this period he was influenced by Trotsky's* writings, particularly *The History of the Russian Revolution* and *The Revolution Betrayed*. He is a well-known Trotskyist and has been closely associated with the Fourth International. He was a member of the Revolutionary Socialist Party between 1953 and 1981, but resigned from the RSP in 1981. At present he is affiliated with the Communist League, an Indian section of the Fourth International. He is one of the most influential Marxist scholars among the various extant left groups in India.

Desai is one of the first Marxist sociologists to use historical materialism to analyze the structural transformation of Indian society during the British and postindependence periods. He shows that Indian nationalism was generated by the political subjection of the Indian people by the British. For their own imperial interests, the British introduced capitalist norms of production. It established a new type of centralized state based on capitalist needs and introduced modern education, modern means of communications, and other institutions that resulted in "the growth of a new social class and the unleashing of new social forces unique in themselves" (*Social Background of Indian Nationalism*, p. 15). The rise of an Indian bourgeoisie and an educated middle class came into conflict with British imperialism and became the basis of, and motive for, the rise and development of Indian nationalism.

In his various writings, Desai refutes the theory of the "two-stages revolution" propounded by major left parties such as the Communist Party of India, the Communist Party of India (Marxist), and the Communist Party of India (Marxist-Leninist). These parties argued that India must pass through two stages of development. The first stage will entail a "national democratic," "people's democratic," or "new democratic" revolution. The second stage will commence thereafter and will take the form of a socialist revolution. Desai argues that India has already followed a capitalist path of development under British rule. The native Indian bourgeoisie that now governs is, according to Desai, historically weak. Moreover, it functions at a time of general crisis in the world capitalist system. Desai exposes, with empirical data, the inherent limitations of the welfare state, which has been adopted as a strategic means to save Indian capitalism. He examines both the rural and urban tensions that have appeared in the wake of India's capitalist path of development, as well as various indigenous aspects of Indian society, e.g., caste, class, family, tribe, and religion. He concludes that even elementary bourgeois democratic tasks cannot be attained by the present bourgeoisie. Under capitalism it is simply not possible to liquidate mass poverty, mass unemployment, mass illiteracy, and mass ignorance. These tasks can only be attained through a socialist revolution. Desai argues that Indian social and economic conditions have ripened to the point that this noncapitalist alternative is now both desirable and necessary.

BIBLIOGRAPHY:

A. *Social Background of Indian Nationalism* (New York: Oxford University Press, 1948); *Slums and Urbanization* (Bombay: Popular Prakashan, 1970); *A Positive Program for Indian Revolution* (Bombay: Popular Prakashan, 1974); *State and Society in India* (Bombay: Popular Prakashan, 1975); *Peasant Struggles in India* (Bombay: Oxford University Press, 1979); *Urban Family and Family Planning in India* (Bombay: Popular Prakashan, 1981).

GHANSHYAM SHAH

DIAZ, JOSÉ (1896–1942). A baker by trade, José Diaz was a member of an anarchist labor union, Confederación Nacional de Trabajadores, when, after being jailed in 1925, he came in contact with the Communist Party. Together with several anarchists from Seville he joined the Spanish Communist Party (PCE) in 1927, thus forming one of the few labor groups of the then minority party. The accusations of the representatives of the Third Communist International* against the leaders of the Party, then headed by José Bullejos, brought about the Seville group's domination of the Party's Political Bureau during the Fourth Party Congress, which met in Seville in March 1932. In October of that year, as a result of what was considered improper conduct on the part of the Communist leadership when faced with a military uprising, the International decided to expel Bullejos and bring in José Diaz and his cohorts to head the Secretariat of the PCE. Diaz immediately became secretary general.

Although the official history of the PCE may have presented the rise of Diaz and Ibárruri* as the origin of the "*gran viraje*" (great swing) attributed to Spanish communism, the truth is that, during 1933 and until the first half of 1934, the new leaders of the Party continued the same policies of the previous leadership: radical rejection of the Republic and accusations of Spanish socialism as really being social fascism. Only in September 1934, with the entry of the PCE into the Alianza Obrera (Workers' Alliance), did there begin (due to pressure from the International and under an evident French influence) the political swing that led the PCE into forming a popular front with the Socialists and the leftist Republican parties.

José Diaz, an affable person, had passed into the history of Spanish communism as the leader who best personified the ideal of the Popular Front. Although Jesus Hernandez was, undoubtedly, the leader who explained more rigorously the new policy, Diaz had to convince a Communist Party noted for its leftist politics of the need for a popular front. On his return from the International's Seventh Congress (where he was elected a member of the Executive Committee) he gave several speeches, which contributed no new ideas concerning official policy formulation but which did carry great conviction. Because of the general policy of the Popular Front (and under Diaz's direction), the PCE was able to increase its membership from 300 in 1932 to between 50,000 and 60,000 in the spring of 1936.

During the Civil War Diaz stayed on as Secretary General of the Party, from which position he tried to maintain a balance between the continued pressure exerted by the International and the needs of the leftist coalition that governed the Republic. However, his capacity to lead the Party effectively was diminished, due in part to the clear hegemony of the International and also to the breakdown of his health. He was exiled to the Soviet Union at the end of the Civil War, and his authority was further diminished, while that of Dolores Ibárruri rose. She criticized him severely before the International's Secretariat, further reducing his authority.

Because of Nazi advances he was transferred to the Caucasian city of Tbilisi, where he was hospitalized, isolated, and able to see only a few relatives and the secret police. He ended his life by jumping from a window on 19 March 1942.

BIBLIOGRAPHY:

A. *Tres años de lucha* (Paris: Col. Ebro, 1971).

B. Jane Degras, ed., *The Communist International, 1919–1943* (London: Oxford University Press, 1956–65); Julius Braunthal, *History of the International* (New York: Praeger, 1966); Fernando Claudín, *The Communist Movement, from Comintern to Cominform* (New York: Monthly Review Press, 1975).

SANTOS JULIÁ

DOBB, MAURICE HERBERT   (1900–1976). Maurice Dobb was born on 24 July 1900 in London. Dobb received his M.A. in 1922 from Pembroke College of Cambridge University, where he had become a member of Keynes's Political Economy Club. From 1922 to 1924, with a research studentship, Dobb worked in the graduate program of the London School of Economics and Political Science. There he wrote a Ph.D. thesis that was later to function as a beginning sketch for his magnum opus of 1946, *Studies in the Development of Capitalism*. Dobb began teaching in 1924 as a university lecturer at Cambridge University. In 1948, he was elected a fellow and lecturer of Trinity College at Cambridge University. It was at this time that he started his collaboration with Piero Sraffa in editing the *Works and Correspondence of David Ricardo*. In 1959 Dobb was appointed a reader in economics at Cambridge University, a post he shared with economists of such high repute as Kaldor and Joan Robinson. Upon his retirement from teaching in 1967, Dobb was elected a reader emeritus. In addition to his posts at Cambridge University, Dobb held visiting positions at the University of London, School of Slavonic Studies (1943–46) and at the University of Delhi, India (1951). In autobiographical notes written in 1965 and published in a Maurice Dobb memorial issue of the *Cambridge Journal of Economics* (June 1978), Dobb credited his stay in India for an interest in problems of development, which culminated in 1960 in his publication of *An Essay on Economic Growth and Planning*. Dobb received honorary degrees from the Charles University of Prague, from the University of Budapest, and from the University of Leicester. He was a member of the British Communist Party from 1922 onward. He participated in many political activities: speaking in workers' circles, doing antifascist work in the 1930s, and writing political pamphlets. He remained in the Communist Party through the 1956 events in Hungary; significantly, though—as he mentions in his autobiographical notes—at the 1957 Congress of the British Communist Party he seconded an amendment to the effect that " 'dogmatism' (in place of 'revisionism') was the main danger to be combatted."

Dobb was without a doubt one of the most prominent Marxist Western economists of his time, and certainly the most prominent British Marxist economist. His work was wide ranging (covering economic history, planning, development, economic theory, and the history of economic thought) and almost always path-breaking. The work that alone would have sufficed to ensure the inclusion of Dobb's name in a list of important contributors to Marxism is his *Studies in the Development of Capitalism*. In this work, Dobb provided a flesh of historical facts to the Marxist skeletal thesis that historical developments are to be understood in terms of class relations and struggles. Dobb's immensely important contribution to the Marxist theory of history was his clear and innovative thesis that the transitional process between social formations has to be understood in terms of changes in the mode of surplus extraction and distribution. Specifically, Dobb presented the transition from feudalism to capitalism in terms of the various struggles that developed around forms of rent (feudal forms of surplus extraction and distribution). It is a measure of the importance of Dobb's book to Marxist theory that its appearance sparked a long discussion in Marxist circles about whether the transition to capitalism was best understood as a result of forces internal to the feudal "mode of production" or a result of external forces (trade) impinging on and dissolving feudal relations of production.

Dobb's contribution to Marxism is not as momentous, but is nonetheless very important, when it comes to "pure" economic theory (theory of value, theory of crises), rather than economic history. Dobb contributed to the development of Marxist theory most in his 1937 *Political Economy and Capitalism*. In this book he not only summarized superbly the structure of Marx's economic theory but also, in an article on the place of frictions and expectations in a market economic system, provided an early statement of the relevance of the Keynesian/Kaleckian* critique of neoclassical theory to Marxist theory. Dobb's article could have functioned as a kind of prescient statement of an explicit and self-conscious Marxist research program on the specific class processes that entail economic crises. Unfortunately, this research program did not come into being as a Marxist program, with the result that the Marxist theory of crises is not as fully developed as it could have been. Dobb himself failed to pursue his insights of the 1930s. In the 1940s his attention was taken up with the writing of *Studies*, and in the 1950s he developed an interest in problems of development and growth. Most importantly, in the late 1940s he began cooperating with Sraffa on editing the *Works and Correspondence of David Ricardo*, a task that, for better or worse, drew him more and more into emphasizing the relations of continuity between

Marx and the classical economists and that thus made the task of developing a distinctly Marxist theory of value and of crises a less than urgent task. Dobb's view of the relationship of Marxist theory to classical economics (and, hence, to neoclassical economics) is most completely and masterly presented in his book on the history of economic thought, *Theories of Value and Distribution Since Adam Smith* (1973).

The last of Dobb's contributions to Marxist thought that needs to be mentioned is in the field of socialist planning. Dobb's analyses of socialist planning are particularly important because they present a clear example of how his theoretical and his more explicitly political work affected each other. Dobb's work extended to some of the more technical problems in the theory and practice of planning in socialist countries, covering the so-called Marx-Feldman model of the relationship between the investment goods sector and the consumption goods sector of the economy (the two sectors in Marx's reproduction schemes), and reading critically the Soviet planning experience, both Stalinist and post-Stalinist, in terms of this model. It was in the 1960s that Dobb developed this critical attitude toward the Soviet planning experience, a critical attitude that contrasts with his earlier work, which had been supportive, although not unreservedly so, of Soviet planning. The reason for Dobb's change in attitude was not wholly theoretical but partially, and perhaps more importantly, a matter of practical politics. As he mentions in his autobiographical notes, Dobbs was very much influenced in 1956 by the "Poznan events" in Poland, which he witnessed in person. He came to think that "contradictions were possible in a socialist society" and that, in Soviet history, mistakes—both theoretical and political—had been made, with serious negative consequences.

Maurice Dobb died on 17 August 1976. He has received the universal, if not uncritical, approbation of Marxist students and theoreticians. In the words of Alexander Erlich, a contributor to the *Cambridge Journal of Economics* Maurice Dobb memorial issue, for those "who admired the work and the man, a sense of keen regret for the things left undone will always be overshadowed by gratitude for what he did."

BIBLIOGRAPHY:

A. *Studies in the Development of Capitalism* (New York: International, 1963); *Welfare Economics and the Economics of Socialism* (Cambridge: Cambridge University Press, 1969); *Political Economy and Capitalism*, 2d ed. (London: Routledge and Kegan Paul, 1972); *Theories of Value and Distribution Since Adam Smith* (Cambridge: Cambridge University Press, 1973).

B. *Cambridge Journal of Economics*, 2, no. 2 (June 1978), an entire issue devoted to the work of Maurice Dobb.

ANTONIO CALLARI

DUBČEK, ALEXANDER   (b. 1921). From 1949 to 1960 Alexander Dubček was a district and regional Communist functionary in Slovakia, mainly in the Party apparatus. During that time he completed the College of the Central Committee of the Communist Party of the USSR in Moscow. After 1960 he was active in central Party functions: from 1960 to 1962 as Secretary of the Central Committee of the Communist Party of Slovakia; in 1962–63 as Secretary of the Central Committee of the Czechoslovak Communist Party and a member of the Presidium of the Central Committee; in 1963–68 as First Secretary of the Central Committee of the Slovak Communist Party; in 1968–69 as First Secretary of the Central Committee of the Czechoslovak Communist Party; and 1969 as chairman of the Federal Assembly; and from autumn 1969 as ambassador to Turkey. In 1970 Dubček was expelled from the Communist Party of Czechoslovakia, and he is now employed as a clerk in Bratislava.

Dubček's political career was typical of most of the workers in the Party apparatus. He began as a district functionary and slowly worked his way upward. Nevertheless, he had a few peculiarities. First of all, he made it to the top—the office of First (now General) Secretary of the Central Committee of the Czechoslovak Communist Party. Secondly, he was well aware of the Soviet reality. Prior to World War II his family lived in the Soviet Union, where they went to find work during the Great Depression. Thirdly, he had the courage to oppose the General Secretary of the Central Committee of the Czechoslovak Communist Party (Novotny) and criticize him. His stand was an important factor in the recall of Novotny in 1967–68 and the advent of the Prague Spring.† The motives for Dubček's criticism of Novotny were not related to ambitions for power. Indeed, his election to the highest office in January 1968 took place against his wishes. Power was one of the most serious problems of Dubček's political career. In contrast to other leading Communist officials, the excessive power that he acquired as the head of state encumbered him; he did not want it, nor did he know how to use it. During the democratic reforms of 1968 this unusual trait was hidden because he contributed significantly to breaking down the social isolation of the political leadership and the Communist Party, and he strengthened the political authority of both Party and government. However, unbeknownst to most observers, he was unable to utilize power to protect the democratization process against its opponents.

Dubček became the symbol of the Prague Spring of 1968. When he became head of state in January 1968, no one, including himself, had a clear notion of the path the democratization process would take. His program was gradually and spontaneously developed, and it acquired specific form in the Action Program of the Czechoslovak Communist Party of April 1968. The program contained both an analysis of the state of the Czech socialist society (focusing on factors that were inhibiting its development) and defined the goals of Czech democratization as well as the most urgently required reforms. This program was the first stage in the proposed Czech transition from a totalitarian to a democratic socialist regime. It contained an expansion and guarantee of the democratic rights of Czech citizens, including their guaranteed participation in governmental policy making; it defined the organizational form by which workers and farmers could exercise these political rights; it guaranteed the rights of citizens to be fully informed and to engage in scientific and cultural activities; and it simultaneously maintained and respected the leading role of the Communist Party in the state. The Action Program was a daring experiment by which the Communist Party would use its monopoly of power for democratic purposes, with the support and confidence of the Czech citizenry, who would act autonomously to balance the power and influence of the Communist Party. It was and is to Dubček's credit that he placed this most significant experiment in democratic socialist reform at the head of his political agenda, and worked hard to realize it.

The Prague Spring was liquidated by the military occupation of Czechoslovakia by five countries of the Warsaw Pact, together with the Soviet Union. Dubček and his leaders underestimated the danger of Soviet intervention and did not adequately utilize popular support and unity to defend his policies. Dubček's belief that the democratic reforms could be partially maintained even after Soviet occupation proved to be an illusion. His was a vain effort, a path of constant concessions and little resistance to Moscow's pressure. The first step on this road backward was the Moscow Protocol of August 1968, which a hesitant Dubček finally signed under pressure from his political allies. It continued with Dubček's departure from the office of head of state in April 1969, also with his acquiescence to legal restrictions (August 1969) aimed at his supporters. It ended with his being cut off entirely from political life and with the persecution of his supporters. The broad front of functionaries and supporters of the Prague Spring were gradually scattered by the Soviet occupation, and it became impossible to regroup them into a meaningful oppositional political force. Dubček chose not to use his great authority to oppose the Soviets. Figuratively speaking, he could not escape his background an an obedient Party member. Dubček, the politician and the symbol of the Prague Spring, quietly became a private citizen. Neither Moscow nor the new Prague leader were able to force Dubček to self-criticism or a public condemnation and repudiation of the Prague Spring and the program of democratization. He remained passively faithful to it.

M. KAREL KAPLAN

E

ENGELS, FRIEDRICH   (1820–1895). Born on 28 November 1820 in the German city of Barmen, Friedrich Engels was the eldest son of a textile manufacturer. Brought up as a devout Calvinist and trained to be a merchant, Engels was slowly taken by Hegel and the Young Hegelian movement that flourished in the 1830s around Bruno Bauer. In 1842 Engels moved to England to work in his father's firm in the city of Manchester. Already a communist, his contacts with factory workers in England distanced him from the idealist Hegelians and convinced him of the proletariat's potential as a revolutionary class. He met and collaborated with Marx* on the anti-idealist *The Holy Family*. By his own admission, Engels played only a peripheral role in the maturation of Marx's work on political economy, despite his collaboration on the book that first proffered this new conception, *The German Ideology*. Between 1845 and 1850 Engels collaborated with Marx on scholarly and practical political activities in Brussels and Paris. They both joined the German League of the Just (later renamed the Communist League) and coauthored the *Communist Manifesto*. After the 1848 Revolution Engels worked with Marx on the *Neue Rheinische Zeitung*. After a year's stay in France, Engels returned to Germany to help resist the counterrevolution. Engels traveled in Switzerland and London before settling, in 1850, in Manchester to rejoin the family firm. Here he stayed until 1870, financially subsidizing Marx and continuing their scholarly and political collaboration. Engels retired in 1870, moved to London, and took over the daily operation of the First Inernational* from an ailing Marx. For the next decade or so Engels established his professional reputation as a major philosopher with works like *Anti-Dühring*, *Origin of the Family*, and *Ludwig Feuerbach*. When Marx died in 1883, Engels devoted himself to editing and publishing volumes two and three of *Capital*, as well as helping establish the Second International.* Engels died on 5 August 1895 of cancer while working on the fourth volume of Marx's *Capital*, which was subsequently published as *Theories of Surplus Value*.

Friedrich Engels connected Marx's materialism to contemporary social theory, providing Marxism with the philosophical evidence that Marx himself ignored and drawing ontological and epistemological implications of both historical materialism and dialectics. Scientifically active at a time of pioneering experimentation yielding dramatic hypotheses concerning human evolution, the conservation and transformation of energy, organic cellular structure, and even the measurement of mental phenomena, Engels was in the mainstream of mid-nineteenth-century European culture, believing the unity of life is expressible in impersonal scientific laws. He based these, however, on materialist, not empirical, evidence.

Engels saw the philosophical dialogue in Europe pitting idealism against materialism, and he explicitly favored the latter. Idealism conjures immaterial principles, spiritual beings that use body organs but are essentially independent of matter. Echoing *The German Ideology*, Engels believed that mind is an attribute of matter (that is, the human body) organized in a specific, materially determined way. All mental functions depend on appropriate bodily organs; hence, intelligence and creativity are qualities traceable to matter via the human body. Mind is therefore the product of a historical process in which animals gradually develop nervous systems that evolve into complex forms of matter we call brains. These allow animals to interpret reflexes meaningfully and connect disparate physical activities mentally. "Higher" cognitive activities reflect the brain's progressive evolution. Thought merely "translates" matter into the brain's historically developed functions. This form of materialism, known as "monism," rejects the "dualist" assertion that consciousness, although part of matter, is something other than matter. Reinforced by political factors, this subtle distinction was ammunition for Georgii Plekhanov's* later struggle with Lenin.*

Engels defined matter as the physical world directly perceived by the senses, apart from speculation of any kind. All aspects of this world, including space and time, are composed of dynamic, changing matter. Engels felt that matter in motion evolves into ever higher qualities or forms of being. Thus, social movement is qualitatively different—more progressive—than the movement, for example, of plants. Mechanistic materialism, reducing everything to a universal mechanical motion, is therefore ill equipped to reveal life's progressive movement, which marks nature as well as human history and thought. Mind's subjective movement, consequently, merely reflects nature's own objective process, because mind is matter that has taken a particular progressive form. Dialectics scientifically explains the movement of matter and the study of that movement. It is thought imitating nature. However, since mind is originally a form of natural matter, dialectical thought—dynamically evolving throughout human history— is an inevitable by-product. Truth is a correspondence between ideas and objective reality. Knowledge consists of true ideas. Engels merely fulfills history's promise by assisting in the realization of dialectical human knowledge.

Engels predictably viewed economics as the key to society's material determination. Matter's dialectical movement is expressed in the changing patterns of human productive techniques. Each mode progresses to its own destruction and assimilation in higher productive forms. Class antagonisms are reflected culturally in competing ideas and institutions. Social and economic progress coincide as each successive class seizure of the productive apparatus alters the quality of social life. Marx described matter's dynamic movement concretely, rejecting theoretical discussion of any kind. Engels completes Marx's unfinished picture. Dialectics, for Engels, embodies three universal laws that govern matter in motion: the law of the transformation of quantity into quality, and vice versa; the law of the interpenetration of opposites; and the law of the negation of the negation. These three principles explain reality and generate an apt method of social inquiry.

The first dialectical law, the transformation of quantity into quality, means perceived qualitative changes occur only by the quantitative addition or subtraction of matter in motion. Engels defined quantity as those states that are measurable on the same scale (for example, temperature, pressure, weight, speed, and so on), and quality as those not adequately expressed in figures only. As quantities of matter increase or decrease, they alter qualitatively. A numerical increase in atoms, for example, transforms a molecule into a substance with new properties. A change in temperature produces melting or freezing; the accumulation of cooperative human labor alters the environment; an increase in workers and a decrease in capitalists inevitably yield a qualitatively new form of social life. Engels distinguished his dialectical materialism from mechanism, which defines changes in quality as perceived illusions, mechanically caused by "primary" units to which everything is reduced. Although composed of elementary units of matter, a quality, Engels argued, is also more than the sum of its material parts.

Nature consists of bodies in motion, constantly interacting through attraction and repulsion. From these two subforms of matter—attraction and repulsion, positive and negative—various qualities present in the universe (for example, heat, electricity, light, magnetism, and sentiments) are derived. Motion is therefore a primordial natural substance. It appears materially in the measurable forms of attraction and repulsion, and cognitively as the qualities experienced in life. The world is therefore a unity of opposites, hence the second dialectical principle: the interpenetration of opposites. Each perceived item, and nature itself, is a tense amalgam of antagonistic, interpenetrating motions, which at any one time are empirically invisible. Progress emerges from this opposition and interpenetration. Engels considered this principle to be the decisive refutation of formal (bourgeois) logic, especially its principle of noncontradiction. Since nature, including space and time, is a dynamic unity of antagonistic forms of matter, empirical facts are defined by what they are not, that is, their past, future, and encompasssing environments. Revolution, then, is as true and inevitable as a morning's sunrise or a subway ride to work, even though it is empirically nonverifiable at this particular moment in an apparently peaceful society. Everything contains within itself its own opposite, which, as a result of laws one and three, emerges and is itself surpassed.

The law of the negation of the negation serves as the linchpin in Engels's sytem. It is absolutely certain that every object, thought, or condition will turn into its opposite. This "negation" of the original phenomenon is then negated, producing a new reality synthesizing primary qualities of the first two stages and preserving them in a more perfect—or progressive—form. The progressive residue survives in a synthetic unity, which resolves thesis and antithesis. Engels's laws are manifest on every level of life. A seed, for example, develops into a plant (its negation), and the plant produces new seeds and dies. These new seeds, the negation of the negation, propagate the original's most useful or strongest traits but also introduce new ones that increase the second plant's life chances. History is similarly governed: Property relations evolve from common ownership in primitive society, to private ownership in capitalism (the negation of the negation). Socialism is thus heir to the residual best from both previous stages. Even philosophy begins as primitive materialism, is negated by idealism, and is resolved in the more perfect form of dialectical materialism. The negation of the negation energizes nature and society, where inner contradictions generate quantitative changes that promote ever more perfect qualitative forms. It is "an extremely general . . . law of development of nature, history, and thought; a law which . . . holds good in the animal and vegetable kingdoms, in geology, in mathematics, in history, and in philosophy" (*Anti-Dühring*, p. 179).

These laws function impersonally. Valid knowledge, natural and human, results from cognitively perceiving and willingly adopting them. But reality, an interpenetration of opposites, is not explained by contemplation alone. Impersonal dialectical laws are defined and expressed by everyday facts, hence the final test of knowledge is practice. In other words, does knowledge help us effectively alter the environment to satisfy real material needs? If so, knowledge is verified. Mental speculation is passive and therefore scientifically inadequate. Practice is not only a criterion of knowledge but also its source. Real needs propel us to certain fields of scientific inquiry and shape experimental questions. Prevalent forms of scientific inquiry are therefore motivated by the concrete needs of those having the inclination and resources to make science a tool for maintaining privilege, that is, the dominant economic class. Practice is both the purpose and verification of scientific inquiry. If practical consequences—manifest in social practice—satisfy the original, founding need, the science is valid. Knowledge, therefore, is objective (reflecting matter) and practical (satisfying a need), confirming its dialectical character.

Engels never openly repudiated this version of materialism but late in life may possibly have lost the courage of his convictions. In a series of letters written in response to questions regarding the meaning of historical materialism, Engels reclaimed the significance of nonmaterial factors. He admitted that he and Marx may have overemphasized the historical role of economics. Ideas are, indeed, important. Moreover, crude economic determinists are nondialectical. However, Engels could retreat only so far before losing credibility among materialists, which he was not prepared to do. He utimately asserted both the dialectical interpenetration of all phenomena and a concrete material process that, "in the last resort," determines. History's dialectic remains impersonal, objective matter in motion.

Engels, nonorthodox neo-Marxists argue, vulgarized Marxism with an indefensible metaphysics of nature and history, transforming Marxism into a reductive
epistemology that turns humanity into passive, helpless products of autonomous
laws. He is atavistic, naively defending traditional bourgeois metaphysics. His
tragic misinterpretation, the argument goes, is directly responsible for oppressive
Soviet and Eastern European institutions.

Certainly Marx rejected Engels's type of philosophical speculation. But Marx
and Engels may have purposely divided their labors to avoid needless repetition.
Engels's ontological and epistemological exegesis and Marx's more concrete
analysis of historical materialism and capitalism together complete the totality
that a materialist social theory must encompass. Marx and Engels jointly believed
that matter is prior to thought. For both, the dialectic is an attribute of dynamic
matter in history. Engels was probably correct in claiming to have read the entire
manuscript of *Anti-Dühring* to an approving Marx, who even collaborated on
the tenth chapter. Materialists now also claim that the major themes of *Dialectic
of Nature* were discussed by Engels and Marx "many times."

The situation is actually a good deal more complicated than most Marxists
care to admit. Materialist Marxism has become reductionist and now rationalizes
oppressive institutions, and this is traceable directly to Engels. But Engels did
not pervert Marxism; he merely expressed philosophically principles that Marx
hypothesized in concrete terms. Marxists who condemn Engels do so as nonmaterialists. They, of course, can and do cite potentially anti-Engelsian remarks
from Marx, but Marx's invisible philosophy and cursory remarks concerning
epistemology are vague and contradictory. Marx confirmed *and* denied Engels's
dialectical materialism. Materialists, including the mainstream orthodox movement, approvingly recognize Engels's important contributions to revolutionary
social theory. Nonmaterialists see Engels as the first Stalinist.* Claiming, however, that Engels distorted or misinterpreted Marx requires that we ignore a
significant portion of Marx's work that Engels himself chose not to.

In any case, the Second International eventually recognized Engels as Marxism's official philosopher. "Dialectical materialism," first coined by Engels,
became the philosophy of orthodox Marxism, and Party members continually
praised *Anti-Dühring* for providing the theoretical analysis that Marx ignored.
Significant second-generation materialists—especially Kautsky* in Germany and
Plekhanov, Bukharin,* and Lenin in Russia—are philosophically Engels's children. At the turn of the twentieth century Marxian philosophy was visible only
in Engels's brand of materialism.

BIBLIOGRAPHY:

A. *Socialism: Utopian and Scientific* (New York: Scribners, 1892); *Dialectic of Nature*
(New York: International, 1940); *Ludwig Feuerbach and the End of Classical German
Philosophy* (New York: International, 1941); *The German Peasants War* (Moscow: For-
eign Language Press, 1956); *The Origins of the Family, Private Property and the State*
(New York: International, 1972); *Anti-Dühring* (Peking: Foreign Language Press, 1976).

B. S. Marcus, *Engels, Manchester and the Working Class* (New York: Random House,

1974); W. O. Henderson, *The Life of Friedrich Engels* (London: Frank Cass, 1976); David Mclellan, *Engels* (New York: Viking Press, 1977); Terrell Carver, *Engels* (New York: Oxford University Press, 1981), and *Marx and Engels:The Intellectual Relationship* (Brighton: Harvester, 1983).

ROBERT A. GORMAN

EVANGELISTA, CHRISANTO   (1882–1943). Chrisanto Evangelista, born in 1882(?), is considered the father of Filipino communism. As early as 1906 he formed a Marxist-oriented printers' union. In 1913 he became one of the leaders of the Filipino Workers' Congress (COF), the country's largest labor federation. In 1924, Evangelista established the Workers' Party (Partido Obrero), which in 1927 affiliated with the Comintern's Pan Pacific Trade Union Secretariat (PPTUS). In 1929 Evangelista established the Association of Workers (KAP), a Marxist labor federation. The following year, on 26 August 1930, Evangelista established the Communist Party of the Philippines (PKP). At its First Congress in May 1931 a manifesto was adopted that declared the Philippines Revolution to be in a "bourgeois democratic stage" and the Party's objectives to be the achievement of independence for the Philippines, the implementation of an agrarian revolution, and an improvement in workers' conditions. In September 1931, however, Evangelista was arrested and sentenced to eight years' imprisonment for subversion. On the outbreak of the Pacific war, Evangelista called for the creation of a united front against fascism. In January 1942, following the Japanese invasion, Evangelista and other prominent PKP leaders were again arrested. He died in prison in 1943.

BIBLIOGRAPHY:
   B. Jose Lava, *Milestones in the History of the CPP*, (Manila: Mimeo, 1950); Alfredo B. Saulo, *Communism in the Philippines* (Manila: Ateneo, 1969).

MICHAEL C. WILLIAMS

F

FIRST INTERNATIONAL (1864–1876). The First International, organized in 1864 by representatives of Western Europe's labor movement as the International Working Men's Association (IWMA), succeeded the smaller League of Communists and functioned as a public forum for workers' issues and as a means of mobilizing and radicalizing Europe's organized workers. Led by Marx* (1864–72) and Engels* (1870–72) the First International admitted both individual members as well as local and national organizations and recruited liberal British trade unionists and continental followers of Proudhon, Mazzini, and Lasalle. Its governing institution, the General Council, was located in London. By 1868 the International's strategy had progressed from supporting liberal causes to advocating public ownership of large national industries, mines, and arable lands. Support for the Paris Commune of 1871 and the expansion of working-class suffrage throughout Europe both pushed the International into partisan political activities. The London Conference of the International in 1871 proposed the creation of a working-class political party, and with Marx's energetic support this proposal was officially adopted at the Hague Conference of 1872.

Notwithstanding Marx's opposition to anarchism, Bakunin's International Alliance for Socialist Democracy was admitted into the IWMA in 1869, and there followed three years of bitter conflict between Marx and Bakunin regarding the International's organization and the strategy of involving workers in national politics. Bakunin condemned the IWMA's institutionalized authoritarianism and favored a transfer of power to secret, hierarchical societies controlled by himself. In this he was supported by delegates from Britain and several European nations. Marx and Engels argued, in response, that the International could survive only by expanding the General Council's powers. The Hague Conference of 1872 ratified Marx's program and expelled Bakunin. It also moved the headquarters of the General Council to New York. The weakened and divided organization was officially dissolved in Philadelphia in 1876. Its legacy, however, included the ensuing growth of national workers' parties throughout Western Europe. The International's post-1871 strategy bore fruit posthumously.

Other than its manuscripts supporting the Paris Commune (especially Marx's

The Civil War in France, which was sponsored and published by the International) and condemning anarchism, the First International produced little of theoretical significance. It did, however, struggle nobly with the thorny problems of formulating apt strategies for revolutionary national working-class movements throughout the world. These problems remain, and the Marxist movement since 1876 has also given a substantial portion of its time, energy, and ability to solving them.

BIBLIOGRAPHY:

A. *Documents of the First International*, 5 vols. (London: Lawrence & Wishart, 1963–68).

B. Henry Collins and Chimen Abramsky, *Karl Marx and the British Labour Movement: Years of the First International* (New York: St. Martin's Press, 1965); Julius Braunthal, *History of the International* (vols. 1–2, New York: Praeger; vol. 3, Boulder, Colo.: Westview Press, 1966–80).

ROBERT A. GORMAN

FLYNN, ELIZABETH GURLEY   (1890–1964). A labor and radical activist, Elizabeth Gurley Flynn was born in Concord, New Hampshire. She joined the Industrial Workers of the World, the radical anarcho-syndicalist union romantically known as the Wobblies in 1906 at the age of sixteen. Throughout her lifetime she was a prominent activist, organizer, and spokesperson, first in the radical labor movement and then as a member of the American Communist Party.

Her career as an activist was defiantly confrontational in nature. She was arrested for her part in the IWW's Missoula (Montana) and Spokane (Washington) free speech fights in 1908 and 1909. In Spokane she had tried to delay her arrest by chaining herself to a lamppost. She was a strike leader at the Lawrence (Massachusetts) and Patterson (New Jersey) textile strikes in 1912 and 1913. She was active in the defense of Wobbly minstrel Joe Hill before his execution in 1915. In 1918 she was arrested along with many other Wobbly and radical leaders under the wartime criminal syndicalism laws.

After leaving the IWW Flynn became interested in Soviet communism. She joined the American Communist Party in 1937, became a Communist board member in 1939, contributed regularly to the Party newspaper, *The Daily Worker*, ran for the U.S. Congress on the Communist ticket in 1942, and by the late 1950s was a member of the National Committee headquartered in New York City. In 1956 she was arrested and convicted, under the provisions of the Smith Act, as a member of a subversive organization. During the trial she was cited for contempt for steadfastly refusing to implicate her friends and associates as Communists.

In 1961 Flynn was named chair of the American Communist Party. Before her death in 1964, she had become the foremost woman activist in America, having outlived Ella Reeve Bloor and "Mother" Mary Jones.* She died at the age of seventy-four while visiting Moscow. *Izvestia* devoted half its front page to her obituary, and Mrs. Nikita Khrushchev headed her full-scale state funeral. Back in the United States, her death was remembered less gloriously by a modest memorial service in New York City's Community Church.

Although her theoretical contributions were of little importance, as a labor activist she did contribute to the theory of sabotage, which she defined as the nonviolent disruption of capitalist production by workers interfering with the quality or quantity of production. However, her major contribution to the Marxist tradition in America came more through her tireless zeal as an organizer and soapboxer proselytizing for the cause of traditional Marxism-Leninism. She was notorious as a fiery and effective public speaker. Of her, the Socialist Norman Thomas once said, "She put life into a meeting as practically no other speaker could."

BIBLIOGRAPHY:

A. "The Free Speech Fight at Spokane," *International Socialist Review*, 10 (December 1909), p. 483; "The Truth About The Patterson Strike," Manuscript in the Labadie Collection, University of Michigan Library, ca. 1913; "Sabotage: The Conscious Withdrawal of Workers' Industrial Efficiency," Pamphlet (Cleveland, Ohio: I.W.W. Publishing Bureau, 1915); *I Speak My Own Piece: Autobiography of "The Rebel Girl"* (New York: Masses and Mainstream, 1955), reissued as *The Rebel Girl: My First Life (1906–1926)* (New York: Publishers International, 1973); *The Alderson Story: My Life as a Political Prisoner* (New York: International, 1972).

B. Mary Heaton Vorse, "Elizabeth Gurley Flynn," *Nation* (17 February 1926), pp. 175–76; Benjamin H. Kizer, "Elizabeth Gurley Flynn," *Pacific Northwest Quarterly*, 34 (July 1916), pp. 110–12; Joyce L. Kornbluth, ed., *Rebel Voices: An I.W.W. Anthology* (Ann Arbor: University of Michigan Press, 1964); Rosalyn Fraad Baxandall, "Elizabeth Gurley Flynn: The Early Years," *Radical America*, 8 (January-February 1975), p. 98; Philip S. Foner, *Women and the American Labor Movement: From Colonial Times to the Eve of World War I* (New York: The Free Press, 1979).

CHARLES W. HAMPTON

FONSECA AMADOR, CARLOS (1936–1976). The principal leader and theorist of the Sandinista Revolution in Nicaragua, Carlos Fonseca was born in humble circumstances in Matagalpa. An active anti-Somoza leader since his secondary school days, he continued to organize students against the Somoza dictatorship when he began university studies in law. He initiated a student group that began to study Marxist thought and was one of the few students to associate with the orthodox Marxist party in Nicaragua (Partido Socialista Nicaragüense). A dedicated nationalist who fondly remembered Augusto César Sandino's guerrilla war against conservative politicians and U.S. Marines (1927–33) he helped found the New Nicaragua Movement in 1957. He began to study carefully Sandino and the struggle waged by his Army to Defend National Sovereignty. Inspired by the struggle initiated by the Cuban nationalists in the Sierra Maestra, he was one of a small group of Nicaraguans who began to wage guerrilla warfare against the dictatorship in the late 1950s. By 1960 he had been severely wounded and had already been in prison several times. Undaunted, he, Tomás Borge,*

Silvio Mayorga and a few other militants founded the Sandinista National Liberation Front in July 1961. Inspired by Sandino and disgusted with the dogmatic, unrevolutionary sectarianism of the Nicaraguan Socialist Party, they began armed struggle based on the popular concepts of guerrilla warfare. As the movement evolved through several stages, Fonseca Amador emerged as the prinicpal leader and ideologue. Trips to other Central American countries, Cuba, Western Europe, and the Soviet Union exposed him to other ideas, but only seemed to strengthen his fundamental Nicaraguan identity. Much of the movement's later successes are credited to the careful study of the original Sandino's ideology and tactics that he developed and the emphasis he placed on organization and the education and mobilization of the masses. A determined advocate of the importance of armed struggle, he was killed in battle in 1976, less than three years before the FSLN's final victory.

Fonseca was among the first members of a new generation of Latin American radicals who used Marxist-Leninist thought to develop a profoundly nationalist understanding of their Third World reality. He came to be very critical of the Moscow-oriented Nicaraguan Socialist Party because their understanding of the national reality was so painfully inadequate that they classified Sandino as nothing more than a petit bourgeois populist and—following the Soviet-inspired internationalist line—thought that the level of economic development in Nicaragua precluded any revolutionary armed activity. Consequently, they called for cooperation with bourgeois politicians. Even before the Cuban Revolution evolved a Marxist ideology, Fonseca Amador was carefully studying local conditions in light of Marxist theory so as to understand both better. His independence and firm nationalist roots helped him develop a brand of FSLN ideology that was very much part of the Nicaraguan context. "He understood clearly, lucidly, that the international revolutionary doctrines are useless unless they combine with national revolutionary thought and practice" (Tirado López, pp. 4–6). Like Latin America's first original Marxist thinker, the Peruvian José Carlos Mariátegui,*he believed that Marxism-Leninism should provide the basis for national analysis and ideology, but that national conditions would shape form and precise content. He looked to internationalist doctrine and the popular struggles waged in Vietnam, China, and Russia to gain necessary perspective and insight, but believed that the FSLN's ideology must be firmly rooted in the Nicaraguan reality. Like many young Latin American revolutionaries in the early 1960s, he was drawn to Che Guevara's* formula for guerrilla warfare. Several bitter defeats and the death of many close comrades emphasized the fact that although in some ways similar, Nicaraguan conditions were not Cuban conditions and that the FSLN needed an ideological orientation that was very much its own and that could generate its own revolutionary strategy. This prompted an even more intensive study and updating of the ideology, military tactics, and political organization of Augusto César Sandino and the guerrillas he led. Fonseca not only advocated the intensive study of the original Sandinistas, but began to circulate studies about and quotes from their leader (see *Sandino, guerrillero proletario*, and

Augusto César Sandino, ideario político). Several important lessons emerged from Fonseca's analysis: Armed struggle was important, but must be tightly linked to effective political organization and should only occur *after* some political education had begun; the vanguard must stay tightly linked to the masses and must never allow itself to become separated from its mass base; mass mobilization through popular people's war was the most effective way to overthrow the dictatorship; careful popular organization provided the organizational mechanism to incorporate the masses in the struggle; the guerrilla fighter must meet the peasant as an equal, learn from him, and carefully integrate him into the guerrilla army at all levels; and finally, if properly approached, the peasants and laboring masses would form the backbone of the revolution. These lessons, his flexible approach to theory and tactics, and the ability to learn from mistakes helped to carry the FSLN to final victory and opened a whole new horizon for revolutionaries in Central and Latin America.
BIBLIOGRAPHY:
A. Ed., *Augusto César Sandino, Ideario político* (San José, Costa Rica: Porvenir, 1979); *Escritos* (Managua: Sandinist Popular Army, Cultural and Political Education Section, 1979); *Sandino: guerrillero proletario* (Managua: FSLN National Secretariat of Propaganda and Political Education, 1979 or 1980).

B. Victor Tirado López, *El pensamiento político de Carlos Fonseca Amador* (Managua: FSLN National Secretariat of Propaganda and Political Education, 1979 or 1980); Harry E. Vanden, "The Ideology of the Insurrection," in *Nicaragua in Revolution*, ed., Thomas W. Walker (New York: Praeger, 1982).

HARRY E. VANDEN

FRIEDMANN, GEORGES   (1902–1977). The son of a banker, born in 1902 in Paris, Georges Friedmann went from the Lycée Henri IV to the Ecole Normale Supérieure and then into teaching. By 1920, he was a member of *Clarté*.* He joined the French Communist Party (PCF) in 1929, helped to fund the *Revue marxist*, and was active in the *Philosophies* group*, which supported the review. In 1932 he became an assistant at the Centre du Documentation Social of the Ecole Normale Supérieure, where he was responsible for studying the influence of machines on worker mentality. He returned to teaching in 1935, but the Vichy laws forced him out of his post during the war and he became a member of the Resistance. In 1945 he was appointed inspector general of technical education and later professor of the history of work at the Conservatoire des Arts et Métiers. In 1949 he became the director of the Sociology Centre of the Centre National de la Recherche Scientifique (CNRS), president of the International Association of Sociology in 1956, president of the Latin American Social Sciences faculty created by UNESCO in 1958, director of the Ecole Practique des Hautes Etudes, and codirector in 1960 of *Annales*. He died in 1977.

Friedmann was a specialist in industrial and agricultural sociology, concentrating on the effects of the machine age on workers. The general focus of his work was the change from what he called the *"milieu naturel"* to the *"milieu* *technique.*'' His particular contribution to Marxist thought was his analysis of alienation and class consciousness in the modern work context. This reinterpretation of Marx led him into occasional conflicts with others on the left, from Paul Nizan* in the 1930s to fellow members of the PCF in the postwar years. (He was, for a short period, the Party's expert on labor questions.)

An indefatigable traveler, he visited the Soviet Union three times in the period 1932–36, and in his works *Problèmes du machinisme en URSS et dans les pays capitalistes* and *De la sainte Russie à l'URSS* he exhibited his very complex views on the established socialist states. He attacked both of the groups in opposition to Stalin,* yet he strongly criticized the sterile dogmatism of Stalinism and the price paid for the great agricultural and industrial plans in the lack of food and goods available to the masses. He said that it was unreasonable to expect the establishment of a perfect socialist system in a country which was still ''Holy Russia,'' and yet he also traced part of that failure to the fact that, in Marxist terms, Stalinism was still a long way from true socialism. In 1938 he defended the outcome of the purges and trials because he claimed that those who had been condemned were against popular fronts, the League of Nations, and the peace movement. His general line was to defend the Stalinist state as an entity and a positive step toward socialism, while criticizing it for not eliminating the root causes of worker oppression—the alienation produced by the nature of modern machine labor—a failure that seemed more important to him than the other totalitarian aspects of the regime.

In the post-war period he increasingly exalted the values of ''the humanist heritage of the West,'' and in his books *Où va le travail humain?*, *Humanisme du travail et humanités* and *Le travail en miettes* he took a much more idealistic and individualistic stance on questions of alienation and exploitation. He was one of the founders of the new study of the sociology of work and an early proponent of the theory of the ''new working class'' (*Traité du sociologie de travail*, with Pierre Naville,* and *Sept études sur l'homme et la technique*). This was to inspire the younger generation of postwar sociologists who sought radical alternatives to orthodox Marxist interpretations of labor and recognized, as did Friedmann, that the nature of work had so drastically changed since the end of the nineteenth century that it was the social and psychological alienation of automated work that produced class consciousness rather than the pure economic exploitation of the capitalist productive system.

BIBLIOGRAPHY:

A. *L'Adieu* (Paris: Gallimard, 1932); *Problèmes du machinisme en URSS et dans les pays capitalistes* (Paris: Gallimard, 1934); *La Crise du progrès, équisse d'histoire des idées: 1893–1935* (Paris: Gallimard, 1936); *Humanisme du travail et humanités* (Paris: Gallimard, 1950); *Où va le travail humain?* (Paris: Gallimard, 1950); *Le Travail en miettes* (Paris: Gallimard, 1958); *Les problèmes d'Amérique Latin*, 2 vols. (Paris: Gallimard, 1959–60); with Pierre Naville, *Traité du sociologie de travail* (Paris: A. Colin, 1961); *Sept études sur l'homme et la technique* (Paris: Gouthier, 1966); *La Puissance et la sagesse* (Paris: Gallimard, 1970).

B. N. Imbert, *Livre d'or des valeurs humaines* (Paris: de Sales, 1972); *Une Nouvelle Civilisation: hommage à Georges Friedmann* (Paris: Gallimard, 1973).

JOHN C. SIMMONDS

FUKUMOTO KAZUO (b. 1894). Fukumoto Kazuo was the leading theoretician of the newly rebuilt Japanese Communist Party in 1926–27. Born in Tottori Prefecture of a wealthy landlord, Fukumoto attended a local middle school, the First Higher School in Tokyo, then studied political science in Tokyo Imperial University's Department of Law. He graduated in 1920, became a professor at the newly established Matsue Higher School, and in 1921 was sent abroad for two years by the Ministry of Education to study in England, Germany, the United States, and France. During these years, he became engaged in the study of Marxism, reading works of Marx,* Engels,* Lenin,* Luxemburg,* and others. In 1924 he returned to Japan after joining the German Communist Party and resumed teaching at Yamaguchi Higher School in 1925.

Beginning in December 1924, Fukumoto began to publish in rapid succession a series of articles on Marxism in the journal *Marxism*, the editorial staff of which he joined shortly thereafter. He boldly and harshly criticized the economic methodology of such leading Marxist scholars as Kawakami Hajime,* Fukuda Tokuzō, and Kushida Tamizō,* and published the details of the struggle over organizational theory between Lenin and Luxemburg. In October 1925 he published a widely influential essay in *Marxism* in which he attacked the doctrine of a single proletarian political party. Before such a political party could be formed, it was necessary to separate and crystallize a high level of Marxist revolutionary consciousness among those who would form the vanguard. In this "separation before unity" theory, Fukumoto advocated fierce theoretical struggle within the ranks of the proletariat against non-Marxist elements. In a highly acerbic manner that alienated his peers, Fukumoto went on to denounce the views of Akamatsu Katsumaro, Takahashi Kamekichi* and others working for a proletarian party as "trade unionist" and "economistic." In 1926, Fukumoto directed his attacks against the Japanese movement's leading theoretician, Yamakawa Hitoshi,* calling his advocacy of a united front political party a mere compromise between economic struggle and political struggle. Meanwhile, Fukumoto resigned his position at Yamaguchi and went to Tokoyo to join the effort to rebuild the now-dissolved Communist Party. He then launched his own journal *Under the Banner of Marxism* (*Marukishizumu no hata no moto ni*). Leftists in the General Federation of Labor (Sōdōmei) under attack from the right eagerly grasped Fukumoto's ideas as a weapon of theoretical struggle, and "Fukumotoism" quickly replaced Yamakawaism as the leading theory in the movement.

In the Third (or Reconstruction) Congress of the Japanese Communist Party in December 1926, Fukumoto drafted the sections of the proclamation on the history of the development of Japan's bourgeoisie, proletariat, and Communist movement. Thus Fukumoto became the Party's ideological leader, serving on its Central Committee and as head of the political department. The Comintern, however, called Fukumoto, Tokuda, and Watanabe Masanosuke to Moscow to discuss strategy and tactics in Japan, and then severely criticized Fukumoto's organizational theory in its July 1927 Theses as dogmatic and sectarian and his theory of the imminent demise of Japanese capitalism as incorrect. Roundly denounced for helping to drive a wedge between the new Party and the masses, Fukumoto thereupon lost his position as the Party's theoretical leader, losing his Central Committee post but remaining on the agitation-propaganda committee. After escaping the March 1928 roundup, he was arrested for his Party activities in June of that year and sentenced to ten years' imprisonment. After fourteen years in prison, he was released in April 1942 and *tenkō*ed (defected from the Party) during the war.

After the war Fukumoto joined the revived Communist Party, lost an election bid for the Senate in 1950, was arrested in September 1951 by occupation authorities, but was released because of insufficient evidence. He renewed his activities by forming a Japanese Communist Party Unity Council in opposition to Tokuda's allegedly paternalistic leadership. Although the council dissolved in July 1955, Fukumoto and several of its members formed a Peasants' Social Gathering, which published its own organ as well as the *Marxist Review* (*Marukusu-shugi kōron*). Because of his opposition to the Party central's line, he was expelled in 1958, and thereafter concentrated on writing on socialism and the history of Japanese capitalism.

BIBLIOGRAPHY:

A. *Keizaigaku hihan no hōhōron* (The methodology of economic criticism) (Tokyo: n.a., 1926); *Shakai no kōsei narabi ni henkaku no katei* (Social organization and the process of revolution) (Tokyo: n.a., 1926); *Riron tōsō* (Theoretical struggle) (Tokyo: n.a., 1926); *Fukumoto Kazuo shōki chosaku-shū* (Collected early works of Fukumoto Kazuo), 4 vols. (Tokyo: n.a., 1976–77).

GERMAINE A. HOSTON

G

GARCIA QUEJIDO, ANTONIO (1856–1927). The son of a Madrid dyer, Garcia Quejido received a lay education in accordance with the democratic and republican ideas of his father. He became an apprentice typesetter. As such, he joined the Asociacion del Arte de Imprimir Madrileño (Madrid Association of the Printing Arts). He also formed part of the socialist nucleus within that association that would later become the Partido Socialista Obrero Español (PSOE). He became acting secretary of the Socialist Party at its clandestine organizational session in Madrid (1879). From then on Garcia Quejido played important roles in the socialist labor and political organizations, not only in Madrid but also in Valencia and Barcelona, where he emigrated in the 1880s in search of work. Upon the formation of the Unión General de Trabajadores (UGT) in 1888, mostly on his initiative, he was elected its first president. Upon his return to Madrid in 1897, he occupied high positions in the national committee of the party as well as in the UGT, until the early part of the twentieth century. In the first two decades of this century he worked mainly to modify the statutes of the Madrid Act and of the National Federation of Printers, in order to introduce the "*base multiple*" (multiple base) in those organizations. Garcia Quejido was widely known by socialists because his labor organizational acumen could be observed in national as well as international congresses in which he participated. That is why his decision to join the Spanish Communist Party (PCE) when it expelled the PSOE (of which he was a member of the Executive Committee) had important repercussions. That is also the reason why, although Garcia Quejido remained in the PCE until his death (he was elected secretary in 1922–23), the PSOE lauded him as a socialist organizer and propagandist when he died.

Unlike most other Spanish socialists, Garcia Quejido was at least concerned with key questions of socialist ideology. In 1892 he tried, unsuccessfully, to publish *La nueva era*, a socialist magazine dedicated to promote debate on salient ideas. In 1897–98 he published in Spanish, for the first time, the first volume of Marx's *Capital*, editing it himself based on a translation by the Argentine Juan B. Justo.* He was unable to publish the other two volumes, as he had wished, but in 1901 he was finally able to publish *La nueva era*. Here, Garcia

Quejido railed against the errors of the "Bronze Law" as it related to the prevailing salary scales for writings and speeches by Spanish socialist leaders. His constant preoccupation with Marxist theory is evident in subsequent articles, including the translation of Eleanor Marx's* version of the *Communist Manifesto*, which Garcia Quejido did shortly before his death.

Garcia Quejido, in brief, was one of the few Spanish labor leaders who constantly studied Marxist theory in depth and criticized the most obvious errors in contemporary versions done in his own country.

BIBLIOGRAPHY:

B. Juan José Moralo, *La cuna de un gigante: historia de la Asociación General del Arte de Imprimir* (Madrid: Edicusa, 1925), pp. 275–90; Juan José Moralo, *Lideres del moviemiento obrero español 1868–1921* (Madrid: Edicusa, 1972), pp. 255–305; Manuel Perez Ledesma, ed., *Antonio Garcia Quejido y la Nueva era* (Madrid: Ediciones del Centro, 1975); Santiago Castillo, "La labor editorial del PSOE en el siglo XIX," *Estudios de Historia Social*, no. 8–9 (1979), pp. 181–95.

S. CASTILLO

GHIOLDI, RODOLFO   (b. 1897). Rodolfo Ghioldi was born in 1897 in Buenos Aires, Argentina, where at age sixteen he worked to form a socialist youth group. He later joined the anti-imperialist, anti-World War I movement that helped keep Argentina out of that conflict. Between 1910 and 1921 he led Argentina's League of Teachers. In response to the Socialist Party, which he criticized as reformist, he co-founded the International Socialist Party, forerunner of Argentina's Communist Party. After a 1921 visit to the Soviet Union, he became a lifelong supporter of Leninism* and Argentine interpreter of the Communist Party position. The Comintern sent him to Brazil to organize the National Liberation Alliance, an activity that brought him close to Luis Carlos Prestes,* whom he served as an ideological mentor. After World War II, the regime of Juan Perón forced him into exile. He subsequently returned and served as a Communist Party delegate to his nation's Constituent Assembly.

As a political thinker Ghioldi was known for his opposition to the strong current of positivism that existed in Argentina. To him, positivists erroneously believed that moral order presupposes human freedom and the existence of God. He also challenged the existentialism popularized in Argentina by the works of Spanish philosopher José Ortega y Gasset. He believed that Ortega was neither scientific nor materialistic, and worked against the anti-imperialist and agrarian revolutions needed in Latin America. He criticized Ortega's *Revolt of the Masses*, which depicted the masses as causing chaos and violence, as an extension of Nietzsche who, unlike Marx,* believed that elites will always be needed to lead the masses.

In his *Federalismo y autonomías provinciales*, Ghioldi assailed the belief that the nineteenth-century conflict, between the residents of Buenos Aires and those from the interior, over the benefits of Argentina's tax revenues from the port city hindered the nation's progress. He asserted that what most severely damaged

Argentine society was the alliance of foreign imperialists with the ruling oligarchy against the working class, not the conflict between the city and the provinces. To him the people of the former and the latter were national allies against the common enemy.

BIBLIOGRAPHY:

A. *La política en el mundo* (Buenos Aires: Futuro, 1946); *Acerca de la cuestión agraria Argentina* (Buenos Aires: Fundamentos, 1953); *Escritos*, vols. 1–2 (Buenos Aires: Anteo, 1975–76).

SHELDON B. LISS

GHOSH, AJOY   (1909–62). Born in India in 1909, Ajoy Ghosh was a member of the central leadership of the Communist Party of India (CPI) from 1936 or 1937 until 1962; its General Secretary from 1951 to 1962; a member of its Politburo, with breaks due to imprisonment, illness, or resignation in protest against its policies, from 1948 until 1951. Ghosh pioneered in articulating a view in 1947, which was then highly unorthdox among Marxists, that the bourgeois-democratic aim of complete political independence and sovereignty (although not economic independence) for India could be, and was about to be achieved, regrettably under bourgeois hegemony or leadership, albeit in the form of the states of India and Pakistan in a partitioned India. Under pressure from the strident protests of the majority of Indian (and foreign) Communists and Marxists (including such Indian Communist leaders, prominent then or later, as P. C. Joshi and E. M. S. Namboodiripad, as well as from Josef Stalin* on behalf of the Communist Party of the Soviet Union) Ghosh retracted to write of India's "so-called freedom" in 1950 (Rao, p. 948), and then of the need for "achieving full freedom" in 1951 (Sen, p. 19). But he edged cautiously back from 1952 onward, stressing in 1952 "the need to defend national independence and national sovereignty" (ibid., p. 110), which implied that these had been won, visibly and obviously under bourgeois leadership, and was not a bourgeois illusion or myth. By 1955–56, the retraction of the retraction of his 1947 initiative was complete, except for the refinement that he was now writing of "the attainment of political freedom . . . under the hegemony of the 'big bourgeoisie' " (ibid., pp. 435, 531). The exact meaning of the term "big bourgeoisie" was left unclear.

Ghosh's 1947 thesis that it is possible to achieve political freedom under bourgeois-democratic leadership is now a commonplace among Indian Marxists, except for some strong echoes from the 1947 and 1950–51 controversies and from the debates of the early 1960s, when the Chinese Communist Party reopened the question and many Indian Communists agreed with them. But it was not so in 1947. In fact, in 1947 Ghosh's thesis was up against a powerful contrary thesis, i.e., that political independence for all colonies and semicolonies from monopoly capitalist imperialism could be achieved only under working-class (Communist) hegemony or not at all. Indeed, this counter-thesis had hardened into an unquestioned axiom.

Marx* himself, in 1853, on the eve of the first Indian revolt against British rule in 1857, had foreseen the possibility of the "Hindus" throwing off the English yoke altogether by themselves. But he had left the question of class hegemony in such a revolt open, to be decided by history. Lenin,* in working out the implications of his analysis of capitalist imperialism for the national colonial movements, similarly left open the question of class hegemony over the national movement, although Lenin's formula tilted against the bourgeoisie of the oppressed countries. However, mainly on the initiatives of the Indian member, and of Otto Kuusinen, the Finnish-Soviet member of the Comintern executive, by 1928 the notion that "the mission of freeing India has been conferred by history on the Indian workers and peasants" (Adhikari, p. 429) had emerged as a Euclid-like Comintern axiom. It implied the impossibility of political independence for India under bourgeois hegemony. So strong was the hold of this axiom that the CPI Politburo's "Proletarian Path" resolution of 1939 (probably authored by Ghosh) declared that "the revolutionary realization of the war crisis for the achievement of national freedom" could be achieved only by "breaking through the shackles of the Gandhian (bourgeois) technique" and by "realizing the proletarian hegemony over the national movement" by "putting the proletarian impress on the struggle" (Roy, pp. 125, 134–35). Later, in 1942, when Indian Communists began to extend support to the "people's war" fought under the leadership of the Soviet Union, an unusually convoluted argument was advanced in the CPI Politburo that neither could the war be brought to an end, nor the defeat of fascism in the war achieved, in the absence of India's freedom from British rule, secured on the basis of an Indian Communist hegemony over the national movement, albeit exercised mainly "from below." This alone, it was argued, would force the Congress and Muslim League bourgeois leaderships to unite and wrest freedom from British imperialism. Thus Ghosh's 1947 thesis challenged a deeply entrenched doctrine that had survived several unorthodox twists and turns of Indian Communist policy.

Ghosh's new Marxian doctrine that political freedom under bourgeois leadership was possible reopened many major and minor questions that had been the subject matter of controversies within the CPI. One such question—a major one from 1947 until around 1980—was whether Communists should extend general support to the Congress regime in India, since political independence had been achieved under Congress bourgeois-democratic leadership. When Ghosh put forward his novel thesis in 1947, neither he nor others who supported him at the time advocated general support to the Congress regime. However, by 1956 Ghosh adopted the view that Indian Communists should function as a critical but loyal opposition, or act as an internally nonaligned political force willing to support such political initiatives and economic reforms proposed by the Congress regime as it considered to be progressive. In this crucial change of position, Ghosh was supported by a minority of those who supported his 1947 thesis. But it left dissatisfied others—among whom the most influential was Bhalchandra

Ranadive*—who had agreed with his 1947 thesis, convinced that the Indian bourgeoisie, precisely because it had secured independent political power, must be opposed at all costs by Indian Communists.

BIBLIOGRAPHY:

B. M. B. Rao, ed., *Documents of the History of the Communist Party of India*, vol. 7 (New Delhi: People's Publishing House, 1976); Subodh Roy, ed., *Communism in India: Unpublished Documents, 1935–1945* (Calcutta: National Book Agency, 1976); Mohit Sen, ed., *Documents of the History of the Communist Party of India*, vol. 8 (New Delhi: People's Publishing House, 1977); Gangadhar Adhikari, ed., *Documents of the History of the Communist Party of India*, vol. 3–c (New Delhi: People's Publishing House, 1982).

ARUN BOSE

GIAP VO NGUYEN, (b. 1910). Vo Nguyen Giap was born in Quang Binh Province in Vietnam in 1910 and at the age of sixteen participated in the student movement of 1926. Arrested in 1930 and jailed for two years, Giap subsequently studied law and history at the University of Hanoi. During the Popular Front period (1936), he agitated in various semilegal Communist organizations, writing in the journals *Le Travail, Notre voix, En avant* and others. In 1940, Giap went with Pham Van Dong* to work under Nguyen Ai Quoc (Ho Chi Minh*) in southern China. On 22 December 1944, Giap created, organized, and led the nucleus of the later Vietnam People's Army (VPA) (then known as the Armed Propaganda Brigade for National Liberation). Its slogan "Politics takes command" remained the governing principle of the army. In August 1945, Giap became Minister of Defense of the Democratic Republic of Vietnam (DRV), and the following year chairman of the DRV's Military Committee. He remained Defense Minister and commander-in-chief of the VPA throughout the first Indochina War against France. Giap was the architect of the VPA's most brilliant victory, the encirclement and defeat of the French Army at Dien Bien Phu in 1954, and later masterminded the war against the United States in South Vietnam.

Giap was elected to the Politburo of the Vietnamese Workers' Party in 1951 and became vice premier in 1955. He gave up the vice premiership in 1976 and the defense portfolio in 1980. He resigned from the Politburo in March 1982 to devote himself to heading the State Science and Technology Commission.

Giap was the foremost military strategist of the Vietnamese Communist Party over a period of almost four decades. His writings borrowed much from existing Marxist works on revolutionary warfare, and especially Mao Zedong.* Another inspiration was traditional Vietnamese revolutionary experience. An early work that Giap wrote with Truong Chinh* in 1938, *The Peasant Question*, argued that the peasants were ripe for revolutionary organization, although the study stopped short of holding that the peasantry could be the revolution's principal social base. From this beginning, Giap forged a distinctly Vietnamese contribution to Marxist theories of revolutionary war. Thus the August Revolution is depicted by Giap as neither a carbon copy of the Bolshevik Revolution nor of the protracted Chinese revolutionary war but a sophisticated combination of the two. The unique character of the August Revolution lay in its adroit coordination of political and armed struggle. In later years, Giap continued to argue that the success of the Vietnamese Communist Party lay first in its carefully orchestrated balance of political and military struggle. Second, the Party's success lay in its ability to operate in both the cities and the countryside. Where the Bolshevik Revolution had been for the most part urban and the Chinese Revolution primarily rural, the Vietnamese Communist Party had combined the two approaches in a single integrated strategy. Throughout his writings, Giap constantly stressed the spirit of self-reliance and creativity without copying foreign experiences and without being complacent about acquired revolutionary experience.

BIBLIOGRAPHY:

A. *People's War, People's Army* (New York: Praeger, 1962); Truong Chinh and Vo Nguyen Giap, *The Peasant Question*, trans. Christine Pelzer White, Data Paper no. 94 (Ithaca: Cornell Southeast Asia Program, 1974); *Unforgettable Days* (Hanoi: Foreign Languages Publishing House, 1975); *Selected Writings* (Hanoi: Foreign Languages Publishing House, 1977).

MICHAEL C. WILLIAMS

GOES, FRANK VAN DER   (1859–1939). Frank van der Goes (who also used the names Ontheusden and Hack) was a Dutch Marxist and essayist whose international reputation is based primarily on his translation of the first volume of Mark's *Capital* into Dutch. He was a member of F. D. Nieuwenhuis's* Social Democratic Federation (SDB), and later joined P. J. Troelstra* in his opposition to the antiparliamentary actions of the SDB and its propagation of absolute expropriation. Of the so-called twelve apostles who founded the Dutch Social Democratic Workers' Party (SDAP) in 1894 (on the basis of the Erfurt Program of 1891), van der Goes was the only Marxist. Within the SDAP he belonged to a group left of center but not to the radical Tribunists* (D. Wijnkoop, J. C. Ceton, and W. Ravesteijn). Van der Goes founded *De Nieuwe Tijd*, the SDAP party paper of which Antonie Pannekoek,† Herman Gorter,† Willem van Ravesteijn, and Henriëtte Roland-Holst* would be editors. After the expulsion of the Tribunists, from 1909 to 1919, van der Goes edited *Het Weekblad*, a weekly supplement to the SDAP daily *Het Volk*, for which he was foreign correspondent from 1912 to 1925. After 1932 van der Goes aligned himself with the Dutch Independent Socialist Party (OSP), which published *De Fakkel*. He collaborated closely with the International Bureau for Revolutionary Socialist Unity (London Bureau), the International Labor Party (ILP), the Partido Obrero de Unificación Marxista (POUM), and the German Social Democratic Party. In 1935 he founded the Federation of Revolutionary Socialists, which published *De Socialist*. Van der Goes's theoretical contributions to Marxism are insignificant.

BIBLIOGRAPHY:
A. *Collected Essays* (Amsterdam, 1898).
B. *De Grote Winkler Prins* (Amsterdam: Elsevier, 1974).

TINEKE RITMEESTER

GOTTWALD, KLEMENT   (1894–1953). Klement Gottwald was a member of the Communist Party of Czechoslovakia since its origin in 1921, holding positions on its Central Committee and Politburo since 1925. In 1929 he became General Secretary of the Communist Party of Czechoslovakia and member of the National Assembly. From 1928 to 1943 he was a member of the Executive Committee of the Communist International, and from 1936 to 1943 a member of its Secretariat. From 1939 to 1945, while in exile in the Soviet Union, Gottwald was a leading functionary in the foreign management of the Czechoslovak Communist Party. In 1939 he was criticized by the Communist International for mistakes in Party policy during the Munich Crisis in 1938. From 1945 to 1953 Gottwald was chairman of the Czechoslovak Communist Party. His government positions included Prime Minister (1946–48) and President (1948–53) of the Republic.

Gottwald was an adept Communist politician who was nurtured by the Communist International. His activities mirrored both the growth of the Comintern and the democratic conditions of prewar Czechoslovakia. He rose to the forefront of the Party as a relatively young and still little-known functionary who proved his competence by unquestioningly obeying the instructions of the Comintern. Gottwald mastered the methods of communist power, politics, and social struggle and learned to adapt them to Czechoslovak conditions. Consequently, the Czech Communist Party was able, for twenty years, to survive legally despite a marked drop in membership. The experience gained in the Communist International cultivated in Gottwald an awareness of the need for unconditional subordination to its decrees and resolutions. This conviction indelibly colored his political thinking. After the Comintern's dissolution he was transferred to Moscow by Soviet leaders.

During the years 1948–53 Gottwald developed a deference to Stalin* and a fear of his Soviet political surroundings. Particularly after the excommunication of the Yugoslav Communists Gottwald would decide important questions only after consultation with his Soviet advisors, often accepting their advice even when he knew it was incorrect and even contrary to the needs and interests of Czechoslovakia. Gottwald lacked courage and fortitude in pushing his own positions. In internal politics, on the other hand, he behaved as a hard and ruthless Communist leader. For the last three years of his life he was a completely broken man, increasingly isolated from his political surroundings and responsible for a series of ruthless political intrigues and murders involving his closest friends and colleagues. As early as 1933, prompted by Comintern directives, he soundly condemned and removed from the Party a member of its top circle, Josef Guttmann,* for his views on the German question, which, ironically, resembled the decision later taken by the Comintern. After 1949 he agreed with Stalin's directive to arrest his closest coworker and colleague, the General Secretary of the Czechoslovak Communist Party, Rudolf Slansky. Gottwald himself proposed his execution, with that of ten other leading Communists, during the trial. Gottwald's political path resembled that of most Communist leaders in the Soviet bloc countries: he began it as a young promising functionary and concluded it as a broken and ruthless dictator, subordinate to Moscow and responsible for mass political persecution and murder.

Gottwald was a practical politician, by no means a theoretician. However he could "interpret" the general directives of the Comintern in a manner that respected Czech national peculiarities. This was the case, for example, when he led the strikes by unemployed Czechs during the economic crisis of the mid-1930s, or formulated a nationalist political line during the Nazi threat to Czechoslovakia in the years 1935–38. Gottwald never gave up his goal of attaining a Communist monopoly of power, nor did he ever have any concept of a socialist society other than the Soviet one. The years 1945–48 presented the opportunity of achieving this goal peacefully by political means, one of which was obtaining a Communist majority in parliamentary elections. Gottwald called this method, suggested by Stalin in 1946, the Czechoslovak path to socialism. Gottwald's method of achieving power required three stages: (1) an increase in Communist parliamentary representation (the Communists obtained almost 40 percent of the votes in 1946); (2) the internal breakdown of noncommunist parties and their being taken over by "leftists," whom the Communists had deliberately groomed; (3) organized mass unrest among Czech workers and farmers, in order to exert political pressure against coalition partners, as well as the popularly elected Parliament. The parliamentary representatives of several noncommunist parties gave Gottwald a golden opportunity to achieve his power monopoly. On 20 February 1948 they resigned, precipitating a government crisis. Gottwald used organized social protest to break the noncommunist parties and eventually control them with obedient "leftists." In comparison to the decisive Communist struggles in other countries of the Soviet bloc, the Gottwald method differed primarily in the fact that by "mobilizing the masses" he obtained the active support of a large proportion of Czech citizens. During the ensuing years he rapidly lost this support.

BIBLIOGRAPHY:

A. *Works*, 15 vols. (Prague: Svoboda, 1951–54).

M. KAREL KAPLAN

GROSSMANN, HENRYK   (1881–1950). Henryk Grossmann was born in Cracow on 4 April 1881 and died in Leipzig on 24 November 1950. After earning his doctorate in law at the University of Cracow, he practiced law in Vienna until the outbreak of World War I, during which he served as an officer in the Austro-Hungarian Army. In 1922 he was named professor of political economics at the Free Polish University in Warsaw, but at the end of 1925 he moved to Frankfurt, where he was associated with the Institute for Social Research. Appointed extraordinary professor of economics at the University of Frankfurt in 1930, he emigrated to Paris in 1933, later moving on to London and then New York. In 1949 he accepted an appointment at Leipzig University, where he lectured on economic and social history until his death.

Grossmann achieved prominence primarily through his efforts to defend and elaborate upon Marx's* theory of the declining rate of profit. Building upon Marx's schematic analysis in *Capital* of the problems created by the necessity of maintaining an equilibrium between the producer and consumer goods sectors of the economy, he calculated that although the economic collapse predicted by Marx had been postponed, largely through imperialist exploitation of less developed areas of the world, between three and four decades after the capitalist system reached maturity the rate of profit would necessarily decline to the point that it would no longer be sufficient to support continued production.

BIBLIOGRAPHY:

A. *Das Akkumulations—und Zusammenbruchs—gesetz des kapitalistischen Systems* (Leipzig: C. L. Hirschfeld, 1929); *Marx, die klassische Nationalökonomie und das Problem der Dynamik* (Vienna: Europa, 1969).

B. *Neue Deutsche Biographie*, vol. 7 (Berlin: Duncker und Humblot, 1966), pp. 158–59.

KENNETH CALKINS

GUESDE, JULES (1845–1922). Jules Guesde was born in 1845 in Paris, was educated in his father's private school, and became a journalistic opponent of the Second Empire. To avoid embarrassing his father, he abandoned his family name of Bazile and worked under the pseudonym of "Guesde." A journalist and editor for the *Droits de l'homme* in Montpelier, he wrote a series of articles in praise of the Commune in 1871 and was later forced to flee to Switzerland to escape jail. Here he joined the anarchist inspired Federation Jaurassien, but returned to France in 1876, before the Communard amnesty, as a Marxist. He joined the Café Soufflet group and founded the radically left-wing L'Egalité in 1877. The paper was banned a year later, and Guesde was arrested for attempting to organize a socialist congress, but he was nevertheless very influential when the first socialist congress did take place in Marseilles in 1879. A founder member of the Federation des Ouvriers Socialistes de France, which emerged from the congress, he visited Marx* in London and with the help of Paul Lafargue* he persuaded its successor Parti des Travailleurs Socialistes de France to adopt a Marxist program. His influence was soon surpassed by that of Brousse, and Guesde broke away from those he condemned as "possibilists" in 1882 to form the Parti Ouvrier Français (POF).

A deputy from 1893 to 1898 in the Nord, he took over the influential *Petite Republicaine* and excluded all non-Marxists from its columns, including Jean Jaurès.† During the various attempts at unity, Guesde took an orthodox Marxist position on parliamentarianism, and he led the opposition to Millerand, joining the Waldeck-Rochet ministry in 1899. In 1905 the socialists unified under pressure from the International around a program that showed considerable Guesdist influence. He was a member of the SFIO leadership commission from 1905 and a deputy again from 1906 to 1922. In 1914 he became a Minister of State without portfolio in the Union Sacrée government, where he remained until 1916, after which he took an increasingly less active part in both Parliament and the Socialist Party.

Guesde was a popularizer of Marxism who staunchly maintained that he was a revolutionary socialist, even when he had succumbed to the Jacobin patriotism of 1914 and joined a thoroughly bourgeois government. He had a catastrophist view of capitalism and was a strident advocate of the class war, which he saw as inevitable in a rather mechanistic way. He maintained that Parliament was a bourgeois distraction and that entering elections was only justifiable as a means of propagandizing the revolution and disturbing the political process. He thought that unions were little more than revolutionary training schools, and he insisted that reforms were only acceptable if they were ''revolutionary.'' This contradictory element in his thinking can also be seen in his desire to unite the peasantry and petit bourgeoisie with the working class and in his pursuit of parliamentary alliances after the POF successes in 1893. He was sustained through these and other compromises by his rather simplistic belief that the expropriation of the expropriators was inevitable after mass action by the working class, and one of his last major speeches included the famous phrase, ''We must mount guard around the Russian Revolution.'' This despite the fact that he stayed with the SFIO in 1920 and helped compose its first manifesto in 1921.
BIBLIOGRAPHY:

A. *Collectivisme et révolution* (Paris: Oriol, 1879); *Services publics et socialisme* (Paris: Oriol, 1884); *Le Problème et la solution* (Paris: Le Socialiste, 1893); *Le Socialisme au jour le jour* (Paris: Giard, 1899); *Les Deux Méthodes* (Lille: Lagrange, 1900); *Double Réponse a MMde Mun et Deschanel* (Paris: Bellais, 1900); *Jules Guesde: textes choisis*, ed. C. Willard (Paris: Editions Sociales, 1959).

B. A. Zaeves, *Jules Guesde* (Paris: Marcel Riviere, 1929); A. Compere-Morel, *Jules Guesde. Le Socialisme fait l'homme 1895–1922* (Paris: Editions Internationales, 1937); S. Lacore, ed., *Jules Guesde* (Paris: Editions du Centenaire, 1946); C. Willard, *Les Guesdistes* (Paris: Editions Sociales, 1965).

JOHN C. SIMMONDS

GUEVARA DE LA SERNA, ERNESTO (CHE) (1928–1967). Che Guevara was born in Rosario, Argentina, on 14 July 1928, and died in Bolivia on 8 October 1967. He graduated from the University of Buenos Aires with a degree in medicine in 1953 and then traveled extensively throughout Latin America. He was in Guatemala in 1954 when the CIA orchestrated the overthrow of President Jácopo Arbenz. Che resisted and was forced to take refuge in the Argentine Embassy. He spent 1955 and 1956 in Mexico City, where he met Fidel Castro.* He sailed on the *Granma* with Fidel Castro in December of 1956 and survived the first disastrous weeks as the guerrillas made their way from the coast of Cuba into the Sierra. He became a major in the rebel forces and one of Castro's most trusted associates. After the rebels came to power, Che served as President of the National Bank, Minister of Industries, and Director of the Industrial Development Section of the National Institute of Agrarian Reform. On 14 March 1965, Guevara left Cuba and made his way into the Bolivian back country. His efforts to stimulate revolution in that country were largely unsuccessful. In October of 1967 his guerrilla band was ambushed, and he was wounded and taken prisoner. The following day he was executed by Bolivian military authorities.

Guevara adapted Marxism to what he perceived to be the reality of Latin America. He rejected the notion common in Latin American Communist parties of his time that argued for supporting national-democratic bourgeois revolutions as precursors to socialist revolution. Instead he insisted that it was the duty of revolutionaries to make revolution, that individual people are the catalysts of history and the role of vanguard groups is to help create the conditions necessary for worker-peasant takeover of the state apparatus. Guevara wrote in *Socialism and Man*, "Our aspiration is that the party will become a mass party, but only when the masses have reached the level of the vanguard, that is, when they are educated for communism" (p. 19). Revolutionaries must not wait for the masses to demand revolution, they must lead them to it. The starting point for revolution would be with guerrilla bands operating in rural areas. Military activity would take precedence over political activity. He wrote that "revolutionary theory, as the expression of a social truth, surpasses any declaration of it; that is to say, even if the theory is not known, the revolution can succeed if historical reality is interpreted correctly and if the forces involved are utilized correctly" (ibid.). Praxis must precede theory or ideology.

Guevara believed that the end of Marxism was not social change in itself, but rather the development of a new "socialist" person. "What is really involved," he wrote, "is that the individual feels more complete [in the Communist system], with much more internal richness and much more responsibility" (ibid., pp. 19–20). The manifestation of this new humanity would be proletarian internationalism, i.e., the bonding together of the working people of the world. Freedom, that is, the rational control of nature and social life by people, would be the product of proletarian internationalism. But total freedom, he asserted, could not come about until communism existed on a world scale.

Guevara was also a forceful advocate of socialist planning in the economy. He argued that the development of the productive forces in a society would not, of necessity, lead to the breakdown of capitalist structures in a society in transition to socialism. Revolutionary leaders must take active measures to ensure the destruction of the vestiges of capitalism.

BIBLIOGRAPHY:

A. *Che Guevara Speaks: Selected Speeches and Writings* (New York: Grove Press, 1968); *Reminiscences of the Revolutionary War* (New York: Monthly Review Press, 1968); *Socialism and Man* (New York: Pathfinder Press, 1978).

B. Roberto F. Retamar, ed., *Obra revolucionaria* (Mexico City: Era, 1968); Robert Scheer, ed., *Diary of Che Guevara* (New York: Bantam Books, 1968); J. Mallin, ed., *Che Guevara in Revolution: A Documentary Overview* (Miami: University of Miami Press, 1969); Michael Lowy, *The Marxism of Che Guevara* (New York: Monthly Review Press, 1973).

KELLY AINSWORTH

GUILLÉN, ABRAHAM (b. 1913). A native of Corduente, Guadalajara, Abraham Guillén was born on 13 March 1913. He became active in politics during the Spanish Civil War of 1936–39, when he joined the anarcho-syndicalist National Labour Confederation (CNT) and Iberian Anarchist Federation (FAI) and rose from the Republican ranks to become commissar of the Fourteenth Division and later of Cipriano Mera's Fourth Army Corps. He participated in several major battles and in the defense of Madrid. Captured at the end of the war, a death sentence was commuted to imprisonment, and he managed to escape from Spain in 1945.

After three years of political exile in France, Guillén went to Argentina, where he worked as a journalist, contributing to *Economía y finanzas*, *El laborista*, and Cooke's *De frente*. His books began to appear in the early 1950s, and the anti-imperialist line contained both there and in his articles soon made it harder for him to find employment (although he was employed briefly as an economic consultant in the Argentine Senate in 1960). Accusations of links with the Uturunco guerrilla group led to three months' imprisonment in 1961 and general police harassment, which persuaded him to move to Montevideo in 1962.

In Uruguay Guillén wrote for José Batlle's newspaper, *Acción*. It was there that he developed his influential urban guerrilla strategy in association with exiled Argentine guerrillas including José Luis Nell and "Joe" Baxter, leaders of the Tacuara Revolutionary Nationalist Movement (MNRT). He met Che Guevara* in 1962, but their differences over guerrilla strategy only increased as a result. Guillén and the Argentines strongly influenced the nascent Tupamaros (and they were even detained on charges of instructing them), but Guillén's own ideas were more precisely reflected by the tiny Revolutionary Popular Organization (OPR-33), a guerrilla unit of the clandestine Uruguayan Anarchist Federation (FAU).

Outside Uruguay, Guillén's influence spread to the Argentine People's Revolutionary Army (ERP) through Baxter and to the Montoneros through Nell. In Brazil he influenced Carlos Marighela's* *Minimanual of the Urban Guerrilla* (1969) and his Action for National Liberation (ALN), as well as Carlos Lamarca's Popular Revolutionary Vanguard (VPR). During the early 1970s Guillén returned to Argentina, but soon had to leave following threats from the Triple A death squad. He worked for UNESCO in Peru as a specialist on cooperatives and self-management. Only after the death of Franco was Guillén able to end his long term of political exile by returning to Spain in 1976.

Guillenismo has been summarized as signifying: "the feasibility, desirability, and necessity of urban struggle; the integration of rural guerrilla warfare, urban guerrilla warfare, and mass-line organizing (combined struggle); continental revolution; and . . . the socialism of workers' control'' (Kohl and Litt, p. 187). Guillén's literary output amounts to more than twenty books, which reflect three phases in his evolution. From 1952 to 1964, Guillén went through what he called his ''neo-Marxist'' period of applying Marx's* dialectical method, materialist conception of history, and analysis of capitalism to contemporary events; from 1965 until the early 1970s his writing exhibited more of a Bakuninist emphasis upon direct action; and subsequently he attempted to reconcile Marxist and anarchist ideas through some form of ''anarcho-Marxism.''

The anarchist spirit has always been foremost. Even during the ''neo-Marxist'' stage, Guillén was using Michael Bakunin's concept of ''technobureaucracy''to characterize the Soviet regime, and he has always been a fervent admirer of the Spanish anarchist militia chief, Buenaventura Durruti (1896–1936). Guillén's writing naturally points to contradictions within capitalism and imperialism and between capitalist and socialist systems, but also to intersocialist and intrasocialist antagonisms—the former based on Soviet military and political imperialism, and the economic gulf between developed and underdeveloped socialist countries; the latter derived from the emergence of a new ruling and exploiting class in the socialist states, the ''technobureaucracy,'' which excludes workers from management of their enterprises.

Guillén's view of revolution is internationalist. For Latin America he has advocated the establishment of a ''continental strategic command'' to direct revolutionary movements in a struggle against feudalism, imperialism, and monopoly capitalism. Successful liberation fronts, he argues, must be led by the proletariat, which needs also to ally with the peasantry and attract middle-class support. The revolution will bring liberation not only from imperialism but also from ''Soviet revisionism'' and the national bourgeoisies.

It is only on questions of strategy that Guillén has been truly influential, although it should be noted that guerrillas in Latin America, both rural and urban, have often improvised, only to discover who their ''mentors'' were long after the initiation of revolutionary warfare. Guillén's strategic writing draws upon studies of the seizure of Petrograd in 1917, the defense of Madrid in 1936, and the battle for Santo Domingo in 1965, as well as upon classical military theory. He often cites Clausewitz, whose appeal to guerrillas lay especially in his discussion of the comparative advantages of defensive forms of warfare in which the central aim is to exhaust the enemy while avoiding decisive battles.

Guillén's strategy envisages warfare by the ''people in arms,'' combining operations by a rurally based liberation army and guerrilla activity against the enemy rear guard in the cities. The two elements are complementary, for it is only if the enemy is harassed in its heartland that it will be unable to deploy its full repressive might against rural insurgency. Warfare can be initiated by a handful of revolutionaries but can only succeed if the political conditions are right and if popular support for the urban guerrillas is forthcoming. While they hold down enemy troops and resources in the cities, their rural counterparts have an opportunity to establish "liberated zones" and develop into a people's army. This view of the rural element, along with an insistence upon a single political-military command structure for the revolutionary war, are conceptions which already figured in Cuban strategic theorizing. What set Guillén apart from it, early on, was his idea of "total war" (as opposed to the Guevara- Debray†stress on rural *foquismo*), and later his preference for urban over rural guerrilla warfare.

Urban guerrillas were not yet Guillén's priority when he wrote his *Teoría de la violencia*. There he urged a "total war: economic, social (strikes), demonstrations, protests against the cost of living, isolated violent actions, well-directed propaganda, and a coherent international policy, but all combined with the liberation army and the guerrilla (located at the enemy's back)" (p. 230). However, by 1966, in his *Estrategia de la guerrilla urbana*, Guillén was depicting the cities as the main arena of insurrectional warfare for highly urbanised Argentina and Uruguay, and he added Brazil to the list in 1972. During the early 1960s rural guerrillas had suffered defeats in many parts of Latin America. Guillén now realized that developments in the technology of repression had nullified many classical theses concerning rural guerrilla warfare, but he maintained that urban warfare was still possible, for that technology could not be used so tellingly in the cities. There the enemy could not use its heavy weaponry and numerical strength to their full advantage, nor could it use napalm.

Urban guerrilla warfare flourished briefly in the early 1970s in Uruguay and Argentina, but in the long run all the organizations that accepted Guillén's prescriptions were destroyed. Urban guerrilla warfare failed both in Latin America and in Guillén's own country. Not all the urban guerrilla defeats can be attributed to him. He did warn against the terrorism that some of his devotees fell into as states responded to insurrectional challenges with terrorist methods themselves. He criticized the Tupamaros for developing into something resembling a counter-state without counter-institutions to sustain it. And he further rebuked the Tupamaros for having too weak a mass line.

However, experience has shown the latter to be an invariable feature of urban guerrilla warfare. The theory has never given rise to successful coordination of guerrilla group and mass activity. Since they chose to operate "behind enemy lines," the urban guerrillas had for security reasons to isolate themselves to an extreme degree even from the working class. The strategy was far too demanding for most workers. It was embraced mainly by students and graduates whose relatively privileged financial and social circumstances enabled them to make the necessary commitment, which for many combatants involved a totally clandestine existence. Indeed, the evidence indicates that the strategy tended to be too demanding for people of all classes once they had reached their late twenties, when family and job considerations made security more attractive. Although urban guerrilla warfare arguably contributed to the downfall of the Argentine military regime of 1966–73, it was unable to bring about a socialist alternative.

In Uruguay in 1972–73 and Argentina in 1976, urban guerrilla activity was used as a pretext for reactionary military coups, and the armed forces stayed in power long after the guerrillas had been defeated.

BIBLIOGRAPHY:

A. *La agonía del imperialismo* (Buenos Aires: Sophos, 1957); *Teoría de la violencia* (Buenos Aires: Jamcana, 1965); *Estrategia de la guerrilla urbana* (Montevideo: Manuales del Pueblo, 1966); *Dialéctica de la política* (Montevideo: Cooperative Obrera Gráfica, 1967); *Philosophy of the Urban Guerrilla*, trans. and ed., Donald C. Hodges (New York: Morrow, 1973).

B. James Kohl and John Litt, *Urban Guerrilla Warfare in Latin America* (Cambridge: MIT Press, 1974); Richard Gillespie, "A Critique of the Urban Guerrilla: Argentina, Uruguay and Brazil," *Conflict Quarterly* (New Brunswick) (Fall 1980); idem, *Soldiers of Perón (Argentina's Montoneros)* (Oxford: Clarendon Press, 1983).

RICHARD GILLESPIE

GUTTMANN, JOSEF (1902–1958). Josef Guttmann was born into a bourgeois family in 1902 in the city of Tabor. He left school in order to join the Czech Communist Party (PCT) after it was established in 1921, and became from then on a professional militant and a political journalist. His impressive intellect and his exceptional skills allowed him to rise rapidly in the Party apparatus. Representing, with Šverma* and Slanský, the "left tendency" of the local Prague Party, he was selected to serve on the national Central Committee by the Third Party Congress in March 1925; in August 1928 he became a delegate to the Sixth Congress of the International, meeting in Moscow. After his friend Klement Gottwald* was installed as head of the PCT, Guttmann, despite his youth, became a powerful Party official: serving in the Party's political office and as editor-in-chief of the Party's major journal, *Rudé Právo*. In April 1931 Guttmann was selected to be the Secretary of the Presidium of the Executive Office of the Communist International. As a leader of the PCT, and with the support of Gottwald and Jan Šverma, Guttmann, in August 1932, presented a fundamental criticism of several of the International's policy positions. In particular, Guttmann condemned the Stalinist* thesis that social democrats had become "social fascists" and were not reliable allies. Guttmann claimed (correctly, as it turned out) that Nazism could be defeated only when workers, social democrats, and Communists joined in opposition. The Stalinist counter-offensive to Guttmann's remarks aimed either to defeat Guttmann and the other leftists and Trotskyists* or at least to isolate them. Pressure was exerted on Gottwald and Šverma to abandon Guttmann and his leftist line. Gottwald and his comrades eventually yielded, composed the standard self-criticism, and accused Guttman of misleading them. Guttman was removed from all of his Party posts and arrested by the Czech police in September 1933. From prison, Guttmann composed a "Memorandum" developing his own arguments and refuting those of his Communist enemies. Termed a Trotskyist and counterrevolutionary, Guttmann was expelled from the party on 31 December 1933. He continued to oppose Stalinism by writing polemics, organizing leftist opposition movements, and associating

with Trotsky aides such as Erwin Wolf and Jan Frankel. In 1936, Guttmann
changed tactics, aiming to create a "new Party" and a "new International"
instead of reforming the old ones. With his friend Záviš Kalandra,† he published
anti-Stalinist polemics and formed the opposition journal *Worker*. He also tried
to unite several left opposition groups into the new Socialist Revolutionary Party
of Czechoslovakia in 1938. He finally left Czechoslovakia the day after the
Munich Agreement was signed. He traveled first to Denmark and then to London,
where, with J. Kopp, he helped publish the Trotskyist journal *Jiskra*. He arrived,
ultimately, in the United States, where he allied himself with Max Shactman*
and others who rejected the elitism and bureaucratism that stained the Soviet
Union, the Fourth International, and most orthodox Communist parties. In America he soon associated with ex-Trotskyists and non-Marxist intellectuals, even
collaborating with Dwight Macdonald's *Partisan Review*. He usually published
under the pen names Gordon or Peter Meyer and, as the latter, collaborated on
a major study of Czech anti-Semitism. He lived in New York City until his
death in 1958.

Guttmann's contributions to Marxism are those not of a grand theorist but of
a politically active Marxist of incomparable lucidity. There are three important
issues Guttmann focused on: first, the Communist International's responsibility
for the Nazi defeat of the German proletariat; next, the significance of the Czech
national question and the inability of the PCT to propose an effective international
revolutionary strategy; finally, the crisis of the Czech state and the political
dynamics characterizing the Soviet Union's relationship to the Czech Communist
Party during the era of Munich.

Regarding the errors of the Communist International's German policy in the
1930s, Guttmann was the only leader of a national Communist Party to contest
the International's assertion in 1933 that a Nazi victory constituted "a progressive
step in the battle for socialism" and was "inevitable." Guttmann argued that
Nazism should have been actively resisted by a united front of workers, social
democrats, and Communists led by a Communist Party that steered the masses
toward the necessity of defeating Hitler and, ultimately, abolishing capitalism.

On the Czech national question, Guttmann argued that in Czechoslovakia
between the two world wars the major contradiction was not between social
classes but between ethnic conflicts of different nationalities. These conflicts
were fueled by the Versailles settlement (subordinating native ethnic interests to
the defense and economic needs of Western capitalist states) and the Soviet-
inspired policies of the PCT (which increasingly alienated itself from the interests
of non-Czech nationalities). Guttmann called for a new Party strategy that recognized and resolved the ethnic difficulties in Czechoslovakia. None was
forthcoming.

Guttmann felt that the Czech imperialist bourgeoisie, the class controlling
Czechoslovakia during the interwar years, was divided. The first group, led by
President Beneš, felt another world war was inevitable. They would willingly
accept a temporary military defeat and exile in order to reattain power when the

Western democracies emerged victorious. The other group, led by the banker Dr. Preiss and agrarian leader Beran, were opportunists willing to bow to, and cooperate with, the powerful Germans. After France and the Soviet Union capitulated to Germany's annexation of the Sudetenland, Czechoslovakia was immediately seized by popular anger and protests. The Czech government and police were immobilized. Guttmann argued that the time was ripe for the Czech Communist Party to seize power. But the Party refused, fearing the internal battle that Guttmann felt they would surely have won. Moreover, the Soviet Union was not interested in supporting a revolutionary war at this time and wished to maintain stable relations with France. Hence the Czech Party, under orders from Moscow and led by Klement Gottwald, encouraged the masses to return home and support the new, opportunistic military regime, which would continue the policy of appeasement. Guttmann condemned the Party for supporting the new military government of "national defense," which was, he opined, really a government of "national capitulation."

BIBLIOGRAPHY:

A. *Ústřednímu výboru Komunistické strany Československa*, vol. XIX, no. 21 (1933); with Záviš Kalandra, *Odhalení Tajemství Moskevského Procesu* (Prague: n.a., 1936); with Záviš Kalandra, *Druhý Moskevský Proces* (Prague: n.a., 1937); Jan Buchar (pseudonym), *Zur nationalen Frage in Mitteleuropa* (Exile papers of Leon Trotsky, Houghton Library, Harvard University, bMRus 13–1, 15896), excerpted in *The New International*, no. 7 (July 1939); Peter Meyer (pseudonym) and Bernard D. Weinryb, *The Jews in the Soviet Satellites* (Syracuse: Syracuse University Press, 1953).

B. Zdenek Hradilák, "Josef Guttmann: Konflikt rozumu a svědomí," *Dějiny Socialismu* (Prague), no. 5 (1968); Jacques D. Rupnik, "Conflits au sein du mouvement communiste en Tchécoslovaquie au début des années trente: L'affaire Guttmann," *Revue française de science politique*, no. 4 (1976); Pierre Broué, "Sur l'histoire du Parti Communiste Tchécoslovaque," *Revue française de science politique*, no. 2 (1982).

M. KAREL KOSTAL

H

HAYWOOD, WILLIAM D.   (1869–1928). A labor activist and socialist, William Haywood was active around the turn of the century in the leadership of the Western Federation of Miners (WFM) and the Industrial Workers of the World (IWW) before defecting to the Soviet Union in 1920. Known affectionately as "Big Bill," he was an awesome, towering figure, well over six feet tall, big-boned and brawny, with a rugged, mean look that came partly from the effects of his long, hard-working, roughneck life as a miner, cowboy, and homesteader, and partly from being blind in one eye, the result not of a mining accident as was popularly believed, but a childhood injury. Haywood possessed a genuine proletarian charisma. He was a self-educated man who had risen from the ranks, deeply and defiantly class-conscious, but activist to the point of being oblivious to ideology.

Haywood was active in the WFM from 1896 to 1905. He was elected to the Executive Board in 1899 and named secretary-treasurer in 1900, a post he held for the next five years. He participated in a series of WFM-inspired strikes in Colorado after 1901. By 1905, when he became involved in the founding of the IWW, he had built a solid reputation as a seasoned, militant activist and organizer, well known among the nation's labor and socialist leaders. And the views he would cling to for the rest of his life had already crystallized out of his experiences as a miner and mine worker organizer.

These views, which Haywood brought to the founding of the IWW, may be briefly summarized as follows: Something was fundamentally wrong in the structure of American society that could only be corrected through the "direct action" of a united working class, and not through political or electoral action. The union movement in America should be organized industrially and not by craft. The goal was one overarching union of all workers, instead of a plurality of small elite groups of skilled workers. Haywood insisted that such a union would cater to the unskilled masses and include women and minorities. In 1905 Haywood promised the delegates at the founding convention of the IWW that they would go "down into the gutter to get at the mass of workers and bring them up to a decent plane of living." Haywood also considered himself a socialist, having joined the Socialist Party of America in 1901. But his political concerns were for the plight of his fellow workers and not with questions of ideology.

Big Bill Haywood, like the roughnecks he personified and represented, caused a great deal of controversey with the imagery of violence that stubbornly clung to his public character. When provoked, he was willing to use physical violence. On one occasion in 1903, for example, he was involved in a scuffle with three deputies in Denver and settled the whole affair by shooting one of the deputies three times with the 38-caliber revolver he was carrying for just such occasions. And in 1906, just six months after the founding of the IWW, he was arrested, tried, and acquitted in a sensational and nationally publicized murder trial, involving the terrorist-style bombing death of the ex-governor of Idaho. But, as a rule, and as a matter of principle, Haywood never advocated the use of violence as a political strategy, and, especially after the establishment of the IWW, he almost always advised against it. His view of direct action—his "folded arms" philosophy—was distinctly nonviolent, based on a strategy of passive resistance. "When we strike now," he said in 1913, "we strike with our hands in our pockets. We have a new kind of violence, the havoc we raise with money by laying down our tools."

Haywood was an important and romantic figure in the IWW from 1905 to 1920. In 1912 and 1913 he was in the forefront of the IWW strikes at Lawrence, Massachusetts, and Patterson, New Jersey. From 1916 to 1918, he held the post of secretary-treasurer of the IWW and was a leading participant in the Joe Hill Defense Campaign of 1915. In September 1917 he was arrested and convicted under the Federal Espionage Act. In 1920 he jumped bail and fled to the Soviet Union, where he worked for a while as the leader of the American Kuzbas Colony in Siberia.

But his exile was not a happy one. He felt useless, out of place, and homesick. And although he never rejected Soviet communism, as some have argued mistakenly, he was never very comfortable with the ideological orthodoxy of the Soviets. He said of his Russian experience: "The trouble with us old Wobblies is that we all know how to sock scabs and mine guards and police or make tough fighting speeches to a crowd of strikers, but we aren't so long on this ideological stuff as the Russians."

He died in April of 1928 in Moscow at the age of fifty-nine, after suffering a stroke.

BIBLIOGRAPHY:

A. "Industrial Unionism," *Voice of Labor* (June 1905); with Frank Bohn, *Industrial Socialism* (Chicago: Charles H. Kerr, 1911); "On the Patterson Picket Line," *International Socialist Review*, 13 (June 1913), pp. 847–51; "Sentenced To Be Shot—Act Quick," *International Socialist Review*, 16 (August 1915); *Bill Haywood's Book: The Autobiography of William D. (Big Bill) Haywood* (New York: International, 1929).

B. Some of the best secondary sources on Haywood are the memoirs of his friends and associates, including Emma Goldman, *Living My Life* (New York: Knopf, 1931); Mabel Dodge Luhan, *Intimate Memories*, vol. 3, *Movers and Shakers* (New York: Harcourt, Brace, 1933); Elizabeth Gurley Flynn, *I Speak My Own Piece* (New York: Masses and Mainstream, 1955); and Ralph Chaplin, *Wobbly: The Rough and Tumble Story of an American Radical* (Chicago: University of Chicago Press, 1948). The following scholarly sources include discussions of Haywood: Paul F. Brissenden, *The I.W.W.: A Study of American Syndicalism* (New York: Columbia University Press, 1920); Joyce L. Kornbluh, ed., *Rebel Voices: An I.W.W. Anthology* (Ann Arbor: University of Michigan Press, 1964); Philip S. Foner, *History of the Labor Movement in the United States*, vol. 4, *The Industrial Workers of the World, 1905–1917* (New York: International, 1965); and especially Joseph R. Colin, *Big Bill Haywood and the Radical Union Movement* (Syracuse: Syracuse University Press, 1969).

CHARLES W. HAMPTON

HILFERDING, RUDOLF   (1877–1941). Rudolf Hilferding was born in Vienna into a Jewish merchant family. Although he studied medicine and practiced as a pediatrician for a few years, his real vocation became political economy. He contributed regularly to the socialist journal *Neue Zeit* edited by Karl Kautsky,* taught at the party school of the Social Democratic Party of Germany (SPD), and became an editor of the SPD central newspaper *Vorwärts*. An early opponent of the SPD's decision to vote in favor of war credits, Hilferding joined the dissidents who founded the Independent Social Democratic Party of Germany (USPD) in 1917. He served briefly as a military doctor in the Austrian Army, then returned to Berlin, where he eventually became a German citizen. During and after the November 1918 revolution he worked as an editor of the USPD newspaper *Freiheit* and as a leader of the right wing of the new party. He was also a prominent figure on the two government-appointed Socialization Commissions, which considered state takeover of various industries. The fragile coalition governments of the early Weimar Republic, however, ignored the commissions' recommendations.

Hilferding's expertise as a political economist and his distrust of the Communists helped him to gain support in the upper ranks of the SPD after a major segment of the USPD rejoined its sister party in 1922. In August 1923 he was selected to become minister of finance in the Great Coalition government headed by Gustav Stresemann, where he earned a reputation for deliberation at a time (hyperinflation) when quick action was prized. He was forced to resign within months. Hilferding again held the same office in 1928–29, under Chancellor Hermann Müller, with unfavorable results. In between and afterward, he served on the SPD's parliamentary executive and executive committee. He also edited the socialist journal *Gesellschaft*. After the collapse of the Great Coalition government in March 1930, Hilferding became one of the most prominent advocates of the SPD's policy of tolerating the Brüning government as the lesser evil to Nazism. From the mid-1920s on, Hilferding was one of the most influential figures within the party elite and more or less official party theorist.

In March 1933, after the Nazi takeover, Hilferding and his wife Rose escaped to Switzerland. They chose to settle in Austria but had to flee in 1938 to France, where they were trapped, along with Toni and Rudolf Breitscheid,* when the

Germans invaded in 1940. In February 1941 Vichy authorities arrested Hilferding and Breitscheid in Arles and turned them over to the Germans in Paris. Hilferding, of Jewish origin, apparently took a fatal dose of veronal and thus prevented the Nazis from bringing him back to Berlin. Breitscheid was taken to Berlin, then imprisoned in Sachsenhausen and Buchenwald, and was apparently killed by an SS guard in the midst of an Allied bombing raid in August 1944.

Hilferding's two major theoretical works were *Böhm-Bawerk's Marx-Kritik* (1904) and *Finanzkapital* (1910). The former was, in effect, a defense of Marxism; the latter, in some respects, an adaptation of Marx's *Capital* to changed economic circumstances. Hilferding discussed the increasingly close relationship between investment banks and industry, the role of cartels in eliminating competition in industrial production and sales, and the importance of new investment opportunities as a driving force behind imperialism. Perhaps his most important achievement was to present a more realistic Marxist depiction of the state's role in the modern industrial economy. During World War I Hilferding speculated that this "organized capitalism" might be capable of avoiding economic crisis and collapse, even if its potential remained inferior to that of a socialist economy. This possibility called for a new and more flexible political strategy on the part of the proletariat, whose triumph was by no means assured. By 1922 Hilferding concluded that a democratic state was not an enforcement mechanism for an oppressive economic order, but the representative body of all groups and interests in society. The organized working class was the only group whose interest was identical with that of society as a whole—freedom from the interlocking elite of industrialists, merchants, and bankers.

Although Hilferding saw a great tension between a democratic state and huge, privately controlled corporations, his solution was to reassert the supremacy of the state through political action. Use of the parliamentary system provided the best means for the proletariat to capture power and implement its socialist aims. Hilferding had become a democratic socialist. By the mid-1920s Hilferding placed considerable importance on the beneficial effects of economic stabilization. Organized capitalism, with its principles of planning, research, and scientific management, was already a step toward socialism. Yet Hilferding was vague about how the economic process could be pushed further in the direction of socialism. His own financial policies were far from radical. He feared budget deficits and inflation and worked to reduce government spending. He believed that some sort of worker participation in management would have to precede full-scale nationalization; otherwise, workers would not be prepared for their eventual role in a socialist economy. Many of Hilferding's political addresses to SPD party congresses represented theoretical justifications for the party's future participation in coalition governments.

Even with a less than controlling influence in the state, Hilferding told the 1927 party congress, the working class could exert significant economic influence and gain direct material benefits. The weekly wage rate depended in part on the strength of the parliamentary representation of the SPD. Moreover, democracy always possessed the potential of effecting social change.

Hilferding failed to draw the full consequences from his own theory of the stabilization of capitalism. Despite his warning that socialism would not develop by itself out of capitalism, he relied essentially on a view of social structure and class consciousness that assumed unduly favorable results over time and on a concept of parliamentary democracy that remained abstract and institutional. His political patience corresponded to his personality—deliberate, unemotional, somewhat fatalistic. He was in this respect representative of the German Social Democratic Party leadership.

BIBLIOGRAPHY:

A. *Das Finanzkapital*, 2 vols. (Frankfurt: Europäische Verlagsanstalt, 1968); *Karl Marx and the Close of His System, by Eugen von Böhm-Bawerk, and Böhm-Bawerk's Criticism of Marx, by Rudolf Hilferding*, ed. Paul M. Sweezy (New Jersey: Kelley, 1977).

B. Wilfried Gottschalch, *Strukturveränderungen der Gesellschaft und politisches Handelin in der Lehre von Rudolf Hilferding* (Berlin: Buncker und Humblot, 1962), pp. 268–73; Minora Kurata, "Rudolf Hilferding: Bibliographie seiner Schriften, Artikel und Briefe," *Internationale Wissenschaftliche Korrespondenz zur Geschichte der deutschen Arbeiterbewegung* (September 1974), pp. 327–44.

RICHARD BREITMAN

HIRANO YOSHITARŌ (1897–1980). Hirano Yoshitarō was a leading Japanese Marxist of the Kōza-ha ("feudal") faction, which remained loyal to the Japanese Communist Party after the party split in December 1927, in a dispute over revolutionary strategy and tactics. Born in Tokyo, Hirano attended the First Higher School and graduated from the prestigious Tokyo Imperial University Department of Law in 1921. He then became an assistant professor in the same department and, already a Marxist, by 1925 had published "Class Struggle in the Law" ("Hōritsu ni okeru kaikyū tōsō"). The following year Hirano joined the Industrial Labor Research Institute (Sangyō rōdō chōsasho), then headed by Nosaka Sanzō. While studying abroad that year in France and Germany, Hirano reported on Japan's proletarian students at the April 1928 meeting of a pedagogical workers association in Leipzig. The following year, Hirano joined Katayama Sen to participate in the Second Congress of the International Anti-Imperialist League. In returning to Japan, he was arrested on charges of violating the Peace Preservation Law.

That year, Hirano began planning the seven-volume *Symposium on the History of the Development of Japanese Capitalism (Nihon shihon-shugi hattatsu shi kōza)*, resigning his post at Tokyo Imperial University. The original purpose of the *Kōza* was twofold. First, it was intended to offer scholarly support to the two-stage strategy of revolution the Comintern had prescribed for Japan in its 1927 Theses that were immediately adopted by the Japanese Communist Party. Arguing that feudal remnants, particularly in the countryside and in the political superstructure (e.g. the emperor system), persisted, the Theses maintained that it was necessary to complete the bourgeois-democratic revolution begun by the Meiji Restoration before proceeding to the proletarian-socialist revolution. The dissident Rōnō (Labor farmer) faction, led by Yamakawa Hitoshi* and Inomata Tsunao,* left the party in opposition to the Theses and to Comintern leadership, arguing that Japanese capitalism was sufficiently highly developed to warrant an immediate socialist revolution. Noro Eitarō* and contributors to the *Kōza* defended the view that feudal remnants in Japan were sufficiently strong to require the completion of the bourgeois-democratic revolution first. Their scholarship served a second purpose, however, in responding to the need for comprehensive indigenous analysis of Japanese economic and political development. If Yamada Moritarō's* work best systematized the Kōza-ha's interpretation of recent Japanese economic history, Hirano's essays in the *Kōza* analyzed the implications of these economic developments for changes in the political sphere. Hirano focused on the incomplete character of the Meiji Restoration, which failed to result in a true bourgeois democracy in Japan. Continued backwardness in the agrarian sphere, mostly attributable to the long-term impact of "Asiatic characteristics," was reflected in authoritarian elements in the political arena, e.g., the absolute authority of the emperor, who was given exclusive sovereignty in the Meiji Constitution, and the role of the *genrō*, Privy Council, and military in rendering parliamentary government ineffective. Hirano was most innovative in writing about the Asiatic mode of production and the process of bourgeois-democratic revolution on the basis of the comparison of the experiences of England, France, Germany, and Japan. In the Japanese case, he stressed the structural interdependence of old "semifeudal" and capitalistic factors shaping the Japanese state. Hirano's essays in the *Kōza* were collected in a single volume and published as *The Structure of Japanese Capitalist Society* (*Nihon shihon-shugi shakai no kikō*) (1934).

In 1936, Hirano was detained at length in the Communist Academy Incident; during the Sino-Japanese War, he *tenkō*ed (defected from the Communist Party) and engaged in research on the Chinese countryside and on Southeast Asia. After the war, Hirano founded his own China Research Institute (Chūgoku kenkyūjo), headed the League for the Support of Democracy (Minshu-shugi yōgo dōmei), and in concert with the World Peace Congress convened in Paris in 1949, cofounded (with Ōyama Ikuo) the Japan Peace Committee. He also founded and became vice-chair of the Japan-China Friendship Association when the People's Republic of China was founded in 1949 and became an advocate of the civil rights of Koreans living in Japan. Hirano remained active both academically, continuing his writing on the state, and politically until his death in 1980.

BIBLIOGRAPHY:

A. *Burujoa minshu-shugi kakumei* (The bourgeois-democratic revolution) (Tokyo: Nihon hyōron-sha, 1948); *Kokka kenryoku no kōzō* (The structure of state power) (n.a.: Riron-sha, 1954); *Nihon shihon-shugi shakai to hōritsu* (Japanese capitalist society and the law) (Tokyo: Hōse, daigaku shuppan-Kyoku, 1955); Moriya Fumio, *Nihon shihon-*

shugi bunseki no kyoshōtachi (Great craftsmen in the analysis of Japanese capitalism) (Tokyo: Hakuseki shoten, 1982).

GERMAINE A. HOSTON

HOBSBAWM, ERIC J.   (b. 1917). Born in Alexandria, Egypt, in 1917, Eric Hobsbawm was educated in Vienna, Berlin, London, and King's College, Cambridge. He was a fellow of King's College (1949–55) and reader (1959), then professor (1970–) at Birkbeck College, University of London. He was a member of the Communist Party Historians' Group (1946–56), and a founding member of the magazine *Past and Present*.

Professor Hobsbawm is a leading social historian of his generation. His most enduring concern has been the history of the British working class, a subject he has done much to reorient in postwar Britain, both by striking new emphases and by opening up new areas of research. His writings have typically pushed beyond the bounds of institutional labor history, trying to place "the labour movement" more firmly into the broader setting of working class life and thought. Thus his first work, a sourcebook titled *Labour's Turning Point 1880–1900* (1948), presented a wide array of documents from the period, highlighting the new unionism but also the diversity of ideological positions within the working class, the Irish element, the influence of religious models on aspects of the labor movement, and so on; the intent was generally "to broaden the scope of labour movement history as then available to students" (*Labour's Turning Point*, p. i). *Labouring Men: Studies in the History of Labour* (1964) collected a series of seminal articles Hobsbawm produced over the subsequent decade and a half on aspects of nineteenth-century social and labor history; again, while not ignoring working-class organizations and their leaders, Hobsbawm cast his eye more widely to discuss traditions, customs, and rituals in the working class, the unskilled, machine-breaking, the standard of living in the industrial revolution, Methodism, and other diverse topics.

Primitive Rebels: Studies in Archaic Forms of Social Movement in the Nineteenth and Twentieth Centuries (1959) was an offshoot from and an elaboration on certain of these themes. Influenced notably by social anthropology and stimulated doubtless by such contemporary events as the Mau-Mau rising in colonial Kenya, it examined in turn social banditry, mafia, millenarianism, and insurrectionary mobs as varieties of "primitive" (generally prepolitical) social movements. The underlying claim of the book is that such archaic movements are not only important and interesting in themselves but provide some of the background to more modern labor and socialist agitations. *Primitive Rebels* can thus be seen as an argument about the bases of revolutionary and rebellious activity.

Hobsbawm has written a number of important pieces on Marxism and historiography, including "Karl Marx's Contribution to Historiography" (*Diogenes*, 64 [1968]) and an introduction to Marx's *Pre-Capitalist Economic Formations* (1964). He is also an editor, since 1979, of the international collaborative *History of Marxism*.

BIBLIOGRAPHY:
   A. *Labour's Turning Point, 1880–1900* (Rutherford, N.J.: Fairleigh Dickinson University Press, 1948); *Primitive Rebels: Studies in Archaic Forms of Social Movement in the Nineteenth and Twentieth Centuries* (New York: Praeger, 1959); *The Age of Revolution* (New York: New American Library, 1962); *Labouring Men: Studies in the History of Labour* (New York: Basic Books, 1964); *Industry and Empire* (London, Weidenfeld & Nicolson, 1968); *Bandits* (London, Weidenfeld & Nicolson, 1969); *Captain Swing* (New York: Pantheon Books, 1969); *Revolutionaries* (New York: Pantheon Books, 1973); *The Age of Capital* (London: Weidenfeld & Nicolson, 1975); *The Forward March of Labour Halted?* (London: New Left Books, 1981).

                                                                                          MICHAEL DONNELLY

HO CHI MINH   (1890–1969). Ho Chi Minh (also known as Nguyen Ai Quoc), the founder of Vietnamese communism and its recognized leader throughout virtually all his life, was born on 19 May 1890 at Kim-Lien in the province of Nghe An in central Vietnam. He attended *lycée* in Hue before going to Saigon to teach French. In 1912, Ho left Vietnam and worked for several years as a seaman on French ships. He spent several years in England and also apparently visited the United States, which led him several years later to write a pamphlet on the position of blacks there, *La Race noire*. In 1917, Ho moved to France and joined the French Socialist Party. In 1919 he petitioned the Versailles Peace Conference for Vietnamese independence and the following year became a founding member of the French Communist Party. In 1921 Ho founded the Intercolonial Union in Paris and edited its newspaper *Le Paria*. In this period he also wrote his famous pamphlet, *Le Procès de la colonisation française*, the first work directly appealing in Marxist terms to the Vietnamese people. Between 1922 and 1924, Ho worked in Moscow with the Comintern and was also vice president of the short-lived Krestintern (Peasant International). At the Fifth Congress of the Comintern in 1924, Ho made an impassioned intervention on behalf of the colonized peoples, criticizing the European leaders of the Comintern for their failure to understand the importance of the revolutionary movement in the colonies.

   In 1925, Ho moved to Canton and established the Revolutionary Youth Association (Thanh Nien), which served as the first vehicle for spreading Communist ideas among Vietnamese. Thereafter, no single person was to play a more important role than Ho Chi Minh in the introduction, adaptation, and leadership of the Communist movement in Vietnam from 1925 to his death in 1969. In February 1930, Ho established the Indochinese Communist Party, its first meeting taking place in a football ground in Hong Kong. The term "Indochinese" was apparently preferred by the Comintern. This was the first unified Communist Party in Vietnam founded after various Communist groupings had been riven by factionalism for many years. Again in 1941, Ho Chi Minh reshaped the Indochinese Communist Party after it had suffered tremendously from French colonial repression. In 1945 he led it successfully in a seizure of power in the August Revolution and thereafter was president of the Democratic Republic of

Vietnam until his death in 1969. He had been chairman of the Indochinese Communist Party since 1935.

From the moment he embraced communism, Ho Chi Minh saw his mission to bring about a fusion of Vietnamese patriotism and internationalism. The instrument of this fusion was to be the Communist Party. He desired the closest working relationship between the Comintern and the anti-imperialist movement in the colonies, while at the same time maintaining that every effort should be made to adapt communism creatively to local conditions. The key issues for Ho were the structure of the Party, the principles of urban insurrection, and its relationship both to the countryside and to the international context. Not the spontaneity of the masses but organization was, Ho believed and argued, the reason for the success of the Vietnamese revolution.

BIBLIOGRAPHY:

A. *Oeuvres choisies*, 4 vols. (Hanoi: Foreign Languages Publishing House, 1960); *Selected Works*, 2 vols. (Hanoi: Foreign Languages Publishing House, 1960); (Nguyen Ai Quoc), "The Party's Military Work Among the Peasants," in *Armed Insurrection*, ed., A. Neuberg (Franz Neumann) (London: New Left Books, 1970).

B. Jean Lacouture, *Ho Chi Minh: A Political Biography* (New York: Random House, 1968).

MICHAEL C. WILLIAMS

HUBERMAN, LEO   (1903–1968). Leo Huberman was coeditor and cofounder of the independent socialist journal *Monthly Review* and the Monthly Review Press. Before founding *Monthly Review* in 1949, Huberman taught in public and private schools from 1922 to 1933, edited *Scholastic* magazine in 1934–35, was chairman of the Department of Social Sciences at New College, Columbia University, from 1938 to 1940, and served as labor editor of the newspaper *PM* in the 1940s. Also from 1942 to 1945 he was director of public relations and education for the National Maritime Union. Throughout his life Huberman wrote or coauthored eleven books, coedited six books (with Paul Sweezy*), and wrote hundreds of magazine articles and pamphlets.

Leo Huberman was instrumental in popularizing Marxist interpretations of political and economic history, disseminating an intelligible Marxist critique of American capitalism, and making available to Americans an assessment of the progress of the Cuban Revolution. In *We, the People*, originally published in 1932, Huberman provided a model for "people's history" long before historians and activists of the 1960's rediscovered the idea that history all too typically was written about the ruling classes to the exclusion of oppressed and exploited classes. *We, the People* was an American history written from the bottom up in class terms with a lively style accessible to the general public. *Man's Worldly Goods* (1936) was an economic history that described to a mass audience feudalism and its transformation into capitalism. *The New Yorker* called this volume "the most successful attempt to date to humanize the Dismal Science and link the history of man to the history of economic theory." It sold 500,000 copies in the United States and thousands more in other countries.

As editor and contributor to *Monthly Review*, a journal written to disseminate socialist ideas and analyses of the contemporary world, Huberman wrote articles on the concrete meaning of socialism. The Monthly Review Press published *Introduction to Socialism*, a series of essays written by Huberman and Paul Sweezy addressing "The ABC of Socialism," "The Responsibility of the Socialist," and other essays lucidly defining socialism and its historical antecedent capitalism.

Perhaps Huberman's last major contribution to an American socialism (along with his coauthor Paul Sweezy) involved the publication of two books on the Cuban Revolution. *Cuba: Anatomy of a Revolution* (1960) explained how and why the Cuban Revolution succeeded in its initial seizure of state power in January 1959. It also described for concerned Americans the early phases of socialist construction in Cuba and its growing harassment by the U.S. government. *Socialism in Cuba* (1969), published after Huberman's death, described the major economic achievements of the Cuban Revolution during its first decade as well as its shortcomings, such as the legacy of the single-crop economy.

In each of these cases, as in his labor writings (*The Labor Spy Racket*, 1937, and *The Truth About Unions*, 1946) information about history, the nature of capitalism and socialism, and people's struggles was presented to facilitate knowledge *and* action. As a writer for people in general and as editor and publisher of a people's press, Huberman helped rekindle the idea of socialism in the United States in the 1950s and 1960s.

BIBLIOGRAPHY:

A. *We, the People: The Drama of America* (New York: Monthly Review Press, 1932); *Man's Worldly Goods: The Story of the Wealth of Nations* (New York: Monthly Review Press, 1936); *The Labor Spy Racket* (New York: Monthly Review Press, 1937); *The Truth About Unions* (New York: Reynal and Hitchcock, 1946); with Paul M. Sweezy, *Cuba: Anatomy of a Revolution* (New York: Monthly Review Press, 1960); with Paul M. Sweezy, *Introduction to Socialism* (New York: Monthly Review Press, 1968); with Paul M. Sweezy, *Socialism in Cuba* (New York: Monthly Review Press, 1969).

HARRY TARG

HYNDMAN, HENRY MAYERS   (1842–1921). Founder of the pioneering Marxist organization in Great Britain, the Social Democratic Federation, Henry Hyndman remained active in the movement until his death. He was unsuccessful in several attempts to win a parliamentary seat. Hyndman greatly influenced the reception of Marxism in Great Britain. Converted through a reading of *Capital* in 1880, he brought to the task of propagating Marxist teachings his experiences as a journalist and company promoter and a political outlook that drew on conservative, liberal, and radical traditions. From the outset his emphasis on the Marxist doctrines of the class struggle and the materialistic conception of history was combined with a strong patriotism and, indeed, a belief in the civilizing mission of the British Empire. And this bent, together with his failure to give Marx* credit in his first exposition of the new ideas, gained him the enduring enmity of Friedrich Engels.*

Hyndman's leadership of the Social Democratic Federation was marred by a somewhat autocratic temperament and policies in which political opportunism and dogmatic theory were curiously blended. Hence the series of defections and schisms that marked the development of the Federation. Some, most notably William Morris,† departed because they believed that the socialist vision was being hopelessly compromised; others because Hyndman failed to see the practical importance of the trade unions and other working-class organizations. These deficiencies in Hyndman's outlook help to explain the success of the Fabian Society and the Labour Party in formulating the political strategies for the British working classes.

Hyndman's organization, to which he devoted much of his life and his resources, was the most important vehicle for Marxist ideas in Britain during the period before World War I. It found significant pockets of working-class support—in London, Lancashire, and Scotland—and served as a kind of socialist conscience for the wider movement. Hyndman attempted in 1909 to draw his Marxist followers and the disaffected of other socialist groups together in the British Socialist Party. But his intense patriotism, expressed in a campaign to warn the British people of the dangers of German rearmament, and his vigorous support for the war effort after 1914, led to new divisions among the Marxists. Until he died in 1924, however, Hyndman remained faithful to a form of Marxism that condemned the capitalistic system without, however, approving the revolutionary strategy of the Bolsheviks or the tactics of the young British Communist Party.

BIBLIOGRAPHY:

A. *England for All* (London: Gilbert & Rivington, 1881); *The Historical Basis of Socialism in England* (London: K. Paul, Trench & Co., 1883); *The Record of an Adventurous Life* (London: Macmillan, 1911).

B. Chushichi Tsuzuki, *H. M. Hyndman and British Socialism* (London: Oxford University Press, 1961).

STANLEY PIERSON

I

IBÁRRURI, DOLORES   (b. 1895). Dolores Ibárruri was born on 9 December 1895 in the mining locality of Gallarta in the Basque provinces of Spain. She was the granddaughter, daughter, sister, and finally, wife of miners. She remembers having a very devoted mother and attending school until the age of fifteen, intending to become a teacher. She could not, however, fulfill her aspirations, instead becoming an apprentice in a dressmaker's shop. She married when she was twenty and moved to Somorrostro, an important mining center. Five children were born to her there, only two surviving. One of the two surviving children, Rubin, was killed in the Battle of Stalingrad during World War II.

After 1918 Ibárruri wrote for the newspaper *El minero vizcaine* (The Basque Miner) using the pseudonym, which was to become famous, "Pasionaria" (Passion Flower). Later, the socialist group of Somorrostro joined the Spanish Communist Party (PCG), and Dolores became a member of the provincial committee of the PCE in Biscay in 1920. She was a delegate from her province to the first and second congresses of her Party, where she was elected a member of the Central Committee of the so-called Pamplona Conference, which, however, was held in Bilbao in 1930. In 1931, enjoying a political career definitely not typical for a Spanish woman, she was called to Madrid to work as an editor in *Mundo obrero*, the official organ of the PCE. Although she was jailed on several occasions, her appointment to the Central Committee was ratified at the Congress of Seville in March 1932. She was also appointed to the Secretariat of the PCE after the expulsion of José Bullejos in October of that year.

In November 1933 she organized the Group of Antifascist Women, and as a result of the Asturias insurrection in 1934, she became conspicuous for her work in defense of the prisoners, to the extent that she was considered to be an Asturian. At the Seventh Congress of the Communist International, at which José Diaz* was present, she was appointed, together with Diaz, to the Executive Committee. Upon her return she became a fervent propagandist for the Popular Front and obtained certification as a delegate from Asturios in the elections of 1936.

During the Civil War the PCE was known as the party of José Diaz and Dolores Ibárruri, who was by then known as Pasionaria. Her continued visits to the front, her warm speeches, and her leadership of the Comision de Auxilio Feminine (Women's Help Commission) made her one of the figures and symbols of the Republican resistance. After the war she went to Toulouse, Paris, and finally Moscow, where in 1942 she was sponsored for the position of Secretary General of the PCE, thus putting an end to the rivalry between Vicente Uribe and Jesús Hernandez (the two Communist members of the Republican governments) to succeed José Diaz.

Elected and ratified as Secretary General of the PCE at the Fifth Congress held in November 1954, her star began to wane. The death of Stalin,* the admission of Spain to the United Nations, and the fact that she was far from the headquarters of the PCE (now located in Paris) all contributed to her decline, and the leadership fell more and more upon the shoulders of the "young ones" headed by Santiago Carrillo.† Not entirely convinced of the wisdom of the political initiatives undertaken by Carrillo (national reconciliation and a peaceful nationwide general strike), she preferred to resign her position rather than serve as a figurehead or symbol for the new policies. At the PCE Sixth Congress, in January 1960, she finally gave up the position of Secretary General and was, in turn, chosen for the new and symbolic position of President of the party. From this position she has always made the weight of her moral authority felt by those who have tried to create new factions, despite the fact that her stance might create difficulties for her before the Soviet authorities, as was the case when Santiago Carrillo denounced the invasion of Czechoslovakia.

Ibárruri has an honorary doctorate from the University of Moscow and is also a holder of the Order of Lenin.

BIBLIOGRAPHY:

A. *Autobiography* (New York: International, 1976); *El unico camino* (Moscow: Progress, 1976).

B. Teresa Pamies, *Una española llamada Dolores Ibárruri* (Barcelona: DOPESA, 1976); P. Erratita and Luis Haranburu, *Dolores Ibárruri* (Bilbao: Siglo, 1977).

SANTOS JULIÁ

IGLESIAS, PABLO   (1850–1925). The son of semi-illiterate parents, Pablo Iglesias became the most outstanding Spanish Socialist leader since the party's emergence. His father died when Pablo was a child, and he moved to Madrid with his mother. There, at the public orphanage, he learned the typesetting trade. He escaped from the orphanage at age twelve, and started working as an apprentice, then as a typesetter, in several printing establishments. Iglesias became a charter member of the first Spanish typesetters union that was organized in March 1870. He collaborated in the preparation and editing of its papers, *La solidaridad* and *La emancipación*. He also held several positions in the Federal Council of the AIT.

As a writer for *La emancipación*, Iglesias followed the Marxist line in regard to the expulsion of the AIT in the years 1872–73. The fall of the First Republic drove the international labor movement underground. Iglesias joined the Asociación General del Arte de Imprimir, the Madrid typesetters union. He was elected president of same and was responsible for making it a resistance organization. Clandestinely, in 1879 (together with other typesetters and workers in related fields), he founded the first socialist nucleus for the PSOE. As soon as the party was legalized in 1881, Iglesias became a key figure. He became editor of *El socialista*, a party journal. He was a distinguished leader not only of the Partido Socialista Obrero Española (PSOE) (president since the First Congress in 1888) but also of the Unión General de Trabajadores (UGT) syndicate, whose president he was from the late 1890s until his death.

Iglesias was a regular speaker at Socialist meetings, becoming, in 1916, the first Socialist delegate to the Spanish Parliament. His important positions in labor organizations, as well as his prestige and influence and his constant participation in national and international Socialist congresses, made him an important figure in the early twentieth-century debates between Spanish Socialists and Communists.

Iglesias wrote many articles and made numerous speeches at meetings, conferences, and in Parliament. But in general they were Marxist propaganda or practical advice for particular labor organizations. His writings are pragmatic, lacking theoretical depth or subtlety. What theory there is is based on a variety of influences, including French "Guesdism"* as well as orthodox materialism. The result, predictably, is theoretical inconsistency. Formulations completely foreign to Marx,* such as the so-called Bronze Law of salaries, would take more than two decades to disappear from the work of Spanish leftists. Iglesias's role with respect to Marxist theory is therefore that of a great propagandist rather than an original or consistent thinker.

BIBLIOGRAPHY:

A. M. Perez Ledesma and S. Castille, eds., *Pablo Iglesias: escritos*, vol. 1 (Madrid: Azuso, 1975); M. Cabrera et al., eds., *Paglo Iglesias: escritos*, vol. 2 (Madrid: Azuso, 1975).

B. Juan José Morato, *Pablo Iglesias, educador de muchedumbres* (Madrid: Espasa Calpe, 1931); Julian Zugazagaitiá, *Pablo Iglesias; de su vidor y de su obra* (Valencia: Cuadernos de Cultura, 1931); Julian Zugazagaitia, *Pablo Iglesias, vida y trabajo de un obrero socialista* (Madrid: Edit Fenix, 1935).

S. CASTILLO

IKUMI TAKU'ICHI   (b. 1901). Ikumi Taku'ichi, a Japanese economist and Marxist theoretician, was born on 1 April 1901 in Shiga Prefecture near Kyoto. After attending middle school and the First Higher School in Tokyo, Ikumi entered Tokyo Imperial University for the purpose of studying medicine. After studying medicine for only one year, Ikumi changed his field of concentration, and he was graduated from the German literature course in the Literature Department in 1925. Ikumi joined the Toyama Higher School as a lecturer and was promoted to professor in 1926. At this point, Ikumi's interest in social science was sparked by a pamphlet written by one of the Japanese Communist Party leaders, Sakai Toshihiko, and Ikumi followed up this interest by taking a leadership role in the newly formed Social Science Research Association at the Toyama Higher School. He then went to Tokyo to pursue his studies and become a lecturer at Japan University in 1927. Ikumi's political activities in the Japanese Labor-Farmer Party led him in 1929 to become active in the Marxist Industrial Labor Research Bureau (Sangyō Rōdō chōsasho), where he doubtless encountered Noro Eitarō* and Inomata Tsunao,* who were both engaged, on opposite sides, in the Marxist debate on Japanese capitalism. As Ikumi became more and more deeply involved in the movement, he was drawn into the debate on the side of the Kōza-ha ("feudal" school), led by Noro. In 1930 Ikumi changed his Japan University affiliation to its Department of Economics, so that there was a greater convergence between his teaching and research interests. Ikumi's involvement in the active political movement led to his arrest in April 1930, on charges of offering shelter and money to Communist Party members driven underground by the police. Although he was arrested for a violation of the Peace Preservation Law, he was released in April 1931. After this brief absence, Ikumi returned immediately to the Industrial Labor Research Bureau and with Noro's encouragement joined the Communist Party itself and organized a Communist Party faction within the Bureau.

At this juncture, Ikumi was prepared to take major steps in establishing his reputation as a Marxist. Accordingly, he became one of the few Communist Party members who helped Noro to plan the seven-volume *Symposium on the History of the Development of Japanese Capitalism*, published in 1932–33. Once again Ikumi was arrested in June 1933, released in 1936, rearrested in 1937, and after his release in December of that year joined the Riken Industrial Group, working as a manager of Riken Mining. After the war, in 1946, Ikumi became a research associate with Keidanren, the Federation of Economic Organizations, and a director of National Association for Economic Research (Kokumin keizai kenkyū kyōkai). He resumed teaching in 1956, when he joined Takasaki Economic *tandai* as professor, then moved in 1958 to Tokyo Economic University, where he subsequently was selected president of the university in 1967.

It was in the postwar period that Ikumi made his theoretical contribution to Japanese Marxism. After launching a critique of his own former Kōza faction, Ikumi developed his own "Ikumi theory" as a result of studies on the theory of the business cycle, contemporary capitalism, and the theory of state monopoly capitalism. This last theory became the basis for Ikumi's "theory of structural reform." After the critique of Joseph Stalin* in 1956, Ikumi became a leading figure in the so-called contemporary Marxist school, which opposed the Japanese Communist Party and endeavored to update Marxism to meet the needs of postwar Japan. Thus, during the 1960s, Ikumi established his own publishing house and (on two separate occasions) launched the journal *Contemporary Theory* (*Gendai no riron*) and continued to write on issues in contemporary Marxist theory.

BIBLIOGRAPHY:

A. *Gendai shihon-shugi to keiki junkan* (Contemporary capitalism and the business cycle) (Tokyo: n.a., 1961); *Kokka dokusen shihon-shugi ron* (The theory of state monopoly capitalism) (Tokyo: n.a., 1971).

GERMAINE A. HOSTON

INOMATA TSUNAO (1889–1942). Inomata Tsunao was the leading theoretician of the dissident Rōnō faction of the Japanese Communist Party. Born in Niigata Prefecture, he attended middle school in Nagaoka, until family financial hardship forced him to work as a substitute teacher and private tutor. From 1909 to 1911 he was enlisted in the Sixteenth Artillery Regiment; for a year he served on the reserve list as an officer. In 1913 he graduated from the private Waseda University and pursued graduate work there in law and economics until 1915. In that year he was sent to the United States by the university and studied economics and philosophy at the University of Wisconsin for three years, finishing his Ph.D. in 1920. In 1920 and 1921 he also studied at the University of Chicago and Columbia University. During this period, he specialized in Marxist studies, drew close to American socialists, and, through his association with Katayama Sen, participated in study groups for Japanese socialists in the United States. He was heavily influenced toward socialism by the Polish student Bertha Bronstein, whom he married. In October 1921, Inomata returned to Japan and became a lecturer at Waseda, and in the following year joined the newborn Japanese Communist Party.

Inomata quickly gained prominence in the left-wing movement. He chaired the discussion of the 1922 Theses at the Shakujii meeting in March 1923, was imprisoned briefly in the June 1923 arrests of Party members, and by late 1926 had already published several translations and a commentary on Rudolf Hilferding's* *Finance Capital*. He had also joined the Industrial Labor Research Institute (Sangyō rōdō chōsasho) in June 1925 to study imperialism. Like former Japanese Communist Party leader Yamakawa Hitoshi,* Inomata did not participate in Comintern-sponsored efforts to rebuild the Party after its dissolution under police pressures in 1924. Thus, in December 1927 Inomata readily followed Yamakawa, Sakai Toshihiko, and others out of the party in protest against the Comintern's (July) 1927 Theses prescribing a two-stage revolution for a Japan that was still "feudalistic" in many respects. With his fellow dissidents, Inomata founded the organ *Rōnō* that would give the faction its name and published regularly theoretical essays and analyses of current events in defense of the Rōnō-ha's call for immediate socialist revolution. In his essays on "The Present Political Position of the Japanese Bourgeoisie" and "The General Strategy of the Japanese Proletariat," he offered the theoretical backing for Yamakawa's "united front" political strategy. In opposition to the Comintern line, Inomata argued that Japanese capitalism was sufficiently highly developed to warrant an immediate socialist revolution. Drawing on Hilferding's *Finance Capital* and Nikolai Bukharin's* work on the advanced capitalist state, he maintained that one could detect the formation of state capitalist trusts in Japan in the late 1920s, as state capital increasingly merged with rising concentrations of private capital in leading *zaibatsu* (financial cliques). Inomata applied what contemporary Western Marxists would recognize as an "instrumentalist approach" to the state to analyze the ruling bourgeoisie's use of the state as a tool of class interests. More significantly, Inomata recognized the remnants of "feudal absolutism" in Japan's emperor system, but argued that the problem did not require the two-step revolution demanded by the Comintern. Rather, Inomata maintained that these forces would disappear as the by-product of a proletarian revolution that embraced "bourgeois-democratic tasks."

As a Rōnō-ha leader, Inomata also participated actively in the Labor-Farmer Party (Rōdō nōmintō), and subsequently the Proletarian Masses Party as a member of its Executive Committee. In November 1928, he launched the semimonthly *Labor-Farmer News*. After criticizing the Proletarian Masses Party for being insufficiently leftist, he was expelled along with Suzuki Mosaburo in May 1929. Shortly thereafter, Inomata also opposed Yamakawa's united front argument, which placed primacy on unity, and left the Rōnō-ha in October 1929. Thereafter, Inomata penned independent analyses of Japanese capitalism and imperialism, writing in such journals as *Central review* (*Chūō kōron*) and *Reconstruction* (*Kaizō*). After his break with the Rōnō-ha, Inomata's work, notably his *Introduction to the agrarian problem* (*Nōson mondai nyūmon*) (1937), attributed greater significance to factors in Japanese development more commonly stressed by the Rōnō-ha's opponents of the Kōza-ha, e.g., continued backwardness of Japanese agriculture because of the lingering impact of the Asiatic mode of production. An earlier book on *Agrarian Poverty* was the result of a survey of conditions in eighteen prefectures. Inomata was arrested and imprisoned in December 1937 in the Popular Front Incident. He was released when he became seriously ill in February 1939, but died in January 1942.

BIBLIOGRAPHY:

A. *Teikoku-shugi kenkyū* (Studies in imperialism) (Tokyo: Kaizō-sha, 1927); *Gendai Nihon kenkyū* (Studies on contemporary Japan) (Tokyo: Kaizō-sha, 1929); *Nihon no dokusen shihon-shugi* (Japan's monopoly capitalism) (Tokyo: Nanboku shoin, 1931); "Inomata Tsunao kenkyūkai," *Inomata Tsunao kenkyū* (Studies on Inomata Tsunao), Tokyo, nos. 1–16 (1970–74).

GERMAINE A. HOSTON

J

JAGAN, CHEDDI   (b. 1918). Cheddi Jagan was born on 22 March 1918, in Port Mourant, British Guiana (Guyana). His parents were Indian immigrants who came to Guayana as very young children as part of the great wave of Asian agricultural workers looking for employment in the Caribbean. Raised a Hindu, Jagan received his primary and secondary schooling in Guyana. In 1936, unable to secure a position in Georgetown, Jagan was sent by his family to the United States for advanced study. During his seven years in the United States, Jagan attended Howard, Northwestern, and the Chicago YMCA College. Although he eventually received a professional degree from Northwestern in dentistry, it was the Chicago YMCA College that most shaped his later life. At this school, Jagan took courses in history and economics, and it was here that he fell under the influence of teachers deeply involved in India's struggle for independence. After marrying in the United States, Jagan returned to Guyana in 1943 to start a dental practice, a profession that he has engaged in sporadically ever since.

Once back in Georgetown, Jagan became active in national politics. In 1946 he formed the Political Affairs Committee to discuss contemporary issues, particularly the questions of independence and social reform. Convinced that a more formal political organization was needed, Jagan—together with his wife Janet and L. F. S. Burnham—launched the People's Progressive Party (PPP) in 1950, patterned after the Progressive Party of Henry Wallace in the United States and the People's National Party in Jamaica. The PPP considered itself to be a socialist party and wanted to break Guyana's colonial ties with Great Britain. In the PPP's first election in 1953, Jagan's party won control of the colonial government, but it governed only 133 days before being removed by Great Britain because of the purported threat of internal disorder. Nevertheless, Jagan's party was the first Marxist party to win office democratically in Latin America. In 1955, the PPP split along personal and racial lines. Jagan continued the PPP (supported mainly by Indo-Guyanese), and Burnham formed the People's National Congress (supported principally by Afro-Guyanese). The PPP won control of the government again in 1957, and Jagan governed the colony until 1964, when the British imposed a new constitution that had the effect of removing Jagan's party from control. Since that time, he has led the PPP as the major opposition party to the government of L.F.S. Burnham.

Nationalism and Marxism have always been the twin pillars of Jagan's political philosophy. As a young student, Jagan found the writings of Charles Beard, Matthew Josephson, Jawaharlal Nehru, and Karl Marx* particularly enlightening in forging a perception of the political world. After World War II, Jagan followed with great interest the independence struggle of the Indian National Congress and the same fight among the British Caribbean islands—especially that of Eric Williams in Trinidad. Jagan has steadfastly labeled himself a socialist and Marxist, but he has argued since 1969 that most parties on the left must look to the Soviet Union for leadership. His political experience in leading Guyana and his labors in heading the chief opposition party have convinced him that socialism could not be achieved in Guyana as long as "imperialist" nations had the power to interfere in Guyana's domestic affairs. Although Jagan and his party have been denied a realistic opportunity of returning to power through democratic means (primarily because of the PNC's manipulation of the electoral process), his opposition to the government has been tempered in recent years by the threat to Guyana's territory of Essequibo by neighboring Venezuela and by the fact that the ruling PNC also considers itself to be a socialist party.

BIBLIOGRAPHY:

A. *Forbidden Freedom* (New York: International, 1954); *The West on Trial* (New York: International, 1966).

JAMES A. LEWIS

JIANG QING   (b. 1913). Born in 1913 and reared by her servant mother, Jiang Qing rose from her humble beginnings as a poor child in a broken family to become arguably the most important woman in twentieth-century China. Having chosen acting as a career and failed in three marriages, Jiang Qing escaped the Japanese invasion of 1937 by retreating to the Communists' cave headquarters at Yenan, where she met Mao Zedong.* Party leaders eventually sanctioned Mao's divorce from his loyal wife and marriage to Jiang Qing on the condition that Jiang stay out of politics for thirty years. This term of forced political inactivity expired at the start of China's Cultural Revolution. Mao turned to Jiang for help in mobilizing the Chinese to the Cultural Revolution's radical principles, and she then supervised the revolutionary purification of China's theaters. There is as yet no valid method of ascertaining Jiang's influence over Mao. Some argue that she had enormous powers and helped shape this turbulent period of Chinese history. Jiang herself claimed, during her trial "Everything I did, Mao told me to do. I was his dog; what he said to bite, I bit" (quoted in *New York Times*, 4 March 1984, sec. 4, p. 12). In any case, less than a month after Mao's death his successors arrested Jiang along with the other members of the so-called Gang of Four, and in their show trial of 1980 only Jiang defiantly asserted her innocence. Jiang is now in prison inside China for what will likely be a life term. Although it is highly unlikely that Jiang was a theoretical mastermind behind the events of China's Cultural Revolution, her notoriety, visibility, and relationship to Mao make her a force scholars of modern China must reckon with.

BIBLIOGRAPHY:

B. Ross Terrill, *The White-Boned Demon: A Biography of Madame Mao Zedong* (New York: Morrow, 1984).

ROBERT A. GORMAN

JOBET, JULIO CÉSAR   (1912–1980). During the early 1930s Julio César Jobet joined the newly formed Chilean Socialist Party and subsequently became one of its ideological mentors and one of his nation's outstanding economic historians. He tried to build a strong Marxist historiographical tradition in Chile. His efforts began to prove successful by the 1950s with the publication of a number of profound Marxist works that diverged from narrative chronology and moved toward class-oriented history that analyzed the causes and effects of Chile's social development. Before such treatments became popular elsewhere in the Americas, Jobet and his followers produced studies that examined society from the bottom up, did not glorify Chile, and told about its people's pain and misery. Unlike the mainstream of Chilean historians of his era, he categorized the nation as semifeudal, semicolonial, and extraordinarily dependent. He did not paint the traditional picture of Chile as a bastion of constitutional democracy as did the conservative and liberal academicians, who he felt deluded themselves into believing that their scholarship was objective and free of ideology.

Jobet saw Latin America as an organic entity that through continental unity could replace capitalism and imperialism with its own type of socialism. He maintained that each Latin American country should pursue independent economic development, but with the intent eventually to integrate the nations politically and economically. He contended that this was the only way to eliminate the imperialist control over the region's primary resources exercised and perpetuated by white oligarchs who promoted nationalism.

BIBLIOGRAPHY:

A. *Ensayo crítico del desarrollo económico-social de Chile* (Santiago: Universitaria, 1951); *Recabarren: los origines del movimiento obrero y del socialismo chilenos* (Santiago: Prensa Latino-Americana, 1955) *Los fundamentos del marxismo* (Santiago: Prensa Latino-Americana, n.d.).

SHELDON B. LISS

JONES, MARY   (1830–1930). "Mother" Jones was a nationally renowned, charismatic American labor activist, socialist, and Wobbly, and perhaps the most prominent and effective woman activist in the history of the American left. Mother Jones is also one of the few American radicals around which a significant body of legend and myth has accumulated (from Gene Autry's 1931 country recording of "The Death of Mother Jones," to the late 1960s SDS splintergroup the Mother Jones Revolutionary League, to the 1970s popular radical magazine

Mother Jones), but one who has attracted surprisingly little serious scholarly research. Born on 1 May 1830 in Cork County, Ireland, she came to North America when her family emigrated to Canada in 1835. The family settled in Toronto, where Mary studied elementary education and dressmaking. In 1861 she accepted a teaching position in Memphis, eventually marrying a Memphis ironworker and Knights of Labor organizer, Frank Jones. After the loss of her husband and four children during the yellow fever epidemic of 1876, she devoted the rest of her life to labor organizing, taking the American working classes as her new family. Her first activist experiences were with the Knights of Labor, and then with the United Mine Workers of America, the Socialist Party of America, the Social Democratic Party, and the Industrial Workers of the World. She participated in many of the classic struggles, strikes, and confrontations of the early labor movement in America: Chicago's Haymarket Riot of 1886; the Pullman Strike of 1894; the Pennsylvania athrocite strike of 1902; the Ludlow, Colorado, massacre of 1913; and the nationwide steel strike of 1919.

She was a fiery and captivating public speaker, always more of a soapboxer than a political philosopher, long on proletarian sentimentality and short on dialectics. Her approach to radical politics was decidedly dramatic and symbolic, and yet she was an innovator in the area of tactics, famous for mobilizing the wives of striking workers to parade, protest, and picket on behalf of their men and for organizing children to march in protest of child labor abuses. But her greatest contribution to the American left was not the force of her ideas or even her determined activism; her great contribution and legacy was her image as labor's "mother," leading her working-class children in the continuing struggle against capitalist tyranny.

Seeing old news photos of this slight, grandmotherly figure, wearing wire-rimmed glasses and schoolmarmish attire, with snow-white hair and a stern, deeply lined face, it is easy to understand how the socialist and labor movements of the early part of this century dubbed her the patron saint of the picket lines. Although she was seventy years old at the turn of the century, and an elderly woman during the most productive years of her career, she remained politically active well into her nineties. However, during the last decade of her life, old age did finally manage to keep her away from direct participation. And yet, even while bedridden, she continued to speak out against class injustice and to involve herself in the factional bickering among the various socialist and labor organizations of the 1920s. She died in her hundredth year in 1930. A funeral train ceremoniously carried her remains from Washington, D.C., to Mt. Olive, Illinois, for burial in the Union Miners' Cemetery.

BIBLIOGRAPHY:

A. *The Autobiography of Mother Jones*, ed. Mary Field Parton (Chicago: Kerr, 1925).

B. Irving Werstein, *Labor's Defiant Lady* (New York: Crowell, 1969); Keith Dix, "Mother Jones," *People's Appalachia*, 1 (June 1970), p. 6; Dale Featherling, *Mother*

Jones, the Miners' Angel (Carbondale: Southern Illinois University Press, 1971); Philip S. Foner, *Women and the American Labor Movement* (New York: Free Press, 1979).

CHARLES W. HAMPTON

JUSTO, JUAN BAUTISTA   (1865–1928). Argentine physician and professor of medicine, Juan Bautista Justo became acquainted with socialism while studying in Europe and began to explore the relationship between the human biological struggle for existence and the battle for political solidarity. He founded the socialist journal *La vanguardia* in 1894. The following year he helped organize a Socialist Party committed to evolutionary parliamentary ideals and also translated *Das Kapital* into Spanish. In 1912 Justo was elected to Argentina's Congress as a Socialist deputy.

Justo disagreed somewhat with the Hegelian idea of the ever-present dialectic being the route to progress. He was a materialist who felt that Marx* had become lost in abstractions and had neglected the practical ways of rectifying social inequities. He rejected Marx's assumption that scientific socialism was inevitable and claimed that man had to experiment to find out how, most scientifically, to alter society. Justo argued that foreign capital was necessary to develop Argentina, because the nation's inept middle class could not do it alone. He believed that foreign investment would accelerate the evolutionary process, which laid the foundations for eventual socialization of the means of production. He deviated from Marxist emphasis on the role of the proletariat. In adopting socialism to Latin American and Argentine conditions, he emphasized that the rural sector, where over three-fourths of the population owned no land, needed restructuring. He contended that, although an industrial proletariat did not exist in Argentina, a mass basis for socialism existed in the rural towns. He advocated the mobilization of all wage earners, rural and urban, lower and middle class. He stated that the ruling landlord class had created an urban proletariat, not by industrialization, but by excluding workers from access to the land and forcing them to the cities. He noted that Marx's observation that the supply of exploitable labor made industrial capitalism possible could pertain to the undernourished rural population of Latin America.

BIBLIOGRAPHY:

A. *Teoría práctica de la historia* (Buenos Aires: Lotitio & Barberis, 1915); *Socialismo* (Buenos Aires: La Vanguardia, 1920); *Internacionalismo y patria* (Buenos Aires: La Vanguardia, 1933).

B. Richard J. Walter, *The Socialist Party of Argentina, 1890–1930* (Austin: University of Texas Press, 1977).

SHELDON B. LISS

K

KALECKI, MICHAL   (1899–1970). Michal Kalecki was born on 22 June 1899 in Lodz, and died in Warsaw on 17 April 1970. A noted economist, Kalecki spent the years 1929–36 at the Institute for the Study of Economics and Prices in Warsaw. From 1936 to 1939 he studied in Sweden and England. He also worked at the Oxford Institute of Statistics (1940–44) and the Economic Division of the United Nations in New York (1946–54), and from 1955 to 1964 was an advisor to the government of the Polish Peoples' Republic and professor at the Main School of Planning and Statistics in Warsaw.

Inspired by the works of Karl Marx* and Rosa Luxemburg,* Kalecki created a theory of the economic cycle that anticipated several theses of Keynes's General Employment Theory. Kalecki's theory hinges on the dependence of the level of production (as well as profit and employment) on the expenses (in investment and consumption) of capitalists. In brief, Kalecki believed that capitalists will receive as much as they spend and workers will spend as much as they earn. The paradox of investment is that it generates economic growth during its development but the market situation deteriorates when the production apparatus is actually increased. His theory of the capitalist political cycle opposed the optimistic theory of full employment. According to Keynes, full employment engenders in capitalists the desire to suppress the workers, to discipline them. Therefore, for Kalecki, capitalists direct the state into deflationary politics, which will eventually lead to worker discontent.

In the 1950s Kalecki created a theory of "dynamic capitalism." Over long periods of time, the decision-makers of dynamic capitalism are not the internal power sources but rather semi-exogenous factors. For example, technical innovators as well as the discoverers of new sources of raw materials shape the character of investments, and hence the economic growth of capitalism. Kalecki's view of capitalist prices and profits, like Marx's, is based on the relative level of monopolization. In contemporary capitalism, Kalecki argued, prices are fixed not by free competition in the market place but rather by corporations. Their price mark-ups are based on their changing costs of production, which, because of their monopoly strength, they can indirectly control. This theory significantly influenced the American Marxists Paul Baran* and Paul Sweezy.*

Kalecki sacrificed the last fifteen years of life mainly to fruitlessly formulating a theory of socialist economic growth, focusing on the limiting effects of multinational corporations.

BIBLIOGRAPHY:

A. *Theory of Economic Dynamics: An Essay on Cyclical and Long-Run Changes in Capitalist Economy* (London: Allen & Unwin, 1954); *Selected Essays on the Dynamics of the Capitalist Economy* (Cambridge: Cambridge University Press, 1971); *Selected Essays on the Economic Growth of the Socialist and Mixed Economy* (Cambridge: Cambridge University Press, 1972).

B. George Feivel, *The Intellectual Capital of Michal Kalecki* (Knoxville: University of Tennessee Press, 1975).

TADEUSZ KOWALIK

KAUTSKY, KARL (1854–1938). Born on 16 October 1854 in Prague, Karl Kautsky studied history, philosophy, and economics at the University of Vienna. In 1875 he joined the Austrian Social Democratic Party and published articles in the socialist press while still in graduate school. In 1880 he moved to Zurich, where he befriended Eduard Bernstein,† and from 1885 to 1890 he lived in London and collaborated with Friedrich Engels.* When the Anti-Socialist Law was repealed Kautsky returned to Germany, where he became the leading theorist in the Social Democratic Party (SPD) and wrote the theoretical section of the Erfurt Program in 1891. Kautsky, like other Marxists who eventually opposed World War I, left the SPD in 1917 to join the leftist Independent Social Democratic Party (USPD), but rejoined the SPD after the war in 1922. Kautsky was the leading theorist of the Second International* from 1889 to 1914. After 1883 he edited *Die Neue Zeit*, translated and edited various works of Marx,* and became Marxian orthodoxy's major defender against revisionism. Nevertheless he ran afoul of Lenin* with his critique of bolshevism, opposition to the dictatorship of the proletariat, and support of parliamentary democracy. Hence his later years were spent, for the most part, out of public life. He emigrated to Prague in 1934 and died in exile in Amsterdam on 17 October 1938.

Kautsky's materialism is a scientific, deterministic form of inquiry, and his four volumes of historical analysis unflinchingly defend historical materialism. Similarly, his two theoretical volumes adopt Engels's dialectical materialism as the philosophical rationale of proletarian revolution. Kautsky secured his prominent position in history as a systematizer and applier of Marxist materialism, not as an original theorist. His one original contribution to orthodoxy consists of grafting Darwin's theory of evolution onto Marxism.

Natural and human development, Kautsky stated in *Ethik und materialistische Geschichtsauffassung* (1906), are generated by living organisms interacting with environments. As Darwin unmistakedly proved in his theory of natural selection, the best-adapted organisms survive and transmit useful traits to their offspring, assuring a genetically determined movement of history toward higher, ever more progressive developmental stages. The competition for survival among species creates a universal interspecies instinct of aggression and an intraspecies instinct for solidarity. Presumably, then, human beings are aggressive toward lower species and instinctively caring and cooperative with each other. Kautsky connected these theories of biological determinism and universal instincts to a rigidly orthodox rehash of historical and dialectical materialism. Human beings appear in history after an impersonal material process of natural selection, their survival assured because of toolmaking skills and an ability to communicate through language. The same distinguishing attributes, however, lead inexorably to higher social forms and eventually to institutionalized private property. Humanity, then, is propelled by an inner material dynamic toward economic and social inequality, class antagonism, revolution, and finally sublation in higher, more progressive ways of living. The entire process leads to workers seizing the means of material production, eliminating the source of contradiction, and creating democratic socialism, where harmony and peace prevail.

Kautsky's input within the Second International* on questions of revolutionary strategy was shaped by this Darwinian Marxism. Predictably, he argued that consciousness evolves like any other natural or social phenomenon, a determined product of objective matter. Hence, scientific socialism reflects and expresses matter and is unrelated to spontaneous working-class perceptions and beliefs. Revolutionary theory is cognitively grasped by historical and social "scientists," who then formulate authentic working-class consciousness. Ironically, Kautsky's analysis theoretically justified Lenin's closed, dictatorial workers' party, despite the fact that Kautsky, by inclination and argument, was a democrat who later emerged as Lenin's most insistent antagonist. By understanding and accepting dialectical materialism literally, Kautsky believed socialism can appear only after capitalism matures and economic classes polarize. Workers, in other words, can successfully seize political power only in ripe economic conditions. He admiringly repeated Marx's critique of classical political economy, that is, the inevitability of capitalist overproduction, increasing unemployment, and social anarchy. His calm faith in historical determinism indicated the folly of "rushing" history, capitulating to subjectivist schemes for action at any cost. The proletariat, without seeking shortcuts, will carry capitalism to its objective conclusion. They create needed skills and class consciousness and simultaneously exacerbate capitalism's inherent contradictions by working slowly to enact partial economic, social, and political reforms. These, however, are no substitute for the objectively necessary workers' revolution. Since base and superstructure are reciprocally linked, effective working-class reformism promotes concrete economic change, even though base is primary "in the last resort"—a phrase borrowed, untouched, from Engels. History's unavoidable workers' revolution will yield a democratic socialist society, where humanity's needs are satisfied. Here, the masses run their own affairs, with the state restricted to coordinating material production and distribution, not ruling people. Although everyone benefits from socialism, history requires the struggle be fought only by workers.

His disagreement with Lenin was primarily strategic, not theoretical, but this dulls neither its intensity nor its fury. Kautsky claimed that Marx's "dictatorship of the proletariat" refers to the postrevolutionary government's social content, not its form. Marx used the term, claimed Kautsky, to describe the Paris Commune, which defended basic democratic principles such as free speech, free elections, and open party access to electoral politics. The workers' revolution liberates people to run their own lives, guided by principles of socialist equality. Kautsky questioned whether Russia's revolution should have occurred in the first place, given the unripe, precapitalist surroundings. It certainly could not depend on workers governing themselves, for as a class they were neither skilled nor ideologically mature. Lenin was forced to create a secretive, hierarchical party that, upon reaching power, instituted a new and ruthless dictatorship. Sadly, this would lead to bureaucratic exploitation and a tyranny worse than capitalism's, where workers could at least express divergent points of view. Party dictatorship also increased the likelihood of a strong individual eventually seizing control and subverting Party principles. Finally, Lenin's revolutionary strategy could consume itself by encouraging "Thermidor," a desire by workers for more traditional values and institutions.

Kautsky earnestly contended that no single party should monopolize truth or suppress discussion. Given his theoretical orthodoxy, however, this belief is hollow and naive, built on a boundless faith in history's material laws rather than principle. It was inconceivable to Kautsky that workers in mature capitalism are anything but revolutionary Marxists, and it is similarly inevitable that all nations pass through a capitalist developmental stage. The belief in worker self-government reflected his own assurance that self-governing workers will be Marxists, that is, passively recognizing and following authentic, true needs. Kautsky rejected even the possibility of a conflict between material truth and subjectivity.

While Westerners can sympathize with Kautsky's surface democratic sheen, they should also detect a philosophical naiveté. His crude dialectical materialism and simplistic assumption that worker self-government will take only one (socialist) form has had paradoxical consequences for Europe's social democratic parties. Especially after Stalinism,* Kautskyite socialists realized that materialism, emphasizing inviolable objective truth, does not necessarily support worker self-expression and democracy, and is easily transformed into totalitarianism. Marxist social democracy was burdened with antagonistic legacies inherited from Kautsky. When their reformist tactics effectively altered the most brutal aspects of capitalism, they discarded dialectical materialism as a threat to socialist democracy. Kautsky's workers' parties remained only superficially loyal by turning his democratic reformism from a means of realizing worker self-government to an end in itself. They are now established participants in capitalist political systems, the same systems that Kautsky felt history—working through his social democratic parties—would obliterate.

BIBLIOGRAPHY:

A. *Bernstein und das sozialdemokratische Programm: Eine Antikritik* (Stuttgart: Dietz, 1899); *The Road to Power* (Chicago: S. A. Bloch, 1909); *The Class Struggle* (Chicago: C. H. Kerr, 1910); *The Social Revolution* (Chicago: C. H. Kerr, 1916); *Ethics and the Materialist Conception of History* (Chicago: C. H. Kerr, 1918); *The Dictatorship of the Proletariat* (Ann Arbor: University of Michigan Press, 1919); *Terrorism and Communism* (Westport, Conn.: Hyperion, 1920); *Foundations of Christianity* (New York: International, 1925); *Die materialistische Geschichtsauffassung in der Staat und die Entwicklung der Menschheit* (Berlin: Dietz, 1927).

B. Gary P. Steenson, *Karl Kautsky, 1854–1938* (Pittsburgh: University of Pittsburgh Press, 1979).

ROBERT A. GORMAN

KAWAKAMI HAJIME (1879–1946). The Japanese Marxist pioneer Kawakami Hajime was born in Iwakuni in Yamaguchi Prefecture, the eldest son of a former village headman. After attending primary and high school locally, Kawakami was sent to the Yamaguchi Higher School, where he developed an interest in literature. In 1898, however, when Kawakami entered Tokyo Imperial University, he decided to major in the law course, where he heard lectures by such eminent socialists as Kinoshita Naoe, and Abe Isō. After graduating from the university in 1902, Kawakami tried in vain to gain a position as a newspaper reporter, and joined Tokyo University's Agricultural College in 1903 as a lecturer, teaching at various other schools as well, including the Peers' School.

In 1905 Kawakami began what would become his life's work in disseminating socialist thought in Japan. Beginning in October of that year, he serialized an essay entitled "Review of Socialism" ("Shakai-shugi hyōron") in the daily *Yomiuri* newspaper. There, criticizing both the dominant school of social policy and socialists, Kawakami offered his own theory of humanistic socialism, which combined traditional ethical values with Western socialist thought in the manner that characterized Kawakami's approach to Marxism throughout his life. Several months later, Kawakami pursued the ethical dimensions of his thought more deeply by resigning his university position and entering Itō Shōshin's Buddhist spiritual cultivation group at the Garden of Selflessness (Muga-en). Kawakami left the Garden of Selflessness in early 1906, worked briefly as a reporter for *Mainichi shinbun*, then launched his own journal, the *Japanese Economic Review* (*Nihon keizai shinshi*), as he vigorously pursued research in Marxist economics. In 1908, Kawakami accepted an academic appointment at Kyōtō Imperial University, was sent to Europe in 1913, and returned to Japan to be awarded a doctor of laws degree in 1914 and to be promoted to professor in February 1915. In 1916, Kawakami serialized his influential *Tale of Poverty* in the *Ōsaka Asahi shinbun*, exposing the wretched conditions of laborers in newly industrialized

Japan. Shortly thereafter, in response to severe criticism by Kushida Tamizō*
for a "bourgeois" approach to economics, Kawakami immersed himself in
Marxist economic studies. In 1919 he launched the journal *Studies on Social
Questions* and thereafter became embroiled in debate with future Marxist leaders
Sakai Toshiko, Kushida, and Fukumoto Kazuo* on such issues as materialism
and the theory of value.

During the 1920s, Kawakami solidified his position as a leading Marxist
teacher and scholar at Kyōtō Imperial University, and although he as yet had
no affiliation with the Japanese Communist Party, he too came to suffer the
effects of increasing police repression directed against the Party. In 1926 and
1927, Kawakami became active in the Social Science Research Society, began
to publish the *Symposium on Marxism* (*Marukusu-shugi kōza*) with Ōyama Ikuo,
and engaged in practical politics by supporting the latter in his candidacy for
office in the first universal suffrage election of 1928. By April 1928, however,
Kawakami was forced to resign from the university because of his participation
in these activities.

Thereafter, Kawakami continued his scholarly writing, but also thrust himself
increasingly into political activism. Thus, he published his *Introduction to Capital* and *Outline of Economics* and serialized his "Second Tale of Poverty" in
the magazine *Reconstruction* (*Kaizō*) by 1930. In the meantime, Kawakami also
helped rebuild the Labor-Farmer Party in 1928 and 1929 and allowed the party
to run him unsuccessfully for office in the second universal suffrage election of
1930. Later that year, he was expelled along with others from the Labor-Farmer
Party for advocating that the party be dissolved and its members rally to the
support of the Japanese Communist Party. In July 1932, he was then entrusted
by the Communist Party to translate the Comintern's 1932 Theses; and it was
only the following month at the age of fifty that Kawakami fully committed
himself to revolutionary Marxism by joining the now underground Japanese
Communist Party. Kawakami was soon arrested, however, in January 1933, and
was sentenced in August to five years' imprisonment. Unlike hundreds of other
imprisoned Marxists, Kawakami, having made his revolutionary commitment
slowly and painfully, now steadfastly refused to *tenkō* (renounce the Communist
Party) during his term in prison. After his release from prison in 1937, Kawakami
lived a quiet secluded life, first in Tokyo then in Kyōtō, writing his memoirs
until his death of pneumonia at the age of sixty-eight.

BIBLIOGRAPHY:

A. *Jijōden* (Autobiography), 5 vols. (Tokyo: Iwanami shoten, 1952).

B. Gail Lee Bernstein, *Japanese Marxist: A Portrait of Kawakami Hajime, 1879–1946*
(Cambridge: Harvard University Press, 1976); Amano Keitarō, *Kawakami Hajime Hakushi bunkenshi* (Bibliography of Kawakami Hajime) (Tokyo: Nihon hyōron shin-sha,
1956); Sumiya Etsuji, *Kawakami Hajime* (Tokyo: n.a., 1962); Òuchi Hyōe, *Kawakami
Hajime* (Tokyo: n.a., 1966).

GERMAINE A. HOSTON

KHIEU SAMPHAN (b. 1929). Khieu Samphan was born in 1929 in Koh
Sothin, Kompong Cham Province, Kampuchea (Cambodia). He was educated

at the Sisowath Lycée in Phnom Penh. In 1953, he went to Paris to study and became active in the Association of Khmer Students, becoming its Secretary General. In 1959 he obtained a doctorate in law and economic science with a dissertation on "The Cambodian Peasantry and Its Problems with Industrialization." Returning to Cambodia, he taught in Phnom Penh University Law Department and edited a review, *L'Observateur*, which spread left-wing ideas. In 1962, Khieu Samphan accepted a post as Secretary of State for Commerce in Prince Sihanouk's government. He resigned after a few months and returned to opposition politics, remaining a member of the National Assembly. In April 1967, following a peasant uprising in Battambang Province, Khieu Samphan went underground and joined the nascent revolutionary movement known as the Khmer Rouge. In 1970, Khieu Samphan became National Defense Minister in the Royal Government of National Union of Cambodia formed in exile by Prince Sihanouk following his overthrow by General Lon Nol. At the same time, he was commander-in-chief of the Liberation Armed Forces and together with Pol Pot* the central revolutionary figure in the Khmer Rouge. In 1976, following the Khmer Rouge victory of the previous year and Sihanouk's abdication, Khieu Samphan became President of Democratic Kampuchea.

Khieu Samphan appears to have become a committed Marxist during his student days in France in the early 1950s. On his return to Cambodia, he assisted Pol Pot in founding the Kampuchean Communist Party, largely consisting of returned students from France, fiercely nationalistic and opposed to the Kampuchean Revolutionary Party, which was considered to be pro-Vietnamese. Proceeding on the basis of views already outlined in his thesis, Khieu Samphan argued that the only way Cambodia could be independent and self-sufficient would be to cut itself off from the international economy for a period of time. Urban dwellers who were unproductive should be transferred to productive sectors of the economy, basically to agriculture, and organized into cooperatives. In this process, a new Cambodian man would be forged. The basis for this revolutionary movement, however, was to be solely the Cambodian peasantry. Unlike even Mao Zedong,* who accorded a place in his revolutionary schema for the proletariat, in the eyes of Khieu Samphan only the peasantry were fit to lead the revolution, for only they were untainted by the bourgeois and alien world of the cities.

BIBLIOGRAPHY:

A. *Cambodia's Economy and Industrial Development*, trans. Laura Summers (Ithaca: Cornell University Southeast Asia Program, 1979).

B. Ben Kiernan and Chanthou Boua, eds., *Peasants and Politics in Kampuchea 1942–1981* (London: Zed Press, 1982).

MICHAEL C. WILLIAMS

KHRUSHCHEV, NIKITA SERGEVICH (1894–1971). Nikita Khrushchev was the preeminent leader of the Soviet Union for nearly a decade. A Stalinist* apparatchik for much of his career, he had seen service as a responsible Party official for the city of Moscow, for the Republic of the Ukraine, and for the national network of Party secretaries and staff personnel responsible for agriculture before achieving the post of First Secretary in 1954. In that early training he had supervised the construction of the Moscow subway, finished the job of collectivization and Party purging in the Ukraine in the late 1930s, and performed a troubleshooter function during World War II. However, upon the death of Stalin he became a ''reformer'' Soviet-style by championing de-Stalinization, pressing for structural reforms in the Communist Party of the Soviet Union's (CPSU's) organization, and using his powers of office as chairman of the Council of Ministers (especially after 1957) to promote his country's international position and to satisfy the demands of the Soviet population through greater investment in consumer goods industries. He made policy mistakes as well as political errors in his treatment of subordinates; as a consequence, he was forced to resign in October 1964, when both the Presidium and Central Committee voted against him. He retired to a dacha in the Moscow area and played no role in Soviet politics thereafter. He became a ''nonperson,'' his name disappearing from print in a matter of hours. He was never seen at Party meetings and only rarely seen in public, usually at the opera or the polling place. Only the sudden mysterious appearance of his memoirs in the West in 1970 interrupted the obscurity of his last years.

Khrushchev as a bureaucratic-political leader endorsed several new ideas about socialism in the Soviet Union and the state of the world under contemporary conditions. His major work is his ''Secret Speech'' in March 1956, wherein he denounced the ''cult of personality'' of Josef Stalin. That speech is notable not only in providing details of the personal complicity of Stalin in the arbitrary use of coercion against Party and masses, but also in the implicitly non-Marxian idea that personal psychology may have a great impact on the entire fabric of socialist society. No attempt was made to indict the institutions that allowed such a personality to come to hold great power, but the later actions and statements of Khrushchev do imply precisely such an indictment. ''Socialist legality'' (restricting secret police and court repression), ''communist public self-government'' (bringing the general population into policy implementation to contain bureaucratic isolation that feeds personal power at the top), and ''state of all the people'' (with its counterpart ''Party of all the people,'' meaning an end to class struggle and a new period of social peace) are all concepts to be found in the 1961 Party Program that was the capstone of Khrushchev's ideological work. It is in force today.

On the international side, Khrushchev endorsed the all-encompassing struggle between the ''world capitalist system'' and the ''world socialist system.'' That struggle was to be social, economic, political, ideological, and, within one major limit, even military. (That exception is conflict with a nuclear power that might lead to devastation of both sides.) Of course, this is the concept of ''peaceful coexistence'' that has been proclaimed to be the CPSU's main line in foreign policy since the death of Stalin. ''Imperialist wars'' are no longer seen as inevitable as long as the "world socialist system" is ideologically united, militarily strong, and politically agile. The socialist states are seen as benefiting from an advantageous "correlation of forces" that allows for a relatively peaceful global transition from capitalism to socialism. This transition involves detaching "Third World" states from the world capitalist system, supporting "wars of national liberation" in capitalist colonies, and mobilizing bourgeois allies into a global "zone of peace." The confrontation between capitalism and socialism is thereby transformed from an international struggle between classes in the many extant states into a competition of states with putatively different class bases and class interests.

BIBLIOGRAPHY:

A. *For Victory in Peaceful Competition with Capitalism* (New York: Dutton, 1960); "Program of the Communist Party of the Soviet Union," in *Essential Works of Marxism* (New York: Bantam, 1961); Khrushchev's "Secret Speech," in *The Crimes of the Stalin Era* (New York: The New Leader, 1962); *Krushchev Remembers* (Boston: Little Brown, 1970).

B. Edward Crankshaw, *Khrushchev* (New York: Viking, 1960); Roy and Zhores Medvedev, *Khrushchev* (New York: Norton, 1978).

THOMAS OLESZCZUK

KOLLONTAI, ALEKSANDRA M.   (1872–1952). Kollontai was born Aleksandra Domontovich into an aristocratic Russian family of liberal dispositions. In 1890 she briefly attended the Bestuzhev course for women students in St. Petersburg. In 1893 she married Vladimir Ludvigovich Kollontai, with whom she had a son in 1894. Early in her marriage she began to participate in quasi-legal education projects with workers. Desiring more independence and education than was possible in the confinement of her country and her domestic situation, Kollontai left her husband and traveled to Zurich in 1898. Her departure marked the beginning of a life-long involvement in working-class and revolutionary politics.

In Western Europe Kollontai established contacts with European Social Democrats and Russian exiles. She became a member of the Russian Social Democratic Labor Party, siding with the Menshevik faction in the 1903 party split. The same year she published *The Life of the Finnish Workers*, an orthodox Marxist account with special attention to the question of the peasantry. By 1904 she had become a public speaker in St. Petersburg and a teacher of socialism in workers' study circles. Although the high-status roles of speaker and writer were less open to women, early in her political career Kollontai displayed theoretical ambitions and gravitated toward the intellectual side of revolutionary politics. She generally abstained from internecine party politics, working in the ensuing years with members of both party factions. Nevertheless, she continued to have reservations about the Bolshevik approach to trade unions and factory committees. In 1905, in two pamphlets—*On the Question of Class Struggle* and *Who Are the Social Democrats and What Do They Want?*—Kollontai defended socialism as a "living real necessity" against charges of utopianism, but also denied Lenin's* vanguard theory of the party. She identified the untutored "class psychology" of the workers as the greatest weapon in the historical process (Clements, p. 32).

The year 1905 was a turning point for Kollontai: from that date forward she concentrated her energies on the creation of a socialist women's movement. Kollontai drew inspiration from the living example of the German Social Democratic party's women's movement under Clara Zetkin's* leadership. She enthusiastically participated in the 1907 founding conference of the international socialist women's movement in Stuttgart, hoping to forge strong ties with the German women's movement and to replicate their successes in her own party. There she pledged to defend against the spread of feminism. Indeed, Kollontai's frequent denunciations of feminist groups for their bourgeois outlook and program seemed to derive from a concern that the feminists might out-organize socialists among their natural constituency, working-class women. In 1908, Kollontai responded to the feminists' call for an All-Russian Women's Congress with the pamphlet, *The Social Basis of the Woman Question*, in which she rejected "the existence of a special woman question separate from the general social question of our day" (*Selected Writings*, p. 58). She insisted on the class divisions among women, objecting to the feminist claim of women's unity. Moreover, she wrote, "Class instinct—whatever the feminists say—always shows itself to be more powerful than the noble enthusiasms of 'above-class' politics" (ibid., p. 73). Kollontai emphasized the Marxist view that economic revolution must precede sexual revolution, but she stressed that female emancipation meant more than simply the reforms outlined in the Social Democratic Party platforms. She admitted that the personal realm—marriage, the family, and sexuality—was an arena where no general agreement existed among socialists. She urged socialists to consider a future in which women, as independent female workers, would also be "independent personalit[ies], free in love" (ibid., p. 63). In orthodox Marxist fashion, Kollontai looked beyond the bourgeois family, but in a new vein she sought the basis for a revolution that would transfigure human relationships by removing all possessiveness in love and creating genuine community.

Kollontai was forced to battle on a second front for her vision of socialist feminism: not only against feminists on the outside, but inside the party against male resistance to a feminist program. Although Russian social democracy was formally committed to the German-inspired socialist feminist program (women's suffrage, legal equality, full funding of maternity benefits and child-care provisions, and working conditions tailored to protect women's health), the party resisted Kollontai's efforts to organize a women's bureau on the German model. In 1910, her demand for maternity insurance through taxation for all (wed and unwed) mothers was defeated by the International. In "Sexual Morality and the Social Struggle" (1911) and "The New Woman" (1913) she addressed these obstacles by way of an exploration of the ideological and moral dimension of the class struggle. She looked forward to the birth of a new female personality, emancipated womanhood in the social and sexual arena. She insisted that a new morality was part of the class struggle. Clements characterizes Kollontai's socialist feminism as a two-pronged effort: advocacy of reforms for women achieved by women's organizations; and an exploration of the psychology of subordination (Clements, p. 75).

Drawing closer to Lenin, in 1915 Kollontai joined the Bolsheviks. Within the Party and the revolution she continued her struggle to achieve a socialist feminist program. In 1917 she was elected to the Party's Central Committee and organized the first Petrograd conference for working women. After the October Revolution, Kollontai was named Commissar of Social Welfare, a post she resigned in March 1918. As a delegate of the Central Commission for Work Among Women, she urged the Party to commit itself to the image of a new woman: "a woman freed from family cares, not tied to marriage, part of the work force, a member of the soviet" (Farnsworth, p. 168). In 1919, when the commission was reorganized as the Section for Work Among Women (the Zhenotdel), Kollontai joined the efforts to promote socialist feminist goals within the revolution. She succeeded to the Zhenotdel's directorship upon the death of its first leader, Inessa Armand, in 1920. Through agitation, education, and a delegate system, the Zhenotdel sought to overcome women's political backwardness and to lobby for women's demands within the Party. In 1921 Kollontai temporarily suspended her work in the Zhenotdel to become involved in the Workers' Opposition, the movement for which she is perhaps best known in the West. She authored the pamphlet, *The Worker's Opposition*, and argued the case for working-class power against the developing bureaucratization of the Party and the state in Soviet Russia. She insisted that the unions, as true class organs, must create the Communist economy. She expressed a vibrant concern for the decline of democracy within the Party.

Following the defeat of the Worker's Opposition, Kollontai was appointed to the first of many diplomatic posts in which she served until her death in 1952. Except for a brief and unsuccessful political intervention in support of more progressive provisions within the proposed marriage laws of 1926, Kollontai retreated from any direct political role. Throughout the 1920s in stories and articles, and later in her autobiographical account, Kollontai continually elaborated her perspective on socialist sexual morality. She explored the contradictions between public political goals and personal freedom. She insisted on the need to view morality as a political issue. In that respect, "Kollontai was pioneering a new line of enquiry. She was raising the question of the connections between the personal and the political" (Alix Holt, commentary to *Selected Writings*, p. 209).

BIBLIOGRAPHY:

A. *Sexual Relations and the Class Struggle: Love and the New Morality* (Bristol: Falling Wall Press, 1972); *Women Workers Struggle for Their Rights* (Bristol: Falling Wall Press, 1973); *The Autobiography of a Sexually Emancipated Communist Woman*

(New York: Schocken Books, 1975); *Love of Worker Bees* (London: Virago, 1977); *Selected Writings of Alexandra Kollontai*, ed. Alix Holt (London: Allison & Busby, 1977); *A Great Love* (New York: Norton, 1981); *The Worker's Opposition*, Solidarity Pamphlet, no. 7 (London, n.d.).

B. Richard Stites, *The Women's Liberation Movement in Russia: Feminism, Nihilism, and Bolshevism, 1860–1930* (Princeton: Princeton University Press, 1978); Barbara Evans Clements, *Bolshevik Feminist: The Life of Aleksandra Kollontai* (Bloomington: Indiana University Press, 1979); Beatrice Farnsworth, *Aleksandra Kollontai: Socialism, Feminism, and the Bolshevik Revolution* (Stanford: Stanford University Press, 1980); Cathy Porter, *Alexandra Kollontai: The Lonely Struggle of the Woman Who Defied Lenin* (New York: Dial Press, 1980).

JOAN LANDES

KOLMAN, ARNOŠT (1892–1979). Born in the city of Prague in 1892, Arnošt Kolman became a naturalized citizen of the Soviet Union. He studied mathematics at the University of Prague and received a Ph.D. in 1914. As a prisoner of war in Russia, Kolman joined the Bolshevik Party and eventually became a political commissar in the Red Army during the Russian Civil War. During the 1930s Kolman was put in charge of several Soviet opinion-forming institutions: he was director of a section of the Marx-Engels-Lenin Institute, director of the Department of Sciences at the Institute of Soviet Education, and member of the presidium of the Communist Academy. In 1934 he became a professor of philosophy at Moscow University. Kolman returned to Czechoslovakia in 1945 and was appointed professor of philosophy at Charles University in Prague. In 1948 he was arrested because of his political activities and ideological radicalism and deported to the Soviet Union. He was granted his liberty and politically rehabilitated after Stalin's* death. Kolman returned to Prague in 1959 and was named director of the Institute of Philosophy of the Czech Academy of Sciences. After once again angering Czech political authorities he returned to the Soviet Union in 1964 and retired from professional activities. However, for openly sympathizing with the Prague Spring† movement Kolman was continually harassed by Soviet authorities. In 1976, while on a trip to Sweden, Kolman finally broke with Marxism-Leninism by addressing a critical open letter to Brezhnev* and returning therein his Communist Party membership card, which he had held for over sixty years. He died in Stockholm in 1979.

Kolman's literary work is voluminous, but consists primarily of commentaries on a vulgarized, Stalinist version of dialectical materialism and polemical articles on one or another of Stalin's ideological campaigns. However, one can detect in Kolman's work a lucidity and spiritual openness that distinguished him from his Soviet colleagues. He was fascinated by the philosophical problems of modern logic and staunchly defended the new science of cybernetics, which other Stalinist philosophers condemned as a ''false imperialist science.'' He was considered a heretic by official Soviet intellectuals because he contested diamat's rejection of the notion of an infinite universe while simultaneously arguing that the contrary thesis is entirely compatible with Marxist-Leninist philosophy.

BIBLIOGRAPHY:

A. *Cybernetics* (New York: U.S. Joint Publications Research Service, 1960); *Die verirrte Generation. So hätten wir nicht leben sollen. Eine Biographie* (Frankfurt am Main: Fischer, 1979).

LUBOMIR SOCHOR

KONRAD, KURT (1908–1941). Born on 15 October 1908 in the city of Trebic, Kurt Konrad was a noted Czech Communist journalist, historian, aesthetician, literary critic, and activist. He graduated from secondary school in Brno, then studied historiography at Prague University. He was active in the international Communist movement, visited several Western European countries, and wrote political commentaries for the Czech Communist press. From the early 1930s he was editor of *Tvorba*, *Rude Pravo*, and *Halo*. He worked with a Marxist historical group founded in Prague in 1936. After the Communist press was shut down at the end of 1938, he worked for a short time at the Soviet Embassy in Prague. Because of his participation in the illegal movement against the German occupation of Czechoslovokia he was arrested and executed in Dresden on 25 September 1941.

Konrad's literary work, prematurely interrupted by death, touches several subjects. As a Communist journalist he studied revolutions of the past—particularly revolutions in Spain, Hus's revolution, and the European revolutions of 1848. He became a pioneer of Czech Marxist historiography. His knowledge of Marxist classics and German idealistic aesthetics, especially Hegel's, gave Konrad the theoretical background and inclination to tackle the abstract problems of aesthetics. In his study *Contention of Content and Form: Marxist Observations of the New Formalism* (1934), he proffered an analysis and critique of both Russian formalism, especially Sklovsky's theory of prose, and the early phases of Czech structuralism, particularly the work of Jan Mukařovský.† Konrad pointed out the scientific contributions of these authors to the studies of aesthetics and linguistic construction in literary works and contrasted both to classical idealism's belief in autonomous artistic structures—with its implication that people's practical activities are isolated from each other and from history. *Category Formation* (1935) dealt with Konrad's interpretation of socialist realism. Like Bedrich Vaclavek,† Konrad understood socialist realism as a synthesis of revolutionary proletarian trends and artistic contributions of the avant-garde in the period between the two world wars, which he felt intensified human relations with reality. Konrad also wrote critically acclaimed commentaries on surrealism and on the Czechs V. Nezval and K. Teig.†

Konrad's published work on theoretical problems in Marxist aesthetics, while not voluminous, can be favorably compared to the aesthetic ruminations of M. Lifschitz and G. Lukács.†

BIBLIOGRAPHY:

A. *Španělské revoluce* (Prague: Naše vojsko, 1949); *Na prahu války* (Prague: Svoboda, 1951); *Ztvárněte skutečnost* (Prague: Československýspisovatel, 1963); *Dějiny husitské revoluce* (Prague: Nakl politické lituratury, 1964).

B. K. Chvatík, *Bedřich Vaclavek a výoj marxistické estetiky* (Prague: akademie věd, 1962); S. Strohs, *Marxisticko-leninská filosofie v Československu mezi dvěma světovými válkami* (Prague: akademie věd, 1962); J. Brabec, "Preface" to Konrad's *Ztvárněte skutečnost* (Prague: Československý spisovatel, 1963).

K. CHVATÍK

KOSAMBI, DAMODAR DHARMANAND   (1907–1966). Damador Kosambi was born on 31 July 1907, at Kosben in Goa (then a Portuguese colony). His early education was in "British" India at Poona. Between 1918 and 1925, he studied at Cambridge Grammar School and Latin High School, Cambridge, Massachusetts, where his father, Professor Dharmanand Kosambi, was teaching at Harvard University. Between 1925 and 1929, Damodar Kosambi studied at Harvard University and graduated with an S.B.. At Harvard, although his principal subject of study was mathematics, he also studied physics, theoretical and applied statistics, classical and contemporary European languages, and, under the influence of his father, took a great deal of interest in history, Indology, and Buddhist studies. On his return to India, Kosambi taught mathematics at Banaras Hindu University, Aligarh Muslim University, and Fergusson College, Pune. From 1947 to 1962 he worked at the Tata Institute of Fundamental Research, Bombay, and in 1965, the title of "scientist emeritus" was conferred on him by the Council of Scientific and Industrial Research, New Delhi. On 29 June 1966, Kosambi passed away in his sleep at Pune.

During his fifty-nine years Kosambi did pioneering work in many areas in mathematics, statistics, demography, genetics, numismatics, archeology, anthropology, linguistics, applied physics, ethnography, epigraphy, and history. Kosambi was the first person to be awarded the Ramanujam Memorial Prize in 1934 for his work on mathematics. Subsequently, he received the Special Bhabha Prize in 1947. As a UNESCO Fellow he carried out research work on electronic calculating machines (computers) in the United States and United Kingdom in 1948–49 and taught path-geometry in 1949 as a visiting professor at Chicago. In the same year, as a guest of the Institute of Advanced Studies at Princeton, he held several technical discussions with Albert Einstein on his unified field theory and with O. Veblen on tensor analysis. In 1955, he was invited by the Soviet Academy of Sciences to lecture and to attend the first conference on peaceful uses of atomic energy. He also went to China on an invitation from the Academia Sinica to suggest statistical methods for the forecasting of food crops and quality control in industry. After his visit to China, he made useful suggestions in India on appropriate technology, small dams, and the harnessing of alternative sources of energy, including solar power. His most invaluable work toward the understanding of history and culture was largely published in the last few years of his life.

Kosambi was a committed Marxist intellectually and in terms of his own social praxis, but he could not appreciate the rigid straitjacket of Party politics that "official Marxists" subjected themselves to and remained a nonparty Marxist.

He was an activist in the world peace movement and was a member of the World Peace Council.

In terms of contribution to Marxist theory and/or practice, it would be wrong to outline Kosambi's work separately in the areas of pure and applied natural sciences on the one side and his writings in the field of social sciences on the other. He successfully spanned the two cultures and understood the organic relationship between the two. It is significant that in both his principal interest lay in developing methodologies of analysis, mathematical and historical, not exclusively applied to respective fields but used to understand reality as a whole. Thus, he applied mathematics and statistics to study human actions through brilliant exercises in, for instance, numismatics and demography, and a historical study of ancient trade and trade routes was used creatively in the areas of civil engineering, dam and road construction. By demolishing the methodological boundary imposed by orthodox Marxism between "dialectical materialism" on the one side and "historical materialism" on the other, Kosambi made a significant contribution to these otherwise much-abused concepts, which had in many respects lost their methodological incisiveness on account of having been simplistically reduced to mere cant.

In studying history, although Kosambi followed the Marxist methodology, he did not hesitate in questioning and critically examining observations made by Marx* himself. Kosambi held that "the adoption of Marx's thesis does not mean blind repetition of all his conclusions (and even less, those of the official, party-line Marxists) at all times" (*Introduction to the Study of Indian History*, p. 10). Kosambi strongly refuted the general statement of Marx that "Indian society has no history at all . . . What we call its history, is but the history of successive intruders," and Marx's blanket observations on "Oriental despotism" and the "Asiatic mode of production." Kosambi refuted the contention that "India has some episodes, but no history" and attempted to reconstruct a history without episodes—without undue concern with "lists of dynasties and kings, tales of war and battle spiced with anecdote," history defined as the presentation, in chronological order, of successive developments in the means and relations of production (ibid., p. 1). Weaving together the methodologies of several disciplines, creating "combined methods" of Indology in particular and of history in general, and creatively applying Marx's historical method, Kosambi contradicted Marx himself: "The (Indian) village did not exist 'from time immemorial.' The advance of plough-using agrarian village economy over tribal India is a great historical achievement by itself." (ibid.) Indeed, one great insight Kosambi provided on the intricate questions of composition of caste and class in India, questions that are still vexing for Marxists, was in introducing an understanding of the role of tribes and tribal institutions in that context: "The entire course of Indian history shows tribal elements being fused into a general society" (ibid., p. 27). This concern led him to another brilliant methodological exercise—the study of history backward, starting from an understanding of the contemporary present and searching for its roots in previous times (*The Culture and Civilization of Ancient India in Historical Outlines*, pp. 1–25).

In this sense, Kosambi's work on "history" and his observations on "contemporary" phenomena cannot be separated. His critique of the Asiatic mode and positing an explanation of "feudalism from above" and "feudalism from below" (*Introduction*, pp. 295–405) on the one side went hand in hand with his attempt to understand contemporary Indian society, in which he saw the bourgeoisie coming of age (*Exasperating Essays*, pp. 10–31). For him the totality of India was not composed of discrete "semifeudal" and "semicolonial" sectors but was a woven tapestry of interrelated phenomena. Another important area of Kosambi's work was critical historical analysis of myths that are components of organized religion (*Myth and Reality*). All these together enabled him to get a historical overview of Indian society, economy, and popular culture and with this also an appreciation of the influence of social phenomena on scientific advances and vice versa, all these exercises geared toward the search for an alternative humane and egalitarian society.

BIBLIOGRAPHY:

A. *An Introduction to the Study of Indian History* (Bombay: Popular Book Depot, 1956); *Exasperating Essays: Exercise in the Dialectical Method* (Poona: People's Book House, 1957); *Myth and Reality: Studies in the Formation of Indian Culture* (Bombay: Popular Prakashan, 1962); *The Culture and Civilisation of Ancient India in Historical Outline* (London: Routledge and Kegan Paul, 1965).

B. *Science and Human Progress: Essays in Honour of Prof. D. D. Kosambi* (Bombay: Popular Prakashan, 1974); *Indian Society: Historical Probings in Memory of D. D. Kosambi* (New Delhi: People's Publishing House, 1977).

ARVIND N. DAS

KUN, BÉLA   (1886–1939). Béla Kun was born in the Transylvanian village of Lele on 20 February 1886. Raised in a lower middle-class family, Kun discontinued his university education and became a journalist for a radical daily in 1906. In 1910 he was employed as a clerk in the Workers' Insurance Bureau in the city of Kolozsvar, and quickly rose to managing director. Kun was elected as a delegate to the 1913 congress of the Hungarian Social Democratic Party and began reading the works of Marx,* Engels,* Eduard Bernstein,† and Karl Kautsky.* He was more an activist than a philosopher, and his interest in Marxian theory was always secondary to his practical aspirations within the socialist movement. During World War I Kun served on the Russian front, was taken prisoner in Tomsk in 1916, and while in a prison camp became an avid Bolshevik supporter. Kun became leader of the newly established Hungarian Section of the Bolshevik Party and focused on revolutionary strategy for Germany and Central Europe. His key contributions to Bolshevik tactics included advocating nationalism as a necessary ingredient in Central European proletarian revolutions and supporting the participation of national petit bourgeoisies in the first, anti-monarchic, and anti-German phases of the revolutions. Always, however, he worked from an orthodox and at times leftist and dogmatic Marxist-Leninist worldview. By 1918 he had become a confidant of Lenin* and a leader among Bolsheviks, despite his non-Russian nationality.

In 1918 the Communist Party of Hungary was reestablished in Budapest with Kun as head and Moscow as its chief sponsor. A thwarted Communist-led coup (which Lenin had opposed) led to Kun's imprisonment in 1919. However, Hungary's liberal government soon collapsed, and on 21 March 1919 Kun was invited into a coalition government with the Social Democrats that rapidly turned into a Soviet-style "dictatorship of the proletariat" led by Béla Kun and consisting of Communists and Socialists. The Hungarian Soviet Republic lasted a mere 133 days. Against Lenin's wishes, Kun insisted on a program of total nationalization of all industrial and land resources. The resulting economic chaos, combined with a heavy-handed foreign policy, quickly doomed Hungary's socialist experiment.

In August 1920, after a year of political exile in Austria, Kun was allowed passage to Petrograd where he wrote and fought in the Russian Civil War. After being named chairman of the Crimean Soviet, Kun ordered the execution of almost 20,000 White Russian officers, apparently violating a general amnesty that was in force. This moral and political blunder by a foreigner convinced many Bolsheviks—including Lenin, Trotsky,* and Stalin*—that Kun was not to be trusted. Nevertheless, with Zinoviev's support and Lenin's acquiescence, in 1921 Kun was appointed a Comintern emissary to help Bolshevize the German Communist Party and was also given a position on the Small Bureau of the Comintern Executive. In Germany Kun sponsored—against the wishes of prominent German Communists—the ill-fated March putsch in which 145 workers died and almost 3,500 were imprisoned. Kun escaped back to Moscow, although most of his subordinates perished. Discredited by Hungarian Communists centered around Landler and Lukács,† Kun nevertheless managed to survive a Comintern investigation in the fall of 1921. Still the head of Hungary's Communist Party and a Comintern official, he was appointed head of the propaganda department of the Ural Bureau of the Bolshevik Party and in the ensuing years gained a reputation in the Comintern for his servile obeisance to Stalin.

Kun wrote prolifically as a journalist (18 monographs and 250 articles) but almost all of these dealt with factional disputes in Hungary, Germany, and Russia. From 1921 until 1934 Kun combined a career as a Comintern bureaucrat with minor responsibilities in the Comintern's AgitProp Department with frequent official trips abroad. His downfall began in 1929, when a Stalinist historian condemned his leadership of the Hungarian Soviet Republic of 1919. After 1934 Kun—a Hungarian, a leftist, and a Jew—was inevitably caught up in Stalin's purges. By 1936 the Hungarian Communist Party was disbanded by Stalin, and Kun's position as Party leader abolished. Kun was arrested by the NKVD in 1937, incarcerated for twenty-nine months in Butyrka Prison in Moscow, where he was psychologically and physically tortured and executed on 30 November 1939.

BIBLIOGRAPHY:
    A. *Revolutionary Essays* (London: British Socialist Party, 1919); *Válogatott irások és beszédek* (Selected writings and speeches), 2 vols. (Budapest: Kossuth, 1966).
    B. Rudolf Tökes, *Béla Kun and the Hungarian Soviet Republic* (Stanford, Calif.: Hoover Institute, 1967); Iván Völgyes, ed., *Hungary in Revolution 1918–1919* (Lincoln: University of Nebraska Press, 1971).

ROBERT A. GORMAN

KUSHIDA TAMIZŌ   (1885–1934). Kushida Tamizō, a Japanese Marxist economist commonly associated with the Rōnō-ha (Labor-Farmer faction), wrote extensively on the Japanese agrarian economy and the theory of rents. Born in an agrarian household in Fukushima Prefecture, because of his family's financial difficulties Kushida was forced to change middle school several times, and finally graduated in 1908 from the German course in the Tokyo Foreign Language School. Kushida then entered the political science course at Kyoto Imperial University, where he studied under the future Marxist pioneer Kawakami Hajime.* After graduating in 1912, he became a graduate student at Tokyo Imperial University, studying economics, and then advanced to the position of assistant in the university's seminar on economic statistics. Because Kushida had not been promised advancement to assistant professor and professor, he remained in the same position until 1916, doing additional lecturing at Chūō and Senshū universities. He joined the editorial staff at *Ōsaka Daily News* briefly, resigning after only a year because of a conflict with the editor-in-chief. He then joined Dōshisho University as a lecturer, then professor, and later planned reforms as head of the Law Department, but resigned this position in February 1919.

    That same fall, Kushida returned to Tokyo Imperial University as lecturer and began to branch out into more politically oriented activity. He helped to edit the newly launched leftist magazine *We* (*Warera*) and also began to work part time at the Ōhara Institute for the Study of Social Problems (Ōhara shakai mondai kenkyūjo). When fellow economist Morito Tatsuo was suspended from his professorship at the university because of his role in disseminating socialist thought, Kushida, who had also become a Marxist at this point, resigned and in August 1920 became a full research scholar at the Ōhara Institute. In October he was sent to Germany by the Institute to study Marxism and gather materials on socialism and political economy on behalf of the Institute. On returning to Japan, Kushida wrote prolifically in the Institute's journal and in *We* on historical materialism and on value and rent theory. One of the first Japanese Marxists to explore these topics in depth, Kushida applied his training in Marxian economics to explore the pressing agrarian problem in Japan. This work brought him into often intense conflict with other Marxists, including former teacher Kawakami and the Kōza-ha ("feudal faction") in the 1930s. This conflict was heightened by Kushida's rumored links with the so-called dissolutionist faction (*kaitō-ha*) of Asano Akira, a group that renounced both the Japanese Communist Party and the principle of the subjection of Japan's socialist movement to international leadership. The group went on, in the late 1920s, to argue in favor of a Japanese socialism built on the existing imperial household.

The crucial point at issue in Kushida's debate with Kōza-ha scholars Noro Eitarō* and Hirano Yoshitarō* was whether agrarian rents in the 1920s were essentially capitalistic or feudalistic. The Rōnō-ha's basic view of Japanese economic development was that the Meiji Restoration (1868) had constituted Japan's bourgeois-democratic revolution and that Japanese capitalism had developed sufficiently to warrant immediate socialist revolution. The Kōza-ha maintained the Comintern and official Japanese Communist Party view that feudal remnants, particularly in the agrarian sector of the economy and political superstructure, were still so powerful that the bourgeois-democratic revolution would have to be completed before the Japanese proletariat could embark on a socialist revolution. In addressing this issue, Kushida focused on the larger question of the transition from feudalism to capitalism in the countryside. Although agrarian rents remained high in the 1920s and 1930s, often as high as feudal ground rents levied in the Tokugawa era, Kushida maintained, these were no longer feudal rents but capitalistic rents determined by forces of supply and demand for scarce land. A crucial point in the transition was the imposition of the land-tax reforms in the Meiji period. These reforms destroyed old feudalistic relations of production; feudal personalistic relations of obligation had been replaced by impersonal capitalist contracts. In making this argument, Kushida delved into the theoretical complexities of Marx's economic theory on the question of the source of differential rent, in an effort to challenge the claim of non-Marxist economists Hijikata Seibi and Takada Yasuma that Marx's* labor theory of value and theory of differential rent were inconsistent. It was in this theoretical aspect of the controversy that Kushida is acknowledged to have made a significant contribution to Japanese Marxism.

BIBLIOGRAPHY:

A. *Kushida Tamizō zenshū* (Complete works of Kushida Tamizō), 5 vols. (Tokyo: n.a., 1935).

B. Ōuchi Hyōe, *Kushida Tamizō* (Tokyo: n.a., 1949).

GERMAINE A. HOSTON

L

LABRIOLA, ANTONIO   (1843–1904). Antonio Labriola was born in Cassino on 2 July 1843, and died in Rome on 2 February 1904. He completed his university studies in Naples, where he met and studied under the Hegelian Bertrando Spaventa. In 1874 he became an untenured professor of moral philosophy and pedagogy at the University of Rome; in 1879 he began to associate with radical and socialist groups, which marked the beginning of a political commitment that would continue to grow and would have an echo even in his university teaching, so that in 1889 a course of his on the French Revolution would be suspended as a result of criticism provoked by elements of the right. Before that, in 1887, he gave a preliminary lecture (*prelezione*) for a course in the philosophy of history, a lecture that was an important turning point, a synthesis of his preceding development and a signal of his adoption of a new historical methodology. In 1890 he came to know Filippo Turati, a leader of Italian socialism. At the same time he carried on a correspondence with Friedrich Engels* that lasted until 1895 and was of significant importance for Italian Marxism. He had contacts with all the leaders of international socialism, from Karl Kautsky* to Wilhelm Liebknecht,* Victor Adler, August Bebel and Paul Lafargue,* and he contributed to the principal German reviews. He was very active in preparations for the constitutive congress of the Socialist Party in 1892 in Genoa. In 1895 the first of his essays on the materialist concept of history appeared, published by invitation of Georges Sorel† in *Devenir social* and followed by two others before 1897. Having become engaged in a controversy with Turati, who accused him of wanting to make socialism "likable" and of watering down class struggle in favor of socialism, he dedicated himself to theoretical polemics regarding the revisions of the Second International* and the "crisis of Marxism" occurring at the end of the century. Among the targets of his anti-revisionist polemic was his old disciple—and later the editor of his works—Benedetto Croce. But in reality his last years found him isolated and defeated.

"In Naples, in private circles from 1840 to 1860 and then publicly at the university from 1860 to 1875, there was a rebirth of Hegelism," wrote Labriola himself, as he reconstructed his own intellectual development in a letter to Engels on 14 March 1884.

I was born in this milieu. At nineteen I wrote an invective against Zeller favoring the return to Kant (introductory lecture at Heidelberg). All the Hegelian and post-Hegelian literature was familiar to us. . . . I studied Feuerbach in 1866–67 and then the School of Tuebingen. . . . All that is over, because our country is a cesspool of history. Now the positivistic demimonde dominates. Perhaps—no, very definitely—I became a Communist because of my (rigorous) Hegelian education, after having studied the psychology of Herbart and the Voelkerpsychologie of Steinthal and others.

Even if Labriola accentuates the influence of Hegelianism, as has been recently emphasized, above all by Garin, this autobiographical sketch signals some of the more significant influences in the intellectual development of Labriola, influences that remained decisive even after his adoption of Marxism. Spinoza and Hegel furnished him with the basis for a polemical objectivism toward all subjectivism and rhetorical humanism; Herbart and the reflection on German culture of 1860–80—in particular the debate on history and historiography (from Droysen to Bernheim), as well as positivism—show him the need for the construction of defined scientific knowledge (and specifically the new sciences in particular) and precise language.

He considered whether philosophy of history can be this type of defined scientific knowledge: it is the subject of the *prelezione* of 1887 on *Problemi della filosofia della storia*. Once one has rejected the monism typical of absolute idealism and of the Hegelianism that was then fashionable and that reduces the facts of historical knowledge to rigid deductions of abstract metaphysical categories, the task is to investigate history's real principles, going beyond every type of dull empiricism and establishing a foundation on the scientific principle of "difference," that is, explaining nondogmatically the connections and complexities of activity comprising human history. One then arrives at something that Labriola defines as an "epigenetic theory of civilization," i.e., a theory that permits revelation of the ways in which the "spirit," creating new developments in the course of the historical process, comes to be the motive force of the historical process itself. The essential instrument of such a theory is social psychology, once it is cleansed of generic and abstract analogies and of excessively rigid and specific distinctions. Labriola believed that all psychic dynamics are characterized by the fact that they both reflect surrounding conditions and are conditioned by personal assumptions, but are not simply mechanically caused.

It is after all his reflection on the possibility of establishing a science of history that brings Labriola to Marxism, and, on the other hand, it is through him that Marxism is introduced into Italy. He sees historical materialism as a scientific philosophy of history, capable of surpassing idealism and of having as its subject concrete forces, human beings embedded in real social situations that are characteristic of them. Historical materialism performs the revolutionary function of turning historical explanation into an almost natural, scientific process. In any case, Marxism is also always philosophy, and self-sufficient philosophy: Labriola wants to confirm it forcefully against every revisionist and idealist reduction.

Marxism, and its science of historical materialism, is an accurate depiction of history's objective, unified tendencies, which also critically rejects all pretense toward absolute metaphysical certainty. The nondogmatic, empirically based tendency to monism is therefore directly opposed to the total monism of the "common evolutionists" and the "decadent Hegelians" and those who support rigid economic determinism. As a matter of fact, historical materialism corrects monism through the fact that it is based on praxis, that is, on the development of industriousness. Since it is the theory of the man who works, Labriola thus considers science itself a form of work. Marxism, therefore, is philosophy of praxis, the overcoming of every common opposition between theory and practice. Moreover, philosophy of praxis is the core of historical materialism. The latter is immanent in the very objects about which it philosophizes. Hence it originates in life and conditions thought. It is born in concrete human activities, and shapes abstract theory. Historical materialism is generated by, and explains, the inner psychological states that follow the satisfaction or dissatisfaction of human material needs. Free inquiry and methodical observation, in particular voluntary and technically correct empirical experiment, characterize the philosophy of praxis.

After all, Labriola considers Marxism to be a unitary synthesis of three related elements: first, Marxism is a "philosophic tendency" that is expressed in a general view of life and the world; second, it is a criticism of political economy, in that it is a critical analysis of the capitalistic bourgeois social structure, historicized and therefore removed from absolutization in an hypothesized eternal natural order; third, it is an interpretation of politics, and above all of that which is necessary and useful to the direction of the workers' movement toward socialism.

BIBLIOGRAPHY:

A. *Essays on the Materialist Conception of History* (Chicago: C. H. Kerr, 1904); *Socialism and Philosophy* (Chicago: C. H. Kerr, 1907); *Opere* (Milan: Feltrinelli, 1959–62); *Scritti filosofici e politici* (Turin: Einaudi, 1973).

B. Luigi dal Pane, *Antonio Labriola: la vita e il pensiero* (Rome: Roma, 1935); Stefano Poggi, *Introduzione a Labriola* (Bari: Laterza, 1981).

VITTORIO DINI

LAFARGUE, PAUL   (1841–1911). Paul Lafargue was born in Cuba in 1841, but his family moved to France for his education in 1851 and eventually to Paris, where he studied medicine. He met Karl Marx* in 1865 through his membership in the First International,* was expelled from medical school and moved to London, where he took his degree and married Marx's second daughter, Laura. A member of the Commune in Bordeaux, he fled briefly to Spain, helped secure the exclusion of Bakunin from the International at the La Haye congress, and eventually moved to London. He returned to France in 1882 after the Communard amnesty and joined Jules Guesde* to form the breakaway Marxist Parti Ouvrier Français (POF). From 1891 to 1898 he was deputy for Lille and contributed to a large number of journals. He and his wife committed suicide in 1911 to escape the indignities of senility, and at his funeral Lenin* called him "one of the most important and profound propagators of Marxist ideas."

He wrote many articles and pamphlets on a wide range of topics, and his ideas were more a vague adaptation of Marxism rather than an interpretation or development of it. He believed that perception of the material world was the basis for all ideology and used Locke, Diderot, and Condillac to support his argument. He thought that the bourgeoisie had suppressed rationalism and used romantic mysticism to delude and subjugate the working classes, so he attempted to "use" rationalist concepts to "prove" Marxism. His materialism was vulgar and mechanistic to the point of determinism; indeed, Lafargue didn't recognize the existence of free will or the search for ideals, and saw man only as an animal with hands. In *La Droit à la paresse* he posited the idea that work was a mystical fixation produced by the romantic and pseudo-moralistic propaganda of the bourgeoisie. Man, he felt, should regain the right to be idle, which was the first step toward the arcadian utopia of Lafargue's socialist state. His own romanticism and his view of society as a series of sensual perceptions ran counter to the Marxist dialectic in many ways, and for a short time he was seduced by Boulangism, but his imagery was very influential in winning a section of the working class to Marxism before World War I.

BIBLIOGRAPHY:

A. *Le Communisme et l'évolution économique* (Lille: Delory, 1892); *Idéalisme et matérialisme* (Paris: Spartacus, 1892); *Idéalisme et matérialisme dans L'histoire* (Lille: Delory, 1893); *The Right to Be Lazy* (Chicago: Kerr, 1907).

B. J. Varlet, ed., *Paul Lafargue: Theoricien du marxisme* (Paris: Editions Sociales, 1933); G. Stolze, *Paul Lafargue, militant du socialisme* (Paris: Nouveau Promethée, 1937); J. Bruhat, "Paul Lafargue et la tradition du socialisme révolutionaire français," *Cahiers internationaux* (July-August 1949), pp. 38–56.

JOHN C. SIMMONDS

LANGE, OSKAR RYSZARD   (1904–1965). Oskar Ryszard Lange was born on 27 July 1904 in Tomaszow Mazowiecki, and died 2 October 1965 in London. He was a noted economist, statistician, socialist theorist, and political activist. Lange taught at several universities in Poland and the United States, was ambassador of the Polish Peoples' Republic in Washington, and was a Polish representative to the United Nations Security Council. From 1957 to 1962 Lange chaired the Economic Council for the Polish Peoples' Republic, and from 1957 to 1959 he chaired the European Economic Council. As a specialist in planning he was an advisor to the governments of India, Ceylon, and Iraq.

Lange's original ideas concerning the economic theory of socialism (1936–38) brought him world renown. Lange argued that rational socialist economies could be based on following the marketplace through trial and error. Asserting that the main difficulties of socialism are the dangers of economic centralization and bureaucratization, he looked for ways to create socialist economic institutions that would ensure a high level of effectiveness and democratic planning. During the 1956 Polish October he stood as a symbol of reformist tendencies.

He published several developmental studies synthesizing neoclassical and Keynesian theories. Many times he undertook the project of synthesizing Marxist and bourgeois economics under the aegis of the former. For him economics was part of a theory of social development, understood as the science of the most general rules governing dynamic social structures. Lange emphasized the special importance for economic theory of what he called praxeology: the theory of efficient and rational economic decision making. In his later years Lange tried to translate the traditional categories of dialectical materialism into the language of contemporary cybernetics. Both the totality (i.e. the system and its structures) as well as development (i.e. contradiction and change) could, he argued, be mathematically explained by certain rules of movement and social development. Knowledge of these rules would generate a socialist system characterized by popular self-regulation and self-direction of the economic, social, and political systems. Based on these considerations he criticized mechanized socialist bureaucracies.

BIBLIOGRAPHY:

A. *On the Economic Theory of Socialism*, ed. B. Lippincott (New York and Toronto: University of Minnesota Press, 1938); *Political Economy* (London: Pergamon Press, 1963); *Wholes and Parts: A General Theory of System Behavior* (London: Pergamon Press, 1965).

B. *On Political Economy and Econometrics: Essays in Honor of Oskar Lange* (Warsaw: PWN, 1964); S. Wellisz, "Oskar Lange," in *International Encyclopedia of Social Science*, vol. 9 (New York: Macmillan, 1968).

TADEUSZ KOWALIK

LARGO CABALLERO, FRANCISCO   (1869–1946). Born in Madrid on 15 October 1869, Largo Caballero started working at age eight as an apprentice in a factory making cardboard boxes. A year later he became a carpenter's apprentice, a job he held until 1904, when he began to devote his time to labor and political activities. He was a member of the Unión General de Trabajadores (UGT) beginning in 1890, and of the Partido Socialista Obrero Española (PSOE) after 1894, and he held all major leadership positions of the labor organizations both in Madrid and throughout Spain. He was Secretary General of the UGT (1918) as well as president of the PSOE (1932), resigning this position in December 1933, after a serious confrontation with Indalecio Prieto.* He was also a councilman in Madrid and a provincial delegate to the Cortes (1918). He participated in the steering committees that directed the general strikes of 1917, 1930, and 1934, activities for which he was jailed. He was named State Counsellor by dictator Primo de Rivera, and Labor Minister in the first Republican administration. From these positions he was able to push forward a corporate system of labor relations. Having become disappointed at the results of the alliance with the Republican parties, he began to defend, beginning in 1933, the need for a revolutionary movement that would overthrow the Republic and give power to the working class led by the Socialist Party. Following the failure of the labor rebellion of October 1934, Largo Caballero approved, with reservations, the "Prietista" policy of reestablishing an alliance with the Republicans, although he imposed on this policy a merely electoral scope, preventing the formation of a Socialist–Republican government until the Civil War made this inevitable. He was appointed Head of Government and Minister of Defense, positions he had to abandon after the crisis of May 1937. His unsuccessful attempt to return to politics with the help of the UGT embittered the last years of his life, which came to an end in Paris on 23 March 1946, after a brief stay in a Nazi concentration camp.

While Prieto represented, better than anybody else, the political swing of Spanish socialism in the period between the two world wars, Largo Caballero was, during the same period, the principal leader of the labor union movement. He was not a well-read man, and his system of ideas was the result of personal experiences, coated with the ideological message of the intellectuals who worked side by side with him. What was important to him was the good health and growth of the UGT, to which he sacrificed everything else, including the question of who should govern Spain. He organized the UGT on the basis of national industrial federations. The labor union method, of which he was a tenacious defender, was characterized by an emphasis on internal discipline, caution, and the need to avoid involving the organization in risky actions. As a determined believer in the presence of labor unions whenever the fate of the working class was discussed, Largo Caballero formulated the ideology of labor corporatism, which resulted in the UGT supporting the Organización Corporativa Nacional, an institutional system of labor relations involving independent labor input into public policy making, established by the Primo de Rivera dictatorship in 1926 and reinforced by the Second Republic.

The same concerns that led him to defend that kind of corporatism also explains his progressive radicalization, which began in 1933. Ideologically supported by the Juventudes Socialistas (Socialist Youth), who began to call him the Spanish Lenin,* and by the radicalized intellectuals of the PSOE, Largo Caballero announced in his speeches to the workers the immanence of a labor revolution as a defensive maneuver against a likely fascist attack on the Republic. Although he was mainly responsible for this revolutionary union movement, he was unable to furnish it with a coherent body of ideas or an efficient organization. Following the inevitable failure of the insurrection he became more prudent in his threats, and he limited himself to the obstruction of the Republican–Socialist alliance led by Prieto and Azaña. His conversion to an ideology that defended labor isolation and independence while simultaneously exalting revolutionary insurrections was not substantial enough, however, to comprise an acceptable alternative policy to the International's* alliance with the Republicans. Moreover, his timid attempts at uniting labor were met with the traditional distrust that he inspired among anarchist labor unions.

BIBLIOGRAPHY:

A. *Presente y futuro de la Unioń General de Trabajodore* (Madrid: Pedreño, 1925); *Discursos a los trabajadores* (Madrid: Gráfica Socialista, 1934); *Mis recereados* (Mexico: Alianza, 1954).

B. Santos Juliá, *La izquierda del PSOE, 1935–36* (Madrid: Siglo XXI, 1977); Andres de Blas, *El socialismo radical en la II república* (Madrid: Tucar, 1978).

SANTOS JULIÁ

LE DUAN   (b. 1905). Le Duan was born in Haiphong in Vietnam in 1905. He appears to have joined the Indochinese Communist Party in the early 1930s and was a political prisoner on Poulo Condore. After the August 1945 Revolution, he was a key political commissar in the South, emerging eventually as the most important authority on Southern problems within the Vietnamese Communist Party. From this position, as chairman of the Regional Committee for the South, Le Duan argued in 1956–57 that North Vietnam, following the Geneva Peace Agreement, should step up aid to the revolutionary forces in the South. Le Duan summarized his views in a document that was to assume pivotal importance in the history of the Vietnamese Communist Party, *The Path of Revolution in the South*. He argued that building socialism in North Vietnam could not be separated from liberating the South. In 1957 Le Duan became acting Secretary General of the Party, and at its Third Congress in 1960 he was made Secretary General and appointed a member of both the Politburo and the Party Secretariat. He retains these positions until the present day.

Le Duan emerged as one of the foremost theoreticians of the Vietnamese Communist Party in the late 1950s. His views are most decisively expressed in *The Vietnamese Revolution: Fundamental Problems, Essential Tasks*. Le Duan argued that although most of the external forms of the Party, such as its front organizations, are subject to constant change in response to changing conditions, the internal structure of first the Indochinese Communist Party, then the Vietnamese Communist Party, was to remain unchanged. Indeed, organization was one of the key weapons in the ICP's seizure and retention of power in 1945. Organization, propaganda, and agitation—these basic operational features of the Indochinese Communist Party—complemented each other.

BIBLIOGRAPHY:

A. *Forward Under the Glorious Banner of the October Revolution* (Hanoi: Foreign Languages Publishing House, 1965); *On the Socialist Revolution in Vietnam*, 2 vols. (Hanoi: Foreign Languages Publishing House, 1965); *The Vietnamese Revolution: Fundamental Problems, Essential Tasks* (Hanoi: Foreign Languages Publishing House, 1970).

B. William J. Duiker, *The Communist Road to Power in Vietnam* (Boulder, Colo.: Westview Press, 1981).

MICHAEL C. WILLIAMS

LENIN, VLADIMIR ILICH   (1870–1924). The man known to history as Lenin was born Vladimir Ilich Ulianov in 1870 in the Russian city of Simbirsk (subsequently renamed Ulianovsk), the son of a school inspector who had achieved the status of minor nobility. Expelled from Kazan University in 1887 for student radicalism, Lenin read for the law on his own, passing his legal examinations in 1891. Drawn to revolutionary thought, Lenin joined a Marxist group in the Russian capital of St. Petersburg in the early 1890s and was arrested and exiled to Siberia, where he authored his first Marxist study of the Russian economy. Leaving Russia early in the new century, Lenin became a coeditor of the Russian Marxist journal *Iskra* (The Spark), contributing his own version of Marxism in *What Is to Be Done?* in 1902. The following year Lenin led a successful struggle to split the fledgling Russian Social Democratic Labor Party (RSDLP) at its London Conference, with Lenin's followers adopting the name "Bolsheviks," which means "majority" in Russian. During the next decade, Lenin attempted to instill rigid centralism within the Bolshevik movement, edited several new journals, and founded the journal *Pravda* in 1912. A few weeks prior to the outbreak of the spring, 1917 Russian Revolution, Lenin informed a group of workers in Switzerland, where he was in exile, that it appeared unlikely that his generation of Russians would live to see the revolution. Returning to Russia in April 1917, Lenin immediately plunged into radical politics, arguing that all power ought pass from the just-formed liberal Provisional Government to the Soviet of Soldiers and Workers Deputies. In the fall of 1917, the Bolsheviks took power in a second revolution, and in the next seven years Lenin attempted to establish a viable worker-peasant state while awaiting a Western socialist revolution, which would end Russia's new isolation. Lenin's death in January 1924 sparked a struggle for power among his colleagues that ended only after the bloody purges of the 1930s.

It is difficult to summarize the intellectual development and contributions of a man whose collective works run well over forty volumes, a man who led a successful revolution and became prime minister of the world's largest country. But of the two areas of concern, intellectual and practical, there is little doubt that Lenin always subordinated the former to the latter. Lenin's efforts to adopt socialist thought to the changing realities of early twentieth-century Europe resulted in several significant revisions of earlier Marxism and the emergence of a new synthesis of radical thought aptly known as Marxism-Leninism. Each component of this synthesis was inspired by a practical problem confronting this Russian revolutionary.

The first dilemma facing Lenin upon completion of his exile in 1900 was the obvious and bitter diversity that existed both in the Russian socialist movement and within the European movement as a whole. Two key problems appear to have guided Lenin's political and intellectual activities at this time: how might one account for the apparent decline in worker class consciousness since Marx's* death; and how was it possible that real wages for European workers had risen, given Marx's prediction of gradual impoverishment? The initial question was addressed in Lenin's major work *What Is to Be Done?* Rejecting Marx's confidence in the ability of the working class to master revolutionary theory and action, Lenin argued that, left to themselves, workers could reach only a trade union consciousness adequate for extracting economic concessions but leaving the basic structures of capitalism intact. Only the organization of a small, tightly knit Marxist party could bring the required enlightenment and direction to the workers. It was the issue of the Party's role as defined by Lenin that led to the 1903 split in the Russian Social Democratic Labor Party.

During the 1905 Russian Revolution, Lenin, in exile in the West, issued a position paper for his followers back home analyzing the general revolutionary situation. While this lengthy pamphlet ("Two Tactics of Social Democracy in the Democratic Revolution, 1905") conceded that the ongoing Russian revolt ought to lodge power in the hands of the Russian middle class, Lenin did suggest one possible alternative that might allow rapid movement toward socialism. If the alliance of peasants and proletariat that he exhorted his followers to form should shift to a more narrow alliance of poor peasants and proletariat, a transition to socialism might be possible. The formation of such a government, however, would require the spread of revolutionary uprisings to the more advanced Western states, and the subsequent willingness of such Western socialist states to assist their more backward Russian class allies in economic advancement and military defense. Although the course of the 1905 Revolution failed to create even the first stages of Lenin's peasant and proletariat alliance, his analysis of the possibilities open to the Russian working class broached the notions of permanent proletariat-peasant dictatorship in a backward society and a "permanent revolution" linking feudalism directly to socialism. These notions would assume a central place in Lenin's thinking during the 1917 Revolution.

In the period after the abortive 1905 Revolution, Lenin continued his study of Marxism and his efforts to bring ideological and organizational harmony to the Russian socialist movement. In 1908, Lenin authored his sole book-length examination of modern currents of philosophy (*Materialism and Empirio-Criticism*, 1908). Directed largely against the theories of Ernest Mach and Richard Avenarius, and their Russian followers such as Alexander Bogdanov (Alexander A. Malinovsky), Lenin castigated recent advances in scientific philosophy as idealist. Maintaining that philosophy, unlike the individual sciences, possesses no independent object of analysis, Lenin argued that the entire history of philosophical speculation could be grouped within the idealist–realist dichotomy, with only the latter possessing revolutionary potential. Lenin defined idealism as epistemological subjectivism, the mind creating ideas and using them to evaluate and explain reality. In capitalism, idealism stresses the priority of subjectivity both theoretically and practically. Individuals are legally free to speculate and choose the most attractive world view. The apparent battle of ideas is really a unanimous consensus on bourgeois values and institutions, for these intellectual freedoms are also necessary to preserve liberal democracy and capitalism, and to reinforce elitism. Idealism engages in an endless series of subjective intellectual games whose sole practical purpose is to maintain class domination. Materialism, on the other hand, defines human cognition as the mental reflection of actual objects which exist materially, independent of mental counterparts. Lenin's so-called "copy theory" of perception presumes all sensations are photocopies, imitations of the real thing. Objective matter exists outside the mind, determining what we perceive but not coextensive with mental processes. Sensations, for Lenin, are "images" or "reflections" of real things. The mind is a correlative of matter: the latter exists only in relationship to mind. Lenin's "dualism" presupposes two realities, the objective material world and its cognitive mirror image. Plekhanov*, and the orthodox school generally, are "monists" because they define mind in material terms only, as matter determined by the physical world. Mind, in other words, is complex matter that is part of material reality in the same way that trees, stars, or subhuman animals are. The external perceived object is the content or data of perception. Since mind is passively determined matter, there is no intervening mode of cognition which reflects or mirrors reality. Why, then, did Lenin diligently accumulate Engels's* scattered comments on cognitive "reflection" and construct a potentially confusing concept, which from his own materialist viewpoint is probably superfluous? Lenin, it seems, was a materialist who was unwilling to accept the passive, noncreative role assigned to social actors. By describing a subject's cognition as "reflecting" matter, he implicitly condemned orthodox Marxism for denying mental reality altogether. If everything, including mind and its contents, is reducible to physical properties, then Marxian materialism is indistinguishable from the vulgar non-Marxist predecessor. Our role in history requires meekly awaiting the inevitable revolution, which will appear independent of unique desire or intentions. This attitude was obviously unsuitable to Lenin's temperament and the circumstances of a decaying czarist Russia. Lenin's dualism, then, is his materialist defense of ideas and intentional action, resurrecting subjectivity and simultaneously denying its autonomy.

Encouraged by his reading of Hegel during the war years, Lenin continued searching for a revised, subjectively relevant dialectical materialism. The *Philosophical Notebooks*, published posthumously in the Soviet Union as volume 38 of the *Collected Works*, consists of speculative writings completed after 1914, and are invaluable for understanding Lenin's domestic tactics. His goal in these essays was to examine Hegel's dialectic and salvage what could fruitfully be applied to materialism. All phenomena, including material objects and human minds, embody universal (abstract) and particular (material or concrete) qualities. Perceived objects, therefore, are never completely understood, for they express an infinite number of perceptions. Moreover, in perceiving an object, I also express abstract and concrete meanings. The world, as Lenin sees it in the *Notebooks*, is infinitely complex, with all of its parts interconnected and interrelated. Since absolute truth requires perceiving reality's infinite dialectical linkages—an impossible task—human knowledge is always fragmentary. Each particular cognitive reflection is incomplete and exhibits internal contradictions between universal and particular elements, the variety of abstract and concrete meanings it simultaneously expresses. As knowledge increases, these contradictions are surpassed and replaced by new ones. This cycle continues endlessly: Incomplete and contradictory knowledge is resolved by continued learning, but reappears at more advanced levels and pushes us to learn even more. Truth, never absolute, is generated by this process of resolving contradictions. In *Materialism and Empirio-Criticism*, Lenin unequivocally rejected idealism as false, misleading, and oppressive. In the *Notebooks*, Lenin had mellowed somewhat. Idealism merely overemphasizes or absolutizes truth's abstract component at the expense of its particularity. Idealism, in other words, has gnoseological roots and cannot be ignored or simplistically dismissed. There is some truth in all knowledge, including idealism. Lenin, however, also persists in seeing the dialectic as a property of reflective knowledge *and* an objective trait of nature. History and society are therefore governed by nature's dialectical laws, which exist prior to human perception or will. Capitalism dissolves into its opposite as surely as did feudalism; proletarian revolution inevitably resolves bourgeois contradictions. Incontrovertably, Lenin remains a dialectical materialist.

In retrospect, the *Philosophical Notebooks* transforms dialectical materialism from a frozen formula into a dynamic process. Lenin reactivates subjectivity as a complex unity of abstract and concrete processes rather than, as before, stuffed bodies manipulated by impersonal forces. Yet these incredibly complex human agents also express and reflect objective universal laws governing all human and nonhuman phenomena. He is defending the integrity of irreducible subjects as well as the epistemological priority of an objective material dialectic. This project is also nurtured by other orthodox Marxists, many of whom are troubled by the numbing consequences of their own materialism. In any case, whether Lenin's unrealized philosophical dream is a cause or consequence of his revolutionary tactics, Leninist theory and practice are mutually supportive. Unlike Plekhanov and Kautsky,* he is not willing to await history's dénouement passively. Social actors are more than automatons. History's dialectical process includes real live subjects reflectively perceiving and creatively altering the world. But history is not arbitrary; it unfolds dialectically. Society passes through developmental stages leading inexorably to workers' revolution. History's truth, in other words, is expressed in creative activity by reflective, knowledgeable people. However, only "correct" actions are justifiable. Here is the rationale for Lenin's voluntarism. While Leninist tactics are shaped by concrete circumstances, they also express his unique epistemology. Successful revolutionary strategies embody creative, goal-oriented actions by knowledgeable agents generating history's objective process. By having it both ways epistemologically, that is, defending irreducible, innovative subjects and a determining, objective dialectic, Lenin can creatively modify historical materialism's reductionism and impose a rigid dictatorship of scientists.

Following the outbreak of war in 1914, Lenin spent less time on theory and instead returned to his earlier, more practical problems concerning rising wages and declining worker class awareness. In a major study written in 1916 (*Imperialism, the Highest Stage of Capitalism*), Lenin resolved these questions while providing an account of the origins of modern war. Capitalism, he argued, at a definite (objective) stage in its natural development required the export of capital so as to prevent or postpone the cyclical pattern of expansion and depression described by Marx. Such capital sent abroad to lesser developed parts of the globe returned huge profits, allowing the capitalists in the home nation to raise workers' wages and to "bribe" an emerging aristocracy of labor. This movement of capital abroad and profits back to the mother country was reflected in studies showing a rise in real wages, an increase gained only by workers in the imperialist states. When the millions of new workers in the colonies were taken into consideration, it became apparent that real wages for the world's working class had indeed fallen, just as Marx had predicted. The decline of worker class consciousness within Europe was a logical result of the repatriation of profits that increased domestic wages as well as social mobility. Imperialism, a clear and objective stage of capitalism, was to Lenin the last gasp of a dying system. Whereas the generation of profits within capitalism appeared potentially unlimited, the opportunities for investment abroad were restricted by the earth's finite land surface. Britain and France, having industrialized before other European states, had passed to the stage of imperialism prior to the division of colonies. The subsequent growth of capitalism in Germany, Austria, Italy, and Russia produced new pressures for foreign investment at a moment when lands available for domination were declining. The resulting tensions, Lenin charged, led to the military alliances so prevalent before 1914, and finally to war. World War I was the inevitable and necessary result of the historic laws that compelled capitalism to pass to its higher stage of imperialism. Once this fateful connection was made clear to the European working class, whose members filled the ranks of the opposing armies, the way would be clear for a European, perhaps a worldwide revolution. To Lenin, the growth of antiwar feelings in Germany, France, Austria, and Russia in 1917 suggested that the lesson was being learned and that revolution was possible. Returning to Russia in the spring of 1917, Lenin called upon the workers and peasants to seize power, maintaining that the uneven development of capitalism in the era of imperialism transferred the loci of rising class consciousness to the more backward and exploited regions, such as Russia.

In the fall of 1917, Lenin became head of the world's first workers' and peasants' dictatorship, eagerly observing Western Europe for indications that the Russian example would be followed. When the Western working class failed to behave as anticipated, Lenin devoted his efforts to institutionalizing and justifying (via the theory of "democratic centralism") a Party dictatorship in a country whose working class made up less than 5 percent of the population. In early 1924, Lenin, exhausted by two serious strokes and a life utterly devoted to revolution, died. The failure of the Western socialists to seize power, and the unproven wisdom of Lenin's decision to terminate the period of middle-class rule in Russia after only a nine-month reign in 1917, despite the backward state of Russian industry, bequeathed an ambiguous legacy to his successors. His followers were to resolve their own disagreements in the next decade not by the subtleties of philosophy and debate, but by the executioner's blade.

BIBLIOGRAPHY:

A. *Collected Works* 45 vols. (Moscow: Foreign Language Publishing House, 1960–70); *Two Tactics of Social Democracy in the Democratic Revolution* (New York: International, 1963); *Materialism and Empiriocriticism* (Moscow: Progress, 1964); *What Is to Be Done?* (New York: International, 1969); *Imperialism, the Highest Stage of Capitalism* (Moscow: Progress, 1970).

B. Nadezhda Krupskaia, *Memories of Lenin (1893–1917)* (London: Lawrence and Wishart, 1942); Alfred Meyer, *Leninism* (Cambridge: Harvard University Press, 1957); Louis Fischer, *The Life of Lenin* (New York: Norton, 1975).

MICHAEL M. BOLL AND ROBERT A. GORMAN

LI DAZHAO   (1889–1927). Li Dazhao was born into a peasant family in northern China. He studied political economy in Japan and achieved prominence during the New Culture Movement after 1915. As librarian and professor at Beijing University, he exerted considerable influence on Chinese youth. He was a founding member of the Communist Party in 1921 and served as the leader of its northern branch in Beijing until his death in 1927.

Li was one of the most distinguished intellectuals of his generation and was the first Chinese intellectual to profess commitment to Marxism (in 1919). China's first Marxist, he was not as orthodox as some who followed him into Marxism, nor was he the most knowledgeable Marxist of his times. Li's significance as a Chinese Marxist lay in his reading of Marxism, which anticipated themes central to Chinese Marxism, especially the Marxism of Mao Zedong.* Most important among these themes was the relationship between the national and the social revolution. Li was a revolutionary patriot before he discovered Marxism; Marxism provided him with a theoretical justification for his nationalism, as well as a political guide for the reconstitution of China as a nation. To Li, China was a "proletarian nation," which implied that the Chinese people as a whole suffered from oppression by imperialism. But unlike other proponents of this view (such as Guomindang ideologues), Li did not use it to deny the existence of internal class exploitation and oppression. The Chinese nation he spoke of was not a given, a legacy to be preserved, but an entity to be created. His hope lay with the "people," especially the agrarian population, who had to remold themselves through a social revolution to fulfill the promise of China as a nation.

This hope gave Li's Marxism a strongly populist cast. Li shared with populists elsewhere a faith in the ability of the people to regenerate themselves, as well as an anti-urban, anticapitalist outlook. Nevertheless, it would be simplistic to interpret Li's faith in the common people as an unqualified reaffirmation of the people as they were; if the common people were to become the subjects of the new nation (and the new world), they needed to be liberated from the past's hold upon them. Li saw in Marxism, especially the idea of social revolution embodied in the Russian Revolution, the means to achieve this goal.

Li applied an activist reading to Marxism. While he lauded the materialist conception of history as a theory that had revolutionized historical thinking by drawing attention from the activities of individuals to the underlying forces of history, Li did not take this to mean human activity was historically irrelevant. Revolutionary will (or consciousness) was necessary not just to carry out the revolution but also to transform society. He saw the Russian Revolution of 1917 as the "dawn" of a new age of social revolution that would complete the mission of creating a new world by resolving the question of "bread." It was not abstract forces in history but human activity that would bring about this social revolution.

Li pursued the cause of revolution with consistency, but more as an intellectual leader than as an organization man. His writings do not reveal any breakthroughs in Marxist theory. Rather, they are revealing as a reading of Marxism by a Third World intellectual striving to reconcile national with social goals. Li's Marxism was further animated by a vision of "mutual aid" as the goal of history, which he owed to Kropotkin's anarchism. Indeed, his understanding of social revolution was permeated by the vocabulary of anarchism, which, as late as the early 1920s, dominated Chinese conceptions of socialism.

Li was murdered by the soldiers of a warlord during the counterrevolutionary terror of April 1927.

BIBLIOGRAPHY:

A. *Li Dazhao xuanji* (Selected works of Li Dazhao) (Beijing, n.a., 1978).

B. Maurice Meisner, *Li Ta-chao and the Origins of Chinese Marxism* (Cambridge: Harvard University Press, 1967).

ARIF DIRLIK

LI LISAN   (1899 or 1900–1967). A labor organizer and one of the early leaders of the Chinese Communist Party (CCP), Li Lisan was born in Hunan Province in 1899 or 1900. After participating in the student work study program in France in the years 1919–21, Li returned to China, where, as a member of the fledgling CCP, he became an active trade union organizer in central China. He gained national prominence as a leader of the Shanghai General Labor Union during the anti-imperialist May 30th movement of 1925. Following the CCP's debacle of 1927, Li became the de facto head of the Party at its Sixth Congress in Moscow in 1928, a position he retained until he was criticized and removed from power in early 1931, after a bitter policy dispute involving the Comintern (see below). He sojourned in Moscow for fifteen years, returning in 1946 to China, where he again served as a leader of the CCP-directed trade union federation and as Minister of Labor in the PRC between 1949 and 1953. Thereafter, Li was demoted to secondary positions and made to engage in severe self-criticism at the Eighth Party Congress in 1956. During the Cultural Revolution beginning in 1966, Li was again subjected to attack. He apparently died on 22 June 1967, although the cause of death remains unclear. Perhaps Li was an early victim of that violent era.

Li's career is noteworthy in three respects. First, he personifies the earliest generation of CCP leaders who were urban- and trade union-oriented and who had substantial foreign experience (in France and the Soviet Union). Second, his stewardship of the CCP (1928–30) gave rise to a continuing controversy over the so-called Li Lisan line. In essence, Li, who believed that the Chinese Revolution could spark a world revolution, interpreted Comintern pronouncements of late 1929 concerning an imminent revolutionary upsurge as an immediate call for action. On his own initiative he ordered the Chinese Red Army to attack urban centers, but the results were disastrous. The Li Lisan line was condemned by Moscow and later by Mao Zedong* as an example of revolutionary adventurism or putschism. Third, Li's post-1945 career demonstrates how Mao rendered impotent a potential rival by co-opting, then demoting him, obscuring his early importance by rewriting history to serve his own purposes, and finally destroying him.

BIBLIOGRAPHY:

B. Benjamin I. Schwartz, *Chinese Communism and the Rise of Mao* (Cambridge: Harvard University Press, 1951); Tso-liang Hsiao, *Power Relations Within the Chinese Communist Movement, 1930–1934* (Seattle: University of Washington Press, 1961); Richard C. Thornton, *The Comintern and the Chinese Communists, 1928–1931* (Seattle: University of Washington Press, 1969).

STEVEN LEVINE

LIEBKNECHT, WILHELM   (1826–1900). Born in the German Grand Duchy of Hesse-Darmstadt on 29 March 1826 of well-rooted, middle-class Protestant stock, Wilhelm Liebknecht nevertheless became one of the principal founders of the social democratic movement in Germany. Baptized into revolution and imprisonment during the 1848 Revolution, he subsequently spent a dozen years in exile in London. There he met Karl Marx,* who became his tutor in revolutionary theory. After returning to Germany in 1862, Liebknecht helped to organize the socialist movement there. At first he worked with Ferdinand Lassalle's faction, but the authoritarian and pro-Prussian policies of Lassalle and his successors repulsed Liebknecht. So in 1865 he joined and helped to expand a rival working-class party based in Saxony. Ten years later, at the Gotha Congress, Liebknecht did more than any other individual to unite these two hostile segments of German socialism. For the next twenty-five years, he continued to lead this united and growing party as its principal journalist and public speaker and as a dominant member of its Reichstag delegation. He also played an important part in resurrecting the Second International* in 1889, and for the next decade he was Germany's most important figure in that organization. On 7 August 1900, Liebknecht died, to his contemporaries perhaps the most famous and respected social democrat of his generation.

Liebknecht pioneered the accommodation of Marxist theory to the daily, legal operation of a mass-based political party. Many of the issues he confronted appear more practical than theoretical, but practical decisions can have immense implications for Marxist theory. For example, consider Party organization. Should it be closed and conspiratorial or open and democratic? Liebknecht always built his parties according to the latter prescription, ordaining democratically elected annual congresses as the highest authority among Social Democrats. According to Liebknecht, delegates to these congresses should be chosen by Party comrades, from whom only a minimal commitment—paying monthly dues or subscribing to a party newspaper—and no knowledge of theory were required. Continuing in this democratic, nondirective vein, in his own area of special competence, the Party press, Liebknecht edited his newspapers to mirror rather than to guide member opinions. When he was criticized for the indecisiveness that resulted from such practices, he asserted that his comrades were too firmly committed to democracy to tolerate the intellectual autocracy implicit in a press code of orthodoxy.

As an agitator in the field, Liebknecht's programmatic statements were influenced considerably by the circumstances he confronted. As circumstances changed, so did Liebknecht's stance. He rationalized the resulting tergiversations by saying that the issues in question involved only *tactics*, not *principles*. As an example of his flexibility, in the mid-1860s, when the issue of German national unification dominated the political scene, Liebknecht allied himself with the left liberals and bitterly opposed any constructive work in Bismarck's Reichstag. At that time he believed these tactics offered the best hope for progressive developments in Germany. By the early 1870s, however, the left liberals had been exposed as impotent, and the imperfect Reichstag promised to be a permanent fixture. So Liebknecht discarded his temporary allies in the middle class, reasserted working-class independence, and at the same time fashioned a somewhat more positive attitude toward Germany's elected legislature. But Liebknecht's attitude toward parliamentarism would and did change again, according to volatile circumstances. In interpreting his theoretical comments on this or any other issue, it is always necessary—more so than would be the case in reviewing the thoughts of a reclusive theoretician—to consider their political context.

If the context is carefully considered, consistencies are clear in Liebknecht's thought. Regarding parliamentarism, he rejected the mere facades of popular sovereignty that were offered by Bonaparte and Bismarck, but he endorsed an ideal parliamentarism, where the will of the people would find free expression and effectiveness. Although he recognized the potential for political manipulation available in universal suffrage, he nevertheless retained the early Marxist conviction that an enlightened working class would come spontaneously toward socialism. Consequently, democracy and socialism meshed comfortably in his world view, and he never subscribed to any version of Marx's revolutionary dictatorship of the proletariat or of an elitist role for the party.

Regarding the means for implementing socialism, Liebknecht never ruled out the possibility that a gradual and fundamental reform might suffice. But he doubted that such a peaceful process could be completed without provoking violent resistance from the old ruling class. In Liebknecht's scheme of analysis, he expected the next revolution to originate with a counterrevolutionary coup from above. In preparation for that moment, he advocated agitation, education, and organization as the proper activities for social democrats. Whenever less patient comrades proposed new tactics to hasten the party's acquisition of political power, Liebknecht repudiated them. Thus, in the 1890s he rejected both the antiparliamentary tirade of Die Jungen and the revisionism advocated by Eduard Bernstein.† Although hindsight makes Liebknecht's position look sterile and passive, given the steady advance of socialist vote tallies and the plotting of counterrevolution in high government circles that characterized imperial Germany, his tactics are perhaps defensible for the environment in which he worked.

Liebknecht wrote his most important party program in 1875 for the Gotha Congress. This Gotha Program was based upon Liebknecht's draft, but it also included several significant concessions to Lassallism, concessions that Liebknecht personally found distasteful. He accepted such theoretical imperfections because he thought working-class unity was worth that price. His mentor, Marx, disagreed and made the Gotha Program a foil for his famous *Critique*. Since Marx's objections have become so well known, it ought to be emphasized that the Gotha Program committed German social democracy to a platform of unequivocal socialism, which included denunciations of capitalism, a call for collective ownership of the means of production, and prescriptions for proletarian self-reliance and international solidarity.

The Gotha Program and Liebknecht's later interim draft for the Erfurt Program embody the insights of an agitator rather than a pure theoretician. Designed to incite action from their readers, these platform proposals presented a provocative indictment of current society and then urged the socialist party to remedy the specified evils. These documents accordingly downplayed the impersonal economic forces in the present order that constituted the seeds of its *Aufhebung*. Stated differently, Liebknecht remained uncomfortable with the deterministic variety of Marxism that more theoretically oriented individuals like Karl Kautsky* introduced into German social democracy.

Liebknecht's brand of socialism was voluntaristic. It also battled as hard against the authoritarian temptation as it did against capitalism. It denounced militarism and narrow nationalism, whatever the rationale. And it exercised a flexibility and tolerance of dissent that, although sometimes irritating to theoreticians who observed the struggle from afar, served well in making the Social Democrats Germany's largest political party.

BIBLIOGRAPHY:

A. "On the Political Position of Social Democracy Particularly with Respect to the Reichstag: No Compromises, No Election Deals" (Moscow: Foreign Languages Publishing House, n.d.); "Wissen ist Macht—Macht ist Wissen" (Berlin: Vorwärts, [1872] 1894); *Zur Grund - und Bodenfrage* (Leipzig: Genossenschaftsbuchdruckerei, 1876); *Karl Marx: Biographical Memories*, trans. Ernest Untermann (Chicago: C. H. Kerr, 1906);

Socialism: What It Is and What It Seeks to Accomplish, trans. May Wood Simons (Chicago: C. H. Kerr, 1901).

B. Vadim Chubiniski, *Wilhelm Liebknecht: Soldat revolutsii* (Moscow: Mysl, 1968); Raymond Dominick III, *Wilhelm Liebknecht and the Founding of the German Social Democratic Party* (Chapel Hill: University of North Carolina Press, 1982).

RAYMOND DOMINICK

LIN BIAO (1907–1971). Lin Biao distinguished himself as one of the foremost Communist commanders during the Chinese Revolution. He began to achieve eminence after 1959, when, as Defense Minister, he came to Mao Zedong's* support against the critics of Mao's policies. During the Cultural Revolution he acquired sufficient power to be ranked number two after Mao in the Communist hierarchy.

In its popularized form, Cultural Revolution ideology reduced Marxism to an atavistic ideology of action, the cornerstone of which was "Mao Zedong thought." At its best, this ideology served as an inspiration for unreflective pragmatism in selfless service to goals defined by the leadership; at its worst, as a source for mindlessly proclaimed slogans. While Lin made no significant contribution to the theoretical articulation of Cultural Revolution ideology, he played an important part in its production and promotion. As head of the Peoples Liberation Army (PLA) after 1959, Lin launched an ideological reeducation of the Chinese military in accordance with Mao's thought. The PLA was to become a model for revolution during the Cultural Revolution, and Lin, as Mao's "closest-comrade-in-arms," was well placed to extend to society at large the ideological campaign that had been formulated for the PLA. He was responsible for the compilation of aphorisms from Mao's writings in "the little red book," which came to symbolize Chinese communism during the Cultural Revolution. The model revolutionaries who were held up as examples for emulation during the Cultural Revolution were for the most part PLA soldiers who had dedicated themselves to selfless service in the cause of Mao's thought, the "people," or the Chinese nation. Finally, Lin gained fame (or notoriety, as the case may be) outside of China for his espousal of "people's war," which represented the extension of the Chinese revolutionary experience to global revolution and, for a while in the 1960s, determined China's stance in international politics.

The ideological orientation Lin fostered was consistent with his background as a military man. Lin did not claim ideological originality, and indeed his ideas were derivative of the views of Mao Zedong, whom he claimed to represent. In Lin's hands, however, Mao's thought lost much of its historicity and analytical concreteness and was reduced to a few essentials, which Lin made into universal principles of socialist revolution in an age of imperialism. Mao's thought, which was consistently action-oriented, lent itself easily to such reductionism. Mao's own analyses, however, were marked by a basic tension between the requirements of theory and the exigencies of revolutionary action. The tension was lost in Lin's interpretation of Mao, which retained few traces of theory but was concerned primarily with tactical exigencies in the formulation of revolutionary strategy. The vision of socialism, or even consciousness of its material basis, disappeared from sight when revolution was reduced to a military operation, where the distinction between a socialized military and a militarized society was abolished. Lin is noted for his ideologizing of the PLA. Equally, if not more, important was his militarization of Marxist ideology, a tendency that was inherent to a Chinese Marxist ideology that had been fashioned out of a revolution that was at every point also a military struggle.

Certain basic elements of Cultural Revolution ideology reflected this ideological militarization. As an ideological text, *Quotations from Mao Zedong*'' (the little red book) contained little more than maxims extracted from Mao's writings to guide behavior. These maxims encouraged disciplined self-reliance and tactical flexibility in the resolution of practical problems, but did nothing to promote ideological sophistication. The model heroes of the Cultural Revolution were striking mainly for their total internalization of goals set for them by their leaders; as in any militarized conception of society, self-fulfillment in this case implied an unquestioning commitment to fulfillment of the roles to which they had been assigned.

The militarized conception of socialism was most evident in the idea of people's war, which reduced the problem of revolution to a matter of strategy and tactics in a global war of ''rural'' against ''urban'' societies. People's war was the most prominent example of the ''guerrilla socialism'' that achieved prominence in the 1960s under the impact of national liberation movements. The idea drew heavily upon Mao's articulation of the guerrilla strategy that had carried the Chinese Revolution to success. Nevertheless, the democratic claims of guerrilla socialism sounded false under conditions where policy no longer responded to guerrilla dependence on the people, but was rather utilized by those in power to manipulate the population in accordance with organizational prerogatives. Without such a democratic impulse, guerrilla socialism easily degenerated into a militaristic conception of revolution where tactical necessity (a revolutionary pragmatism that recognized no end beyond itself) took precedence over the goals and purposes of revolution. Revolution, as war, was made into an end in itself.

Lin died in a plane crash while trying to escape from China following an abortive *coup d'état*. With him was the top leadership of the PLA.

BIBLIOGRAPHY:

A. *Mao Tse-tung and Lin Piao: Post-Revolutionary Writings,* ed. K. Fan (New York: Anchor Books, 1972).

B. Martin Ebon, *Lin Piao* (New York: Stein and Day, 1970).

ARIF DIRLIK

LIU SHAOQI   (1898–1969). Liu Shaoqi was born in Huagongdang, Nandang, in Ningxiang County, Hunan Province, in 1898, the youngest in a family of four boys and two girls. His father was a primary school teacher. He attended local schools through middle school, joined the newly founded Socialist Youth

League in Shanghai, then left for a brief study sojourn in Moscow, where he joined the Chinese Communist Party (CCP). Upon his return he plunged into the organization of urban trade unions, under the auspices of the United Front between the Communist and Nationalist (Kuomintang, or KMT) parties; this activity focused not only on undermining the hegemony of the warlords who controlled most of China at the time but on improving the material livelihood of the workers. When this fragile coalition disintegrated upon Chiang Kai-shek's successful unification of the country in 1926–27, Liu continued his efforts in China's cities clandestinely, as the KMT sought to throttle Communist organizational activities. The Japanese invasion of China proper in 1936, however, forced the CCP and KMT into a reluctant second united front, and Liu Shaoqi became the leading organizer of underground Communist base areas behind Japanese lines, where he succeeded in promoting a major expansion of Communist influence in some of the most populous and economically advanced regions of China before Japan was finally forced to capitulate in the summer of 1945. Thus when the second united front dissolved shortly after V-J day, the CCP was in a much stronger strategic position vis-à-vis the rival KMT than when the first united front had collapsed. As a reward for his organizational achievements (and for his political support for Mao Zedong's* accession to power over Moscow-trained intraparty rivals), Liu became second in command and Mao's heir apparent in the post-Liberation regime. A rift however soon developed between these ideologues concerned primarily with sustaining revolutionary momentum and the organization specialists intent upon consolidating previous advances and facilitating rapid economic growth, placing Mao and his heir apparent on opposing sides. Thus Mao seized the opportunity of the chaotic Cultural Revolution (1966–76) to blame Liu for "revisionist" deviations from long-term Communist ideological objectives: Liu was criticized and actively opposed frequently and intensively over the next two years, culminating in his purge from all leadership positions and from the CCP itself at the Twelfth Plenum of the Eighth Central Committee in October 1968. This exemplary disgrace no doubt contributed to his rapid physical decline, and Liu died in Kaifeng, Henan, on 12 November 1969, too soon to witness the rehabilitation of his associates or policies that would follow Mao's own death in 1976. Liu's posthumous rehabilitation in the spring of 1980 in effect placed the last nail in the casket of the Cultural Revolution and ensured the survival of his political legacy.

Because he has been the object of intense and recurrent controversy, any attempt to arrive at a reasonably objective assessment of Liu Shaoqi's contribution to Marxism is confronted by unusual methodological difficulties. In the pre-Cultural Revolution period, he was generally regarded as a gray and faceless bureaucrat, but few suspected policy differences between him and Mao. During the Cultural Revolution, he became the archetype of Maoist revisionism, "China's Khrushchev,"* who threatened to suspend further progress toward communism and lead the nation down the "capitalist road." Following his rehabilitation in May 1980 he was identified as the representative of a mixture of ideological orthodoxy and economic pragmatism that incidentally reflected the Deng Xiaoping* regime's priorities.

In the pre-Cultural Revolution period, Liu Shaoqi made significant contributions in the realm of organization theory. During the Zhengfeng (rectification movement) in Yanan (1942–44), he wrote a number of articles defining the functions and procedures of Communist organization that have since become classics, including *How to Be a Good Communist* and *On Inner-Party Struggle*. The former featured a conflation of Marxism-Leninism with indigenous belief systems, which probably coincided nicely at the time with Mao's simultaneous attempt to adapt Marxism to Chinese conditions. From Confucianism Liu borrowed the concept of "self-cultivation" to define the ethical self-realization of the model Party member, attempting to broaden the term from its original idealistic concerns to include revolutionary praxis and social consciousness. His preachments envisioned a synthesis of morality and politics more individualistic, incremental, and procedurally self-conscious than Mao's bold iconoclasm. The second essay conceived of inner-Party struggle as a legitimate and indeed unavoidable reflection of class struggle, but attempted to provide a set of rules for the proper conduct of such struggle so that it might result in a consensual solution of problems rather than in heated and acrimonious controversies. These rules provided a theoretical basis and organizational forum for limited political pluralism within the Party, and their adoption helped to facilitate the longest uninterrupted period of apparent intra-Party consensus in its history.

During the Chinese Cultural Revolution, Liu Shaoqi was defined as the touchstone of Maoist revisionism, identified with the economic and political experiments being pursued at the time in Eastern Europe and the Soviet Union. There were four tenets of "revisionism." First, following the redistribution of property in the postrevolutionary period, class struggle dies out, as classes can no longer be defined by their relationship to the means of production. All people, all classes may be treated equally in legal and political terms, depending on how well they cooperate in achieving the regime's current policy objectives. Second, socialism is not merely a brief transition period en route to communism but a stable and semipermanent condition, with its own laws, such as "to each according to his work, from each according to his abilities." The leadership is also a permanent entity that should not be expected to fade away soon, although it may redefine itself as a "whole people's" state and Party rather than a dictatorship of the proletariat. Third, in the progress of socialism toward ever-higher forms of association, the forces of production essentially set the pace for the relations of production: only after the forces of production have fully matured (defined in terms of economic productivity) are further changes in the relations of production or the ideological superstructure objectively possible. Finally, science and technology are defined as components of the forces of production rather than the ideological superstructure. Indeed, the role they will play in further progress toward economic modernization is deemed extremely significant. In terms of policy, this leads to an attempt to co-opt the intelligentsia and to foster a non-repressive ideological "hegemony" in the cultural realm while utilizing the scientific-technological component of the intelligentsia to enhance economic productivity.

The rehabilitation of Liu Shaoqi in the spring of 1980 resulted in a selective synthesis from both pre- and post-1966 versions of his contribution to Chinese Marxism. His theoretical contributions to Communist organization theory have been reaffirmed, in an interpretation of these writings that is if anything somewhat more conservative than the pre-1966 interpretation. Once again acclaimed as classics, *On the Party*, *How to Be a Good Communist*, and *On Inner-Party Struggle* are once again broadly disseminated as part of the attempt to enforce organizational discipline and Communist morality. His theoretical revisions as caricatured in the Cultural Revolution polemics were repudiated on the whole, tacitly accepted however in some particulars. For example, although his loyalty to Mao is reaffirmed, it becomes clear that he did not really understand the purpose of the Cultural Revolution and opposed Mao's plans therefore, and that he had little use for the "personality cult" that contributed to Mao's immense public prestige. The charge that he favored the dying out of class struggle, a possibly nonviolent transition to socialism, the incorporation of science and technology into the productive forces, the primacy of productive forces over production relationships (and the consequent coronation of economic growth as the regnant desideratum in postrevolutionary socialism) are all tacitly admitted, and in some cases theoretically rationalized. On the other hand, it is also tacitly conceded that Liu made too many concessions to China's capitalist classes in the immediate post-Liberation period (for example, in his notorious speeches to the Tianjin business elite, which are conspicuously absent from his *Selected Works*). The selected version of "Liuism" that emerges in its officially legitimated form is of course no longer considered "revisionist" but quite ideologically orthodox, identical with the policy line chosen by the Deng Xiaoping regime.

Who was the "real" Liu Shaoqi? A comparison of the materials released during the successive segments of his career suggests that he was far more orthodox than the ideological renegade criticized during the Cultural Revolution, yet somewhat more pragmatic than the "iron Bolshevik" depicted in the pre-1966 media. Certainly he was a professional revolutionary and not a liberal, and the amount of tolerance he was willing to afford ideological experimentation was much more narrow than the Red Guard polemicists had assumed. He fully supported the violent seizure of power by the CCP and helped to operationalize it, whatever allowance he may have later made in strictly theoretical terms for nonviolent accession to power under other conditions. Although there may have been differences of opinion concerning the relative priority of productive forces and production relationships, he also fully supported and helped to realize the socialization of the means of production after Liberation. In sum, Liu Shaoqi emerges as an orthodox Leninist* in ideological and organizational questions, albeit certainly a quite flexible and adaptive one; on economic questions he was more willing to experiment, although it remains unclear whether these experiments were simply makeshift adaptations to short-term economic exigencies or more theoretically ambitious undertakings that would result in fundamental changes in the Communist developmental program. Always he was intent upon preserving the ideological purity of the Party, however willing he might be to countenance such heterodox innovations as rural free markets, competitive material incentive systems, and Eastern European enterprise organization systems into the economy. There was of course an implicit contradiction between this particular combination of orthodoxy and heterodoxy that never emerged in Liu's lifetime because the whole Liuist paradigm was cut short by the Cultural Revolution. But this contradiction survives in the Deng Xiaoping regime, and whether it can be satisfactorily resolved remains to be seen.

BIBLIOGRAPHY:

A. *Collected Works*, 3 vols. (Hong Kong: Union Research Institute, 1968–69); *Liu Shao-ch'i wen-t'i tzu-liao chuan-chi* (A special collection of materials on Liu Shao-ch'i) (Taipei: Chinese Communist Problems Research Center, 1970); *Liu Shaoqi Xuanji*, vol. 1 (Liu Shaoqi's Selected Works) (Beijing: People's, 1981).

B. Lowell Dittmer, *Liu Shao-ch'i and the Chinese Cultural Revolution* (Berkeley: University of California Press, 1974).

LOWELL DITTMER

LOMBARDO TOLEDANO, VICENTE   (1894–1968). Mexican labor organizer, peace activist, and champion of national political and economic self-determination, Vicente Lombardo Toledano believed that many of the social goals of the Mexican Revolution had been forgotten by the corrupt politicians and property holders who controlled the nation. His career included writing many books, articles, and pamphlets and founding socialist journals. He organized the Popular Party (PP) in 1948, the first political group in Mexico to articulate the theory that the state bureaucracy had lost some of its political autonomy to the middle class, but without damaging Mexico's ruling party, a doctrine abandoned by its successor organization the Popular Socialist Party (1960), which Lombardo headed. He also launched the Confederation of Latin American Workers (CTAL) a leftist trade union organization.

Lombardo believed that social justice could be achieved in Latin America by the unification of intellectual and manual workers and their alliance with international labor. He explained to the workers that the Mexican Revolution did not have a socialist orientation, but was a capitalist movement pervaded by socialist rhetoric. He felt that Mexican nationalism was sincere, but that the nation was controlled by a few profit-seeking natives and foreigners. He believed that land tenure questions, along with foreign economic incursions, were Mexico's greatest problems. In *El problema del indio* (*The Indian Problem*) he noted that originally communal land and subsoil resources belonged to the people and that a current need existed to incorporate the Indians into Mexico's collective farm system. His program for Indians rejected Social Darwinism on the grounds that Mexico's class struggle emanated from colonial dependency, not racial problems. He saw making the Spanish language dominant as injurious to the indigenous cultures and claimed that the Indian's way of life did not have to be destroyed for them to understand how they were being exploited, that they could comprehend how capitalism affected them by eliminating their ignorance, not their culture.

In debates with Mexican philosopher Antonio Caso, Lombardo demonstrated scientifically how idealists took sanctuary in religion and metaphysics. He contended that man could bridge the gap between the organic and inorganic worlds, and thought of the unity of time, space, and matter as a mystery that science could solve. To him, a reciprocal relationship existed between man's material and spiritual needs, and meeting one would in turn benefit the other.

BIBLIOGRAPHY:

A. *Escritos filosóficos* (Mexico City: México Nuevo, 1937); *La batalla de las ideas en nuestra tiempo* (Mexico City: UNAM, 1937); with Antonio Caso, *Idealismo vs. materialismo dialéctico* (Mexico City: Universidad Obrera de México, 1963); *El problema del indio* (Mexico City: Sep Setentas, 1973).

B. Robert P. Milton, *Mexican Marxist: Vicente Lombardo Toledano* (Chapel Hill: University of North Carolina Press, 1966).

SHELDON B. LISS

LORA, GUILLERMO (b. 1922). A figurehead of postwar Bolivian Trotskyism,* Guillermo Lora is one of the few exponents of this current to have exercised a consistent and critical influence on the politics of his country. As the principal author of the Thesis of Pulacayo (1946), he succeeded in gaining the backing of the powerful miners' union for what was in effect a translation of the Fourth International's Translation Program to Bolivian conditions. The following year he became leader of the miners' representatives in congress, seven revolutionaries who attempted with some success to emulate the Bolsheviks' example of parliamentary intervention. However, Lora's party, the Partido Obrero Revolucionario (POR), failed to match its ideological influence with a strong organizational presence in the working class and was overtaken by the nationalist Movimiento Nacional Revolucionario (MNR), which finally took command of the 1952 Revolution, although Lora played a key role in maintaining the early leftward impetus of the popular movement. Lora's study of the MNR regime marked a refinement in his work and established him as a major political writer with its powerful critique of populism and reformism.

His consistent rejection of the popular front, the guerrilla foco, and nationalism recouped support for the POR in the 1960s, making it one of the strongest Trotskyist forces in the world. Its central role in the 1971 Asamblea Popular indicated a growing constituency for Lora's concept of tactical anti-imperialist fronts and the notion that oppressed nations can only be liberated under the leadership of the proletariat. Although ostracized by the various currents of the Fourth International, Lora remains a force in Bolivian politics and has sustained a remarkable output of political analysis in addition to his very detailed and sensitive history of the working class.

BIBLIOGRAPHY:
    A. *Tesis de Pulacayo* (La Paz: Masas, 1978); *La revolución bolivana* (La Paz: Difusión, 1964); *Formación de la clase obrera*, 6 vols. (La Paz: Masas, 1966–80); *Contribución a la historia política*, 2 vols. (La Paz: Ediciones ISLA, 1979).

JAMES DUNKERLEY

LUNACHARSKY, ANATOLI V.   (1875–1933). Lunacharsky was born in 1875 in Poltava, the son of a Russian civil servant. Familiar with Marxist thought since fifteen, Lunacharsky began his university studies in the 1890s in Zurich, where he became acquainted with Georgii Plekhanov,* the best known of the Russian Marxists living abroad. In 1899, Lunacharsky returned to Moscow in the company of Lenin's* sister, joining a Marxist circle and being arrested shortly thereafter. Following his release, Lunacharsky wrote for several Marxist journals both in Kiev and in Western Europe, soon coming under the influence of the Russian Marxist philosopher Alexander Bogdanov (A. Malinovsky) and joining a movement of radical philosophers known as "God-builders" due to their glorification of the proletariat and their efforts to harness the traditional spirituality of the Russian intelligentsia to the coming revolution. Vacillating between the Russian Bolsheviks and Mensheviks in the period after the 1903 party congress, Lunacharsky adopted an "internationalist" position upon the outbreak of the war and became coeditor along with Trotsky* of the Paris-based, Russian journal *Our Word*. Following the spring 1917 Russian Revolution, Lunacharsky adopted a Bolshevik stance and attempted to convince his friends to accept Lenin's position. After the successful Bolshevik uprising in the fall of 1917, Lunacharsky was appointed the first Soviet Minister of Education. In 1933, following the consolidation of Stalin's* leadership within the party, Lunacharsky was appointed ambassador to Spain, dying in Paris on his way to his new assignment.

BIBLIOGRAPHY:
    A. *On Literature and Art* (Moscow: Progress, 1973).
    B. Sheila Fitzpatrick, *The Commissariat of Enlightenment, Soviet Organization of Education and the Arts under Lunacharsky, October 1917–1921* (Cambridge: Cambridge University Press, 1970).

MICHAEL M. BOLL

LUXEMBURG, ROSA   (1870–1919). Rosa Luxemburg was born in 1870 in the small Polish town of Zamosc near the Russian border into an assimilated Jewish merchant family. She was the victim of a childhood hip ailment, which left her body frail and twisted and made her limp noticeably. From the beginning, Luxemburg exhibited an unquenchable thirst for knowledge and culture of all kinds. She drew, painted, wrote poetry, studied anthropology, history, botany, and geology, and read voluminously. At sixteen she graduated at the top of her class from the girls' gymnasium in Warsaw and three years later fled (for the first and only time in her life) to Switzerland to avoid arrest for her rebellious demeanor and activities. She earned two doctorates from the University of Zurich, one in law, the other in philosophy, and worked with Russian exiles such as Georgii Plekhanov,* Paul Axelrod, and Lenin.* In Switzerland she also met and began a life-long relationship with a fellow Polish exile and radical, Leo Jogiches. Luxemburg traveled to France and then Germany, where she opportunistically married the German Gustav Luebeck in order to escape her designation as a foreigner. She used her married name, "Frau Rosa Luebeck," only when required to legitimize her political activities. This arrangement apparently satisfied Herr Luebeck as well. A noted writer for theoretical and popular journals in Germany, she rose quickly in the German Communist Party. She contributed to the Party's theoretical organ, *Neue Zeit*, and later became assistant to its founder and editor Karl Kautsky.* She became editor of several radical provincial dailies and of the Party's daily paper, *Vorwärts*, and became a teacher of Marxian economics at the Central Party Training School. From 1905 until her death in 1919 Luxemburg was a leader of the extreme left wing of the German Marxian movement. Notable for her courageous unwillingness to flee public authorities in order to avoid prison terms, Luxemburg steadfastly opposed Germany's entrance into World War I and later, during the Spartacus uprising in Germany, the centralizing tendencies of the German Communist movement. Outvoted by her Party, Luxemburg hesitantly supported a doomed "putsch," which had neither the arms nor popular support required for success. She refused to leave Germany, hid for two years while reconstructing the Party, and was finally seized and arrested with Karl Liebknecht and Wilhelm Pieck. She and Liebknecht were brutally murdered by Prussian officers while being taken to prison.

Luxemburg was primarily a strategist and political economist, not a theoretician. Her tactical influence on the European working-class movement was enormous, and certainly no reasonable observer can deny the magnitude of her personal courage and commitment to proletarian democracy. *Die krise der Sozialdemokratie* (1915), commonly known as the *Junius Pamphlet*, became an ideological signpost for the Spartacus League and, through the league, the future German Communist Party (KPD). *Die russische Revolution* (1922) graphically presented the outrage that democratic socialists experienced as Leninism turned dictatorial. The ensuing condemnation and rejection by Lenin, more than any other single factor, doomed Luxemburg to a secondary position in the litany of Marxism.

Capitalism, described in *Die Akkumulation des kapitals* (1913), can survive only as long as it has noncapitalist markets—internal and external—to support it. It ineluctably breeds the accumulation of surplus value and the continual increase in constant capital (that is, the reproductive apparatus). Surplus value, however, must be changed into money by selling commodities. For this new markets are continually needed, for workers cannot consume enough to keep up with the incessant drive for accumulation. Capitalism is thus pushed into a frantic search for backward lands and rural economies to assimilate economically. Ironically, this expansion sucks dry the lifeblood by which capitalism survives. When accumulation becomes impossible because new markets can no longer be found, then capitalism itself becomes unfeasible. For Luxemburg, imperialism is the last-ditch struggle among capitalists to gain control of untapped markets. It marks the final stage in capitalism's development. *The Accumulation of Capital* defines the precise economic circumstances under which capitalism becomes untenable. Luxemburg condemned Marx's ambiguity on this subject, his vague assertion that capitalism's increasing concentration of capital and worker impoverishment would precipitate a revolution. Hers is, therefore, a scientific elucidation and verification of Marx's economic theories. *The Accumulation of Capital* proved, at least to its author, that capitalism will self-destruct because of inherent material processes. The inexorable tendency toward compound accumulation means that capitalism reflects impersonal matter, independent of human intention. This work established Luxemburg's materialist credentials. Her Marxism in 1913 was deeply rooted in the epistemology of Friedrich Engels* and Kautsky. As a result she firmly, some might say inflexibly, defended the orthodox condemnation of reformism and nationalism, holding both to be reactionary and unjustifiable in any circumstance.

There is, however, another side to Rosa Luxemburg, one that dominated the later years and is effectively expressed in *The Russian Revolution* (1922) and *Leninism or Marxism?* (1924). Although revolution is necessary and inevitable, it actually occurs only when the prediction itself becomes part of history, that is, when workers self-consciously realize it. Luxemburg maintained that revolutionary theory had already been promulgated by Marx,* Engels, and the others. What was needed now was proletarian revolutionary consciousness, which occurs spontaneously, without coordination or prior direction. A revolutionary party is unable either to launch or to prevent revolution because it cannot control human cognition. It must cooperate with workers, for they are the working-class movement. The Leninist party emasculated this group by depriving them of responsibility and initiative. Revolutionary tactics fall meaninglessly on deaf ears when formulated by this kind of insulated party bureaucracy.

Luxemburg was convinced after examining the Russian Revolution of 1905 and other workers' uprisings that mass strikes are the most useful form of revolutionary action. They are spontaneous, uncoordinated, leaderless outbreaks, not controlled by parties. Revolutionary organization is a product of spontaneous action, not its source, so in the course of its struggle workers will spontaneously unite and form needed organizations and institutions. Through such actions, workers realize their objective and collective interests and proceed to a full-scale revolution. The Party's role is to help cultivate a collective revolutionary consciousness. If successful, it becomes superfluous, and workers complete their project as independent, free, unguided actors. A Communist Party, therefore, should consist only of active workers who easily slip back into battlefront positions. They must transform scientific theory into revolutionary action by encouraging spontaneous worker strikes. Theory and action blend in the thoughts and actions of workers spontaneously realizing the truth.

The Bolsheviks correctly seized power in Russia but were misusing it by casting, from above, a uniform revolutionary consciousness. By destroying democratic institutions in Russia, Lenin and Trotsky* eliminated the only means by which workers could act collectively to support their revolution. Lenin did not understand that socialism lives not by administrative fiat but in workers themselves, through free self-expression. Luxemburg believed that workers control their revolution only in circumstances of unlimited democracy, which includes basic liberal freedoms of election, speech, public opinion, press, association, artistic expression, and so on. Although a Leninist-type dictatorship of the proletariat is justifiable under adverse conditions as a temporary means of survival, its success is measured by how quickly it dissolves into a workers' democracy. By this criterion, bolshevism was a dismal failure.

Luxemburg's mature writings indicate that she was aware of the theoretical links between materialism and Bolshevik tyranny. Her pamphleteering, however, never surpassed livid critique, and her assertions regarding revolutionary spontaneity are philosophically unsupportable. She was driven, in other words, to the untenable position of defending materialist orthodoxy while denying the one institution (the Leninist party) charged with realizing it. She believed in both the materialist predetermination of history and the essentiality of working-class spontaneity. Epistemologically, this is inconsistent and unconvincing. However, in terms of the historical reemergence of Hegelian Marxism, Luxemburg perceived materialism's inability to explain worker oppression effectively and mobilize working-class support. Her critique of bolshevism lifts subjectivity above material process. Workers possess, Luxemburg implied, an innate, collective essence that must and will be realized consciously before the revolution can succeed. This spiritual renewal is generated by spontaneous strikes, unplanned collective activities that galvanize oppressed workers into authentic consciousness and assure democratic working-class institutions. Although material conditions must be ripe for such a transition to occur, Luxemburg suggested that workers consciously experience a transcendent historical truth that simultaneously manifests practical action. Luxemburg's implicit Hegelianism foreshadows the more sophisticated work of George Lukács,† Karl Korsch,† and Antonio Gramsci.†

BIBLIOGRAPHY:

A. *The Accumulation of Capital* (New York: Modern Reader Paperbacks, 1968); *Selected Writings*, ed. Dick Howard (New York: Monthly Review Press, 1971); *The Russian Revolution* and *Leninism or Marxism?* (Ann Arbor: University of Michigan Press, 1976).

B. J. P. Nettl, *Rosa Luxemburg* (Oxford: Oxford University Press, 1966); Paul Frölich, *Rosa Luxemburg: Her Life and Work* (New York: Howard Fertig, 1970); Lelio Basso, *Rosa Luxemburg* (New York: Praeger, 1975).

ROBERT A. GORMAN

M

MACLEAN, JOHN (1879–1923). John Maclean was born on 24 August 1879 in Pollockshaws, near Glasgow. He died in his beloved Glasgow on 30 November 1923. He was the son of Daniel Maclean, a potter, and Anne Maclean (née MacPhee). His family were of highland origin. Victims of the infamous Highland Clearances in the 1840s, they ended up as manual workers in the industrial lowlands of Scotland. Described as "a Scot of Scots," John Maclean had to fend for himself at an early age. Daniel Maclean died in 1888, when John, the second youngest of seven children, was only eight years old. As a result of the death of her husband at an early age, Anne Maclean was compelled to return to her original occupation as a weaver.

Anne Maclean had inherited the traditional Scottish working-class passion for education. Although she wanted John to become a Presbyterian minister and sent him to a Presbyterian Teachers' Training College in Glasgow, it was not to be. While training as a teacher at the Presbyterian Teachers' Training College, he was converted to Marxian socialism. At the same time, he attended the University of Glasgow, where he studied political economy and Latin. Graduating with the degree of M.A. in 1903, he subsequently sought to raise the educational and intellectual level of the activists in the labor movement.

An outstanding socialist internationalist, John Maclean fought for a Scottish Parliament and proportional representation some years before World War I. From the commencement of his career as a socialist in the west of Scotland in 1903, after the dissident elements in the Social Democratic Federation in Scotland had broken away to form the DeLeonite* Socialist Labour Party, he devoted most of his energy to the task of educating Scottish working women and men in the principles of Marxian socialism. Although the stimulus of the momentous events engendered by the war induced Maclean to sharpen his position on the Scottish national question, it was already foreshadowed in his agitational and educational work before the outbreak of the war.

World War I propelled John Maclean into national and international prominence. The "Red Clydeside" and John Maclean became synonymous. Appointed by Lenin* as the Bolshevik consul in Glasgow in 1918, Maclean soon became an uncompromising champion of a Scottish Socialist Republic, the Russian Revolution, and Irish independence. Although he always attached great importance to socialist education and developing a socialist counterculture, he never wavered in his support of agitations for socialism from below rather than from above. A socialist educator of international stature, he also regarded the land question as one of the major problems confronting socialists in Scotland.

The major intellectual source in shaping John Maclean's agitation for real (or "participatory") democracy and Irish independence was Sylvia Pankhurst's weekly newspaper, the *Workers' Dreadnought*. In articles denouncing British imperialism in Ireland and Africa, Herman Gorter,† the Dutch socialist, and Claude McKay, the West Indian poet and novelist, contributed articles to the *Workers' Dreadnought* during the same years as John Maclean. Both John Maclean and Claude McKay were critical of the racism and chauvinism of the leaders of the British Communist Party. Rather than join the Communist Party, they initially opted to cooperate with the internationalist opposition grouped around Sylvia Pankhurst.

John Maclean did not produce any original ideas, except perhaps in relation to the Scottish national question. He was a teacher of basic socialist concepts between 1903 and the outbreak of World War I. Thereafter until his death in 1923, he became famous for his practical rather than theoretical work. During the war he became notorious for his antimilitarism and antiwar speeches on street corners throughout Britain as well as within the labor movement. Between the outbreak of the war and his death, he was imprisoned on four separate occasions on various charges, including sedition. From 1917 on he devoted much of his free time to mustering mass support for the Russian Revolution, although very often with skepticism and a critical stance.

John Maclean also agitated for the cause of Irish independence. A friend of James Connolly* before the outbreak of World War I, he was deeply influenced by Connolly's stance in Dublin in the Easter Rebellion of 1916. Although he attracted much more support among the Irish and those of Irish origin in the west of Scotland than among the native Scots, he did have some influence within the Scottish labor movement. Through his pamphlet, *The Irish Tragedy: Scotland's Disgrace*, he sought to break the influence of British imperialism within the Scottish labor movement.

An uncompromising opponent of bourgeois nationalism, he was very critical of the authoritarian nature of the Scottish educational system. Although he failed to produce a thorough critique of traditional educational methods, he taught Marxian economics to working women and men in evening classes financed by the authorities before World War I. Perhaps his most important—and certainly his most concrete—practical achievement was the foundation of the Scottish Labour College in Glasgow in 1916. The main purpose of the Scottish Labour College was to provide full-time trade union students with an education in socialist history and theory.

Despite his failure to produce an original contribution to socialist theory, John

Maclean became a folk hero soon after his death. Scottish poets and novelists have constantly kept his memory and example of self-sacrifice alive. Although he was said to lack humor, he made and kept many friends as a result of his warmth, compassion, and hatred of injustice.

BIBLIOGRAPHY:

A. *The Greenock Jungle* (Glasgow: John Maclean, 1907); *Co-operation and the Rise in Prices* (Glasgow: John Maclean, 1911); *The War After the War* (Glasgow: Scottish Labour College, 1918); *Sack Dalrymple and Stevenson: Let Labour Revenge Bloody Friday* (Glasgow: John Maclean, 1919); *The Irish Tragedy: Scotland's Disgrace* (Glasgow: John Maclean, 1920); *The Coming War with America* (Glasgow: BSP Scottish District Council, 1920); *The Glasgow Police Murder Hush Up* (Glasgow: John Maclean, 1920); *In the Rapids of Revolution* (London: Allison & Busby, 1978).

JAMES YOUNG

MAGDOFF, HARRY   (n.a.). Harry Magdoff has been coeditor of the independent socialist journal *Monthly Review* since 1969. He received a B.A. in economics from New York University. During the 1930s, Magdoff supervised statistical productivity studies for the Works Progress Administration National Research Project on Reemployment Opportunities and Technical Development. During this government service he designed the method of measuring production and productivity still used by the Department of Labor. During World War II, Magdoff was chief of the Civilian Requirements Division of the National Defense Advisory Commission. He was in charge of planning and controls for the metalworking machinery industries during the war. He also served as head of the Current Business Analysis Division in the Department of Commerce and as a special assistant to the Secretary of Commerce. Along with writing and editing for *Monthly Review* and the Monthly Review Press, he has lectured at universities around the world.

Magdoff's writings on the history, theory, and practice of imperialism have been a major contribution to Marxist scholarship. His two leading works, *The Age of Imperialism* (1969), and *Imperialism: From the Colonial Age to the Present* (1978), have been influential in bringing Marxist-Leninist renditions of imperialism to newer audiences and have contributed to the interpretation of the relevance of those analyses of imperialism to the post–World War II period.

The first volume, *The Age of Imperialism*, appeared at a time, 1969, when radical scholars and anti-Vietnam War activists were searching for a way to understand U.S. foreign policy, particularly toward the Third World. This volume argued that there was a connection between monopoly capitalism and imperialism. Rather than relying on one or another variable in the Leninist* equation to explain the drive toward expansion by the major imperialist powers, Magdoff argues that markets, capital export, raw materials acquisition, and cheap labor all bear on the behavior of core capitalist states. These "principal levers," which also include political and military considerations, are "associated with the new stage of monopoly and the essential ways monopoly operates to achieve, wherever and whenever feasible, domination and control over sources of supply and over markets (pp. 39–40).'' The bulk of the volume describes U.S. imperialism and the significance of its pattern of foreign investments, its aid and trade, and the international monetary system that it created and from which it benefits. The identification of U.S. expansionism within a broader historical development of monopoly capital served as a stimulus for scholars and activists to understand policies like the Vietnam War in new and more systemic ways.

Imperialism: From the Colonial Age to the Present, published almost ten years later (1978), is a collection of essays written over time that address the issues raised by the Leninist theory of imperialism since the publication of Magdoff's first book. In this volume, Magdoff argues that imperialism must be understood in its historical complexity. He challenges Marxists who too readily accept one or another element of Lenin's ideas as the root cause of capitalist expansion overseas: underconsumption, the falling rate of profit, resource scarcities, etc. His own view is that each of these elements may be particularly relevant at given points in time for given capitalist powers but that ultimately all of these variables are interconnected features of the general logic to expand in monopoly capitalism. In this light, multinational corporations are the major carriers of economic expansion in the modern world. They guide, nurture, and are nurtured by the nation-states from which they come. Consequently, the new globalism of the multinational corporations does not presage an integration of these giant economic actors. Rather, the protection they get from the state reinforces the competition and conflict that occurs between them through their states. Magdoff, in this volume, criticizes bourgeois scholars who have written ''imperialism''and ''exploitation'' out of scholarly discourse because these are emotional and not scientific terms. He argues to the contrary that the theories from which they come provide the best tools to understand the modern global system. Magdoff also criticizes Marxist scholars who address the question as to whether imperialism is necessary to capitalism and what Lenin wrote about this subject. To Magdoff, Marxists must analyze what happened, not what logically might have been. The task of Marxist scholarship is to develop theoretical insights that make history rational to a contemporary understanding.

As editor of *Monthly Review*, Magdoff has written many articles over the years addressing such issues as the international political economy, the international financial system, inflation and unemployment in advanced capitalist countries, and the nature of productivity under capitalism. Ultimately, Magdoff's major contribution rests on his interpretation and application of the Marxist-Leninist theory of imperialism to the contemporary era.

BIBLIOGRAPHY:

A. *The Age of Imperialism: The Economics of U.S. Foreign Policy* (New York: Monthly Review, 1969); with Paul M. Sweezy, *The End of Prosperity: The American Economy in the 1970s* (New York: Monthly Review, 1978); *Imperialism: From the Colonial Age to the Present* (New York: Monthly Review, 1978); with Paul M. Sweezy, *The Deepening Crisis of U.S. Capitalism* (New York: Monthly Review, 1982).

HARRY TARG

MALDONADO-DENIS, MANUEL   (b. 1933). Born in Santurce, Puerto Rico in 1933 Manuel Maldonado-Denis received a B.A. from the Universidad de Puerto Rico (UPR) and his M.A. and Ph.D. in political science from the University of Chicago. Maldonado-Denis has been teaching political science at the UPR, Rio Piedras, since 1959. He has been an active supporter of Puerto Rican independence and has worked with the Partido Socialista Puertorriqueño. In the late 1960s and early 1970s Maldonado-Denis was involved in anti-ROTC and antimilitary activity, which ultimately resulted in riots, on the UPR campus.

Maldonado-Denis has been a prolific scholar. His best-known book is *Puerto Rico*, originally published in Spanish in 1969, which provided a historical narrative of Puerto Rico's long colonial past from a dependency–Marxist perspective. This was presented as a popular rather than a strictly scholarly work, although it was carefully researched and remains a valuable critical introduction to understanding Puerto Rico. His theoretical perspective has evolved toward a more orthodox Marxist position as revealed in his book on emigration, which analyzes the massive migration of Puerto Ricans using Marx's* concepts of various fractions of the reserve army of labor. His major contribution has been in reinterpreting and rediscovering aspects of Puerto Rico's past and his exemplary scholarly methods.

BIBLIOGRAPHY:

A. *Puerto Rico: Mito y realidad* (Barcelona: Peninsula, 1969); *Puerto Rico: A Socio-Historic Interpretation* (New York: Random House, 1972); *The Emigration Dialectic: Puerto Rico and the USA* (New York: International, 1980).

JAMES DIETZ

MANDEL, ERNEST   (b. 1923). Born in Belgium in 1923, Ernest Mandel joined the Belgian affiliate of the Fourth International (FI, founded by Trotsky* in 1938) when he was seventeen and has been a member of the Central Committee of this organization since 1941. He was active in the anti-Nazi resistance and was arrested and sent to a German prison camp in 1944. The Second World Congress of the FI, held after the war, elected him to a leadership position, which he has since maintained. During the 1950s and 1960s, when the Trotskyists operated within the Belgian Socialist Party, Mandel worked in the Economic Studies Commission of the Belgian Trade Union Federation, writing a report on economic concentration. He was expelled from the Socialist Party for opposing its coalition with the Christian Socialists and its acceptance of antistrike legislation. Mandel has been barred at various times from entering the United States, France, Switzerland, and Germany, where he nonetheless earned a doctorate in political economy at the Free University of Berlin. In 1978 he delivered the Alfred Marshall Lectures at Cambridge University.

In addition to his prolific activity as an editor and writer for the Trotskyist and other leftist press, Mandel has published several volumes of political essays. By and large he has remained faithful to classic Trotskyist politics, calling (in Europe at least) for a united front of the FI with the Socialist and Communist parties in the formation of a "bourgeois workers' government," with an eye to its eventual replacement, once the revolutionary insufficiency of the latter parties is seen by the masses, by a government of "transition to socialism" by the FI alone. The socialism to be established is conceived of as a matter of a nationalized economy with workers' control operating to the "technologically feasible" extent. In this the Bolshevik Revolution in Russia has shown the way, although the Stalinist*-bureaucratic distortions of the socialism established by Lenin* and Trotsky may require a political revolution to establish a workers' government answering to the socialist economy already in place.

Outside of Trotskyist circles, Mandel's main impact has been as an economic writer. He is the author of books on the economic competition between Europe and America and on capitalism's recent difficulties: his little *Introduction to Marxist Economics* is said to have sold several hundred thousand copies. His main contributions have been the two-volume *Marxist Economic Theory* (1962) and the massive *Late Capitalism* (1975). The former aims to show that it is possible, on the basis of the scientific data of contemporary science, to reconstitute the whole economic system of Karl Marx.* It thus consists, on the one hand, of the compilation of an enormous mass of data and descriptive material bearing on the nature and history of capitalism and, on the other, of an attempt to integrate parts of bourgeois economics along with elements of the many conflicting Marxist schools into one comprehensive theory. The book includes a consideration of the Soviet economy as exemplifying the "transition to socialism," marred though it is by Stalinist distortions.

Late Capitalism more particularly strives to explain the contemporary history of capitalism by its immanent laws of motion. "Late capitalism" is seen as characterized by the dominance of the multinational firm and by the involvement of the state in the national and international economy. Despite these modifications, however, capitalism remains under the sway of the crisis tendency diagnosed by Marx. As in the earlier book, Mandel's explanation of this tendency involves the combination of a number of seemingly incompatible theories in a "multifaceted" approach, although at base Mandel follows Roman Rosdolsky in holding to a form of underconsumption theory. A novelty is Mandel's attempt to integrate his eclectic conception into a version of the Kondratiev "long wave" theory of fifty-year cycles of upturns and downturns: this is used, finally, to explain both the long period of prosperity capitalism enjoyed after the last world war and its recent economic misfortunes.

BIBLIOGRAPHY:

A. *Marxist Economic Theory* (London: Merlin, 1962); *Europe Versus America* (London: New Left Books, 1970); *Late Capitalism* (London: New Left Books, 1975); *The Second Slump* (London: New Left Books, 1978); *From Stalinism to Eurocommunism* (London: New Left Books, 1979); *Revolutionary Marxism Today* (London: New Left Books, 1979); *Long Waves of Capitalist Development* (Cambridge: Cambridge University Press, 1980).

B. Paul Mattick, "Review Essay on *Marxist Economic Theory*,"*Radical America*, 3, no. 4 (1969), pp. 12–19; Paul Mattick, *Economic Crisis and Crisis Theory* (White Plains, N.Y.: M. E. Sharpe, 1981).

PAUL MATTICK, JR.

MAO ZEDONG   (1893–1976). Mao Zedong was born into a peasant family in Hunan in 1893. He participated in the First Congress of the Communist Party of China in 1921 and played an important role in the revolutionary movement of the 1920s. His rise to power came after the Communist revolution was driven to the countryside after 1927. In 1935, he became the leader of the Party and retained that position until his death in 1976. Although his role in the revolution has been downgraded by his successors, he is recognized to this day as the foremost political and theoretical leader of the Party during the years of revolution.

Mao is easily the most original and, therefore, the most controversial figure among China's Marxists. Mao did not devise the strategy of the Chinese Revolution single-handedly, as some of his more enthusiastic followers have claimed on occasion. Nevertheless, it has been generally accepted that he did more than anyone else to articulate the general principles that guided revolutionary strategy.

Mao's Marxism stands today as a classic articulation of Third World Marxism, a product of protracted struggle for national liberation from imperialist domination. After 1945, Mao was credited in Chinese Communist ideology with having "Sinified" Marxist theory, in other words, having integrated the "universal" truths of theory with the concrete practice of the Chinese Revolution. This synthesis of theory with the specific conditions of different societies was, in Chinese eyes, to provide a model for societies in circumstances similar to that of China. As Lu Dingyi remarked in 1951, the Chinese Revolution was a prototype of revolutions in colonial and semicolonial countries. By the time of the Cultural Revolution in the 1960s, Mao was credited with having advanced Marxism-Leninism to "a new stage." In 1966, Lin Biao* hailed Mao's thought as Marxism-Leninism in the era in which imperialism is heading for total collapse and socialism toward worldwide victory.

Whether or not we accept these claims in their entirety, Mao's significance as a Third World Marxist is indisputable. Mao's Marxism provides a cogent illustration of the theoretical developments within Marxism in response to the challenges of revolution in the Third World. These developments are of significance for Marxism in general. The globalization of Marxism in the twentieth century has raised questions concerning the central assumptions of Marxist revolutionary theory, especially questions of who makes revolutions and why. Mao's thinking confronted these questions with a directness that has few parallels.

Mao's Marxism was practice-oriented. Marxism provided Mao with a political test; and like a good student, he used theory critically, with a flexibility that took account of the need to bridge the gap between social reality and the abstractions of theory. At its most theoretical, Mao's Marxism abstracts general principles from the experience of the Chinese Revolution, rather than pursue theoretical questions in the abstract. His writings serve as a guide to the problems Marxist revolutionaries in China faced in pursuing their revolutionary cause in an environment that was socially and culturally foreign to the original premises of theory. The confrontation was to transform both Chinese society and Marxist theory. "Sinification" does suggest the parochialization of the Marxist revolutionary idea. At the same time, its underlying assumptions present a challenge to theory to demonstrate its universality by providing explanations to the particular circumstances of different societies.

The first problem was the reconciliation of Marxist to Chinese goals. Mao viewed Marxism from the perspective of China's revolution for national liberation from foreign hegemony. Marxism provided theoretical guidelines to resolve the twin problems of how to achieve national liberation and how to rebuild China following liberation. The idea that Marxism should serve national ends was as old as the history of Chinese Marxism (see Li Dazhao*). What Mao brought to this idea was a conviction that the language of Marxism must be rephrased in the idiom of the Chinese Revolution if Marxism was to serve as an effective guide to that revolution. It was not coincidental that Mao's views of Marxism, and of its relevance to the Chinese Revolution, were articulated most explicitly during the years of Chinese resistance to Japan, which was the high point of China's national crisis. Mao himself proved to be very adept at the task of translating Marxism into a Chinese idiom. His analysis of the Chinese Revolution was cast in terms of basic Marxist categories of social and political analysis; his presentation of those categories, however, was exclusively in the terms of Chinese historical experience, in particular the experience of revolutionary struggle. Mao's views on a "nationalized" Marxism were most clearly expressed in his idea of "new democracy," which served as guide to the political strategy that brought the Communists to power in 1949. New democracy stressed class alliance under Communist leadership over class struggle, advocated a mixed economy that would secure rapid national economic development under state leadership, and urged the creation of a revolutionary but national culture.

It is evident that for some among Chinese Marxists, Marxism has been instrumental in achieving national ends. Mao himself stopped short of instrumentalizing Marxism. The idea of new democracy to Mao did not imply abandonment of the social goals of Marxism, but was intended as a stage in the progress toward socialism. Mao believed that socialism must take its own autonomous course for China, but he also believed that Chinese society must be transformed in accordance with Marxist goals. Mao's idea of China was empirical: the Chinese nation was not a given but an entity to be created in the course of struggle. Marxism would be present at the creation.

The exigencies of protracted guerrilla warfare in an agrarian setting reinforced Mao's inclination to modify theory as required by specific circumstances. Guerrilla warfare reinforced the lesson that Mao, and others among Chinese Communists, had learned from Lenin*: that class and class consciousness were not spontaneous products of "objective" economic relationships, which were too complex to yield a one-dimensional consciousness, but would be produced in the process of revolutionary struggle. Guerrilla struggle, more than any other kind of revolutionary struggle, presupposed that revolutions are made not by abstract historical forces but by revolutionaries. Revolution, Mao frequently reminded his audiences, required a fine-tuned analysis of the dialectic between the goals set by abstract analysis and the empirical conditions of revolution. Mao believed, with Lenin, that "objective" class consciousness was a potential that could be realized only in the course of a total social struggle that was at once economic, political, and cultural. On the other hand, the simple demands of guerrilla survival, as well as the populist links forged between revolutionaries and the people in the course of the struggle, required that revolutionaries take account of the complexities of everyday social relations and consciousness, complexities that remained invisible as long as social existence was viewed through abstract theoretical categories. Mao perceived society as a structure in constant flux under the force of universal and multifaceted contradictions. Successful revolutionary activity required thorough understanding both of long-term historical trends *and* of the conjuncture of contradictions at any particular time. Only then could revolutionaries adjust their abstract goals to the concrete demands of everyday life without losing sight of their ultimate goals. The organizational expresssion of this "guerrilla socialism" was the "mass line," which sought to translate the dialectic between theory and social reality into the relationship between revolutionary goals and popular aspirations.

Guerrilla socialism presented problems of its own. The fundamental problem, which is central to Mao's Marxism, was how to reconcile the goals of revolution with the "objective conditions" of Chinese society. To Mao, theoretical categories were guides to social analysis and transformation, not substitutes for the realities of social existence. Marxism in Mao's hands was converted into a means of policy analysis that was reminiscent in its pragmatism of bourgeois policy analysis. What distinguished this policy analysis from its bourgeois counterparts was its underlying commitment to the revolutionary social goals prescribed by Marxist ideology. Without this faith, revolutionary pragmatism would easily be converted into a positivistic affirmation of the empirical order at hand. Mao's pragmatism escaped this fate because it was guided (even after 1949) by a faith in immanent social transformation, not immanent order. In the hands of some of Mao's followers, especially after 1949, when the immediate goals of revolution had been achieved, the pragmatism Mao had established as a model would take just such a nonrevolutionary course (see Deng Xiaoping*).

Mao, however, glossed over some of the other problems that grew out of the experience of guerrilla socialism. Whatever the claims of the Party to "control the gun," guerrilla socialism implied the militarization of politics, in the sense that guerrilla survival took priority at all times over the political goals of revolution. This enhanced the potential for manipulation of both political principle and the people for contingent needs. The goal of the mass line, ultimately, was not to guarantee democratic participation in politics to the people but to mobilize mass support for the revolutionaries. Although it encouraged Party responsiveness to popular aspirations when the Party needed the population, it could also be used as a means to manipulate the population in service of Party goals. Mao provided no clear resolution to this contradiction, which would surface in Chinese politics with all its tragic implications during the Cultural Revolution.

Finally, Mao's Marxism reveals the theoretical problems created by the fact that socialism in China had to be molded out of a precapitalist agrarian society. Mao was committed to the idea that socialism must undertake the task of developing productive forces not only as a Marxist who believed that socialism presupposed a high level of development of the material forces of production but also as the leader of a national revolution in pursuit of autonomy from imperialist hegemony. That China was a precapitalist society reinforced Marxist notions about the material prerequisites for socialism; the underlying urge of the Chinese Revolution to achieve economic autonomy through rapid economic development coincided with the Marxist urge to secure liberation from capitalism. Nevertheless, the two goals were also in contradiction: the development of the forces of production, so dear to Chinese nationalists of all political orientations, did not necessarily guarantee the socialist development of the relations of production. It is a tribute to Mao's socialist commitments that he refused to distinguish these two goals. Mao did not, as is sometimes claimed, sacrifice the goals of national development to a utopian vision, but he did seek to redefine national development in such a way as to further socialist relations of production. He believed, in the first place, that transformation of the relations of production was itself a means to developing the forces of production, since the one was not absolutely separable from the other—a position that is certainly consistent with the basic assumptions of Marxism even if it is not universally shared by Marxists. Secondly, China's very economic backwardness did create possibilities, in Mao's eyes, that were foreclosed to more advanced capitalist societies: economic backwardness implied the absence of a capitalist structure that might serve as an obstacle to the creation of socialist relations of producton. Indeed, Mao believed that socialism in countries such as China should devise its own course of development rather than follow unthinkingly models of development created by capitalism that give priority to forces over the relations of production. Developmental goals, as well as the need to overcome capitalist ideological hegemony, were incorporated in Mao's thinking in a coherent if uneasy partnership.

How uneasy this partnership was became clear once again after 1949, but especially during the years after 1956, from the Great Leap Forward through the Cultural Revolution, when Chinese backwardness was on occasion portrayed not simply as a source of new possibilities but as *the* point of departure for socialism. In the hands of a Lin Biao, Mao's rejection of urban hegemony over rural society was made into an assertion of the priority of agrarian over urban society as a necessary means for establishing a socialist world.

Unlike many Third World (and Third Worldist) Marxists, Mao appreciated the difficulties posed by the attempt to create a revolutionary language that expressed the mutual incorporation of socialist goals with the particular aspirations of the Chinese Revolution. Mao's view of revolution as an unending dialectic, rather than a break in time, revealed his appreciation that the dialectic between abstract categories and empirical conditions, between the universalistic assumptions of Marxism and the specific disposition of Chinese society, between distant goals and immediate needs, could be sustained only through continued effort on the part of revolutionaries. It is not surprising that the hallmark of Mao's Marxism, one that was dramatically brought forward during the Cultural Revolution, was its stress on conscious revolutionary activity as a means to social transformation.

Mao's preoccupation with consciousness predated his Marxist days. Marxism, with its emphasis on the social constraints on voluntary activity, tamed but did not abolish Mao's belief in the ability of revolutionary will to mold society. Indeed, the exigencies of the Chinese Revolution, with its conflicting aspirations, reinforced Mao's preoccupation with revolutionary consciousness. The need to create a language of revolution, which would be cast in Chinese idiom but derive its grammar from Marxism, created a burden for revolutionary consciousness. It might even be suggested that Mao's sensitivity to contradictions (in his own words, both "antagonistic" and "nonantagonistic; i.e., conflicts between revolutionaries and reactionaries, and within the revolutionary class, respectively) within the revolution was a product of the contradictions that beset his own consciousness as a Marxist Chinese revolutionary. Revolution appeared to Mao not simply as a political activity but as education in its broadest sense, education both for the revolutionary steeped in ideology, who had to translate ideology into everyday practice, and for the people, who had to transcend the limitations of everyday social consciousness through the aid of ideology. Revolutionary transformation, in other words, implied not only social and political transformation but also a cultural transformation that would change the language of politics and, with it, the principle of hegemony in society. Consciousness and conscious activity, as keys to this goal, held a place of primary significance in Mao's thinking: As he said:

But whatever is done has to be done by human beings; protracted war and final victory will not come about without human action. For such action to be effective there must be people who derive ideas, principles, or views from the objective facts, and put forward plans, directives, policies, strategies, and tactics. Ideas, etc. are subjective, while deeds or actions are the subjective translated into the objective, but both represent the dynamic role peculiar to human beings. We term this kind of dynamic role "man's conscious dynamic role." ("On Protracted War," in *Selected Works*, vol. 2, p. 151)

Revolutionary consciousness was to Mao the key to the dialectical resolution of contradictions. In practice, however, the dialectical resolution of contradictions has appeared in the course of the Chinese Revolution as oscillations between contradictory aspirations. As a summation of the experiences of the Chinese Revolution, Mao's Marxism embodied the very contradictions that it set out to resolve. The problems his Marxism presents are a cogent illustration of the problems that revolution in the Third World presents to Marxist theory.

BIBLIOGRAPHY:

A. *Selected Works of Mao Tsetung*, 5 vols. (Beijing: Foreign Language Press, 1965–77).

B. Stuart Schram, *Mao Tse-tung* (Baltimore: Penguin Books, 1967); John B. Starr, *Continuing the Revolution: The Political Thought of Mao* (Princeton: Princeton University Press, 1979); Robert A. Gorman, *Neo-Marxism: The Meanings of Modern Radicalism* (Westport, Conn.: Greenwood Press, 1982).

ARIF DIRLIK

MARIÁTEGUI, JOSÉ CARLOS   (1894–1930). The dean of Latin American Marxists, José Carlos Mariátegui was born in the small southern Peruvian town of Moquegua. The circumstances of the family were so humble that he never attended school beyond the eighth grade and was forced to begin to help to support the family when he was fourteen. Soon becoming one of Lima's best-known newspapermen, he evolved from a fascination with elite culture to a growing interest in working-class movements and socialism. His growing political involvement soon angered the authoritarian Leguía regime and Mariátegui fled to Europe from 1919 to 1923. Drinking in the revolutionary culture of France and Italy, he studied classical Marxist works and closely followed political events in Italy, where he spent three years, married, and was exposed to Antonio Gramsci's† thought. While in Europe he followed events in the Soviet state that Lenin* and the other Bolshevik leaders were consolidating. Returning to Lima, he spent the remaining seven years of his life writing, editing his famous magazine *Amauta*, and engaging in revolutionary organizing to implant socialism in Peru. He was confined to a wheelchair after 1924. Speaking at workers' universities and union meetings to augment his broadly circulated newspaper articles, he began to organize a working-class movement that culminated in the formation of the General Confederation of Peruvian Workers in 1929. He had simultaneously created the conditions that made possible the foundation of the Peruvian Socialist Party in late 1928. Mariátegui served as the first Secretary General of the Marxist-Leninist party and insisted on a high degree of national and tactical autonomy in his relations with the Third International,* as seen in theses he sent to the First Meeting of Latin American Communist Parties in 1929. Police searches, brief imprisonments, and an even greater workload occasioned by rural and peasant organization finally provoked a complete physical relapse that resulted in the Peruvian's death in April 1930.

Mariátegui was both Latin American nationalist and international Marxist. For many years he was the only major Latin American Marxist thinker to adapt Marxist thought successfully to local conditions. He never lost sight of his Peruvian or Latin American/Third World identity and mixed insights gained from radical nationalist and *indigenista* writers who glorified the Incas and Indian culture with those provided by Marx,* Lenin, and Gramsci. Unlike many subsequent orthodox Marxists in Latin America, he flexibly employed Marxist and non-Marxist sources to study carefully the reality of his own nation so as to understand it better and eventually change it. *Seven Interpretive Essays on Peruvian Reality* (1928) is a comprehensive study of Peru that uses insights gained from Marxist theory to analyze multiple aspects of the nation. It employs general concepts (exploitation, economic imperialism, racism, Europeanism, and upperclass elitism) to elucidate Peruvian history, social structure, and culture and draws heavily on statistical data and a new generation of radical pro-Indian writers and artists in Peru and Mexico. Mariátegui was one of the first Latin Americans to employ the concept of dependent development and anticipated the empirically founded radical analysis that has distinguished Latin American social scientists in recent years. His post-1920 writings have been collected in some twenty volumes of *Collected Works*, but with the exception of the *Seven Essays*, have not been translated into English. His less-known political and union writings are found in *Ideología y política* and *Defensa del marxismo* and attest to his creative use of Marxism and Leninism in the national context. Mariátegui's organizational activity is still not well understood, although glimpses can be found in editorials in *Amauta* and *Labor* (his short-lived working-class newspaper) and in as yet unpublished letters found in the Mariátegui family archive. He was one of the first Third World Marxists to understand the full potential of the peasantry for socialist revolution and began Marxist peasant organization in the late 1920s.

BIBLIOGRAPHY:

A. *Obras completas de José Carlos Mariátegui*, 20 vols. (Lima: Biblioteca Amauta, 1959–72); *Defensa del marxismo, polémica revolucionaria* (Lima: Biblioteca Amauta, 1967); *Seven Interpretive Essays on Peruvian Reality* (Austin: University of Texas Press, 1971); *Ideología política* (Lima: Biblioteca Amauta, 1972).

B. Harry E. Vanden, "The Peasants as a Revolutionary Class—An Early View from Peru," *Journal of Inter American Studies and World Affairs*, 20, no. 2 (May 1978), pp. 191–209; Harry E. Vanden, "Marxismo, Comunismo and Other Bibliographic Notes," *Latin American Research Review*, 14, no. 3 (Fall 1979), pp. 61–86; Jesús Chavarría, *José Carlos Mariátegui and the Rise of Modern Peru, 1890–1930* (Albuquerque: University of New Mexico Press, 1979); Aníbal Quijano, *Reencuentro y debate, una introdución á Mariátegui* (Lima: Mosca Azul, 1981).

HARRY E. VANDEN

MARIGHELA, CARLOS (n.a.–1969). Details of Carlos Marighela's early life are not available. In the course of thirty years of militancy in the Brazilian

Communist Party (Partido Communista Brasileiro, PCB), Carlos Marighela rose to membership of its Executive Committee and came to lead the Party in São Paulo, Latin America's leading industrial city. He became critical of the PCB's ineffective peaceful strategy after the 1964 military takeover and soon became a convert to armed struggle. In that year he led a minor assault on an officers' club in São Paulo and was later wounded and arrested, but he managed to escape from a hospital in May. Deeply influenced by the revolutionary appeal that issued from Havana after the Tricontinental Conference in January 1966, Marighela resigned from the Executive Committee of the PCB on 10 December 1966.

When the PCB decided to boycott the Havana conference of the Organization of Latin American Solidarity (OLAS, an attempt to rally genuine revolutionists behind a strategy of armed struggle) in July-August 1967, Marighela broke loose. He attended the conference, supported its resolutions, resigned from the PCB's Central Committee, and broadcast to Brazilians a call to arms over Havana radio. He resigned from the Party upon his return to Brazil, taking with him other São Paulo Communists.

Disagreeing with those Communist dissidents who wanted to create a new party, Marighela stressed instead the urgency of armed activity. His group took the name Action for National Liberation (Ação Libertadora Nacional, ALN) and in February 1968 called for the initiation of urban armed struggle. Before being destroyed by ruthless counterinsurgency forces, the ALN kidnapped ambassadors from the United States and Switzerland in September 1969 and December 1970. Marighela himself was trapped and murdered by death squadron chief Sergio Paranhos Fleury on 4 November 1969. His successor, Joaquim Câmara Ferreira, was killed in October 1970.

Marighela's break with the PCB was partly a reflection of political differences, for he disputed the Party's contention that the bourgeoisie would lead an anti-feudal, anti-imperialist, national, democratic revolution. He accepted the PCB's characterization of the Brazilian revolution but differed in arguing the need for proletarian leadership of it. Moreover, without portraying them as identical, he pointed to the interdependence of anti-imperialist and anticapitalist struggles. Marighela envisaged the Brazilian dictatorship being overthrown by an armed alliance of workers and peasants, backed by sectors of the middle class, and with the revolutionary struggle passing through three phases: a preparatory stage in which the urban guerrilla would seize matériel, train, and build its infrastructure; a rural guerrilla phase in the countryside, which would be the decisive theater of operations; and a final stage during which the rural guerrilla would develop into a people's army and defeat the armed forces of the regime in rural battles.

On the question of organization, Marighela reacted so drastically against PCB bureaucratism that he came close to relying upon spontaneity and at times seemed an advocate of action for action's sake: "Take the initiative, assume the responsibility, do something. It is better to make mistakes doing something, even if it results in death" (quoted in Kohl and Litt, p. 29). He called for the creation of tiny "firing groups" of four to five fighters, in such a way as almost to invite infiltration and court anarchy. Groups and *francs tireurs* were conceded absolute freedom of action as long as they accepted the ALN's general strategic and tactical principles. Leaders, so as to merit the confidence of fighters, were expected to participate in the most dangerous activities.

In Brazil, Marighela's strategic line and example of combat were more influential than his organizational doctrine. Partly because he presented his ideas in the form of a manual, his tactical advice was heeded and translated into various forms of direct revolutionary action by groups in Spanish America, the United States, and Europe. The Brazilian guerrillas failed because a very weak social base left them vulnerable to a ruthless military regime. They emerged at a time when mass movements had been pacified and when the regime was at peak strength. Marighela's followers increased their isolation by rejecting mass activity: only "mass front" work was countenanced by the ALN, and this was to involve armed actions oriented toward the mass movement rather than actual involvement in mass forms of opposition to the regime. The ALN was doomed to fail, for its methods were highly militaristic and aggressive in a period when the requirements of the Brazilian left were defensive. By the end of the 1960s the armed revolutionary groups, having lost the advantage of the "surprise effect," were in the process of being destroyed.

BIBLIOGRAPHY:

A. *For the Liberation of Brazil* (Harmondsworth: Penguin, 1971).

B. João Quartim, *Dictatorship and Armed Struggle in Brazil* (London: New Left Books, 1971); James Kohl and John Litt, *Urban Guerrilla Warfare in Latin America* (Cambridge: MIT Press, 1974).

RICHARD GILLESPIE

MARINELLO, JUAN   (b. 1898). Cuban Juan Marinello initially gained national prominence in 1923 when he joined the Protest of the Thirteen against the corrupt government of Alfredo Zayas. During the 1930s he directed the magazine *Masas*, dedicated to awakening Cubans to their plight as pawns in an international game controlled by foreigners. He predicted that a second world war would occur as a result of competition for international markets. He saw the end of World War II as the start of a new era in U.S. imperialism and realized that wartime conditions had shifted much of Latin America's economic dependence from Europe to the United States, a situation that the latter would try to exploit. After the war he worked to maintain the visibility of Cuba's Communist Party. By 1956, when Fidel Castro* began his battle against the regime of dictator Fulgencio Batista, Marinello headed Cuba's Communist Party. After Castro's victory in 1959, Marinello reconciled the Party with Cuba's revolutionary forces.

Marinello wrote numerous pamphlets on such topics as politics and international economics, but he specialized in literary criticism and the roles of writers in the revolution. He was particularly interested in nineteenth-century Cuban freedomfighter and political thinker José Martí, whose works he interpreted. He showed how Martí's liberalism served as a precursor of Cuban socialism. To him, Martí took the initial step toward eliminating Cuba's oppression by advocating the solidarity of the people of Latin America. Marinello contended that Martí defied categorization, and referred to him as a poet who expressed reality in a unique fashion and who transformed it within himself and made it part of his inner conflict.

Marinello's thinking approached that of the new left, which years later stood for "unitary democracy," which one distinguishes from the "adversary democracy" of liberalism by its distrust of representative institutions and which prefers participation by all citizens in political deliberations and decisions that require a consensus. "Unitary democracy" is predicated to some extent on Aristotle's idea of the polis as an association for the expression of civic friendship, rather than the modern concept of the state as an instrument serving private ends.

BIBLIOGRAPHY:

A. *José Martí escritor Americano: Martí y el modernismo* (Mexico City: Grijalbo, 1958); *Once ensayos martianos* (Havana: Comisión Nacional Cubana de la UNESCO, 1964); *Contemporáneos* (Havana: Universidad Central de las Villas, 1964); *Literatura hispanomericana: hombres meditaciones* (Mexico City: Universidad Nacional, n.d.).

B. Trinidad Pérez and Pedro Simón, eds., *Recopilación de textos sobre Juan Marinello* (Havana: Casa de las Americas, 1979).

SHELDON B. LISS

MARTÍ, AGUSTIN FARABUNDO   (1894–1932). Born at Teotepeque in the department of La Libertad, El Salvador, in 1894, the son of wealthy parents who owned two haciendas, Farabundo Martí received a privileged education from the Salesians and later at the University of El Salvador. He always associated with the common people, however, whether the offspring of laborers on his father's land early on or the workers in San Salvador subsequently. Before he could graduate as a lawyer, Martí was deported by the government of Jorge Meléndez for denouncing the latter's quasi-charitable Liga Roja as a demagogic ploy to win votes. The expulsion merely consolidated an attraction to Leninist* ideas that had grown while he was at the university.

It is unlikely that Martí fought as a sergeant in the Red Battalions in Mexico, as folklore suggests. Before being expelled from Guatemala in 1925 for his role in founding the short-lived Central American Socialist Party, he worked as a farmhand, baker, and bricklayer and reputedly lived for a while with the Indians of El Quiché. His life over the next six years was one of nomadic proselytism and agitation, expulsions from Central American states, jailings, and successful hunger strikes to secure his release. During this period he worked briefly for the Anti-Imperialist League in New York and became the representative of the Caribbean Bureau of International Red Aid in El Salvador, which the Communists developed as a broad front organization.

Today's Salvadoran revolutionaries recall Martí's collaboration with Augusto

César Sandino and his "crazy little army" in Nicaragua, but they ignore the confrontation with which the relationship ended. Martí joined Sandino in May 1928 and became his personal secretary while also fighting with the rank of colonel against the National Guard and U.S. forces in the northern mountains of Las Segovias. However, Martí distrusted Sandino's theosophic and masonic ideas and became increasingly impatient of his refusal to go beyond national liberation goals to lead a social revolution. He was sacked by Sandino in August 1929, and in January 1930 the Nicaraguan nationalist leader denounced Communist activities "on his behalf."

Early in 1930 Martí returned to El Salvador from Mexico, only to be imprisoned by the government of Pío Romero Bosque and thus miss the formal founding of the Salvadoran Communist Party (Partido Comunista de El Salvador, PCS) on 28 May 1930. A hunger strike and public campaign produced his expulsion from the country in December 1930, but he returned secretly in February 1931 and used the relative freedom of the Araujo presidency, chosen in the country's last free elections, to proselytize and organize the workers. Given the overall level of organization and preparation, he was not optimistic about the prospects of the imminent armed insurrection, yet with other Communist leaders was forced to stand at the head of a powerful movement of largely spontaneous peasant insurgency. He did not in fact lead the insurrection of 22 January 1932, which was drowned in blood in eight days by the dictatorship of General Maximiliano Hernández Martínez. Together with Alfonso Luna and Mario Zapata, he was arrested on the nineteenth, tried by a Council of War, and shot in the Cemetery of San Salvador on 1 February 1932. He was thirty-eight years old.

"El Negro" Martí became the symbol of that revolution. A man of action and an international revolutionary, he was no typical Communist. He was an admirer of Leon Trotsky,* whose image appeared in the red star he often wore on his lapel. Martí's name was invoked by the tiny group of dissident Communists led by Salvador Cayetano Carpio* that broke with the PCS over guerrilla warfare in 1970 and that in 1972 announced the formation of the Farabundo Martí Popular Liberation Forces (FPL). When El Salvador's fissiparous guerrilla movement finally united in October 1980, it took the name of the Farabundo Martí National Liberation Front (Frente Farabundo Martí para la Liberación Nacional, FMLN), whose largest contingent was supplied by the FPL. The PCS only came around belatedly to the strategy of armed struggle, endorsing it at its clandestine seventh Party Congress in April 1979.

As an international revolutionary and leader of the first Communist Party of the Americas to attempt an armed revolution, Farabundo Martí left an example to be followed by future generations, but he did not write much apart from proclamations. His maxim has been adopted by the FMLN: "When history cannot be written with the pen, it must be written with the rifle."

BIBLIOGRAPHY:
B. Mauricio de la Selva, "El Salvador: tres décadas de lucha," *Cuadernos americanos* (Mexico) (January-February 1962); Roque Dalton, *Miguel Mármol* (San José: Editorial Universitaria Centroamericana, 1972); Jorge Arias Gómez, *Farabundo Martí* (San José:

Editorial Universitaria Centroamericana, 1972); "Las rutas de Farabundo Martí," *Revista Farabundo Martí* (Costa Rica), no. 2 (September 1980); "Interview with Miguel Mármol, Comrade of Farabundo Martí," *Granma Weekly Review* (Havana) (8 March 1981); Richard Gillespie, "From Farabundo Martí to FMLN," *Communist Affairs*, no. 1 (January 1982).

RICHARD GILLESPIE

MARTÍNEZ DE LA TORRE, RICARDO   (ca. 1901–1969). As a young man Ricardo Martínez de la Torre was one of the small group of Peruvian intellectuals and workers who gathered around Peru's principal Marxist thinker, José Carlos Mariátegui.* He was strongly influenced by Mariátegui's independent Marxism and his analysis of national conditions. One of the founders of Peru's Marxist movement, he tried to continue the nationalist line formulated by his mentor. A founder of the Peruvian Socialist Party, he resigned when, after Mariátegui's death, E. Ravines and other Party members surcame to directives from the Communist International to change the name to the Peruvian Communist Party.

As one of those who advocated independent national Marxism, he helped to span the gap between Mariátegui and Hugo Blanco,* Aníbal Quijano and others who began to emphasize the necessity of autonomous analysis and action in the period after the Cuban Revolution and the Andean peasant uprisings in the mid-1960s. Heavily involved in leftist politics and the labor movement through most of his life, he assembled a comprehensive four-volume collection of documents that chronicle left and labor history from 1919 to the late 1940s. *Notes for a Marxist Interpretation of Peruvian Social History* is required for all who want to understand Peruvian politics or labor history during this period.
BIBLIOGRAPHY:

A. *El movimiento obrero en 1919* (Lima: Amauta, 1928); *La teoría del crecimiento de la miseria aplicada a nuestra realidad* (Lima: Amauta, 1929); *Apuntes para una interpretación marxista de historia social del Perú*, 2d ed., 4 vols. (Lima: Empresa Editora Peruana, 1947–49).

B. Sheldon B. Liss, *Marxist Thought in Latin America* (Berkeley: University of California Press, 1984).

HARRY E. VANDEN

MARTOV, JULIUS L.   (1873–1923). Julius Martov was born Iuri O. Tsederbaum into a prosperous Jewish family in 1873. In 1895, Martov joined with Lenin* and others to form the St. Petersburg Union of Struggle for the Liberation of the Working Class, being arrested the same year. In 1900, Martov again joined with Lenin to publish the Marxist journal *Iskra* (The Spark), designed to bring ideological unity to the young Russian Marxist movement. By 1903 and the Second Congress of the Russian Social Democratic Labor Party in London, Martov and Lenin found themselves in serious dispute as to the desired nature of the Russian Marxist party, Martov leading the debate for the Mensheviks (Minority) in support of party membership open to supporters of the Marxist ideals. During World War I, Martov adopted an "internationalist" position, supporting termination of the conflict without victory. Returning to Russia shortly after the spring 1917 revolution, Martov refused to side with the main Menshevik opinion, which favored continuation of the war until German monarchism was defeated. As a result, Martov soon lost influence among the Mensheviks, although he retained his seat in the Petrograd Soviet of Workers and Soldiers Deputies. Following the Bolshevik Revolution in the fall of 1917–an uprising he opposed—and with the failure of Lenin to establish a coalition government, Martov emigrated to Germany, where he became a major figure of the Menshevik Party in exile. Julius Martov died in 1923 in a sanitorium in the Black Forest.

BIBLIOGRAPHY:

A. *Geschichte der russischen Sozialdemokratie* (Berlin: Dietz, 1926).

B. Israel Getzler, *Martov: A Political Biography of a Russian Social Democrat* (Cambridge: Cambridge University Press, 1967).

MICHAEL M. BOLL

MARX, KARL HEINRICH   (1818–1883). Karl Marx was born on 5 May 1818 in the Rhenish city of Trier, son of a successful Jewish lawyer of conservative political views who converted to Christianity in 1824. He studied law at the University of Bonn in 1835 and at the University of Berlin in 1836, changing his course of study in that year to philosophy, under the influence of Ludwig Feuerbach, Bruno Bauer, and the young Hegelian movement. Marx completed his doctorate in philosophy in 1841. With the accession of Friedrich Wilhelm IV in 1840, however, the young Hegelians came under attack from the government, and Marx lost all chance of an academic career in philosophy. Between 1842 and 1848, Marx edited radical publications in the Rhineland, France, and Belgium. Marx married his childhood sweetheart Jenny von Westphalen in 1843; despite their exceedingly hard life after 1850 the marriage was a happy one, and lasted until her death in 1881. Jenny Marx aided her husband in his writing, regularly preparing his (virtually illegible) manuscripts for publication. In 1844, while in Paris, Marx was introduced both to the working-class movement and to the study of political economy by his former fellow student at Berlin, Friedrich Engels,* with whom he began a lifetime of collaboration. While in Brussels, Marx first formulated the materialist conception of history, which was expounded in the unpublished manuscript *The German Ideology,* jointly authored by Marx and Engels. Marx returned from Belgium to Paris in 1848, after the revolution, and then went back to the Rhineland, where he worked as a publicist in behalf of the insurrection there. In the same year, Marx and Engels played a key role in founding the Communist League (which lasted until 1850), writing the *Communist Manifesto* as part of their activity in the League. After successfully defending himself and his associates in a Cologne court on charges of inciting to revolt, Marx was expelled from Prussian territories in 1848. After a brief stay in Paris, Marx took up residence in London, where he lived the rest of his life. The first years in England were a time of bitter, brutal poverty for the Marx family: three of their six children died of want, and Marx's health suffered a collapse from which it never fully recovered. For much of the 1850s Marx's only regular source of income was Horace Greeley's *New York Tribune*, for which he served as European correspondent, receiving a fee of one pound per article. Later Marx's family was supported largely by Engels. Throughout the 1850s and 1860s, when not confined to bed by illness, Marx regularly spent ten hours every day at the British Museum studying and writing. After returning home, he often wrote far into the night. His first scientific work on political economy, *Contribution to a Critique of Political Economy*, was published in 1859; the preface to this work contains a succinct statement of the materialist conception of history, usually regarded as the definitive formulation of that doctrine. This was only a prelude to Marx's definitive theory of capitalism, *Capital*, which Marx regarded as his life's work. Volume one of *Capital* was published in 1867, but two more volumes were left uncompleted at his death. Engels edited them and published them in 1884 and 1893, respectively. Marx was instrumental in founding the International Workingmen's Association in 1864 and guided it through six congresses in nine years. The demise of the First International* in 1876 was brought about by a combination of factors, notably the organization's support for the Paris Commune (see Marx's *The Civil War in France*) and internal intrigues by Mikhail Bakunin (expelled in 1872). Marx died of longstanding respiratory ailments on 13 March 1883 and is buried next to his wife in Highgate Cemetery, London.

Marx's interest in philosophical materialism is evident as early as his doctoral dissertation, on the philosophy of nature in Democritus and Epicurus. But the dissertation's focus on Epicurus's philosophy of self-consciousness and its historical significance equally displays Marx's education in German idealist philosophy and his preoccupation with its themes. As a philosopher Marx selfconsciously sought to marry the tradition of German idealism, especially the philosophy of Hegel, with the scientific materialism of the radical French Enlightenment. This was to some extent the tendency of the young Hegelian movement generally, but Marx's emphatic admiration for English and French materialism in contrast to the young Hegelians' deprecation of it is displayed in a well-known passage from *The Holy Family* (1844).

Of greater significance for Marx's later thought is the way in which his famous Paris manuscripts of 1844 address to the "materialistic" science of political economy a set of issues that Hegel and his followers had treated as questions of religious subjectivity. German idealism was concerned with problems of human selfhood, the nature of a fulfilling human life and with people's sense of meaning, self-worth and relatedness to their natural and social environments. They saw modern culture as both a scene of "estrangement" or "alienation" (*Entfremdung, Entaeusserung*) for human beings from themselves, their lives, and others, and also as holding out the promise of the conquest or overcoming of alienation. Hegel, however, saw the task of self-fulfillment and reconciliation as a philosophical-religious one. It was Marx in the Paris manuscripts who first attempted to see it as fundamentally a matter of the social and economic conditions in which people live, of the kind of laboring activities they perform and the practical relationships in which they stand to one another. Marx's concern with the plight of the working class was from the beginning a concern not merely with the satisfaction of "material needs" in the usual sense but fundamentally a concern with the conditions under which human beings can develop their "essential human powers" and attain "free self-activity."

The Paris manuscripts view human beings in modern society, human beings as they are understood by the science of political economy, as alienated from themselves because their life-activity takes an alien, inhuman form. Truly human and fulfilling life activity is an activity of free social self-expression. It is free because it is self-determined by human beings themselves; it develops and expresses their humanity because, as Hegel had realized, it is the nature of a spiritual being to create itself by objectifying itself in a world and then comprehending this world as its adequate expression, as the "affirmation," "objectification," and "confirmation" of its nature; and it is social because it is the nature of human beings to produce both with others and for others and to understand themselves in light of their mutual recognition of one another and their common work. The social relationships depicted by political economy, however, are relationships in which the life activity of the majority, the working class, is increasingly stunted, reduced to meaningless physical activity that, far from developing and exercising their humanity, reduces them to abstract organs of a lifeless mechanism. They do not experience the products of their labor as their expression, or indeed as theirs in any sense. For these products belong to a nonworker, the capitalist, to whom they must sell their activity for a wage that suffices only to keep them alive so that they may sustain the whole absurd cycle of their lives. Political economy, moreover, depicts human beings whose social life and relationships are at the mercy not of their collective choice but of an alien, inhuman mechanism, the marketplace, which purports to be a sphere of individual freedom but is in fact a sphere of collective slavery to inhuman and destructive forces.

Hegel had earlier conceived of alienation in the form of the "unhappy consciousness," of a misunderstood Christian religiosity that experiences itself and the whole changeable natural world as empty and worthless, and places everything valuable in a supernatural "beyond." The cure for alienation in Hegel's view is the recognition that finite nature is not the absence of infinite spirit but its expression. Feuerbach brought to light the latent humanism in Hegel's view and attacked all forms of religion (and even Hegel's speculative metaphysics) as forms of alienation. The true being of human individuals, he maintained, is in the enjoyment of sensuous nature and of loving harmony with other human beings. What both Hegel and Feuerbach had in common was the perception of alienation as fundamentally a form of false consciousness, whose cure was a correct perception or interpretation of the world. Alienated consciousness contains both a lament that our natural human life is unsatisfying and worthless and also the hope of consolation in the beyond. Hegel and Feuerbach agree that the illusion of alienated consciousness consists in its negative attitude toward earthly life; the comforting assurances of religion, according to both philosophers, contain the truth, if only we know how to put the right philosophical interpretation on them. To Marx, however, alienation becomes intelligible as soon as we adopt just the reverse supposition: that the alienated consciousness tells the truth in its laments, not in its consolations. Religion, according to Marx, gives expression to a mode of life that is in fact empty, unfulfilled, degraded, devoid of dignity. Religious illusions have hold on us because they provide a false semblance of meaning and fulfillment for a mode of life that without this illusion would be seen for the unredeemed meaninglessness that it is. For Marx, then, religious misery is both an expression of actual misery and an attempt to flee from it into a world of imagination: it is the "opium of the people." The way out of alienation is not, as Hegel and Feuerbach thought, a new philosophical interpretation of life, but a new form of earthly existence, a new society in which the material conditions for a fulfilling human life would no longer be lacking. "The philosophers have only *interpreted* the world in different ways; the point is to *change* it" (*Theses on Feuerbach*, no. 11).

This concern with the conditions for fulfilling human life and with the "alienated" condition in which they are absent remained with Marx throughout his life. But the theory of society and history adumbrated in the 1844 manuscripts was soon to undergo significant development. In the 1844 manuscripts, Marx gave expression to three related ideas that anticipate his mature social theory. First, there is a complex interconnection between the various ills and irrationalities to which people in modern society are subject. Second, what is basic to this system of irrationalities (which Marx called "alienation") is something about the kind of labor or social production in which people are engaged ("alienated" laboring activity). Third, this alienated kind of labor is characteristic of a transitory but critical stage in the generally progressive course of human history. "Alienation," says Marx, "is founded in the essence of human development" (*Collected Works*, vol. 3, p. 281).

In the materialist conception of history, formulated for the first time in *The German Ideology* of 1845, the interconnection is not "alienation" but the "form of intercourse" (*Verkehrsform*) or economic structure of capitalist society. The materialist conception of history traces it not to "alienated labor" but to the exercise of society's productive powers at a determinate stage of their historical development. And finally, the course of historical development is not something predetermined by the essence of the human species, as it was in the 1844 manuscripts, but the historical path taken under contingent circumstances by the relentless expansion of these productive powers.

For the materialist conception, then, the fundamental thing in human history is the productive powers of society and their tendency to grow. Whether the materialist conception is a "technological" theory of history depends on how broadly the concept "productive powers" is to be interpreted. Marx indicates, however, that under this heading he understands not only the arsenal of tools and means of production and the human skills required to employ them but also the theoretical knowledge of nature involved in production and even forms of human cooperation, insofar as they play a direct role in the techniques of the human mastery of nature and the satisfaction of human needs. Productive powers at a given stage of development determine the nature of human laboring activity because labor consists in the exercise of precisely those powers. A given set of productive powers, however, also thereby favor certain "material relations of production," forms of human cooperation, or division of labor, that are not directly part of them but that facilitate their employment to a greater degree than rival forms would do. They thereby also favor certain "social relations of production," systems of social roles relating to the control of the production process and the disposition of its fruits. It is this system of social relations of production that the 1859 preface calls the "economic structure of society," which forms the "real basis" of social life on the materialist theory, conditioning "superstructures" such as the political state and legal forms of property ownership and the "ideological" forms of consciousness found in religion, philosophy, morality and art. The "real basis," however, itself rests on the productive powers of society, to which social relations of production must "correspond."

Marx's primary aim in formulating the materialist conception of history is to sketch an account of periodic large-scale social change. Within the framework of any system of social relations of production, society's productive powers expand at a greater or lesser rate, depending on the historical circumstances, including the social relations themselves. Eventually, however, a given set of social relations of production are outgrown or rendered obsolete by the productive powers. The prevailing relations either make it difficult to employ the existing powers or else fetter the further development of these powers. Powers and relations of production thus come into conflict or "contradiction"; an "epoch of social revolution" begins. The outcome of the conflict is the transformation of the relations of production to bring them into line with the productive powers so as to facilitate the further expansion of these powers. Changes in the superstructure of society, including its political and legal institutions, are to be explained in terms of the required changes in the social relations of production.

The 1859 preface does not mention the mechanism by which these adjustments are to be carried out, but other writings do, and this mechanism is one of the most characteristic features of Marxian social theory: the class struggle. Social relations of production divide society into groups distinguished by their degree of control over production. These groups are not directly classes in the strict sense, but they become classes as soon as they are organized and represented by a political movement that defines and promotes their class interests. Class interests are dependent on the common situation of a class's members, and especially by their hostile relation to other classes, which arises from the fact that the social relations of production assign effective control over production to some at the expense of others. Those who have this control have a common

interest in retaining it, and those who are excluded have a common interest in
wresting it from those who have it. But class interests proper are not just shared
or common interests but "general" interests, which are distinct from the particular interests shared by the class's members, and can sometimes demand the
sacrifice of individual interests. These class interests are the interests of the
political movement that represents the class; ultimately, they are identified with
the establishment and defense of a particular set of social relations, those which
give social dominance to members of the class in question. At a given stage of
history, that class is victorious whose class interests consist in the establishment
of that set of production relations that best suits the productive powers at that
stage.

On the materialist theory, the political state is superstructural: its form and
its actions are to be explained by their correspondence to the economic structure
of society. By the same token, however, the political state is also seen as a tool
of the ruling class: it is a mechanism by which that class effects its dominance
over the rest of society and gives the stamp of universality and legitimacy to the
economic relations constituting its rule. Religion, morality, philosophy, and art
are "ideological": that is, the socially prevalent forms of these intellectual
activities are to be explained in terms of the way they promote class interests,
and competing ideas in terms of competing class interests they represent. As
Marx depicts them, a class ideology typically distorts social reality by seeing
everything only from one class's perspective, and presenting the conditions for
that class's rule as conditions in which the general welfare or universal interests
of the whole of society are satisfied.

How is the materialist conception of history related to Marx's philosophical
materialism? This question is difficult (perhaps impossible) to answer, for at
least two reasons. First, Marx never presented in any detail or specificity the
type of "philosophical materialism" to which he subscribed. Except for passages
from the Paris manuscripts and *The Holy Family* (1844) and the celebrated but
brief and obscure *Theses on Feuerbach* (1845), we find in Marx's writings no
exposition of philosophical materialism. We do find such expositions in the
writings of Engels, but it is a matter of controversy how far such views may be
attributed to Marx himself. Second, although Marx does describe his view as
the "materialist" conception of history, he never tells us in what sense the term
"materialist" is being used in this description, and any of several quite different
meanings might reasonably be intended. It is possible that Marx thought his
conception of history consonant only with a materialist (as opposed to spiritualist
or idealist) world view; if he did think this, he never gave us his reasons. Or
he may have named his view materialist because it sees human labor (the in-
terchange between the human body and its material environment) rather than
philosophical thought as the key to human history. Or he may have been referring
to the central place of people's material (as distinct from their supposed spiritual)
needs in the explanation of their behavior as historical agents. Yet it is also
possible that "materialist" refers only to the role given in Marx's theory to

productive "matter" (the social exercise and development of productive powers) in explaining social "form" (social relations of production). If this is what Marx had in mind, then the "matter" in historical materialism is opposed not to mind or spirit but to social form, and there is in fact no connection at all between Marx's materialist conception of history and whatever form of philosophical materialism Marx may have held.

The materialist conception of history is a general program of historical research, an explanatory sketch that Marx hopes and believes will prove sound when it is applied to particular societies and large-scale social changes. Although Marx occasionally (for example, in the *Grundrisse* of 1857–58) applies it to premodern societies and brings considerable empirical evidence to bear in such applications, the sketch itself was obviously suggested to him by the rise of capitalism. And Marx envisions the overthrow of capitalism and the rise of socialism by applying the same sketch to capitalism's decline, which accounts for its triumph. The rise of capitalist social relations is the work of the bourgeois class, throwing off the yoke of feudalism and permitting the rapid creation of the new productive powers of modern industrial society. (This process is described briefly in part one of *The Communist Manifesto*; it is described in more detail in *Capital*, volume one, part eight.) By the same token, the rise of socialism will be the work of the proletariat, throwing off the yoke of capitalism, and enabling the human powers of production to continue their growth.

If historical materialism is a program for empirical research and theory construction, it is also a philosophy of history, a theory that relates the history of the human species to a certain conception of the human essence. Human beings for Marx are practical or socially productive beings whose nature is to transform the world around them so as to make it satisfy their needs and express themselves as free conscious contemplators of their own work. The ultimate tendency of history for Marx is the Promethean drive of the human species to develop its "essential human powers," its powers of production. Under capitalism these powers, and the complex network of human cooperation through which they are exercised, have for the first time grown far enough to put within the reach of human beings themselves the collective, rational control of the social form of their own production: the human species has for the first time acquired the capacity to determine its own destiny rationally, to produce in a way that is self-conscious, self-determined, and therefore free. But human beings under capitalism are alienated because capitalist social relations, by dispossessing the vast majority of producers and subjecting the form of social production to the market mechanism, frustrates this collective self-determination. The historic mission of the proletariat, as Marx sees it, is to actualize the capacities for human freedom that the capitalist mode of production has put within our reach by abolishing class society and subjecting the social form of production to the rational might of united human individuals. In this way, the materialist conception of history becomes not only a program for theoretical research but also a weapon in the hands of the proletarian class. It gives this class a full conscious understanding of its historic mission, so that unlike previous ruling classes, it may fulfill this mission consciously and thus truly enable the human species to master itself and its destiny. The materialist conception of history thus serves as the link between Marx's concern with the conditions for human fulfillment, his theoretical enterprise as economist and historian, and his practical activity as a working-class organizer and revolutionary.

The materialist conception of history has implications for the way we should conceive of revolutionary social change and of our own historical agency in bringing it about. The goals of a class movement according to this theory are determined not by the whims of its members but by the set of production relations they are in a position to establish and defend. This implies that historically conscious revolutionaries should not proceed by setting utopian goals for themselves and then looking around for means to achieve them. Revolutionary practice is rather a matter of becoming a part of an already developing class movement, helping to define its own goals and to actualize them through the use of the weapons inherent in the class's historical situation. The definition of these goals, moreover, is an ongoing process, a task relative to the class's stage of development. It is pointless to speculate about the precise system of distribution that a revolutionary movement will institute after its victory when the movement itself is still in its infancy.

Marx's own attitude toward various styles of socialist theorizing exhibits the influence of these consequences of historical materialism. Marx believed that future society would see the abolition of classes, the abolition of private ownership of means of production, and even commodity production (production of goods and services for exchange or sale), and the elimination of all systematic social causes for alienation and human unfulfillment. Yet he never thought of future society as an unchanging state of perfection. On the contrary, he thought of the end of class society as the true beginning of *human* history, of the historical development of human society directed consciously by human beings. Above all, Marx never attempted to say in any detail what distribution relations in future socialist or communist society would be like, scorning the project of "writing recipes for the cookshops of the future" (*Capital*, vol. 1, p. 17). He scorned equally those who concerned themselves with formulating principles of distributive justice and those condemning capitalism in their name. Marx's historical materialism treats justice as closely connected with the superstructural institutions of law and the state and with the moral ideologies attendant upon them. Marx conceives the justice of economic transactions as their correspondence to or functionality for the prevailing mode of production. Given this conception of justice, Marx very consistently (if rather surprisingly) concluded that the inhuman exploitation practiced by capitalism against the workers is not unjust and does not violate workers' rights. This conclusion, of course, constitutes no defense of capitalism, but it does constitute part of Marx's attack on the use of moral conceptions such as right and justice within the proletarian movement. Marx saw the task of the proletarian movement in his time as one of self-definition and growth through organization, discipline, and self-criticism based on scientific self-understanding. He left for later and more mature stages of the movement the task of planning the future society that it is the movement's historic mission to bring to birth.

BIBLIOGRAPHY:

A. In listing the principal writings of Marx, there are two main sources: *Marx Engels Collected Works* (New York: International, 1975–), hereafter CW; and *Marx, Engels, Selected Works in One Volume* (New York: International, 1968), hereafter SW. Except in the case of *Capital*, dates given are those of composition rather than publication. *Difference Between the Democritean and Epicurean Philosophy of Nature* (1841), CW, vol. 1; *Economic and Philosophic Manuscripts of 1844*, CW, vol. 3; with Friedrich Engels, *The Holy Family* (1844), CW, vol. 4; with Friedrich Engels, *The German Ideology* (1845), CW, vol. 5; *The Poverty of Philosophy* (1846), CW, vol. 6; with Friedrich Engels, *Manifesto of the Communist Party* (1847), CW, vol. 6; *Wage Labor and Capital* (1849), CW, vol. 9; *The Class Struggles in France, 1848 to 1850* (1850), CW, vol. 10; *The Eighteenth Brumaire of Louis Bonaparte* (1851), CW, vol. 11; with Friedrich Engels, *The Great Men of the Exile* (1852), CW, vol. 11; *Revelations Concerning the Communist Trial in Cologne* (1852), CW, vol. 11; *The Grundrisse (1857–8)*, trans. Martin Nicolaus (Harmondsworth: Penguin Books, 1973); *Contribution to a Critique of Political Economy* (1859) (New York: International, 1970); *Herr Vogt* (1860), CW, vol. 17; *Theories of Surplus Value*, 3 vols. (1862–63) (Moscow: Progress, 1963); *Wages, Price and Profit* (1865), SW; *Capital* (New York: International, 1967), vol. 1 published 1867, vol. 2, ed. Friedrich Engels, published 1884, vol. 3, ed. Friedrich Engels, published 1894; *The Civil War in France* (1871), SW; *Critique of the Gotha Program* (1875), SW.

B. Shlomo Avineri, *The Social and Political Thought of Karl Marx* (Cambridge: Cambridge University Press, 1968); David McLellan, *Karl Marx* (London: Penguin Books, 1973); M. Morishima, *Marx's Economics* (Cambridge: Cambridge University Press, 1973); A. Cohen, *Karl Marx's Theory of History* (Princeton: Princeton University Press, 1978); Jerrold Seigel, *Marx's Fate* (Princeton: Princeton University Press, 1978); Allen W. Wood, *Karl Marx* (London: Routledge and Kegan Paul, 1981); Richard Miller, *Analyzing Marx* (Princeton: Princeton University Press, 1984).

ALLEN W. WOOD

MAURÍN JULIA, JOAQUÍN   (1896–1973). Joaquín Maurín Julia, a prominent Marxist thinker and organizer during the 1920s and 1930s, is renowned for having been the principal founder of one of the most controversial political parties of the Spanish Civil War, the Partido Obrero de Unificación Marxista, (POUM). Maurín began his political education while teaching history and geography at the Liceo Escolar in Lerida. After joining the republican youth group, Juventud Republicana, he became a writer for its daily organ, *El ideal*. The Bolshevik Revolution of 1917, however, so profoundly influenced the young Maurín that he decided to commit himself to a life of left-wing radicalism. From his readings of socialist and syndicalist literature at this time, Maurín concluded that the Spanish proletariat would never fulfill their own revolutionary ambitions as long as the working-class movement was dominated by the two opposing doctrines of anarchism and socialism. In Georges Sorel's† brand of revolutionary syndicalism, Maurín believed that he had found a theory that synthesized the progressive elements in both of these ideologies, and indeed, it was this belief that shaped his thinking for the next few years.

When he joined the predominantly anarchosyndicalist Confederación Nacional del Trabajo (CNT) in 1920, Maurín belonged to a small group of young radicals, known as the communist-syndicalists, who were likewise infatuated with the Bolshevik Revolution and who, despite their exiguous numbers, were briefly able to exert considerable influence within the CNT. Maurín himself edited the leading communist-syndicalist mouthpiece in Catalonia, *La lucha social*, and also served as the secretary of the CNT's provincial committee in Lerida. The following year, Maurín, along with other like-minded militants, such as Andreu Nin* and Hilario Arlandis, formed part of the Spanish delegation of the CNT that was sent to Moscow to attend the Third Congress of the Comintern and the founding congress of the Profintern (Red International of Trade Unions, RILU).

Maurín's experiences in the Soviet Union helped to confirm in his own mind the tactics and strategies he should pursue as a communist-syndicalist. At the RILU congress, for example, he supported the Leninist* resolution that called for the Comintern and Profintern to be "organically linked," which essentially meant subordinating the latter to the former. When he returned to Spain, Maurín was determined to orient the CNT toward Moscow. To this end, he organized a tiny Bolsheviklike faction within the organization, the Comités Sindicalistas Revolucionarios (CSR) and simultaneously brought out a Marxist trade union weekly, *La batalla*. Maurín's proselytizing efforts, though, threw him into conflict with the majority of *cenetistas*, who were inveterately opposed to having their organization "bolshevized." As a result, he decided to leave the CNT at the end of 1922.

After the installation of Primo de Rivera's military dictatorship in 1923, Maurín was obliged to abandon his strategy of using the CSR as a means of penetrating the CNT, and accordingly, he turned increasingly toward the Spanish Communist Party (PCE) as a base for his political activities. During the summer of 1924, he attended the Third Congress of the Profintern in Moscow, and that same year he formally joined the Catalan section of the PCE, the Federación Comunista Catalano-Balear (FCCB, popularly called the Catalan Federation).

Between 1925 and 1930 Maurín suffered the fate common to many political activists of his day: he was relentlessly persecuted by the authorities, imprisoned for over two years, and finally exiled to France. Soon after he returned to Barcelona in 1930, Maurín, who now directed the Catalan Federation, broke with the PCE over several fundamental issues, not least of which was the question of the PCE's relation to the Comintern. Maurín particularly objected to the way in which the Comintern exercised complete control over the PCE, which he argued violated the Leninist principle of "democratic centralism." Moreover, his attempts to put the Catalan Federation on an independent footing flagrantly contradicted the Comintern policy that called for the "bolshevizing" (i.e. centralizing) of the PCE. Although several notable Comintern officials, including

J. Humbert-Droz, tried to woo Maurín and the Catalan Federation back into the PCE, their efforts were to no avail, and in June 1931 they were officially expelled from the Party.

Parallel to these developments, Maurín had been preparing the ground for the creation of an independent Marxist movement. He revived *La Batalla* in the summer of 1930, and later that year he founded a Marxist theoretical journal, *La Nueva Era*. In November, Maurín met with Jordi Arquer, Victor Colomer, and other members of the nonaligned Marxist Partit Comunista Català (PCC) to lay plans for the consolidation of their two parties. The product of these negotiations was the formation in March 1931 of the Bloque Obrero y Campesino (BOC), of which Maurín served as secretary general.

To the left of Maurín among the Spanish Marxists was the tiny but vociferous Trotskyist* Left Opposition faction, Oposición Comunista de España (OCE). Led by Andreu Nin,* who also returned to Barcelona in 1930, the OCE group was at first content to work alongside Maurín and the Catalan Federation, largely because Nin believed that their respective theoretical positions were compatible. After the creation of the BOC, however, collaboration between the two groups was no longer possible. Their final break arose over a problem that had long vexed Marxists, namely, how to relate nationalist feelings in a country to the socialist movement. On the one hand, Maurín contended that the nationalist (i.e. regionalist) movements in Spain, particularly those in the Basque and Catalan provinces, were so far advanced in their development that they were inextricably bound up with the workers' and peasants' causes. For this reason he and the BOC envisaged the Spanish revolution developing along nationalist lines, ultimately resulting in the formation of a Union of Iberian Socialist Republics. On the other hand, Nin and the OCE followed Trotsky in arguing that Maurín had failed to grasp the true significance of the national question. According to them, the nationalist movements in Spain were simply expressions of ''petit bourgeois'' nationalism, and as such their aims were inconsistent with those of the working classes. Nin and the OCE thus concluded that the policies of Maurín and the BOC would lead not to the creation of a federation of socialist republics but rather to the political and economic dismemberment (''Balkanization'') of Spain.

What clearly emerged from Maurín's disputes with both the PCE and the OCE was that, unlike them, he did not feel obliged to import a purely Russian style of Marxism into Spain. For Maurín, Marxism was an all embracing view of the development of human society, and as such, the tactics and strategies derived from it could not be defined solely in terms of one nation's experience. Thus while he was deeply influenced by the ideas of Bolsheviks like V. I. Lenin* and Nikolai Bukharin,* he believed that their revolutionary strategies, grounded as they were in circumstances peculiar to Russia, could not properly address the problems of the Spanish revolution, where historical circumstances had been altogether different.

For Maurín, the fundamental problem facing Spain was how to attain the bourgeois-democratic revolution so that the proletariat could achieve their own revolutionary destination. His attempts to resolve this led him to suggest a significant, albeit vague idea, that of the "democratic-socialist" revolution, by which he meant that the Spanish proletariat had to assume a leadership role in the historical process by accomplishing first the bourgeois revolution and then the socialist one.

How precisely the proletariat was to make this "historical leap" was a problem that occupied Maurín's thinking throughout the first two years of the Second Republic (1931–33). Yet by the spring of 1933, Maurín believed that he had contrived a tactic that could, in a variety of ways, play a decisive role in bringing about the "democratic-socialist" revolution. The Alianza Obrera (AO), as this tactic came to be known, was a united front of workers and peasants organizations that, according to Maurín, would provide the divided Spanish left a rampart against the growing menace of fascism. Maurín also thought of the AO as a vehicle that the proletariat could utilize both for mounting a counter-offensive against the bourgeoisie and for exercising political power during the transitional period between the bourgeois and socialist revolutions. Above all, it had to be led by a Marxist party, such as his own Catalan Federation (renamed the Federación Comunista Iberia in 1932), which clearly understood the historic mission of the Spanish working classes.

In the following months, Maurín struggled to keep the Alianza Obrera movement alive. In order to do this, he endeavored to expand the influence of the BOC, which until then had largely confined its activities to the Catalonian region. Although his overtures to the CNT and Spanish Socialist Party (PSOE) fell on deaf ears, his policies did appeal to the ICE, which had recently broken with Trotsky and thereupon dissociated itself from the international Left Opposition movement. The two groups finally merged in September 1935 to form the POUM, with Maurín becoming secretary general.

Despite their criticisms of the Popular Front alliance, as postponing working-class hegemony, the POUM nevertheless felt compelled to join it during the elections of February 1936. At the time, Maurín, as well as other leading POUM-ists, justified their decision on the grounds that it saved them from being completely cut off from the powerful prodemocratic movement among the masses. In any case, Maurín was the only POUM member to win a seat in the Cortes.

When the Civil War broke out in July 1936, Maurín found himself trapped behind nationalist lines. Although he briefly managed to elude his enemies by assuming several false identities, he was eventually arrested under his real name and kept prisoner for the remainder of the war. Meanwhile, thanks to an apocryphal article that appeared in the London *Times* on 17 September 1936, reporting his capture and execution by the Francoists, Maurín became the left's first important martyr. Not only was a street named in his honor, but the Independent Labour Party of Great Britain (ILP) formed a "Joaquin Maurín" ambulance unit. Maurín was freed from prison in 1946, and he subsequently took up residence in the United States. Although his active political career ended in 1936, Maurín continued writing on political and social themes from an anti-Soviet perspective for the rest of his life.

BIBLIOGRAPHY:

A. *Hacia la segunda revolución* (1935), re-edited as *Revolución y contrarevolución en España* (Paris: Ruedo ibérico, 1966); *Los hombres de la dictadura* (Barcelona: Anagrama, 1977); *La revolución española* (Barcelona: Anagrama, 1977); Joaquin Maurín Archives, Stanford, Calif.: Hoover Institution.

B. Victor Alba, *El marxismo en España, 1919–1939*, 2 vols. (Mexico City: B. Costa-Amic, 1973); Jules Humbert-Droz, *De Lenine à Staline* (Neuchatel: la baconniere, 1973); Gerald Meaker, *The Revolutionary Left in Spain: 1914–1923* (Stanford: Stanford Univ. Press, 1974); Victor Alba, *Dos revolucionarios: Andreu Nin/Joaquin Maurín* (Madrid: Seminarios y Ediciones, 1975); Jeanne Maurín *Cómo se salvó Joaquín Maurín* (Madrid: n.a., 1979).

GEORGE R. ESENWEIN

MEEK, RONALD LINDLEY   (1917–1978). Ronald Meek was born on 27 July 1917 in Wellington, New Zealand. He died on 18 August 1978 in Leicester, England. Meek received an M.A. at Victoria University College, New Zealand, in 1946. He then moved to England to read for his Ph.D. under Piero Sraffa at St. John's College in Cambridge. He received his Ph.D. in 1949. Meek taught at the University of Glasgow from 1948 to 1963 and at the University of Leicester from 1963 to 1978. Meek was a member of the British Communist Party until 1956, when he ended his membership to protest the Hungarian events. Noteworthy in Meek's public life are his founding of the Center for Public Economics at the University of Leicester and his membership on the East Midlands Regional Economic Planning Council.

Ronald Meek's intellectual work can best be understood as guided by a concern to bridge the theoretical gap between Marxist and non-Marxist economists, especially those guided in their interests by the works of the classical political economists and of Keynes. Until 1959, Meek devoted some of his energies to providing information to Western scholars about the nature, and development through time, of the discipline of economics in the Soviet Union. Meek's primary interests and contribution were in the history of economic thought. Meek's goal was to provide a "materialist" reading of economic theories, and particularly (but not exclusively) of pre-Marxian political economy—physiocracy, Smith, Ricardo. Meek interpreted the analytical structures of these systems of political economy as expressions of the concurrent class relations and of the political-economic conflicts to which these class relations gave rise. For example, he explained the differences between the economics of physiocracy and those of Adam Smith—on the question of whether the surplus took the form of rent or of rent and profits—on the grounds that capitalist class relations had penetrated the sphere of industrial (as opposed to simply agricultural) production to a much greater extent in Britain than in France in the mid- to late eighteenth century.

In tracing the history of economic thought, Meek drew on, systematized, and popularized as well as further developed material that can be found in Marx's* *Theories of Surplus Value*. His work nonetheless retains a mark of originality and an unquestioned seal of scholarly excellence, especially as regards his concern to reread Marx and to reaffirm his contribution in the light of modern developments in economic theory. Meek, for example, was quite willing to acknowledge the contribution and relevance of Sraffa's work to Marxist economic theory without exhibiting any tendency to participate in exercises that denude Marxist theory of its critical perspective on the work of Ricardo.

Meek's work can be seen best as an attempt to demonstrate that Marx's economic and social theoretical breakthroughs, although momentous and original, were brilliant developments—continuations—of the traditions of classical political economy and physiocracy. Hence, Meek spent much of his intellectual life discovering the origins of Marx's ideas on value, capital accumulation, economic reproduction, and socio-economic development in the works of Marx's "precursors," especially in the writings of Adam Smith. Meek's approach to Marx's contributions partly explains his continued interest in Smith, as can be seen in his coeditorship of a recently discovered version of Smith's *Lectures on Jurisprudence* and in his several articles and texts on the development of Smith's thought. Meek sought to extract from Smith's work early versions both of Marx's theory of value and of what he considered the "materialist" view of historical development, i.e., the "four-stages" theory of socio-economic development. According to this "four-stages" theory, societies have been structured by the prevalent mode of subsistence (production). Meek interprets Marx's historical materialism as a schema in which transformations in the modes of subsistence bring about transformations in other economic and noneconomic relations, thus, eventually, producing successive transitions to higher and more developed socio-economic structures. This reading of Marx's theory of history, strikingly similar to L. H. Morgan's concept of social evolution, allows Meek to find an important anticipation of Marx in Smith's discussion (along with that of Ferguson, Montesquieu, and others) of the historical stages constituted by the hunting and gathering, pastoral, agricultural, and commercial modes of subsistence. Meek's reading of Marx's breakthroughs can be contrasted with the readings of Louis Althusser† and others who have stressed the theoretical rupture that Marx effected between his work and that of the classical political economists.

BIBLIOGRAPHY:

A. "Teaching of Economics in the USSR and Poland," *Soviet Studies* (Winter 1959); *Economics and Ideology and Other Essays: Studies in the Development of Economic Thought* (New York: Barnes and Noble, 1967); *Social Science and the Ignoble Savage* (Cambridge: Cambridge University Press, 1976); *Studies in the Labor Theory of Value* (New York: Monthly Review Press, 1976).

ANTONIO CALLARI

MELLA, JULIO ANTONIO   (1903–1929). Cuban Julio Antonio Mella first attained recognition as a political activist by organizing, in 1922, the Federation of University Students, which served as a forerunner to similar movements in Cuba, including the one from which Fidel Castro* emerged some thirty years later. Mella helped form José Martí Popular University, which integrated students, workers, and professors and served to denounce inhuman working conditions and U.S. imperialism in Cuba. After the Popular University was closed by the state, Mella, who considered the clergy to be reactionary and opposed to scientific thinking, founded an Anti-Clerical League to combat Church influence in Cuban schools. Mella and Carlos B. Baliño* started the Cuban section of the liberal-radical Anti-Imperialist League of the Americas, which campaigned against the region's dictators, whom they viewed as subservient to international capitalism. Within the league Mella became known as Cuba's expert on the Leninist* concept of imperialism. He and Baliño went on, in 1925, to organize the Constitutional Congress of the Communist Party of Cuba. Agents of Cuban dictator Gerardo Machado assassinated Mella in Mexico in 1929.

Mella had a talent for writing provocative, not highly theoretical, essays and polemics that got across the socialist message in a precise and inspirational fashion. In 1925 he wrote *Glosas al pensamiento de José Martí*, which exhorted Cubans to follow Martí's anti-imperialist, antifeudal, prointernational, and pro-black rights thinking. He demonstrated how Martí's love of Cuba fit into the idea of international solidarity for workers. In essence, Mella reconciled Cuban nationalism with internationalism. Following the tradition of Martí, but from a Marxist point of view, Mella left his imprint on Cuba. His ideas have been translated into the reality of the 1959 Cuban Revolution and the Constitution of 1976, particularly aspects pertaining to domestic relations, property rights, land reform, anti-imperialism, the value of literacy, and equal rights for Cubans of all colors and sexes.

BIBLIOGRAPHY:

A. *Julio Antonio Mella en el Machete: antología parcial de un luchador y eu momento histórico* (Mexico City: Fondo de Cultura Popular, 1968); *Escritos revolucionarios* (Mexico City: Siglo XXI, 1978).

B. Erasmo Dumpierre, *J. A. Mella: biografía* (Havana: Editorial de Ciencias Sociales, 1977).

SHELDON B. LISS

MENJÍVAR, RAFAEL   (b. 1936). Rafael Menjívar was rector of the National University of El Salvador until his exile in 1972, and thereafter professor of economics and sociology, University of Costa Rica, San José. He is the leader and principal theoretician of Salvador's Bloque Popular Revolucionario (BPR), as well as founder, member, and driving force of the Movement of Independent Professionals and Technicians. He is also the leading figure of the Frente Democrático Revolucionario (FDR). One of the most prominent Marxist economists to analyze postwar developments in Central America, Menjívar has always displayed an ability to refine new concepts within a framework of empirical rigor. His 1975 essay on the region's agricultural organization effectively challenged the orthodox notion of the peasantry as a static and unrevolutionary class, emphasizing the growth of a large rural proletariat as a result of the increasing capitalization of agriculture and the shift from labor rent to wage labor and money rent. Similarly, his work on the Salvadorean proletariat is less a formal history than a sharp political analysis derived from a sensitive socio-economic appreciation of the forms and dynamics of a working class in a backward capitalist country dominated by agrarian production. Since 1979 Menjívar has concentrated on political work, adopting a firm radical stance within the FDR. His lucid, historically based work is the most complete and incisive produced by the Salvadorean left; in many respects he is the heir to Roque Dalton.*

BIBLIOGRAPHY:

A. "Los problemas del mundo rural," in *Centroamérica Hoy* (Mexico City: Siglo XXI, 1975); *Crisis del desarrollismo* (San José: EDUCA, 1977); *El Salvador: el eslabón más pequeño* (San José: EDUCA, 1980); *Acumulación ordinaria y dessarrollo del capitalismo en El Salvador* (San José: EDUCA, 1980).

JAMES DUNKERLEY

MONDLANE, EDUARDO CHIVAMBO   (1920–1969). Born in 1920 in Gaza Province of Mozambique, Eduardo Chivambo Mondlane came from a traditional African village background. At the insistence of his mother, he attended Portuguese government schools and later Swiss Presbyterian mission instruction before going to the capital, Lourenço Marques (now Maputo), to enroll in a course in dryland farming. In 1948, Mondlane secured a scholarship that enabled him to register in South Africa's Witwatersrand University. At the end of his second year, the South African government switched its policy and dismissed him from the university for being a "foreign native."

Back in Lourenço Marques, he helped organize an association of Mozambican students (Núcleo dos Estudantes de Moçambique) that resulted in confrontation with Portuguese authorities. To cure his "embryonic spirit of black nationalism," the colonial government allowed him to pursue his education in Portugal. At the University of Lisbon (1950–51), he associated with African students from Angola and Guinea-Bissau, some of whom became nationalist leaders. With the aid of a scholarship Mondlane continued his studies in the United States, graduating from Oberlin in 1953 with a B.A. and earning a Ph.D. at Northwestern University. After a year spent in research at Harvard, Mondlane served as a research officer in the United Nations until 1961. Using a UN passport, Mondlane and his American wife visited Mozambique, which convinced him of the need for Mozambican independence.

Taking a position as an assistant professor at Syracuse University to provide himself more time, Mondlane began an active interest in Mozambican political developments. By 1960 the southeastern African country had witnessed the growth of a number of small, often exiled, political groups. The independence of neighboring Tanzania saw three of the larger parties establish headquarters in Dar es Salaam, where Mondlane assisted in the formation of a merger of the three parties to form the Frente de Libertacão de Moçambique (FRELIMO) in 1962. He became the movement's first president. Two years later FRELIMO launched a guerrilla war in the northern provinces, which culminated in independence in 1975, six years after Mondlane's assassination.

A revolutionary leader, political activist, and guerrilla organizer, Mondlane was also a man of revolutionary thought. His political ideas were directed toward four goals: formation of a political movement capable of military conflict; independence from Portugal; development of a national consciousness in a multiethnic society; and reconstruction of Mozambique along egalitarian lines under the direction of FRELIMO. Conflicts had already begun in Portugal's two other African territories—Angola and Guinea-Bissau—and Mondlane was convinced only armed struggle would bring independence to Mozambique. He believed that the reason for the racial socio-economic structure typifying the Portuguese colonial society was that African people had lost their political power from the very beginning of their relations with the Portuguese. He believed that a protracted conflict with Portugal would force Lisbon to negotiate the independence of Mozambique—a scenario that proved correct. As the third goal for FRELIMO, Mondlane stressed its role in fusing the various ethnic and regional elements of Mozambique into a unified and politically conscious nation. He maintained that ethnic divisions were often the result of the Portuguese, whose colonialism perverted traditional power structures and encouraged elitist elements. To Mondlane and other Marxist-influenced nationalists, these "elitist elements" had vested interest in perpetuating colonial rule and furthering ethnic and class divisions so as to maintain their privileged position in the colonial hierarchy. Mondlane wrote that the guerrilla war and revolution would lessen ethnic splits, an unfulfilled goal still today. Mondlane's fourth and most sweeping objective centered on the social and economic reconstruction of postindependence Mozambique. The president of FRELIMO envisioned an egalitarian, self-governing society. In the era after independence, Mondlane advocated strong central planning to develop Mozambique and to prevent the concentration of wealth by privileged groups. FRELIMO's role, as Mondlane saw it, was to act as a guide to people to assert their freedom and independence.

Before Mondlane's death in 1969, FRELIMO had moved in a radical direction. It had a Central Committee with a burgeoning cell organization system; it adopted Marxist phraseology and "democratic centralism"; and it looked for model and direction to North Vietnam, Cuba, and the Soviet Union. Mondlane's analysis of Portuguese colonialism borrowed heavily from Marxism and Leninism. But unlike Lenin,* who held ambivalent views toward the peasantry, the FRELIMO president followed the teachings and lessons of Mao Zedong* on the preeminence of the rural regions in a people's war. Despite the vigor with which he pursued his far-reaching goals, Mondlane was viewed as moderate and pro-American by some journalists, a few Mozambicans, and even some Portuguese. It is generally believed that the Portuguese secret police had Mondlane assassinated; another interpretation, however, holds that more radical elements in FRELIMO killed him. Whatever the truth, FRELIMO became a thoroughgoing Marxist party after his death and rules an independent Mozambique today along conventional Marxist-Leninist lines.

BIBLIOGRAPHY:

A. "The Struggle for Independence in Mozambique," in *Southern Africa in Transition*, ed. John A. Davis and James K. Baker (New York: Praeger, 1966); "Conversations with Eduardo Mondlane," *Africa Report* (November 1967); "Mozambique War," *Venture*, 20, no. 7 (July-August 1968), pp. 9–10; *The Struggle for Mozambique* (Baltimore, Md.: Penguin Books, 1969).

B. Thomas H. Henriksen, "The Revolutionary Thought of Eduardo Mondlane," *Geneve Afrique*, 12, no. 1 (July 1973), pp. 37–52; Thomas H. Henriksen, *Mozambique: A History* (London: Rex Collings, 1978); Thomas H. Henriksen, *Revolution and Counterrevolution: Mozambique's War of Independence, 1964–1974* (Westport, Conn.: Greenwood Press, 1983).

THOMAS H. HENRIKSEN

MONTAÑA CUÉLLAR, DIEGO   (1910–n.a.). Born in 1910, Colombian lawyer Diego Montaña Cuéllar received a degree in law and political sciences in 1934. He held the posts of professor and rector of the Universidad Libre (Free University) and professor of American sociology at the National University. Montaña also acted as legal advisor to two confederations of Colombian petroleum workers. He is the author of numerous works on the petroleum industry, agrarian problems, law, political parties, economic development, and worker and student organizations.

Montaña Cuéllar viewed Marxism-Leninism as the only route to revolution in Latin America. He adopted Lenin's* characterization of imperialism as the highest phase of capitalism, and his works frequently analyze the effects of imperialism on Colombia. He notes that despite Colombia's vast oil supplies, national demand is satisfied only by importation. Although international monopolies profit from the exportation of the major part as crude, only a small portion is refined for local consumption. The required importation of gasoline and other petroleum derivatives produces an outflow of capital. Montaña argues that because national capitalists have joined with the foreign capitalists to exploit petroleum, there exists no independent national bourgeoisie. This conclusion leads Montaña to his first departure from orthodox Marxism: as a result of its weak and dependent nature, Montaña contends, the national bourgeoisie is incapable of initiating an anti-imperialist revolution. The revolution, therefore, cannot be a bourgeois-democratic revolution in which the proletariat serves as an auxiliary force. Rather, the revolution must be led by the revolutionary vanguard with the proletariat playing the principal role. Also included, however, would be workers, university sectors, peasants, intellectuals, the most progressive factions of the national bourgeoisie, and even conservatives.

Montaña also deviates from classical Marxism in his view of economic determinism. He notes that although the economic base normally determines the political superstructure, the contrary occurs in periods of crisis. That is, the political structure determined by the crisis in turn determines the base. The political dimension assumes an essential role in the socio-economic formation, becomes integrated in history, and determines whether society moves backward or forward. During the imperialist stage, especially, the political dimension dominates the economic for a prolonged period. According to Montaña, the social turmoil that plagues Latin America, particularly Colombia, springs from the constant lack of correspondence between the potentially dynamic productive forces and conservative relations of production, especially when previous socio-economic formations are not overcome. For this reason, according to Montaña, in Colombia the political dimension determines the economic.

BIBLIOGRAPHY:

A. *Sociología americana* (Bogotá: Universidad Nacional de Colombia, 1950); *El petróleo de Colombia para los colombianos* (Bogotá: Ediciones Suramerica, 1958); *Colombia: país formal y país real* (Buenos Aires: Platina, 1963).

DAWN FOGLE DEATON

MORA VALVERDE, MANUEL   (b. 1910). Manuel Mora was born in San José, Costa Rica, on 27 August 1910. His first formal association with radicalism came in 1929, when as a young law student he associated himself with the Revolutionary Association of Labor, a group dedicated to the study of Marxist theory and advocating political action in Costa Rica against economic and social injustice. This group was a precursor to the Costa Rican Communist Party, which Mora and other radicals founded in June 1931. Since then Mora has been the only significant leader that the Costa Rican Communist Party has ever had. He has served, for example, as the Party's secretary general from 1931 to the present. In addition, Mora has represented the Party as a congressional deputy (1934–48 and 1970–74) and as the Party's presidential candidate in 1940 and 1974.

Manuel Mora's contributions to Marxism in Costa Rica involve practice rather than theory. Mora's leadership role in the 1934 banana workers strike and his alignment with the government of Calderon Guardia during the 1940s represent, perhaps, the periods of greatest influence that Mora and the Communist Party have enjoyed in Costa Rica. While generally following a conservative Moscow line, Mora has managed to establish a respectable place for himself and his party in the Costa Rican political system. The Costa Rican establishment views Mora as one of the nation's leading intellectual figures and accepts the Communist leader's repeated assertions that he will work for change within the structures of the Costa Rican democratic system. Mora's somewhat tame "Costa Rican" brand of Communism has led, within the last generation or so, to a series of schisms within the nation's Marxist movement. Younger militants advocate a much more stringent Party line, and it appears as if Mora's influence, so significant over the past fifty years in Costa Rica, is finally beginning to wane.

BIBLIOGRAPHY:

B. Vladimir de la Cruz, *Las luchas sociales en Costa Rica, 1870–1930* (San José: Editorial de Costa Rica, 1980); Jorge Mario Salazar, *Politica y reforma en Costa Rica,*

1914–1958 (San José: Porvenir, 1981); Charles D. Ameringer, *Democracy in Costa Rica* (New York, Praeger, 1982).

RICHARD V. SALISBURY

MUSSO   (1897–1948). Musso was born in 1897 in Kediri, East Java, Indonesia. He was educated in Batavia (Jakarta). An early member of the ISDV (Indies Social Democratic Association) of Sneevliet*, he was imprisoned in 1919–23 for nationalist activities. Emerging from prison, he became one of the most important leaders of the Indonesian Communist Party (PKI). He became first secretary of the Batavia branch, then moved east to Surabaya, where he became editor of the newspaper *Proletar* and secretary of Sarekat Postel (the Postal Workers' Union). By 1925, Musso had become a Central Executive member of the PKI and was one of the main architects of the revolt planned by the Party for the following year. Musso himself journeyed to Moscow in a vain attempt to secure the agreement of the Comintern to this abortive revolt.

Following the failure of the 1926 revolt, Musso remained in Moscow for most of the next two decades. He attended the International Lenin School and in 1928 represented the PKI at the Sixth Comintern Congress, when he was elected a member of the Executive Committee (ECCI). In 1935, Musso journeyed briefly to Indonesia to establish a clandestine party organization, generally referred to as the "illegal PKI." This party, on Musso's instructions, urged its members to join the non-Communist nationalist parties and encourage the formation of an antifascist front. In August 1948, Musso returned from the Soviet Union armed with what he referred to as his "Gottwald* Plan." He assumed leadership of the PKI and directed the Party in a new radical path, making clear that he hoped to duplicate in Indonesia what Klement Gottwald had just achieved in Czechoslovakia. On 18 September the PKI rose in revolt against the Republican government of Sukarno, but the rebellion was quickly crushed and Musso shot to death on 31 October 1948.

BIBLIOGRAPHY:

    B. George McTurnan Kahin, *Nationalism and Revolution in Indonesia* (Ithaca: Cornell University Press, 1952); D. N. Aidit, *Menggugat Peristiwa Madiun* (Jakarta: Jajasan Pembaruan, 1964); R. T. McVey, *The Rise of Indonesian Communism* (Ithaca: Cornell University Press, 1965).

MICHAEL C. WILLIAMS

N

NAVILLE, PIERRE (b. 1904). As a sociologist and writer, Pierre Naville's entire career has been spent at the Centre National de la Recherche Scientifique (CNRS) in Paris (1947–74). He has also acted as director emeritus of the CNRS. Born in Paris on 1 February 1904, Naville studied at the Ecole Alsacienne and the Faculté des Lettres in Paris. He received his *docteur èn lettres* as well as a diploma from the Institut d'Orientation Professionnelle. During the 1920s and 1930s Naville was influenced by the radical surrealist literati and their rebellion against the bourgeoisie. He became attracted to communism, but eventually moved with other radical intellectuals to Trotskyism.* Before World War II he edited *La Verité*, an official French organ of the Trotskyist Fourth International. After the war he abandoned the organization and began working at the CNRS, established under the Popular Front government. During the postwar period, he wrote for *L'Observateur*, a left-wing biweekly for independent Marxists with a small readership. Today he lives in Paris, works primarily as a sociologist, and writes prolifically on issues of labor.

Like many Trotskyists, Naville's contribution to Marxist theory has come largely from his struggle against the bureaucratic and authoritarian elements of the Stalinist* form of communism. Much of Naville's life has been spent criticizing the powerful Stalinist influence in the French Communist Party (PCF) and rejecting the bureaucratic Soviet version of Marxism in general. During the 1940s and 1950s he remained an admirer of the October Revolution as the epitome of Marxist revolution, while still critical of Stalinism. His obsession with the bureaucratic forces of oppression in Stalinist Marxism led Naville in the 1950s and 1960s to lose faith in any automatic organic fusion of socialism and proletarian democracy and to turn as a Trotskyist sympathizer to empirical studies of the labor process and automation in hopes of revising Marxism.

Naville's philosophical contributions have been minor and have not deviated far from the positivist orthodoxy in Marxist theory. From his earliest days as a Trotskyist, Naville has attacked any view that consciousness can be liberated before the radical transformation of social structures. That kind of determinism is rooted in his early materialism and positivism of the 1940s and 1950s. In a major work on the French Enlightenment materialist D'Holbach, Naville strives to renew materialism as a serious method of analysis by recovering its philosophical roots. Indeed, his strong attachment to forms of rationalism, scientism, and positivism led Maurice Merleau-Ponty† after World War II to link Naville with the Stalinists on the grounds of common positivist methods and sentiments.

Naville's highest visibility came in 1956 when he attacked Jean-Paul Sartre's† defense of the PCF (which he saw as equating authentic Marxism with the Communist Party). The attack, which came in the work *L'Intellectuel communiste*, centered on the ambiguity in Sartre's existentialism as the root of his idealist and uncritical relations with the PCF. Naville's attack was harsh, and after 1956 Sartre never again defended the PCF. Since then, Naville has concentrated his efforts on numerous empirical studies of automation, the need for greater labor mobility and task diversity in large-scale industry, economic nationalization, worker self-management, and modern problems of class struggle.

BIBLIOGRAPHY:

A. *D'Holbach et la philosphie scientifique au XVIIIe siècle* (Paris: Gallimard, 1943; rev. ed., 1967); *L'Intellectuel communiste* (Paris: Rivière, 1956); *De l'aliénation à la jouissance* (Paris: Rivière, 1957), vol. 1 of the six-volume *Le Nouveau Léviathan*, (1957–77); *Temps et technique* (Geneva: Droz, 1972); *Sociologie d'aujourd'hui* (Paris: Anthropos, 1981).

SCOTT A. WARREN

NEGRIN, JUAN (1889–1956). The son of a wealthy family living in the Canary Islands, where he was born in 1889, Juan Negrin studied medicine in Madrid and continued his studies in Germany. At a very young age, in 1921, he became a professor of physiology at the University of Madrid, where he was instrumental in the construction of the University City. He became a socialist and was affiliated with the Partido Socialista Obrero Español (PSOE) in the final years of the dictatorship and was a delegate of the Canary Islands to the Constitutional Cortes in 1931. Although he did not hold any leadership office in the party, he always supported the political positions of Indalecio Prieto.* Recommended by Prieto for the position of Minister of Public Finance in Francisco Largo Caballero's* cabinet, he was responsible for the transfer (for deposit) of over 500 million metric tons of gold to the Soviet Union as a guarantee of payment by Spain for war material bought from the Soviet Union by the Spanish Republic.

After the fall of Largo Caballero in May 1937, Negrin was called by Azaña to preside over the Cabinet or Council of Ministers, a position he held until the end of the Civil War. Roughly treated by Largo Caballero (whom he succeeded in the presidency) and by Prieto (whom he fired as Minister of Defense in April 1938), he was accused of being the *hombre de paja* (straw man) of the Communists. Later history, however, emphasizes his qualities of great energy and independence, his vast culture, and his enormous capacity for work. Having no inclination at all toward theoretical problems, he is remembered for his decision to resist at any price and prolong the Civil War to the last possible moment. In this decision he relied, above all, on the firm support of the Communists, although he never felt beholden to them, nor could he be considered their political puppet. After the war he tried, unsuccessfully, for a reconciliation with Prieto, who invariably rejected his offers of friendship. Negrín died in Paris on 14 November 1956.

BIBLIOGRAPHY:

A. *Epistalario Prieto y Negrin* (Paris: Maspero, 1939).

B. Hugh Thomas, *The Spanish Civil War* (Harmondsworth: Penguin, 1965); Gabriel Jackson, *The Spanish Republic and the Civil War* (Princeton: Princeton University Press, 1967); Angel Viñas, *El gro de Moscu* (Barcelona: Grijalbo, 1979).

SANTOS JULIÁ

NETO, AGOSTINHO   (1922–1979). Agostinho Neto was born in 1922 in Bengo (Catete), a Mbundu village sixty miles from the capital of Angola, Luanda. The son of a respected Methodist minister, he was brought up in Luanda, where he went to secondary school, successfully competing for one of the few places available to Africans. He was one of a handful to qualify for a university place. He worked for the Luanda Public Health Service for three years before leaving, on a Methodist scholarship, to train as a medical doctor in Portugal. There he was soon politically active, eventually becoming a member of the Central Committee of the anti-Salazar youth movement, the MUD-J, a broad democratic political front with links to the Communist Party. He also made his mark as a poet, a literary talent he was to cultivate successfully later. His political activity and his anticolonial poetry made him a prime target for the Portuguese secret police. He was arrested for ninety days in 1952 and again sent to jail from February 1955 to June 1957. Nevertheless, he managed to qualify as a doctor in 1958 and returned to Angola the following year with his Portuguese wife. He set up practice in Luanda, where he immediately joined nationalist politics. In June 1960 he was arrested once more and sent in exile to Cape Verde. The protest that followed his arrest in Luanda was brutally suppressed, leaving several dead. In 1962 he escaped from Portugal, where he had been transferred and entered full-time politics as the leader of the Angolan nationalist movement, the Movimento Popular de Libertação de Angola (MPLA). He remained the leader of the MPLA throughout the war of national liberation (1961–75) and became the first president of independent Angola in 1975, when the Portuguese withdrew. The MPLA's success came after fifteen years of difficulties, during which Neto's leadership was not always secure. Until 1966, the MPLA was almost totally ineffective as it was confined to the Congo and, harassed by its rival the FNLA in Zaire, could not secure regular access to Angola. Its only success was in the Cabinda enclave. Between 1966 and 1970 it made good progress in Eastern Angola, setting up liberated areas under its political control and linking up with its isolated fighting group in the Dembos Mountains (near Luanda). It managed to lay down the foundations of a new administration and to carry out political mobilization. After 1970, internal political splits and more intense Portuguese counterattacks drastically reduced the MPLA's effectiveness and left Neto with a much weakened rump party. But Neto's political and diplomatic skills ensured that he represented the MPLA in the tripartite independence negotiations in 1975. Following the Portuguese withdrawal, the MPLA managed to gain control of Luanda and twelve out of the sixteen provinces, successfully holding off the FNLA's military challenge. South Africa's invasion prompted Neto to call on Cuban assistance. Today the FNLA is finished, but UNITA, a third movement under the leadership of Jonas Savimbi (originally the FNLA's "foreign secretary"), continues guerrilla operations against the MPLA government. Neto died from cancer in September 1979 while undergoing medical treatment in the Soviet Union. He was replaced by the First Vice Prime Minister and Minister of Planning, Jose Eduardo dos Santos.

Neto became a Marxist while a student in Portugal, but he always remained, like many of his lusophone colleagues, a nationalist rather than a communist. The movement that he came to lead, the MPLA, had clear Marxist antecedents, as it included within its ranks some members of the short-lived Angolan Communist Party. It was always likely, throughout the war of national liberation, that the MPLA, partly because of Neto's leadership and partly because of its historic support among the working class and *musseques* (slums) of Luanda, would evolve a Marxist ideology and would move toward a Marxist-Leninist state after independence. Although Marxist ideology was toned down before independence for the sake of unity, it reasserted itself quickly afterward. In October 1976, the MPLA Central Committee officially adopted the doctrine of scientific socialism and Marxism-Leninism and endorsed the aims of establishing a people's democracy, all code words marking the creation of a Marxist state. The workers were seen as the "leading force" of the revolution and the peasants the "principal force" in a worker–peasant alliance. It called for planned economic development as a necessary condition for building a socialist society. Centralized planning would cover all sectors of economic and social life, and Marxism-Leninism would serve as the ideological base of the state. Finally, in December 1977, at the First Party Congress, the MPLA converted itself into a vanguard Marxist-Leninist "labor party." The party was now described as a "party of the working class, a solid alliance of the workers, peasants, revolutionary intellectuals, and other working people dedicated to the cause of the proletariat." The MPLA was to become a strict vanguard party, very limited in membership. Although the orientation taken by the MPLA in 1977 was to some extent a result of the Nito Alves "ultra-left" coup attempt, there is little doubt that Angola's firm move toward Marxism-Leninism (one of the first states in Africa officially to do so) derives directly from Neto's thinking.

Neto's reluctance to admit his Marxist inclination during the nationalist struggle did not detract from the strength of his faith in socialism. He believed that socialism could be established in Angola without passing through a capitalist phase, a belief that went beyond a strictly "Bolshevik" position. Neto's conception of Marxist politics was, however, close to the Soviet model, in that the MPLA, despite its success in Eastern Angola and in the Mbundu hinterland, was and substantially remains an urban-based movement. Reference to class struggle and to the political primacy of the working class worked to ensure support in the urban areas for an MPLA always concerned to defuse racial opposition to a largely mulatto and *assimilado* leadership and to preempt working-class opposition to a more privileged, petit bourgeois leadership. The MPLA's contribution to Marxist practice during the war lay in the establishment of what is referred to as *poder popular* (people's power) in the form of village (or urban quarter) action committees, new political structures informed by socialist ideology set up to administer the liberated areas. The MPLA's efforts in moving *poder popular* along distinctly socialist lines involved attempts at setting collective forms of agricultural production and distribution. These were not, however, as successful as those in Mozambique, both because the MPLA was not, like its Mozambican counterpart (FRELIMO), a party strongly rooted in the countryside and because, as a movement of national liberation, the MPLA never overcame the political, military, ethnic, and personality problems that stood in the way of an effective people's war. The final phase of decolonization, the tripartite civil war, the involvement of South African and Cuban troops, the need to defend Luanda, and the MPLA's ultimate reliance on its most loyal and effective source of support among the workers of the capital, all combined to reinforce Neto's penchant for a "Bolshevik" approach to the construction of socialism in Angola. The uncertain, and to some extent dangerous nature (from the point of view of the party's political grip) of *poder popular*, essentially a grass-roots movement, and the lack of firm MPLA organization in large areas of the Angolan countryside led Neto, especially after the Nito Alves coup attempt, to restructure the MPLA very tightly into a vanguard party and to increase the dominance of the state over local centers of democratic power. The continuing civil war in Angola, largely fueled by South Africa's support of UNITA, works further to strengthen the centralizing, statist, *dirigiste* policy. Neto's most significant legacy is an internally consistent Marxist ideology advocating development from above and supporting the dominant role of the MPLA within a strong party-state.

BIBLIOGRAPHY:

A. In *Antologia da poesia negra de expressão portuguesa*, ed. Mario de Andrade (Paris: Oswald, 1958); *Wir kämpfen für die ungeschränkte Unabhängigkeit* (Frankfurt: Deutscher Studenschriften, 1969); "Who Is the Enemy? What Is Our Objective?" *Ufahamu*, 4, no. 3 (1974).

B. Peter Benenson, *Persecution 1961* (Harmondsworth: Penguin, 1961); John Marcum, *The Angolan Revolution I* (Cambridge: MIT Press, 1969); Basil Davidson, *In the Eye of the Storm* (London: Longman, 1972); John Marcum, *The Angolan Revolution II* (Cambridge: MIT Press, 1978).

PATRICK CHABAL

NIN, ANDREU   (1892–1937). Andreu Nin, a preeminent Spanish Marxist during the 1930s, was a founder-member of the controversial Partido Obrero de

Unificación Marxista (POUM) who attracted international attention when he mysteriously disappeared at the hands of NKVD agents during the Spanish Civil War. Born into the modest household of a shoemaker in El Vendrell, Catalonia, Nin trained to become a schoolmaster before moving to Barcelona in 1910. There he was immediately drawn into the rich and complex milieu of the industrial working classes, where he divided his time between teaching at *ateneos* (workers' cultural centers) and writing for various left-republican newspapers and Catalan cultural digests. Nin's early exposure to such literary and political activities exercised a profound influence on him, for throughout his life he strove to combine his interests in both of these areas.

Although initially attracted to republican and Catalan nationalist groups, he soon left their reading circles for socialist ones, joining the Agrupación Socialista de Barcelona in 1913. In the wake of the Bolshevik Revolution, however, Nin deserted the socialist party for the Confederación Nacional del Trabajo (CNT), which he then regarded as the most important revolutionary workers' organization in Spain. Despite the fact that the CNT was a predominantly anarchist organization, Nin himself did not become an anarcho-syndicalist but rather converted to a brand of revolutionary syndicalism that was inspired by Leninist* ideas. From the beginning, Nin played a leading role in the CNT. After organizing a professional union, El Sindicato de Profesiones Liberales, he was designated to replace Evelio Boal as secretary general of the National Committee of the CNT, and in 1921 he formed part of the CNT delegation sent to Moscow to attend the Third Congress of the Comintern and the founding congress of the Profintern (Red International of Labor Unions, RILU).

Nin's trip to Moscow was a fateful one, for he was to remain there as a political exile for the next nine years. On the strength of his abilities as a writer and organizer, he earned a key post in the Profintern as the secretary in charge of the Spanish-speaking countries. In his new role, Nin saw himself as a revolutionary Marxist-Leninist whose task it was to imbue the international syndicalist movement with a Communist perspective. His writings at this time, which are aimed at countering anarcho-syndicalist and fascist influence, slavishly conform to Comintern policy, and as such they reveal his doctrinaire attitude toward syndicalist matters.

Nin's decision in 1926 to join the Trotskyist* Left Opposition faction inevitably strained his relations with the Stalinist*-dominated bureaucracy. He nevertheless continued working in the Profintern until he was forced to resign in the early part of 1928, with his formal expulsion from the Communist Party coming later that year. Isolated from the mainstream of political activity and under a form of house arrest at the Hotel Lux, Nin set himself several ambitious writing projects. A planned biography of the Spanish federal, Piy Margall was never completed, but there was a prodigious output of translations of Russian works into Spanish and Catalan, including Dostoevsky's *Crime and Punishment* (1929), Pilniak's *The Volga Flows Into the Caspian Sea* (1930), as well as the classic Marxist studies by Lenin and Georgii Plekhanov.* Perhaps most important, though, was the fact that Nin now found the time to rekindle his interest in Spanish politics.

By the time he left Russia in 1930, Nin was no longer the "fanatic for action" he had been during his early days in the Profintern. Over the years his zeal for revolutionary syndicalism had given way to a more cautious and systematic way of thinking as he gradually assimilated the teachings of the Russian school of Marxists. In particular, his writings after 1928 demonstrate that at least by then he had mastered the principles of Marxism as defined by his principal mentors, Lenin, Plekhanov and Trotsky. For example, in a series of articles for the Catalan periodical *L'Opinió* (1928), Nin utilizes the Marxian theory of historical materialism to explain why anarcho-syndicalism had successfully taken root in Catalonia.

Most Spanish Marxists at this time maintained that the development of anarcho-syndicalism in Catalonia was attributable both to the absence of a revolutionary Marxist tradition there and to the fact that for years, mass numbers of anarchist workers had migrated to Catalonia from the poorer areas of Spain. Nin argued, though, that its fundamental cause lay elsewhere. Following Lenin and Plekhanov, Nin held that a society's economic "base" ("productive forces") determined the development of its political ideologies, culture, and the like. Thus, Nin claimed, the "utopian" theories of the anarchists had flourished among the Catalonian working classes essentially because the society itself rested on an agrarian (i.e. "backward") economic foundation. It followed, Nin went on to say, that the progressive industrialization of the region would be accompanied by a decline in the strength and influence of a rudimentary theory such as anarcho-syndicalism.

Like so many radicals of his day, Nin believed that he had found in Marxism a tool with which he could lay bare the complexities of society. Accordingly, he employed its methodology not only to analyze political "phenomena" like anarcho-syndicalism but above all to predict their final outcome. In any event, however, the anarcho-syndicalist movement in Catalonia was not linked to the rhythm of the economy in quite the way Nin had imagined, for despite the upsurge of industrialization there, anarcho-syndicalism, instead of deteriorating, actually grew in size and significance.

In April 1930, Nin met in Paris with other leading Trotskyists, including Alfred Rosmer and Kurt Landau, in order to establish the International Bureau of Left Opposition. At the conference, Nin was named as secretary of the group's Spanish section. Among other things, the Oppositionists believed that communism had languished in Spain primarily because the Stalinist Partido Comunista de España (PCE), had deviated from the "true path" of Marxism and was therefore incapable of leading the working classes. Consequently, when Nin arrived in Barcelona in September, his chief objective was to promote the Left Opposition platform as a means of reforming (and hence revitalizing) the Communist movement.

Lacking a political organization of his own, Nin's initial strategy was to try to reorient the PCE by operating through the Catalan branch of the Comintern, the Federación Comunista Catalano-Balear, or FCCB, popularly known as the Catalan Federation. And despite some opposition, Nin did manage briefly to use the organization as a vehicle for his designs, not only promulgating the Trotskyist line in its widely circulated organs, *La Batalla* and *L'Hora*, but also influencing policy decisions through his collaboration with the Catalan Federation's leader and his lifelong friend, Joaquin Maurín.*

By 1931, Nin was pursuing a new course of action that ultimately led to the creation of an independent Trotskyist party. For Nin, it was axiomatic that the more one deviated from orthodox Marxism, as derived from the Bolshevik experience, the less one understood the so-called true forces that shaped social reality. Hence, when Maurín argued that the Russian model of revolution should be rejected in favor of one suited to the pecularities of Spanish society, Nin branded him a "confusionist," that is, one who advocated a spurious form of Marxism.

Meanwhile, Nin's relations with Trotsky were foundering over tactical disagreements. But despite his problems with Trotsky in the 1931–34 period, Nin remained committed to the cardinal principles of his doctrine, and he also accepted the validity of Trotsky's critique of Stalinism. In fact, even after he had broken with him, Nin continued to subscribe to Trotsky's notion of the permanent revolution, according to which the Spanish revolution would develop, not through distinct stages as the Stalinists maintained, but as a continuous process, passing directly from the democratic phase to the socialist one.

Between 1934 and 1935 the political trajectory of Nin and the Izquierda Communista de España (ICE) more and more paralleled that of Maurín and the Bloque Obrero y Campesino (BOC). By the end of September 1935 their policies were so much in accord that the two groups merged to become the POUM, with Maurín as secretary general and Nin, Andrade, and other ICE members serving on the Secretariat. The POUM, which stood for the principles of Marxism-Leninism, refused to identify itself with the Stalinist–Trotskyist controversy, which was then dividing the international Marxism movement, preferring instead to adhere to the non-aligned London Bureau for Revolutionary Socialist Unity. For maintaining an independent stance, the POUM was—both before and during the Civil War—frequently assailed by Trotskyists and Stalinists alike.

When the military uprising began in July 1936, Maurín was trapped behind Francoist lines, where he was to remain for the duration of the war. In his absence, Nin assumed the leadership of the POUM, although, significantly, he ruled not as secretary general but as political secretary of the party. As the new party leader Nin faced a number of obstacles, not least of which was the fact that he lacked the popular support his predecessor had enjoyed. From the outset of the war, Nin and the POUM joined the CNT—the most powerful revolutionary organization in Catalonia—in arguing that the war and revolution were inseparable issues. In so doing, they placed themselves in opposition to the ever increasing numbers of antirevolutionary forces in the Republican camp, who insisted that the revolution give way to the war effort. Above all, Nin believed that it was vital for all revolutionary groups to conquer political power so that they could implement their radical programs. By joining the Generalitat, the ruling body in Catalonia after September 1936, Nin and the POUM thought that they could achieve their aim of establishing a workers' and peasants' dictatorship that ruled entirely in the interests of the proletarian class. Nin took the first step toward this goal when he served as a councillor of justice in the Generalitat between September and December 1936. While in office he advocated a "proletarian form of justice" (i.e. dispensing with judicial procedures inherited from the Republic) in the hope of ensuring the hegemony of the workers in the region.

Before long, however, Nin and the POUM steadily lost ground to their numerous adversaries. Led by the Communist-controlled Partit Socialista Unificat de Catalunya (PSUC), this group effectively undermined the POUM's position by discrediting their political motives, accusing them, among other things, of serving the interests of international fascism. The campaign against the POUM culminated with the notorious May events of Barcelona in 1937, following which the POUM was vigorously persecuted by the Communists under the Negrín government. Nin was one of the first POUMists who fell victim to their witch hunt; he was taken prisoner in June and later secretly assassinated.

Nin's disappearance sounded the death knell for the POUM movement, for despite the fact that some of its militias continued operating, the party apparatus was bereft of all of its principal leaders, who had been either forced underground, killed or imprisoned. Who exactly was responsible for Nin's execution remains a mystery, for although postwar revelations from ex-Communists like Jesús Hernández and Alexander Orlov suggest that he was killed on orders from Moscow, more recent investigations place the blame at the door of the PCE itself.

BIBLIOGRAPHY:

A. *Els moviments d'emancipació* (Paris: P.U.F., 1970); *Los problemas de la revolución española* (Paris: P.U.F., 1971); *Los problemas de la revolución española (1930–1937)* (Barcelona: Ibérica de Ediciones y Publicaciones, 1977).

B. Julián Gorkin, *El proceso de Moscú en Barcelona: el sacrificio de Andrés Nin* (Barcelona: Aymá, 1974); Victor Alba, *Dos revolucionarios: Andreu Nin/Joaquin Maurín* (Madrid: Seminarios de Ediciones, 1975); Pelai Pagès, *Andreu Nin: su evolución política (1911–1937)* (Barcelona: Hacer, 1975); Fancesc Bonamusa, *Andreu Nin y el movimiento communista en España (1930–1937)* (Barcelona: Hacer, 1977); Pelai Pagès, *El movimiento trotskista en España (1930–1935)* (Barcelona: Hacer, 1977).

GEORGE R. ESENWEIN

NIZAN, PAUL   (1905–1940). Born the son of a railway engineer in Tours in 1905, Paul Nizan went to the Lycée Henri IV, where he befriended Jean-Paul Sartre,† and thence with him to the Lycée Louis le Grand in 1922 and the Ecole Normale Supérieure in 1924. He also joined the *Philosophies** group in 1924, but although a friend of Politzer, he kept his distance from the other members, who he felt were undisciplined and anarchistic. He "escaped" on a voyage of self-discovery to Aden in 1926–27 and later in that year, on his return to France, married, with Sartre and Raymond Aron as witnesses. At this time he took up political activism, joining the French Communist Party (PCF), writing for *La Revue marxiste* (1929), and editing *Bifur* and *Commune* with Louis Aragon (1933). From 1931 until 1933 he taught at the *lycée* in Bourg and then on his return to Paris threw himself once again into political activity. He taught at the Université Ouvrière and at the PCF's central school, ran the *L'Humanité* bookshop, published *Morceau choisis de Marx*, and became involved in the Association des Ecrivans et Artistes Révolutionnaires, which led to the editorship of its journal, *Commune*.

In 1934–35 he spent nearly a year in the Soviet Union, attended the Soviet Writers Congress of 1934, and edited pieces for *International Literature*. In 1936 he made journeys to Spain, both before and after the outbreak of Civil War, as a journalist for the Communist press and in 1937 attended a writers conference in Madrid. By 1938 he was codirecting the PCF evening daily paper *Ce Soir* with Aragon, and he followed the prewar crisis very closely for this and other journals. In response to the German-Soviet Pact of August 1939 he quite suddenly resigned from the PCF, sending a letter of resignation to *L'Oeuvre*, the only newspaper to protest the banning of the Communist press. Called up in 1939, he was killed at Audrincq (Pas de Calais) in May 1940.

Nizan's political initiation took place during his voyage to Aden, where he was shocked to see what he denounced in *Aden-Arabie* as the inhuman exploitation of imperialism. His view of the decay and corruption of European capitalist society was reinforced by his opposition to orthodox philosophy in France, which can be seen in his attacks on Bergsonianism in *La Revue marxiste* and his later condemnation of orthodox philosophers in *Les Chiens de garde* (1932). This reply to Julien Benda, who had criticized committted intellectuals in his *La Traison de clercs*, attacked "bourgeois" philosophy for its concentration on the history of ideas, which had resulted in its defense of the Third Republic and its capitalist system. Philosophers, said Nizan, had to tackle contemporary problems and become committed proponents of social change, rather than state watchdogs. For Nizan, this commitment was best expressed through militancy in the PCF, which he felt provided intellectual discipline, a sense of duty, and a means of nonegoistic expression. His attack on orthodox philosophy also contained elements of existentialism and surrealism. In his early years he flirted with Trotskyism,* but his constant theme was commitment, and he did much to influence Sartre toward committed literature.

Nizan was not an original theorist of Marxism, but he was a sophisticated and effective popularizer, whether in novel form—as in the alienation of *Antoine Bloye*—or document form, with the publication of *Morceaux choisis de Marx*. He defended the Soviet Union as a new society experiencing difficulties in the early stages of development and was silent on the question of the show trials. Indeed, for a period in the mid-1930s he became an official apologist for the PCF, although his novel *La Conspiration* (1938) portrayed a young idealist who thought the Communist Party too moderate, and his description of the international scene in *Chronique de septembre* was far broader than that of the PCF.

Nizan had a constant preoccupation with death, which colored much of his work and made it often both fatalistic and pessimistic. He was a great influence on the most notable left-wing thinkers of the 1930s, and although many of them attacked him in 1939 for his "betrayal," men like Sartre, Henri Lefebvre,† and Politzer were all inspired by Nizan's writing.

BIBLIOGRAPHY:

A. *Les Chiens de garde* (Paris: Rieder, 1932); *Antoine Bloye* (Paris: Grassee, 1933); *Le Cheval de Troie* (Paris: Gallimard, 1935); *Aden-Arabie* (Paris: Rieder, 1936); *Chronique de septembre* (Paris: Gallimard, 1938); *La Conspiration* (Paris: Gallimard, 1938).

B. J. J. Brochier, *Paul Nizan: intellectuel communiste* (Paris: Maspero, 1917); Jean-Paul Sartre, "Paul Nizan," in *Situations* (Paris: Gallimard, 1964); A. Ginsbourg, *Nizan* (Paris: Editions Universitaires, 1966); W. D. Redfern, *Paul Nizan* (Princeton: Princeton University Press, 1972).

JOHN C. SIMMONDS

NORO EITARŌ (1900–1934). Noro Eitarō was the innovative young Marxist whose analysis of Japanese economic development formed the theoretical basis of the loyalist Kōza-ha ("feudal faction"). While in primary school in his native village in Hokkaidō, Noro suffered severe arthritis, had his right leg amputated below the knee, and used an artificial leg thereafter. Because of his disability, he did not attend a public middle school, but graduated from a private school in 1920, when he entered the preparatory course at Keiō University in Tokyo. In 1923, influenced by a lecture on the "world socialist movement" by prominent Communist Party member Nosaka Sanzō, Noro then entered the regular undergraduate course of the Economics Department. The following year Noro joined the Industrial Labor Research Institute (Sangyō rōdō chōsasho), helped to establish the Mita Social Science Research Association (Mita shakai kagaku kenkyūkai), and as lecturer at the Sōdōmei union-run Labor School, taught Marx's *Capital*. After graduating from the university with a thesis on the history of Japanese capitalism, in April 1926, he was arrested for his role in the "Kyoto University Incident" of December 1925. He was sentenced in May 1927, but released on bail pending appeal.

While teaching at the Labor School, Noro cultivated an interest in Japanese social history and economic change, and these became the themes of his short life's work. By 1930 he had revised and published his thesis, entitled *History of the Development of Japanese Capitalism* (*Nihon shihon-shugi hattatsu shi*) and penned additional pieces on "The Historical Conditions of the Development of Japanese Capitalism" ("Nihon shihon-shugi hattatsu no sho jōken") and "Contradictions of the Present Stage of Japanese Capitalism" ("Nihon shihon-shugi gendankai no sho mujun"). Noro, along with Inomata Tsunao,* thus was among the first to respond critically and comprehensively to Takahashi Kamekichi's* thesis of "petty imperialism," which used a Marxian analysis of Japanese development to justify Japanese expansion onto the Asian mainland.

During the "petty imperialism" debate, Noro also critiqued Rōnō-ha spokesman Inomata Tsunao's* interpretation of Japanese capitalism. Inomata, Yamakawa Hitoshi,* and others had left the Japanese Communist Party in protest against the Comintern's 1927 Theses prescribing a two-stage revolution for a Japan that was still significantly backward. Noro provided the theoretical leadership for the defense of the two-stage strategy by the Marxist faction that remained loyal to the Communist Party. Although he himself did not join the Party until 1930, the following year he joined Ōtsuka Kinnosuke, Hirano Yoshitarō,* Yamada Moritarō,* and others to plan the seven-volume *Symposium on the History of the Development of Japanese Capitalism* (*Nihon shihon-shugi hattatsu shi kōza*). While he led the Kōza-ha in the "debate on Japanese capitalism," Noro never lived to see this project completed. From 1931 to 1933 Noro remained active in the affairs of a Communist Party that was increasingly repressed by police under the rising fervor following the Manchurian Incident. He headed the Party's peasant department, served on, then chaired, the Central Committee and Politburo, and took over the leadership of the Party after the *tenkō* (defection) of its imprisoned leaders Sano Manabu† and Nabeyama Sadachika. Shortly after marrying in May 1933, he was arrested in November of that year. He fell ill under repeated interrogation and died in North Shinagawa Hospital on 19 February 1934. Although Noro did not have the opportunity fully to systematize his ideas, his writings postulated an intricate structural linkage and interdependence between the "Asiatic" "feudal" elements of Japan's agrarian sector and the advanced capitalist elements in the urban areas. His views were elaborated in the *Kōza* by Hirano, Yamada, and others.

BIBLIOGRAPHY:

A. *Noro Eitarō zenshu* (Complete works on Noro Eitarō) (Tokyo: Shin Nihon shuppan-Kai, 1965).

B. Nosaka Sanzō, Hani Gorō, and Kazahaya Yasoji, *Noro Eitarō to minshu kakumei* (Noro Eitarō and the democratic revolution) (Tokyo: n.a., 1946).

GERMAINE A. HOSTON

O

ORTEGA SAAVEDRA, DANIEL (b. 1945). Currently a Sandinista leader and coordinator of the junta that runs the postrevolutionary Government of National Reconstruction in Nicaragua, Daniel Ortega was born in Libertad, Nicaragua, on 11 November 1945. Completing secondary studies in Managua, he began to study law at the Central American University, but soon became heavily involved in political and organizational activities. In 1962 he entered the Sandinista National Liberation Front (FSLN) to take charge of the Secondary School Student Movement. Undaunted by several brief stays in prison, he became more heavily involved in the Sandinista Front, moved into the national leadership, and was placed in charge of military operations for the internal front in 1966. Captured by Somoza security agents, he was imprisoned and tortured until his comrades forced his release with the famous Christmas party ransom in December 1974. After helping to build international support for the revolution, he returned to Nicaragua in 1976 once again to direct the internal front. As the military intensity of the revolution increased, he assumed leadership of first the northern Carlos Fonseca Amador* Front, and then the Southern Benjamín Zeledón Front. With the victory of the FSLN, Ortega became first a member and then the coordinator of the governing junta. He traveled to numerous countries and appeared before the UN and the Nonaligned Movement to represent Nicaragua.

Like the other Sandinista leaders, Ortega sees the utility of many aspects of Marxist theory to understand and organize society, but is strongly nationalist and far from dogmatic in his use of ideology. Before the reunification of the three different Sandinista tendencies (Protracted Popular Warfare, Proletarian Tendency, and Third Way/Insurrectionalists), Ortega and his brother Humberto (now Minister of Defense) led the Social Democratic Terceristas, who pushed for popular insurrection and the incorporation of diverse sectors of Nicaraguan society in the revolution. Dedicated nationalists, he and the other Sandinista leaders have repeatedly asserted Nicaragua's nonaligned status and argued that the FSLN did not find its ideology in theories that were exported from another country but in Nicaragua's own history—in Sandino and the Nicaragua people. (see *La revolución a través de nuestra dirección nacional* and Vanden).

BIBLIOGRAPHY:

A. With others, *La revolución a través de nuestra dirección nacional* (Managua: FSLN National Secretariat of Information and Political Education, 1980); with others, *Habla la dirección de la vanguardia* (Managua: FSLN Department of Information and Political Education, 1981).

B. Tomás Borge et al., *Sandinistas Speak* (New York: Pathfinder, 1982); Harry E. Vanden, "The Ideology of Insurrection," in *Nicaragua in Revolution*, ed. Thomas Walker (New York: Praeger, 1982).

HARRY E. VANDEN

ŌTSUKA HISAO   (b. 1907). The Japanese Marxist economic historian Ōtsuka Hisao is the head of the school of historiography heavily influenced by both Marxism and Max Weber's work on comparative religion. Born in Kyōtō on 3 May 1907, Ōtsuka attended the Third Higher School and then Tokyo Imperial University, where he concentrated in economics. After graduating in 1930, he became assistant professor, then full professor at Hōsei University in Tokyo; and in 1939 he became an assistant professor of economics at Tokyo Imperial University. By 1947, Ōtsuka had become a full professor at the University of Tokyo, where he remained until his retirement in 1968. During these years, Ōtsuka came under the influence of Christianity, participating in the Tokyo University Bible Society. After his retirement from the University of Tokyo, he joined International Christian University as a professor.

In his early years as a scholar in the prewar period, Ōtsuka focused on the transformation of the earliest forms of capital, merchant and usury capital, to industrial capital as the former lose their irrational aspects. The results of this work appeared in his book *On the Category of So-Called Early Capital*. Ōtsuka then moved to study the unique formation of industrial capital in England and published his *Preface to the Economic History of Europe* (1938). At this point Ōtsuka began to treat what would become a major theme of his work—the contradiction between weaving or textile manufacture in villages and in cities. In the face of the facts gleaned by his own research, Ōtsuka became critical of the classic theories of Evgenii Kosminsky and Michael Postan on agricultural history and the manorial system. More importantly, Ōtsuka was influenced by Weber's *Protestant Ethic and the Spirit of Capitalism*. Thus, his 1941 work on *The Position of Commerce in the History of the Development of Capitalism* and subsequent works on the *Preface to the Economic History of Modern Europe* (1944), *The Ancestry of Modern Capitalism* (1946), and *Religious Reform and Modern Society* (1948) presented Ōtsuka's historical theory on the basis of a merger of Marx's materialism and Weber's sociology.

In the postwar period, Ōtsuka concentrated more on the economic aspects of his work, partly in response to heavy criticism of his earlier work. Influenced by Marx's *Precapitalist Economic Formations*, Ōtsuka published his *Basic Theory of the Kyōdōtai* (Community). This had become a subject of considerable interest in Japan in the prewar period, since it was on the basis of communal structures that Marx differentiated between Germanic, Slavonic, and Oriental communities. During the debate on Japanese capitalism, from 1927 to 1937, many in the Kōza-ha had sought to present a Marxian analysis of Japanese (and Chinese) economic and political development from antiquity to the prewar period and found it useful to refer to the development of the *kyōdōtai* and the notion of the Asiatic mode of production. Now Ōtsuka argued that, in the emergence of modern bourgeois society, the growth of class differentiation within the *kyōdōtai* led to the establishment of local marketing areas.

Finally, since about the 1960s, Ōtsuka's work began to take yet another new direction, prompted by his political role in opposing the security treaty in 1960 and his advocacy of a *People's Economy* (*Kokumin keizai*) (1965). In his 1959 work *Religious Revolution and Modern Society* (*Shūkyo kaikaku to kindai shakai*), Ōtsuka had argued that an ossified bureaucracy is a consequence of modernity and a danger to be considered seriously as a theoretical problem. Thus, Ōtsuka undertook a comparative study of Marx's work on alienation and Weber's ''sociology of domination'' and produced a rethinking of the *Method of Social Science* (1966), which he would in subsequent years also apply to the study of less developed countries in the Third World.

BIBLIOGRAPHY:

A. With others, eds., *Seiyō keizai shi kōza* (An economic history of the West), 5 vols. (Tokyo: Iwanami shoten, n.d.); *Ōtsuka Hisao chosaku shū* (Collected writings of Ōtsuka Hisao), 10 vols. (Tokyo: Iwanami shoten, n.d.).

GERMAINE A. HOSTON

ŌUCHI HYŌE   (b. 1888). The Japanese economist Ōuchi Hyōe was born on 29 August 1888 on the island of Awajishima in the Inland Sea. He attended the Fifth Higher School and was graduated from the economics course of Tokyo Imperial University's Faculty of Law in 1913. Ōuchi then joined the prestigious Ministry of Finance, which sent him to the United States in 1916 to pursue a year of study of trusts. On returning to Japan, Ōuchi resigned from the Finance Ministry and was appointed a lecturer, then, in 1919, assistant professor at Tokyo Imperial University, where he taught finance in the Economics Department. However, Ōuchi's tenure at the university was cut short when he was implicated in the Morito Incident of January 1920. Professor Morito Tatsuo was forced out of the university because of his publication of articles on socialism in popular magazines. Ōuchi, as nominal publisher of the premier issue of one magazine in which Morito's essays had appeared, *Studies in Economics*, was also charged with violating the publication laws, and left his position at the university. In 1921, using his own funds, Ōuchi traveled to Germany to study under the German economist Emil Lederer at Heidelberg, and at the same time Ōuchi began to study in depth the writings of Rudolf Hilferding* on finance capital and other Marxist works. While abroad, he was reappointed to Tokyo Imperial University in 1922, and returned to take the post in 1923.

After a few years teaching finance, Ōuchi had already begun to develop his own unique approach to the subject, one that was represented in the two-volume *Outline of the Study of Finance*, which Ōuchi published in 1930 and adopted for classroom use. During the 1920s the dominant perspective in the field was that of the "social policy school," which was heavily influenced by German economics since the Bismarck era. Ōuchi presented a critique of this school and took "scientific socialism" as the point of departure for his own study of finance. Because of his reliance on Marxist texts in his teaching and research and his personal association with many known members of the dissident Rōnō (Labor-Farmer faction) of the Japanese Communist Party, Ōuchi came to suffer the effects of the increasingly severe police repression of the 1930s. Ōuchi himself repeatedly denied that he was a member of the Rōnō-ha. However, in 1938, along with the Uno Kōzō* and others, Ōuchi was arrested on charges of violating the Peace Preservation Law in the Professors' Group Incident. In 1939 Ōuchi was released on bail, and in 1944 a court of appeals acquitted him, but he was not restored to his university position until after the war, in 1945. During these years Ōuchi published on *Japanese Finance* (1932) and translated Adam Smith's *Wealth of Nations*, Malthus on population, and other Western works.

Ōuchi retired in 1949 from the University of Tokyo, but not before he had helped to create a cadre of distinguished Marxist economists, including Arisawa Hiromi and Takahashi Masao. In addition, after the war Ōuchi continued to write prolifically on contemporary economic issues like inflation and land reform. He served as head of the Conference on the Social Security System and as president of Hōsei University from 1950 to 1959. In the meantime, Ōuchi played an active role in the revived socialist movement. He helped to found the Socialist Association in 1950, and along with Rōnō-ha leaders Sakisaka Itsurō* and Yamakawa Hitoshi* exerted a heavy influence over the left wing of the Japanese Socialist Party. After the Socialist Association split in 1967, he helped Sakisaka to rebuild the group. At the same time, Ōuchi also organized a Research Group on Constitutional Issues and was a representative on the National League to Support the Constitution in order to avert any effort to revise the renunciation of war out of the Constitution.

BIBLIOGRAPHY:
A. *Meiji zaisei keizai shi bunken kaidai* (Explication of Documents on the History of Meiji Finance and Economics) (Tokyo: Iwanami shoten, 1933); *Ōuchi Hyoe chosaku shū* (Collected works of Ōuchi Hyoe) 12 vols. (Tokyo: n.a., 1972).

GERMAINE A. HOSTON

ŌUCHI TSUTOMU (b. 1918). The Marxist economist Ōuchi Tsutomu is the eldest son of another Japanese Marxist, Ōuchi Hyōe.* Ōuchi Tsutomu was born in Tokyo on 19 June 1918. After attending the First Higher School, he graduated from Tokyo Imperial University's Department of Economics in 1942 and became affiliated with the Japanese Agriculture Research Institute. After the war, Ōuchi was appointed assistant professor in the Institute of Social Science at the University of Tokyo. In 1957 he moved to the Economics Department, and in 1960 he became a full professor, after studying in the United States from 1957 to 1959. In the 1970s Ōuchi lectured on Japanese economic theory in the United States, the Soviet Union, India, Pakistan, and Europe. In recent years, Ōuchi retired from active teaching. However, as a specialist on agriculture, Ōuchi has served in rice policy discussions and as a member of the Central Council on Employment Stabilization.

Ōuchi Tsutomu has established himself among both Marxist and non-Marxist scholars in Japan and abroad as one of Japan's leading economists. A student of Uno Kōzō,* the theoretician and founder of the Uno School of Japanese economics, Ōuchi has also been associated with the Rōnō (Labor-Farmer) faction, although Ōuchi himself has denied membership in the latter group. Ōuchi established his reputation through his work on Japanese agriculture on the basis of Uno's theory and empirical methodology, designed to overcome the weaknesses of both the prewar Rōnō-ha and Kōzā-ha ("feudal" faction). Thus, Ōuchi's *Agricultural Problems in Japanese Capitalism* (1948) is recognized as a seminal work in the field. In addition to agriculture policy, Ōuchi has also worked on the theory of "state monopoly capitalism" and its applicability to Japan.

BIBLIOGRAPHY:

A. *Nihon nōgyō no zaiseigaku* (The finance of Japanese agriculture) (Tokyo: n.a., 1950); *Nōgyō kyōkō ron* (A theory of agricultural panic) (Tokyo: n.a., 1954).

GERMAINE A. HOSTON

P

PENG PAI (1896–1929). A Chinese Communist peasant organizer, Peng Pai was born into a leading landlord family in Haifeng, Guangdong Province, and studied in Japan during the period 1918–21. Upon returning to China he joined the Chinese Communist Party (CCP) and became active in peasant affairs in Guangdong, where in 1923 he founded a provincial peasant association. The following year he was named director of the Peasant Movement Training Institute in Canton (nominally under Kuomintang (KMT) control) and emerged as the CCP's leading spokesman on peasant issues. After the collapse of the CCP–KMT united front in 1927, Peng established two soviet governments in his native region, but they were quickly suppressed by KMT forces. Peng thereupon fled to Shanghai, and in the following year he was elected to both the Central Committee and the Politburo. In 1929 he was betrayed to the Nationalist authorities by a fellow Party member and executed shortly thereafter, at the age of thirty-three.

Peng Pai's historical significance lies in the fact that he was the first prominent Chinese Communist leader to take a serious interest in the peasant movement and the first to establish a soviet type of government in China. His interest was probably sparked by his three years at Waseda University in Japan, where radical faculty and students favored organization among the peasant masses over work among the small Chinese urban working class. Peng's activities among the peasants had two dimensions: on the one hand, self-help efforts involving arbitration, education, and sanitation and, on the other, campaigns to reduce rents, harass unpopular landlords, and pressure local government for reform. These activities soon brought unfavorable notice from the provincial authorities, who broke up the peasant associations and forced Peng to flee the area.

In 1925, under the aegis of the CCP–KMT united front, Peng returned to the Haifeng region and revived the peasant associations, which soon took over most of the functions of local government in an increasingly chaotic situation. When the united front collapsed in April 1927, Peng set up soviet governments in Haifeng and Lufeng counties and carried out a series of radical policies involving rent reduction, land expropriation, harassment of local officials, and increasing

violence against landlords. The soviets lasted from November 1927 to February
1928, when they were destroyed by Nationalist armies. Peng's soviets were the
first such governments established by the Communists in China, although they
have since been overshadowed in historical significance by those of the 1930s
and 1940s (e.g. Jiangxi, Yan'an). Likewise, Mao Zedong* has eclipsed Peng
as the CCP's leading peasant strategist and the creator of the distinctive peasant-
based revolution that has since become the hallmark of Chinese communism.
Nonetheless, Peng's earlier efforts have received due recognition from the CCP,
and he remains a respected figure in official Party history.

BIBLIOGRAPHY:

A. *The Haifeng Peasant Movement* (Canton: n.a., 1926).

B. Donald Holoch, *Seeds of Peasant Revolution: Report on the Haifeng Peasant
Movement* (Ithaca: Cornell University Press, 1973); Roy Hofheinz, Jr., *The Broken Wave:
The Chinese Communist Peasant Movement, 1922–1928* (Cambridge: Harvard University
Press, 1977).

RAYMOND F. WYLIE

PETKOFF, TEODORO   (b. 1931). The son of radical middle-class immi-
grant parents, Teodoro Petkoff represents a new breed of Venezuelan Marxist.
He gained political prominence through the Communist Youth Group at Caracas's
Central University. After fighting against dictator Marcos Pérez Jiménez, who
controlled Venezuela between 1948 and 1958, Petkoff moved into national politics, became a guerrilla leader in the struggle to forge socialism, then rejected
extreme vanguardism in which the revolution is interpreted as an act of will. In
1970 Petkoff founded the parliamentary-oriented Movement to Socialism (MAS)
political party, which calls for a peaceful transition to socialism, rejects popular
frontism, and respects socialist democratic pluralism and the tenets of Eurocommunism. The party pursues a neutral foreign policy, including friendly relations
with the United States, to which it looks as a market for Venezuelan petroleum
and as a supplier of technology. Petkoff serves the party in Venezuela's Congress.

Petkoff's strength lies in his ability to criticize socialism as well as capitalism.
He has rejected both the Soviet and Cuban models for Venezuela, which he
knows must combat a form of representative government, rather than dictatorship
or autocracy. He believes that the right wing too often correctly accuses the left
wing of pursuing a revolution with foreign (Cuban, Soviet, or Chinese) thinking.
In so doing, the right defends nationalism and blames foreigners for social and
political distress. The left then acts as if these criticisms were true by defending
internationalism and identifying with foreign socialists. Thus, he asserts, the left
confuses solidarity with the ideas of the parties that rule in socialist nations. By
using foreign models, the left also displays a colonial mentality, which it has to
defend constantly. He argues for a flexible leftist approach and accuses the left
of using syllogistic logic. For instance, it assumes that the state is the machinery
by which one class oppresses another, and that Venezuela is dominated by the
United States and follows its orders. Thus the Venezuelan state exists to execute

United States commands. If this is so, then when Venezuela accomplishes some good for its people, the left has no explanation, and because of its rigidity, rather than search for valid explanations, it says that the good that occurred is a plot to deceive the people.

BIBLIOGRAPHY:

A. *¿Socialismo para Venezuela?* (Caracas: Domingo Fuentes, 1970); *Razón y pasión del socialismo* (Caracas: Centauro, 1973).

SHELDON B. LISS

PHAM VAN DONG   (b. 1906). Pham Van Dong was born in 1906 in Quang Ngai Province, Vietnam. He studied at Whampoa Military Academy in China. Early on, he became one of the closest collaborators of Ho Chi Minh.* He joined various revolutionary youth groups in his twenties, and in 1929 he was arrested by French colonial authorities and imprisoned in the infamous Poulo Condore. Released in 1936, he helped form the Indochinese Democratic Front and in 1941 the Vietnamese Independence League (Viet Minh) with Ho Chi Minh and Vo Nguyen Giap.* Following the August 1945 Revolution, Pham Van Dong became Minister of Finance of the Democratic Republic of Vietnam (DRV) and headed the Vietnamese delegation to the Fontainbleu Peace Conference of 1946. He was elected a member of the Indochinese Communist Party Central Committee in 1949 and simultaneously appointed vice premier of the DRV. In 1954 Pham Van Dong headed the Vietnamese delegation at the Geneva Conference and was subsequently appointed Prime Minister, a post he holds to this day. He was elected to the Politburo of the Vietnamese Communist Party in 1951.

MICHAEL C. WILLIAMS

PHILOSOPHIES.   The Philosophies group was founded in 1924 by Henri Lefebvre,† Georges Politzer, Pierre Nodier, Norbert Guterman, Pierre Morhange (the editor of its journal), and the group's sponsor, Georges Friedmann.* The revue and the group set out to challenge the conventional teaching of philosophy in higher education from a socialist standpoint. The revue changed its title to *L'Esprit* in 1926 and *La Revue marxiste* in 1929, under which title it had some success in the mass diffusion of Marxist ideas. This change of policy to modern but orthodox interpretations of Marxism was partly a result of the maturing of the group and partly because Politzer, Lefebvre, and Paul Nizan* joined the French Communist Party in 1928–29.

It was originally very much concerned with the philosophical questions arising from the experience of war, a fixation with death, anguish over the "lost generations," and violent opposition to the bankrupt orthodox philosophy of Bergson, Brunschvicg, and Larelle, which it felt had so manifestly failed Western civilization. The group was eclectic in its early days, seeking a new mysticism on the one hand, while carrying out gratuitous acts of theft as a challenge to bourgeois property on the other hand. Through its rejection of bourgeois materialism and its concept of philosophical commitment the group moved rapidly toward Marxism and more structured ideas. *La Revue marxiste*, which was the culmination of this trend, became an influential and sophisticated journal with important articles by Politzer, Nizan, and other leading Marxists. It also published some of Marx's early texts and helped to stimulate interest in them. In the more relaxed atmosphere after 1932, the revue was able to speculate more freely on the relationship of Marxism to wider national and international questions, and together with a companion journal, *La Revue de psychologie concrète*, it made overtures toward existential and phenomenological schools of thought.

JOHN C. SIMMONDS

PIJADE, MOŠA (1887–1957). Moša Pijade was born on 22 December 1887 of middle-class Sephardic Jewish parents in Belgrade in the kingdom of Serbia. His first career was art, and he studied painting in Paris, Munich, and Vienna between 1906 and 1910. Upon his return to Belgrade Pijade became a promising impressionist painter, poet, and journalist. Today he is considered one of Yugoslavia's important artists. Prior to World War I he joined the nationalist Black Hand and was the editor of its underground newspaper, *Pijemont.* After the war Pijade founded the first trade union of journalists in Serbia and published the socialist newspaper *New World*. He joined the new Yugoslav Communist Party in 1920 and was named to its Executive Board at the Vukovar congress in the same year. In 1925 he set up an underground Communist press and published three issues of the Party newspaper, *Komunist*, before he was arrested. He was imprisoned from 1925 to 1939 and twice again in 1940–41. During World War II Pijade along with Josep Broz Tito,* Milovan Djilas,† Alexander Ranković, and Edvard Kardelj became one of the leaders of the Yugoslav revolution. In 1943 he was chosen vice president of the Anti-Fascist Council for the National Liberation of Yugoslavia (AVNOJ), which later became the Provisional Government. After the war Pijade also was elected to the Central Committee and Politburo of the Yugoslav Communist Party and served as President of the Federal Assembly of Yugoslavia from 1953 until his death in 1957. He was given a state funeral in Belgrade and was buried in the Crypt of the National Heroes in Kalemegdan Park.

As for many revolutionaries, imprisonment was a very important experience for Pijade. With some collaboration from Rodoljub Colaković (N. Bosanac) and August Cesarec, Pijade (Comrade "Marko" Porobić) carried out the first Serbo-Croation translation of Marx's* *Das Kapital*; it was smuggled out of prison and published in Belgrade, beginning in 1932. This translation established Pijade as the first major ideologist of Yugoslav communism. His ideological impact was broadly felt. Pijade exercised the principal influence on the early communism of Tito, Djilas, Ranković, and other future leaders of Yugoslavia, many of whom he first met in prison.

First as a doctrinaire Stalinist,* and then as a Titoist after the Soviet–Yugoslav split in 1948, Pijade helped to establish Yugoslav communism in power after World War II. Whereas Djilas, Kardelj, Boris Kidrić, and others sought to explain and justify the Yugoslav position, Pijade also often attacked the Soviet Union more directly. For example, in his many speeches and writings he consistently compared Soviet imperialism to that of tsarist Russia and Nazi Germany, and Stalin to Hitler in their treatment of small nations. Pijade also was a leading advocate of Yugoslav nonalignment, pointing out that Yugoslavia's rapid progress outside the Soviet sphere made his country a model for others. In 1953, as Vice President of the Federal Assembly, Pijade also led the excommunication of his old comrade-in-arms Djilas and replaced him as president. He attacked Djilas's deviationist views (finally fully crystallized in *The New Class* in 1957) as "political pornography." Thus, until his death Pijade remained Tito's chief advisor and a high priest of Yugoslav communism.

BIBLIOGRAPHY:

A. *Izbrani govori i članci, 1941–1947* (Selected speeches and articles, 1941–1947) (Belgrade: Kultura, 1948); *Izbrani govori I članci, 1948–1949* (Zagreb: Kultura, 1950).

B. Slobodan Nešović, *Moša Pijade i negovo vreme* (Moša Pijade and his times) (Belgrade: Kultura, 1968); Milovan Djilas, *Memoir of a Revolutionary* (New York: Harcourt Brace Jovanovich, 1973); Milovan Djilas, *Wartime* (New York: Harcourt Brace Jovanovich, 1977).

DENNIS REINHARTZ

PLEKHANOV, GEORGII V. (1856–1918). G. V. Plekhanov, often referred to as the father of Russian Marxism, was born in 1856 in the Russian province of Tambov, the son of a member of the local gentry. Initially drawn to agrarian socialism (narodnichestvo) while a student in St. Petersburg in the 1870s, Plekhanov left Russia for a thirty-seven-year exile to Western Europe in 1880, during which he established himself as the foremost Russian Marxist abroad. Forming the Emancipation of Labor group in 1883 in Geneva, Plekhanov wrote numerous books and pamphlets in an attempt to shift the existing radical movement in Russia toward Marxism. In the words of V. I. Lenin,* Plekhanov "reared a whole generation of Russian Marxists." In addition to providing intellectual guidance for the fledgling Russian Marxists, Plekhanov was active in refuting what he considered to be the main heresies of leading European socialists such as Eduard Bernstein.† Joining with Lenin and Julius Martov* to found the Russian journal *Iskra* (The Spark) in 1900, Plekhanov refused to support Lenin's efforts to overthrow the existing Provisional Government and took no part in the subsequent Bolshevik uprising. Ten weeks after Lenin's advent to power in the fall of 1917, Plekhanov's journal *Edinstvo* (Unity) was banned. Plekhanov died in May 1918 in a Finnish sanitarium.

Although Plekhanov's place in the history of Marxist thought is associated mainly with his efforts to convince fellow Russians that their nation's future fit the Marxist mode, his writings were also important in the broader area of West European socialism. Philosophically, Plekhanov accepted and publicized the orthodox version of Marx's* and Engels's* ideas. His reputation rests on this, as well as on his applying these ideas to areas of philosophical speculation heretofore ignored by Marxist intellectuals. His most significant contribution to Marxist theory came in the area of epistemology, where he set forth the hieroglyphic theory of knowledge, which maintained that human sensations and resulting ideas are not simple copies of things existing in the real world but are arbitrary signs or symbols that represent them. This position was later attacked by both Lenin and Aleksandr Bogdanov.

BIBLIOGRAPHY:

A. *Sochineniia* (Collected works), 24 vols. (Moscow: International, 1923–27); *In Defense of Materialism: The Development of the Monist View of History* (London: Lawrence and Wishart, 1947); *Essays in the History of Materialism* (New York: Fertig, 1967); *Selected Philosophical Works* (Moscow: Progress, 1976).

B. Samuel H. Baron, *Plekhanov: The Father of Russian Marxism* (Stanford: Stanford University Press, 1963).

MICHAEL M. BOLL

POL POT   (b. 1928). Pol Pot was born Saloth Sar in Prey Sbeuv in the Kompong Thom region of Kampuchea (Cambodia) in 1928. He was educated at a secondary school in Phnom Penh and in 1949 attended the Ecole du Livre in Paris, where he studied radio electronics. He was active in the Association of Khmer Students in France. Returning to Cambodia, he taught at a private school, the Kamputh Both. He was one of the main organizers of the Kampuchean Communist Party (KCP) formed in 1960, which broke ties with previous pro-Vietnamese Communist groups. He became its secretary general two years later. In 1963, Saloth Sar went underground and began forming the band of guerrillas that eventually became known as the Khmer Rouge. From 1970 he was vice chairman of the People's National Liberation Armed Forces of Kampuchea. Following the Khmer Rouge victory of 1975, Pol Pot (using this name for the first time) was appointed Prime Minister of Democratic Kampuchea on 14 April 1976. He stepped down as Premier in December 1979, following the Vietnamese invasion of the country. Since then he has remained commander-in-chief of the National Army and chairman of the Supreme Military Committee of Democratic Kampuchea.

It was only in September 1977, two years after the Khmer Rouge took power, that Pol Pot first publicly revealed that Democratic Kampuchea was ruled not just by the Angka (the organization) but by a Marxist government led by a Leninist party, the Communist Party of Kampuchea. Previously, existence of this party had never been acknowledged. In a long statement, the most important made by Pol Pot, he stressed self-reliance and collectivism and spoke in strong terms of the persecution that the Khmer Communists had faced and overcome. He also acknowledged the growing rift with Vietnam. Because of this, Kampuchea's only way forward was to build and develop its own resources. Formal education as such was to be abolished. Moreover, Kampuchea was the first socialist country to claim to have abolished contradictions between urban and rural dwellers, between physical workers and intellectuals, as all now worked

and lived together. It has since been learned that in abolishing these contradictions—in abolishing what Pol Pot perceived as the urban vestiges of Western
imperialism—Pol Pot initiated a forced total migration from Phnom Penh that
led to the deaths of hundreds of thousands of innocent Cambodians. Thousands
more were executed in the countryside, their only crime, apparently, was being
"infected" by Western ideas and education. Ironically, Pol Pot also described
with bitterness the ruthlessness with which former ruler Prince Sihanouk's police
and army had pursued the Khmer Rouge in the 1960s, and he emphasized the
theme that the war and the revolution had unleashed a vast anger accumulated
during long years of persecution.

BIBLIOGRAPHY:

A. *Discours prononcés par le camarade Pol Pot, sécretaire du Comité Central du
Parti Communiste du Kampuchea au meeting commémorant le 17ème anniversaire de la
fondation du Parti Communiste du Kampuchea et à l'occasion de la proclamation so-
lonnelle de l'existence officielle du Parti Communiste du Kampuchea*, Phnom Penh, 27
September 1977.

B. Ben Kiernan and Chanthou Boua, eds., *Peasants and Politics in Kampuchea 1942–
1981* (London: Zed Press, 1982).

MICHAEL C. WILLIAMS

PONCE, ANÍBAL (1898–1938). Argentine essayist Aníbal Ponce wrote in
the fields of education, medicine, philosophy, psychology, and sociology. Initially a positivist, he became a member of the Socialist Party and later made the
transition to orthodox Marxism. While professor of psychology at Argentina's
National Institute of Secondary Education, he coedited the *Revista de filosofía*.
In 1930 he founded the Free College of Advanced Study and in 1936 directed
the journal *Dialéctico*, dedicated to rigorous social analysis.

In his 1935 book on bourgeois and proletarian humanism (republished in Fidel
Castro's* Cuba), he stated that humanism characterized by a return to the study
of the classics was a prologue to the Renaissance, from which there emerged
an intellectual elite with an excessively abstract view of man. To him, Erasmus's
bourgeois humanism proclaimed the freedom of man, but only freed man to
serve those who owned the means of production. He felt that Marxist humanism
viewed people as living beings, not abstractions, and contended that humanity
can only flourish if class distinctions are eliminated. He felt that this could be
done by creating a love for the humanities and a classless culture with which
all could identify. He saw a correlation between transmitting the classics to the
masses and eliminating poverty, between opening up universities to all, enabling
everyone to comprehend how exploitation works in order to eliminate it. He
considered Shakespeare's works, such as *Richard III* and *Julius Caesar*, model
realistic creations through which the class system could be identified. He spoke
about "socialist realism," or the factual history of events seen through the
classics, which demonstrated how societies interacted and exposed the reality
of life to be, not its dreams, but its forces and how they operate.

Ponce's volume on education and the class struggle (also reprinted in Cuba) showed how the dominant class directed the state's social organization through education, which conveyed selected information but did not teach people to think for fear that they might then question their system. He also condemned the concept of the "neutral" scholar and pointed out the dangers of those who maintain that their judgments are objective and value-free.

BIBLIOGRAPHY:

A. *Educación y lucha de clases* (Havana: Imprenta Nacional de Cuba, 1961); *Humanismo burgués y humanismo proletario* (Havana: Imprenta Nacional de Cuba, 1962).

B. Américo Ghioldi, *Juan B. Justo: sus ideas históricas socialistas, filosóficas* (Buenos Aires: Monserrat, 1964).

SHELDON B. LISS

PONLAJAN, ASANI   (b. 1918). Asani Ponlajan came from the family of a wealthy aristocrat and official, but even as he was scoring brilliantly in the best schools of Thailand he was writing sharp attacks on the economic and social injustice practiced by his own class. A talented poet and linguist, he wrote novels and verse in seven languages. While working as a provincial attorney he escaped arrest in a 1953 purge of radical writers, mysteriously disappearing. Later it became known that he had joined the underground Communist Party of Thailand (CPT). By the mid-1960s he had become a member of the CPT Politburo. But defectors from the party said his role was confined to art, propaganda, and literature. Asani's translation of Mao Zedong's* *Collected Works* remains the CPT's most important document.

But Asani's own writing emphasized the importance of art and culture rather than the military-political stress of Maoist doctrine. He wrote that "the revolution of literature is one of the ways that leads to socialism, therefore the content of literature must agree with socialism." (*From Lor and Sri Burapa*, pp. 110–11). Along with Jit Pumisak,* he was one of the first Thai radicals to attack the exploitation of women in traditional Thai society. The marriage certificate "was like buying a woman by using a ticket" (*Some Thought from Literature*, p. 198). Asani's writing has had a great impact on radicals and students but little on the CPT, which remains committed to an armed peasant guerrilla war.

BIBLIOGRAPHY:

A. *Kor kid jag wannakadi* (Some thought from literature) (Bangkok: Student Center of Thailand, 1974); *Rau chana laew mae ja* (We have won, mother) (Bangkok: Kon Num, 1974); *Jag pra lor lae sriburapa* (From Lor and Sri Burapa) (Bangkok: Sahai Rag, 1975); *Silapagarn haeng garb glon* (The art of poetry) (Bangkok: Jaroenwit Garnpim, 1975).

B. Chontira Gladyu, *Wannakadi puangchon* (People's literature) (Bangkok: Aksornsarn, 1974).

YUANGRAT WEDEL

PRADO, JÚNIOR CAIO   (b. 1907). Born in 1907 in São Paulo, Júnior Prado distinguished himself as author, historian, social critic, and politician. He was a founder of the publishing house Editora Brasiliense and editor of the well-known Marxist social science journal *Revista brasiliense*, published during the 1950s and early 1960s. He also was a member of the Brazilian Communist Party and was elected as a Communist deputy to the Brazilian Congress.

Prado's major work focuses on the colonial formation of Brazil. He believes that the discovery and colonization of America was an episode in the history of European maritime expansion after the fifteenth century. He argues that the Brazilian economy was characterized by a high concentration of wealth in the large-scale agrarian organization of large estates, slave labor, and monoculture; in addition, the externally oriented economy was based on production of commodities for the international market, a reflection of Portuguese policies aimed at enriching the mother country's trade. As such, Brazilian relations with the outside world involved not only dependence on Portugal because of colonial subjection but also ties to an international market.

Prado believes that socialism would arise from capitalism. He argues that Marxism, with its dialectical method, offers the possibility of a new historical interpretation and analysis. The Brazilian revolution, however, could not follow the traditional struggle against feudalism because feudalism never existed in Brazil. This position allowed him to attack the interpretation of the Communist Party, which had called for a bourgeois-democratic revolution of antifeudal and anti-imperialist direction. He also criticizes the idea that a national bourgeoisie of progressive capitalists could resist imperialism and bring about the national revolution. Thus, only a radical revolutionary course toward socialism remained. Dependence and submission to imperialism could only be broken by revolutionary struggle and national liberation.

BIBLIOGRAPHY:

A. *O mundo socialista* (São Paulo: Editora Brasiliense, 1962); *Formacão do Brasil contemporaneo: colonia* (São Paulo: Editora Brasiliense, 1963); *A revolução brasileira* (São Paulo: Editora Brasiliense, 1966); *The Colonial Background of Modern Brazil* (Berkeley: University of California Press, 1967).

RONALD H. CHILCOTE

PREOBRAZHENSKY, EVGENY ALEXEYEVICH   (1886–1937). The Russian economist Evgeny Alexeyevich Preobrazhensky was born in Oryol Province in 1886. In 1903 he joined the Russian Social Democratic Party and worked for the Bolsheviks until the end of the Civil War. His loyalty and efforts were rewarded in 1920, when he was chosen a full member of the Central Committee and one of three Party secretaries. He was a leader of the post-Civil War Left Opposition, which advocated industrialization, criticized the bureaucratization and centralization taking place under Stalin,* strived to achieve proletarian political and economic democracy, and argued that the success of Soviet socialism is inextricably linked to successful socialist revolutions elsewhere in Europe and the world. These attitudes got him expelled from the Party. However, Preobrazhensky abandoned Trotsky* and the Left Opposition generally after Stalin* began his program of rapid industrialization. He was, in rapid order, readmitted to the Party, expelled again in 1931, and readmitted in 1932. He was finally arrested in 1935 and, on Stalin's orders, shot while in prison in 1937.

Preobrazhensky was not a philosopher or social theorist. He implicitly accepted the orthodox, Engelsian* versions of historical materialism and dialectical materialism and devoted himself, instead, to formulating an apt economic program that would secure the political and economic maturation of Soviet socialism. As a scholar, he studied the dynamics of economic growth and inflation in underdeveloped economies and argued that a desired increase in industrial investment would generate an inflationary spiral that might limit real economic growth. His solution was to finance large-scale heavy industry by making agriculture bear the heaviest financial burden. State trading monopolies would purchase agricultural goods at depressed prices and sell farmers industrial goods at inflated prices, thereby stimulating industrialization, punishing the alarmingly high number of wealthy peasants, and hence inhibiting the growth of rural capitalism and keeping inflation down. Preobrazhensky called this mechanism of state-controlled unequal exchange "primitive socialist accumulation." It was considered by him to be the economic regulator appropriate to growing socialist states, playing a role analogous to that which the "law of value" plays in maintaining capitalism.

BIBLIOGRAPHY:

A. *The New Economics* (Oxford: Oxford University Press, 1965); *From NEP to Socialism* (London: New Park, 1973); *The Crisis of Soviet Industrialization: Selected Essays*, ed. Donald A. Filzer (London: Macmillan, 1980).

B. Alexander Erlich, *The Soviet Industrialization Debate, 1924–1928* (Cambridge: Harvard University Press, 1960); Wlodzimierz Brus, *The Market in a Socialist Economy* (London: Routledge and Kegan Paul, 1972); R. B. Day, "Preobrazhensky and the Theory of the Transition Period," *Soviet Studies*, 8, no. 2 (April 1975); Donald A. Filtzer, "Preobrazhensky and the Problem of the Soviet Transition," *Critique*, 9 (Spring-Summer 1978); P. R. Gregory and R. C. Stuart, *Soviet Economic Structure and Performance* (New York: Harper & Row, 1981).

ROBERT A. GORMAN

PRESTES, LUIS CARLOS   (b. 1898). Born on 3 January 1898 in the southern Brazilian state of Rio Grande do Sul, Luis Carlos Prestes was for almost forty years the head of the Brazilian Communist Party. Prestes was educated in a Brazilian military college, where he eventually graduated as an army engineer. In 1922 he joined an abortive rebellion known as the Lieutenants' Movement, and in 1924 he led a small army of radical cavalry and foot soldiers that was soon called Prestes' Column and that survived for two years in the Brazilian jungles. From this adventure Prestes earned the nickname "Knight of Hope." Prestes escaped to Bolivia in 1926, where he studied Marxism. In 1931 he traveled to Moscow, where he studied for three years and became a Marxist loyalist who henceforth would always defend Moscow's line. In 1934 Prestes returned to Brazil, directed an unsuccessful Communist-led uprising in the armed forces, and was arrested. Named Communist Party Secretary General while in prison, Prestes was released in 1945 and won an election as a federal senator. When the Communist Party was officially banned in 1947, Prestes was forced into hiding, which lasted, off and on, until 1964. Prestes's consistently radical line eventually generated conflict between himself and Party colleagues. In 1971, on instructions from the Brazilian Central Committee, Prestes again moved to Moscow. He returned in 1979, was ousted by colleagues as Secretary General, and was eventually expelled from the Party.

Prestes is not a theorist. His influence in Latin America is based on his dogmatic commitment to working-class revolution, even when others on the left perceive this dogmatism as self-defeating. His loyalty to Moscow is apparently undaunted, even though Moscow now maintains cordial relations with the same Central Committee of the Brazilian Communist Party that expelled Prestes for unquestioningly supporting Moscow.

BIBLIOGRAPHY:
A. *The Struggle for Liberation in Brazil* (New York: Workers Library, 1936); *Documentos de Luis Carlos Prestes* (Buenos Aires: Tiempos Nuevos, 1947); *A situação politica e a luta por um govêrno nacionalista e democratico* (Rio de Janeiro: Vitoria, 1959).

ROBERT A. GORMAN

PRIETO, INDALECIO (1883–1962). Indalecio Prieto was born in Oviedo, Spain, on 30 April 1883. As a child he roamed the streets of Bilbao selling papers. He worked as a stenographer for *La voz de Viscaya* (The voice of Biscay). He then joined the editorial staff of *El liberal*, where he would later become its director and owner. In 1903 he founded the Socialist Youth of Bilbao. His policy of collaboration with the Republicans led to a confrontation with Facundo Perezagua, a labor leader whom he succeeded in the leadership of the Bilbao socialist movement. He was a councilman and vice-mayor in the City Council of Bilbao. He became a delegate to the Cortes in 1919 and, after 1923, was a declared foe of the socialist collaboration with the dictatorship of Primo de Rivera. This led to another confrontation with the labor leadership within the Spanish socialist movement. He participated actively in the work of the committee formed to overthrow the monarchy in 1930, and when this revolutionary movement failed in December of the same year, he fled to France. He was Minister of Finance in the first Republican government (1931), and later Minister of Public Works. In this position he was an advocate of hydraulic power and railroad access to the larger cities. Implicated in the insurrection of October 1934, he fled again to France, directing from there the restoration of the political alliance with Republicanism. When the Popular Front coalition won in 1936, Francisco Largo Caballero* and other labor leaders prevented him from becoming head of the government, a position to which he had been appointed by Manuel Azaña. As the Minister of the Air Force and Navy in the government of Largo Caballero (September 1936), he took over as Minister of Defense in the Juan Negrin* government (May 1937), from which he resigned when Teruel was lost. He died on 11 February 1962, after reconciling with the monarchist groups in order to overthrow Franco's regime.

Indalecio Prieto used to say of himself that he had arrived at socialism more by sentiment than by reason, and as a matter of fact, it was his deep democratic convictions, rather than a system of socialist ideas, that carried him to the leadership of the most political faction of Spanish socialism. His passionate defense of democracy and freedom, in the context of the chaos of the political system of the Restoration, was invariably based on the advocacy of a political alliance with the Republicans and a moderate labor policy. In his political analyses, Prieto departed from the axiom of the *abulia*, or apathy of the Spaniards, from which only the Unión General de Trabajadores (UGT) labor organization and progressive middle-class democrats would be saved. For Prieto, it was not the time, then, for the Socialists (a minority within Spain) to try the takeover of the government by themselves, but rather to join forces with the Republicans in order to reestablish a regime based on freedom and democracy.

This political scheme of Prieto led to direct confrontations with the labor leadership, but it is to him that the socialists owed their presence, at last, in the movement that culminated in the reestablishment of the Republic. Prieto was the leader of the democratic and republican orientation of Spanish socialism, which would reemerge in 1935, after the bitter results of the 1934 insurrection. In his writings of that year Prieto returned to the fundamentals of his traditional policies, although on this occasion his defense of democracy and the Republic would pit him not only against the labor leadership, but also against the Juventudes Socialistas (Socialist Youth), as well as the radical wing of intellectuals, who accused him of being a centrist and who tried to remove him from the leadership of the Socialist Party. The political and ideological debate thus opened between *prietistas* and *caballeristas* presented all the characteristics of a deep cleavage in the bosom of the Socialist Party, which was avoided by the sudden eruption of the Civil War, thus postponing *sine die* the Congress scheduled for October 1936.

BIBLIOGRAPHY:

A. *Del momento, posiciones socialistas* (Madrid: Indice, 1935); *Discursos fundamentales*, ed. Edward Malefakis (Madrid: Turner, 1977); *De mi vida* (Mexico: Oasis, 1968–70).

B. Juan Pablo Fusi, *Politica obrera en el pais vasco 1880–1923*(Madrid: Turner, 1975); Paul Preston, *La destrucción de la democracía en España* (Madrid: Siglo XXI, 1977); Santos Juliá, *Origenes del frente popular en España* (Madrid: Siglo XXI, 1979).

SANTOS JULIÁ

PUIGGRÓS, RODOLFO   (1906–1980). Born in Buenos Aires in 1906, Rodolfo Puiggrós later edited the magazines *Brújula* and *Argumentos*, the daily *El norte* of Jujuy, and *Clase obrera*, organ of the Communist Workers Movement (Movimiento Obrero Comunista, MOC). As a leader of the Argentine Communist Party (PCA), he negotiated with Perón's representative, Admiral Teisaire, in

1945, when Perón was courting left-wing support. Following Perón's election as president the following year, Puiggrós led a dissident fraction within the PCA that opposed the Codovilla* leadership and its extreme anti-Peronist line. He broke with the PCA and founded the MOC in 1947, and four years later he formed with Perón the Movement of Men of Good Will. The MOC, which was the first serious split from the PCA in twenty years, won over many of the Party's trade union militants and played a leading role in the railmen's strike of January 1951. Puiggrós's reputation derives from his political conversion, numerous books and articles (including a six-volume political and social history of Argentina in the nineteenth and twentieth centuries), and his latter-day association with the Peronist left. With the support of the latter, he briefly became rector of the University of Buenos Aires when Perón returned to office in 1973, and he attempted to turn the place into a "national and popular university." His resignation, engineered by the Peronist right in October 1973, provoked major student demonstrations. In September 1974, with right-wing Peronists having gained control of the government, threats from the Triple A death squad prompted him to accept a Mexican offer of political asylum.

The whole Puiggrós family was deeply affected by Argentina's ugly political violence of the 1970s: his daughter Adriana had her house dynamited by the right; his grandson was the subject of an attempted death squad kidnapping; and his son Sergio, a leading Montonero who commanded a huge guerrilla operation in the northern city of Formosa in 1975, was killed resisting abduction in 1976. While in exile Rodolfo Puiggrós strengthened his ties with the Montoneros, the leading armed organization of the Peronist left. He became First Secretary of the Professionals, Intellectuals, and Artists Branch of the Montonero Peronist Movement (MPM) when it was launched in Rome in 1977. Three years later, after some seventy Montoneros had been killed in a disastrous "counteroffensive" against the military regime in Argentina, Puiggrós was promoted to the leadership of the Montonero Party, based in Havana, where he died of a heart attack on 13 November 1980.

Unlike most of his former Communist Party comrades, who initially characterized Peronism as a fascist movement, Puiggrós maintained that Peronism merited support as a progressive national movement in an underdeveloped country. Without renouncing the PCA belief that Argentina was in need of an anti-oligarchic, anti-imperialist revolution, he argued that the left should support Peronism because of its economic nationalism and enhancement of working-class influence. Basing itself on the position of the Chinese Communists during the early days of the Kuomintang, his MOC attempted to influence Peronism from within. Its organ, *Clase obrera*, presented Perón as the chief of an emancipatory national revolution. Less publicly, its sponsors viewed Perón as an empiricist and hoped by working alongside him to provide the philosophical and ideological foundations of his regime.

Puiggrós attributed the downfall of early Peronism in 1955 to the decomposition of the "national front" it represented and to the lack of revolutionary working-class leadership. He regarded a national front and an independent work-ing-class organization as mutually indispensable, so his prescriptions after the 1955 coup involved the rebuilding of the former and the establishment of the latter as its axis. He also envisaged a resuscitation of the army–labor alliance put together by Perón in 1945, feeling that both the military and the masses could be won to his ideology of "popular revolutionary nationalism" and a program including "mass democracy," the dissolution of political parties, the nationalization of certain industries, and an independent foreign policy. Puiggrós is also renowned for his criticisms of Argentina's traditional left, condemned for possessing a "colonial consciousness," for following foreign models of the transition to socialism, and for always having depicted popular revolutionary nationalist currents (particularly Yrigoyenism and Peronism) as reactionary or fascist. In turn, Puiggrós and his tendency were attacked by the far left for subordinating the political independence of the proletariat to the bourgeois na-tionalist leadership of Peronism, through participating in the Peronist movement and accepting the strategic leadership of Perón. Among Peronists he was widely regarded as the most prominent of those recruits from the left who had come to understand the "national question."

BIBLIOGRAPHY:

A. *Historia crítica de los partidos políticos argentinos* (Buenos Aires: Argumentos, 1956); *El proletariado en la revolución nacional* (Buenos Aires: Trafalc, 1958; Buenos Aires: Sudestada, 1968); *El peronismo: sus causas* (Buenos Aires: Cepe, 1969); *Las izquierdas y el problema nacional* (Buenos Aires: Cepe, 1973).

RICHARD GILLESPIE

PUMISAK, JIT   (1931–1966). Jit Pumisak was born in a small town in eastern Thailand. A brilliant scholar, Jit wrote his own encyclopedia of the Thai language while still in high school. In 1957, after being expelled once for his radical writings, Jit graduated from prestigious Chulalongkorn University. He created a sensation by refusing to accept his diploma from the King. Trained as a linguist, Jit's mind ranged broadly, and he poured out Marxist-influenced works on Thai history, art and literature, linguistics and social ills. In 1958 he was jailed as a Communist for nearly six years. In prison he continued his writing and helped organize a prison commune on Marxist lines. Shortly after his release he slipped into the jungle to join the Communist Party of Thailand and its armed insurgency. Jit's more sophisticated understanding of Marxism clashed with the Maoist* dogma of Party leaders, and the frail, bespectacled scholar was relegated to a village propaganda unit. Jit was shot dead by border patrol police on 5 May 1966. After his death Jit's reputation continued to grow. His works on the role of women, Thai history, and political theory were central to the thinking of later generations of radicals.

Jit was the first writer to make an extensive Marxist reinterpretation of Thai history. He wrote that contrary to the official chronicles, Thailand's history was one of class struggle between the oppressor and the oppressed. (*Art for Life, Art for People*, p. 196). His brilliance lay in adducing linguistic and cultural evidence to support this standard Marxist view from a body of history and literature compiled by aristocrats with an antithetical world view. Adapting Marxist analysis to the undeveloped capitalism in Thailand, Jit used it to attack the feudalist structures and elites that continued to wield great power in modern Thailand. Jit called on workers, intellectuals, and peasants to unite and overthrow the semifeudal, semicapitalist ruling class, but he did not emphasize revolutionary political action. Jit's thought focused on the ruling class's control over the minds of the people. Although trained in the Thai classics, he called for a new literature based on the lives and the needs of the masses of common people. A talented poet, Jit himself produced some of the finest pieces of the new literature, "art for life, art for the people," as he called it. He wrote that the oppression of the people began with the control of their minds and thus allowed a small elite to exploit the labor of the vast majority. Control of the means of production, in turn, allowed the ruling classes to use religion, culture, and art to maintain their position in a tight ring that the revolution must destroy. If the people would stop living their lives through the false myths and with the exploitive values of the ruling class, then the day of total revolution would be brought near. But, he argued, if the revolution did not discard the values of class superiority, social inequality, and power morality, then even a successful political revolution would be meaningless.

BIBLIOGRAPHY:

A. *Karl Marx* (Bangkok: Maharat, 1973); *Bot Wipark Wardouy Silapa Wattanatham Kong Jit Pumisak* (Critique of Art and Culture) (Bangkok: Jaroenwit Garnpim, 1974); *Silapa Pur Chewit Silapa Purt Prachachon* (Art for life, Art for People) (Bangkok: Srimeung Garnpim, 1974); *Bod Wikro Wannakadi Yook Sakdina* (The *Critique of Literature in the Sakdina Period) (Bangkok: Pikanet, 1976); Chom Nar Sakdina Thai* (The Face of Thai Feudalism) (Bangkok: Chomrom Nangseu Sang Tawan, 1976); *Kwam Penma Kong Kam Siam, Thai, Laos/Khom Lae Laksana Kong Sangkom Kong Chue Chon Chart* (The Origin of the Words Siam, Thai, Laos and Khom/The Nature of Society According to Race) (Bangkok: Krung Siam Garnpim, 1976); *Pasa Lae Niruktisat* (Language and Etymology) (Bangkok: Srimeung Garnpim, 1979); *Ong Garn Chaeng Nam Lae Kor Kid Mai Nai Prawatsart Thai Lum Nam Chao Phraya* (Ong Garn Chaeng Nam and New Ideas on Thai History in Chao Phraya River Basin) (Bangkok: Duang Kamol, 1981).

B. Suchart Sawaddisri, ed., *Jit Pumisak, Nak Rob Kong Roon Mai* (Jit Pumisak: The Warrior of the New Generation) (Bangkok: Sangkomsart Paritad, 1974).

YUANGRAT WEDEL

Q

QUINTERO RIVERA, ANGEL G. (b. 1947). Born in San Juan, Puerto Rico in 1947, Quintero Rivera studied at the Universidad de Puerto Rico (UPR) and the London School of Economics and Political Science, where he received his Ph.D. He is employed as a research associate in the Centro de Investigaciones Sociales at the UPR. Quintero was one of the founders, and remains an intellectual leader, of the Centro de Estudios de la Realidad Puertorriqueña (CEREP). CEREP has been the principal research organization from which the great bulk of new Marxist research on Puerto Rico has come, and it is through this organization that Quintero has had his major impact as an intellectual. Nearly all of the young generation of Marxist scholars have been associated with CEREP in one way or another, although CEREP itself is not associated with any political party or tendency.

Quintero was one of the first of a new generation of Puerto Rican scholars to begin to examine Puerto Rico's history from a Marxist perspective. His early work was quite theoretically advanced. While the debate about the place of dependency analysis within Marxism occupied center stage of theoretical debate among much of the left in the 1970s, Quintero was using the concept of mode of production (or articulation) analysis; he explicitly rejected dependency analysis as an analytical tool. Quintero's major contributions have been in advancing a historical analysis of nineteenth- and twentieth-century Puerto Rican history that uses Marxist categories and class struggle as organizing concepts. His focus has been on the history of those "without" a history, particularly the working class. His series of essays on the working class are fundamental sources for beginning to understand the role of working-class politics in Puerto Rico. Quintero is one of the most prolific authors among the newer generation of Latin Marxist scholars.

BIBLIOGRAPHY:

A. "Background to the Emergence of Imperialist Capitalism in Puerto Rico," pp. 87–117, in *Puerto Rico and the Puerto Ricans*, ed. Adalberto Lopez and James Petras (Cambridge, Mass.: Schenkman, 1974); "La clase obrera y el proceso politico en Puerto Rico," *Revista de ciencias sociales*, 10, nos. 1–2 (1974), pp. 145–98; nos. 3–4, pp. 61–107; "El Partido Socialista y la lucha politica triangular de las primeras decadas bajo la dominación norteamericana,'' *Revista de ciencias sociales*, 9, no. 1 (1975), pp. 47–100); ''La disintegración de la politica de clases (2 partes),'' *Revista de ciencias sociales*, 9, no. 3 (1975), pp. 261–300; 10, no. 1 (1976), pp. 3–48; *Conflictos de clase y politica en Puerto Rico* (Rio Piedras, Puerto Rico: Huracan, 1976).

JAMES DIETZ

QUIROGA SANTA CRUZ, MARCELO   (1931–1980). Celebrated as one of the most outstanding speakers and popular figures of the Bolivian left in recent years, Marcelo Quiroga was more of an active politician than a theorist. Nonetheless, it was as a novelist and increasingly radical critic of the Movimiento Nacional Revolucionario (MNR) regime (1952–64) that he came to occupy a key position on the left, embracing Marxist ideas late in his political life. As the minister who ordered the nationalization of Gulf Oil (1969) and leader of the Partido Socialista-Uno (since 1971) he developed an increasingly sensitive understanding of the mechanisms of political economy in the peripheral states and produced a number of incisive studies on this subject centered on the experience of Bolivia. Concerned centrally with building a genuinely radical and popular anti-imperialist movement, Quiroga drew heavily on Bolivia's Trotskyist* heritage but sought with success to avoid its more sectarian excesses. His strong antimilitarist stance and remarkable rhetorical ability, employed to great effect in Congress, earned him almost universal respect and account for his assassination at the hands of the military in the first hours of the 1980 coup.
BIBLIOGRAPHY:
   A. *La victoría de abril sobre la nación* (La Paz: n.a., 1959); *El saqueo de Bolivia* (Buenos Aires: Ediciones de crisis, 1972); *Otra vez Marzo* (La Paz: n.a., 1980); *Oleocracia o patria* (Mexico City: Siglo XXI, 1982).

JAMES DUNKERLEY

QU QIUBAI   (1879–1935). A Chinese Marxist-Leninist theorist and Chinese Communist Party (CCP) leader, Qu Qiubai was born into a declining gentry family in Zhangzhou, Jiangsu Province, and his family's misfortunes made him a harsh critic of traditional Chinese society. From 1921 to 1923 he was the Moscow correspondent for a major Peking newspaper; he joined the CCP there in 1922 and on his return to China he worked in Shanghai and elsewhere as a Central Committee member (appointed 1923), a leading propagandist, and the editor of several Party journals. In early 1927, following the breakup of the CCP–KMT united front, Qu was elected to the Politburo and shortly thereafter named Secretary General of the CCP. Later that year he launched a series of abortive rural and urban uprisings culminating in the so-called Canton Commune in December. He was thereupon criticized for ''left opportunism'' and removed from the Party's top post at the CCP Sixth Congress in Moscow in 1928, but he remained a prominent figure in both the Party and the Comintern. Returning to China in 1930, Qu lost out in a power struggle with the Moscow-backed ''Returned Student'' faction and was relegated to the sidelines. Always the activist, he plunged into theoretical and literary debates among left-wing circles in Shanghai during the years 1931–33, when he became closely associated with Lu Xun, China's most prominent writer, who was known to be sympathetic to the Communists. In the years 1933–35 Qu served as educational commissioner in the Jiangxi Soviet, but following its destruction by KMT forces he was captured and executed a few months later.

Qu Qiubai's life was characterized by an unstable tension between literary abilities and political drives, and his intense but short-lived career is testimony to this duality. First as newspaper reporter and then CCP propagandist, Qu introduced an entire generation of young Chinese to Russian literature, Soviet political and social conditions, and Marxist-Leninist theoretical ideas. He was not an uncritical admirer of the Bolsheviks, but he respected their spirit of self-sacrifice and their determination to bring about radical change along socialist lines. His admiration of willpower at times colored his own approach to politics, as, for example, when he attempted the hopeless insurrections against overwhelming odds in late 1927. Interestingly, Mao Zedong* was in charge of one of these (the Autumn Harvest Uprising in Hunan Province), and the two men in fact shared a strong streak of what one writer has called "voluntarism" in their attitude toward revolutionary politics. It is doubtless this affinity with Mao that has helped ensure Qu's continuing respectability in the CCP's official history, the only previous top leader to be so honored.

As a creative thinker Qu Qiubai was more at home in literature than politics, but, ironically, it was his literary theories that provided the basis for later political innovation by others. In the early 1930s he developed an approach to literature that differed sharply from the common view in Chinese left-wing circles that new political contents (i.e. Marxism-Leninism) demanded new literary forms (i.e. Western models). On the contrary, Qu argued that traditional Chinese literary forms could be given new content and suggested in particular that the old historical epics could be used as a literary model for conveying modern revolutionary history. For example, he said, one could envisage a new epic entitled "The Canton Commune" in which Marxist-Leninist political ideas would be brought to China's literate public in this popular, traditional literary genre. From here it was but a short jump to the proposition that Marxist-Leninist theory, if it were to be readily assimilated by the Chinese masses, should be divested of its exclusively European and Soviet referents and discussed in the context of Chinese history, culture, and revolutionary experience.

Qu Qiubai did not arrive at this conclusion explicitly, but others in the CCP did, most notably Chen Boda,* who worked closely with Mao in formulating the concept of the "Sinification of Marxism" in the late 1930s. Although this terminology was subsequently dropped the CCP to this day interprets "Mao's thought" as the creative synthesis of Marxist-Leninist theory and Chinese revolutionary practice; that is, it is "Sinified Marxism." Thus, Qu's literary ideas were of considerable influence in helping shape the CCP's attitude toward incorporating Western Marxism-Leninism into Chinese intellectual constructs.

BIBLIOGRAPHY:

A. *The Chinese Revolution and the Chinese Communist Party* (Moscow: International, 1928); *Collected Works of Ch'ü Ch'iu-pai* (Peking: Foreign Language Press, 1953–54).

B. Paul G. Pickowicz, *Marxist Literary Thought in China: The Influence of Ch'ü Ch'iu-pai* (California: University of California Press, 1981).

RAYMOND F. WYLIE

R

RAMOS, JORGE ABELARDO   (b. 1921). A writer and political leader born in 1921 in Buenos Aires, Jorge Abelardo Ramos has long been the main representative of Argentina's Izquierda Nacional (National Left). As a student during the 1930s he became active in the country's disunited Trotskyist* movement, supporting a fraction that favored "entrism" in the Socialist Party. The National Left developed as a tendency from the mid-1940s, when the left had to respond to the rise of Perón. Ramos wrote for *Frente obrero*, edited *Octubre* (1945–46), and gave critical support to Peronism's "national revolution." While other Argentine Trotskyists, along with Communists and Socialists, opposed Perón, the pro-Peronists were described by an unsympathetic Fourth International as being "more Catholic than the Pope and more Peronista than Perón." During the early Perón period (1946–55) Ramos and his tiny group embarked upon a popular nationalist revision of Argentine history and invested most of their energies in writing and publishing. His first book (1949) was seized by a parliamentary commission headed by a conservative Peronist. Under the pseudonym Víctor Almargo, Ramos wrote for the Peronist paper *Democracía*. He also edited the theoretical journal *Izquierda* (1954–55) and was associated with the publishing house Editorial Indoamérica. In 1954–55 his group formed a minority within the pro-Perón scission from the Socialists, the Socialist Party of the National Revolution (PSRN), and published *Lucha obrera*.

After the coup of 1955, with the PSRN suppressed, the Ramos tendency spent seven years almost entirely devoted to propagating its ideas. It established the Coyoacán publishing house and brought out the magazine *Política*(1958). In 1957 Ramos published his main work, a fresco of key events in Argentine history interpreted from a national-popular standpoint. This literature influenced young socialist groups and a few dissident Peronists who in July 1962 combined with the National Left to form the Socialist Party of the National Left (PSIN). It launched the magazine *Izquierda nacional* to publicize its theses, and Ramos became its chief collaborator and later its editor. The PSIN was succeeded by the Popular Left Front (FIP) in September 1971, but the latter failed in its bid to regroup the Argentina left. Presided over by Ramos, the FIP won almost

70,000 votes in March 1973, and its nominal vote rose to 889,000 the following September, when it gave voters the chance to vote for Perón on a FIP ticket. The Ramos tendency became increasingly distant from Trotskyism. In 1975, faced with impending military intervention against the right-wing Peronist government of Isabel Perón, Ramos and the FIP called not only for the defense of democratic institutions but also for support for Isabel (*Izquierda Nacional*, September 1975). When the electoral authorities provided details of party membership registration on 30 March 1983, the FIP, with Ramos still its president, had 34,426 members.

Ramos originally based his pro-Perón line on an interpretation of the works of Lenin* and Trotsky and the theses of the first three congresses of the Communist International, which differentiated between oppressive and oppressed countries and backed nationalist movements in the latter. He regarded Peronism as a progressive national bourgeois movement that confronted imperialism and politically developed the working class. Though the National Left retained its organizational autonomy, this attitude to Peronism led to a severing of links with the international Trotskyist movement. Subsequently Ramos attempted to knit together Marxist categories, the Lenin–Trotsky interpretation of the Russian Revolution, and a national-popular perspective on Argentine and Latin American history.

Ramos maintains that Latin America is a single country. Another characteristic of his writing is a constant effort to discredit the Socialists and Communists by presenting them as an *izquierda cipaya*, a sepoy left that has sold out to foreign interests and has ignored Argentina's specific characteristics and problems. At times the attacks have bordered on xenophobia. Ramos's volume on the Communists (1962) and National Left critiques of the Socialists come close to saying that the traditional left failed because it was "foreign." Thus, the failure of the Communists is attributed to Soviet influence alone, and there is no consideration of the real domestic obstacles faced by the Argentine left in its early years. The traditional left is condemned for not supporting the popular presidents Yrigoyen and Perón, yet the former was no champion of the workers and neither leader was a consistent anti-imperialist.

Nevertheless, Ramos's ideas helped to reconcile part of the Argentine left with Peronism. His main book (1957) had sold over 25,000 copies by 1974 and was popular among students, despite Montonero condemnation of Ramos as a CIA agent, presumably because of his equation of urban guerrilla warfare with terrorism. The real elaboration of National Left ideology took place in the 1940s, and subsequently it became ossified, with increasingly less radical political implications. In spite of the reactionary role played by the Argentine armed forces since 1955, Ramos has continued to praise their "Sanmartinian" traditions and has argued that, since they reflect the composition of society as a whole, they can still perform a national liberation role and form part of a national front with Peronism.

BIBLIOGRAPHY:

A. *América Latina: un país* (Buenos Aires: Octubre, 1949); *Revolución y contrarre-volución en la Argentina* (Buenos Aires: Plus Ultra, 1957); *Historia del stalinismo en la Argentina* (Buenos Aires: Coyoacán, 1962); "Con Jorge Abelardo Ramos," Interview, *Confirmado* (Buenos Aires) (29 February 1972); "La Izquierda: sus grupos y tendencias," *Cuarto poder* (Buenos Aires), no. 4 (August 1972).

B. Robert J. Alexander, *Trotskyism in Latin America* (Stanford: Hoover Institution Press: 1973).

RICHARD GILLESPIE

RANADIVE, BHALCHANDRA TRIMBAK   (b. 1903). Born in India, Bhal-chandra Ranadive was a member of the central leadership of the Communist Party of India (CPI) from 1936 to 1950. Elected its Secretary General in 1948, he resigned in 1950. He has been a member of the Central Committee and Politburo of the Communist Party of India (Marxist) (CPI[M]) since its foundation in 1964 and a leader of Indian trade unions organized and led by the CPI(M).

For the past forty years Ranadive articulated a powerful argument for working-class hegemony over Indian politics, through Communist politicization of the working class. In recent years he has increasingly denied that the Indian bourgeoi-sie either aims at an acceleration of Indian capitalist development or is capable of doing so on the basis of its own hegemony over Indian politics, or that there is evidence that it is actually doing so. That is why he wonders why it is that Indian workers are unaware of their progressive function in Indian society.

Ranadive has persistently insisted that the Indian bourgeoisie resists imperi-alism politically in order to secure the best terms for economic cooperation for exploiting the Indian masses economically, and oppressing them politically. However, in recent years Ranadive has been stressing more and more that al-though "the Indian bourgeoisie has embarked upon the capitalist path . . . its alliance with [feudal] landed interests is preventing the liquidation of precapitalist relations in agriculture" ("Working Class Hegemony," p. 4); and powerful Indian (and foreign) capitalist monopolies have emerged which jointly or com-petitively restrict capitalist development. It follows as a corollary that "an an-tifeudal, anti-imperialist, antimonopoly revolution, with the agrarian revolution as the crux" (ibid., p. 43) has to be initiated and carried through under the hegemony of a Communist-led working class. The next stage of this revolutionary movement will require the advance to socialism.

BIBLIOGRAPHY:

A. *Political Thesis* (adopted at the Second Congress of the CPI) and *Strategy and Tactics in the Struggle for People's Democratic Revolution in India*, in *Documents of the History of the Communist Party of India*, ed. M. B. Rao, vol. 7 (New Delhi: People's Publishing House, 1976); "Working Class Hegemony," *The Marxist*, 1 (July-September 1983), pp. 22–60.

ARUN BOSE

RANGEL, DOMINGO ALBERTO   (b. 1923). Venezuelan professor, con-gressman, and political economist Domingo Alberto Rangel was the leading inspiration behind, and ideological mentor to, the Movimiento de la Izquierda Revolucionario (MIR) a political party formed in the late 1950s, inspired by the Black Revolution advocate Frantz Fanon,† and espousing Cuban-style social revolution.

His two-volume *Capital y desarrollo* (Capital and development) explained how the oil industry transformed Venezuela from self-sufficiency to a dependent importer of foodstuffs. He viewed Venezuelan underdevelopment as a condition emanating from the colonial system, not a passing phase, and as a fundamental part of the dependency that accompanies imperialism. He pointed out that in the 1920s, when oil replaced coffee as the nation's major export and capital-producing product, the rural sectors became subordinate to the cities, and political power in his country shifted from the landed gentry to urban elites. Petroleum also helped develop Venezuela's first organized working-class consciousness but heightened class antagonisms by increasing discrimination against oil workers by greedy petroleum producers. Capitalism based on oil needed national unity and centralized institutions. To attain and maintain them, Rangel asserted that Venezuela developed a more professional military, which became a dominant political force in the country and a major pillar of support for the middle class, which has struggled to put the petroleum economy under its own control, rather than that of foreigners.

Rangel explained that after World War II, Latin America replaced Europe and Asia as major suppliers of raw materials for the United States. This led to U.S. military and ideological control in the region and the use of negative feelings toward communism as an excuse to halt any activities that Washington deemed objectionable by labeling them "Communist-inspired." While United States ideological hegemony grew in Venezuela, according to Rangel, the country moved toward control of its own resources, culminating in the nationalization of oil in 1976. Then Venezuela became more dependent upon international capital and technology.

BIBLIOGRAPHY:

A. *La revolución de las fantasías* (Caracas: OFIDO, 1958); *Historia económica de Venezuela* (Caracas: Pensamiento Vivo, 1962); *Capital y desarrollo*, 2 vols. (Caracas: Instituto de Investigaciones Económicas y Sociales, 1969–70); *Los mercaderes de voto: estudio de un sistema* (Valencia, Venezuela: Vadell Hermanos, 1973).

B. Sheldon B. Liss, *Diplomacy and Dependency: Venezuela, the United States and the Americas* (Salisbury, N.C.: Documentary Publications, 1978).

SHELDON B. LISS

RECABARREN, LUIS EMILIO   (1876–1924). A Chilean who excelled at turning theory into practice, Luis Emilio Recabarren had enormous impact upon Latin America's workers' movement. A typographer by trade, he believed that socialist literature was a vital and effective tool, and he contributed to it as a journalist, pamphleteer, playright, and poet. He organized Chile's poor into unions and educated them politically through his work as editor of the newspaper

El trabajador and the periodicals *El proletario, La vanguardia*, and *El grito popular*. In 1906 he was elected to Congress representing the mining district of Antofagasta, but denied his seat for refusing to take an oath of office that included swearing allegiance to God. After creating the first significant Marxist labor movement in Latin America in Chile's nitrate mining region, he founded, in 1912, the Socialist Labor Party. He unsuccessfully sought Chile's presidency in 1920. The following year he was elected to Congress as a member of the Socialist Labor Party, a position he later held under the banner of the Chilean Communist Party, which he also helped organize.

Recabarren's ideas on worker control were unique in Chile. He advocated a system of unions with primary roles, at all levels, for workers in the governance of Chile. His ideal constitution had three basic governmental divisions: (1) industrial assemblies, made up of workers from each geographical sector who would represent all agricultural, industrial, and service areas; (2) municipalities run by delegates from each industrial assembly and governed by commissions that would assume responsibility for the well-being of their inhabitants; (3) a national assembly with delegates from each municipal territory with over 10,000 inhabitants and run by committees that would legislate for the entire nation. Under this system all citizens over eighteen years of age could participate in the government.

In *La materia eterna e inteligente* (Eternal matter and intelligence), he postulated a time and space theory that refuted the concept of a supreme creator and stated that material, or the universe, always existed in infinite space and time. To him the material, which could be visualized, was the only truth. He felt that humans could solve the mysteries about themselves. He also noted the differences between dialectical materialism and Christian metaphysics and questioned how the existence of a supreme being could account for cultural, racial, moral and religious diversity in the world. He contended that the only explanations were environmental and evolutionary.

BIBLIOGRAPHY:
A. *Obras escogidas* (Santiago: Recabarren, 1965); *Le pensamiento de Luis Emilio Recabarren*, 2 vols. (Santiago: Austral, 1971).

B. Julio César Jobet, *Recabarren: los origines del movimiento obrero y del socialismo chilenos* (Santiago: Prensa Latino-Americana, 1955).

SHELDON B. LISS

REDDY, TARIMELA NAGI (1917–1976). Born on 11 February 1917 in a wealthy farming community in Andhra Pradesh, Tarimela Reddy was a colorful personality in the Indian Communist movement. He was the brother-in-law of the former President of India, Neelam Sanjiva Reddy. Late in life Reddy became a Maoist,* which in Indian parlance is called a Naxalite. The Naxalite movement takes its name from a city in West Bengal State called Naxalbari, where its founders lived. Reddy joined the Communist movement as a student in 1940, after being arrested by the British government. He was secretary of the Regional

Committee of the Communist Party in the area called Rayala Seema in Andhra Pradesh State from 1947 to 1951, and then became a member of the National Council of the Indian Communist Party. The Communist Party split in 1964, and Reddy became a member of the more radical Communist Party of India (Marxist) (CPI[M]), and also fully supported Mao Zedong's harsh critique of revisionist Soviet policies. He believed that China's socialist path was also applicable to the Indian revolution. Following Mao's principle that power flows from the barrel of the gun, Reddy believed that Indian workers and peasants should be mobilized for the violent confrontation with Western imperialism and Indian capitalism. In 1969 he resigned his sixteen-year membership in the State Assembly of Andhra Pradesh.

Nagi Reddy and his group held that the Indian bourgeoisie is comprador in character and acted as a lackey of U.S. imperialism. Modern India has witnessed the increasing dominance of foreign monopoly capital and the strengthening of feudal and semifeudal relations. Reddy believed India remained a semicolonial and semifeudal country, like China before the revolution. Its principal contradiction, therefore, is between the masses of Indian people and feudalism; the secondary contradiction involves nationalism and imperialism. Revolution in India must occur in two stages: bourgeois democratic and socialist. This is akin to the *Two Tactics* of Lenin.* India's revolutionary agenda must include the fight for national liberation as well as a strategy for conquering U.S. imperialism and its allies, the comprador bourgeoisie and the landlords. Only an armed uprising by the mobilized masses could accomplish these goals.

After the 1964 split in the Indian Communist movement into the CPI and the CPI(M), Reddy became embroiled in the internecine disputes of the more radical CPI(M). By 1968 he was being accused by radical Maoists of revisionism and obstructing the armed struggle, which in parts of India had deteriorated into campaigns of terror and murder. Reddy opposed this left adventurism and argued that the armed struggle can begin only after the agrarian revolution began solving fundamental questions of land distribution and Indian peasants were ripe to rebel. Hence he opposed Charu Mazumdar and his program to annihilate landlords. He also opposed the Maoist tendency to interpret every economic struggle of the poor peasantry as a glorified struggle for political power. This could only lead to a war for which the poor masses were unprepared. He was also not prepared to accept the Chinese Communist Party's characterization of the Soviet Union as social imperialists. Reddy's own characterization of the Indian state and revolution is stated in his "Immediate Programme," which was adopted by his wing of the Andhra Pradesh Revolutionary Communist Committee in 1969. It argues that India is a "neocolony." Its people are suffering from exploitation by U.S. imperialism, British imperialism, and Soviet revisionist neocolonialism. Internally, India is still plagued by feudalism, which, like imperialism, exploits its landless peasants and workers. India is thus awaiting its antifeudal, anti-imperialist, democratic revolution. Its people should be organized for an armed struggle. He proposed the forceful liberation of villages, towns, and eventually urban areas, but emphasized the necessity of first redistributing land and educating the proletariat in self-government.

BIBLIOGRAPHY:

A. *India Mortgaged: A Marxist-Leninist Appraisal* (Anantapuran, Andhra Pradesh: Tarimela Nagi Reddy Memorial Trust, 1978).

K. SESHADRI

REVUELTAS, JOSÉ   (1914–1976). One of Mexico's most distinguished writers and political activists of this century, José Revueltas was born on 20 November 1914 in the state of Durango, Mexico. A prolific writer, he produced novels, collections of short stories, plays, and several works on Mexican politics, literature, and cinema theory. Revueltas combined a literary career with political activities. Becoming involved with leftist politics in Mexico City at the age of fourteen, he was sent to a reformatory a year later for his part in a demonstration in the capital and at the age of twenty was deported to Islas Marias for Communist activities. These were the first in a long series of imprisonments for illegal political activities. These early experiences are recounted in some detail in his *Los muros de agua* (1941). In 1961, after a life-long association with the Mexican Communist Party, Revueltas left the Party to help found the Spartacus Leninist League, but he quickly became disillusioned with this party also. His last imprisonment, a result of his participation in the 1968 student demonstrations, contributed to his failing health.

Revueltas's principal contributions were literary and political rather than theoretical. His best-known novel, *El luto humano* (1943), received the National Literary Prize. Written as a series of monologues, it is an account of the flight and struggle of a group of Mexican *peóns* and their priest. This novel was translated into English and was published as *The Stone Knife* in 1947. In it the author identifies with the common man and demonstrates his idealism and commitment to the nation's exploited working class. This theme remains constant in his works despite prolonged confrontations with the authorities and with some elements of the Mexican left.

In his *Ensayo sobre un proletariado sin cabeza* (Essay on a proletariat without a head), Revueltas attacked the Mexican Communist Party and democratic revisionism. Revueltas concluded that the Mexican working class desperately needed a "Leninist"-style leadership instead of a middle-class democratic ideology. Previously, Revueltas had espoused the necessity of unifying the various Mexican Marxists into a working-class party. Now, more ideological purity and a dedicated, disciplined group was required to create a true "class" party and to avoid the pitfalls of growing bureaucratization. *Ensayo* signaled the formation of the Spartacus Leninist League founded in part by the ubiquitous Revueltas. In *Los errores* (1964), one of his most successful later novels, Revueltas (perhaps incongruously) rails against a dogmatic political party that constricts the individual and warns of the dangers inherent in such a rigid approach. In his last

years, Revueltas grappled with the problem of how to modify Leninist theory
to fit the Mexican experience, but never clearly articulated an effective alternative. He died in Mexico City on 14 April 1976.

BIBLIOGRAPHY:

A. *The Stone Knife* (originally, *El luto humano*) (New York: Reynal, 1947); *Ensayo
sobre un proletariado sin cabeza* (Mexico City: Logos, 1962); *Los errores* (Mexico City:
Fondo de Cultura Económica, 1964); *Obra literaria* (Mexico City: Empresas Editoriales,
1967).

B. James E. Irby, *La influencia de William Faulkner en cuatro narradores hispa-
noamericanos* (Mexico City: Editorial Mimeógrafo de Juan Velazco, 1957), pp. 40–131;
Sam L. Slick, *José Revueltas* (Boston: G. K. Hall, 1983).

CARL A. ROSS AND ALLEN WELLS

RICHTA, RADOVAN   (1923–1983). Born in 1923 in the city of Prague,
Radovan Richta was a well-known activist who took part in the Czech resistance
movement during World War II and was eventually imprisoned by the Nazis.
He studied at the Faculty of Arts and Sciences in Prague. After having worked
as a journalist in the official press of the Czech Communist Party, he later became
a researcher at the Institute of Philosophy of the Czech Academy of Sciences.
One of his first projects was an orthodox Marxist-Leninist critique of the philosophical and sociological work of T. G. Masaryk, a founder of the Czech
Republic. In the early 1960s he directed a group of Czech scholars in examining
some of the social problems generated by the postwar scientific and technological
revolution in Europe, including its short- and long-term consequences for socialist
regimes. His ideas influenced the moderate Communist reformers who initiated
the Prague Spring.† Richta became an advisor to Alexander Dubček,* and is
reputed to have created the popular slogan "Socialism with a Human Face."
He was elected a member of the Central Committee of the Czech Party at the
Fourteenth Party Congress, which met clandestinely during the first days of the
Soviet occupation in August 1968. As the Soviet-directed period of "normali-
zation" began, Richta supported the orthodox Party line of G. Husak, helping
to reestablish order and, as director of the Institute of Philosophy and Sociology,
to purge revisionist scholars.

Richta's theory of "the new revolution in science and technology," whose
radical impact on socialist countries was said to have exceeded even that of the
nineteenth-century industrial revolution, was derived from several sources. It
was inspired in part by the work of Karl Marx* (particularly the *1844 Manuscripts*
and the *Gründrisse*) and Marxian theorists like Friedrich Pollock† and Georges
Friedmann,* as well as by non-Marxist theories such as W. W. Rostow's analysis
of the stages of economic growth. Richta's ideas must also be seen in the context
of both the ideological crisis experienced by post-Stalinist socialist regimes and
the domineering mood of reformism, even utopianism, created by Nikita Khrushchev's* de-Stalinization program (e.g., his unrealistic promise, written into the
new program of the Soviet Communist Party, to fully achieve communism by

1980). The spirit of Khrushchevian reformism influenced Czechoslovakia dramatically, even after Khrushchev's removal, and directly shaped the ideas of Richta and other reformers (cf. the project of economic reform elaborated by O. Šik).

The point of departure for Richta's theory of the new revolution in science and technology is his redefinition of society's forces of production. Contrary to the Stalinist* interpretation, which reduced productive forces to their material components (i.e. the instruments of production and the work force) and hence favored the development of heavy industry, Richta emphasized the subjective components of the forces of production, above all scientific knowledge, creativity, the quality of life, workers' freedom, everyday habits and practices, and the crucial role of intellectuals. A new investment policy was now required: one focusing on "gray matter," the scientific and technological research that will push the new revolution in a socialist direction toward the emancipation of all humanity. Richta's ideas promoted the following policy proposals: an increase in workers' leisure time; transforming work into creative activity; stressing quality rather than quantity in the satisfaction of human needs; reformulating the social composition of the working class; and transforming the manner in which leadership is exercised. In Richta's own words:

With the onset of the scientific and technological revolution and its accompanying complexities and confusions, it will no longer suffice to administer society in a manner appropriate only to the period of industrialization. It is a question of finding, with the help of science, appropriate regulations (i.e. systems of rules that facilitate certain necessary, automatic processes associated with technological development) to govern all spheres of social life, including the economic, social, political, juridical, moral, psychological, anthropological, etc. Those regulations will shape all objective and subjective conditions, ranging from religious activity to the application of cybernetic techniques, thereby opening the possibility of balancing individual and collective needs, and uplifting plans for developing society to a new and superior level. (*Civilization at the Crossroads*, pp. 355–56)

Richta's theory of the new scientific and technological revolution, particularly its critical dimension, was, at first, received with distrust by the intellectual and political leaders of the Soviet Bloc. After the Soviet military suppression of the Prague Spring, however, the theory was purged of potentially nonconformist elements and assimilated by the official ideology of "authentic socialism." Having lost its initial critical spirit and its social base of support in the defeated Czech reformist movement, the theory was transformed into a rationale for the political and social stagnation of the Brezhnev* epoch. As a component of the official Czech ideology, the theory of the new scientific and technological revolution is increasingly in flagrant contradiction with the reality of the Soviet regime, which does not inspire technical innovation and is unable to develop alternative economic growth models.

BIBLIOGRAPHY:

A. *La civilisation au carrefour* (Paris: Anthropos, 1969); *Civilizace na rozcestí: spo-lečenské a lidské souvislosti vědeckotechnické revoluce* (Prague: Svoboda, 1969).

LUBOMIR SOCHOR

RIZZI, BRUNO   (1901–1977). Bruno Rizzi was a member of the Communist Party of Italy as a young man, but he distanced himself from it in order to support the Trotskyite* Fourth International. Research on the social nature of the Soviet Union became the center of his attention; he succeeded in eluding the fascist censors and published an analysis of Trotsky's *The Revolution Betrayed*, under the title *Dove va l'URSS?* in 1937. He went to London and to Paris to communicate to the Trotskyites the results of his analysis and the expectation of a Hitler–Stalin* pact and to publish his book on bureaucratic collectivism. The book finally appeared in Paris in 1939 under the title *La bureaucratisation du monde*, but it remained little known and the subject of limited discussion. Eventually its theses became material for outright plagiarism or unacknowledged reference (for example, the celebrated book entitled *The Managerial Revolution* by James Burnham, which appeared in the United States in 1946; and later works by Max Shachtman,* Milovan Djilas†, Pierre Naville,* Gilles Martinet, Sto-janovic† and others).

After the fall of fascism, in August of 1943, he returned to Italy and attempted again to propagandize the results of his own analysis of the Soviet Union. He returned to the ranks of the Communist Party, but left it again after only a few weeks. As an "independent socialist" and in spite of his commercial activity as a shoe manufacturers' representative, he continued his own research, ex-panding it through macrohistoric comparisons (e.g. of ancient and feudal de-cadence), often publishing at his own expense. The social nature of the Soviet Union, according to Rizzi, is characterized by bureaucratic collectivism: the ownership of the means of production is no longer private and personal, but belongs to one social group, the bureaucracy. This type of ownership does not eliminate the features of domination and exploitation typical of capitalism, even though Soviet society is no longer capitalistic. Bureaucratic collectivistic society is therefore regressive, not progressive, closer to feudalism than to capitalism, and certainly not socialist. This brings Rizzi to question the Marxian principle of the contradiction between social relationships of production and ownership of the means of production: the Soviet Union shows that there can be collective, state ownership of the means of production without however eliminating the exploitation of one class by another class, and indeed increasing the despotic nature of power. In his later writings Rizzi attempts to show the planetary character of such a tendency: the increase in state interference in the economy— common to the Soviet Union, to fascism, to Nazism, and to the New Deal— pushes industrial societies toward totalitarian domination by the bureaucracy and assimilates them to the historical forms of oppression, of total and absolute power, typical of ancient slavery and of feudalism. The agent of this new do-

minion and exploitation is the bureaucracy, a new and unique class, and not—as Trotsky asserted with the intention of defending the formula of the "degenerated worker state" applied to the Soviet Union—an abnormal outgrowth based on the social power of the proletariat and therefore capable of being eliminated by political struggle and merely reforming the relationships of production.
BIBLIOGRAPHY:

A. *Il collettivismo burocratico* (Imola: Galeati, 1967); *La rovina antica e l'età feudale* (Bussolengo: Razionalista, 1969–71).

B. Antonio Carlo, *La natura sociale dell'URSS* (Milan: Centro Studi Terzo Mondo, 1975); Giorgio Galli, "Bruno Rizzi e la nuova classe," *Mondoperaio*, no. 2 (1977).

VITTORIO DINI

ROA GARCÍA, RAUL (1907–1982). Raul Roa was born on 18 April 1907 in Havana and died in the same city on 8 July 1982. He was a leading student radical of the late 1920s and early 1930s and served on the committee that ran the Directorio Estudiantil Universitario (Student Directorate). He wrote articles critical of the Cuban government in the left-wing journal *Línea*. In 1931 Roa was imprisoned because of his political activities. He supported the overthrow of Machado in 1933, participated in a general strike directed against the Batista government in 1935, and was forced into exile in the United States. Roa was a Guggenheim fellow during 1945–1946 and in 1948, while serving as Dean of Social Sciences in the University of Havana, was appointed Director of Culture by then Cuban President Carlos Prío Socarrás. Roa was arrested and jailed after the *coup d'état* that brought Batista back to power in 1952. He again went into exile. On his return to Cuba in 1957, he was arrested and imprisoned a third time, although he was not formally affiliated with Fidel Castro's* July 26 Movement. Castro appointed Roa García Foreign Minister in 1959. He served in that position until 1976, after which he was the Vice-President of the National Assembly and a member of the Council of State. He retired in 1981 and died the following year.

Roa was not a member of any political party in 1959 and had denounced the Soviet invasion of Hungary in 1956. In 1959 he wrote, "The Cuban Revolution had its own roots, programs, and curriculum. It does not stem from Rousseau, George Washington, or Marx." (*Cuba tiene la razón*, p. 41). Roa was, however, a strong opponent of colonialism and imperialism. He saw the heritage of the former and the existence of the latter as the chief contradictions in Cuban society. He believed that internationalism was a fundamental feature of the Cuban Revolution, i.e., that Cuba was duty-bound to contribute to the liberation struggles in Africa and Latin America.
BIBLIOGRAPHY:

A. *Historia de las doctrinas sociales* (Havana: Universidad de Havana, 1948); *Cuba tiene la razón* (San José, Costa Rica: Sociedad de Amigos de la Revolución Cubana,

1960); *Retorno a la alborada* (Las Villas, Cuba: Universidad Central, 1964); *Aventuras, venturas y desventuras de un mambi* (Havana: Instituto del Libro, 1970).

KELLY AINSWORTH

ROCA, BLAS (FRANCISCO CALDERIO)   (b. 1908). Blas Roca was born on 24 July 1908 in Manzanillo, Cuba. He was an early member of the Cuban Communist Party (PCC) and served as its secretary general between 1934 and 1960. During much of this time, the Party was referred to as the Partido Socialista Popular (PSP). Roca was the editor of the party newspaper, *Hoy*,during the 1960s. In the late 1960s and 1970s Roca chaired the PCC committees responsible for the people's power experiment in Matanzas and the reform of the legal system. He also served as president of the Commission for Constitutional Studies of the PCC. He has held a membership in the Party Secretariat since 1965. Before the success of the revolutionary movement in 1959, Blas Roca and the PSP failed to ally themselves with Fidel Castro's* July 26 Movement. During the 1960s and 1970s Roca developed a reputation as an orthodox Marxist-Leninist and virulent enemy of Trotskyism.* He argued that revolutionary leadership had created the mass consciousness necessary for the transformation to socialism.
BIBLIOGRAPHY:
   A. *The Cuban Revolution: Report to the Eighth National Congress of the Popular Socialist Party of Cuba* (New York: New Century, 1961); *Cuba's Socialist Destiny* (New York: Fair Play for Cuba Committee, 1961); *Los fundamentos del socialismo en Cuba* (Havana: Imprenta Nacional, 1961).

KELLY AINSWORTH

RODNEY, WALTER A.   (1942–1980). Walter Rodney was born in Georgetown, Guyana on 23 March 1942, and remained a Guyanese citizen. He attended the University of the West Indies, Jamaica, graduating in 1963, and received his doctorate in African history from the School of Oriental and African Studies of the University of London in 1966, with a dissertation on ''A History of the Upper Guinea Coast, 1540–1800.'' He was greatly influenced by both C. L. R. James† and Amilcar Cabral* at this time. A major part of the research for the dissertation was done in Portugal using original sources. He taught history at the University College, Dar es Salaam, Tanzania, during the years 1966–67 and 1969–74, and at the University of the West Indies, Jamaica in 1968. Rodney was an early advocate of and leader in the black power movement in the Caribbean, and he worked among the Jamaican people teaching about black power and African history, which led Jamaica to block his reentry into the country when he tried to return from a conference in October 1968. His writings were also banned. After a few months' stay in Cuba, Rodney returned to Tanzania to teach, but he maintained his contacts with the Caribbean. He was later offered a position in the Department of History at the University of Guyana, but upon his return to Guyana in 1974 his appointment was canceled by the government of Forbes Burnham, and he was barred from teaching. Rodney participated in the formation of the Working People's Alliance (WPA) in 1975, a multiracial and militant political party. The activities of the WPA and Rodney's active leadership role in opposing the repressive rule of Burnham ultimately led to his political assassination by bomb explosion in Georgetown on 13 June 1980.

It is impossible to separate Rodney's political commitments from his scholarly activity, which was shaped by his political outlook. His most important early work was on African history. Rodney applied class analysis to Africa's history, particularly to understanding slavery, which he argued was differentiated by outside forces—in fact, he argued, slavery was primarily a European-imposed institution—and the role and sophistication of the state in different African societies. At the time he was making this argument, cultural nationalism was much more in vogue and Marxist analysis less in evidence in African studies. After returning to Guyana, although he did not give up his interest in Africa, Rodney increasingly focused his analysis on his own country. His recent study of Guyanese workers is a magnificent political economic analysis that uncovers from a new perspective the history of "those without history." His contribution was not in new theoretical categories, but in his impeccable scholarship, commitment to liberation, and his personal and political example, best expressed in his work with the WPA.

BIBLIOGRAPHY:

A. *A History of the Upper Guinea Coast, 1540–1800* (Oxford: Clarendon Press, 1970); *How Europe Underdeveloped Africa* (Washington, D.C.: Howard University Press, 1974); *A History of the Guyanese Working People, 1881–1905* (Baltimore: Johns Hopkins University Press, 1981).

B. Edward A. Alpers and Pierre-Michel Fontaine, eds., *Walter Rodney, Revolutionary and Scholar* (Los Angeles: Center for Afro-American Studies and African Studies Center, University of California, 1982).

JAMES DIETZ

RODRÍGUEZ, CARLOS RAFAEL   (b. 1913). Carlos Rodríguez was born on 23 May 1913, in Cienfuegos, Cuba. He was educated at Havana University, where, in 1939, he received doctorate degrees in law and the social, economic, and political sciences. He was a member of the radical Directorio Estudiantil de Cienfuegos between 1930 and 1933. In 1933 he was elected mayor of Cienfuegos. Rodríguez joined the Communist Party of Cuba in 1936. He was a member of the Central Committee between 1940 and 1952 and a member of the Executive Committee between 1953 and 1960. He served as a minister without portfolio during the Batista government of the early 1940s. Rodríguez was the representative of the Partido Socialista Popular (Communist Party) to Fidel Castro's* July 26 Movement in the Sierra Maestra during 1958. After the rebel forces came to power, Rodríguez became the editor of the Communist Party paper *Hoy* (1959–62). He was the President of the National Institute of Agrarian Reform and Minister of Agriculture and Animal Production between 1962 and 1965. He became the Vice-President of the Council of State in 1976. He is among the most trusted and closest advisors to Fidel Castro.

Rodríguez has argued that imperialism was the principal contradiction in Cuban society before the revolution. He claimed that Marxism-Leninism was the only basis for addressing that contradiction. He believed that the national bourgeoisie was incapable of directing an anti-imperialist revolution, although "middle" bourgeoisie could be conditionally worked with in both the agricultural and industrial spheres. Nevertheless, unlike other members of the prerevolutionary Cuban Communist Party, he did not believe that a long bourgeois-democratic phase must precede the transition to socialism.

BIBLIOGRAPHY:

A. *La Clase obrera y la revolución* (Havana: Vanguardia Obrera, 1960); *Cuba en el tránsito al socialismo (1959–1963); Lenin y la cuestión colonial* (Mexico City: Siglo XXI, 1978).

KELLY AINSWORTH

ROLAND-HOLST, HENRIETTE (1869–1952). Henriette Roland-Holst was a Dutch poet, militant activist, and Marxist historian. She joined Pieter Jelle Troelstra's* Socialist Democratic Workers' Party (SDAP) in 1897 together with her friend Herman Gorter† and her husband, the artist Richard Roland-Holst. By 1900 Roland-Holst had aligned herself with the radical left within the SDAP, a group that would later be known as the Tribunists,* who strongly opposed the revisionist course of the party leadership. When in 1909 the Tribunists defied party orders to cease publishing their oppositional paper *De Tribune*, they were expelled. That same year they founded the Dutch Social Democratic Party (SDP), which earned the support of Lenin* and which in 1919 would become the first Dutch Communist Party (CPH). From the Marxist editors of *De Nieuwe Tijd*, the SDAP monthly for theory and criticism, Herman Gorter and Antonie Pannekoek† were the only ones to join the Tribunists. Despite urgent pleas from Gorter, Roland-Holst refused to join the Tribunists and stayed in the SDAP. Her friendship with Rosa Luxemburg* helped convince Roland-Holst to leave the SDAP in 1911, the year the "mass strike" debate culminated in the German Social Democratic Party. Until 1915 Roland-Holst was politically unaffiliated, but soon she had aligned herself with the Zimmerwald movement and in 1916 with the Zimmerwald Left, which, under the influence of Lenin and Radek, sought to organize against the war. Roland-Holst and Pannekoek, under the editorial control of Karl Radek, put out *Die Vorbote*. This time also witnessed a reconciliation between Roland-Holst and the Tribunists. For two years Roland-Holst was a leader of the Revolutionary Socialist League (RSB), a pacifist socialist organization. It merged with the SDP in 1916. It was during World War I that Roland-Holst reached the peak of her political activism. She became a member of the Dutch Communist Party, and in 1921 she was the representative of the CPH at the Third Congress of the Comintern. She was also a member (with Gorter, Pannekoek, and others) of the executive of the West European subbureau of the Comintern in Amsterdam, for the few months that it existed. Roland-Holst stayed in the CPH until 1927, when she founded the Independent

Communist Party (OCPN). During the last years of her life she severed all ties with the Communist movement in favor of a nonaligned religious socialist pacifism. Roland-Holst, finally, must be remembered for her valuable contributions to the internationalization of the European workers' movement.

BIBLIOGRAPHY:

A. *Kapitaal en arbeid in Nederland* (Rotterdam: Brusse, 1902); *Josef Dietzgens Philosophie, gemeinverständlich er lautert in ihrer Bedeutung für das Proletariat* (Munich: Verlag der Dietzgenschen Philosophie, 1910).

TINEKE RITMEESTER

ROTHSTEIN, THEODORE (1871–1953). Theodore Rothstein was born in Kovno, Russia, the son of a Jewish apothecary, and was educated at the Poltava Gymnasium. He came to England in 1891, although he remained a Russian citizen. He made his living as an author and journalist, correspondent for several Russian radical papers, and for *The Tribune, The Daily News, The Manchester Guardian*, and the *Neue Zeit*, organ of the Second International.* He was for many years a member of the National Union of Journalists. Rothstein joined H. M. Hyndman's* Social Democratic Federation in 1895. By 1901 he was elected its chief executive, a position in which he served until 1906. From 1906 to 1914 he edited the *Socialist Annual* for the Social Democratic Federation and its successors. He was a frequent contributor to the SDF paper *Justice*. As a refugee from both tsarist autocracy and the virulent Russian anti-Semitism of the 1880s, Rothstein was one of a group of Russian emigrés to Britain who brought to British socialism a higher degree of revolutionary consciousness than previously existed in Britain, and also a pronounced internationalist commitment as well as international contacts. Rothstein was a good friend of the German Social Democrat Karl Kautsky.* In 1907, when the exiled Russian Social Democratic Party held its annual conference in London, Rothstein helped them find their expenses by negotiating a loan from Joseph Fels, a Russian-born soap millionaire. During World War I he served as a translator of foreign press reports and as a special advisor on Russian affairs to Lord Balfour, until Hyndman succeeded in getting him fired as an alleged German agent. Although he was probably not a police spy, he was known to talk too freely, and he was the indirect source of much Cabinet Office information about the flow of Russian money and influence to the British left. He played a decisive role in the founding of the Communist Party of Great Britain, which was consummated on 1 August 1920. Ten days later he left Britain for Moscow as a member of the Soviet trade delegation to report possibly on trade or more likely on the possibility of revolution in Britain. The British authorities refused to let him return to Britain, so he became an official of the Soviet government: chairman of the Universities Reform Commission (1920–21); Soviet minister to Persia (1921–22); and a member of the Collegium of the People's Commissariat for Foreign Affairs (1922–29). In 1920 he was also made a member of the Communist Party of the Soviet Union "as from 1900." He was the brother-in-law of Zelda Kahan, another active Russian emigré socialist in Britain, and the father of Andrew Rothstein, prominent figure in the British Communist Party. He died in Moscow on 30 August 1953.

Rothstein's career reflected the classic socialist dilemmas of the dialectical relationships between practical politics and revolutionary transcendence, and between ideological clarity and the task of mobilizing an inert, recalcitrant working class. Against Belfort Bax's† attempt to rescue the SDF from sterile mechanical dogma and to appeal to a broader concept of culture, Rothstein argued that the monism of Marxism must be preserved in its scientific and dialectical rigor. But he also warned against the sectarianism of "impossibilist" critics of Hyndman, whom he dubbed "the unholy Scotch current" and who founded the Socialist Labour Party in 1906. Doctrinal purity could not be preserved by guarding it from the real world. Socialists could not simply preach their principles at the working class. Rather the party must come off its pedestal and lead the masses in the day-to-day struggles of their lives. But this praxis of engagement and sound doctrine always rested on a delicate balance. By 1908 Rothstein helped voice many Socialists' growing impatience with the reformism of the Labour Party. He conceded that the Social Democratic Party was not adhering to that permanent and intimate cooperation with the masses that Marx* and Engels* advocated, but he insisted that the hope of revolutionizing the immature workers "from within" was a delusion. In 1912, amid the great "labour unrest" and the national coal strike, Rothstein had welcomed the new combativeness among workers and the syndicalist spirit, which, although not Socialist consciousness, provided a basis from which that consciousness could be built. But Hyndman soon steered the new British Socialist Party, which succeeded the Social Democratic Party in 1912, away from its flirtation with industrial syndicalism and ultimately into support for the British war effort. By 1916 the internationalist section of the BSP—Rothstein, E. C. Fairchild, and John Maclean*—felt ready to challenge Hyndman's prowar stance. They launched a rival to *Justice* named *The Call*, and at the party's annual conference in April they in effect expelled Hyndman. Maclean and Rothstein hoped to move the Clyde Workers' Committee and the shop stewards' movement toward revolutionary antiwar actions such as a general strike in the munitions industry, but these hopes foundered on the shop stewards' craft preoccupations and their loss of economic and political leverage at the end of the war.

Rothstein's greatest significance was his pivotal role in the formation of the Communist Party of Great Britain—in circumstances that helped to weaken the Party from birth. For reasons unclear, when Maxim Litvinov, official Soviet representative of the Bolshevik Revolution, was deported from Britain in 1918, Rothstein succeeded him as the chief representative of the Third (Communist) International.* For the British left, the Russian Rothstein embodied the tremendous moral prestige of the Russian Revolution and its organ, the Communist International. He had not always been a Leninist. In 1907 he had supported Georgii Plekhanov* and the right wing of the Russian Social Democrats against the Bolsheviks. He and Lenin continued to disagree up to 1917, and Rothstein continued to side with the Mensheviks up to the time of the Bolshevik coup. But his section of the BSP was inspired by the Bolshevik example and the vision of workers' soviets springing spontaneously out of the "revolutionary instincts" of the masses. As Stanley Pierson suggests, they did not fully grasp the disjunction between their Marxist principles and the Leninist party they were to form in connection with the Third International.

As the conduit for Comintern funds to the British left, Rothstein distributed almost £15,000 as wages for militants and subsidies for socialist papers. That considerable leverage helped shape the new Communist Party as an alien creature that failed to incorporate several vital elements of British left-wing socialism. Despite the Comintern's original invitation to five British groups and to John Maclean by name, Rothstein insisted on building the new Party around his section of the BSP, which had split first with Hyndman and then with the moderate internationalists. When the CPGB insisted on seeking affiliation with the Labour Party, hoping to revolutionize it from within, the Socialist Labour Party, mostly militant Scots who had closely identified with the Bolsheviks, drew back from the new party. The Labour Party rejected the application for opposite reasons. Most serious, however, was the exclusion of John Maclean, the greatest of the Clydeside Socialists. When he came to London to make contact with Rothstein, the two quarreled bitterly. Maclean refused to accept the job Rothstein had assigned him in the "Hands off Russia" campaign, insisting that his work mobilizing British workers was more important. Maclean came to despise Rothstein personally. They also had political differences. Rothstein wanted to gather all potential sympathizers into the new Communist Party, including reformists in the Labour Party and the trade unions. He even offered a considerable subsidy to the Labour newspaper, *The Daily Herald*. Maclean insisted that such dilution would play into the hands of their enemies and lead to reformism. The split between the two made it unlikely that the new party would gain strength in Scotland.

Finally, and oddly, the founding conference of the CPGB was held at the same time as the Second Congress of the Third International in Moscow, so that many strong native-born leaders of the British left were not present, leaders generally opposed to Rothstein's BSP nucleus. The upshot was that while the new Party represented one of the authentic ideological possibilities to be precipitated out of the history of British Marxism, its personal and political factionalism helped to isolate it and prevent it from playing a more important part in British politics.

BIBLIOGRAPHY:

A. *From Chartism to Labourism: Historical Sketches of the English Working Class Movement* (London: Martin Lawrence, 1929).

B. W. Kendall, *The Revolutionary Movement in Britain, 1900–21: The Origins of British Communism* (London: Weidenfeld and Nicolson, 1969); R. Challinor, *The Origins of British Bolshevism* (London: Croom Helm, 1977); Stanley Pierson, *British Socialists:*

The Journey from Fantasy to Politics (Cambridge: Harvard University Press, 1979); Keith Nield, "Theodore Rothstein," in Joyce M. Bellamy and John Saville (eds.), *Dictionary of Labour Biography*, VII (London: Macmillan, 1984), pp. 200–209.

JOHN BOHSTEDT

ROY, MANABENDRA NATH   (1887–1954). Narendranath Bhattacharya (the original name of Manabendra Nath Roy) was born at Arabalia in West Bengal, India, to a Brahmin schoolteacher of a reformist outlook. In his checkered political career, Roy was first a national revolutionary, then a Marxist, and thereafter a radical humanist. As a national revolutionary, he worked as a lieutenant of the Bengali militant nationalist, Jatin Mukherji, and spent twenty months in jail for his involvement in terrorist activities against the British. During World War I, Roy went to Batavia, Java, Japan, and China in order to secure arms and funds from Germany to be used against the British in India. Unsuccessful in his efforts, he, disguised as a Christian theological student, went to the United States.

While in New York, he read the works of Karl Marx* in the public library. When America joined the war, Roy, fearing arrest, escaped to Mexico, where he received huge amounts of money from the Germans for the purpose of engineering an anti-British revolution in India. But disappointed by delays in receiving some promised German arms, and influenced by the 1917 Bolshevik Revolution, he made a sudden jump from die-hard nationalism to communism. He became General Secretary of the Mexican Socialist Party in 1918, which, in the following year, became the first Communist Party outside Soviet Russia. By this time, he had become an intimate friend of Michael Borodin, an agent of the Communist International. On Borodin's recommendation, Roy was invited to the Second Congress of the Communist International. On his way to Moscow, he stayed in Berlin for a while, where he met Edward Bernstein,† Karl Kautsky,* Rudolf Hilferding,* and others.

In Moscow, Lenin* asked him for "criticism and suggestion" on his Draft Thesis on the National and Colonial Question. Roy was unhappy with Lenin's strategy and tactics of Communist revolution in the colonies. Lenin believed that in the colonies and semicolonies, imperialism rested heavily on native feudal forces and that therefore the Communists should support any bourgeois-democratic liberation movement as a transitional stage to a Communist revolution. Roy maintained that Lenin underestimated the strength that the bourgeoisie had already acquired in the colonies. The bourgeois-democratic phase, Roy seemed to say, was almost over. He said that British imperialism was already making concessions to the Indian bourgeoisie and that the latter was showing tendencies toward compromise with the former. While Roy concurred with the strategy of a "united front" with the bourgeois-democratic forces, he wanted the Communists to rely more on the workers, peasants, and petit bourgeoisie. These, he said, should be enabled to acquire the leadership of the revolution. Heeding Roy's suggestion, Lenin's final draft of the thesis stipulated that the Communists should support "the revolutionary liberation movements" and not, as was in the original draft, "the bourgeois-democratic liberation movement."

Another point of difference between Roy and Lenin centered around the relationship between the Communist movements in the East and those in the West. Roy emphasized that since colonial extractions from the East had become the mainstay of imperialist regimes in the Western countries, Communist revolutions in the East had a priority over those in the West. This view was not fully shared by Lenin and other Russian Communists. The Second Congress of the Communist International, however, adopted Roy's thesis as a supplementary thesis. Roy also was made a full voting member of the Executive Committee of the Communist International in 1924.

In 1926, Roy wrote *The Aftermath of Non-Cooperation*, in which he maintained that the Indian noncooperation movement against the British failed because the bourgeoisie was too afraid to follow a revolutionary path. He reiterated that the imperialist and native bourgeois forces were making compromises with each other. The proletariat alone, he said, was truly revolutionary. He proposed the formation of a broad-based People's Party of all the oppressed classes of India, i.e., the petit bourgeoisie, the peasantry, and the proletariat. According to him, the petit bourgeois intellectuals, if united with the proletariat, would provide a revolutionary intellectual leadership.

In 1927, Roy went to China as the head of a delegation of the Communist International in order to advise the Chinese Communists whether to support the nationalist, landholding Kuomintang or to foment a peasant revolution. At that time, the government of Wuhan was in the hands of an alliance between the left wing of the Kuomintang and the Communists. Roy proposed radical agrarian changes and a peasant revolution in the countryside. But his plan misfired because most of the higher-level political workers and soldiers of the Kuomintang left, who were landholders, acted quickly and expelled the Communists from the ruling alliance. Roy returned to Moscow with a diminished stature. Before long, he was expelled from the Comintern, partly on account of the China debacle and partly on account of his unorthodox view that the subimperialist industrialization of the colonies would bring about the voluntary transfer of power to the native bourgeoisie. According to his theory of decolonization, the Communists were to work in collaboration with the national bourgeoisie. This was contrary to Stalin's* newly developed ultra-leftist program of anti-imperialist proletarian struggle. One of the factors singled out by Roy for his expulsion was that he had been opposed to the control of the Indian Communist movement by the Communist Party of Great Britain.

Roy returned to India in 1930 and was jailed for six years on charges of involvement in two earlier Communist conspiracy cases. On his release from jail, he joined the Indian National Congress, under whose aegis he formed the League of Radical Congressmen. He regarded the Congress as composed of a rank and file that had much revolutionary potential and a leadership that was largely conservative. He maintained that its Gandhian ideology was utopian and reactionary. He also felt that the Gandhian stress on religion was unscientific and that fascism was inherent in nationalism. Believing that the socio-cultural and political situation in India was like that of France before the French Revolution, he advocated a twentieth-century Jacobinism, or radical democracy, as a preparatory stage for a social revolution in India. The preparatory work he had in mind was the dissolution of the religious mode of thought represented by Gandhi. Accordingly, Roy left the Congress in 1940 and formed the Radical Democratic Party, which was to be a broad, united front of workers, peasants, and petit bourgeoisie. He maintained that any sharpening of class differences within this block should be avoided in order to combat the combination of the imperialist-feudal-capitalist forces. Largely because of its unorthodox and unpopular views on religion and nationalism, Roy's Radical Democratic Party failed to make a dent in Indian politics. In 1948 he dissolved the party and founded a new movement called radical or new humanism.

Roy maintained that a humanist appeal, rather than an appeal to class interests, was relevant to Indian society, in which, he said, decomposed feudal relations were inextricably interwoven with weak capitalist relations. Class struggle, he held, is not the sole source of socio-historical changes; there is a social interest that binds classes together.

Roy justified these unorthodox "extensions" of Marxism by claiming that the rejection of all dogmas is the fundamental methodological principle of Marxism. While in his orthodox Marxist phase, he endorsed the Marxist assumption that consciousness is determined by being; in his "new humanist" phase he averred that cultural values have intrinsic historical significance, transcending time and space. He discovered the essence of Marxism in the idea that man is God and, therefore, the master of history. He maintained that Marxism has its foundation in rationalism and that its message for India is that the nation needs a renaissance movement. Moreover, Roy now deduced morality from man's innate rationality.

Human life, according to Roy, must be guided by a moral philosophy that is rational and as comprehensive and permanent as humanity itself. Moral man, rather than mere economic man, becomes the crucial actor in this philosophical revolution. Both fascism and communism, he said, sacrifice individual freedom on the altar of collectivity. He extolled the ideals of spiritual freedom as being both prior to and beyond political and social freedom. In other words, he regarded the moral transformation of the individual as being both the prerequisite to and the fulfillment of economic and political freedom. In place of the structural or institutional approach to the creation of the good society, he adopts an individual, moral approach.

What is more striking in Roy's new humanism is its outright rejection of the doctrine that the end justifies the means and its adoption of the Gandhian view about the integral relationship between means and ends. Accordingly, Roy maintains that the dictatorship of the proletariat cannot be the means to any truly free, humanist society. Freedom, in this view, requires that we look beyond communism.

BIBLIOGRAPHY:

A. *India in Transition* (Geneva: Da la Librairie J. B. Target, 1922); *Scientific Politics* (Calcutta: Renaissance, 1942); *Materialism: An Outline of the History of Scientific Thought* (Calcutta: Renaissance, 1951); *Reason, Romanticism and Revolution* (Calcutta: Renaissance, 1955); *Politics, Power and Parties* (Calcutta: Renaissance, 1960); *Memoirs* (London: Allen and Unwin, 1964).

B. G. Adhikari, ed., *Documents of the Communist Party in India*, vol. 1 (Delhi: People's Publishing House, 1971); J. P. Haithcox, *Communism and Nationalism in India: M. N. Roy and Comintern Policy, 1920–1939* (Princeton: Princeton University Press, 1971); M. Shiviah, *New Humanism and Democratic Politics: A Study of M. N. Roy's Theory of the State* (Bombay: Popular Prakashan, 1977).

THOMAS PANTHAM

S

SAKISAKA ITSURŌ   (b. 1897). Sakisaka Itsurō, now spiritual leader of the Marxist left wing of the Japanese Socialist Party, first established his reputation in the 1930s as an economist and a leading theoretician for the Rōnō-ha (Labor-Farmer faction) of the Japanese Marxist revolutionary movement. Born in Fukuoka Prefecture, the son of an employee for the Mitsui Products Company, Sakisaka entered the Fifth Higher School in 1915. There he was influenced by reading Kawakami Hajime's* *Tale of Poverty* (*Binbō Monogatari*), which exposed the depths of distress suffered by Japan's urban industrial workers, and thereupon Sakisaka resolved to study economics. In 1918 he entered the economic course in the Law Department of Tokyo Imperial University, where he encountered as a classmate the future Marxist economist Uno Kōzō,* who encouraged Sakisaka's interest in Marxism. The two became active in radical campus politics when Professor Morito Tatsuo was suspended from the university for disseminating Marxist ideas in popular journals.

In 1922, as a condition to his appointment to the Law and Literature Faculty of Kyūshū Imperial University, Sakisaka was sent to study in Berlin. There, for two years he studied the Marxist classics, then returned to Japan to lecture on principles of economics. In the mass arrests of Communists of 15 March 1928, Sakisaka was chased out of the university and fled to Tokyo, where he earned a living by writing until he could resume his professorship after the war in 1946. During this interim, Sakisaka not only helped publish the world's first complete edition of Marx's* and Engels's* writings (published by Kaizō-sha), but also wrote extensively on Marxian economic theory in debate with anti-Marxists. These writings focused particularly on *Capital*, and he contended on the correct interpretation of the theory of rent with Kōza-ha Marxists Noro Eitarō* and Yamada Moritarō.* In the debate on Japanese capitalism, which engulfed the movement from 1927 to 1937, Sakisaka embraced the position of the Rōnō-ha dissidents, whom Yamakawa Hitoshi* had led out of the Japanese Communist Party in December 1927. Against the Comintern and official Communist Party espousal of a two-stage revolution, the Rōnō-ha argued that Japanese capitalism was so highly developed that an immediate socialist revolution was possible.

Along with Inomata Tsunao,* Sakisaka and Kushida Tamizō* offered Marxist analyses of Japanese capitalism to support the Rōnō-ha's revolutionary strategy. Kushida was not as closely identified with the faction, however, so after Inomata split with Yamakawa circa 1930, Sakisaka became the Rōnō-ha's leading theoretician in the 1930s. In the early part of the decade, he wrote extensively on *Studies in the Theory of Rent* (1933) and on the *Current Agrarian Problem* (1936), and in 1937 he published his seminal work, *Problems of Japanese Capitalism*. Sakisaka is now recognized as the leading Japanese Marxist economist of the prewar years for his analysis of rent: He argued that Marx's theory of differential rent was fully consistent with the Marxist theory of value, and he demonstrated the operation of the law of market value in relation to different land characteristics. In his view, differential rent resulted when surplus value was redistributed by means of commodity circulation.

As police repression silenced increasing numbers of Japan's Marxists in the late 1930s, Sakisaka too fell victim to the pressure of the state. Arrested in the Popular Front Incident of December 1937, he was imprisoned for almost two years. After his release, he could not publish and made his living as a farmer until the end of the war. In 1946 he resumed his post at Kyūshū University, which he held until his scheduled retirement in 1960. In the meantime, he also resumed his political activities in the socialist movement, launching the revived Rōnō-ha's organ *Forward* (*Zenshin*) with Yamakawa. The journal ceased publication as early as August 1950, however, when its staff split over the issue of Japan's rearmament and the critique of the Soviet Union. Sakisaka and Yamakawa thereupon founded the Socialist Association (Shakai-shugi kyōkai), and published the journal *Socialism*. Sakisaka played a central role in drafting the program adopted by the Left Socialist Party in 1954, and in the same year helped to found the Socialist Party Labor University, of which he became Dean. After Yamakawa's death sapped the energy of the Socialist Association, Sakisaka rebuilt it and increased its influence over the Japanese Socialist Party and the labor movement. The objective of the group, as formulated by Sakisaka, is to execute a peaceful socialist revolution in Japan, and this remains the goal of the left wing of the Socialist Party.

BIBLIOGRAPHY:

A. *Studies in the Theory of Rent* (Tokyo: Kaizō-sha, 1933); *Problems of Japanese Capitalism* (N.p.: Ikusei-sha, 1937); *Keizaigaku hōhōron* (Economic methodology) 3 vols., (Tokyo: n.a., 1950); *Marukusu keizaigaku no hōhō* (The method of Marx's economics) (Tokyo: n.a., 1959).

B. Hidaka Hiroshi et al., *Nihon no Marukusu keizaigaku* (Japan's Marxian economics) 2 vols., (Tokyo: n.a., 1968); Makoto Itoh, *Value and Crisis: Essays on Marxian Economics in Japan* (New York: Monthly Review Press, 1980).

GERMAINE A. HOSTON

SECOND INTERNATIONAL   (1889–1914). Like the First International,* the Second International was founded by representatives of Europe's organized labor movement, this time at the Marxist-inspired International Workers' Congress in Paris in July 1889. Its members included all of Europe's major working-class political parties and trade unions, although it was largely dominated by German social democracy. Camille Huysmans headed the International Socialist Bureau, established in Brussels in 1900 to administer the organization. While most member organizations were Marxists, other ideologies were also represented. Anarchist groups were officially expelled in 1896. After Engels's* death in 1895, the Second International unofficially adopted the orthodox outlook of Karl Kautsky* and Georgii Plekhanov.* Meetings were usually held every two to four years and were used to debate strategy and adopt common tactics.

The ideological split of most national workers' parties into right, center, and left was duplicated in the Second International and shaped the latter's debates on issues such as the advisability of joining or cooperating with bourgeois governments (the Paris Congress of 1900 gave qualified approval), the legitimacy of Eduard Bernstein's† revisionism (the Amsterdam Congress of 1904 condemned Bernstein, while permitting revisionists to remain members of the International), and colonialism (which the Stuttgart Congress of 1907 unequivocally condemned in a close vote after intense, emotional debate). However, the issue that dominated the Second International almost from its beginning, and that intensified after 1907, was that of war. It was resolved after much debate at the Stuttgart Congress of 1907 and reiterated at later congresses. The chosen formula was framed by Lenin,* Rosa Luxemburg,* and Julius Martov* and provided that while the labor movement exert "every effort" to prevent war, if it should occur workers must use the resulting political and economic crises to hasten the downfall of capitalism. The actual outbreak of war in 1914 saw the leading parties of the Second International support the war efforts of their own national governments. The Second International, broken and embarrassed, collapsed immediately. Several efforts by leftist parties in neutral nations to revive it (including the "Berne International" in 1919) failed. So did the efforts of ten larger parties in 1921 (who formed, briefly, the International Working Union of Socialist Parties—the "Vienna Union"—nicknamed the "Second-and-a-Half International"). The Labour and Socialist International, which encompassed the remnants of the Vienna Union and the Berne International, was formed in 1923 and folded in 1940. The Socialist International, which exists today as a loose alliance of Socialist and Social Democratic parties centered in London, is a legacy of the Labor and Socialist International.

The Second International, like the First, produced no major works on theory. Apart from its severe critique of revisionism, it merely applied Marxist orthodoxy—as it was evolving in works by Engels, Kautsky, Plekhanov, Lenin, Luxemburg, and others—to the conditions of prewar Europe in an effort to mobilize workers. This stress on strategy rather than philosophy would dominate the Marxist movement even further after the success of the Russian Revolution and the systematic formulation of Marxism-Leninism.

BIBLIOGRAPHY:
B. James Joll, *The Second International, 1889–1914* (London: Routledge and Kegan Paul, 1955); Julius Braunthal, *History of the International* (vols. 1–2, New York: Praeger; vol. 3, Boulder, Colo.: Westview Press, 1966–80).

ROBERT A. GORMAN

SEN, MOHIT   (b. 1929). Mohit Sen was born in Calcutta on 24 March 1929 into an enlightened and aristocratic family of Bengal. His father A. N. Sen was justice of the Calcutta High Court, and his mother Mrinalini was the niece of Lord Sinha of Raipur, the first Indian to be raised to that position by the British government. Mohit Sen is married to Dr. Vanaja Iyenagar, a mathematician and now Vice-Chancellor of the Women's University, Tirupathi, in Andhra Pradesh.

Mohit Sen had his early education at Calcutta University, where he did his B.A. in history and then proceeded to Cambridge, in the normal pattern established by upper-class Bengalis. He did his Tripos in history in 1950 and then his M.A. in 1953. He obtained his diploma from Charles University, Prague, in 1953. While in his teens he was exposed to the Communist Party and its activities by his eldest brother, the late P. C. Sen. In Cambridge he befriended and was influenced by Maurice Dobb,* Eric Hobsbawm,* and E. M. Foster. Eventually he was attracted to the Party by its dialectical logic and the courage it displayed during World War II. A word about this is necessary in order to understand Sen's motives. Following the Nazi invasion of the Soviet Union in June 1941, Communists throughout the world characterized World War II as a people's war. Earlier, Mahatma Gandhi and the Indian Congress Party had demanded independence for India, with the whole-hearted support of India's Communist Party (CPI). The British government prevaricated. On 9 August 1942, Gandhi finally called the Indian nation to oppose the British government and demand that the British "Quit India." India's Communists, because of the changed international configuration, opposed Gandhi's move and refused to join the national struggle. As a result Indian Communists were humiliated by what nationalists termed their rank betrayal of India's anti-imperialist "revolution." They still have not fully recovered from this faux pas. It was a classic instance of a political party defending an unpopular tactic in order to serve a higher moral purpose. At this time Indian Communists also worked day and night during the unprecedented manmade famine in Bengal when some 3.5 million people died while the British government callously ignored the tragedy. These facts favorably influenced Mohit Sen, so in 1945 he joined the student wing of the Party—the All India Student Federation—and in 1947 was given probationary membership in the Party itself. In 1948 the Indian Communist Party blundered again. At the Second Party Congress in Calcutta, inspired by the "Zhadanov line," they resolved to overthrow the Nehru government by armed insurrection. This led to the Party being driven underground and forced a change in Party leadership. Many Indian Communists were imprisoned, and many more lost their lives during the ferocious counter-measures Prime Minister Nehru unleashed on them. During this period Sen helped the Party by carrying secret papers to London, where he befriended Rajni Palme Dutt of the British Communist Party (CPGB). In England Sen was soon appointed chairman of the Communist Party branch at Cambridge University. He traveled to China during the period of land reform and worked closely with Liu Shaoqi.* After 1953 he devoted his energies to working for the Communist Party of India, proofreading for the Party press and serving as secretary of the Party Centre Branch. In 1966 he was elected to the National Council of the CPI and in 1971 was elected to the Chief Executive Council. He was principal of the Central Party School from 1973 to 1976 and worked on the editorial board of the Party's journal. He also attended the Party congresses of Lebanon, the GDR, and Czechoslovakia as official representative of the CPI. At present he is organizing workers in the state of Gujarat, the home state of Mahatma Gandhi, where the CPI has traditionally been impotent. Tactical disagreements between Sen and the CPI leadership have recently diminished his stature among Party members.

Following the 1964 split of the Indian Communist movement into the Communist Party of India and the Communist Party of India (Marxist), Mohit Sen became one of the important theoreticians of the Communist Party of India. He has argued that India's revolution must eventually travel a noncapitalist path, but at present the Congress Party and other progressive and national bourgeoisie must be supported. This characterization of the Indian bourgeoisie and the present stage of the Indian revolution is in contrast to the more radical one propounded by the Communist Party of India (Marxist). Hence, during most of the 1970s, the chasm between the two parties has been wide. Sen is propagating a dialectical approach to India's current government —a strategy of "Unity and Struggle." He argues that Indian Communists must support its progressive measures in the international arena, its pro-Soviet stance, and its antifeudal and anticommunal policies, while simultaneously struggling to achieve more progressive reforms. Although Sen's party eventually withdrew its support from Mrs. Gandhi before her assassination, Sen continues in his analysis of the progressive role of the national bourgeoisie and the real dangers posed by the threat of world war and nuclear holocaust. He still advocates a united front with the Congress Party. He fears the hideous consequences of Western economic, political, and cultural imperialism and argues that leaders of the anti-imperialist national bourgeoisie should be considered allies.

BIBLIOGRAPHY:

A. *Aspects of the CPI Programme* (New Delhi: Peoples' Publishing House, 1966); *Maoism and the Chinese Revolution* (New Delhi: Peoples' Publishing House, 1975); *Revolution in India: Problems and Prospects* (New Delhi: People's Publishing House, 1977).

K. SESHADRI

SHACHTMAN, MAX   (1904–1972). Born in Warsaw, 10 September 1904, Max Shachtman was brought to America as an infant by his Jewish parents. A charter member of the Communist Party, he was expelled in 1928 as a Trot-skyite.* For the next twelve years he was one of the leaders of the Trotsky movement in America. He broke with his colleagues in 1940 over their support of the Soviet Union's invasion of Finland and formed the Independent Socialist League. He joined the Socialist Party in 1958 and died on 4 November 1972.

Shachtman's major theoretical contribution to Marxism was his theory of bureaucratic collectivism, which held that when the state owned the means of production, those who controlled the state became the ruling class. The Soviet bureaucracy, uncontrolled by the people, was a new ruling class and the Soviet Union was not a progressive historical force. One implication of Shachtman's views, later developed by Milovan Djilas,† was that democracy had to be part of a socialist society.

BIBLIOGRAPHY:

A. *The Bureaucratic Revolution* (New York: Donald Press, 1962).

RICHARD KLEHR

SILVA HERZOG, JESÚS   (b. 1892). The renaissance man of the Mexican Revolution, Jesús Silva Herzog was born on 14 November 1892 in San Luís Potosí. Author, poet, educator, economist, social critic, historian, businessman, politician, founder of the Fondo de Cultura Económica (Mexico's principal press for economic publications), and for over thirty years editor of *Cuadernos amer-icanos*, Silva Herzog has played an integral role in twentieth-century Mexico. After primary studies in San Luís Potosí and secondary schooling at the Paine Uptown Business School in New York City (1912–14), he received a degree in economics from the National Autonomous University of Mexico (UNAM) in 1923. Like many young intellectuals of the day, he had his studies interrupted by the violent phase of the Mexican Revolution (1911–20). During this time, Silva Herzog was a supporter of the interim President Eulalio Gutiérrez. Because of his political activities, he was jailed in 1916 for four months. After the end of hostilities, he returned to his studies to complete his graduate education at UNAM. Silva Herzog's most outstanding accomplishments as an educator in-clude his role in the founding of the National School of Economics at UNAM (serving as director, 1940–42) and the National School of Agriculture (professor, 1923–38). At UNAM he was professor of economic thought from 1931 to 1959, and in 1960 was named professor emeritus at that institution. From 1918 to 1948 he held a number of governmental posts. He served as President Cárdenas's economic advisor during the petroleum conflict in 1937–38, which led to the nationalization of the oil industry. Later he was named general manager of the National Petroleum Company (1939–40), the forerunner of Petroleos Mexicanos (PEMEX). Other posts held during this period include director of economic studies for the National Railroads of Mexico, Minister to the Soviet Union (1928–30), and various positions within the Finance Ministry. Finally, Silva Herzog returned to public service during the Echeverría administration (at the age of eighty) to serve as Director General of the National Housing Institute.

In addition to his role in government service and education, Silva Herzog's written works are voluminous, and he has been a spokesman for the democratic left in Mexico. A self-proclaimed heterodox Marxist, Silva Herzog blames the world capitalist system for the underdevelopment of Latin America. Unlike many Marxists, however, he argues that the correct path for Mexico and Latin America is democratic socialism, a society where the liberty of man to think, act, and create is respected. According to Silva Herzog the ills of communism lie in the dogmatism and fanaticism that necessarily accompany it. He questions whether all of history has been a class struggle and argues that the proleteriat's working conditions have in fact improved over time. On the other hand, he agrees with many tenets of Marxism, including the Marxist materialist conceptualization of history, the notion of surplus value, and the organic composition of capital. These ideas are expressed in "México a cincuenta años de su revolución." However, critics have countered that Silva Herzog's vision conforms all to closely to the static rhetoric espoused by Mexico's ruling party, the PRI (Partido Revolucionario Institucional). Given the author's intimate working relationship with various presidential administrations, the charge may not be unfounded.

One of Silva Herzog's most notable accomplishments is his role as ongoing editor of *Cuadernos americanos*, a leading Latin American interdisciplinary journal. For over thirty-five years, this review has served as an international forum for the exchange of ideas on Latin American society. Along with the author's seminal publications on the history of the Mexican Revolution, his work with *Cuadernos americanos* may prove to be his most lasting achievement.

BIBLIOGRAPHY:

A. *Breve historia de la Revolución Mexicana,* 2 vols. (Mexico City: Fondo de Cultural Económica, 1960); "México a cincuenta años de su revolución," *Cuadernos americanos,* 132 (January-February1964), pp. 7–30.

B. James W. Wilkie and Edna Monzon de Wilkie, *México visto en el siglo XX: entrevistas de historia oral* (Mexico City: Instituto Mexicano de Investigaciones Económicas, 1969), pp. 697–720.

CARL A. ROSS AND ALLEN WELLS

SISON, JOSÉ MARIA   (b. 1939). José Maria Sison was born on 8 February 1939 in Cabuago, Ilocos Sur, the Philippines. He attended high school in Manila and graduated from the University of the Philippines in 1959. He studied Indonesian language and literature in Djakarta in 1962 and returned to teach in Manila the following year. In 1964 he founded the Kabataang Makabayan (KM, National Youth) and was its national chairman until 1968. Sison succeeded in linking the activities of the KM with labor unions and especially with the Workers' Party (Lapiang Manggagwa), of which he also became general secretary. In 1966, he became the founding general secretary of the Movement for the Advancement of Nationalism (MAN), a united front organization for national independence and democracy that sought to include support from the national bourgeoisie. From 1963 to 1968, Sison was also editor of the journal *Progressive Review.*

Sison became founder and chairman of the Central Committee of the Communist Party of the Philippines (Marxist-Leninist) from 1969, a breakaway from the older Communist Party of the Philippines (PKP), following a "Congress of Reestablishment of the Communist Party of the Philippines" held in Southern Tarlac Province, Luzon, between 26 December 1968 and 7 January 1969. In March 1969, under Sison's direction, the CPP(M-L) organized the Party's military wing, the New People's Army (NPA). Since then, the NPA has waged guerrilla warfare on Maoist* lines against the government of President Marcos. Sison, until his arrest in November 1977, remained the principal CPP(M-L) theoretician and NPA tactician. He has since been detained on charges of subversion and conspiracy to commit rebellion.

Prior to its effective reestablishment by Sison in 1969, the Philippines Communist Party had lost the influence and prestige that it gained during the Japanese occupation of 1942–44 and the Huk rebellion of the late 1940s. As chairman of the reestablished Party, Sison undertook a comprehensive class analysis and strategy for revolution, which he outlined in his *Philippine Society and Revolution*. From the beginning, the CPP(M-L) and later the NPA adopted a separate article in its Constitution on the "territorial organization" of the Party, which effectively gave local Party units self-government. The Central Committee, Sison argued, should only put forward the "general line." Initiative was to be left to regional Party organizations in accordance with local conditions. Centralized leadership was always to be accompanied by "dispersed operations." At the same time, Sison argued for the need for "liaison teams" to operate between the masses and the NPA. The teams were charged with establishing close contact with the public at large "through various flexible methods" and the conducting of "social investigation."

BIBLIOGRAPHY:

A. *Struggle for National Democracy* (Quezon City: Progressive Publications, 1967); Amado Guerrero (Sison), *Philippine Society and Revolution* (Hong Kong: Ta Kung Pao, 1971).

MICHAEL C. WILLIAMS

ŠMERAL, BOHUMIR   (1880–1941). Born on 25 October 1880 in Trebici, Bohumir Šmeral studied law at Charles University in Prague. From 1901 to 1918 he was the editor of the principal socialist democratic daily *Pravo lidu*. Even before World War I he had become a prominent figure in the Czech Socialist Democratic Party. From 1921 to 1929 and from 1936 to 1941 he was a member of the Central Committee of the Czechoslovak Communist Party. From 1921 to 1924 he was a member of the Party's Executive Committee, and from 1924 to 1929 a member of the Politburo. From 1922 to 1935 Šmeral was a member of the Executive Committee of the Comintern, from 1922 to 1928 (except for 1923) a member of its Presidium, and after 1935 a member of the Comintern's International Control Commission. After 1926 he lived primarily in Moscow and worked in the Executive Committee of the Comintern. He died on 8 May 1941 in Moscow.

Before World War I Šmeral formulated the nationality program of Czech socialist democracy. An attempt was made to stop the progressive breakdown of the all-Austria socialist democracy. Šmeral repudiated the formation of an independent Czech state and saw the solution in the radical democratic federal reorganization of Austria, equality of national rights, and cultural autonomy. This program applied the ideas of Karl Renner and Otto Bauer† to the specific conditions under which Czech socialist democracy operated. Šmeral never abandoned his pro-Austrian orientation.

After the formation of the Czechoslovak Republic, Šmeral quickly became a representative of the leftists in the party and made contact with the Comintern. In discussions with Bolshevik leaders, however, he advocated delaying the founding of the Communist Party until he could win over as many members of the Social Democratic Party as possible. As a result, the Communist Party of Czechoslovakia did not formally come into existence until 1921, and it acquired two-thirds of the members of the Czech Social Democrats. In contrast to the Bolshevik approach of a nucleus party, comprised only of highly active members, Šmeral advocated a large and heterogeneous party, within which the "nucleus" principle could take shape. In Party discussions regarding a "workers government" in 1922, he expressed the view that such a loose coalition of leftists could exist for a long period, and he proposed that the Communist Party formulate a program for its implementation. After 1924, when the Comintern declared that a "workers government" was merely a synonym for a dictatorship of the proletariat, Šmeral gradually turned away from an active political life.

BIBLIOGRAPHY:

A. *Pravda o sovetovém Rusku* (Prague: Práce, 1920); *Historické práce, 1908–1940* (Prague: státni nakl. politické literatury, 1961).

B. J. Galandauer, *Bhumir Šmeral, 1880–1914* (Brno: Blok, 1979).

M. MILOS HÁJEK

SNEEVLIET, H. J. F. M.   (1883–1942). Henk Sneevliet was born in Rotterdam, Netherlands, on 13 May 1883. He was an early activist in the Dutch Social Democratic Workers' Party (SDAP). In 1913, he left Holland for the Dutch East Indies and the following year established the first Marxist party in colonial Asia, the Indonesian Social Democratic Association (ISDV), later to become the Indonesian Communist Party (PKI). In 1920, Sneevliet was elected secretary of the Commission on National and Colonial Questions at the Second Congress of the Comintern and a member of the Executive Committee of the Comintern. Sneevliet became the representative of the Comintern in the Far East and Southeast Asia in 1921 and assisted that year in the founding of the Chinese Communist Party (CCP). In 1927, Sneevliet broke with the Comintern and in 1929 founded the Dutch Revolutionary Socialist Party (RSP), one of the few independent Marxist parties with popular support outside the Third International.* He was active in the resistance during the German occupation of Holland after 1940. Sneevliet was arrested and executed by the Gestapo in 1942.

Sneevliet's profound understanding and sympathy for Asian nationalism and his direct experience made him an unparalleled figure in the early Comintern. Although the early membership of the ISDV in Indonesia was almost entirely Dutch, Sneevliet was acutely conscious of the urgent need to attract Indonesians if the Party was to become a viable and potent force. Within a few years it had done so and recruited, among others, Tan Malaka.* Sneevliet realized, however, that if Marxism was to make an impact on Asian society, it had to draw support from the peasantry as well as the working class. Like Lenin,* Sneevliet was deeply aware that if the rising nationalist tide in Asia could be linked to the socialist movement, its political repercussions would be revolutionary.

For Sneevliet, the nationalist Sarekat Islam (Islamic Association) presented the ideal vehicle through which the ISDV could advance a program of revolutionary socialism. This strategy, later referred to as the "bloc within," was the first concrete example of a Marxist party attempting to infiltrate another party and form cells within it as a means of developing its own propaganda and contacts among the masses. As a result of the success of this policy, the PKI, by 1921, was the largest Marxist party in Asia.

At the Second Congress of the Comintern in 1922, Sneevliet, with Lenin's support, advocated the necessity for the infant Communist movement in Asia to ally itself with nationalist parties. The Lenin–Sneevliet view dominated the policy of the Comintern in Asia over the following years. In China, Sneevliet was decisive in persuading the infant Chinese Communist Party to pursue a "bloc within" strategy and to work inside the nationalist Kuomintang (KMT) from 1922. This resulted in a great expansion of the CCP in the labor movement. However, after Sneevliet's departure from China in 1923, the strategy of the CCP became increasingly subordinate to Soviet foreign policy. Events in China in 1926–27 and the debacle of the Communist Party hastened Sneevliet's break with the Comintern. Sneevliet continued to defend the strategy provided Communist parties were able to preserve their freedom of organization and propaganda and not be subject to Soviet interests.

BIBLIOGRAPHY:

B. Fritjof Tichelman, *Henk Sneevliet, Een Politieke Biographie*(Amsterdam: Van Gennep, 1974); Max Perthus, *Henk Sneevliet: Revolutionair Socialist in Europa en Azie* (Nijmegen: Sun, 1976); Michael Williams, "Sneevliet: A Comintern Odyssey," *New Left Review*, 123 (September-October 1980), pp. 81–90.

MICHAEL C. WILLIAMS

SODRÉ, NELSON WERNECK   (b. 1911). One of the most profound Marxist writers and thinkers in Brazil, Nelson Werneck Sodré graduated from his country's military academy and rose to the rank of general. He has written over thirty books that use Marxism as a heuristic device and take note of the role of class struggle and imperialism in the history of Brazil. His volumes have stood for years as models of scholarship for Brazilian Marxists. They cover such diverse topics as racism, the ideology of colonialism, modernization, military history, and Marxist aesthetics.

Ofício de escritor dialéctica da literatura (The Writers' Profession: The Dialectic of Literature) contains Sodré's penetrating insights into the relationship of art and society. To him, writers search for social reality, truth, and beauty and also recreate them through interpretations. Writers demonstrate societies' perpetual conflicts and dialogues, which are often class struggles. In this work and others, Sodré also distinguished between the technicians who transmit facts or practical knowledge and intellectuals who stimulate ideas that reshape society. To him, art dominated by technology becomes obedient and loses purity, autonomy, and value as art.

Sodré feels that artists must destroy fantasies of false hope and express the realities that the future holds. To him, hope is visible through revolution, not dreams. The militant artist must convey hope for revolution, and therefore for humanity, through creativity. Sodré shows the basic liberty in communication, its propaganda value, and its authoritarian potential, but insists that art remains one of the best ways to search for truth. He contends that socialist artists retain individuality and creativity while producing for mass audiences, that social consciousness can be retained in the course of doing an individual piece or book. Art, he asserts, should be constructed to liberate the mind, must reflect social conditions, and has to encourage and bring about change to foster independence. In particular, he views written art as a form of consciousness, which can free the mind and then produce deeds.

BIBLIOGRAPHY:

A. *Formacão histórica do Brasil* (São Paulo: Brasiliense, 1962); *Ofício de escritor dialéctica da literatura* (Rio de Janeiro: Civilização Brasileira, 1965); *História da burguesia brasiliera* (Rio de Janeiro: Civilização Brasileira, 1967); *Fundamentos da estética marxista* (Rio de Janeiro: Civilização Brasileira, 1968); *História da literatura brasileira* (Rio de Janeiro: Civilização Brasileira, 1976).

SHELDON B. LISS

STALIN, JOSEF VISSARIONOVICH (1879–1953). Born Josef Vissarionovich Dzhugashvili on 21 December 1879 in the Georgian city of Gori, Josef Stalin was the son of a cobbler who rose to lead the Soviet Party and state. Expelled in 1899 from a theological seminary in Tbilisi for nontraditional and unacceptable interests (e.g. Victor Hugo's novels) Stalin became a professional revolutionary who identified as early as 1904 with Lenin* and bolshevism and rose gradually in Russia's Marxist movement until he was appointed to the Bolshevik Central Committee in 1912. After 1902 Stalin was frequently arrested, imprisoned, and exiled by tsarist forces for his revolutionary activities. After the Bolshevik Revolution in October/November 1917, Stalin was elected as an original member of the Party Politburo. In April 1922, with Lenin ill, Stalin was appointed General Secretary of the Russian Communist Party. After Lenin's death, in January 1924, Stalin quickly consolidated his power, defeating potential opposition forces rallying around Leon Trotsky,* Alexander Zinoviev, and Nikolai Bukharin.* By 1929 he was the supreme and unchallenged leader of the Soviet Union. He supervised the industrialization, purges, and mass annihilations that took place during the 1930s. During World War II he was the commander-in-chief of the Soviet armed forces. Stalin, alone among wartime leaders, managed to maintain power uninterruptedly until his death in 1953.

As a political theorist, Stalin's contributions are miniscule. In 1938 *The History of the Communist Party of the Soviet Union (Bolsheviks), a Short Course* was edited by an anonymous Soviet commission. Stalin was initially credited with writing the fourth chapter, "On Dialectical and Historical Materialism." He later claimed to have written the entire volume. For fifteen years, the *Short Course* was an article of unhesitating truth that literate Soviet citizens read continually. It lauds everything Lenin and Stalin did to foment and preserve the workers' revolution and labels their theoretical and political opponents people's enemies. "On Dialectical and Historical Materialism" smoothly rehashes basic orthodox principles of Engels,* Plekhanov,* Bukharin, and, of course, Lenin. Conceived as a catechism of what Stalin called "Marxism-Leninism," it was written in very simple language with each idea numbered, presumably to facilitate memorization. Under the unacknowledged influence of Plekhanov—a man elsewhere ridiculed—Stalin described dialectical materialism as the general laws governing matter and historical materialism as a special case referring particularly to history and economics. He delineated four unoriginal laws governing nature's dialectical movement (for some unexplained reason ignoring Engels's "law of the negation of the negation") and three already popular principles of materialism and concluded by unimaginatively describing the primacy of material production, the interaction of base and superstructure, the class struggle, ideology, the role of technology, and history's progression of socio-economic systems. Stalin was neither innovative nor prepared for philosophical subtleties: he adopted, for example, Lenin's reflection theory of knowledge but ignored the important issues raised in the *Notebooks*. Praxis, for Stalin, was unquestioningly determined by fixed historical laws.

Stalin's unrivaled, absolute power in the Soviet Union made theory of any kind expendable. He did whatever he wished and later found appropriate quotations; hence, his significant contributions to orthodox Marxist materialism are policies enunciated while consolidating power. The principle of "socialism in one country" (the belief that socialism could be established in the Soviet Union without socialist revolutions occuring elsewhere) was partially intended to raise Party and worker morale at a time of unfulfilled expectations regarding world proletariat revolution. Appearing in *Concerning Questions of Leninism* (1924), only two years after *The Foundations of Leninism* (1922) confirmed the universal validity of Leninism and the necessity of proletariat revolution in the West, "socialism in one country" also legitimated the brutal suppression of those, like Trotsky, who were dissatisfied with Stalin's policies promoting world revolution.

Preceding the violent purge of the Left Opposition in July 1928, Stalin declared that maturing Soviet communism had intensified the class struggle, making Party violence a necessary and acceptable tactic. As purges continued, Stalin declared (12 January 1933) that dialectics required the proletarian state to evolve first into a state of maximum power before finally "withering away." These Stalinist "principles" were obviously premeditated excuses for an unprincipled reign of terror. During this period, Stalin published articles on a variety of scientific and artistic topics, none innovative or theoretically significant. Collectively, they comprised an official "line" and determined what Soviet scholars were permitted to write about. Stalin emerged as head of Lenin's Party, world communism's chief scientist. His actions were objectively justifiable. Potential critics, *ipso facto*, rejected history's valid laws—and Stalin did not tolerate such arrogance. Materialism slid headlong into totalitarianism not because it is inherently anti-democratic—Karl Kautsky,* for one, considered himself a democrat—but because it theoretically emasculated subjectivity, leaving the masses unwilling and unable to defend themselves actively against unscrupulous leaders.

BIBLIOGRAPHY:

A. *Dialectical and Historical Materialism* (New York: International, 1940); Works, 13 vols. (London: Lawrence & Wishart, 1952–55); *The Essential Stalin: Major Theoretical Writings, 1905–1952*, ed. Bruce Franklin (Garden City, N.Y.: Anchor Books, 1972).

B. T. H. Rigby, ed., *Stalin* (Englewood Cliffs, N.J.: Prentice-Hall, 1966); Isaac Deutscher, *Stalin: A Political Biography* (New York: Oxford University Press, 1967); Robert C. Tucker, *Stalin as Revolutionary* (New York: Norton, 1973).

ROBERT A. GORMAN

STERNBERG, FRITZ (1895–1963). Fritz Sternberg was born on 11 June 1895 in Breslau and died on 18 October 1963 in Munich. He studied economics at Breslau and Berlin, receiving his doctorate in 1917. After serving for several years as an assistant under Franz Oppenheimer, he began a career in 1924 as an independent author and journalist. Active after 1931 in the Socialist Workers Party, which broke off from the left wing of the Social Democratic Party in that year, he fled into exile in 1933. After spending the next few years largely in Basel and Paris, he emigrated to the United States in 1939. Although he became a U.S. citizen, he spent his final years in West Germany and Austria.

Although usually considered a disciple of Rosa Luxemburg,* Sternberg criticized both her and Lenin* for failing to recognize the extent to which imperialism had served to ameliorate conditions for the working classes in the industrialized parts of the world. He argued, however, that by the interwar period imperialism had entered a new era in which its stabilizing effects had been much reduced, thus setting the stage for a new series of economic crises. This resulted largely from the tendency of imperialists to ally themselves with feudal agrarian interests in the areas under their domination, thus retarding growth and limiting the ability of the colonial economies to continue to absorb the excess capital and consumer goods produced by the advanced countries.

BIBLIOGRAPHY:

A. *Der Imperialismus* (Berlin: Malik, 1923); *Der Niedergang des Deutschen Kapitalismus* (Berlin: Rowohlt, 1932); *The Coming Crisis* (New York: John Day, 1947); *Capitalism and Socialism on Trial* (New York: John Day, 1950).

B. *Biographisches Handbuch des deutschsprachigen Emigration nach 1933*, vol. 1 (New York: K. G. Sauer, 1980), p. 734.

KENNETH CALKINS

ŠVERMA, JAN   (1901–1944). Born on 23 March 1901 in Mnichove Hradiste, Jan Šverma studied law at Charles University in Prague. In 1921 he joined the Communist Party of Czechoslovakia. From 1926 to 1928 he studied at the Lenin College in Moscow. After 1929 he was a member of the Czech Party's Central Committee and Politburo, and by 1935 was a candidate for the Executive Comintern. From 1936 to 1938 he was the editor-in-chief of *Rude Pravo*, the major journal of the Party. During World War I Šverma fled Czechoslovakia. On 28 September 1944 he flew as a political representative of the party to the insurgent territory in Slovakia. On 10 November he died in flight while passing over the partisan headquarters in the Chabenec Mountains.

In the early 1930s Šverma perceived weaknesses in the Moscow-directed Comintern line. At the twelfth session of the Executive Comintern he, Klement Gottwald,* and Josef Guttmann* criticized the policy of the German Communist Party and sought an alliance with Social Democratic representatives of the workers. Their criticism was rejected. In November 1934 the Central Committee of the Communist Party of Czechoslovakia, encouraged by Šverma, adopted a resolution advocating a coalition government of all socialist parties. This initiative was stopped by the Secretariat of the Executive Comintern. Later, during an absence of General Secretary Gottwald, Šverma bore the principal responsibility for Party policy and tried to accommodate other democratic forces on the left (voting, for example, for some items in the state budget and to support Eduard Beneš against the right-wing candidate in the upcoming presidential election). This policy was criticized in the Comintern as an opportunistic interpretation of the decree of the Seventh Congress.

BIBLIOGRAPHY:

A. *Collected Works*, 2 vols. (Prague: n.a., 1981).

M. MILOS HÁJEK

SWEEZY, PAUL M.   (b. 1910). Born in New York in 1910, Paul Sweezy attended Exeter and Harvard. He received his Ph.D. in economics in 1937, having been a student of Joseph Schumpeter. He did further work at the London School of Economics, in Vienna, and elsewhere on the continent, returning to teach economics at Harvard until 1942, when he failed to gain tenure. He never again had a regular university faculty appointment, although he was a visiting professor at Cornell, Stanford, the New School, and the University of Tokyo, among many schools. Sweezy's lectures on socialism at the University of New

Hampshire led to his investigation in 1956 by the state Attorney General, in the course of which Sweezy testified that he neither had been nor then was a member of the American Communist Party. He spent the years 1942–46 in the U.S. Army (in the OSS), earning a Bronze Star. In 1949 he founded the journal *Monthly Review*, which he has edited since then, first with Leo Huberman* and then with Harry Magdoff*; Paul A. Baran* was a leading contributor and close coworker.

Sweezy's book, *The Theory of Capitalist Development*, has from its publication in 1942 until the present day been widely considered *the* modern introduction to Marx's thought; his later *Monopoly Capital*, coauthored with Baran, was perhaps the central theoretical work of the new left of the 1960s. It might be said that this preeminence was due in part to Sweezy's near monopoly of Marxist publishing during the 1950s and 1960s, as editor of *Monthly Review* and its associated Press. But it more importantly reflects the fact that Sweezy was the first American Marxist to attempt a theoretical rapprochement of Marxist and neoclassical (Marshallian and Keynesian) economic theory.

Thus Sweezy developed Oskar Lange's* distinction between the socio-political and the economic aspects of Marx's theory, arguing that while the concept of value was important in drawing attention to the class character of capitalist society, the price theory of orthodox bourgeois economics provides a superior tool for the analysis of that society's "laws of motion" (*Theory*, pp. 128–29). Adding to this line of thought the assumption that the change from competitive to monopoly capitalism has rendered Marx's value theory of accumulation obsolete, the analysis in *Monopoly Capital* combines neoclassical microeconomics, without the assumption of pure competition, with left-Keynesian macroeconomics.

In the earlier book Sweezy developed an underconsumptionist explanation of capitalist crisis: while the concentration of wealth in capitalism implies an increase in investment relative to consumption, only an equal increase in consumption can match the output of the expanding capacity to produce consumer goods. This suggests the need for unproductive uses of output, such as military spending. A second argument, amplified in the book written with Baran, asserted that monopoly conditions spelled restriction of output and of technological innovation, in the interest of maintaining highly profitable price structures; once again this means economic stagnation except to the extent that waste production serves to absorb the surplus output generated by modern capitalism. Of course, the first argument forgets that producer goods are part of output, alongside consumer goods; the second not only rests on dubious assumptions of static price theory but was disconfirmed by the enormous growth rates of world capitalism in the post-World War II period. However, their very proximity to the tenets of bourgeois theory allowed Sweezy's books to serve as the basis for the development of "radical" or "Marxist" economics within the academic world.

Politically, Sweezy remained more or less a Stalinist,* although an eclectic one, throughout his career. "By 'socialism,' " the editorial statement of *Monthly Review* affirmed, "we mean a system of society with two fundamental characteristics: first, public ownership of the decisive sectors of the economy and, second, comprehensive planning of production for the benefit of the producers themselves. . . . Socialism became a reality with the introduction of the first Five Year Plan in Soviet Russia in 1928.'' While Khrushchev's* "revelations" of Stalin's crimes left Sweezy with faith in the essential soundness of the Soviet regime, he soon shifted his main allegiance to Maoist* China and, in later years, briefly to the North Korea of Kim Il Sung. Here too, therefore, as in his consistent championing of Castro* and the Cuban Revolution, Sweezy's positions were in harmony with the predispositions of the majority of those within the new left who identified themselves with the chief post-1918 tradition of Marxism. The influence of his works, and above all the enormous role played by *Monthly Review* as a journal of the recent American left, is therefore understandable.

BIBLIOGRAPHY:

A. *The Theory of Capitalist Development: Principles of Marxian Political Economy* (New York: Oxford University Press, 1942); *Socialism* (New York: McGraw-Hill, 1949); *The Present as History* (New York: Monthly Review Press, 1953); with Leo Huberman, *Cuba: Anatomy of a Revolution* (New York: Monthly Review Press, 1960); with Paul Baran, *Monopoly Capital* (New York: Monthly Review Press, 1966); *Four Lectures on Marxism* (New York: Monthly Review Press, 1980).

B. Tom Kemp, "Paul M. Sweezy e la teoria dello sviluppo capitalistico,'' pp. 1475– 90, in *Storia del marxismo contemporaneo*, ed. Aldo Zanardo (Milan: Feltrinelli, 1973); Mario Cogoy, "Les théories néo-marxistes, Marx, et l'accumulation du capital,'' *Les Temps modernes*, 29, no. 314–334 (1972).

PAUL MATTICK, JR.

T

TAKAHASHI KAMEKICHI   (1891–1977). Takahashi Kamekichi is a Japanese Marxist best known for the Marxist scholarship on Japanese economic development that he pioneered in the 1920s. He is also heavily criticized in orthodox Marxist circles for his theory of "petty imperialism," which began with a Marxian analysis of Japanese economic history since the Meiji period (1868–1912) and ended with a defense of Japanese expansion onto the Asian mainland in support of proletarian socialist revolution. Takahashi's work both offered a coherent contemporary analysis of the economic factors propelling Japan toward ultra-rightist militarism in World War II and exposed some of the theoretical difficulties that arose from the application of Lenin's* theory of imperialism to the actions of a late-developing country like Japan in a period in which patterns of economic development diverged from those that Marx* traced for England and France in the nineteenth century. Takahashi's Marxist scholarship positing a *yukizumari* (deadlock) in Japan's economy in the face of a changing international context suggested implications similar to those Immanuel Wallerstein† would draw about the economic difficulties encountered by countries developing on the "periphery" and "semiperiphery" of the capitalist "world-system."

Takahashi had an unusual background for a Japanese Marxist theorist in prewar Japan. He was educated at the private Waseda University rather than at the prestigious Tokyo Imperial University, which produced most leading Marxists. Because of financial hardship, Takahashi could not pursue graduate work in law or economics and thus was self-educated in Marxist economic theory. He was an economic reporter at the Tōyō Keizai Shinpō-sha (Oriental Economic News Agency) until 1926, when he became an independent economic historian. In 1932, Takahashi established his own institute for the study of economics and subsequently served as consultant to the Japanese colonial administrations in Manchuguo and Taiwan and to the Japanese government in several positions, including advisor in the Cabinet's War Planning Office. Takahashi wrote prolifically, publishing several dozen works on political economy by 1945.

Takahashi's political activities reflected his theoretical interests. Never a member of the Japanese Communist Party, he nevertheless cultivated ties with leftists like Sakai Toshihiko and Yamakawa Hitoshi,* who founded the Party. After Takahashi helped to establish the left-wing Seiji Kenkyū Kai (Political Studies Association), his rightist inclinations became increasingly apparent. When factionalism in the group resulted in its domination of "right-wing" social democrats by the Communist left, Takahashi left the group. In 1926, he became active in the Japanese Farmers Party (Nihon Nōmintō), which exhibited both leftist and rightist tendencies. After running unsuccessfully for office as a Nōntō candidate in 1928, Takahashi severed all ties with the left-wing movement. After Japan became engaged in full-scale war with China in 1937, he drew close to more explicitly right-wing nationalist groups, like the Shōwa kenkyū kai (Showa Research Association), which supported the government's military policies in Asia.

Takahashi first established his reputation as a Marxist scholar in the mid-1920s, when his scholarship on Japanese economic history produced his thesis of the deadlock (*yukizumari*) of the Japanese economy. Here Takahashi argued that the ingredients that fueled Japan's spectacular growth from the Meiji Restoration (1868) to the end of the Meiji era (1912)—copying of Western technology, exploitation of natural resources, and a supply of cheap labor—had disappeared. As Takahashi wrote his influential *Studies on the Japanese Capitalist Economy* (*Nihon shihon-shugi keizai no kenkyū*) (1924), Japan was experiencing a severe recession, a "deadlock" in its development. Takahashi observed that new domestic and international factors had emerged to impede Japan's development: rising wages in response to labor union activism, rising taxes required to support Japan's expansion abroad, and increasing nationalist resistance to Japanese imperialism in countries like China, which were experiencing indigenous capitalist development and beginning to compete with Japanese industry (e.g. in textiles). Japan's narrow natural materials base and the previous partition of the world into spheres of influence by more advanced capitalist states prevented Japan from easing its internal economic difficulties by means of traditional British-style imperialism.

At this point, Takahashi moved on to posit the central argument of his "petty imperialism" thesis. In evaluating "The Imperialistic Position of Japanese Capitalism" ("Nihon shihon-shugi no teikoku-shugi-teki chi'i) (1927), Takahashi argued that Japan's expansionism was fundamentally different in character—hence less reprehensible—than Western imperialism. Since Japan's capitalist development was so limited, its imperialistic maneuvers could not be explained by Lenin's theory of imperialism, which noted a pattern of heavy industrial development and subsequent expansion in a world of free trade. Given its dearth of raw materials and the obstacles posed by the prior erection of economic spheres of influence in Asia and Africa, Japan was compelled to pursue military expansion rather than expansion via financial-industrial combines. On the basis of its lower level of development, Japan could be merely "petty imperialist," as the petit bourgeoisie is to the haute bourgeoisie. As domestic and international conditions severely constrained Japan's economic expansion, both its benefits and its negative impact on other countries were significantly less than those occasioned by comparable activities by advanced Western countries. Takahashi's conclusion, then, was deeply disturbing for fellow Marxists who adhered to the Comintern's anti-imperialist line. As a disadvantaged, late-developing country, it was essential that Japan resolve its economic deadlock by expanding territorially onto the Asian mainland. Furthermore, such a policy, which so closely resembled the official notion of the Greater East Asia Co-Prosperity Sphere, would help to advance the cause of Karl Marx's* proletarian socialism. Takahashi argued: the "deadlock" broken, accelerated development would bring the dawn of socialism closer. After Takahashi made this argument he suddenly found himself boycotted by the major left-wing journals and publishing houses that had published his work to date. More importantly, his thesis provoked the Marxist "debate on Japanese capitalism" (1927–37) by challenging more orthodox Japanese Marxists to produce a more cogent interpretation of Japanese economic development.

BIBLIOGRAPHY:

A. *Nihon keizai no yukizumari to musan kaikyū no taisaku* (The impasse of the Japanese economy and the countermeasures of the proletariat) (Tokyo: Hakuyō-sha, 1926); *Sayoku undō no riron-teki hōkai: uyoku undō no riron-teki konkyo* (The theoretical collapse of the left-wing movement—the theoretical basis of the right-wing movement) (Tokyo: Hakuyō-sha, 1927); *Nihon shihon-shugi hattatsu shi* (History of the development of Japanese Marxism) (Tokyo: Nihon hyōron-sha, 1928); *Taishō Shōwa zaikai no hendō* (Economic fluctuations in the Taishō and Shōwa periods), 3 vols. (Tokyo: Tōyō Keizai Shinpō-sha, 1954–55); *Takahashi keizai riron keisei no rokujū nen: Nihon keizai gekidō no jidai to watakushi no jinsei* (Sixty years in the formation of Takahashi's economic theory: the era of Japanese economic turmoil and my life), 2 vols. (Tokyo: Tōshi Keizai-sha, 1976).

B. Kojima Hinehisa, *Nihon shihon-shugi ronsō* (The debate on Japanese capitalism) (Tokyo: Arisue, 1976).

GERMAINE A. HOSTON

TAKAHASHI KŌHACHIRŌ   (b. 1912). Born in Fukui Prefecture on 1 June 1912, Takahashi Kōhachirō has emerged as a premier Marxist scholar of comparative political history. In 1935, Takahashi graduated from the course in occidental history in the Department of History at Tokyo Imperial University. After teaching at Keisei University and other colleges during the prewar period, after the war in 1952 Takahashi was appointed professor at the University of Tokyo and subsequently was also appointed to that university's prestigious Institute of Social Science. In 1973, Takahashi followed custom and resigned from the university and then became professor at the private Waseda University. Since the early 1950s, Takahashi has established an international reputation, and his translated work has been included in an anthology on *The Transition from Feudalism to Capitalism* as Takahashi began to participate in the controversy involving Maurice Dobb* and Paul Sweezy.* In 1952 Takahashi was guest professor at the invitation of the French government and helped incorporate Western work on economic history into Japanese scholarship. Finally, since about 1960, Takahashi has been active as an Asian representative to the Secretariat of the head-quarters of the International Historical Association.

The basis for Takahashi's international reputation has been his work in the economic history of the French Revolution. A descendant of the prewar Kōza school (or feudal faction), which emphasized Japan's relative backwardness in comparison with other more advanced capitalist states, Takahashi thus reflected nicely the tendency of Kōza-ha analysts to wield influence on comparative economic history. By 1950, Takahashi had published two works that quickly became classics of Japanese contemporary social analysis in the postwar period: *A Historical Treatise on the Establishment of Modern Society* (1947); and *The Structure of Bourgeois Revolutions* (1950). His basic argument was that the collapse of feudalism and rise of modern capitalist society had to be comprehended in relation to the emergence and dissolution of an independent peasantry. This became a key contribution to the debate on whether the development of world trade was the decisive factor spawning the growth of capitalism in the West. Although Takahashi was critical of the arguments of both Dobb and Sweezy, he moved closer to Dobb when he argued the growth of production forces that in turn necessitated bourgeois-democratic revolution had originated and developed within the feudal system itself and could not be externally originating forces. To focus on the modern dissolution of the direct producer peasant strata was, for Takahashi, to examine such internal forces. The land problem or the peasant problem, and liberation of peasants from feudal bonds, was then the key to the bourgeois revolution and the formation of industrial capital. In a subsequent essay, Takahashi went on to suggest the applicability of Marx's notion of the two paths from feudalism to capitalism to express the difference between the British experience and the Japanese experience. From the perspective of his work on both Japanese and Western economic history, Takahashi suggested that it may have been the Western European and not the Japanese experience that was unique, in that Western feudalism collapsed so readily, preparing the path for capitalist relations.

BIBLIOGRAPHY:

A. *The Transition from Feudalism to Capitalism* (London: New Left Books, 1976); *Shimin Shakai no Kozo* (*The Structure of Bourgeois Revolutions*) (Tokyo: Ochoanomizu shobo, 1980).

GERMAINE A. HOSTON

TAN MALAKA   (1897–1949). Tan Malaka was born in 1897 in Suliki in West Sumatra, Indonesia. While studying in the Netherlands, he came into contact with the Dutch labor movement and became a Marxist. Returning to Indonesia, he quickly became immersed in the activities of the Indonesian Communist Party (PKI). In late 1921, Tan Malaka was elected chairman of the PKI. The following year, however, he was forced to leave Indonesia by the colonial authorities and, traveling once again to the Netherlands, was elected a member of the National Assembly representing the Dutch Communist Party. In August

1922, he represented the PKI at the Fourth Comintern Congress. In December 1923 Tan Malaka was appointed Comintern representative for Southeast Asia, based in Canton. Opposed to what he considered an "adventurist" and putschist rebellion organized by the PKI in 1926, Tan Malaka established his own independent party, PARI (Party of the Indonesian Republic) in 1927. Despite this, he was elected to the Executive of the Comintern at its Sixth Congress in 1928. Having been expelled from the Philippines in 1927 for revolutionary activities, Tan Malaka spent the next fifteen years in China. He returned to Indonesia in 1942 after a twenty-year absence. Following the collapse of the Japanese in 1945, Tan Malaka emerged as one of the most important nationalist leaders and formed a revolutionary opposition to the government of President Sukarno. He was arrested and executed by the Indonesian Army in 1949.

Although a prolific pamphleteer and popularizer of Marxism in the Indonesian language, very little of Tan Malaka's written work has been translated into English. His first pamphlet, *Sovjet atau Parlement?* (Soviet or parliament?), written in 1921, was the first Marxist text in the Indonesian language. A schoolteacher by profession, Malaka's next pamphlet *S.I. Semarang dan Onderwijs* (The Semarang Sarekat Islam and Education) was the first attempt in Indonesian to propound socialist ideas about education. Malaka's main political objective, however, was to obtain the broadest possible support for the PKI and its struggle against imperialism. In particular, he sought to harness the anticolonial spirit of Islam, the main religion of Indonesia. At the Fourth Comintern Congress, Tan Malaka raised the question of pan-Islam, declaring that it was a movement for national independence and hence wholly merited Communist support. He outlined his views on revolutionary organization and the necessity for as broad a united front as possible in a pamphlet in 1926 entitled *Massa Actie* (Mass action). In the 1940s, he wrote a three-volume autobiography aptly entitled *Dari Pendjara ke Pendjara* (From prison to prison).

BIBLIOGRAPHY:

B. Ben Anderson, *Java in a Time of Revolution* (Ithaca: Cornell University Press, 1972); Rudolf Mrazek, "Tan Malaka: A Political Personality's Structure of Experience," *Indonesia*, no. 14 (October 1972); Harry A. Poeze, *Tan Malaka: Strijder voor Indonesie's Vrijheid, Levensloop van 1897 tot 1945* (S'-Gravenhage: Verhandelingen KITLV, Martinus Nijhoff, 1976).

MICHAEL C. WILLIAMS

TEITELBOIM VOLOSKY, VOLODIA VALENTÍN (b. 1916). Volodia Valentín Teitelboim Volosky was born in Chillán, Chile on 17 March 1916. After joining the Communist Party of Chile in 1932, he became a lawyer, journalist, essayist, and novelist. As one of the Party's leading intellectuals, Volodia Teitelboim served on its Central Committee and other key bodies from the 1940s on. In 1961, he won election to the national Chamber of Deputies, and then in 1965 rose to the Senate. Since the 1973 *coup d'état* in Chile,

Teitelboim has been editing cultural journals in Spain and speaking against the dictatorship of Augusto Pinochet. Throughout his career, he has publicly espoused the official positions of the Communist Party.

BIBLIOGRAPHY:

A. *El amanecer del capitalismo y la conquista de América* (Santiago: Ediciones Nueva américa, 1943); *Hijo del salitre* (Santiago: Editora Austral, 1952); *La semilla en la arena* (Santiago: Editora Austral, 1957); *Hombre y hombre* (Santiago: Editora Austral, 1969).

PAUL DRAKE

THIRD INTERNATIONAL   (1919–1943). The Third International was formed in the wake of the Second International's* demise. Seeking to avoid a similar fate, the Third International—also called the Communist International, or Comintern—was founded in Moscow by Lenin* and his victorious Bolshevik Party and was tailored to minimize pluralism and maintain Soviet Communist Party hegemony. From the beginning its primary goals were to support the Soviet Revolution and propagate Soviet-style national dictatorships of the proletariat as alternatives to bourgeois democracies. While its membership ballooned, by 1935, to over three million—including over sixty-five national political parties—it carefully excluded participation by what it perceived as unstable and disloyal social democratic revisionists. Its Twenty-One Conditions stipulated that all members purge their leaderships of reformists and centrists, engage in legal as well as illegal activities, and accept centralized, hierarchical institutions both at home and in the Comintern itself. Practically, this meant establishing the local hegemony of national Communist parties and, internationally, the hegemony of a Soviet-dominated Comintern Executive.

The Comintern's policies vacillated, depending on the needs and perceptions of the Bolsheviks. Under Lenin's stewardship the Comintern's Second Congress (1920) emphasized the need for an anti-imperialist alliance of Third World liberation movements with the Soviet-led European working class. By the Third Congress (1921) Lenin saw the long-term stability of European capitalism and hence the need for a united front of all working-class parties to push for workers' rights. After 1923 the Soviet Party's internal struggles were played out in the Comintern. Trotsky's* opposition to Stalin's* domestic and international policies was debated and repudiated by the Comintern, and Trotsky himself was expelled from the Comintern Executive in September 1927. At the Sixth Congress (1928) the Comintern denounced social democracy as "social fascism" and repudiated the united front policy. The disastrous consequences of this last tactical swing, particularly in Germany, prompted a reversal. The Seventh, and last, Comintern Congress (1935) advocated a popular front uniting all working-class parties to stem the tide of fascism. This policy generated alliances between Communist and non-Communist working-class parties, particularly in Germany, France, and Spain, and support for the Spanish Republic's battle with fascism. The German–Soviet nonaggression pact of August 1939 prompted another Comintern reversal, this time condemning both of the warring sides as reactionary and offering help to neither fascism nor its liberal-democratic enemy. The German attack on the Soviet Union in June 1941 pushed the Comintern forcefully into the Allied camp. All through these tactical twists and turns, the Comintern consistently supported Stalin's purges of the Soviet Communist Party. The Comintern was dissolved in June 1943, at least in part to placate Stalin's Western allies, who were wary of committing men and materiel to defending the world's leading anticapitalist conspirator.

Although seminal theoretical works of Marxism-Leninism were formulated by Lenin, Bukharin,* Trotsky, and others who were also at various times Comintern spokesmen, the institution itself was clearly a tactical instrument by which the Soviet Party exerted control over the worldwide Communist movement. Its tactical shifts and iron-handedness generated among many Communists an unquestioned commitment to orthodox materialism. Differences, when they surfaced, were over practical policies rather than philosophy. Ironically, however, other leftists became so outraged at the Comintern's arbitrary, ineffective, and inhuman policies that they ended up rejecting its theoretical source: orthodox materialism. From the depths of Stalinist orthodoxy emerged a new interest among some Marxists in nonmaterialist alternatives. The Comintern's unintended legacy of neo-Marxism was more than it bargained for.

BIBLIOGRAPHY:

A. Jane Degras, ed., *The Communist International, 1919–1943: Documents*, 3 vols. (London: Oxford University Press, 1956–65).

B. Julius Braunthal, *History of the Internationals* (vols. 1–2, New York: Praeger; vol. 3, Boulder, Colo.: Westview Press, 1966–80); Fernando Claudín, *The Communist Movement: From Comintern to Cominform* (New York: Monthly Review Press, 1970); A. Sobolev et al., *Outline History of the Communist International* (Moscow: Progress, 1971).

ROBERT A. GORMAN

THOMAS, CLIVE YOLANDE   (n.a.). Clive Thomas was born in Guyana and received a Ph.D. in economics from the University of London in 1964. He worked as a research associate in the Institute of Social and Economic Research and taught at the University of the West Indies, Jamaica, until 1969. Thomas, like his countryman, Walter Rodney,* was banned from Jamaica for his political views and political activism. From there he went to the University of Guyana, Georgetown, where he became professor of economics. In 1972–73 Thomas taught economics at the University of Dar es Salaam, Tanzania, and was further influenced by Walter Rodney's teachings. Thomas was the founder of the political journal *Ratoon*, and he cooperated in the publication of others like *Transition* and *Georgetown Review*. Thomas has been a leading member of the Working People's Alliance, the militant and Marxist multiracial party opposed to the rule of Forbes Burnham in Guyana.

Thomas's most important theoretical work is *Dependency and Development*, which provides a critique of neoclassical and socialist economics for their failure to develop an analysis of how to achieve development in the smaller countries that predominate in the Third World. Thomas argues that size is important only if a country is attempting to develop indigenous capitalism. Small socialist economies can overcome their so-called size constraint through industrial transformation based on a growing convergence between domestic demand and resources. Over time, this focus is the only way to create a viable domestic consumption pattern, growing exports, and higher incomes. Trade must not be for trade's sake per se but must be planned to maximize intersectoral linkages. Thomas's book provides both theoretical justifications and policy measures to achieve these goals.

BIBLIOGRAPHY:

A. *Dependence and Transformation: The Economics of the Transition to Socialism* (New York: Monthly Review Press, 1974); " 'The Non-Capitalist Path' as Theory and Practice of Decolonization and Socialist Transformation," *Latin American Perspectives*, 5, no. 2 (Spring 1978).

JAMES DIETZ

TIMPANARO, SEBASTIANO   (b. 1923). Born in Parma, Italy, in 1923, Sebastiano Timpanaro has led a bifurcated existence: on the one hand, he has been absorbed in classical philology and published many works as a Latinist; on the other, he was a rank-and-file militant on the left of the Italian Socialist Party from 1945 until 1964, and since 1964 has been active in parties to the left of the Italian Communist Party (PCI). He has written many essays from a revolutionary Marxist perspective, most of them in polemic with idealist or Freudian tendencies in Marxism and in defense of a rigorously materialist Marxism. He is currently an editor at the Florentine publishing house Nuova Italia.

For Timpanaro, materialism is both a *Weltanschauung* that brings to mind certain inescapable biological givens of human existence and a philosophy that is a call to the scientific investigation of a reality independent of the human mind. In the first instance, Timpanaro's materialism has been greatly influenced by the nineteenth-century Italian poet, Giacomo Leopardi, whose themes of physical suffering, aging, and death reflected a kind of naturalistic pessimism about the human condition. Due regard to the biological determinants of human life is not, however, seen as an alternative to Marx's emphasis on the historicity of socio-economic phenomena; rather, it is a necessary complement to historical materialism. Only a materialist Marxism that reflects the contradictory nature of man as both a natural and a historical being can lay scientific claim to grasp the totality of human experience; for the individual is the product of the totality of society and nature's conditioning effects.

Thus, Timpanaro's materialism leads him into deterministic, anti-free-will positions: external reality injects an element of passivity in experience that imposes itself on everyone. At the same time, his materialism calls for an investigation of concrete objects through concrete methods of analysis. Knowledge of this external world requires the utilization of a scientific method capable of producing verifiable answers to questions. Timpanaro's critique of structuralist and psychoanalytic variants of Marxism rests on his view that they introduce an antiscientific strain ultimately related to atemporal, spiritualistic views of the universe. The propositions they set forth often do not meet scientific standards of verifiability, leading to nonrational, obscurantist modes of thinking.

BIBLIOGRAPHY:

A. *On Materialism* (London: New Left Books, 1975); *The Freudian Slip: Psychoanalysis and Textual Criticism* (London: New Left Books, 1976); "The Pessimistic Materialism of Giacomo Leopardi," *New Left Review* (July–August 1979).

B. Raymond Williams, "Problems of Materialism," *New Left Review* (May–June 1978); Robert A. Gorman, *Neo-Marxism: The Meanings of Modern Radicalism* (Westport, Conn.: Greenwood Press, 1982); Robert Dombroski, "Timpanaro's Materialism: An Introduction," *Journal of the History of Ideas* (April–June 1983).

LAWRENCE GARNER

TITO, JOSIP BROZ   (1892–1980). Josip Broz was born in the village of Kumrovec, Croatia. The seventh of fifteen children, he sought the opportunity to escape the miseries of a hard peasant life. One of the Broz family's nine surviving children, he left home and learned the metal trade in Croatia. Ambitious and upwardly mobile, Broz (Tito is one of his many revolutionary pseudonyms) left less developed Croatia to work in Austrian and German factories. During his first thirty-five years of struggle for power (1910–45) he was not only a good worker but an avid reader of books and a student of languages; he was active in the socialist workers' movement and a connoisseur of good food, clothing, and other bourgeois pleasures of city life. In World War I Tito served as an Austrian noncommissioned officer, volunteering for reconnaissance duty. He fought at first against the Serbian Army on the Drina River front and later against the tsarist Russian army at the Carpathian front. There he was seriously wounded and captured by the Russians. He spent a year recuperating and observing the miserable life of the Russian people. This rekindled Tito's revolutionary socialist spirit, and he became a participant in the Bolshevik Revolution. Following Lenin's* triumphant seizure of power, Tito joined the Communist Party, served in the Communist International* (Comintern), and became one of Stalin's* more daring and skillful leaders of the decimated, faction-ridden Yugoslav Communist Party in 1936. He became a ruthless coordinator and the most successful leader of the Yugoslav partisan national liberation struggle against fascist occupiers (4 July 1941–8 May 1945), triumphing craftily in the bloody civil war over his Serbian nationalist rival, Chetnik leader General Drazha Mihailovich. After a mock trial in 1946, Tito ordered the execution of Mihailovich and his burial in an unmarked grave. With all of his enemies vanquished and the country in ruins, Tito emerged next to Stalin as one of the most prominent Communist leaders, ready to build another socialist state—the mirror image of the Soviet Union.

Tito's reign over Yugoslavia, or the second stage of his manipulation of power (1945–80), was marked by triumphs as well as by real and imagined foreign and internal threats against his lordship. Tito's greatest personal triumph was his total control of Yugoslav destiny for almost four decades. However, Tito's greatest historical achievement was his ability to survive a vicious attack from Stalin in 1948. Tito was the first Communist leader in power to defy his idol and master, Stalin, and live. Thus Tito preserved Yugoslavia's independence and inscribed his own name in history as the David who had stood up to Goliath, or as the "red Martin Luther" who had defied the "red Communist Pope," Stalin. This victory, made possible in part by Western military and economic support, earned Tito a global fame and respect that strengthened his undisputed leadership of the League of the Communists of Yugoslavia (LCY) and his control over Yugoslavia.

Tito's metamorphosis from a ruthless and cunning revolutionary to a pragmatic Communist-dictator-statesman was the result of his break with Stalin. It marks the resurgence of early Western bourgeois tendencies embedded in Tito's character that had been suppressed when he had obsequiously served the cause of the Stalinist Comintern. Forced by Stalin to choose between slavish ideological and physical obedience to the Soviet Union and the Soviet brand of communism, or freedom for himself and independence for national Communist Yugoslavia, Tito chose the latter in 1948. This led to another triumph for Tito and his trusted aides, Kardelj, Rankovich, and Djilas†: the introduction of greater freedom for all Yugoslavs and the liberalization of institutional life as well (1950–70). To reinforce Yugoslav independence Tito and his top aides created a uniquely Yugoslav model of socialism by promulgating, internally, the concepts of market socialism and workers' self-management and, externally, the policy of nonalignment with either of the two superpowers. Tito's decentralized version of socialist economics permitted state-owned factories the flexibility of reacting to local market conditions. Consequently, Yugoslav production decisions were in part determined by the actual economic needs of Yugoslav citizens. Within factories, workers were permitted a role in deciding production and investment quotas, as well as working conditions, and of sharing equally in the economic success of their enterprise. Although Tito and his Communist Party had the final say on national economic decisions, these alterations of the Soviet Union's rigidly centralized economic model influenced Marxists throughout Eastern Europe, particularly in Hungary, Czechoslovakia, and Poland.

Tito's strategy of promoting workers' self-management at home and nonalignment abroad benefited Yugoslavia economically and ideologically. Economically, Yugoslavia could become the active partner of Western economies and export its labor and goods while importing needed Western goods, technology, and capital. Similar policies on a smaller scale (minus export of labor) were conducted with the Soviet Union and its Eastern European satellites. Being nonaligned also meant Yugoslavia could maintain its one-party state while remaining ideologically different from the West as well as politically independent of (and economically dissimilar to) the Communist States of Eastern Europe and the Soviet Union. Tito, as the symbolic and real leader of Yugoslavia, derived personal benefits from this strategic game: he became a statesman known worldwide. However, in maneuvering between East and West he also encouraged some of his closest collaborators to go further in pursuit of certain policies than Tito could tolerate. This resulted in the frequent removal of some of Tito's most trusted and capable collaborators from positions of power. Whenever they rose high enough to match or come close to matching Tito's prestige, they were dismissed. Some were removed via full-scale purges, including the liberal-minded Djilas. Indeed, over 55,000 Party members were purged for these same liberal tendencies. Similar treatment was accorded to former police chief Rankovich and his followers some years later, this time because of their excessive antiliberal or centralist tendencies. Another major shakeup of liberals and national-oriented leaders of the Croatian and Serbian Communist parties was also engineered by Tito in 1971–73. By removing some of the most talented Party and government leaders, Tito exacerbated problems that Yugoslavia has to face now that he is gone.

Tito was not an original thinker or theoretician. He studied Marxism-Leninism in jail and attended formal courses while working as a Comintern employee in Moscow. He relied upon and incorporated the original thoughts of his military and theoretical-ideological collaborators. His voluminous collected works (mostly speeches) reflect momentary concerns and specific tactics to be pursued rather than a continual or complete philosophy.

Tito did prepare, in part, his succession. He tried to preserve intact the dominant role of the LCY but weakened it by introducing the office of rotating one-year collective presidencies of the Party and the state, thus blocking the reemergence of an even moderately strong successor. Tito's tendency for self-aggrandizement also helps explain Yugoslavia's often excessive aid to some nonaligned nations. This policy not only weakened the Yugoslav economic base, but unnecessarily increased the debt owed to the West—a burden that succeeding Yugoslav generations will have to bear.

Tito, the pragmatist, was the superb practitioner of the old adage that necessity is the reason for a successful policy, especially a contradictory one. Once freed from Stalin's grip, Tito became a proponent of neither Stalin's totalitarianism nor Western democracy. Tito favored limited freedom, not Stalinist oppression or Western civil liberties. As always, Tito was trying to practice what would serve first his self-interest as permanent ruler of Yugoslavia and then the self-interest of his socialist subjects. Like Franz Joseph of Austria, Tito made sure that each nationality in Yugoslavia would have something—but never everything—that it liked. Thus, Tito succeeded in combining enlightened aspects of Franz Joseph's absolutism with a tinge of Stalin's totalitarianism and a good dose of liberalism. This concoction, named Titoism, benefited first Tito's needs and then the diverse interests of each Yugoslav nationality.

A man of contradictions, Tito was also a man of many "firsts:" the first to order the shooting down of two unarmed American planes that strayed over Yugoslavia and thus to initiate the hot phase of the cold war; the first to defy Stalin and declare national communism a fashionable ideology and, then, to subvert Soviet hegemony over the international Communist movement and seriously undermine Soviet domination over Eastern Europe; the first to introduce and practice market socialism; the first to argue for peaceful coexistence of the East and West (détente, disarmament, denuclearized zones in Eastern and Western Europe); the first to create an international bloc of nonaligned states; the first to sponsor the entrance of Soviet client states like Cuba, North Korea, and North Vietnam into the nonaligned movement; the first to introduce alternating decentralizing-liberalizing policies that transformed communism into a kind of "one-and-a-half-party state"; the first to resolve a quarrel with the Soviet Union after an apology by Krushchev in 1955, and then condemn the Soviet invasions of Hungary in 1956, Czechoslovakia in 1968, and Afghanistan in 1979 (in each instance Tito restored cooperative relations with the Soviet-sponsored regimes in those countries shortly after his strong condemnation of Soviet interference); and the first statesman to deal effectively with both Communist and non-Communist leaders. Tito was a genuine supporter of world peace because it reinforced the security of Yugoslavia; he supported wars of national liberation because he was ideologically opposed to Western imperialism.

Theoretically, Tito always remained a Marxist-Leninist. However, Titoism sowed the seeds of other schisms within the Soviet orbit: internal dissent in the Soviet Union; Maoism,* Eurocommunism; national communisms. Some view Tito as Moscow's Trojan horse; others as a Westernizer who gently prodded the Soviets toward closer ties with the West. Tito at one time or another played both roles. He died on 4 May 1980, three days before his 88th birthday, after a prolonged, painful, and emaciating illness.

BIBLIOGRAPHY:

A. *Sabrana dela* (Works) (Belgrade: Komunist, 1979).

B. H. Christman, ed., *The Essential Tito* (New York: St. Martin's Press, 1970); V. Dedijer, *The Battle Stalin Lost* (New York: Grosset & Dunlap, 1971); P. Auty, *Tito* (New York: Ballantine Books, 1972); V. Dedijer, *Tito* (New York: Arno Press, 1972); A. Nikolskiy, ed., *Josip Broz Tito* (Moscow: Politizdat, 1973); M. Djilas, *Tito: The Story from Inside* (New York: Harcourt Brace Jovanovich, 1980); F. Maclean, *Tito* (New York: McGraw-Hill, 1980); V. Dedijer, *Novi prilozi za biografiju Josipa Broza Tita*, 2 vols. (Rijeka: Liburnija, 1981).

MICHAEL M. MILENKOVITCH

TOURÉ, AHMED SÉKOU   (1922–1984). Ahmed Touré was born in Faranah (Upper Guinea, then French Guinea) in 1922 of peasant parents, and died of an apparent heart attack on 28 March 1984. A Malinke and a Muslim, he came from the same group (but is not a direct descendant of) Samory Touré, the historical and legendary figure who led an extraordinarily successful (although ultimately doomed) armed resistance against the French in the 1890s. Educated first in a Koranic school, then in the Ecole Professionnelle Georges Poiret in Conakry (the capital), Sékou Touré was unique in being a self-taught man who never received any formal education beyond primary school. His knowledge came from his readings, his work as a trade union leader, and his contacts with French and African politicians. In 1941 he joined the Post Office as a lowly civil servant. By 1945 he had helped to organize its members in the first Guinean trade union. A year later he became the Guinean leader of the local branch of the French trade union, the Confédération Générale du Travail (CGT), a post he held for the next twelve years. Sacked from his job, he attended in 1946 the CGT Congress in Paris. He was briefly jailed in 1947. In France he became acquainted with Socialists and Communists, and he himself took a Marxist position. From 1946 he was a member of the West African political party, the Rassemblement Démocratique Africain (RDA). In 1947 he helped to form its Guinean branch, the Parti Démocratique de Guinée (PDG), in which he became the dominant voice in 1953, following the success of a seventy-three-day general strike demanding the immediate implementation of the Code du Travail. He was elected mayor of Conakry in 1955 and member of the French Parliament in 1956. Between 1956 and 1958 he consolidated his position as the leader of the PDG through the sheer force of his personality and his immense organizational talent. In 1958 he led Guinea to independence following his campaign to vote no to de Gaulle's referendum on colonial constitutional reforms. Guinea was the only territory to vote no. After this he became the undisputed leader of the party and the master of one of the most powerful party-states in Africa. By 1984, the year of his death, he was the longest serving head of state in Africa.

Touré's relation to Marxism, let alone his contribution, is very difficult to assess because his thoughts and actions underwent the most extraordinary series of transformations during the twenty-five years he was in power. Trained as a Marxist unionist through his contacts with the French CGT and the French Communist Party, he evolved between 1946 and 1956 from that orthodox position to an *ouvrièriste* phase and, as a leader of the PDG, eventually to what can only be conceived of as an African populist stand. In Africa, the central theoretical question about which socialists of all shades debate is the existence and political significance of social classes within what is generally recognized as an unsatisfactory definition of the extant modes of production. African socialists have defined themselves along a wide spectrum ranging from the view that indigenous society was classless to the notion that class struggle was the sole determinant of history. Touré traveled virtually the full length of that spectrum, part of it in both directions, over the years. Until 1964, he remained in his ideology closer to "African socialism," a position far from Marxism since it rejects the primacy of class forces. Understandably, in the early years of independence priority was given to national unity. Between 1964 and 1967, Touré moved steadily back toward a more orthodox position, culminating in a strident use of the notion of "class enemy" as the major explicans of Guinea's difficulties. In 1967 he went one step further, calling for the PDG to become a vanguard party and beginning to reorganize it along these lines. For the next ten years he experimented with various forms of Marxist practice, from a Stalinist*-type organization of the party to a Chinese-style cultural revolution. He proclaimed the PDG to have become a party-state, i.e., the "withered" Marxist state; through its new local structures, the *pouvoirs révolutionnaires locaux* (PRLs), which in 1978 were said to number 2,500, each controlling a population of 1,500–2,000. In more recent years Touré, again, toned down the references to Marxism, no doubt because he was not entirely satisfied with the results of the mobilization campaigns. There is, however, little information available here.

Touré's contribution to Marxism was not in the realm of theory despite the endless volumes collecting his every thought and utterance; it was in his attempt to apply Marxist-Leninist concepts to the African context. Touré's understanding of these concepts, colored by his training as a union leader, was severely biased toward the political, and even more the organizational, side of socialist policies. The premise of Touré's action, as far as it can be understood, was that politics can drive and direct development through organization: "politics in command," as the Ottaways have written. Touré's was, then, an extreme "Leninist" vision of Leninism, in that he thought that an all powerful and extremely well-organized political party is sufficient to dictate the course of the country's economic and social development regardless of the existing socio-economic constraints. Since Touré had not made the economy of a revolution, indeed actively avoided moving in that direction since he smashed the powers of the chiefs in Guinea, it was difficult to see how he could successfully use Stalinist methods to transform society. He had neither the ideological commitment nor the political (and police) apparatus. Furthermore, the extremes of the Guinean economy—the world's largest exporter of bauxite, a potentially successful agriculture that no longer feeds the country, and a state marketing system that has driven most exchange of goods to the black market—largely defeated Touré's efforts. His attempts to collectivize and modernize agriculture failed repeatedly (maybe they could not succeed in Africa), and his government proved less able than most in Africa to secure better terms for the exploitation of its mineral ore by foreign firms. Ultimately, then, Touré's failure to evolve a satisfactory Marxist "model" for Guinea stemmed from his neglect, indeed his lack of understanding, of the economic parameters of development. Not only was there little consistency in the shifts in his political stance, but there was not much ideological logic to the various steps the government took to promote (or as the case may be, hinder) economic progress. Touré will be remembered as the leader most successful in politicizing, mobilizing, and organizing an African society galvanized at first by his early nationalist campaign but battered since by his political about-faces and economic incompetence.

BIBLIOGRAPHY:

A. *Collected Works*, 19 vols. (Conakry: Imprimerie Lumumba, 1984).

B. Jean Lacouture, *Cinq hommes et la France* (Paris: Seuil, 1961); Immanuel Wallerstein, "The Political Ideology of the PDG," *Presence Africaine*, 12 (January–March 1962); R. W. Johnson, "Sékou Touré and the Guinean Revolution," *African Affairs*, 69, no. 277 (October 1970), pp. 43–60.

PATRICK CHABAL

TRAN DUC THAO   (n.a.). Born in Vietnam, Tran Duc Thao (also known as Nguyen Khac-Vien) studied in Paris after World War II with Maurice Merleau-

Ponty,† and later at the Husserl Archives in Louvain. He received his doctorate in 1951 with his thesis, later published, "Phénoménologie et matérialisme dialectique."

The young Tran set for himself the double task of purging phenomenology of its Platonism as well as clarifying the humanist side of Marxism, in contrast to the mechanical determinism of Stalin's* dogmatism. His 1946 article "Marxisme et phénoménologie," which phenomenologically examined the concept of superstructure and requested from sympathetic radicals a subjectively revitalized Marxism, established his credentials among the school of prolific radical French existential phenomenologists, which included Jean-Paul Sartre† and Merleau-Ponty. As Tran matured, however, he was unable to resolve the potential contradiction between phenomenological and materialist epistemologies. By 1951, already under pressure from colleagues in the French Communist Party who condemned his infatuation with phenomenology, Tran concluded in *Phénoménologie et materialisme dialectique* that phenomenology was overly abstract and thus had to be abandoned as a valid approach to social inquiry and knowledge. Only dialectical materialism could grasp the movement of concrete reality, of which the human psyche was a determined part.

In later writings, particularly *Recherches sur l'origine de la conscience* (1973), Tran was concerned with establishing the concrete material roots of human personality and consciousness. By reiterating Marx's* early argument regarding Hegel's inversion of subject and object Tran argued that Hegel's idealistic dialectic could be fruitfully analyzed and milked—via the inversion process—for what it can teach us about reality's concrete dialectical movement. In particular, Hegel's theory of desire, i.e., humanity's search for recognition by another consciousness that generates social relations and the struggle for life and death, has been naively accepted by contemporary Freudians. Both Hegelianism and Freudianism posit an indefensible a priori ideal that determines individual and social evolution. Tran contended that modern psychologists and psychoanalysts have neglected the Marxian materialist inversion, which alone is capable of connecting human desire to the material environment. Such an inversion, argued Tran, proves that although animal desire exists as a real product of biological matter, in humans it is conditioned and ultimately superseded by both the objective material conditions of social existence and the human labor that thrives therein. In brief, the Freudian belief in desire as a constitutive component of the human psyche and a generator of individual and social behavior, fails to connect what is called human instinct to its social and historical roots. Tran Duc Thao, like his contemporary Lucien Sève† and others, offers a critical perspective of popular psychological theory as well as a formula for linking historical materialism and psychology.

BIBLIOGRAPHY:

A. *Phénoménologie et matérialisme dialectique* (Paris: Minh Tan, 1951); *El materialismo de Hegel* (Buenos Aires: Siglo Veinte, 1965); *Recherchessur l'origine de la conscience* (Paris: Editions Sociales, 1973).

B. Michael Kelly, *Modern French Marxism* (Baltimore: Johns Hopkins University Press, 1982).

ROBERT A. GORMAN

TRIBUNISTS   (1907–1919). The Tribunists were a group of Dutch radical Marxist intellectuals that formed an opposition to Pieter Jelle Troelstra's* revisionist course and his right-wing followers in the Dutch Social Democratic Workers' Party. In 1907 David Wijnkoop (1876–1941), Willem Ravesteijn (1876–1970), and J. C. Ceton (1875–1943) founded the oppositional paper *De Tribune*. When party officials in 1909 at the SDAP congress in Deventer moved that either the Tribunists cease the publication of *De Tribune* or else be expelled, they chose the latter. That same year they founded the Social Democratic Party (SDP) and were joined by Antonie Pannekoek† and Herman Gorter,† who had been editors at *De Nieuwe Tijd* (the SDAP monthly). They were also supported by Lenin.* Between 1909 and 1916 Herman Gorter was the leading propagandist for the SDP, although party leadership vacillated between Gorter on the one hand and Ravesteijn and Wijnkoop on the other. Whereas Ravesteijn–Wijnkoop represented a narrow-minded orthodox Marxism, Gorter was always fully committed to internationalism. In 1919 the SDP became the first Dutch Communist Party (CPH), with Gorter and Pannekoek as members until 1921. The CPH was represented in the Dutch Parliament from 1918 to 1925 by Wijnkoop and Ravesteijn, who were also Party representatives at the Comintern. In 1926 Wijnkoop briefly formed his own party, but reconciled with the CPH in 1929 and was elected to Parliament for a second term. Wijnkoop was also active in politics at the state and local level in Amsterdam as an elected representative from 1919 to 1940. Willem Ravesteijn was a socialist essayist and contributor to *De Nieuwe Tijd* and editor of the SDAP daily in Rotterdam *Voorwaarts*, and also a member of Parliament from 1918 to 1926 and alderman in Rotterdam from 1919 to 1927. Disagreements with the Comintern caused his expulsion in 1925. No reconciliation took place, and Ravesteijn returned to the SDAP. In 1927 he accepted a position as curator of the municipal library in Rotterdam.
BIBLIOGRAPHY:

A. W. van Ravesteijn, *De wording van het communisme in Nederland 1907–1925* (Amsterdam: Elsevier, 1948).

TINEKE RITMEESTER

TROELSTRA, PIETER JELLE   (1860–1930). Pieter Troelstra was a Dutch politician, lawyer, journalist, and Friesian poet of some international repute. He joined Ferdinand Nieuwenhuis's† Social Democratic Federation (SDB) in 1890 and became editor of the *Sneeker Courant*, a precursor of *De Nieuwe Tijd*, a monthly forum for Marxist discussion and theory (with Antonie Pannekoek,† Herman Gorter,† and Henriette Roland-Holst* among its editors) founded in 1894. Within the SDB Troelstra had become the leading opponent of Nieuwenhuis's politics on antimilitarism and the general strike. The final split occurred in 1894, when the SDB decided on its anarcho-syndicalist course. Troelstra, as one of the so-called twelve apostles, founded the Dutch Socialist Workers' Party, based on the Erfurt Program. From 1897 to 1925 Troelstra was a member of Parliament for the SDAP, representing its right wing. Indeed the SDAP became a popular party under Troelstra, who possessed a great talent for rhetoric. He was a featured speaker at mass meetings, particularly those on the so-called red Tuesdays, that advocated "suffrage," the eight-hour work day, "state pensions," etc., issues that would continue to be priorities for the Dutch socialist movement long after Troelstra's death. Although he was essentially a political figure to the right of center, there were moments of true revolutionary élan, such as in November 1918, when the antimonarchist Troelstra called for a Dutch republic. Troelstra's role in the famous struggle of the Dutch railroad workers in 1903 was less commendable. At its critical moment, just before a general strike was about to be proclaimed, Troelstra pronounced publicly that he would not, and the SDAP should not, support it. The general strike did not take place. In 1925 Troelstra resigned from his post for reasons of health.

BIBLIOGRAPHY:

B. J. Winkler, *Prophet of a New Era: The Life and Work of P. J. Troelstra* (Amsterdam: Elsevier, 1948).

TINEKE RITMEESTER

TROTSKY, LEON   (1879–1940). Leon Trotsky was born Lev Davidovich Bronstein into the family of a prosperous Jewish farmer in the Ukrainian province of Kherson in 1879. Introduced to the then dominant ideas of agrarian socialism (*narodnichestvo*) while a high school student in Odessa and Nikolayev, Trotsky soon graduated to Marxism, becoming a cofounder of the South Russian Workers Union in the late 1890s. Arrested in 1898, Trotsky fled Russia in 1902, joining V. I. Lenin* and the editorial staff of the Russian Marxist paper *Iskra* (The Spark) in London that same year. Initially drawn to Lenin's view of party discipline, Trotsky, upon the 1903 split between Bolsheviks and Mensheviks, adopted an independent stance. In 1905, Trotsky returned to Russia, becoming the chairman of the St. Petersburg Soviet, which had formed to direct the 1905 Revolution. Arrested in December 1905, Trotsky devoted his time in prison to refining his theory of permanent revolution. Escaping from Russia in 1907, Trotsky settled in Vienna until the outbreak of the war. During the war, Trotsky helped organize the Zimmerwald Conference against workers participation in the conflict, edited several Russian-language Marxist journals in France, and left for New York in 1917. Returning to Russia after the spring 1917 revolution, Trotsky discovered a new ideological kinship with Lenin and later joined the Bolshevik Party. As Chairman of the Petrograd Soviet, Trotsky directed the fall 1917 Revolution, which brought the Bolsheviks to power, receiving the position of Commissar of Foreign Affairs in the first Lenin cabinet. Resigning his appointment the following spring due to a disagreement as to the wisdom of accepting a humiliating peace with Germany, Trotsky became Commissar of

War and organizer of the Red Army. With the death of Lenin in 1924, Trotsky found himself in opposition to the new triumvirate of Alexander Zinoviev, Lev Kamenev, and Josef Stalin,* and lost his Party and state positions. In 1927, Trotsky was expelled from the Party and exiled to Soviet Central Asia. Deported to Turkey in 1929, Trotsky began a new eleven-year exile, which took him to various Western European countries before settling in Mexico. As the Stalinist dictatorship strengthened in the Soviet Union, Trotsky became a vocal figure of resistance, eventually forming a Fourth International to oppose Stalin's leadership of the world working class. In August 1940, a Soviet security agent assassinated Trotsky in his home in Coyoacan, Mexico.

Trotsky's writings reveal a wealth of interest and accomplishment and range from discussions of Marxist military doctrine and the nature of proletarian culture to a firsthand analysis of the 1917 Revolution. Moreover, before 1917 and after Lenin's death (i.e. before and after he exercised power in the Bolshevik Party) Trotsky presciently warned that a dictatorial workers' party would evolve into a cruel, self-serving, and exploitative bureaucratic dictatorship. However, Trotsky remains best known for his theory of permanent revolution. First broached in his writings during 1905, Trotsky argued that the uneven development of world capitalism and the incomplete formation of a native Russian bourgeoisie promised that the revolutionary movement in Russia could pass directly to a workers' government without a significant period of middle-class rule. A Russian workers' state, however, would be unable to perpetuate its existence unless the shockwave of the Russian Revolution inspired similar upheavals in the more advanced countries to the west. Without assistance from Western socialist states, world capitalism would crush the first Russian socialist state. Devoid of the skills and ideological steadfastness gained by Western workers in the decades of capitalist development there, the future of a workers' government in backward Russia would be of limited duration. When the fall 1917 Revolution created a workers' and peasants' dictatorship in Russia, Trotsky called for greater efforts to ensure the future of the Russian regime by promoting revolution abroad. When in the mid-1920s, Stalin became the proponent of "socialism in one country," a bitter struggle ensued, with Stalin's masterful control of key Party and state positions eventually producing both Trotsky's exile and assassination.

BIBLIOGRAPHY:

A. *The Permanent Revolution* (London: New Park Publications, 1962); *Terror and Communism* (Ann Arbor: University of Michigan Press, 1963); *The Age of Permanent Revolution: A Trotsky Anthology* (New York: Dell, 1964); *The History of the Russian Revolution* (London: Gollancz, 1965); *Autobiography* (New York: Pathfinder, 1970).

B. Isaac Deutscher, *The Prophet Armed: Trotsky, 1879–1921* (New York: Oxford University Press, 1954); Isaac Deutscher, *The Prophet Unarmed: Trotsky, 1921–1929* (New York: Oxford University Press, 1959); Isaac Deutscher, *The Prophet Outcast: Trotsky, 1929–1940* (New York: Oxford University Press, 1963); Richard B. Day, *Leon Trotsky and the Politics of Economic Isolation* (Cambridge: Cambridge University Press, 1973).

MICHAEL M. BOLL

TRUONG CHINH   (b. 1907). Truong Chinh, whose real name is Dang Xuan Khu, was born in 1907 in Hanh Tien, Nam Dinh Province, northern Vietnam.

He joined the Indochinese Communist Party in 1930, being imprisoned in the same year for revolutionary activities. Released in 1936, Truong Chinh rose rapidly in the Party, becoming its secretary general in 1941. During a sojourn in China in World War II, he adopted the name Truong Chinh ("Long March"). In 1956, Truong Chinh was forced to resign as secretary general of the Vietnam Workers' Party (as the ICP had been called since 1951) following a disastrous land reform campaign in North Vietnam that provoked widespread peasant unrest, leading to revolts in some areas. He subsequently became Vice Premier and Chairman of the State Scientific Research Committee. Since September 1960 he has been a member of the Politburo and Chairman of the Standing Committee of the National Assembly.

Truong Chinh's responsibilities in the Politburo have included the chairmanship of the Commission for the Study of Party History. The commission, under Truong Chinh's guidance, is charged with editing and publishing Ho Chi Minh's* complete works. Truong Chinh was also responsible for overseeing the drafting of the 1980 Constitution of the Socialist Republic of Vietnam. In July 1981 he became Chairman of the Council of State, Vietnam's president.

Truong Chinh has been the chief political theoretician of the Vietnamese Communist Party since the early 1940s. He was to become the virtual embodiment of the principles and techniques of political mobilization upon which subsequent Communist success in Vietnam has been based. Above all, Truong Chinh was associated with a new-found meaning for and identity with nationalism, which led to the formation of organizations for popular participation in politics such as the Vietnam Independence League (Viet Minh) in 1941. His pamphlet, *The Resistance Will Win*, was to be for many years the most important work for Party cadres. It was the first major exposition of Vietnamese revolutionary strategy. At first reading, Chinh's text seems to borrow heavily from Mao's* writings on revolutionary war. While his debt to Mao is apparent, there is also a clear willingness to depart from Chinese teachings.

In the first place, Chinh took issue with Mao's interpretation of the role of terrain in revolutionary strategy. Conceding that terrain was an important factor in protracted war, Chinh claimed that active popular support and a disciplined people's army led by the Communist Party could overcome the disadvantages of geography and colonial status. Chinh also departed from Mao in his view of the preponderant importance of the world situation. From the beginning, the Vietnamese Communist Party laid far greater stress on the importance of the international situation for the success of national revolution than the Chinese Communist Party. Chinh sought to situate the Vietnamese revolution within the context of world revolution. Great importance was attached to the impact of the war on world public opinion and how this would influence French policy and, later of course, U.S. policy. The Vietnamese revolution should actively seek the support of democratic and progressive forces throughout the world. Declining morale and increasing public resistance to the war would ultimately sap French will, as it would later that of the United States. A shift in the world balance of power could also undermine the imperialist order. Chinh concluded, unlike Mao, that ultimate victory was not simply a question of absolute military superiority but a combination of military power with political and diplomatic factors. Increasingly, in later years, Chinh argued not only the importance of international factors to Vietnam's struggle, but also that the Vietnamese revolution was the focal point of the global political struggle between imperialism and revolution.

BIBLIOGRAPHY:

A. *Primer for Revolt* (New York: Praeger, 1963); with Vo Nguyen Giap, *The Peasant Question*, trans. Christine Pelzer White, Data Paper no. 94 (Ithaca: Southeast Asia Program, 1974); *Selected Writings* (Hanoi: Foreign Languages Publishing House, 1977).

MICHAEL C. WILLIAMS

U

UNO KŌZŌ   (1899–1977). Uno Kōzō, Japanese Marxist economist, founded the radical Uno school of Japanese economics. He was born in Kurashiki in Okayama Prefecture of a merchant family. Uno's early interest in socialism led him to pursue economics, and after graduating from the Economics Department of Tokyo Imperial University in 1922, he joined the Ōhara Institute for the Study of Social Problems (Ōhara Shakai Mondai Kenkyūjo) briefly. From 1922 to 1924 he went to study in Berlin and on his return to Japan was appointed assistant professor at Tōhoku University Department of Law and Literature. There Uno taught economic policy and in his research concentrated on Marx's* *Capital*, German capitalism, and the history of world capitalist development. During these years, he endeavored to systematize a theory of economic policy by making a careful distinction between pure theory and practical policy, and between socialist ideology and the scientific effort to understand capitalism. In 1936, he published the first volume of his *Theory of Economic Policies* and developed the basis for his postwar theory of three stages of world capitalist development.

During the debate on Japanese capitalism from 1927 to 1937, although Uno did not ally himself with either the Rōnō-ha (Labor-Farmer faction) or the Kōza-ha faction (loyal to the Comintern-led Japanese Communist Party), he was more critical of what he saw as the latter's mechanistic application of Marx's abstraction of the European experience in *Capital* to the realities of Japanese economic development. In Uno's view, it was not surprising that the Kōza-ha should find Japan economically backward and "semifeudal" on the basis of this kind of simplistic application of theory to reality. This observation became the basis for Uno's innovative postwar work. As presented in the completion of his *Theory of Economic Policies* in 1954, Uno's interpretation argued that Marxist economic research must be done on three levels: the study of the basic pure principles of capitalism, especially as manifested in the development of the nineteenth-century British economy; the analysis of the three stages of world capitalist development, i.e., mercantilism, dominated by British merchant capital, liberalism, dominated by British industrial capital, especially in textiles; and imperialism, dominated by German, British, and American finance capital, and described by Lenin* as the highest and final stage of capitalist development. This second step of Marxist research embraces the development of the world capitalist economy—as opposed to the capitalist development of individual societies—up to World War I. In order to analyze the development of individual national capitalisms and of world capitalism after World War I, Uno argued, Marxist research would occur at the third level: empirical analysis of concrete situations. This "three-step" approach to Marxist inquiry would avoid the Kōza-ha's error of trying to compare abstract theory with concrete reality, and the Rōnō's tendency to see Japan in terms of development toward pure, abstract capitalism and to ignore the peculiar aspects of capitalism in Japan.

In the prewar era, Uno, too, fell under the shadow of police repression and was arrested in connection with the Rōnō-ha Professors' Group Incident in February 1938. An appeal won him acquittal. In 1941, Uno resigned his professorial post at Tōhoku University and joined the Japan Trade Institute of the Japanese Association for the Promotion of Trade. In 1944, he moved to the Mitsubishi Economic Institute, where he became involved in the publication of the institute's organ *Economic Affairs*. After the war, Uno became more deeply involved in journalism, penning articles on inflation and other postwar economic difficulties. In 1947, Uno became a professor at the University of Tokyo's Institute of Social Science and, as head of the Institute beginning in 1949, organized joint research projects on subjects like forestry (1954) and land tax reform (1957, 1958). In the meantime, Uno continued to work in basic Marxist research, producing a rewriting of the three volumes of *Capital* as the two-volume *Principles of Political Economy* (1950–52). In this effort to systematize the abstract principles of "pure capitalism," Uno also produced the *Theory of Value* (1947) and *Studies on the Theory of Value* (1952). These writings on the theory of value are appreciated for their resolution of an old and complex dilemma in Marxist economic theory. Engels,* Rudolf Hilferding,* and others had had to assume the applicability of the capitalist commodity theory of value to a hypothetical precapitalist society. Uno avoided the use of such a hypothetical by demonstrating the concrete necessity for the labor theory of value, arising out of capitalist commodity production. It then became possible to discuss the precapitalist value in terms of precapitalist commodity circulation, without reference to the substance of value as labor. Finally, Uno made a contribution to the theory of crisis in capitalism by emphasizing Marx's view of the absolute overproduction of capital vis-à-vis the labor force.

In the years of disorder in the Marxist movement occasioned by the criticism of Stalin* in 1956, Uno's work gained influence, particularly in the academic circles of the University of Tokyo. Today, Uno Marxists, including Ōuchi Tsutomu* and Hiroshi Iwata, have made additional theoretical contributions to Marxian economics by building on Uno's work. Moreover, the faction also wields political influence through its membership in the Socialist Association (Shakaishugi Kyōkai), which exerts an often decisive impact on the policies of the left wing of the Socialist Party. Uno himself retired from the University of Tokyo in 1958, whereupon he became professor of sociology at Hōsei University. Since then, Uno continued his writing, completing his *Methodology of Economics* (*Keizaigaku hōhōron*). The collaborative publication of the Uno school's eight-volume *Outline of Economics* (*Keizaigaku taikei*) both represented the culmination of Uno's theoretical endeavors and marked the split of the school between "pure capitalism" and "world capitalism" schools.

BIBLIOGRAPHY:

A. *Shihon-ron gojūnen* (Fifty years of Capital), 2 vols. (Tokyo: Hōsei daigaku shuppan-Kyoku, 1970–73); *Uno Kōzō chosakushū* (Collected works of the Uno Kōzō), 10 vols. and supplement (Tokyo: Iwanami shoten, 1973–74).

B. Ōuchi Shūmei, *Uno keizaigaku no kihon mondai* (Basic issues of Uno economics) (Tokyo: Iwanami shoten, 1971); Makoto Itoh, *Value and Crisis: Essays on Marxian Economics in Japan* (New York: Monthly Review Press, 1980).

GERMAINE A. HOSTON

V

VAILLANT, EDOUARD   (1840–1915). Born to a bourgeois family of rural origins who lived near Paris, Edouard Vaillant went to the Ecole Central to train as an engineer (1862) and later gained a doctorate from the University of Paris in sciences and medicine (1865). He studied philosophy at Heidelberg, where he came into contact with German Marxists and the First International,* although at this time he was very much influenced by Proudhon and Feuerbach. He returned to Paris in 1870 and became a leading member of the Commune as Commissioner for Education and a member of the Executive. He worked closely with Frankel and the Internationalists, but was also a friend of the Blanquists and noted for his advocacy of violent measures. On the fall of the Commune he fled to London, where he met Marx* and joined the International, but left it because it wasn't sufficiently revolutionary. He returned to France in 1880 and founded the Blanquist Comité Central du Révolution, although himself moving toward Marxism. A municipal councillor in 1884, he became a deputy in 1893 and formed the Parti Socialiste Révolutionnaire in 1898. After initiating the fall of the Dupuy government in 1899, he violently opposed the entry of Millerand into the Waldeck-Rousseau administration. His opposition to socialist ministers in bourgeois governments drew him closer to Jules Guesde,* with whom he formed the Parti Socialiste de France in 1901. He was one of the architects of the unified socialist party in 1905 and cosponsored the famous antiwar motion of the International with Keir Hardy in 1910. He was a champion of the call for a general strike against war, but supported the Union Sacré government in 1914.

His early ideas were marked by a tendency toward utopianism and violent revolution, which led him to think in terms of insurrectionary elites and direct action. In the 1880s he maintained his antimilitarist and anti-imperialist propaganda, while also mounting a fierce attack on clericalism. He was an ardent Dreyfusard, but increasingly wove Marxist economic concepts into his ideas. These confusions were complicated by his reformist campaign for socialist measures inside Parliament, his ''socialisme municipal'' of devoluted power, and his insistence on pursuing the class struggle and revolution outside the Chamber.

His particular use of surplus value theory to explain proletarian exploitation became a constant theme in his writing, and he turned to the mobilization of the mass as the only way forward to change, marking his move away from Blanquism.
BIBLIOGRAPHY:

A. For the list of Vaillant's many articles and brochures, see the bibliography of M. Dommanget, *Edouard Vaillant* (Paris: La Table Ronde, 1956).

B. J. Howarth, "La Propaganda socialiste d'Edouard Vaillant pendant les années 1880–1884," *Mouvement social*, 72 (1970), pp. 83–119; J. Howarth, "The French Socialists and Anti-Clericalism: The Position of Edouard Vaillant and the Parti Socialiste Revolutionnaire," *International Review of Social History*, 22, no. 2 (1977), pp. 165–83; J. Howarth, *Edouard Vaillant* (Paris: Edi/Syros, 1982).

JOHN C. SIMMONDS

VAILLANT-COUTOURIER, PAUL   (1892–1937). Paul Vaillant-Coutourier was born in 1892 to an artistic family, and after a degree in history and a doctorate in law he joined the bar in 1912. Wounded in World War I, he achieved the rank of sublieutenant and won the Légion d'Honneur. He joined the Socialist Party in 1916 and a year later founded the Association Républicaine des Anciens Combattants together with Henri Barbusse* and Raymond Lefebvre. In 1919 he was elected a deputy, and he voted with the Communist majority at the Tours Congress, becoming a member of the Party's Central Committee upon its foundation in 1920. He took great interest in the Secours Rouge Populaire and in its work in the colonies, particularly Indochina, because of his friendship with Ho Chi Minh.* Voted out of the Chamber in 1928, he became mayor of Villejuif in 1929 and chief editor of *L'Humanité* in the same year. He voyaged in Russia, China, and Spain, founded the Association des Ecrivains et Artistes Révolutionnaires, was reelected as Deputy in 1936, but died in 1937.

His importance as a figure on the French Marxist left was as an eloquent propagandist for Marxist ideas, as a writer of attractive and good quality Marxist prose and verse, and as a commentator on the international scene. During his editorship of *L'Humanité* it developed a breadth of view and seriousness of analysis that it had previously lacked.
BIBLIOGRAPHY:

A. *Lettres à mes amis: 1918–1919* (Paris: Flammarion, 1920).

JOHN C. SIMMONDS

VERA, JAIME   (1859–1918). The son of a distinguished Republican leader, Jaime Vera received an excellent education at the Institucíon Libre de Euséñanza in Madrid. He received many prizes for his scholarly excellence, including the Extraordinary Prize when he graduated in June 1879. By then he had become acquainted with the workers who were clandestinely trying to organize the Socialist Party (PSOE). Vera was the only nonlabor person who participated in the PSOE's constitutional assembly (2 May 1879) who also thereafter remained a member of the party. Vera began, in 1880, a brilliant career as a medical doctor and psychiatrist, obtaining success after success, not only in his private practice but also in research related to his specialty. Vera's prestige was very important to the PSOE, which was characterized by a general lack of intellectuals in its ranks until the first decade of the twentieth century.

Although his principal activity was his medical career, he performed many important tasks in the PSOE after its inception. He wrote the party's report to the comisíon de Reformas Sociales in 1884. He financed the publishing of *El socialista*, the party's newspaper, and he provided needed funds for the party, despite his estrangement (1886–91) because of disagreements over alliance tactics. In spite of poor health, which eventually left him blind, Vera was for many years a Socialist Party candidate in Spanish elections. He also participated in national and international socialist congresses, and his political texts and speeches were published in the socialist press and later reproduced for several decades after his death.

The theoretical importance of Vera can be judged by his first Marxist text, *El informe*, which was the first Marxist text of consequence produced by the Spanish socialists and was adopted by the party as its official text in 1886. Vera offered a sophisticated reading of Marx* interspersed with "Guesdista*" interpretations, of which Spanish socialism was deeply imbued until the latter part of the nineteenth century. During his lifetime Vera continued writing on Marx as well as other socialists, especially Jean Jaurès.† Although Vera's writings do not contribute anything original to Marxian theory, they are, nevertheless, texts in which Vera's knowledge and analytical abilities shone far superior to the other socialist leaders of that time. Vera's texts are indeed far more sophisticated than the mass of socialist writings, which illustrates one of the difficulties limiting the absorption of Marxism by Spanish socialism.

BIBLIOGRAPHY:

A. *Ciencia y proletariado: escritos escogidos de Jaime Vera*, ed. Juan Jose Castillo (Madrid: Edicusa, 1973); "La introducción del marxismo en España: el informe a la Comisión de Reformas Sociales de Jaime Vera," ed. Tomás Jimínez Araya, *Anales de economia*, no. 15 (July–September 1973), pp. 107–49.

B. Santos Juliá, *La izquierda del PSOE 1935–6* (Madrid: Siglo, 1977).

S. CASTILLO

VITALE, LUIS   (b. 1927). Born in Argentina in 1927, Luis Vitale later became a naturalized citizen of Chile, where he was renowned as a writer and professor of history and geography. Prior to the Chilean military coup of September 1973, Vitale taught at the University of Concepción. He was involved in various Trotskyist* movements affiliated with the Fourth International, and he served as national director of the labor Central Unica de Trabajadores de Chile (CUT) from 1959 to 1962. His principal writings fall into two areas, one dealing with questions of whether Latin America is feudal or capitalist and the other focused on a Marxist interpretation of Chilean history.

Vitale vigorously disputed widely accepted premises that feudalism in Latin America had been transplanted from medieval Spain to the New World. He argued that a natural economy was transformed into a monetary economy as Spain moved through the transition from feudalism to capitalism and that Spanish capital of the fifteenth century was a primitive capitalism. Spain conquered America not with the intent of reproducing European feudalism but incorporating the new area into a system of capitalist production. Thus Spanish America was ruled not by feudal lords but by a commercial bourgeoisie whose source of wealth was based on export trade. This line of thinking underlies Vitale's multivolume study on a Marxist interpretation of Chilean history. This work is a grand synthesis of Chilean history from its pre-Hispanic origins to the nineteenth century, and an effort to demonstrate the consequences of imperialism.

BIBLIOGRAPHY:

A. *Esencia y apariencia de la democracía cristiana* (Santiago: Arancibia, 1963); *Interpretación marxista de la historia de Chile*, 3 vols. (Santiago: Prensa Latinoamericana, 1967–71); "Latin America: Feudal or Capitalist?" pp. 32–43, in *Latin America: Reform or Revolution?*, ed. James Petras and Maurice Zeitlin (Greenwich, Conn.: Fawcett, 1973).

RONALD H. CHILCOTE

W

WAISS BAND, OSCAR (b. 1912). Oscar Waiss Band was born in Concepción, Chile, on 16 November 1912. Adopting Marxism in 1928, he became a university student leader with the Advance Group, which protested against the dictator Carlos Ibáñez in 1931. In that same year, he helped found the Communist Left, a Trotskyist* splinter from the Stalinist* party. After receiving a law degree in 1934, Waiss joined most of his comrades in entering the Socialist Party of Chile in 1936. He briefly defected from that party as a member of the Socialist Workers' Party in 1940. That dissident group protested the mother party's involvement in the Popular Front government (1938–41) and consequent neglect of revolutionary Marxism and the proletariat. After returning to the fold, Waiss served on the Central Committee of the Socialist Party from 1946 to 1957. He was expelled from the party in 1961 because of a feud with its Secretary General, Raúl Ampuero.† Following the presidential election of Socialist Salvador Allende* in 1970, however, Waiss became director of the government newspaper.

Within the Socialist Party, he pressed for a Marxist path between the Social Democrats and the Communists. Although rejecting Popular Front reformism and personalistic populism, Waiss also opposed Soviet communism and dogmatic Marxism unadjusted to Chilean peculiarities. Therefore he believed that Marxian socialism had to be blended creatively with popular nationalism to forge mass movements in Latin America. Among foreign models, Titoism* in Yugoslavia most attracted Oscar Waiss.

BIBLIOGRAPHY:

A. *Nacionalismo y socialismo en América Latina* (Santiago: Prensa Latinoamericana, 1954); *Amanecer en Belgrado* (Santiago: Prensa Latinoamericana, 1956); *Los problemas del socialismo contemporáneo* (Buenos Aires: Ediciones Iguazú, 1961).

PAUL DRAKE

WANG MING (1904–1974). A Moscow-trained and supported leader of the Chinese Communist Party in the 1930s, Wang Ming (original name Chen Shaoyu) was born in Anhui Province, China, in 1904. After joining the CCP in 1925, he studied in Moscow for several years, returning to China in 1930 along with other members of the so-called Twenty-eight Old Bolsheviks—a derisive term for the inexperienced Russian-returned students. Through the offices of his Soviet mentor Pavel Mif (Mikhail A. Fortus), Wang Ming was installed as head of the CCP in early 1931, replacing the discredited Li Lisan.* Within a few months, however, he returned to Moscow as CCP delegate to the Comintern. In this capacity, he became a leading spokesman for the united front line of opposition to fascism and Japanese imperialism. Upon his return to China in 1937, Wang Ming continued to promote cooperation between the CCP and Chiang Kai-shek's Nationalists, but he was unable to wrest control of the CCP from Mao Zedong,* who perceived Wang Ming as a rival. Wang was obliquely but severely criticized in an intra-CCP purge of the early 1940s and was given only minor posts after the establishment of the People's Republic of China in 1949. He retired to Moscow in the mid-1950s, where he remained until his death on 28 March 1974. While there, he published a withering criticism of Mao, whom he accused of being a petit bourgeois nationalist, Great Han (Chinese) chauvinist, and a betrayer of Marxist internationalism.

Wang Ming's political career from start to finish was dependent upon foreign (Soviet) support. His evanescent leadership of the CCP originated in Moscow, and he was most successful as a Comintern specialist on Chinese affairs in the 1930s. He apparently had little talent or inclination to engage in intra-Party conflict, and he lacked a domestic political base. Wang Ming served as a convenient target for Maoist attack as an alleged "left deviationist" in the early 1930s and as a supposed "right capitulationist" in the late 1930s. The underlying issues in both cases were power, not policy. Wang's eclipse after the CCP's *zhengfeng* (rectification) campaign of 1942–44 symbolized the triumph of a nativist leadership over a Muscovite group within the CCP. In his Moscow exile, Wang Ming again served as a symbol—to the Soviets he was a pro-Soviet orthodox Chinese Marxist-Leninist; to the Maoists he was a dogmatist and turncoat who was slavishly loyal to the Soviet Union.

BIBLIOGRAPHY:

A. *A Half Century of Betrayal* (Moscow: Progress, 1974).

B. Lyman Van Slyke, *Enemies and Friends* (Stanford: Stanford University Press, 1967); Tetsuya Kataoka, *Resistance and Revolution* (Berkeley: University of California Press, 1974).

STEVEN LEVINE

WEIMANN, ROBERT   (b. 1928). Robert Weimann was born on 18 November 1928 in Magdeburg, Germany, studied philosophy at the Martin Luther University in Halle, and earned the Ph.D. in 1955. Since 1964 he has been a professor of literary theory and English literary history at Humboldt University in East Berlin. He is a member of the Academy of the Arts and of the PEN-Centrum group of writers in the GDR. In 1971 Weimann received the Friedrich Engels* award of the Academy of Sciences and (together with A. Schloesser and M. Lehnert) the National Award for his research on Shakespeare. He is a member of the Central Institute for Literary History at the Academy of Sciences in Berlin. Weimann has received international acclaim for his published studies on English Renaissance literature, especially Shakespeare.

New Criticism und die Enwicklung der bürgerlichen Literaturwissenschaft (1962) offers a critical assessment of modern nondialectical (text immanent) literary methodology. Weimann centers his analysis on the relevance of history to the writing and analysis of literature. The act of writing, for Weimann, is a social act. A literary work can never exist in and of itself, but only in a social context of cause and reaction. This context must also be considered when examining the history of a literary work's reception as well. In his study *Gegenwart und Vergangenheit* (1970) Weimann claims that a historically founded theory of reception must take into account what he calls the dialectic of literary genesis and the history of impact (*Wirkungsgeschichte*). Literature as a creative process, in other words, is also part of a dialectically unfolding historical reality. Weimann has also tried to integrate structuralist literary critique and his own materialist reflection theory.

Weimann is a regular contributor to the two leading journals on literary theory in East Germany: *Sinn und Form* and *Weimarer Beiträge*. He also contributes to English and American journals and has been a visiting scholar to the United States on several occasions.

BIBLIOGRAPHY:

A. *Drama und Wirklichkeit in der Shakespearezeit; ein Beitrag zur Entwicklungsgeschichte des elisabethanischen Theaters* (Halle-Saale: Niemeyer, 1958); *"New criticism" und die Entwicklung bürgerlicher Literaturwissenschaft; Geschichte und Kritik neuer Interpretationsmethoden* (Halle-Saale: Niemeyer, 1962); *Phantasie und Nachahmung. 3 Studien zum Verhältnis von Dichtung, Utopie und Mythos* (Halle-Saale: Mitteldeutscher, 1970); *Structure and Society in Literary History: Studies in the History and Theory of Historical Criticism* (Charlottesville: University Press of Virginia, 1976); *Kunstensemble und Öffentlichkeit. Aneignung-Selbstverständigung-Auseinandersetzung*(Halle-Leipzig: Mitteldeutscher, 1982).

B. *Meyers Taschenlexikon, Schriftsteller der DDR* (Leipzig: VEB Bibliographisches Institut, 1975), pp. 588–89; Sara Lennox (Review), "Robert Weimann, 'New Criticism' und die Entwicklung bürgerlicher Literaturwissenschaft," *New German Critique*, no. 5 (Spring 1975), pp. 169–76.

MAGDALENE MUELLER

Y

YAMADA MORITARŌ   (b. 1897). The Japanese Marxist economist Yamada Moritarō was born in Kisogawa-chō in central Japan, and graduated from the Economics Department at the prestigious Tokyo Imperial University in 1923. After studying briefly in Europe, Yamada was appointed assistant professor at the university. There he studied economic theory, the theory of value, and the theory of reproduction, and in 1931 completed his doctoral thesis, "Introduction to a Schematic Analysis of the Process of Reproduction." As police repression directed against the left intensified, Yamada too left Tokyo University when he was implicated in the 1930 Communist Party Sympathizer Incident. Thereafter Yamada worked as an independent economic scholar, until he joined the East Asian Research Institute (Tō-A Kenkyūjo) after his arrest in the 1936 Communist Academy Incident.

It was during the time Yamada worked without institutional affiliation that he made his most notable contributions to the development of Marxism in Japan. In 1932 and 1933, along with Noro Eitarō,* Hirano Yoshitarō,* and Ōtsuka Kinnosuke, Yamada planned the seven-volume *Symposium on the History of the Development of Japanese Capitalism* (*Nihon shihon-shugi hattatsu shi kōza*), and through his contributions to the *Kōza*, Yamada became the leading representative of the so-called Kōza faction's (Kōza-ha) economic theory. The Kōza originally was intended to fulfill two separate but related objectives. First, Noro and others wished to defend the Comintern and Japanese Communist Party argument that Japan was still sufficiently backward, especially in the agrarian sphere and in its political superstructure, to require the completion of a first-stage bourgeois-democratic revolution before proceeding to a proletarian-socialist revolution. The Rōnō-ha (Labor-Farmer faction), led by Yamakawa Hitoshi* out of the Japanese Communist Party in December 1927, claimed that the Comintern view was incorrect and based on ignorance of the full extent of Japan's capitalistic development. The Rōnō-ha thus espoused a one-stage revolution. In 1931, however, the Comintern's short-lived Draft Political Theses appeared to adopt the Rōnō-ha view, and accordingly, the defense of the old 1927 Comintern line became a less salient goal for planners of the *Kōza*. A second aim gained importance: to produce the kind of comprehensive and systematic structural Marxist analysis of the Japanese economic development that thus far had been produced only by Takahashi Kamekichi,* who had used Marxist analytical method to justify Japanese expansion onto the mainland. Since scholarship emerged as the main goal of the *Kōza*, the project came to reflect the divergent views of its contributors on specific issues. Yet virtually all agreed that Yamada's interpretation of the structural relationship between the capitalist and feudalistic components of the contemporary Japanese economic system offered the definitive statement of Kōza-ha economic theory.

Yamada's *Kōza* essays were gathered and published as the single-volume *Analysis of Japanese Capitalism (Nihon shihon-shugi bunseki)* in 1934. This is a dense and extremely complex work, difficult reading even for current Marxist scholars in Japan. Widely influential among intellectuals in the prewar period, Yamada's *Analysis* bore much unacknowledged similarity to Leon Trotsky's* and Georgii Plekhanov's* interpretations of Russia's late development through revolutions from above inspired by external threats in the international system. Because this external threat forced the Meiji regime to undertake rapid primitive capitalist accumulation, it did so in a manner that strengthened the nation militarily. The state promoted heavy industry, thereby developing "a huge military structure" or "key industry system." Thus, the Meiji state resembled the nineteenth-century Prussian state in its "militaristic semifeudal" absolutist character; it did not complete the bourgeois revolution, as the Rōnō-ha claimed, but merely created the conditions in which a still weak bourgeoisie could develop and prosper. The economic basis of this state, and the source of surplus used to finance rapid industrialization, was a land system that remained semifeudalistic; despite the land tax reforms of the Meiji era, the land taxes were merely the continuation of feudal ground rents from the Tokugawa era. In this view, the Meiji Restoration had simply changed the system from a feudalistic to a semifeudal one by concentrating sovereignty (i.e. landownership) on the highest level, in a single unified imperial state. In this way, Yamada's *Analysis* established the basis for the Kōza-ha argument, best presented by Hirano, that the political superstructure was semifeudalistic also. In addition, Yamada's interpretation of the constraints of late development posed by external factors could also be applied to the analysis of other late-developing states.

After the war, in 1945, Yamada resumed his professorship in the Economics Department of the University of Tokyo. In 1950 he became a doctor of economics and chairman of the department and was elected to the Japan Academy. After retiring from the university at age sixty, Yamada followed normal practice and taught elsewhere, including Tokyo's Senshū University. When the debate on Japanese capitalism was revived, Yamada's *Analysis* became the target of criticism; but Yamada felt that the postwar land reforms affected landlord landownership and proved the historical veracity of his own *Analysis of Japanese Capitalism*. Accordingly, Yamada himself became head of the records committee for the land reforms in 1950 and published *A Detailed Outline of Land Reform*

(1951) and *The Structure of the Forces of Production of Japanese Agriculture* (1960). In addition, Yamada used a diagrammatic representation of interrelationships among various industries to fix the date for the postwar economy's transition to the stage of heavy chemical industry in his *Basic Processes of the Postwar Structure of Reproduction* (*Sengo saiseisan kōzō no kiso katei*) (1972).

BIBLIOGRAPHY:

A. *Nihon shihon-shugi bunseki* (Analysis of Japanese capitalism) (Tokyo: Iwanami shoten, 1934).

GERMAINE A. HOSTON

YAMAKAWA HITOSHI   (1880–1958). Yamakawa Hitoshi was a founding member of the Japanese Communist Party, leading theoretician of the Party in its early years, and leader of the dissident Rōnō-ha (Labor-Farmer faction), which broke with the Party in a policy dispute in December 1927. Born in Kurashiki in Okayama Prefecture, Yamakawa attended the Dōshisha Christian School, where he was converted to Christianity. At age seventeen he renounced Christianity in opposition to Dōshisha's "subservience" to the regime, and left Dōshisha for Tokyo. There he cofounded the magazine *Gospel to Youth* and was arrested and fined on charges of lese majesty for a critical article he published on the marriage of the crown prince in 1900. In prison he educated himself on economic theory, reading Adam Smith, David Ricardo, and Alfred Marshall. On leaving prison, he joined the newly founded Japanese Socialist Party, and at the invitation of anarchist leader Kōtoku Shūsui became a member of the editorial staff of the daily *Commoners' Newspaper* (*Heimin shinbun*). Yamakawa supported Kōtoku's "direct action" doctrine in the party's policy dispute with "parliamentarists." After the party was banned, Yamakawa continued to support Kōtoku's activities, while launching the leaflet *Laborer* (*Rōdōsha*) with Sakai Toshihiko to propagate socialism. In 1908 he was arrested in the Red Flag Incident and sentenced to two years in prison, thus escaping the High Treason Incident of 1910. After a five-year absence from Tokyo after his release from prison in 1910, Yamakawa returned to Tokyo in 1916 to take his place at the forefront of the socialist movement.

In Tokyo, he joined Takabatake Motoyuki† and others in the Baibun-sha and contributed to such journals as *New Society* (*Shin shakai*) and with Sakai cofounded *Studies in Socialism* (*Shakai-shugi kenkyū*). Along with the anarchist Arahata Kanson, Yamakawa formed the Labor Union Study Group (Rōdō Kumiai Kenkyū Kai). As the Japanese movement was revived by the example of the Bolshevik Revolution in Russia, Yamakawa was converted to Marxism, and his writings in these years introduced Marxist thought, news of European labor movements, and developments in the Soviet Union. He was a coplanner of the Socialist League and helped publish its organ *Socialism* in 1920–21, helped to establish the Communist group in April 1921, and participated in the founding of the Japanese Communist Party in 1922.

Yamakawa became the Party's leading theoretician from 1922 to 1924, when

he published the essay, "Change of Direction of the Proletarian Movement" in
Vanguard. Here Yamakawa called for a move from the syndicalist tendencies
that had been dominant in the movement toward a mass-oriented movement led
by a vanguard party. When the Party was weakened by the intensification of
police repression, Yamakawa supported the movement to dissolve the Party and
thereafter worked for the establishment of a single "united front" legal political
party of workers, peasants, and all anticapitalist forces. This conception diverged
from the Comintern's united front strategy in that it rejected the need for a
vanguard party. Thus when the Party was rebuilt in 1926–27, Yamakawa was
heavily criticized by the Comintern as "liquidationist" and surrendered his
position as theoretical leader to Fukumoto Kazuo,* a firm advocate of a steeled
vanguard Party. This conflict laid the groundwork for Yamakawa's final split
with the Japanese Communist Party over the proper interpretation of the revolution in Japan. At the core of the dispute were the Comintern's 1927 Theses,
issued in July of that year. The Theses argued that despite Japan's rapid capitalistic development, significant "semifeudal" remnants remained, particularly
in the countryside and in the form of the emperor system and military-influenced
state. This unevenness in Japan's development required that the Japanese revolution go through two stages, first completing the bourgeois-democratic revolution begun by the Meiji Restoration, then proceeding to the socialist stage.
Yamakawa argued that Japan was sufficiently developed to experience a proletarian-socialist revolution immediately, and he led his followers (including
Sakai, Arahata, and Inomata Tsunao*) out of the Party in December 1927. They
immediately launched the journal *Rōnō* (Labor-Farmer), which gave the faction
its name.

As head of the dissident Rōnō-ha, Yamakawa led the struggle for socialist
revolution under the banner "Towards a Political United Front!" Yamakawa's
faction endeavored to implement his ideas on a single coalition of proletarian
and peasant parties to oppose the "imperialist bourgeoisie." Late in 1931, after
the Manchurian Incident, Yamakawa announced his retirement from the united
front, although he did voice public criticism of events he found disturbing. He
spent a year and a half in prison after being arrested in the Popular Front Incident
in December 1937, and was effectively barred from public life until the end of
the war. In the postwar period, Yamakawa resumed his role as theoretical leader
of the Rōnō-ha, which became the core of the Socialist Party. Along with Ōuchi
Hyōe* and Sakisaka Itsurō,* Yamakawa founded the Socialist Association (Shakai-
shugi Kyōkai), and drafted a program of "peaceful socialist revolution." In
January 1954, this program was adopted as the policy of the left wing of the
Socialist Party and remains so to the present day under Sakisaka's guidance.

BIBLIOGRAPHY:

A. *Yamakawa Hitoshi zenshū* (Complete writings of Yamakawa Hitoshi), 20 vols.
(Tokyo: Keisō-shobo, 1966–).

B. Yamakawa Kikue and Sakisaka Itsurō, eds., *Yamakawa Hitoshi jiden* (Autobiography of Yamakawa Hitoshi) (Tokyo: Iwanami shoten, 1961); Koyama Hirotake and

Kishimoto Eitarō, *Nihon no hi-kyōsantō marukusu-shugisha*(Japanese non-Communist Party Marxist) (Tokyo: San'ichi shobo, 1962).

GERMAINE A. HOSTON

YAO WENYUAN   (b. 193?). Yao Wenyuan was an ideologist and literary censor and member of the Maoist* faction during the Cultural Revolution. He worked in the Propaganda Department of the Shanghai Party Committee in the 1950s and 1960s, where his job was to write articles denouncing "bourgeois tendencies" among writers and artists. He became a leading member of a local Party faction committed to tight ideological controls and opposed to liberalization. His most famous piece was written at the behest of Jiang Qing* (Mao's wife) in 1966. In it he attacked a prominent Peking playright, and this turned out to be the opening shot in the factional battle that erupted into the Cultural Revolution. In late 1966 he was named a member of a Party group in Peking in charge of the movement, and by 1969 he was a member of the standing committee of the Politburo. In October 1976, less than one month after the death of Mao, he was arrested in a purge carried out by other national leaders and was vilified as a member of the "Gang of Four." He was given a long prison term in the show trial of early 1981.

While Yao was a leading proponent of the line of thinking developed by Mao after 1957 that led to his conflict with the rest of the Party leadership, he did little to formalize Maoist thinking during that era. His writings were largely derivative of Mao's formulations after the early 1960s. From his criticisms of authors and playrights, however, one can deduce the main elements of this thinking: that class struggle does not end with the establishment of socialism; that it continues in the superstructure of ideas, laws, and art; that a failure to engage in continued "class struggle" against mistaken ideas would contribute to a restoration of capitalism. Yao's only significant attempt at theory was a 1975 article in which he argued that continuing inequalities in socialist society engender "new bourgeois elements" among the elites within the Party and without. These new bourgeois elements seek to stress production over ideological mobilization, use material incentives to spur the economy, seek to liberalize the Party's censorship of political and artistic expression, and seek to open trade and other contacts with the West. This relaxation of ideological vigilance was seen to lead inevitably to corruption and self-seeking and to a restoration of capitalism, as in the Soviet Union. While stated in general form, the argument in retrospect was clearly aimed at other Party leaders who sought to push these stigmatized policies. It was this insistence that policy differences were linked with class struggle, and his willingness, as demonstrated in the Cultural Revolution, to attack as class enemies those who disagreed with him, that earned Yao and his leftist colleagues the enmity of most of the rest of the Party leadership. Yao should be considered as one of the leading proponents of the Cultural Revolution brand of Maoism now repudiated in Peking.

BIBLIOGRAPHY:

A. "On the Social Basis of the Lin Piao Anti-Party Clique," *Peking Review*, 10 (7 March 1975), pp. 5–10.

B. Hong Yung Lee, *The Politics of the Chinese Cultural Revolution* (Berkeley: University of California Press, 1978).

ANDREW G. WALDER

Z

ZAVALETA MERCADO, RENE (b. 1930). The Bolivian Rene Zavaleta came to adopt the categories of Marxist analysis in his political writings largely as a result of the decomposition of the 1952 revolution, only quitting the ruling Movimiento Nacional Revolucionario (MNR) in the early 1960s. In 1971 he played a major role in founding the Movimiento de la Izquierda Revolucionaria (MIR), but by the end of the decade his positions had converged with those of the Bolivian Communist Party (PCB), of which he became a leading theoretician. The constant theme of this ever-changing political career has been a trenchant critique of Trotskyism.* Zavaleta's principal objectives have been to discern a form in which socialist and anti-imperialist ideas might attract broad popular support and acquire coherent organizational form. In this respect the legacy of Marxist theory may be considered only a part of his intellectual system, which had demonstrated a close understanding of the concrete problems facing revolutionary movements such as that in Bolivia. Nevertheless, his critical study of dual power in Bolivia and Chile is of central importance in comprehending the structural constraints on the socialist experiments in these countries.

BIBLIOGRAPHY:

A. *El poder dual en América Latina* (Mexico City: Siglo XXI, 1974); "Consideraciones sobre la historia de Bolivia (1932–71)," in *América Latina: historia de medio siglo*, ed. Pablo Gonzáles Casanova (Mexico City: Siglo XXI, 1977).

JAMES DUNKERLEY

ZETKIN, CLARA (1857–1933). Clara Eissner was born in a small village in Saxony in 1857. Her mother was an active participant in the early German women's movement. She prepared for a teaching career as a student at the Steyber Institute, a secondary school in Leipzig, where she encountered two prominent members of the women's movement, Luise Otto Peters and Auguste Schmidt. By her graduation in 1878, however, her goals had shifted. She was in close contact with the German Social Democratic Party (SPD), participating in support work for the party after the passage of Bismarck's Anti-Socialist Laws. In Leipzig, she met a Russian revolutionary exile, Ossip Zetkin, whom she followed into exile in Paris in 1882 after his expulsion from Germany. They lived together in common-law marriage, had two sons, and pursued active political lives until his early death in 1889. Her writings from France in the 1880s were widely read and debated in the women's education and trade associations in Germany. Following her husband's death, she participated in the founding congress of the Second International,* presenting a report on the situation of working women under capitalism.

In 1890, after the lapse of the Anti-Socialist Laws, Zetkin returned to Stuttgart, Germany. She then entered one of the most productive periods in her life. She rose to a leadership position in the German Social Democratic Party and within the SPD's women's movement. In 1891 Zetkin became the editor of *Die Arbeiterin*, which she transformed into the socialist women's journal *Die Gleichheit*. For twenty-five years, until her forceable expulsion by the Majority socialists in 1917, Zetkin used her *Gleichheit* editorial position to articulate the goals of the socialist women's movement. Under her leadership, the paper provided a forum for radical perspectives within the increasingly revisionist party atmosphere. Zetkin rose to a leadership position, as well, in the international socialist women's movement, whose first international conference coincided with the 1907 meeting of the Second International. In the international arena, she fought to commit all socialist parties to the principle of universal suffrage and for the establishment of a separate women's bureau to coordinate women's activities between conferences of the International.

Alongside Rosa Luxemburg,* Karl Liebknecht, and Franz Mehring, in 1914 Zetkin opposed her party's voting of war credits, and in 1917 she joined the newly founded independent socialist party, the USPD. During the war, Zetkin committed her energies to oppositional work among socialist women inside the belligerent nations. She organized an international conference of women at Berne. Shortly thereafter she was arrested and imprisoned for almost three months at Karlsruhe. In 1919, Zetkin quit the USPD and participated in the founding conference of the German Communist Party (KPD). She was elected to the Party leadership and made editor-in-chief of *Die Kommunistin*. In the 1920s she served as an elected deputy to the German Reichstag. Zetkin continued her active political life, helping to found and guide the international women's movement within the Third International.* She died in exile in the Soviet Union in 1933.

Zetkin's formulation of a Marxist orientation on women's liberation set the dominant terms for the theoretical and organizational perspectives of international socialist movements within the Second and Third internationals. Theoretically, Zetkin pursued the outlines of Engels's* and Bebel's writings on the "woman question." She linked private property to the rise of the patriarchal order in history and saw its demise as the bellwether for the future emancipation of women. She sought to distinguish socialist feminists organizationally and politically from the bourgeois women's movement, whose attempts to unify women in a sex-based outlook she especially abhorred. She opposed feminist views inside social democracy, and she resisted the inroads of radical feminist groups among working-class women. Zetkin emphasized the class character of the women's movement. She argued repeatedly that proletarian women were exploited as workers of the female sex; their place was beside the men of their class.

Zetkin conceived of women not simply as laborers but as mothers. She accepted the basic sexual division of labor in the family, challenging only the unequal value accorded to women's work by society. Fearing Malthusian prescriptions and because of a tenacious commitment to socialist motherhood, Zetkin opposed contemporary arguments for birth control and abortion. She stressed the potential for women's influence in society. Once freed from their oppression and their exclusion within the domestic realm, women would contribute qualitatively to the full measure of society's cultural goods. In her antiwar work, she sought to build upon women's familial roles and their traditional concern with peace. Thus, despite her strong opposition to organized feminism, Zetkin's maternalistic rhetoric and her emphasis on sexual difference resembled the dominant outlook of the bourgeois movement. For both groups, the abstract claims for women's equality made by natural rights feminists a century earlier failed to account for the social specificity of women's material situation.

In another sense as well, Zetkin's contributions to the socialist women's movement were inspired by feminist goals, although she would likely have declined the comparison. In the organizational arena, Zetkin fought for the political necessity of "special work" among women, that is, agitation, enlightenment, and recruitment of working-class women to the socialist movement. In part this derived from two practical considerations: First, until 1908 in most of Germany, women's political activities were severely restricted. They were barred from voting, joining political groups, even assembling in public. Second, Zetkin operated on the familiar socialist concern that women, being the more "backward" members of the class, would retard the forward movement of the class struggle. And indeed, in Germany familial connections within the party were strong. The women's movement of the SPD was largely a movement of married women, overwhelmingly housewives, rather than of women workers.

In this context, Zetkin struggled to maintain separate forums for working-class women. "If the women of the people are to be won for socialism," she wrote, "we cannot make it without [utilizing] special approaches, for which the directing and driving forces are overwhelmingly women dedicated to the awakening and schooling of women" (quoted in K. Honeycutt, 1981, p. 37). But she remained dedicated to the principles of women's autonomy and participation within the larger Party structure even after 1908, when there were no further barriers to women's full participation in the Party. Indeed, she helped to make independence within the larger Party structure an organizational tenet of the socialist women's movement. In addition to women's groups, there were frequent demonstrations around women's issues, a socialist women's press, and a delegate system whereby women's groups elected representatives to Party bodies. Significantly, within these semi-autonomous female arenas a more radical perspective on social democracy was encouraged. The defeat of left social democracy in the period of World War I witnessed a similar eclipse of the institutional fabric of socialist feminism that Zetkin had nurtured. Many of its tenets, however, were incorporated in the women's organizations of the Bolshevik Party and the Third International during the early 1920s.

BIBLIOGRAPHY:

A. *Ausgewalte Reden und Schriften*, 3 vols. (Berlin: Dietz, 1957–60).

B. Karen Honeycutt, "Clara Zetkin: A Left-Wing Socialist and Feminist in Wilhelmian Germany" (Ph.D. diss., Columbia University, 1975); Richard Evans, *The Feminists: Women's Emancipation Movements in Europe, America and Australasia 1840–1920* (New York: Barnes & Noble Books, 1977); Alfred G. Meyer, "Marxism and the Women's Movement," pp. 85–112, in *Women in Russia*, ed. Dorothy Atkinson, Alexander Dallin, and Gail Warshofsky (Stanford: Stanford University Press, 1978); Jean H. Quataert, *Reluctant Feminists in German Social Democracy, 1885–1917* (Princeton: Princeton University Press, 1979); Karen Honeycutt, "Clara Zetkin: A Socialist Approach to the Problem of Women's Oppression," in *European Women on the Left: Socialism, Feminism, and the Problems Faced by Political Women, 1880 to the Present*, ed. Jane Slaughter and Robert Kern (Westport, Conn.: Greenwood Press, 1981).

JOAN LANDES

ZHANG CHUNQIAO (b. 192?). Zhang Chunqiao was an ideologist and bureaucrat in the Propaganda Department of the Shanghai Party Committee from the early 1950s and one of the most important leaders of the Maoist faction that rose to national prominence in the Chinese Cultural Revolution of the late 1960s. During the 1950s he headed a section of the Shanghai Propaganda Department in charge of monitoring and censoring the activities of writers and artists. He became a leader of the faction that wanted to tighten censorship and ward off liberalization as dangerous to the fate of the revolution. This led him into conflict with more moderate Party officials who sought liberalization. He rose to head the Shanghai Propaganda Department in 1964 and used that position to have published, at Mao's behest, articles critical of the Peking Party establishment. He was named in 1966 to the group of national leaders in charge of overseeing the Cultural Revolution and its dismantling of the Party and state apparatus and emerged from the Cultural Revolution in 1968–69 as one of the top handful of national leaders. By the mid-1970s he was the leading radical Maoist contender to succeed Mao Zedong* as Party chairman. Zhang was arrested in 1976, shortly after Mao's death, and vilified as a member of the "Gang of Four." He refused to cooperate with the show trial of 1981 and was given a death sentence later commuted to life imprisonment. He is currently in jail.

Zhang's distinctive contribution to the body of Maoist thinking that culminated in the Cultural Revolution was in elaborating the notion of "bourgeois right" in relation to the more general Maoist theories about the transition to communism and the perceived dangers of the restoration of capitalism. Although not primarily a theorist, he authored two well-known articles, one (as yet untranslated) in 1958 that called for a material supply system for officials instead of a wage system based on unequal grades. The second, in 1975, represented a concise summary of the Maoist theory of the dangers of backsliding toward capitalism. The central argument was that there is a continual danger of a restoration of capitalism during the transition to communism. Market mechanisms and material incentives are inherently corrupting because they enshrine the principle of bourgeois right to unequal returns from labor. These practices lead to greater inequalities through time that eventuate in the establishment of a new "bourgeois" elite that seeks to restore capitalism. In ideological and artistic realms, these bourgeois interests are expressed in calls for political and artistic liberalization and a stress on practices that raise productivity. The Maoist answer to this danger, Zhang made clear, was to use mass mobilization and moral incentives to develop the economy, continually restrict the growth of inequalities, and continue to practice strict censorship in political and artistic expression. Zhang can perhaps be considered the major proponent of post-1960 Maoism, now repudiated in China.

BIBLIOGRAPHY:

A. "On Exercising All-Round Dictatorship Over the Bourgeoisie," *Peking Review*, 14 (4 April 1975), pp. 5–11.

B. Andrew G. Walder, *Chang Ch'un-ch'iao and Shanghai's January Revolution*, Michigan Papers in Chinese Studies, no. 32 (Ann Arbor: Center for Chinese Studies, University of Michigan, 1978).

ANDREW G. WALDER

ZHOU ENLAI (1898–1976). A Chinese Communist leader and government official, Zhou Enlai was born into a scholar-official family in Huian, Jiangsu Province, and studied in both Japan (1917–19) and France (1920–24). After returning to China he played a prominent role in the Chinese Communist Party–Kuomintang united front, specializing in political and military affairs. When the coalition collapsed in 1927, Zhou, who was elected to the Central Committee and the Politburo the same year, remained active in the upper echelons of the CCP. During the Jiangxi Soviet (1931–34) he vied with Mao-Zedong* for the leading military position, but Mao emerged as the top Party and army leader in early 1935 during the Long March. From that time on Zhou remained subordinate to his former rival and never again challenged Mao's preeminent position. Over the years the two men developed a symbiotic relationship, with Zhou providing the administrative and diplomatic skills to complement Mao's theoretical and leadership abilities. Zhou was prominent in wartime negotiations with the KMT and the United States, and he became a well-known CCP spokesman at home and abroad. After the Communist victory in 1949, he was appointed both premier and foreign minister; he gave up the latter post in 1958 but remained in the top government post until his death in 1976. He was one of the most urbane and well traveled of the CCP's top leaders and was highly regarded abroad as a consummate negotiator and effective Chinese spokesman.

Unlike other prominent Chinese Communist leaders (e.g. Liu Shaoqi*), Zhou Enlai did not establish a reputation as a Marxist-Leninist theoretician. He wrote a great deal during his lengthy career, but most of his output was administrative and technical in nature. Nonetheless, he had a substantial influence in shaping the evolution of CCP theory and practice over the years. To a considerable extent Zhou was the moderate voice of the revolution, tending toward caution and stability in contrast to Mao's more innovative—and destabilizing—experiments in socialist reconstruction. For example, although he worked closely with Mao in the Great Leap Forward (1958) and the Cultural Revolution (1966–69), his primary concern was maintaining minimal social order rather than pushing these radical experiments to their outer limits. Although his influence on theory was indirect, there is little doubt it was real and worked in the direction of moderation and stability.

This is seen most clearly in two specific situations where Zhou Enlai's name became virtually synonymous with new departures in Chinese policy. In 1954, for example, Zhou negotiated with Indian Prime Minister Jawaharlal Nehru the so-called five principles of peaceful coexistence. These principles, which laid the basis for friendly and constructive relations between China and other non-Marxist countries in the Third World, represented a sharp departure from the confrontationist policies of the early 1950s. They reached the peak of their influence during and after the Bandung conference in 1955, at which Zhou emerged as a leading spokesman along with Nehru, Nasser, and Sukarno. By 1958, however, Mao had decided to launch the Great Leap Forward, and this quickly led to increased radicalism in Chinese domestic and foreign policy, thus bringing the brief era of peaceful coexistence to an end.

Zhou's name also became intimately associated with the idea of the "four modernizations," which came to characterize the main thrust of Chinese policy in the immediate post-Mao era. By the early 1970s many Chinese leaders, Zhou among them, had concluded that the Cultural Revolution (whatever its original merits) was theoretically and politically bankrupt. Consequently, Zhou promoted the "four modernizations" in contrast to the more politically oriented theories of the so-called Gang of Four radical leaders surrounding Mao in his declining years. Eschewing the previous emphasis on class struggle and ideological re-molding, the new direction stressed the importance of bringing China up to modern world standards in science and technology, agriculture, industry, and the military. The result was a sharp about-face in Chinese domestic and foreign policy, leading to an abrupt break with the Maoist policies of the past. This in turn placed China more closely in tune with the theoretical and policy perspectives of orthodox Marxism-Leninism as represented by the Soviet Union and its socialist allies. Although Zhou Enlai did not live to see this remarkable transformation, it is closely associated with his name, and he most likely would have approved it.

BIBLIOGRAPHY:
    A. *Selected Works of Zhou Enlai*, 2 vols. (Beijing: Foreign Language Press, 1981).

    B. Kai-yu Hsu, *Chou En-lai: China's Grey Eminence* (New York: Doubleday, 1968); Dick Wilson, *Zhou Enlai: A Biography* (New York: Viking, 1984).

                                                            RAYMOND F. WYLIE

Appendix

Entrants By Nationality

ANGOLA

Agostinho Neto

ARGENTINA

Sergio Bagú
Victorio Codovilla
John William Cooke
Rodolfo Ghioldi
Juan Bautista Justo
Aníbal Ponce
Rodolfo Puiggrós
Jorge Abelardo Ramos

BELGIUM

Ernest Mandel

BOLIVIA

Sergio Almaraz Paz
José Antonio Arze
Guillermo Lora
Marcelo Quiroga Santa Cruz
Rene Zavaleta Mercado

BRAZIL

Carlos Marighela
Júnior Caio Prado
Luis Carlos Prestes
Nelson Werneck Sodré

BULGARIA

Dimitur Blagoev

CAMBODIA

Khieu Samphan
Pol Pot

CHILE

Salvador Allende Gossens
Clodomiro Almeyda Medina
Julio César Jobet
Luis Emilio Recabarren
Volodia Valentín Teitelboim Volosky
Luis Vitale
Oscar Waiss Band

CHINA

Ai Siqi
Chen Boda
Chen Duxiu
Chen Yun
Deng Xiaoping
Jiang Qing
Li Dazhao
Li Lisan
Lin Biao
Liu Shaoqi
Mao Zedong
Peng Pai
Qu Qiubai
Wang Ming
Yao Wenyuan
Zhang Chunqiao
Zhou Enlai

COLOMBIA
José Consuegra Higgins
Diego Montaña Cuéllar

COSTA RICA
Manuel Mora Valverde

CUBA
Carlos B. Baliño
Fidel Castro Ruz
Ernesto Guevara de la Serna
Juan Marinello
Julio Antonio Mella
Raul Roa García
Blas Roca
Carlos Rafael Rodríguez

CZECHOSLOVAKIA
Alexander Dubček
Klement Gottwald
Josef Guttmann
Arnošt Kolman
Kurt Konrad
Radovan Richta
Bohumir Šmeral
Jan Šverma

EL SALVADOR
Salvador Cayetano Carpio
Roque Dalton Garcia
Agustin Farabundo Martí
Rafael Menjivar

FRANCE
Henri Barbusse
Clarté
Georges Friedmann
Jules Guesde
Paul Lafargue
Pierre Naville
Paul Nizan
Philosophies Group
Tran Duc Thao
Edouard Vaillant
Paul Vaillant-Coutourier

GERMANY
Bertolt Brecht
Rudolf Breitscheid

Friedrich Engels
Rudolf Hilferding
Karl Kautsky
Wilhelm Liebknecht
Rosa Luxemburg
Karl Heinrich Marx
Fritz Sternberg
Clara Zetkin
Robert Weimann

GREAT BRITAIN
Edward Bibbins Aveling
Eleanor Marx Aveling
Maurice Herbert Dobb
Eric J. Hobsbawm
Henry Mayers Hyndman
John Maclean
Ronald Lindley Meek

GRENADA
Maurice Ruppert Bishop

GUINEA
Ahmed Sékou Touré

GUINEA-BISSAU
Amilcar Cabral

GUYANA
Cheddi Jagan
Walter A. Rodney
Clive Yolande Thomas

HOLLAND
Frank van der Goes
Henriette Roland-Holst
H.J.F.M. Sneevliet
Tribunists
Pieter Jelle Troelstra

HUNGARY
Béla Kun

INDIA
Gangadhar Adhikari
Jyoti Basu
K. Damodaran
Promode Das Gupta

Akshyay Kumar Ramanlal Desai
Ajoy Ghosh
Damodar Dharmanand Kosambi
Bhalchandra Trimbak Ranadive
Tarimela Nagi Reddy
Manabendra Nath Roy
Mohit Sen

INDONESIA

Dipa Nusantara Aidit
Musso
Tan Malaka

IRELAND

James Connolly

ITALY

Amadeo Bordiga
Luigi Cortesi
Antonio Labriola
Bruno Rizzi
Sebastiano Timpanaro

JAPAN

Fukumoto Kazuo
Hirano Yoshitarō
Ikumi Taku'ichi
Inomata Tsunao
Kawakami Hajime
Kushida Tamizō
Noro Eitarō
Ōtsuka Hisao
Ōuchi Hyōe
Ōuchi Tsutomu
Sakisaka Itsurō
Takahashi Kemekichi
Takahashi Kōhachirō
Uno Kōzō
Yamada Moritarō
Yamakawa Hitoshi

MALAYSIA

Chin Peng

MEXICO

Alonso Aguilar Monteverde
Roger Bartra
Narciso Bassols

Vicente Lombardo Toledano
José Revueltas
Jesús Silva Herzog

MOZAMBIQUE

Eduardo Chivambo Mondlane

NICARAGUA

Tomás Borge Martinez
Carlos Fonseca Amador
Daniel Ortega Saavedra

PERU

Hugo Blanco Galdos
José Carlos Mariátegui
Ricardo Martínez de la Torre

PHILIPPINES

Chrisanto Evangelista
José Maria Sison

POLAND

Henryk Grossmann
Michal Kalecki
Oskar Ryszard Lange

PUERTO RICO

Manuel Maldonado-Denis
Angel G. Quintero Rivera

SCOTLAND

John Maclean

SOVIET UNION

Leonid Ilyich Brezhnev
Nicolai I. Bukharin
Nikita Sergeevich Khrushchev
Aleksandra M. Kollontai
Vladimir Ilich Lenin
Anatoli V. Lunacharsky
Julius L. Martov
Georgii V. Plekhanov
Evgeny Alexeyevich Preobrazhensky
Theodore Rothstein
Josef Vissarionovich Stalin
Leon Trotsky

SPAIN

Julio Alvarez del Vayo
Juan Andrade Rodriquez
Luis Araquistain
Julián Besteiro
José Diaz
Antonio Garcia Quejido
Abraham Guillén
Dolores Ibárruri
Pablo Iglesias
Francisco Largo Caballero
Joaquin Maurín Julia
Juan Negrin
Andreu Nin
Indalecio Prieto
Jaime Vera

THAILAND

Asani Ponlajan
Jit Pumisak

URUGUAY

Rodney Arismendi

UNITED STATES

Paul A. Baran
Earl Browder

Angela Yvonne Davis
Daniel DeLeon
Elizabeth Gurley Flynn
William D. Haywood
Leo Huberman
Mary Jones
Harry Magdoff
Max Shachtman
Paul M. Sweezy

VENEZUELA

Germán Carrera Damas
Teodoro Petkoff
Domingo Alberto Rangel

VIETNAM

Vo Nguyen Giap
Le Duan
Ho Chi Minh
Pham Van Dong
Truong Chinh

YUGOSLAVIA

Moša Pijade
Josep Broz Tito

Contributors

Kelly Ainsworth
History
Virginia State University

John Bohstedt
History
University of Tennessee

Michael M. Boll
History
San Jose State University

Arun Bose
Politics
Kirori Mal College

Richard Breitman
History
American University

Kenneth Calkins
History
Kent State University

Antonio Callari
Economics
Franklin & Marshall College

S. Castillo
Madrid, Spain

Patrick Chabal
Cambridge University

Ronald H. Chilcote
Political Science
University of California, Riverside

K. Chvatík
Slavik Studies
University of Konstanz

Arvind N. Das
Public Enterprises Centre for Continuing Education
New Delhi, India

Dawn Fogle Deaton
Chicago, Illinois

James Dietz
Economics
California State University, Fullerton

Vittorio Dini
Philosophy
University of Salerno

Arif Dirlik
History
Duke University

Lowell Dittmer
Chinese Studies
University of California, Berkeley

Raymond Dominick
History
Ohio State University, Mansfield Campus

Michael Donnelly
European Studies
Harvard University

Paul Drake
Latin American & Caribbean Studies
University of Illinois

James Dunkerley
Latin American Studies
University of Liverpool

George R. Esenwein
Stanford University

Lawrence Garner
Political Science
DePaul University

Richard Gillespie
St. John's College
Oxford University

Robert A. Gorman
Political Science
University of Tennessee

M. Milos Hájek
Náprstkova, Czechoslovakia

Charles W. Hampton
Political Science
University of Tennessee

Thomas H. Henriksen
Hoover Institute
Stanford University

Germaine A. Hoston
Political Science
Johns Hopkins University

Santos Juliá
Madrid, Spain

M. Karel Kaplan
Munich, West Germany

Richard Klehr
Political Science
Emory University

M. Karel Kostal
Grenoble, France

Tadeusz Kowalik
Institute of History of Science, Education & Tech
Polish Academy of Sciences

Joan Landes
Social Science
Hampshire College

Steven Levine
School of International Service
The American University

James A. Lewis
History
Western Carolina University

José Limon
Anthropology
University of Texas at Austin

Sheldon B. Liss
History
University of Akron

Paul Mattick, Jr.
Social Sciences
Bennington College

Michael M. Milenkovitch
Political Science
Lehman College

Austen Morgan
London, England

Magdalene Mueller
Germanic Languages
Washington University

Thomas Oleszczuk
Political Science
Rutgers University

Thomas Pantham
Political Science
University of Baroda

Stanley Pierson
History
University of Oregon

Paul Preston
History
University of London

Vera Blinn Reber
History & Philosophy
Shippensburg State College

Dennis Reinhartz
History
University of Texas at Arlington

Juan Rial
Centro De Informaciones Y Estudios
Del Uruguay
Montevideo, Uruguay

Tineke Ritmeester
Germanic Languages
Washington University

Karen Rosenblum-Cale
Political Science
University of Southern California

Carl A. Ross
History
Appalachian State University

Richard V. Salisbury
History
Western Kentucky University

K. Seshadri
Politics
Jawaharlal Nehru University

Ghanshyam Shah
Social Studies
South Gujarat University

John C. Simmonds
History
California State University, Long Beach

Lubomir Sochor
Arcueil, France

Harry Targ
Political Science
Purdue University

Harry E. Vanden
Political Science
University of South Florida

Andrew G. Walder
Sociology
Columbia University

Scott A. Warren
Political Science
Pomona College

Yuangrat Wedel
New Delhi, India

Allen Wells
History
Appalachian State University

Michael C. Williams
Development Studies
University of East Anglia

Allen W. Wood
Philosophy
Cornell University

Raymond F. Wylie
International Relations
Lehigh University

James Young
History
University of Stirling

Index

About the Editor

ROBERT A. GORMAN is Associate Professor of Political Science at the University of Tennessee, Knoxville. He is the author of *Biographical Dictionary of Neo-Marxism* (Greenwood Press, 1986), *Neo-Marxism: The Meaning of Modern Radicalism* (Greenwood Press, 1982), and *The Dual Vision*, as well as many articles in political science, sociology, philosophy, and history journals.